CU00794768

"Sanity, balance, and sober judgment are all qua
in recent discourse. Even what some might cor
New Testament textual criticism has not been immune from false facts and fake news.
It is against this backdrop that this volume makes an invaluable contribution. Combining care, caution, and rigorous scholarship, the contributors place before readers
the latest research and an accurate account of the state of the text of the New Testament. For those seeking to be reliably informed there will be no better guide than
this book to understand the origins, manuscripts, transmission, collection, and
translations of the writings that form the New Testament. This book replaces ignorance with knowledge, foolishness with wisdom, and angry argument with irenic
debate. Anybody who cares about the text of the New Testament must read this book."

PAUL FOSTER, PROFESSOR OF NEW TESTAMENT AND CHRISTIAN ORIGINS,
SCHOOL OF DIVINITY, UNIVERSITY OF EDINBURGH

"I personally don't think that you can defend the truth and accuracy of Scripture as
the Word of God with untruths and inaccuracies. So I welcome this book that contains an enormous amount of useful information on the text of the New Testament
in a form aimed to help people involved in apologetics. Occasionally there is some
tough love when mistakes and problems are highlighted, but the aim is always to
improve the reader's understanding of the New Testament and thus their witness to
the person of our Lord Jesus Christ and the Scriptures that tell his story."

PETER M. HEAD, WYCLIFFE HALL, UNIVERSITY OF OXFORD

"Early in my work as an apologist, I made an embarrassing number of mistakes when
it came to comments about textual criticism. In almost every instance, a book like
this one would have provided the broader perspective that I needed to speak the
truth with greater precision. What Elijah Hixson and Peter Gurry have provided in
this handbook is a tool that every would-be defender of the Christian faith should
purchase and regularly consult. Sloppy defenses of the truth always end up dimin-
ishing the truth instead of exalting the truth. *Myths and Mistakes in New Testament
Textual Criticism* will equip you to leave behind sloppy defenses of Scripture when
it comes to textual criticism."

TIMOTHY PAUL JONES, C. EDWIN GHEENS ENDOWED CHAIR OF
CHRISTIAN MINISTRY, THE SOUTHERN BAPTIST THEOLOGICAL SEMINARY

"Packed with reliable data, Christian-friendly apologetics, but also critical of exag-
gerations and inaccuracies of some apologists, this rich multiauthor volume is a
valuable resource. Practically every aspect of New Testament textual criticism is
addressed competently and clearly. Highly recommended!"

L. W. HURTADO, EMERITUS PROFESSOR OF NEW TESTAMENT LANGUAGE,
LITERATURE, AND THEOLOGY, UNIVERSITY OF EDINBURGH

"I am delighted that these rising stars in the field of New Testament textual criticism have undertaken to guide the church to more integrity and accuracy in the way we talk about the Bible, especially to outsiders. Students, pastors, and lay leaders will find a great foundation for proper handling of Scripture as well as trustworthy resources for apologetics. The essays are in-depth enough to inform the expert but written in plain language with helpful conclusions and takeaways, so the main points are accessible to any committed reader."

AMY S. ANDERSON, PROFESSOR OF GREEK AND NEW TESTAMENT AT NORTH CENTRAL UNIVERSITY, MINNEAPOLIS

"Informative, fair-minded, and sober. A corrective to the text-critical 'malpractice' of the current age."

JUAN HERNÁNDEZ JR., PROFESSOR OF NEW TESTAMENT AND EARLY CHRISTIANITY, BETHEL UNIVERSITY

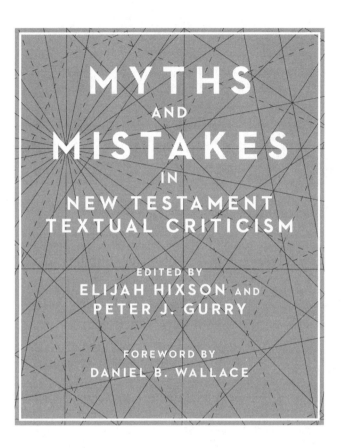

MYTHS
AND
MISTAKES
IN
NEW TESTAMENT
TEXTUAL CRITICISM

EDITED BY
ELIJAH HIXSON AND
PETER J. GURRY

FOREWORD BY
DANIEL B. WALLACE

ivp
Academic

An imprint of InterVarsity Press
Downers Grove, Illinois

InterVarsity Press
P.O. Box 1400, Downers Grove, IL 60515-1426
ivpress.com
email@ivpress.com

©2019 by Elijah Hixson and Peter J. Gurry

All rights reserved. No part of this book may be reproduced in any form without written permission from InterVarsity Press.

InterVarsity Press® is the book-publishing division of InterVarsity Christian Fellowship/USA®, a movement of students and faculty active on campus at hundreds of universities, colleges, and schools of nursing in the United States of America, and a member movement of the International Fellowship of Evangelical Students. For information about local and regional activities, visit intervarsity.org.

All Scripture quotations, unless otherwise indicated, are the authors' translations.

Cover design and image composite: David Fassett
Interior design: Daniel van Loon
Images: Oxy.208 (J 16, 14-22).jpg: Wikimedia Commons / United States public domain
    Papyrus 6 (John 10, 1-10).jpg: Wikimedia Commons / United States public domain
    Papyrus 1 - recto.jpg: Wikimedia Commons / United States public domain

ISBN 978-0-8308-5257-4 (print)
ISBN 978-0-8308-6669-4 (digital)

Printed in the United States of America ♾

InterVarsity Press is committed to ecological stewardship and to the conservation of natural resources in all our operations. This book was printed using sustainably sourced paper.

Library of Congress Cataloging-in-Publication Data
Names: Hixson, Elijah, 1985- editor. | Gurry, Peter J., editor. | Wallace,
    Daniel B., author of foreword.
Title: Myths and mistakes in New Testament textual criticism / edited by Elijah Hixson and Peter J. Gurry ;
    foreword by Daniel B. Wallace.
Description: Downers Grove, Illinois : IVP Academic, an imprint of InterVarsity Press, [2019] | Includes
    bibliographical references and index.
Identifiers: LCCN 2019029450 (print) | LCCN 2019029451 (ebook) | ISBN 9780830852574 (paperback) |
    ISBN 9780830866694 (ebook)
Subjects: LCSH: Bible. New Testament—Criticism, Textual.
Classification: LCC BS2325 .M98 2019 (print) | LCC BS2325 (ebook) | DDC 225.4/86—dc23
LC record available at https://lccn.loc.gov/2019029450
LC ebook record available at https://lccn.loc.gov/2019029451

P	22	21	20	19	18	17	16	15	14	13	12	11	10	9	8	7	6	5	4	3	2	1
Y	39	38	37	36	35	34	33	32	31	30	29	28	27	26	25	24	23	22	21	20	19	

To our teachers

CONTENTS

LIST OF FIGURES AND TABLES

FIGURES

TABLES

FOREWORD

Daniel B. Wallace

WE NO LONGER LIVE IN A BLACK-AND-WHITE WORLD. We never did really, but those who are embroiled in debates about the Bible have often viewed things in such binary hues. These achromatic ideologies can be found on both sides of the theological aisle.

Many who have abandoned the unreflective beliefs they grew up with now cling—just as unreflectively—to unmitigated skepticism toward the New Testament text. The Dan Browns and Kurt Eichenwalds of our world can liken, with a straight face, the scribal copying of Scripture to the parlor game of Telephone. To them, the text has been corrupted so badly that attempting to recover the original wording is like looking for unicorns. It's an impossible task because the search is for something that does not exist.

On the other hand, some apologists for the Christian faith speak of (nearly) absolute certainty when it comes to the wording in the New Testament. And laypeople routinely think of *their* Bible as the Word of God *in every detail.* They are blissfully unaware that Bible translations *change*— because language evolves, interpretations that affect translation become better informed (and all translation is interpretation), and the text that is being translated gets tweaked. Biblical scholarship is not idle. Yet even the publisher of the ESV translation, extremely popular among evangelicals, contributed to this fictive certitude when it declared in August 2016 that "the text of the ESV Bible will remain unchanged in all future editions printed and published by Crossway." The next month it admitted, "This decision was a mistake."[1] When a publishing house tries to canonize its Bible translation,

---

[1]Crossway, "Crossway Statement on the ESV Bible Text," September 28, 2016, www.crossway .org/articles/crossway-statement-on-the-esv-bible-text/.

what does this say to the millions of readers who know nothing of Greek, Hebrew, or Aramaic?

These two attitudes—radical skepticism and absolute certainty—must be avoided when we examine the New Testament text. We do not have now—in our critical Greek texts or any translations—exactly what the authors of the New Testament wrote. Even if we did, we would not know it. There are many, many places in which the text of the New Testament is uncertain. But we also do not need to be overly skeptical. Where we should land between these two extremes is what this book addresses.

The new generation of evangelical scholars is far more comfortable with ambiguity and uncertainty than previous generations. They know the difference between core beliefs and those that are more peripheral. They recognize that even if we embrace the concept of absolute truth, absolute *certainty* about it is a different matter.

One word kept coming to mind as I read this book: *nuance.* The authors understand what is essential and of vital significance in the Christian faith and what is more peripheral. As Stephen Neill argued over fifty years ago and Peter Gurry affirms in this book, "The very worst Greek manuscript now in existence . . . contains enough of the Gospel in unadulterated form to lead the reader into the way of salvation."[2] Andrew Blaski shows that the patristic writers, too, recognized this. Origen, whose concern to recover the original wording of the Bible was worked out with indefatigable exactness, had an even deeper concern. Many Fathers understood that the New Testament—highly valued, revered, even apostolically authoritative—nevertheless pointed ultimately to what is more revered, more authoritative, and more central to our faith: our God and Savior, Jesus Christ.

THE CHASM BETWEEN SCHOLARS AND APOLOGISTS

The authors in this book offer a necessary corrective to decades of overly exuberant apologetic arguments—arguments that have actually hurt the Christian faith. The writers are refreshingly honest, and they do not pull their punches. They observe poignantly that apologetic works on the reliability of the New Testament text have been drifting away from a proper, well-researched, accurately documented scholarship that is anchored to

---

[2]Stephen Neill, *The Interpretation of the New Testament, 1861–1961,* The Firth Lectures, 1962 (London: Oxford University Press, 1964), 63-64, quoted by Peter Gurry in chapter ten.

actual data. Apologists have had a tendency to regurgitate other apologetic works, which in turn are based on other apologetic works. Meanwhile, the scholarship that is supposedly behind the popular declarations in many an evangelical trade book is out of date, misunderstood, or simply ignored.

A classic example of the disconnect between scholarship and apologetics is how textual variants are (mis)counted. A steady stream of apologists for more than half a century have been claiming that variants are counted by wording differences *multiplied by* manuscripts attesting them. Neil Lightfoot's *How We Got the Bible*, a book first published in 1963 and now in its third edition with more than a million copies sold, seems to be the major culprit.[3] Lightfoot claims:

> From one point of view it may be said that there are 200,000 scribal errors in the manuscripts, but it is wholly misleading and untrue to say that there are 200,000 errors in the text of the New Testament. This large number is gained by counting all the variations in all of the manuscripts (about 4,500). This means that if, for example, one word is misspelled in 4,000 different manuscripts, it amounts to 4,000 "errors." Actually, in a case of this kind only one slight error has been made and it has been copied 4,000 times. But this is the procedure which is followed in arriving at the large number of 200,000 "errors."[4]

The only problem with this statement is that it is completely wrong. Chief among the errors, as Elijah Hixson and Peter Gurry point out, is that textual critics "are not counting the number of *manuscripts that attest a variant*; we are counting the number of *variants attested by our manuscripts.*" If variants were actually counted the way Lightfoot suggests, the number of variants among the Greek New Testament manuscripts would be in the tens of *millions.* That this miscalculation has seeped its way, unchecked, into several apologetics books for more than five decades is a telling indictment on the uncritical use of secondary sources by many in this field.

---

[3]Hixson and Gurry note that Warfield's *Introduction to the Textual Criticism of the New Testament*, published in 1899, also produced this miscalculation. But this way of determining the number of variants does not seem to have had much of an impact on apologists until Lightfoot's volume was released.

[4]Neil R. Lightfoot, *How We Got the Bible* (Grand Rapids: Baker, 1963), 53-54. On this see Daniel B. Wallace, "The Number of Textual Variants—An Evangelical Miscalculation," *Daniel B. Wallace* (blog), September 9, 2013, https://danielbwallace.com/2013/09/09/the-number-of-textual -variants-an-evangelical-miscalculation/ as well as the introduction to this volume.

An example of using out-of-date statistics is found in the comparative argument—that is, the argument that compares the number of New Testament manuscripts with those of other Greco-Roman authors. As James Prothro notes, several popular apologists have claimed that there are only 643 manuscripts of Homer's *Iliad*. This number got into apologists' hands, according to Prothro, most likely via a technical book Bruce Metzger authored in 1963. But Metzger repeats the same number of *Iliad* manuscripts in the far-more-accessible first (1964), second (1968), and third edition (1992) of his *The Text of the New Testament*. The fourth and latest edition (2005), coauthored with Bart Ehrman, continues to speak of *only* 643 manuscripts for the *Iliad*! It is not just apologists, then, but sometimes even top-flight scholars who have added to text-critical myths. On the other hand, in the latest edition of *Evidence That Demands a Verdict*, published in 2017 and coauthored with his son Sean, Josh McDowell did his due diligence to update the number of *Iliad* manuscripts by consulting classicists and the Leuven Database of Ancient Books—exactly the right approach.

Other myths that are often touted get some schooling. Jacob Peterson goes into impressive detail on why the "official" number of Greek New Testament manuscripts (i.e., the tally made by adding all the catalogued numbers of papyri, majuscules, minuscules, and lectionaries by the Institut für Neutestamentliche Textforschung), often cited as the *actual* number, is way too generous. But the stats are not static. Peterson commends the work of the Center for the Study of New Testament Manuscripts for adding significantly to our fund with its digitizing of dozens of newly discovered manuscripts.

Gregory Lanier bursts some bubbles about the supposed inferiority of later manuscripts, as though age necessarily corresponds to intrinsic value. He adds that even the later Byzantine manuscripts speak well of "the fidelity of the entire textual tradition." Lanier gives a quite helpful table on the most significant minuscules and, in the spirit of Günther Zuntz, puts forth diagrams that illustrate many facets of transmissional fidelity.

The number of versional manuscripts (those written in other than Greek) has been routinely specified *without documentation* by apologists and some scholars. Jeremiah Coogan reels back the sensationalism and grounds the numbers in what is *known*. He also addresses some key issues in what the versions can and cannot do to aid us in recovering the autographic wording of the Greek New Testament.

Demonstrating sensitivity to the priorities of scholars, translators, *and* faith communities, Edgar Ebojo discusses the dialogue that takes place behind the scenes. The scholarly guild has a say, but it is not the only say in how translations should look and what texts should be included in the translation.

MYTHS AND MISTAKES MADE BY SCHOLARS

Hixson and Gurry tell us that the authors of this book "write primarily as a self-corrective to *Christian* speakers and writers." As I was perusing the manuscript, I came to the conclusion that the editors have defined their readership too narrowly. Precisely because the contributors are up-and-coming scholars—with PhDs (earned or in process) from Birmingham University, Cambridge University, Dallas Seminary, University of Edinburgh, New Orleans Baptist Seminary, University of Notre Dame, and Southern Baptist Seminary—they are up to date on the state of their disciplines. Many have written their doctoral theses on the very topics they explore in this book. These young scholars have something to say—not only to Christian speakers and writers but to non-Christian speakers and writers, and even to New Testament scholars of all stripes.

I have been working for several years on an introduction to New Testament textual criticism. Many of the topics discussed in *Myths and Mistakes* are those I have felt needed some treatment in such an introduction. I was happily stunned to see the depth of discussion, the candid examination, and the up-to-date bibliography in each chapter. Although *Myths and Mistakes* is written in clear, user-friendly prose, the contents are well grounded and perspicacious. I intend to use this volume unapologetically in my introduction as a primary source for several analyses.

There are no sacred cows here. Occasionally, even scholars who have delved into the realm of apologetics have been a bit too enthusiastic, naive, or biased. All of us can learn something from this volume. Craig Evans's view on the longevity of the autographs is perceptively analyzed by Timothy Mitchell; Michael Kruger's link between canon and codex is critiqued by John Meade; Philip Comfort's early dating of papyri is challenged by Elijah Hixson; and I am not immune from censure. Chief among such criticisms (but by no means the sole issue) is my mention of a *first-century* fragment of Mark's Gospel in one of my debates with Bart Ehrman. I had it on good authority that the date was firm and that the papyrus would be published in a year. But at the time I had not seen the manuscript, which should have been critical for me in making any statements about its date. Six years later (!) the fragment was published (April 2018), and it turned out not to be from the first century but was dated to the second or third century by the editors.

Bart Ehrman, a first-rate scholar and an outspoken skeptic about recovering the original New Testament text, comes in for some specific criticisms too. His "early orthodox corruptions" are seen to be less frequent and less severe when Robert Marcello applies a more rigorous method to some key textual problems.

Ehrman's claim that the early scribes were not professionally trained and therefore did not make careful copies is handled by Zachary Cole. Ehrman's view is overly simplistic, presenting a multicolored reality as black and white, and is often factually wrong.

Peter Malik boldly takes on E. C. Colwell, whose studies on method are legendary, by documenting corrections in papyri that "show that scribes strove to improve and revise their work before they handed it to posterity." It is not just what the scribe originally penned but the corrections he or she made to the codex before releasing it to other readers that demonstrate this care.

REQUIEM FOR A DISCIPLINE?

Forty years ago, Eldon Epp published a disturbing article in the *Journal of Biblical Literature*, in which he predicted the end of text-critical studies in America. "New Testament Textual Criticism in America: Requiem for a Discipline" canvasses the trends of a downward spiral pertaining to detailed study of the text and the lack of opportunity for writing a dissertation in textual criticism.[5] He concluded his essay with this gloomy outlook: "I may have pushed too far the figure of speech in the subtitle of this paper when I chose the expression, '*Requiem* for a Discipline.' Yet, that ominous eventuality is all too likely should the clear trends of the recent past continue even into the near future."[6]

Just a decade back, the field appeared almost desolate. At a two-day colloquium held in August 2008 at the Institut für Neutestamentliche Textforschung in Münster, at most a few dozen New Testament textual scholars

---

[5]Eldon J. Epp, "New Testament Textual Criticism in America: Requiem for a Discipline," *JBL* 98, no. 1 (1979): 94-98.
[6]Epp, "New Testament Textual Criticism in America," 98.

were present.[7] I inquired from one of the organizers of the event about the list of those invited. She informed me that all textual critics worldwide were on the list and that only one had declined the invitation. To be sure, the American representation had improved since Epp's requiem, but the numbers were still small.

Samuel Clemens, when rumors that he was on his deathbed were circulating, wrote, "The report of my death was an exaggeration."[8] The same can be said of American—as well as international—scholarship in New Testament textual criticism. A sea change has transpired in the last ten years. Not all the contributors to *Myths and Mistakes* are Americans, of course, but most are. Further, evangelicals in particular have dedicated themselves to this discipline.

Epp spoke of "the growing lack of concern and support for NT textual criticism in America."[9] I was finishing my ThM degree when he wrote these words. As I'm sure that several other graduate students did, I took his requiem to heart. It was a sobering and swift kick in the derrière! I am delighted to report that, forty years later, the scenery has improved markedly. Four of my former students have contributed to this publication: Peter Gurry, Zachary Cole, Robert Marcello, and Jacob Peterson. They either interned at CSNTM, wrote their master's thesis on an aspect of New Testament textual criticism, or both. Elijah Hixson also worked for CSNTM on a digitizing project. Peter Malik collaborated with CSNTM at the Chester Beatty Library as we digitized P47, the topic of Malik's doctoral thesis. Two other interns, Matthew Larsen and Brian Wright, whose doctoral dissertations earn a shout-out or rebuttal in Timothy Mitchell's chapter, also earned their PhDs in New Testament textual criticism or its kin. A certain paternal pride comes with these declarations, but I am hardly alone. Other American professors who specialize in textual studies can claim a measure of mentorship to several of these authors.

---

[7] The group photograph taken on the second day of the conference has fewer than fifty people in it, several of whom were assistants to the scholars in attendance.

[8] Clemens's letter to a reporter, which includes this statement, was published on June 2, 1897, in the *New York Journal*. This wry statement later became embellished to "reports of my death have been greatly exaggerated" (or the like) and included the fictitious backstory that a major American newspaper had printed his obituary!

[9] Epp, "New Testament Textual Criticism in America," 97.

One of Epp's complaints in his requiem is that "the company of trained collators rapidly has disintegrated."[10] Collation is an accurate recording of the exact wording of each manuscript via registering its differences from a base text. At the time that Epp filed this complaint, the number of New Testament books whose manuscripts had been completely collated was *one*. Only the Apocalypse received this honor, a monumental task accomplished by Herman Hoskier in 1929 after thirty years of painstaking labor.[11] Furthermore, virtually nothing has been published on the text of the great majority of codices of the New Testament. A look at Elliott's *Bibliography of Greek New Testament Manuscripts* reveals that less than one-fourth of all extant Greek New Testament manuscripts have even a paragraph published on them. Collations are necessary for every one of these documents.[12]

A collation of a given manuscript not only reveals the differences between said codex and the chosen base text but also unmasks scribal proclivities. The latter is a methodological sine qua non for assessing theological and other tendencies among the manuscripts, as Robert Marcello articulates in his chapter, "Myths About Orthodox Corruption."[13]

Complete collations are not only necessary for individual manuscripts; they are also necessary for each New Testament book. Since Hoskier's work on Revelation some ninety years ago, exhaustive collations have been produced for only two other New Testament books. Tommy Wasserman published his doctoral thesis on the text of Jude in 2006, and Matthew Solomon completed his dissertation on the text of Philemon in 2014.[14] Solomon summarizes his findings in the ninth chapter of *Myths and Mistakes*. Among other observations, he reminds readers that the NA[28] apparatus displays a small fraction of the textual variation in the manuscripts.

Collations of individual documents, when coupled with those of known manuscripts, can reveal something of the rich tapestry of textual history seen in each codex. The textual relations often hint at generations of mixture and influence, opening up intriguing questions on the document's

---

[10]Epp, "New Testament Textual Criticism in America," 97.

[11]Herman C. Hoskier, *Concerning the Text of the Apocalypse*, 2 vols. (London: Quaritch, 1929).

[12]J. K. Elliott, *A Bibliography of Greek New Testament Manuscripts*, 3rd ed. (Leiden: Brill, 2015).

[13]Marcello quotes the well-known yet underimplemented dictum of Hort: "Knowledge of documents should precede judgement on readings."

[14]Tommy Wasserman, *The Epistle of Jude: Its Text and Transmission*, ConBNT 43 (Stockholm: Almqvist & Wiksell, 2006); S. Matthew Solomon, "The Textual History of Philemon" (PhD diss., New Orleans Baptist Theological Seminary, 2014).

transmission history. One of the priorities in collations is work on newly discovered codices. CSNTM posts the images of many such manuscripts, often before they are given a Gregory-Aland number. Graduate students interested in doing original research in the New Testament are encouraged to collate these documents.[15] A recent collation of one of these discoveries, a tenth-century Gospels text, was even used by the editors of the *Tyndale House Greek New Testament*, published in 2017.[16]

COMPLIMENTS AND CAVEATS

I have touched on just a few highlights in *Myths and Mistakes*. There is much, much more here than this bird's-eye view can display. Κῦδος to Hixson for conceiving this work, to both Hixson and Gurry for selecting the contributors, and to all for their unstinting devotion both to this arcane discipline and especially to "the faith that was once for all entrusted to the saints" (Jude 3 NET). The takeaways at the end of each chapter summarize well its relevance for apologetics and anchoring the Christian faith in the text.

Yet the authors do not advance a lock-step apologetic. No doubt, there are several points in this volume that any careful reader will take issue with. More than that, I am sure that not one of the authors will completely agree with all the others. That is part of the book's strength. The pursuit of truth holds greater capital than unity in presentation. The very nature of such a compilation models what the editors intend for the readers to grasp: we may not have an absolutely pure text, nor can we have certainty about everything we do have, but "even the most textually corrupted of our manuscripts and editions still convey the central truths of the Christian faith with clarity and power."

As Michael Holmes has articulated and Zachary Cole attested, the New Testament manuscripts exhibit a text that is overall in excellent shape, but certainly not in impeccable shape; it manifests "microlevel fluidity and macrolevel stability."[17] What the authors of *Myths and Mistakes* insist on

---

[15]Those interested in collating newly discovered manuscripts should contact (info@csntm.org).

[16]Darrell Post, "An Analysis of the Newly Catalogued Gospels Minuscule, GA 2907" (ThM thesis, Central Baptist Theological Seminary, 2012). The manuscript is privately owned in the United Kingdom. CSNTM digitized it in 2009. INTF later assigned it the number Gregory-Aland 2907.

[17]Michael W. Holmes, "From 'Original Text' to 'Initial Text': The Traditional Goal of New Testament Textual Criticism in Contemporary Discussion," in *The Text of the New Testament in Contemporary Research: Essays on the* Status Quaestionis, 2nd ed., ed. Bart D. Ehrman and Michael W. Holmes, NTTSD 42 (Leiden: Brill, 2013), 674, quoted by Cole in chapter seven.

is that it is neither necessary nor even possible to demonstrate that we can recover the exact wording of the New Testament. But what we have is good enough.

ACKNOWLEDGMENTS

THIS BOOK STARTED LIFE AS AN IDEA during our PhD programs. We love the Bible and are fascinated by how it came to be, especially at the level of its textual history. But as we progressed in our studies, we began to see a troubling trend among others who also loved the Bible and wanted to explain how it came to be. What we saw repeatedly were statistics, facts, and arguments meant to bolster confidence in the Bible that were actually having the opposite effect because they were misinformed, misapplied, or misstated. From that experience, Elijah had the idea of putting together a book to help reverse the trend.

One thing became clear: *someone* needed to produce a good resource to correct these errors and provide updated information. Such a task, we quickly realized, was too complex for a single person to be able to handle all of the issues well, and it would be too important to settle for less. We resolved to produce such a book, and we decided that a team effort was the only way to approach the task.

We will say much more about our goal in the following pages, but here we simply want to say thanks to the many others who helped us along the way.

In the first case, our editors at InterVarsity Press have been encouraging from day one—and that despite some hurdles presented by our approach to the book. A special thanks to all who attended and gave us feedback when we presented a preview of the book at the Evangelical Theological Society annual meeting in Rhode Island in 2017, including two distinguished guests from Germany, Holger Strutwolf and Klaus Wachtel. We were especially helped by the feedback from our esteemed panel, which included Peter J. Williams, Michael J. Kruger, Charles E. Hill, Peter M. Head, Timothy Paul Jones, and Daniel B. Wallace. These latter two deserve special thanks for being some of the first to see value in such a book as this and for going the extra mile in helping two greenhorns navigate the wild world of publishing. Other people who encouraged the idea deserve a mention as well, including Amy Anderson, Jeff Cate, Jeffrey D. Miller, and Tawa Anderson. Still others—too many to mention by name—gave of their time and expertise to read individual chapters and offer suggestions. For that, the contributors and we are grateful. Naturally, none of those scholars are responsible for anything they dislike about the resulting book.

Last and most important, we must mention our wonderful wives, whose patience, steadfastness, and joy has come in measure equal to their husband's long hours, eccentricities, and occasional discouragement. For them we are grateful well beyond any words we could write here.

ABBREVIATIONS

ANCIENT

Att.	Cicero, *Epistulae ad Atticum*
De libr. propr.	Galen, *De libris propriis*
Doctr. chr.	Augustine, *De doctrina christiana*
Ep.	*Epistula(e)*
Epig.	Martial, *Epigram(s)*
Fam.	Cicero, *Epistulae ad familiares*
Haer.	Irenaeus, *Adversus haereses*
Hist. eccl.	Eusebius, *Historia ecclesiastica*
Hist. rom.	*History of the Roman Empire*
Hom. Jos.	Origen, *Homiliae on Josuam*
Inst. Or.	Quintilian, *Institutes of Oratory*
P.Amh.	Amherst Papyri
P.Ant.	Antinoopolis Papyri
P.Beatty	Chester Beatty Biblical Papyri
P.Bodm.	Papyrus Bodmer
P.Egerton	Egerton Papyri
P.Köln	Kölner Papyri
P.Mich.	Michigan Papyri
P.Oxy.	Oxyrhynchus Papyri
P.Ryl.	Catalogue of the Greek and Latin Papyri in the John Rylands Library, Manchester
Vir. ill.	Jerome, *De viris illustribus*

MODERN

AB	Anchor Bible
ACW	Ancient Christian Writers
Aeg	*Aegyptus*

AJP	*American Journal of Philology*
AnBib	Analecta Biblica
ANRW	*Aufstieg und Niedergang der römischen Welt: Geschichte und Kultur Roms im Spiegel der neueren Forschung.* Part 2, *Principat.* Edited by Hildegard Temporini and Wolfgang Haase. Berlin: de Gruyter, 1972–
ANTF	Arbeiten zur Neutestamentlichen Textforschung
AÖAW	Anzeiger der Österreichischen Akademie der Wissenschaften
APF	*Archiv für Papyrusforschung und verwandte Gebiete*
ASP	*American Studies in Papyrology*
ASV	American Standard Version
Aug	*Augustinianum*
BASP	Bulletin of the American Society of Papyrologists
BBR	*Bulletin for Biblical Research*
Bib	*Biblica*
BibInt	*Biblical Interpretation*
BibOr	Biblica et Orientalia
BICS	Bulletin of the Institute of Classical Studies Supplement
BSac	*Bibliotheca Sacra*
BT	*The Bible Translator*
BTNT	Biblical Theology of the New Testament
BZNW	Beihefte zur Zeitschrift für die neutestamentliche Wissenschaft
CBQ	*Catholic Biblical Quarterly*
CBR	*Currents in Biblical Research*
CEB	Common English Bible
CEV	Contemporary English Version
ChrÉg	*Chronique d'Égypte*
ClQ	*Classical Quarterly*
ConBNT	Coniectanea Biblica: New Testament Series
CRBR	*Critical Review of Books in Religion*
CRJ	*Christian Research Journal*
CSB	Christian Standard Bible

CSNTM	Center for the Study of New Testament Manuscripts
DSD	*Dead Sea Discoveries*
Dynamis	*Dynamis: Acta Hispanica ad medicinae scientiarumque historiam illustrandam*
EC	*Early Christianity*
ECM	Editio Critica Maior
ESV	English Standard Version
ETL	*Ephemerides Theologicae Lovanienses*
ExpTim	*Expository Times*
FC	Fathers of the Church
GA	Gregory-Aland
GEgerton	Egerton Gospel
Gn	*Gnomon*
GRBS	*Greek, Roman and Byzantine Studies*
GRM	Graeco-Roman Memoirs
HCSB	Holman Christian Standard Bible
HibJ	Hibbert Journal
HTR	*Harvard Theological Review*
HTS	Harvard Theological Studies
INTF	Institute for New Testament Textual Research
JB	Jerusalem Bible
JBL	*Journal of Biblical Literature*
JBTR	*Journal of Biblical Text Research*
JEA	*Journal of Egyptian Archaeology*
JETS	*Journal of the Evangelical Theological Society*
JGRChJ	*Journal of Greco-Roman Christianity and Judaism*
JR	*Journal of Religion*
JRS	*Journal of Roman Studies*
JSNT	*Journal for the Study of the New Testament*
JSNTSup	Journal for the Study of the New Testament Supplement Series
JSSSup	Journal of Semitic Studies Supplement
JTS	*Journal of Theological Studies*

KJV	King James Version
LCL	Loeb Classical Library
LEB	Lexham English Bible
LEC	Library of Early Christianity
LNTS	Library of New Testament Studies
LSTS	Library of Second Temple Studies
MAAR	Memoirs of the American Academy in Rome
MH	*Museum Helveticum*
NA	Nestle-Aland *Novum Testamentum Graece*
NA^{26}	*Novum Testamentum Graece*. 26th ed. Edited by Kurt Aland, Matthew Black, Carlo M. Martini, Bruce M. Metzger, and Allen Wikgren. Stuttgart: Deutsche Bibelgesellschaft, 1979
NA^{27}	*Novum Testamentum Graece*. 27th ed. Edited by Barbara Aland, Kurt Aland, Johannes Karavidopoulos, Carlo M. Martini, and Bruce M. Metzger. Stuttgart: Deutsche Bibelgesellschaft, 1993
NA^{28}	*Novum Testamentum Graece*. 28th ed. Edited by Barbara Aland, Kurt Aland, Johannes Karavidopoulos, Carlo M. Martini, Bruce M. Metzger, and Institute for New Testament Textual Research. Stuttgart: Deutsche Bibelgesellschaft, 2012
NABre	New American Bible revised edition
NASB	New American Standard Bible
NET	New English Translation
NETR	*Near East School of Theology Theological Review*
NHS	*Nag Hammadi Studies*
NIV	New International Version
NKJV	New King James Version
NLT	New Living Translation
NovT	*Novum Testamentum*
NovTSup	Supplements to Novum Testamentum
NRSV	New Revised Standard Version
NSD	New Studies in Dogmatics
NTAbh	Neutestamentliche Abhandlungen

NTS	*New Testament Studies*
NTTS	New Testament Tools and Studies
NTTSD	New Testament Tools, Studies, and Documents
OCT	Oxford Classical Texts
OECS	Oxford Early Christian Studies
OrChr	*Oriens Christianus*
PL	Patrologia Latina [= *Patrologia Cursus Completus*: Series Latina]. Edited by Jacques-Paul Migne. 217 vols. Paris, 1844–1864
PNTC	Pillar New Testament Commentary
PTMS	Princeton Theological Monograph Series
RCT	*Revista catalana de teología*
RevExp	*Review and Expositor*
RSV	Revised Standard Version
RV	Revised Version
SAAFLS	Studi archeologici, artistici, filologici, letterari e storici
SBL	Society of Biblical Literature
SBLDS	Society of Biblical Literature Dissertation Series
SBLMS	Society of Biblical Literature Monograph Series
SBLNTGF	Society of Biblical Literature: The New Testament in the Greek Fathers
SBLRBS	Society of Biblical Literature Resources for Biblical Study
SD	Studies and Documents
SIL	Summer Institute of Linguistics
SNTSMS	Society for New Testament Studies Monograph Series
SO	Symbolae Osloenses
SP	Sacra Pagina
SSEJC	Studies in Scripture in Early Judaism and Christianity
STAC	Studien und Texte zu Antike und Christentum
StPatr	Studia Patristica
SVTQ	*St. Vladimir's Theological Quarterly*
TC	*TC: A Journal of Biblical Textual Criticism*

TCNT	Text and Canon of the New Testament
TCSt	Text-Critical Studies
TENTS	Texts and Editions for New Testament Study
TEV	Today's English Version
TLZ	*Theologische Literaturzeitung*
TRev	*Theologische Revue*
TS	Texts and Studies
TynBul	*Tyndale Bulletin*
UBS	United Bible Societies
UBS³	*Greek New Testament.* 3rd ed. Edited by Kurt Aland, Matthew Black, Carlo M. Martini, Bruce M. Metzger, and Allen Wikgren. New York: United Bible Societies, 1968
UBS⁴	*Greek New Testament.* 4th ed. Edited by Barbara Aland, Kurt Aland, Johannes Karavidopoulos, Carlo M. Martini, and Bruce M. Metzger. New York: United Bible Societies, 1993
UBS⁵	*Greek New Testament.* 5th ed. Edited by Barbara Aland, Kurt Aland, Johannes Karavidopoulos, Carlo M. Martini, Bruce M. Metzger, and the Institute for New Testament Textual Research. New York: United Bible Societies, 2014
VC	*Vigiliae Christianae*
VCSup	Vigiliae Christianae Supplements
VL	Vetus Latina: Die Reste der altlateinischen Bibel
WBC	Word Biblical Commentary
WTJ	*Westminster Theological Journal*
WUNT	Wissenschaftliche Untersuchungen zum Neuen Testament
ZECNT	Zondervan Exegetical Commentary on the New Testament
ZNW	*Zeitschrift für die neutestamentliche Wissenschaft und die Kunde der älteren Kirche*
ZPE	*Zeitschrift für Papyrologie und Epigraphik*

CHAPTER ONE

INTRODUCTION

Peter J. Gurry and Elijah Hixson

WHY THIS BOOK?

PERHAPS, LIKE US, you've had this experience when driving to a new place. You set off, confident that your map or GPS has you headed in the right direction, and you begin thinking about other things. Soon, however, the roads are all the wrong names, and the signs do not seem right. Slowly, you begin to discover that you are lost. But where did you go wrong? Was it the last turn or the turn before that? Was it because you were on the phone, or are the directions wrong? If you're lucky, you manage to answer these questions, get back on the right track, and find your destination. This experience of thinking you know where you are going, only to realize you're lost, can be disorienting and frustrating. It can leave you wondering what else you may be wrong about. Are you sure you turned off the stove? Was the back door locked, or did you leave it cracked again? One doubt easily leads to another.

The problem of getting to the right place by the wrong route is what we address in this book. Not about driving, of course, but about the Bible and about defending its credibility. Unfortunately, some defenders think they know how to get us to the proper destination when in fact they've taken us through several wrong turns along the way. For those who discover that the route is wrong, the realization can be disorienting. Once-trusted guides can turn out not to be as reliable as once thought, and, in the case of defending the Bible, this can sadly lead to greater doubt in Scripture's reliability.

Christians believe and trust the Bible as God's special revelation. That belief is basic to the Christian faith. So, naturally, serious challenges to the trustworthiness of this book are significant and need a response. One challenge to the Bible that has risen to new prominence is the claim that we can't trust the New Testament because we do not even know what it says. This, we are told, is the case because the manuscripts—handwritten copies of the New Testament—are so corrupt from miscopying that we simply cannot know what the original text was. As Bart Ehrman, the scholar whose best-selling book *Misquoting Jesus* has done more than any other to bring this issue to the forefront, has said, "How does it help us to say that the Bible is the inerrant Word of God if in fact we do not have the words that God inerrantly inspired, but only the words copied by scribes—sometimes correctly but sometimes (many times!) incorrectly?"[1] For Ehrman, the answer is clear: it is not much help at all, a conclusion that contributed to his much-publicized loss of evangelical faith.

As Ehrman's public profile has risen, this part of his argument has gained greater traction, often without the benefit of his years of research in the subject area. Just before Christmas in 2014, for example, *Newsweek* published a long-form essay by Kurt Eichenwald titled "The Bible: So Misunderstood It's a Sin." Among a series of provocative claims, Eichenwald tells us, "No television preacher has ever read the Bible. Neither has any evangelical politician. Neither has the pope. Neither have I. And neither have you. At best, we've all read a bad translation—a translation of translations of translations of hand-copied copies of copies of copies of copies, and on and on, hundreds of times."[2]

This notion that the New Testament has been miscopied to the point of near oblivion has reached beyond national news magazines to capture certain parts of the popular imagination. Sometimes it crops up in unexpected places, such as popular fiction. In the bestselling Jack Reacher series written by Lee Child, we find an unexpected presentation of the idea that the original wording of the New Testament is hopelessly lost. In one of his stories, Child presents us with an Anglican priest who meets the protagonist on his way to Yuma, Arizona. On the drive there, the priest offers this lesson on the book of Revelation:

---

[1] Bart D. Ehrman, *Misquoting Jesus: The Story Behind Who Changed the Bible and Why* (New York: HarperCollins, 2005), 7.

[2] Kurt Eichenwald, "The Bible: So Misunderstood It's a Sin," *Newsweek*, January 2015, newsweek .com/2015/01/02/thats-not-what-bible-says-294018.html. Several rebuttals were published online, including one by *Newsweek* itself. Similarly, Gary Wolf writes of textual criticism beginning the demolition job on Christian doctrines nearly two hundred years ago in "The Church of the Non-believers," *Wired*, November 1, 2006, www.wired.com/2006/11/atheism.

> Most of the original is lost, of course. It was written in ancient Hebrew or
> Aramaic, and copied by hand many times, and then translated into Koine
> Greek, and copied by hand many times, and then translated into Latin, and
> copied by hand many times, and then translated into Elizabethan English and
> printed, with opportunities for error and confusion at every single stage. Now
> it reads like a bad acid trip. I suspect it always did.[3]

There you have it. A trippy book made worse by thousands of years of miscopying and mistranslation so that now we do not even know what the
original was. As anyone with a basic introduction to the New Testament
knows, the problems here are obvious and plentiful. For starters, the book
of Revelation was not *translated* into Greek for the simple reason that it was
written in Greek. The many translations we do have of it—both ancient and
modern—are almost all taken directly from Greek. It is true that opportunities for error do come from copying anything of length by hand, but these
have also been accompanied by opportunities for correction and clarification. In short, our traveling priest's view of the matter is about as wrong
as could be. The point here is not to pick on fiction (the appropriate genre
for such misinformation, after all) but to show that views like these are all
too easily consumed and accepted by popular audiences who lack the expertise to see through them. Indeed, it is not too much to say that the view
expressed by the priest in this Jack Reacher novel is held by more and more
people today.

To be sure, most trained scholars ignore such popular nonsense and go
about their work unfazed. Still, when these kinds of conspiratorial claims
find their way to the *New York Times* bestseller list or the cover of *Newsweek*
and *Wired* magazine, Christian scholars and apologists who care about
Christianity's reputation take note. In their justified zeal to defend the Bible
against such misinformation, they have naturally produced a growing
number of books, articles, chapters, study Bibles, and blog posts in response.
With such a proliferation of material, what justification could there be for
yet another publication on the subject?

As it turns out, that very proliferation has caused an unintended problem,
and it is the one this book particularly addresses. A survey of literature reveals a growing gap between good scholarship on the transmission of the

---

[3]Lee Child, *Nothing to Lose* (New York: Bantam Dell, 2008), 434-35. Our thanks to Larry Hurtado
  for this example.

New Testament and its appropriation in the literature aimed at nonspecialists. In some cases, the misinformation is actually more severe on the side of those who want to defend the Bible's reliability (perhaps because they write more often on it). Such treatments often repeat bad or outdated arguments from other authors. In many cases, the treatment ends up worse than the ailment: arguments meant to encourage confidence in the Bible make it look untrustworthy through ignorance, negligence, or worse. This is troubling for those of us who love the Bible and want to know whether it can be trusted.

The contributors to the present volume are convinced that the Bible *should* be loved and that its text *can* be trusted. Like many of those we critique in what follows, we are convinced that the New Testament text provides a more than adequate foundation on which to build the Christian faith. In that, we quite agree with them against Christianity's media-savvy critics. But we often find their reasons inadequate. From our own research, we know that studying the Bible's textual history can be intimidating. For the New Testament, it requires a knowledge of Greek and other ancient languages. It demands experience in reading ancient manuscripts. It draws on elements from classics, church history, and biblical studies. If that were not enough, some of the most important research is published in languages other than English. Those who write for popular audiences should not be faulted if they lack expertise in all these areas, and we certainly do not fault them here. However, the fact remains that many who address the topic from an apologetic angle construct their arguments from information that is at best outdated and at worst patently wrong.

EXAMPLES OF THE PROBLEM

Minor mistakes *should* be avoided, but misleading errors *must* be corrected because they discredit those who make them. At its worst, misinformed apologetics can have the opposite of their intended effect. Although the full story is surely more complicated, atheist Robert Price traces his rejection of Christianity back to this very issue. Despite becoming a Christian at eleven years old and engaging in fervent evangelism, devotional life, and church membership, Price writes, "Ironically, my doubts and questions were a direct outgrowth of this interest in apologetics."[4] He continues,

---

[4]Robert M. Price, *The Case Against the Case for Christ: A New Testament Scholar Refutes the Reverend Lee Strobel* (Cranford, NJ: American Atheist Press, 2010), 9.

Obviously, at first I thought the arguments I was picking up from reading John Warwick Montgomery, F. F. Bruce, Josh McDowell, and others were pretty darn good! But once it became a matter of evaluating probabilistic arguments, weighing evidence, much of it impossible to verify, much of it ambiguous, I found it impossible to fall back on faith as I once had.[5]

That statement is sobering and serves as a warning against irresponsible apologetics. Price traces the beginning of his "deconversion" to bad arguments presented by apologists. Granted, we do not think the question of the textual transmission of the New Testament leaves one's faith hanging in the balance. One could adopt almost any available text of the New Testament and still build a robust, orthodox Christian faith on it. Still, the Bible is worth defending, and that means it is worth defending well. Unfortunately, when it comes to the transmission of the New Testament, misinformation abounds. We can illustrate the problem with three examples.

Outdated information. The first example springs from a problem we all face: keeping up with the deluge of information. Thankfully, textual criticism is a field of study that regularly benefits from new manuscript discoveries. But this blessing becomes a curse for authors who have not kept their arguments updated. We can illustrate from some of our earliest material evidence. The papyri are those manuscripts made using papyrus, a reed plant that flourishes in the Nile River. We get our English word *paper* from this writing material. For the New Testament, the standard scholarly edition (the twenty-seventh edition of the Nestle-Aland *Novum Testamentum graece*, or NA[27]) published in 1993 included all the papyrus manuscripts then known. These were numbered up to P98 (P = papyrus). Fast forward to 2012, and the newest edition (NA[28]) lists papyri up through P127. That is almost thirty new papyri in fewer than twenty years. Moreover, these numbers are already out of date, because more papyri have been added to the official registry of New Testament manuscripts since then.[6] In other words, our

---

[5]Price, *Case Against the Case for Christ*, 9-10. Price cites specifically John Warwick Montgomery, *History and Christianity* (Downers Grove, IL: InterVarsity Press, 1974); F. F. Bruce, *The New Testament Documents: Are They Reliable?*, 5th ed. (Grand Rapids: Eerdmans, 1960); F. F. Bruce, *Tradition: Old and New* (Grand Rapids: Zondervan, 1970); Josh McDowell, *More Evidence That Demands a Verdict: Historical Evidences for the Christian Scriptures* (Arrowhead Springs, CA: Campus Crusade for Christ, 1975).

[6]As of May 2018, the *Kurzgefaßte Liste*, the official list of Greek New Testament manuscripts maintained by the Institut für Neutestamentliche Textforschung in Münster (http://ntvmr.uni -muenster.de/liste), has entries for twelve additional papyri, P128-P139.

knowledge of manuscripts is constantly growing, and it can be hard to keep up. It is understandable when authors do not have the latest and greatest numbers. What is not as understandable and, in fact, a real problem is when the author *does* update the information, but only the part of it that favors the New Testament.

This problem of selective updating has become common in one of the most widely used arguments to defend the New Testament. The argument involves a comparison between the number of New Testament manuscripts and the number of manuscripts for other ancient literature. One of the classic statements of it is found in F. F. Bruce's little book *The New Testament Documents: Are They Reliable?*, in which he tried to demonstrate the reliability of the New Testament using the same methods applied to other ancient documents.[7] In one of his chapters, he directly addresses our concern here about whether the New Testament has been copied reliably. In that context, he shows that many other important works from antiquity lag far behind in comparison to the abundance and quality of the material we have for establishing the New Testament text. Our evidence is both earlier and more abundant. As a trained classicist himself, Bruce was calling skeptics to account for their double standard. As he put it, "If the New Testament were a collection of secular writings, their authenticity would generally be regarded as beyond all doubt."[8] In other words, skeptics were not being consistent, and Bruce's comparison between the New Testament and classical works was meant to expose just how much this was the case. In this use, the argument has a long pedigree. One finds it used centuries ago by one of the great classicists, Richard Bentley (1662–1742).[9] It is not surprising, therefore, that the comparison continues right down to the present. Today it is hard to find a book on apologetics that does not at some point make much of this basic comparison.[10]

---

[7] F. F. Bruce, *The New Testament Documents: Are They Reliable?*, 6th ed. (Grand Rapids: Eerdmans, 1981). In the preface to the sixth edition, Bruce notes that the last thorough update was in 1959 and that he made only minor changes since that time (p. xii).

[8] Bruce, *New Testament Documents*, 6th ed., 20.

[9] Richard Bentley, "Remarks upon a Late Discourse of Free-Thinking," in *The Works of Richard Bentley*, ed. Alexander Dyce (London: Robson, Levey, and Franklyn, 1838), 3:350-52. The same point is made again in B. F. Westcott and F. J. A. Hort, *The New Testament in the Original Greek: Text* (London: Macmillan, 1881), 561-62.

[10] For a representative sample, see Montgomery, *History and Christianity*, 29; Graham Stanton, *Gospel Truth? New Light on Jesus and the Gospels* (London: HarperCollins, 1995), 40; Amy Orr-Ewing, *Why Trust the Bible? Answers to 10 Tough Questions* (Nottingham, UK: Inter-Varsity

The problem with the argument as used today is that the double standard has been reversed so that now it is defenders of the Bible who are guilty of being unfair to the classical literature. In many cases, the number of classical manuscripts is still taken from Bruce's sixty-year-old data, so that comparisons that were once accurate have become inaccurate and thereby misleading. There have been attempts to bring the comparison up to date, but these have gone unnoticed, and in any case they too are now in need of updating.[11] Too often, authors simply take Bruce's numbers for the classical literature for granted even though they dare not do the same for the New Testament. One praiseworthy exception to this trend is Josh McDowell. In the most recent edition of *Evidence That Demands a Verdict* (coauthored with his son Sean McDowell), McDowell and McDowell cite both classicists and the Leuven Database of Ancient Books (LDAB) to give manuscript counts that are even more up to date than Clay Jones's 2012 article.[12]

To give an example of the problem, Bruce tells us that there are only a few papyrus fragments of Herodotus's famous *Histories*, dating nearly four hundred years after he wrote. Beyond that he reports only eight complete copies dating from nearly fourteen hundred years later. For someone familiar with New Testament manuscripts, that is sparse evidence indeed. Today, however, a few minutes with a modern manuscript database such as LDAB reveals forty-three manuscripts for Herodotus's *Histories*, one of which dates as early as the second century BC. For a more famous author such as Homer, the number of manuscripts swells to well over two thousand, the majority of which are papyri.[13] These newer discoveries have not kept

Press, 2005), 42-43; Nicholas Perrin, *Lost in Transmission? What We Can Know About the Words of Jesus* (Nashville: Thomas Nelson, 2007), 142; Darrell L. Bock, "Is the New Testament Trustworthy?," in *The Apologetics Study Bible*, ed. Ted Cabal (Nashville: Holman, 2007), 1452; Craig L. Blomberg, *Can We Still Believe the Bible? An Evangelical Engagement with Contemporary Questions* (Grand Rapids: Brazos, 2014), 35; Greg Gilbert, *Why Trust the Bible?* (Wheaton, IL: Crossway, 2015), 48-49; Stanley E. Porter and Andrew W. Pitts, *Fundamentals of New Testament Textual Criticism* (Grand Rapids: Eerdmans, 2015), 50-51; John Piper, *A Peculiar Glory: How the Christian Scriptures Reveal Their Complete Truthfulness* (Wheaton, IL: Crossway, 2016), 82.
[11]For attempts to update, see Peter M. Head, *Is the New Testament Reliable?*, Grove Biblical Series B 30 (Cambridge, UK: Grove, 2003), 8-11; Clay Jones, "The Bibliographical Test Updated," *CRJ* 35, no. 3 (2012): 32-37.
[12]Josh McDowell and Sean McDowell, *Evidence That Demands a Verdict: Life-Changing Truth for a Skeptical World* (Nashville: Thomas Nelson, 2017), 56-60. Coincidentally, citing classicists and the LDAB (www.trismegistos.org/ldab) are two of the suggestions James B. Prothro makes for using this argument responsibly in chapter four in this volume.
[13]Joachim Latacz and Frank Pressler, "Homerus," in *Brill's New Pauly: Encyclopaedia of the Ancient World; Antiquity*, ed. Hubert Cancik and Helmuth Schneider (Leiden: Brill, 2005), 6:462.

some from adopting Bruce's outdated numbers wholesale without any at-tempt at updating.[14] The problem is made worse by the fact that these same authors do not adopt Bruce's numbers for the New Testament. Instead they rightly try to find more accurate numbers. In the case of Stanley Porter and Andrew Pitts, their zeal for the New Testament seems to have gotten the best of them, as their total is overstated by more than fifteen hundred manu-scripts.[15] How that happened is hard to say, but it is not hard to imagine how a fair-minded reader, to say nothing of a skeptical reader, might think that Christian authors have stacked the manuscript deck in favor of the New Testament. Regardless of intention, the result is lost credibility.

Abused statistics. A second problem in the debate is the widespread abuse of statistics. This is particularly unfortunate because, while statistics can never tell the whole story, they do offer much-needed perspective for nonspecialists. It is, for example, helpful to know how many manuscripts of the New Testament we have, how many differences there may be between them, and how many of the differences affect English translations. However, such information is helpful only if it is accurate and used responsibly. It is at both points that another problem confronts us. The numbers cited are frequently wrong, abused, or both.

The most commonly cited statistic is the number of textual variants. This statistic has been referenced by scholars for over a century, but the number became a staple in the popular literature after Ehrman began claiming that there may be as many as 400,000 variants.[16] Ehrman was one of the first and by far the most prominent scholar to suggest a number that high.[17] Since then, the proposed number has risen even higher, with one prominent scholar venturing that it may be as high as 750,000.[18] This is quite a shocking

---

[14]See Porter and Pitts, *Fundamentals of New Testament Textual Criticism*, 50; Piper, *Peculiar Glory*, 82.

[15]Porter and Pitts, *Fundamentals of New Testament Textual Criticism*, 50; see also 33, 80. Inexpli-cably, their number of majuscules is overstated by more than two thousand, and their number of minuscules is understated by almost six hundred. For an account of this and other errors in this book, see Amy S. Anderson, "Review of *Fundamentals of New Testament Textual Criticism*," *JETS* 59, no. 4 (2016): 846-49.

[16]Ehrman, *Misquoting Jesus*, 89; see also Bart D. Ehrman, "Text and Interpretation: The Exegetical Significance of the 'Original' Text," in *Studies in the Textual Criticism of the New Testament*, NTTS 33 (Leiden: Brill, 2006), 309; Bart D. Ehrman and Daniel B. Wallace, "The Textual Reli-ability of the New Testament: A Dialogue," in *The Reliability of the New Testament: Bart D. Eh-rman and Daniel B. Wallace in Dialogue*, ed. Robert B. Stewart (Minneapolis: Fortress, 2011), 21.

[17]Matthew S. DeMoss suggests "approximately half a million variants" in his *Pocket Dictionary for the Study of New Testament Greek*, IVP Pocket Reference (Downers Grove, IL: IVP Academic, 2001), 127.

[18]Eldon J. Epp, "Why Does New Testament Textual Criticism Matter? Refined Definitions and Fresh Directions," *ExpTim* 125, no. 9 (2014): 419.

number, and it becomes even more so when compared to the number of words in the typical Greek New Testament, which is just over 138,000. As Bart Ehrman is fond of pointing out, this means that "there are more variations among our manuscripts than there are words in the New Testament."[19] The impression is clear: the original New Testament has been lost in a sea of variants. Little wonder, then, that Christians have tried to address this disturbing statistic. Unfortunately, they have not always done a good job.

When we look closely, we find a myriad of problems that accompany all estimates about the number of variants. To begin with, until very recently, no one had bothered to give a reliable account of how they arrived at their number. Estimates were most often rehashed, sometimes accompanied by impressive-sounding but empty phrases such as "some scholars say" or "the best estimates are." What exactly makes one estimate reliable and another unreliable? No one seems to know. Consequently, it is rare that authors explain what it is they count in their estimated number of variants. Do they count spelling differences? Do they count cases in which the scribe has made an obvious mistake and produced something meaningless? Is the estimate meant to include ancient translations and scriptural citations from earlier Christian writers, or is it limited to Greek manuscript evidence alone? These are basic questions one should ask whenever seeing numbers such as 400,000 or 750,000 variants brandished in arguments about the New Testament text.

Recently, however, these problems were addressed in a detailed study with a clear method and open data. The study concluded that there are probably about half a million nonspelling differences among our Greek New Testament manuscripts.[20] Every qualification in that sentence is important. This estimate does not include variants from non-Greek manuscripts or from the quotations of early church writers. Nor does it include what must be a vast quantity of trivial spelling differences. Finally, it estimates differences *between* manuscripts rather than differences *from* the original text, since that original is usually what is up for debate in the first place. (We should emphasize here that it is an *estimate*, not a *count*, since most of our manuscripts remain unstudied in detail.)

---

[19]Ehrman, *Misquoting Jesus*, 90. This comparison is not new to Ehrman. It was used by Erwin Nestle, "How to Use a Greek New Testament," *BT* 2, no. 2 (1951): 54.

[20]Peter J. Gurry, "The Number of Variants in the Greek New Testament: A Proposed Estimate," *NTS* 62, no. 1 (2016): 97-121.

With all the proper qualifications in place, what can this estimate actually tell us? At this point it becomes crucial to think about context. We have already seen Ehrman's statement that variants outnumber the actual words in the New Testament. This juxtaposition, which is numerically true, is offered to support his view that the text comes loaded with uncertainty. The problem is that the comparison itself is meaningless. It makes little sense to compare the number of supposed variants in *all* our Greek manuscripts to the number of words in only *one* manuscript or printed edition. That is a bit like comparing car accidents in the 1930s to car accidents today without factoring in the total number of cars on the road in each era; a crucial variable is left out. As it is, Ehrman's comparison tells us very little about how scribes did in copying the New Testament text.

Unfortunately, many apologists have followed Ehrman in his original comparison without thinking it through, and the results have only made the problem worse. Craig Blomberg, for example, tries to dull the force of Ehrman's estimate by claiming that all our variants are "spread across more than twenty-five thousand manuscripts in Greek or other ancient languages," which, he says, results in a mere sixteen variants per manuscript.[21] This claim is simply not true. As we have already noted, the half a million variants are only among our *Greek* manuscripts, of which there are closer to fifty-three hundred. Even if he were right, the comparison of "variants per manuscript" is not helpful because our manuscripts are of such different sizes. Some are fragments no bigger than your hand, while others are complete copies of the New Testament. As before, the comparison is intrinsically a bad one, as it leaves out a key variable. You do get a number in the end, but it explains next to nothing about the real world. Despite this problem, the comparison continues to be made, and the results can approach the absurd, as, for example, when Stanley Porter's attempt at the comparison draws the conclusion that New Testament manuscript production "nearly rivals that sometimes found today in modern print!"[22] Such a claim certainly grabs attention, but it discredits the larger point.

Another problematic way the number of variants has been addressed by apologists is by addressing how the variants are counted. Some have claimed

---

[21]Blomberg, *Can We Still Believe the Bible?*, 17; see also 27.
[22]Stanley E. Porter, *How We Got the New Testament: Text, Transmission, Translation*, Acadia Studies in Bible and Theology (Grand Rapids: Baker Academic, 2013), 66.

that the number is not as big as it might seem because every textual variant is recounted for every manuscript in which it occurs. If one manuscript has "Peter said . . ." and two thousand others have "*Simon* Peter said . . . ," then we have two thousand variants. If this were true, it certainly would be significant. This way of counting is found in the work of B. B. Warfield and continues down to the present.[23] But, again, it is not right. In the example above, we should *not* count two thousand variants; we should count just two. The reason is that we are not counting the number of *manuscripts that attest a variant*; we are counting the number of *variants attested by our manuscripts*.

Alas, the problems do not end here. More recently, the number of variants has been further mistreated by writers making unfounded claims about *where* these variants occur in the New Testament. Craig Blomberg, in the same book cited above, says that the hundreds of thousands of textual variants "cluster" in "only 6 percent of the New Testament."[24] The implication is that they are less of a problem for Christians since they affect such a small portion of the New Testament. It is true, of course, that some passages lend themselves to variation more than others either because of their significance (such as the words of Jesus) or because of their form (lists are especially easy to mix up).[25] However, one needs to spend only a few minutes with any good, critical edition of the Greek New Testament to see that variants occur throughout. They certainly do not "cluster" in anything like 6 percent of the text.

How did such an erroneous claim get started? In Blomberg's case, the cause appears to be a misreading of his source—a source, it turns out, that itself is unreliable at precisely this point. The original statistic is found in a book by Paul Wegner, who says nothing about variants "clustering" in a certain percentage of the text. Instead, he says that *significant* textual variants affect only about 6 percent of the text. But even this number is unreliable as given. In the only place where Wegner gives absolute figures for it, he says it

---

[23]B. B. Warfield, *An Introduction to the Textual Criticism of the New Testament* (London: Hodder & Stoughton, 1889), 13; Norman L. Geisler, "New Testament Manuscripts," in *The Baker Encyclopedia of Apologetics*, ed. Norman L. Geisler (Grand Rapids: Baker, 1999), 532; Neil R. Lightfoot, *How We Got the Bible*, 3rd ed. (Grand Rapids: Baker, 2003), 95-96; Gilbert, *Why Trust the Bible?*, 50.

[24]Blomberg, *Can We Still Believe the Bible?*, 17. This is repeated without the percentage in Gilbert, *Why Trust the Bible?*, 50-51.

[25]A case of the first category is found in the divorce sayings in Mt 5:32; 19:9; Mk 10:11-12; Lk 16:18. For a case of the second, see those in need of healing in Mt 15:30-31.

is 7 percent—and the numbers behind it are wrong![26] Referring to the well-known UBS fourth edition of the Greek New Testament, he says that it "notes variants regarding approximately 500 out of 6,900 words, or only about seven percent of the text."[27] As a matter of fact, the UBS[4] notes variants affecting over 1,500 words out of a total of 138,020, or only about *1* percent.[28] In this case, the true numbers actually support Wegner's position better than his own numbers. But neither number supports Blomberg's claim about variants "clustering" in 6 percent of the text, whatever that might mean. The best we can say about this example is that it does offer a nice illustration of how texts become corrupted in transmission—and how they can be corrected.

All of this shows how easily statistical problems can spin out of control when left unchecked. In the popular literature, the results can be embarrassing. In the case in Greg Gilbert and his attempt to "debunk silly statements about the Bible," he not only repeats these errors from Blomberg and Wegner but also makes a series of "silly statements" of his own.[29] These bad statistics might be easy enough to ignore if they happened occasionally. And they are certainly excusable in isolation. But when they occur repeatedly and without correction, they become a serious problem that needs to be addressed. In the worst cases, these confident claims about scribes, variants, and manuscripts discredit the very thing they are meant to support: our confidence in the biblical text.

Selective use of evidence. A final error is what we might bluntly call "believing what we want to be true." One place this occurs is in the appeal to

---

[26]Paul D. Wegner, *A Student's Guide to Textual Criticism of the Bible* (Downers Grove, IL: IVP Academic, 2006), 25, 39.

[27]Wegner, *Student's Guide to Textual Criticism of the Bible*, 25; see also 39. Wegner refers to Barbara Aland, Kurt Aland, Johannes Karavidopoulos, Carlo M. Martini, and Bruce M. Metzger, eds., *The Greek New Testament*, 4th rev. ed. (New York: United Bible Societies, 1993). Elsewhere Wegner says that the number of variants in the New Testament is "approximately 10 percent" without saying what it is a percentage of (*The Journey from Texts to Translations: The Origin and Development of the Bible* [Grand Rapids: Baker, 1999], 213).

[28]The introduction to the UBS[4] (p. v) says there are 1,438 places of variation in the edition, many of which involve more than one word. This data may be behind J. Ed Komoszewski, M. James Sawyer, and Daniel B. Wallace's claim that "only about 1 percent of the variants [in the New Testament] are both meaningful and viable" (*Reinventing Jesus: How Contemporary Skeptics Miss the Real Jesus and Mislead Popular Culture* [Grand Rapids: Kregel, 2006], 63), but they do not tell us.

[29]See Greg Gilbert, "Debunking Silly Statements About the Bible: An Exercise in Biblical Transmission," The Gospel Coalition, February 8, 2016, www.thegospelcoalition.org/article/debunking-silly-statements-about-the-bible. This is an excerpt of his book *Why Trust the Bible?*, referenced earlier.

early manuscript evidence. In late 2011 Scott Carroll, at the time a director of the extensive Green Collection of biblical artifacts, tantalized the internet by announcing on Twitter that "For over 100 years the earliest known text of the New Testament has been the so-call[ed] John Rylands Papyrus. Not any more. Stay tuned. . . ."[30] This news went mostly unnoticed until February 2012, when Dan Wallace said during a debate with Bart Ehrman that he could confirm the existence of a first-century fragment of Mark's Gospel, one dated by a renowned (but unnamed) paleographer.[31] This was startling, not only as it would be our earliest New Testament manuscript but also because Mark's Gospel, while probably our earliest, has the poorest attestation when it comes to early manuscript evidence. Wallace went on to report that this new papyrus would be published the next year and suggested that, like our other known papyri, it too would reaffirm the text of the New Testament as we now know it.[32] In time, it became clear that Carroll and Wallace were referring to the same manuscript. Ehrman raised the appropriate question of how much of an impact a first-century copy of Mark's Gospel would make on scholarship. The answer: maybe very little.[33] As one might expect, however, the possibility of new information about early Christianity proved too much to resist, and speculation ran beyond the reach of good judgment.[34]

The yet-unpublished fragment had already begun to appear in published apologetics handbooks as evidence of the reliability of the New Testament. In the most recent update of the classic work *Evidence That Demands a*

---

[30]Scott Carroll (@DrScottCarroll), "For over 100 years the earliest known text of the New Testament has been the so-call John Rylands Papyrus. Not any more. Stay tuned. . . . ," Twitter, December 1, 2011, 11:54 p.m., https://twitter.com/DrScottCarroll/status/142149523391778816.

[31]The initial announcements from Ehrman and Wallace are found in Bart Ehrman, "First-Century Copy of Mark?—Part 1," *The Bart Ehrman Blog: The History & Literature of Early Christianity*, April 6, 2012, https://ehrmanblog.org/first-century-copy-of-mark-part-1-members; and Daniel B. Wallace, "First-Century Fragment of Mark's Gospel Found!?," *Daniel B. Wallace* (blog), March 22, 2016, https://danielbwallace.com/2012/03/22/first-century-fragment-of-marks-gospel-found.

[32]See Daniel B. Wallace, "Earliest Manuscript of the New Testament Discovered?," *DTS Magazine*, February 9, 2012, https://voice.dts.edu/article/wallace-new-testament-manscript-first-century/.

[33]Bart D. Ehrman, "Would a First-Century Fragment of Mark Matter?," *The Bart Ehrman Blog: The History & Literature of Early Christianity*, January 24, 2015, http://ehrmanblog.org/would-a-first-century-fragment-of-mark-matter.

[34]Most recently, in 2015 Craig A. Evans was reported as saying, among other things, that this first-century fragment of Mark would "provide clues as to whether the Gospel of Mark changed over time." See Owen Jarus, "Mummy Mask May Reveal Oldest Known Gospel," *Live Science*, January 18, 2015, www.livescience.com/49489-oldest-known-gospel-mummy-mask.html.

Verdict, Josh and Sean McDowell cite a lecture by Wallace for the following statement: "A recently discovered portion of a Mark manuscript may date as early as c. AD 85–125. However, we must wait for this discovery to go through peer review and publishing before we can establish the dating of this portion with more certainty."[35] It is admirable that they are hesitant with regard to the date—rightly so. However, the date of the fragment was not its only uncertain aspect. A genuine, early fragment of Mark's Gospel could possibly contain a text that differs in some significant aspect from other witnesses of Mark's Gospel, which could be seen as an argument against the reliability of the New Testament rather than for it.

The early Mark fragment was finally published in 2018, and it is not quite so old as many hoped.[36] To the surprise of many, it turned out not to be an item from a private collection but instead was part of the renowned Oxyrhynchus Papyri collection. The early Mark papyrus was edited by Dirk Obbink and Daniela Colomo as P.Oxy. 83.5345, and it was assigned the number P137.[37] Obbink and Colomo admitted, "Dating [its] hand presents even more difficulties than usual," but they assigned it to the late second or early third century. The Egypt Exploration Society issued a statement reporting that Bernard Grenfell and Arthur Hunt had excavated it probably in 1903, according to the inventory number.[38] While some were disappointed that P137 is not a first-century manuscript, it is still a significant discovery—the oldest manuscript of Mark 1 and likely the oldest manuscript of any part of Mark.[39]

What might be surprising to those outside the circle of textual criticism is that P137 is not the first manuscript of the New Testament claimed to be

---

[35]McDowell and McDowell, *Evidence That Demands a Verdict*, 48.

[36]Elijah Hixson was the first to notice the similarities between P137 and the rumors about "first-century Mark" and to suggest that the two manuscripts were probably the same, in "'First-Century Mark,' Published at Last? [Updated]," *Evangelical Textual Criticism* (blog), May 23, 2018, http://evangelicaltextualcriticism.blogspot.com/2018/05/first-century-mark-published -at-last.html. Hixson's suggestion was quickly confirmed by Scott Carroll, Dan Wallace, and the Egypt Exploration Society, as discussed in the updates to the post.

[37]Dirk Obbink and Daniela Colomo, "5345. Mark I 7-9, 16-18," in *The Oxyrhynchus Papyri LXXXIII*, ed. P. J. Parsons and N. Gonis, GRM 104 (London: Egypt Exploration Society, 2018), 4-7.

[38]"P.Oxy LXXXIII 5345," Egypt Exploration Fund, June 4, 2018, www.ees.ac.uk/news/poxy -lxxxiii-5345.

[39]See Elijah Hixson, "Despite Disappointing Some, New Mark Manuscript Is Earliest Yet," *Christianity Today*, May 30, 2018, www.christianitytoday.com/ct/2018/may-web-only/mark -manuscript-earliest-not-first-century-fcm.html.

Figure 1.1. The first-century date assigned to P.Oxy. 83.5345 (P137) before its publication was widely touted by apologists as evidence for the reliability of Mark's account of Jesus; when published, however, it was dated to the second or third century

from the first century. Brent Nongbri points out Schøyen manuscript 2630, a "first-century Mark" papyrus published in 1986 by Anton Fackelmann, son of the Austrian papyrus conservator of the same name.[40] In the original publication, Fackelmann claimed to have deciphered notes used in the composition of Mark's Gospel from the undertext of a rewritten papyrus manuscript.[41] No such undertext has been verified by scholars who have seen the fragment, and the visible writing—the writing that would have been written *after* the notes Fackelmann described—dates to the Ptolemaic period (second or third century BC). Thankfully, no apologists we know of have adopted Fackelmann's outlandish claims about Schøyen manuscript 2630 as evidence of the reliability of the New Testament. The same cannot be said of another alleged "first-century Mark," however.

In 1972, José O'Callaghan, a papyrologist at the Pontifical Biblical Institute in Rome, argued that a manuscript containing Mark 6:52-53 was among the papyrus fragments of the Dead Sea Scrolls found in Cave 7 of

[40]Brent Nongbri, "A First-Century Papyrus of Mark (Probably Not the One You Think)," *Variant Readings* (blog), July 21, 2017, https://brentnongbri.com/2017/07/21/a-first-century-papyrus-of-mark-probably-not-the-one-you-think/; Nongbri, "Some Answers on Fackelmann's 'First-Century Mark' Papyrus," *Variant Readings* (blog), August 3, 2017, https://brentnongbri.com/2017/08/03/some-answers-on-fackelmanns-first-century-mark-papyrus/; Nongbri, "Anton Fackelmann: Conservator and Seller of Antiquities," *Variant Readings* (blog), September 13, 2017, https://brentnongbri.com/2017/09/13/anton-fackelmann-conservator-and-seller-of-antiquities/.
[41]Anton Fackelmann, "Präsentation christlicher Urtexte aus dem ersten Jahrhundert geschrieben auf Papyrus: Vermutlich Notizschriften des Evangelisten Markus?," *Anagennesis* 4 (1986): 25-36.

Qumran.[42] The caves of Qumran were abandoned in AD 68, which means that any manuscripts found in them must have been written before that date,

Figure 1.2. 7Q5 is a small Greek fragment among the Dead Sea Scrolls at Qumran that some still reference as a first-century copy of Mark's Gospel, although scholars today reject this identification

including the fragment in question (designated "7Q5" for Cave 7, Qumran, fragment 5). In the case of 7Q5, the date of this tiny fragment is not what is disputed; the debate is whether it is actually a fragment of Mark's Gospel.

The fragment itself is tiny, "smaller than two standard U.S. postage stamps," as Wallace describes it.[43] The visible text on the papyrus consists of just a handful of letters (see fig. 1.2). The only complete, legible word is καί (*kai*, "and"), which is not a helpful word for identifying the text given how common it

is. Some partial traces of letters are visible, but what ink is left of them is consistent with more than one letter.[44] It was largely on the basis of these uncertain letters that O'Callaghan identified the fragment as Mark 6:52-53. In addition to his reliance on uncertain letters, O'Callaghan's identification requires two unique changes to the text of Mark in order to account for the few letters of 7Q5 that are visible. These changes would make 7Q5 the only manuscript in existence that leaves out the three-word phrase ἐπὶ τὴν γῆν (*epi tēn gēn*, "to the land") in Mark 6:53 and contains a possible but rare misspelling of another word. What makes it highly unlikely is that only two letters of the misspelled word are visible, and one of them constitutes part

---

[42]José O'Callaghan, "¿Papiros neotestamentarios en la cueva 7 de Qumrān?," *Bib* 53, no. 1 (1972): 91-100.

[43]Daniel B. Wallace, "7Q5: The Earliest NT Papyrus?," *WTJ* 56, no. 1 (1994): 173n2.

[44]For example, if we were writing in English, a vertical line could be the first part of a dozen different letters. O'Callaghan identified the letters ννησ (*nnēs*) in the papyrus, which he interpreted as part of the word "Gennesaret." Only the middle two letters are certain, and infrared imaging reveals that there is no fourth letter at all—it is only a dark spot on the papyrus.

of the misspelling. Almost immediately, Gordon Fee, among others, raised problems for O'Callaghan's identification of 7Q5 as Mark's Gospel.[45] Carsten Peter Thiede, on the other hand, continued to defend O'Callaghan's position on 7Q5, despite its rejection by most scholars.[46] In a scathing review of Thiede's book, J. K. Elliott makes an important observation about the temptation to follow the evidence that best suits our desired conclusions:

> Many of those who accepted O'Callaghan's position did so because they were encouraged to date the canonical writings as early as possible on the basis of the specious argument that this would safeguard the veracity of their contents. More than 50 articles were published in the 4 years following the article in *Biblica* [the academic journal in which O'Callaghan's original article appeared]. Most popular writers agreed with O'Callaghan; most scholarly articles rejected his conclusions.[47]

Today, the wider academic community is in almost unanimous agreement that 7Q5 is not a copy of Mark's Gospel.[48] Recently, Hans Förster published a thorough summary and critique of the position, showing how speculative the argument is.[49] Dead Sea Scrolls scholar Timothy H. Lim also rejects O'Callaghan's claims, adding that others have identified the text of the manuscripts in question as 1 Enoch. Lim concludes, "Prudence should guide one to be cautious in reading so much significance out of so little evidence."[50]

---

[45]Gordon D. Fee, "Some Dissenting Notes on 7Q5=Mark 6:52-53," *JBL* 92, no. 1 (1973): 109-12.

[46]The English version of Carston Peter Thiede's work is *The Earliest Gospel Manuscript? The Qumran Fragment 7Q5 and Its Significance for New Testament Studies* (Carlisle, UK: Paternoster, 1992). For critical reviews of Thiede, see Wallace, "7Q5: The Earliest NT Papyrus?"; J. K. Elliott, "Review of *The Earliest Gospel Manuscript: The Qumran Fragment 7Q5 and Its Significance for New Testament Studies*," *NovT* 36, no. 1 (1994): 98-100; Stanton, *Gospel Truth?*, 20-32.

[47]Elliott, "Review of *The Earliest Gospel Manuscript*," 99.

[48]To our knowledge, the only recent attempt to accept 7Q5 as Mark's Gospel is by Austrian theologian Karl Jaroš: "Zur Textüberlieferung des Markusevangeliums nach der Handschrift P.Chester Beatty I (P[45]), zu 7Q5 und zum 'Geheimen Markusevangelium,'" *Aeg* 88 (2008): 71-113; Jaroš, *Die ältesten griechischen Handschriften des Neuen Testaments* (Cologne: Böhlau, 2014). With respect to his work on the dates of early New Testament papyri, Jaroš holds several controversial positions, which are criticized by Pasquale Orsini and Willy Clarysse in their important essay, "Early New Testament Manuscripts and Their Dates: A Critique of Theological Palaeography," *ETL* 88, no. 4 (2012): 443-74.

[49]Hans Förster, "7Q5 = Mark 6.52-53: A Challenge for Textual Criticism?," *JGRChJ* 2 (2001): 27-35. For a more recent treatment of the problems with Thiede's arguments, see Roger S. Bagnall, *Early Christian Books in Egypt* (Princeton, NJ: Princeton University Press, 2009), 25-40.

[50]Timothy H. Lim, *The Dead Sea Scrolls: A Very Short Introduction*, 2nd ed., Very Short Introductions 143 (Oxford: Oxford University Press, 2017), 116.

Unfortunately, the identification of 7Q5 is not the only one of O'Callaghan's and Thiede's claims that was received by popular audiences despite its rejection by the academic community. O'Callaghan also identified several other fragments from Qumran as New Testament texts. Among the scraps of papyrus he also claimed to find manuscripts of Mark 4; James 1; and 1 Timothy 3–4.[51] Additionally, he argued that Acts 27; Mark 12; Romans 5; and 2 Peter 1 were probably attested.[52]

In each case, the tiny fragment in question has only a handful of letters, and one is often required to allow multiple rare or even unprecedented mistakes and changes to the text to "make it work" as a fragment of the New Testament. The unusual errors and changes that O'Callaghan had to propose to account for all the letters on the fragments pose their own problem for Christian apologists tempted to follow him. If O'Callaghan were correct about the fragments in question, it is true that we would have very early New Testament manuscripts, but they would have a text that is unlike anything we have in any of our other copies. Ironically, then, O'Callaghan's view gives him remarkably early manuscripts, but they come at the cost of the text's earliest reliability.[53]

Despite the textual problems these manuscripts would create if they were early witnesses to the New Testament, and despite an academic consensus rejecting O'Callaghan's claims, some Christian apologists continue to cite them. Amy Orr-Ewing, for example, appeals to no fewer than nine of the Cave 7 fragments identified by O'Callaghan in her book on the reliability of the Bible.[54] She does note the presence of debate but still favors the conclusion that supports her larger argument:

> Critics have argued that these are not fragments of New Testament manuscripts but are instead writings produced by the Qumran community which

---

[51]O'Callaghan, "¿Papiros neotestamentarios?"; O'Callaghan, "¿1 Tim 3,16; 4,1.3 En 7Q4?," *Bib* 53, no. 3 (1972): 362-67.

[52]Thiede, *Earliest Gospel Manuscript?*, 46. According to Bagnall, O'Callaghan's identification of several of the Dead Sea Scrolls as New Testament manuscripts "faced immediate withering attacks and was tacitly withdrawn by O'Callaghan already in 1976" (*Early Christian Books in Egypt*, 38).

[53]As George J. Brooke puts it, "I would rather trust the NT evidence on other grounds than on the basis of a supposedly early fragment which has so many discrepancies with what is consistently known from other sources: the discrepancies undermine the integrity of the very text which Thiede for one seems so concerned to establish," in "Review of *Kein Markustext in Qumran: Eine Untersuchung der These: Qumran-Fragment 7Q5 = Mk 6,52-53*, by Stefan Enste," *DSD* 8, no. 3 (2001): 314-15.

[54]Orr-Ewing, *Why Trust the Bible?*, 48-49.

sound similar to New Testament passages. The fact that the fragments are so small makes it extremely difficult to be certain either way. However, if, as seems highly possible, these fragments are pieces of the New Testament, these discoveries are potentially hugely significant.[55]

The shift from what is "extremely difficult to be certain" about in one sentence to what is then deemed "highly possible" in the next is rather stunning here. To the honest reader, it looks as if a desire for evidence to confirm her own view has gotten the best of her.

More problematic still is Brian Edwards's use of O'Callaghan's work in his book on the same subject.[56] Edwards appeals specifically to 7Q5 and 7Q4 ("1 Timothy"), but he dismisses those who object to their identification as New Testament texts as if their own lack of scientific expertise, their critical biases, and even spiritual defects have prevented them from seeing the truth: "Generally, it should be noted, the opposition came from New Testament critical scholars and theologians and not from the scientists."[57] Not to put too fine a point on the matter, but Elliott's warning is again appropriate: "Pots should be particularly self-critical before accusing kettles of blackness."[58]

The controversy over 7Q5 was not the first time someone claimed to have discovered a first-century manuscript of the Gospels. Over a century earlier, Constantine Simonides published an edition of some first-century papyrus manuscripts of the New Testament he had "discovered" in Liverpool.[59] Today Simonides is remembered as the most notorious manuscript forger in history. Not long after his "discovery" in Liverpool, it came to light that he had forged the papyri himself.[60] Dan Wallace gives good advice regarding the use of new, untested discoveries as evidence: "When the next sensational archaeological find is made, should not conservatives and liberals alike ask

[55]Orr-Ewing, *Why Trust the Bible?*, 49.

[56]Brian H. Edwards, *Why 27? How Can We Be Sure That We Have the Right Books in the New Testament?* (Darlington, UK: Evangelical Press, 2007), 189-94.

[57]Edwards, *Why 27?*, 191-92.

[58]J. K. Elliott, "Review of *The Jesus Papyrus* by Carsten Peter Thiede and Matthew d'Ancona and *Gospel Truth* by Graham Stanton," *NovT* 38, no. 4 (1996): 397.

[59]Constantine Simonides, *Fac-Similes of Certain Portions of the Gospel of St. Matthew and of the Epistles of Ss. James & Jude Written on Papyrus in the First Century and Preserved in the Egyptian Museum of Joseph Mayer, Esq. Liverpool* (London: Trübner, 1862).

[60]Simonides also made the outlandish claim that around the year 1840 he had written Codex Sinaiticus himself. For more information on Simonides, see J. K. Elliott, *Codex Sinaiticus and the Simonides Affair: An Examination of the Nineteenth Century Claim That Codex Sinaiticus Was Not an Ancient Manuscript*, Analecta Vlatadon 33 (Thessaloniki: Patriarchal Institute for Patristic Studies, 1982).

the question: Will we fairly examine the evidence, or will we hold the party line at all costs?"[61]

These three cases show the extent of the problem. It is not just that the arguments discussed are wrong; it is that they are misleading. More than that, they are widespread. The result is that the Bible is discredited by the very people who think they are defending it. Their aim is certainly noble, but their knowledge of the subject is not. What celebrated classicist Richard Porson (1759–1808) said about the major Bible controversy of his own day applies here as well: "He, I apprehend, does the best service to truth, who hinders it from being supported by falsehood. To use a weak argument in behalf of a good cause, can only tend to infuse a suspicion of the cause itself into the minds of all who see the weakness of the argument."[62] What we hope to do in the present volume is offer reliable arguments that can be used on behalf of what we heartily agree is a good and noble cause.

RELIABLE ENOUGH FOR WHAT?

If defending the Bible's textual integrity is a noble cause, it remains to offer a working definition of what we mean when we say it is reliable. Simply put, we believe the textual evidence we have is sufficient to reconstruct, in most cases, what the authors of the New Testament wrote. We cannot do this with equal certainty in every case, of course, and the following chapters will discuss places where doubt remains significant. Nor do we think that God has preserved the original text of the New Testament equally well at every point in history or at every place in the world. Some times and places have had better manuscripts, editions, or translations at their disposal than others. This is true today, and it was true in the past. Nevertheless, we do think that even the most textually corrupted of our manuscripts and editions still convey the central truths of the Christian faith with clarity and power. In every age, God has given his people a text that is more than reliable enough to know the saving work he has accomplished through Jesus Christ.[63]

---

[61]Wallace, "7Q5: The Earliest NT Papyrus?," 180.

[62]Richard Porson, Letters to Mr. Archdeacon Travis, in Answer to His Defence of the Three Heavenly Witnesses, 1 John v.7 (London: T. & J. Egerton, 1790), xxv.

[63]In this we agree with influential English reformer William Whitaker, who could readily concede to his Roman Catholic opponents that "the fundamental points of the faith are preserved intact in this Latin edition, if not everywhere, yet in very many places." This despite his opponents' claims that the Latin text had final authority, a claim Whitaker vigorously opposed. See A Disputation on Holy Scripture: Against the Papists, trans. William Fitzgerald (Cambridge: Cambridge

To be sure, the incredible discoveries of the last several hundred years and the enormous labors of textual critics from past eras have done much to identify God's inspired words and to increase our confidence in their recovery. In textual criticism, as in so much else, we stand on the shoulders of giants. Perhaps it would be best, then, to let one of those giants clarify what we mean when we say the text of the New Testament is reliable. Johann Albrecht Bengel (1687–1752) was a student in Germany who became troubled by the variants he encountered in the New Testament. After a lifetime of study and the production of his own important edition of the Greek New Testament, he concluded that these variants shake no pillar of the Christian faith. He writes:

> God's testimony concerning his Son Jesus Christ is truly abundant and worthy of our respect: the main thrust of what God wants us to learn never hangs on one single particle or word. The faith of the saints, accordingly, rests on sure and true foundations. But in the same way that a grain of gold, no matter how small, is nonetheless gold, so the smallest portion of the word which comes from the mouth of God is divine. . . . For this reason, whoever holds in reverence whatever comes from the mouth of God will be bound, in consequence, to seek out the most accurate reading of the New Testament Scripture as well.[64]

We agree with Bengel both in his confidence in the text's ability to support our faith and in the need to continue studying that text to ferret out every "grain of gold" where doubts remain. Our text is more than adequate for what we need, yet the nature of God's Word requires us to seek out its original form to the full extent of our God-given abilities.

PREVIEW

This book is our attempt to bridge the gap between critical scholarship and those who address a popular audience. We do not write primarily for other textual critics; they will know most of what is presented here. Nor is our primary concern to answer Christianity's critics. Although some of that

---

University Press, 1849), 136. Whitaker's original Latin is found in *Disputatio de sacra scriptura contra huius temporis papistas* (Cambridge: Thomas, 1588), 96.

[64]J. A. Bengel, "Introductio ad universam lectionis varietatem dilucidandem," in *Novum Testamentum Graecum* (Tübingen: George Cott, 1734), 372. Translation by Peter M. Head and Philip Satterthwaite, *Method in New Testament Textual Criticism: 1700–1850* (New York: Peter Lang, forthcoming).

naturally occurs in what follows, others have already done that job ably.[65] Instead, we write primarily as a self-corrective to *Christian* speakers and writers. For them and for their audiences, we want to offer an up-to-date, responsible guide to understanding the remarkable history of the New Testament text.

Unfortunately, the task of compiling and presenting correct information is easier said than done. It would be nearly impossible for a single person to gain the required expertise in all the matters we wish to address in this book. For this reason, we have brought together a team of scholars who are willing to contribute to our cause. The contributors are all (relatively) early career academics and all actively involved in academic scholarship of the text of Christian documents. Most received academic training at a time when Bart Ehrman's work was making headlines and topping bestseller lists. Some of the contributors, in fact, were introduced to the discipline of textual criticism through his writing. Though our denominational affiliations and personal convictions differ, we all agree that the New Testament is crucial to the faith and practice of Christians and that our present Greek editions, imperfect as they are, are more than adequate for those needs.

We have organized the book into three broad categories. The first part deals generally with manuscripts, the second with the process of copying, and the third with translation, citation, and canonization. To begin at the beginning, Timothy N. Mitchell explores the starting point of the textual tradition, considering what the autographs were and how long they might have lasted. From there, Jacob W. Peterson plumbs how many manuscripts we have, explaining the difficulties involved in obtaining an accurate count as well as the distribution of manuscripts by content and by age. James B. Prothro picks up on this thread by looking at the widely used comparative argument that pits the vast number of our New Testament witnesses against the supposed pittance of other ancient literature. He details carefully how not to make this comparison and how it can still be of value. Moving on to the question of manuscript dates, Elijah Hixson shows how New Testament manuscripts are assigned a date and warns against falsely accepting our preferred

---

[65]On the issue of textual reliability, we recommend Komoszewski, Sawyer, and Wallace, *Reinventing Jesus*; Timothy Paul Jones, *Misquoting Truth: A Guide to the Fallacies of Bart Ehrman's Misquoting Jesus* (Downers Grove, IL: InterVarsity Press, 2007); and Andreas J. Köstenberger and Michael J. Kruger, *The Heresy of Orthodoxy: How Contemporary Culture's Fascination with Diversity Has Reshaped Our Understanding of Early Christianity* (Wheaton, IL: Crossway, 2010).

date. Having considered our earliest manuscripts, Gregory R. Lanier provides a fresh evaluation of our later manuscripts, showing why the common view that "later is worse" is a caricature that needs to be retired. The upshot is that the appeal to having so many manuscripts by Christian apologists is not entirely "an idle boast" simply because "those numerous MSS are not utilized [by them] to restore the original text," as some have claimed.[66]

Turning from the manuscripts themselves to those who copied them, Zachary J. Cole challenges the claim that our earliest scribes were some of the most careless and "wild." Peter Malik also looks at the work of scribes, particularly what followed their completion of manuscripts. He gives a fascinating tour of how scribal corrections can reveal much more to us than simple mistakes. Panning much wider across the tradition, S. Matthew Solomon provides the rare perspective of one who has collated all the Greek manuscript data for a particular New Testament book, offering insights from his rich study of Philemon. Next, Peter J. Gurry asks about how many variants there are and how much they matter. He qualifies the popular claim that our New Testament text is "99 percent certain" by showing how some variants in that 1 percent really do affect Christian theology and practice. Robert D. Marcello then looks at one type of variant—namely, theologically motivated changes or "orthodox corruptions," showing the validity of the category but raising doubts about how often such occurred.

The final section explores issues beyond the New Testament's Greek form. This includes patristic citations, the canon, and translations ancient and modern. Many popular works address patristic citations of the New Testament, but few address the patristic theology that enlightens their approach to such citation. Andrew Blaski explores the way early Fathers thought about textual criticism, how they dealt with textual variants, and how we can (and can't) use the Fathers in our own textual criticism. John D. Meade answers why the contents of our codices do not always line up with what became the New Testament canon and warns against looking for a canon in the codex. Although many popular-level treatments mention the early translations of the Greek New Testament into other languages, few such discussions are

---

[66]Maurice A. Robinson, "Appendix: The Case for Byzantine Priority," in *The New Testament in the Original Greek: Byzantine Textform*, ed. Maurice A. Robinson and William G. Pierpont (Southborough, MA: Chilton, 2005), 568. Bart Ehrman says, "94 percent of our surviving manuscripts were produced 700 years or more after the originals," in Ehrman and Wallace, "Textual Reliability," 19.

written by someone who works with ancient manuscripts written in those languages. Jeremiah Coogan addresses early Latin, Syriac, and Coptic manuscripts as well as early approaches to translation to assess the value these manuscripts have for recovering the Greek text. Finally, Edgar Battad Ebojo draws from his experience as a trained textual critic and a Bible translator in the field to explain how modern translators work with the textual evidence to produce accurate, reliable translations for Christians around the world.

WHAT THIS BOOK IS NOT

We have explained *what* this book is, and we have explained *why* this book is, but we still need to say a few words about what this book is *not*. It is not meant as a general introduction to New Testament textual criticism. Other books already cover that ground adequately, and readers seeking such an introduction are encouraged to turn to them.[67] This book is also limited to the New Testament. Although we believe these issues arise for the Old Testament as well, few of us are qualified to treat it with the attention it deserves. Indeed, we hope that this book might spur others to take up that task. This book is also not a defense of the New Testament's claims about Jesus, his resurrection, or the apostles' teaching. Rather, this book addresses the more fundamental question of whether we can know what those claims *are*. Finally, this book is not the last word on the subject. The information presented here will become outdated sooner or later, of that we can be sure. More manuscripts will be discovered, methods will be refined, and new editions will be published. That is all to the good of the discipline and, we expect, to the Christian faith as well.

CONCLUSION

It is our sincere hope that this book can help Christians who love the Bible but find the arguments floating around popular culture disturbing. To be sure, there are numerous textual problems that remain unsolved. There are cases where the Bible's text has been corrupted by friend and foe alike. These cases make textual criticism an important discipline for Christians to engage

---

[67]Such as Bruce M. Metzger and Bart D. Ehrman, *The Text of the New Testament: Its Transmission, Corruption, and Restoration*, 4th ed. (Oxford: Oxford University Press, 2005); D. C. Parker, *An Introduction to the New Testament Manuscripts and Their Texts* (Cambridge: Cambridge University Press, 2008).

in. If we believe that God inspired the particular words of Holy Scripture, then it is incumbent on us to do our best to identify those words so that we can preach, teach, treasure, and obey them.

Yet we also hope this book will be helpful to those who have been disturbed to find that not all the arguments they were given about the reliability of the New Testament text are themselves reliable. To them, we hope this book serves as an antidote to cynicism and skepticism. Finally, to our friends who engage in apologetic ministries, we want to express our appreciation for your important work. We hope this book will be a trusted guide and reliable resource as you go about your work. What Richard Porson aimed to do two hundred years ago we want to do again today: to offer a service to truth by keeping it from being supported by falsehood. With that aim in mind, we hope to clear away the myths and mistakes that have grown around the New Testament text and let it shine for all its worth.

Key Takeaways

▶ Information about the reliability of the New Testament in apologetic handbooks is often outdated.

▶ Statistical arguments for the reliability of the New Testament are often unqualified or factually incorrect.

▶ Christians need to avoid the tendency to "believe what we want to be true" about the early manuscripts of the New Testament.

▶ We should be careful not to appeal to exaggerated or sensationalistic claims.

CHAPTER TWO

MYTHS ABOUT AUTOGRAPHS

WHAT THEY WERE AND HOW LONG
THEY MAY HAVE SURVIVED

Timothy N. Mitchell

IN THE MIDST OF NEARLY EVERY discussion of the textual reliability
of the New Testament writings, references to the "autographs," or more
simply "originals," frequently surface. Noted New Testament scholar and
author Bart Ehrman does just this in his bestselling book *Misquoting Jesus:
Behind Who Changed the Bible and Why*, when he writes, "Rather than actually having the inspired words of the autographs (i.e., the originals) of the
Bible, what we have are the error-ridden copies of the autographs."[1] Ehrman
emphasizes the lost "originals" in response to evangelical doctrinal statements, which place God's act of inspiration on the autographs of the New
Testament and not on any one manuscript or manuscript tradition.[2]

The Chicago Statement on Biblical Inerrancy is representative of these
types of doctrinal statements. Formulated in 1978, the International Council
on Biblical Inerrancy held a series of meetings in Chicago, which resulted
in the formulation of the Chicago Statement on Biblical Inerrancy.[3] A central
proposition of this statement is found in article X: "We affirm that inspiration, strictly speaking, applies only to the autographic text of Scripture,

---

[1]Bart D. Ehrman, *Misquoting Jesus: The Story Behind Who Changed the Bible and Why* (New York: HarperCollins, 2005), 5.

[2]See the discussion in John J. Brogan, "Can I Have Your Autograph? Uses and Abuses of Textual Criticism in Formulating an Evangelical Doctrine of Scripture," in *Evangelicals and Scripture: Tradition, Authority and Hermeneutics*, ed. Vincent E. Bacote, Laura Miguelez Quay, and Dennis L. Okholm (Downers Grove, IL: IVP Academic, 2004), 93-111.

[3]Roger E. Olson, *The Westminster Handbook to Evangelical Theology* (Louisville: Westminster John Knox, 2004), 212-15.

which in the providence of God can be ascertained from available manuscripts with great accuracy. We further affirm that copies and translations of Scripture are the Word of God to the extent that they faithfully represent the original."[4]

With a desire to defend a high view of Scripture and in response to the criticisms of scholars such as Bart Ehrman, apologists and theologians often advance arguments advocating that the New Testament manuscript tradition faithfully represents the autographs. In his book *Why Trust the Bible?*, popular author Greg Gilbert writes, "It's more than a little likely that the originals, penned by the authors themselves, would have been preserved and used to make countless new copies over decades or even centuries before they were lost."[5] Gilbert is not the first to make such claims. As he mentions earlier in the chapter, he draws mainly on the work of Craig L. Blomberg of Denver Seminary.[6] While addressing Ehrman's arguments in *Misquoting Jesus*, Blomberg writes, "Second- and third-century New Testament manuscripts may well be copies of the very autographs, or at least copies of those copies."[7]

A similar but much more detailed form of this argument can be found in Craig Evans's article "How Long Were Late Antique Books in Use?"[8] In this study Evans, a professor at Houston Baptist University, contends that because of "the probability that the autographs and first copies circulated and were in use for one century or longer, there really is no justification for supposing that the text of the NT writings underwent major changes in the first and second centuries."[9] This argument is used prominently in the Faithlife documentary *Fragments of Truth*, hosted by Evans, which appeared in American theaters on April 24, 2018.[10]

---

[4]Ronald Youngblood, ed., *Evangelicals and Inerrancy: Selections from the Journal of the Evangelical Theological Society* (Nashville: Thomas Nelson, 1984), 233.

[5]Greg Gilbert, *Why Trust the Bible?* (Wheaton, IL: Crossway, 2015), 48.

[6]Gilbert writes, "For this chapter [chapter 3], I have relied especially on Craig L. Blomberg" (*Why Trust the Bible?*, 43n2).

[7]Craig Blomberg (*Can We Still Believe the Bible? An Evangelical Engagement with Contemporary Questions* [Grand Rapids: Brazos, 2014], 34) bases these statements on Craig Evans's research.

[8]Craig A. Evans, "How Long Were Late Antique Books in Use? Possible Implications for New Testament Textual Criticism," *BBR* 25, no. 1 (2015): 23-37.

[9]Evans, "How Long Were Late Antique Books in Use?," 37.

[10]The Faithlife website, in a description of its film *Fragments of Truth*, declares that Craig Evans "highlights groundbreaking new evidence, demonstrating that the case for the reliability of the New Testament manuscripts is stronger than ever" (https://faithlife.com/fragments-of-truth).

In contrast to the optimism of Evans, Matthew Larsen of Yale University has recently argued against the concept of a finished autograph altogether. Instead, Larsen contends, "We can no longer simply assume that a text was finished and published, especially texts that are not high literature. Unless we can determine that a text was finished, closed and published, which would exclude many of the texts now called the New Testament, traditionally conceived modes of textual criticism may be a square peg for a round hole."[11]

Larsen is arguing that the New Testament writings, more specifically the Gospels, were not the kind of writings that had originals.[12] Thus, Larsen's thesis challenges the very foundation of Evans's optimistic assertions by questioning whether such a thing as a finished autograph existed for the New Testament writings. The conclusions of Evans and Larsen will be addressed throughout the discussion in this chapter, and a rejoinder will follow in the concluding comments.

With all of this talk of autographs and originals, it is of first importance to define these terms. In order to define an *autograph*, it is paramount to understand the Greco-Roman milieu in which the New Testament writings were produced.

GRECO-ROMAN PUBLICATION

The term *book*, used in this chapter to describe the Greco-Roman medium for literature, refers to both the roll or bookroll (often referred to more popularly as a scroll) and the codex, the ancient predecessor to the modern book form. The bookroll was written entirely by hand in columns of continuous text on long sheets of parchment (prepared animal skin) or papyrus and then rolled up with the text on the inside. The codex, in contrast, was made from leaves of parchment or papyrus stacked together, folded down the center, and then stitched along the folded spine with the writing (also by hand) on both sides of the pages.[13]

---

[11]Matthew D. C. Larsen, "Accidental Publication, Unfinished Texts and the Traditional Goals of New Testament Textual Criticism," *JSNT* 39, no. 4 (2017): 379-80.

[12]Larsen, "Accidental Publication," 379n61. For the Gospels not being the kind of texts that had originals, Larsen cites David C. Parker, *The Living Text of the Gospels* (Cambridge: Cambridge University Press, 1997), 7.

[13]On this see William A. Johnson, "The Ancient Book," in *The Oxford Handbook of Papyrology*, ed. Roger S. Bagnall (Oxford: Oxford University Press, 2009), 256-77; Colin H. Roberts and T. C. Skeat, *The Birth of the Codex* (London: Oxford University Press, 1983); Eric G. Turner, *The Typology of the Early Codex* (Philadelphia: University of Pennsylvania Press, 1977), 43-53.

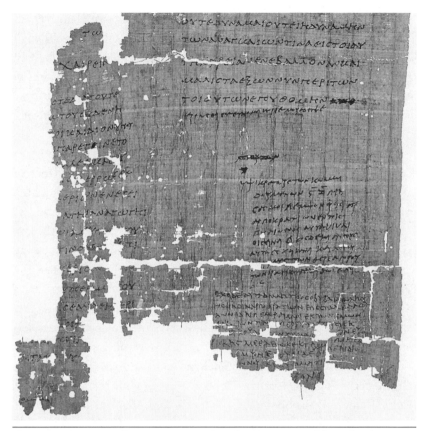

Figure 2.1. P.Oxy. 18.2192 shows postscripts in the right column in two different hands

Modern conceptions of publication, with its copyright laws, rules of plagiarism, the mass production of books by printing presses, and marketing through bookstores, did not exist in the Greco-Roman world. An adequate understanding of the transmission of the New Testament writings in the earliest stages must therefore incorporate the techniques of book production available to the authors of the New Testament and the early communities who copied, circulated, and read these books.[14]

---

[14]The literature on ancient publication is enormous. See Peter White, "Bookshops in the Literary Culture of Rome," in *Ancient Literacies: The Culture of Reading in Greece and Rome*, ed. William A. Johnson and Holt N. Parker (Oxford: Oxford University Press, 2009), 268-87; Jon W. Iddeng, "*Publica aut peri!* The Releasing and Distribution of Roman Books," SO 81 (2006): 58-84; Harry Y. Gamble, *Books and Readers in the Early Church: A History of Early Christian Texts* (New Haven, CT: Yale University Press, 1995), 83-93; Raymond J. Starr, "The Circulation of Literary Texts in the Roman World," *ClQ* 37, no. 1 (1987): 213-23; Kenneth Quinn, "The Poet and His Audience in the Augustan Age," in *ANRW* 30.1, ed. Wolfgang Haase (Berlin: de Gruyter, 1982), 75-180.

In the Roman world of the first and second centuries, two main avenues were used by authors to produce and distribute books of literature. Though likely small in scale, there was a commercial industry of distribution and circulation composed of copyists and artisan craftsmen who sold works of literature in bookshops and city marketplaces. Social contacts and networks of friends and associates who circulated books often played a more pivotal role in the dissemination of literature.[15]

The remains of a letter found in the Roman city of Oxyrhynchus dating to the second century illustrate both the commercial and private circulation of books in striking detail. P.Oxy. 18.2192 is a fragmentary papyrus in which the main body of text no longer survives.[16] All that remains are two postscripts written in a different hand from the text of the letter (see figure 2.1). The first postscript is written by the sender. It is in a different hand likely because the sender, though obviously literate, used a secretary to compose the letter. The first postscript reads, "Have a copy made of books six and seven of Hypsicrates' *Men Who Appear in Commodies* and send it to me. Harpocration says that Pollio has them among his books, and probably others may have them too. And he also has prose epitomes of Thersagorus's *Myths of Tragedy*."[17]

The other postscript is in a different hand and was made by the recipient of the letter, who then dispatched it back to the original sender in reply. It reads, "Demetrius the bookseller has them, according to Harpocration. I have ordered Apollonides to send to me some of my books—which ones you'll find out from him. And if you find any volumes of Seleucus's work on *Tenses/Metrics/Rhythms* that I don't own, have copies made and send them to me. Diodorus's circle also has some that I don't own." This fragmentary papyrus gives a glimpse into the circulation and copying of books among social networks. Here two circles of scholarly acquaintances are exchanging and borrowing books in order to procure copies of them. A bookseller is

---

[15]On the commercial book industry in Rome, see White, "Bookshops in the Literary Culture of Rome," 268-87. On the circulation of books through social networks, see Starr, "Circulation of Literary Texts in the Roman World," 213-23; Iddeng, *"Publica aut peri!,"* 58-84.

[16]Colin H. Roberts, "2192. Letter About Books," in *The Oxyrhynchus Papyri XVIII*, ed. Edgar Lobel, Colin H. Roberts, and E. P. Wegener, GRM 26 (London: Egypt Exploration Society, 1941), 150-52.

[17]The English translations of the postscripts are taken from William A. Johnson, *Readers and Reading Culture in the High Roman Empire: A Study of Elite Communities,* Classic Culture and Society (New York: Oxford University Press, 2010), 180-82. See also Rosalia Hatzilambrou, "Appendix: P.Oxy. XVIII 2192 Revisited," in *Oxyrhynchus: A City and Its Texts,* ed. Alan K. Bowman et al., GRM 93 (London: Egypt Exploration Society, 2007), 282-86.

briefly mentioned, but the circulation of literature occurs mainly by appro-
priating through acquaintances and making personal copies from these bor-
rowed books. Notice that there is no mention of legal or monetary restraints
preventing these scholars from simply transcribing a complete book in order
to possess a copy.

Both the commercial and private circulation of books can be seen in the
letters of Pliny the Younger (ca. AD 61–115), who was governor of Bithynia,
a region that is now part of Turkey.[18] He wrote to the famous Roman historian Suetonius, urging him to publish his work. In this letter Pliny declares
that he wants to hear that the "books of my dear Tranquillus are being copied
out, sold, and read" (*Ep.* 5.10).[19] Here each avenue of distribution is alluded
to. Copying appears to be a reference to the circulation of the work among
Suetonius's associates. Selling must be an allusion to book shops. Reading is
likely a reference to the reading out of the work in a communal setting.[20]

Along with mentioning "publication" more generally, Pliny gives one of
the most detailed descriptions from the Roman era of the editing and releasing process that a work of literature underwent.[21]

> In the first place, I revise my composition in private, next I read it to two or
> three friends, and then give it to others to annotate; if I doubt the justness of
> their corrections, I carefully weigh them again with a friend or two. Last of all
> I recite the piece to a numerous assembly, and this is the time, if you can be-
> lieve me, when I exercise the most rigid criticism; for my attention rises in
> proportion to my solicitude. (*Ep.* 7.17)

Pliny released draft versions to associates and friends in phases of editing,
sharing the edited piece with friends, rewriting in light of the feedback, and
reading out a final draft to a larger group of associates for comment.[22] During

---

[18]For a detailed study of Pliny's life and letters see A. N. Sherwin-White, *The Letters of Pliny: A Historical and Social Commentary* (Oxford: Clarendon, 1966); Eckard Lefèvre, *Vom Römertum zum Ästhetizismus: Studien zu den Briefen des jüngeren Plinius* (Berlin: de Gruyter, 2009).

[19]See also the commentary on this letter in Sherwin-White, *Letters of Pliny*, 337-38. English trans-
lations of Pliny's letters are taken from Pliny, *Letters*, trans. William Melmoth and W. M. L. Hutchinson, 2 vols., LCL (New York: Macmillan, 1915). For a chapter-length discussion of this epistle, see Sean Alexander Gurd, *Work in Progress: Literary Revision as Social Performance in Ancient Rome* (New York: Oxford University Press, 2012), 105-26.

[20]On communal reading (sometimes referred to as public reading), see Brian J. Wright, *Communal Reading in the Time of Jesus: A Window into Early Christian Reading Practices* (Minneapolis: Fortress, 2017).

[21]For a chronology of book 7, see Sherwin-White, *Letters of Pliny*, 37-38.

[22]Starr, "Circulation of Literary Texts," 213-14.

these rewriting stages Pliny assumed that the work in progress would not be circulated beyond this immediate group of friends.[23] Strict control over the draft version did not always occur, and unfinished writings would sometimes circulate before the author desired. Pliny again illustrates this in his letter to Octavius, warning him that portions of his works began to circulate without Octavius's consent (*Ep.* 2.10).

During the draft stages, Pliny often dictated his compositions and notes to a scribe. He wrote to his friend Fuscus that he would close the windows in his Tuscan villa and work on an initial draft, after which, he wrote, "I call my secretary, and, opening my shutters, I dictate to him what I have composed, after which I dismiss him for a little while, and then call him in again and again dismiss him" (*Ep.* 9.36).

Once Pliny was satisfied with the piece, he then "released" the work to be circulated by his associates and acquaintances, either by sending a copy to a dedicatee of the work, giving or lending a copy to a friend upon request, sending a copy to a bookseller, or depositing the book in a library. At this point of relinquishing control of the piece, Pliny signaled that the work was complete and ready to be copied and circulated.[24]

Writing a couple of decades earlier than Pliny, the epigrammatist Martial vividly describes Roman imperial life in the last decades of the first century and often alludes to the publication of his work throughout his epigrams. Martial gives insight into the problem of plagiarizing at the end of the first century. After accusing an anonymous person of plagiarizing his work, Martial warns them, "You must look for private, unpublished work," and this is because "a well-known book cannot change author," and then concludes by declaring that "whoever recites other men's productions and seeks fame thereby, ought to buy—not a book, but silence" (*Epigr.* 1.66).[25]

---

[23]Pliny, *Ep.* 2.10; 7.20; 8.4; Catullus, *Carminius* 35; Cicero, *Att.* 13.21a; 15.27. See especially Galen's comments concerning some of his medical treatises in *De libr. propr.* 19.9.

[24]Starr, "Circulation of Literary Texts," 214-15. See the discussion over the term εκδοσις in Iddeng, "*Publica aut Peri!,*" 64; Eric W. Scherbenske, *Canonizing Paul: Ancient Editorial Practice and the Corpus Paulinum* (Oxford: Oxford University Press, 2013), 17; B. A. Van Groningen, "ΕΚΔΟΣΙΣ," *Mnemosyne* 16 (1963): 1-17. Pliny mentions the releasing of his work throughout his epistles: *Ep.* 1.1, 1.2, 1.8; 3.10; 4.9; 5.12; 6.33; 7.2; 8.3, 8.7, 8.15, 8.19; 9.4, 9.13, 9.18. See Starr, "Circulation of Literary Texts," 215-16.

[25]Martial, *Epigrams, Volume I: Spectacles, Books 1-5*, trans. D. R. Shackleton Bailey, LCL 94 (Cambridge, MA: Harvard University Press, 1993), 87-89. Martial mentions publication in *Epig.* 1.2, 1.3, 1.16, 1.29, 1.66; 2.8, 2.20; 3.38; 5.16; 11.2, 11.3; 14.194 (Iddeng, "*Publica aut Peri!,*" 64n21). For a book-length treatment of Martial and his epigrams, see William Fitzgerald, *Martial: The World of the Epigram* (Chicago: University of Chicago Press, 2007).

Notice here what Martial is declaring: that once a work had been circulated in a community, that writing could not be significantly transformed, either by plagiarizing or altering its text, without these actions becoming widely known. Therefore, an aspiring author who wished to publish another author's work as their own would have to do so from writings not yet in circulation.

Writing at about the same time as Martial, prominent rhetorician Quintilian began to compile his magnum opus, *Institutes of Oratory*, which was a "lengthy dissertation on the finer points of raising a gentleman to the art."[26] In the preface to book one, while dedicating the work to his friend Marcellus Victorius, Quintilian indicates that some of the material in his *Institutes* might be found in an unedited form circulating under his name:

> Two books on the Art of Rhetoric are already circulating in my name, though they were never published by me nor prepared for this purpose. One is a two days' lecture course which was taken down by the slaves to whom the responsibility was given. The other lecture course, which spread over several days, was taken down by shorthand (as best they could) by some excellent young men who were nevertheless too fond of me, and therefore rashly honored it with publication and wide circulation. (*Inst. Or.* 1.prologue.7-8)[27]

Quintilian learned from his circle of acquaintances that his lectures had been copied and were circulating in an unedited form. He knew (or assumed) that Marcellus had read these transcribed lectures and was careful to indicate that the *Institutes* was a new work that supplanted these crude notes.

Several of his speeches had also been copied down by scribes who were expert in shorthand. These scribes made many blunders during the copying process and circulated these poorly transcribed copies for a profit (*Inst. Or.* 7.2.24). The circumstances in which his speeches were copied were different; they were specifically transcribed in order to be sold for a profit.[28] Though

---

[26]Johnson, *Readers and Reading Culture*, 26. Quintilian enjoyed unrivaled fame as an orator, as he was the first to be appointed Rome's official rhetorician and tutored Emperor Domitian's heirs (White, "Bookshops in the Literary Culture of Rome," 278). See also Martial's comments in *Epig.* 2.90.

[27]English translation from Quintilian, *The Orator's Education*, vol. 1, *Books 1-2*, trans. Donald A. Russell (Cambridge, MA: Harvard University Press, 2002), 55-57.

[28]Quintilian's fame created such a demand for his works that in the preface to the *Institutes*, Quintilian writes that the bookseller Tryphon has been pressuring him to finish the *Institutes* (White, "Bookshops in the Literary Culture of Rome," 278). Tryphon appears to have been the same bookdealer who sold Martial's works (*Ep.* 4.72.2; 13.3.4; Gamble, *Books and Readers*, 86).

Quintilian disliked these crudely copied lectures circulating under his name, he was powerless to control the dissemination and copying of them.

Another example comes from physician Galen of Pergamum, who flourished in the last half of the second century, practicing medicine for Rome's social elite and authoring hundreds of treatises, of which around 170 separate works survive.[29] Because many of these treatises circulated haphazardly and without Galen's consent, he wrote two works discussing the composition and publication of his many writings, *De libris propriis* (*On My Own Works*) and *De ordine librorum suorum* (*On the Order of My Own Books*).[30] In *De libris propriis*, Galen provides a unique glimpse into the circulation practices of Greco-Roman society when he complains, "My books have been subject to all sorts of mutilations, whereby people in different countries publish different texts under their own names, with all sorts of cuts, additions, and alterations" (*De libr. propr.* 19.9).

Galen writes that the corruptions of his books occurred when the pupils died and the works were stolen and began to circulate under the names of these plagiarizers. Fortunately, Galen writes, "All these were eventually caught, and many of those who then recovered the works affixed my name to them. They then discovered discrepancies between these and copies in the possession of other individuals, and so sent them to me with the request that I correct them" (*De libr. propr.* 19.10). Apparently, many of Galen's compositions were not meant to circulate as formal works of literature with his name affixed. Instead they were merely Galen's unedited lecture notes. Once these transcripts were given to his students, however, he lost control over their fate, and these writings were then misappropriated and altered by his students' successors.[31]

---

[29]For a detailed study of Galen's life and works, see Susan P. Mattern, *Galen and the Rhetoric of Healing* (Baltimore: Johns Hopkins University Press, 2008). For a full list of Galen's works, see Gerhard Fichtner, *Corpus Galenicum: Bibliographie der galenischen und pseudogalenischen Werke* (Berlin: Berlin-Brandenburgische Akademie der Wissenschaften, 2012). For a discussion on the issues surrounding the date of Galen's death, see Vivian Nutton, "Galen *ad multos annos*," *Dynamis* 15 (1995): 25–39.

[30]Mattern, *Galen and the Rhetoric of Healing*, 12. English translations of Galen are taken from Galen, *Selected Works*, trans. P. N. Singer (Oxford: Oxford University Press, 1997).

[31]See the discussion on Galen's preference for personal instruction and its relation to written texts in Gamble, *Books and Readers*, 30-32; Richard Bauckham, *Jesus and the Eyewitnesses: The Gospels as Eyewitness Testimony*, 2nd ed. (Grand Rapids: Eerdmans, 2017), 21-30. With regard to several of his commentaries on the writings of various philosophers and physicians, Galen wrote, "None of these commentaries was intended for publication" (*De libr. propr.* 19.42-43).

Galen gives a vivid account of a public presentation he facilitated concerning several ancient medical writers. The presentation escalated into a debate between Galen and a follower of Martialius (a contemporary physician). Galen's critical response to the follower of Martialius resulted in admiration from the crowd. As a consequence, Galen writes, a friend begged him to dictate his speech to a scribe trained in shorthand. Galen agreed, and after returning to Rome years later, he discovered that it "was now in the possession of a large number of people" (*De libr. propr.* 19.14-15). Galen was complaining because his lecture notes had circulated and were read more broadly than he had intended. As a result, he vowed never to give a public demonstration for fear that his words would be transcribed and misused (*De libr. propr.* 19.15). He was completely at the mercy of this community to obey his instructions not to circulate a particular writing (*De libr. propr.* 19.42-43).

The sources above reveal that publication, or more accurately, the releasing and circulation of books, occurred only after the author edited and rewrote several times over. It was often a community effort that involved some of the author's closest associates, who gave constructive criticism, suggested changes, and at times used the services of a scribe or secretary to copy down dictation. Once the document was complete, the author signaled to associates that the piece was finished by releasing the work to be copied and circulated through networks of friends and acquaintances, sending the work to a dedicatee, reciting the piece to the community, or by sending a copy to a bookseller or library. Therefore, the concept of "author" can include more than just a single person and more likely included scribes, friends, and others who contributed to the composition. Though these authors used their associates, literate slaves, and scribes to aid in the editing process, the writing was still considered to be the author's own work, a product of his or her creative mind.

In contrast to this view, Matthew Larsen contends that writings such as Galen's accidentally published lecture notes would be better described as a "'living' textual tradition, rather than as a final and fixed book with clean lines of progression that lead back to a pure originary moment."[32] Thus, it is paramount that this "originary moment," or rather, "autograph," be properly understood and defined.

---

[32]Larsen, "Accidental Publication," 375.

A DEFINITION OF *AUTOGRAPH*

Doctrinal statements, apologists, and theologians are typically careful to distinguish between the authorial copies of the New Testament books and the *subsequent* various textual forms and alterations introduced throughout their transmission history. On the other hand, these same theologians and doctrinal statements are not always as clear in distinguishing between the sources used by the New Testament authors, the various stages of composition, and the final form these writings took *before* being released for dispatching to their intended recipients (the Epistles), or for circulation and copying (Gospels, Acts, Revelation).[33]

The word *autograph* means simply "something written or made with one's own hand."[34] Therefore, strictly speaking, included in this definition are any possible early versions and rewritings of a composition while under the control of the author. These draft copies would presumably be in a state of textual fluidity because the author is in the process of composing and editing the document.

Multiple autographs of a petition to Egyptian prefect Publius Ostorius Scapula (ca. AD 3–10/11) illustrate the textual instability of an autographic text.[35] Though the topic at hand concerns literary compositions, P.Mich.inv. 1436 and P.Mich.inv. 1440 provide a rare glimpse of multiple draft copies of the same work (see figs 2.2 and 2.3).[36] Although both papyri were written by the same person, inv. 1436 contains several alterations that favor its identification as the first draft of inv. 1440. Though the text of both papyri is fragmented, lines 2-10 of inv. 1436 are repeated in lines 11-17 of inv. 1440. The scribe revised the text

---

[33]For an exception that carefully considers where the autographic text of the New Testament is found, see P. J. Williams, "Ehrman's Equivocation and the Inerrancy of the Original Text," in *The Enduring Authority of the Christian Scriptures*, ed. D. A. Carson (Grand Rapids: Eerdmans, 2016), 389-406.

[34]"Autograph (n.)," *Merriam-Webster*, www.merriam-webster.com/dictionary/autograph (accessed May 17, 2018).

[35]This discussion of P.Mich.inv. 1436 and P.Mich.inv. 1440 is adapted from Timothy N. Mitchell, "What Are the NT Autographs? An Examination of the Doctrine of Inspiration and Inerrancy in Light of Greco-Roman Publication," *JETS* 59, no. 2 (2016): 302-3. Used with permission.

[36]Ann Ellis Hanson, "Two Copies of a Petition to the Prefect," *ZPE* 47 (1982): 233-43; Hanson, "The Archive of Isidoros of Psophthis and P. Ostorius Scapula, Praefectus Aegypti," *BASP* 21 (1984): 81-83. The fragments of "autographs" discovered in the ancient trash mounds of Oxyrhynchus have largely consisted of documentary papyri; there are many draft versions of "petitions, letters, and accounts" and only a few examples of draft versions of literary papyri (Gurd, *Work in Progress*, 132-33n44). P.Mich.inv. 1436 and P.Mich.inv. 1440 are therefore classified as "documentary" texts rather than strictly "literary" texts.

Figure 2.2. P.Mich.inv. 1436 showing authorial changes

of inv. 1436 above lines 6 and 8, and marked line 9 for deletion; despite this, these alterations were not integrated into the text of inv. 1440.[37]

These two papyri reveal that at the level of "autograph" the author's text can be fluid. The difficulty in this case is that it is impossible to know the completed form of the petition with certainty. This uncertainty would change, of course, if a copy of this petition were known to have been dispatched and was received by the prefect Scapula. Even if a copy were inadvertently released before the author was satisfied with its form, the composition would still be effectively completed since then the author would lose any control over the fate of the document at that point.

---

[37]Hanson, "Two Copies," 233.

With regard to Galen's lecture notes, once they were given over to his students, he lost control over their fate. He could no longer affect the textual form of these writings in the same way without the consent of the students who possessed them. The same is true of the writings of Quintilian; once his students transcribed his lectures and released them for circulation, Quintilian could no longer control the shape of the text as he could before. In both instances, Galen and Quintilian relied on the participation of the community. With Galen's writings, his followers and students informed him of the altered and plagiarized writings, then retrieved and returned them so Galen could edit them (*De libr. propr.* 19.10). Quintilian required the cooperation of Victorius, the dedicatee of his *Institutes of Oratory*, to disregard the other crudely transcribed lectures that were in circulation (*Inst. Or.* 1.prologue.7-8).

This loss of control is important because, in contrast to the views of Larsen, the point at which a document was released beyond the immediate

Figure 2.3. P.Mich.inv. 1440 showing that authorial changes in P.Mich.inv. 1436 were not incorporated into the text of this copy of the petition

control of the author, whether accidentally or intentionally, effectively ended the draft and rewriting stages of the document. This can be seen in the warnings of Pliny to Octavius that his writings were already circulating against his desire (*Ep.* 2.10), in the frustrations of Galen that his writings were widely circulating to unwanted readers (*De libr. propr.* 19.14-15), in Quintilian's explanations of multiple versions of his lectures (*Inst. Or.* 1.prologue.7-8), and in the accusations of Martial to the plagiarizer of his epigrams (*Epigr.* 1.66). The text was fluid in some respects, as Larsen contends, but the authors (in this case Martial, Quintilian, Galen, and Octavius) clearly distinguished between these altered texts and their initially released versions. Even the followers and students of Galen made distinctions between the composing of these documents by Galen and the alterations and mutilations made to them after their release and circulation (*De libr. propr.* 19.14-15).

In light of this, the New Testament writings can be said to be "completed" once they were released by the authors and began to circulate as works of literature. These documents were no longer under the control of their authors and would have circulated as distinct writings. Therefore, in reference to the New Testament, the "autograph," as it is discussed by apologists, theologians, and doctrinal statements, is best defined as the completed authorial work that was released by the author for circulation and copying, and this can and should be distinguished from earlier draft versions or layers of composition.[38]

AUTHOR'S COPIES

Once a New Testament writing was completed and released for circulation, there was a possibility that further copies would be made under the control of the author or authors. Strictly speaking, these copies would also be considered "autographs," for they would be produced by the hand of the author, or at least under the author's direction.[39] The practice of retaining a copy of a writing once published is sometimes referenced by Greco-Roman authors.[40] Though multiple copies of a work may have been produced by the author before or after circulation, as will be seen below, this was not always the case.

---

[38]This definition is adapted from Mitchell, "What Are the NT Autographs?," 306.

[39]Evans, "How Long Were Late Antique Books in Use?," 33.

[40]Roman rhetorician and statesman Cicero (106–43 BC) often retained a copy of his own compositions once they were released for circulation (*Att.* 12.6a; 13.21a; Mitchell, "What Are the NT Autographs?," 295).

The fourfold Gospel. Once completed, a duplicate of a composition might be retained in the personal collection of the author or the author's community. With regard to the Gospels Matthew, Mark, Luke, and John, this is one possibility. The Shepherd of Hermas, likely composed in Rome sometime in the early to mid-second century, may help to illustrate the circumstances surrounding the publication of each of the four Gospels and perhaps Revelation.[41] At one point the narrative features an "elderly woman" (who represents the church) instructing Hermas to distribute copies of the message contained in a "little book" he had been given through very specific means:

> Therefore you will write two little books, and you will send one to Clement and one to Grapte. Then Clement will send it to the cities abroad, because that is his job. But Grapte will instruct the widows and orphans. But you yourself will read it to this city, along with the elders who preside over the Church"(Shepherd of Hermas Vision 2.4).[42]

In this reference, three copies of the "little book" were produced by Hermas. A copy was dispatched to Clement, who then made duplicates to be distributed to various cities. A second copy was sent to Grapte to use for instructing widows and orphans. A third copy was retained by Hermas in order to read communally in "this city" (possibly a reference to Rome). Therefore, it is possible—though we do not know—that multiple copies of the Gospels were made by their authors in order to distribute them through the Christian communities.

In some circumstances, however, an author may not have produced duplicates of a work. It was common practice in the Greco-Roman world for an author to dedicate a composition to a superior, a patron, or a friend.[43] Galen shares a circumstance in which he composed several works dedicated to a friend, Boethus (*De libr. propr.* 19.16). This friend left Rome for Syria with these writings in his possession, apparently before Galen felt they were finalized. It was some time later, after Boethus's death, that Galen was able to reacquire these books and complete them.[44]

[41]Bruce M. Metzger, *The Canon of the New Testament: Its Origin, Development, and Significance* (Oxford: Oxford University Press, 1987), 63-65; Michael W. Holmes, ed., *The Apostolic Fathers: Greek Texts and English Translations*, 3rd ed. (Grand Rapids: Baker Academic, 2007), 442-47; Charles E. Hill, *Who Chose the Gospels? Probing the Great Gospel Conspiracy* (New York: Oxford University Press, 2010), 97-98.
[42]Holmes, *Apostolic Fathers*, 468-69.
[43]Iddeng, *"Publica aut Peri!,"* 66, 70; Gamble, *Books and Readers*, 84-85; Starr, "Circulation of Literary Texts in the Roman World," 214-25.
[44]Johnson, *Readers and Reading Culture*, 87.

In another work, Galen laments the loss of an entire collection of his books, which were kept in storehouses in Rome. A fire on the Sacred Way destroyed several libraries, archives, and book collections along with Galen's own. He writes that he had made duplicates of some of his compositions, which he had sent to friends, but others were not so fortunate. Apparently, he had lost several of his own writings, of which he possessed only a single copy (*De indolentia* 20-22).[45]

Paul's letters. In the time of Paul in the first century, it was common practice for a copy to be made of a letter before it was dispatched and retained in the sender's archives.[46] From these archived copies, if the author was famous or influential, a collection of letters might be gathered, edited, and circulated as a literary unit. With regard to his collection of letters, Pliny the Younger writes to Septicus, "You have frequently pressed me to make a select collection of my Letters (if there be any which show some literary finish) and give them to the public. I have accordingly done so; not indeed in their proper order of time, for I was not compiling a history; but just as they presented themselves to my hands. Farewell" (*Ep.* 1.1). The first nine books of letters, as *Epistle* 1.1 indicates, Pliny collected and circulated on his own initiative, whereas the final book of correspondence between Pliny and Emperor Trajan was likely published posthumously.[47] Pliny illustrates how Paul's epistles could have been gathered together and circulated as a collection.

Although Evans writes, "In late antiquity, no one produced a single exemplar of a work and then circulated it," it is quite possible that Paul did not have copies of his more personal letters, such as those to Timothy and Titus.[48] This occurred in the case of Cicero's (106–43 BC) personal correspondence with his longtime friend Atticus. Apparently these letters were collected from the family archives of Atticus and published around a hundred years after Cicero's death. Cicero's other letters had already been collected from

---

[45]For an English translation of Galen's *De indolentia*, see Clare K. Rothschild and Trevor W. Thompson, "Galen: 'On the Avoidance of Grief,'" *EC* 2, no. 1 (2011): 110-29. See also Galen's references to books and libraries in his *De indolentia*, in Matthew C. Nicholls, "Galen and Libraries in the *Peri Alupias*," *JRS* 101 (2011): 123-42.

[46]In a letter to his friend D. Paeto, Cicero mentions that he made a copy in his notebook before dispatching the letter (*Fam.* 9.26; see also *Att.* 13.6, *Fam.* 7.25; 9.12).

[47]Hans-Josef Klauck, *Ancient Letters and the New Testament: A Guide to Context and Exegesis*, trans. Daniel P. Bailey (Waco, TX: Baylor University Press, 2006), 146. At least some of Paul's epistles circulated as a collection in the first century, for the author of 2 Peter makes reference to a collection of Paul's epistles that were already considered Scripture (2 Pet 3:15-16).

[48]Evans, "How Long Were Late Antique Books in Use?," 33.

Cicero's personal copies and published in books by his secretary Tiro.[49] Thus, it cannot be said for certain that there were multiple autographic copies of every New Testament book produced by the authors.

THE LONGEVITY OF THE AUTOGRAPHS

Having considered the question of what the autographs were, we turn now to consider how long they may have been in use. George Houston, in his work *Inside Roman Libraries*, surveys book collections in antiquity and analyzes their contents, the date of composition, and the rough date of the discarding of the collection or the last known period of use. From these data Houston concludes that the useful life of papyrus bookrolls was on average 100 to 125 years and in extreme cases 300 to 500 years.[50] Using Houston's research as a foundation, Craig Evans argues that the New Testament autographs were likely in use into the second and third centuries.[51] From this, he suggests that the autographs probably had a controlling influence on the textual transmission of the New Testament. To properly evaluate this claim, we should consider both the longevity and the loss of ancient manuscripts.

Longevity of ancient manuscripts. In the ancient Roman city of Oxyrhynchus in Egypt (modern el-Behnesa), thousands of fragments of papyri were recovered in the late nineteenth and early twentieth centuries. Some of these excavations were headed up by Bernard Grenfell and Arthur Hunt, and the findings were published in the famous series the Oxyrhynchus Papyri.[52] During their excavation of the trash mounds and in later discoveries made by others, a few concentrations of documents were revealed that probably represented several distinct collections.[53] Though Grenfell and Hunt did not reveal how they ascertained the date these collections were discarded, the paleographical dating of the bookrolls gives a general period of time these books were used. This period is roughly from 75 to 250 years.[54]

---

[49]Klauck, *Ancient Letters*, 157-58.

[50]George W. Houston, *Inside Roman Libraries: Book Collections and Their Management in Antiquity* (Chapel Hill: University of North Carolina Press, 2014), 257.

[51]Evans, "How Long Were Late Antique Books in Use?," 30. Evans makes similar statements in the Faithlife documentary *Fragments of Truth*.

[52]See Alan K. Bowman et al., eds., *Oxyrhynchus: A City and Its Texts*, GRM 93 (London: Egypt Exploration Society, 2007).

[53]Houston, *Inside Roman Libraries*, 130.

[54]Grenfell and Hunt do not give a reason why they state that the first book collection they discovered was discarded in the third century. Houston presumes that "they found the materials within a stratum of third-century documents" (*Inside Roman Libraries*, 142n54). Houston tabulates these collections and the useful life of the books (*Inside Roman Libraries*, 175).

Houston also examined the remains of the extensive library found in the Villa of the Papyri in the Roman city of Herculaneum, which was destroyed during the eruption of Vesuvius in AD 79.[55] Many papyrus bookrolls were preserved by carbonization in the intense heat. Judging by the paleographical date of when the books were copied and when they were destroyed by the eruption, a general useful date for these rolls ranges from 120 to 350 years.[56] Taking the data from these two studies, Houston, as previously mentioned, calculated the average lifespan of the papyrus bookroll at around 100 to 125 years and in extreme cases 300 to 500 years.

Evidence from the Caesarean library tentatively supports Houston's findings. Living in Bethlehem in the later part of the fourth century, Jerome wrote that the successors of Eusebius of Caesarea labored to copy the library's aging and damaged papyrus bookrolls onto parchment codices. Jerome writes, "Euzoius was educated as a young man at Caesarea along with Gregory, the bishop of Nazianzus, under the rhetor Thespesius and later became bishop of the same city; with very great toil he attempted to restore on parchment the library of Origen and Pamphilus that had been damaged" (*Vir. ill.* 113).[57] Some of these manuscripts that were restored in the middle of the fourth century, if they were from Origen's original collection, would have been nearly 150 to 200 years old. If some of these damaged bookrolls were from the hand of Pamphilus or from his collection, the bookrolls would have been 75 to 100 years old at the time of their replacement by Euzoius.[58] At least in this instance, when a book collection was kept in a large library, the useful life of a papyrus bookroll lasted from 75 to 200 years. This is in general agreement with Houston's study.

Loss due to climate, persecution, and so on. Though Houston's findings reveal a long useful life for bookrolls, these averages likely represent best-case scenarios. Papyrus did not fare as well in the more humid environments of the rest of the Mediterranean world. Galen expressed some exasperation at his attempt to make personal copies of important books stored in the libraries on the Palatine in Rome. Galen writes, "These (books), then, did not cause me a small pain when copying them. As it is, the papyri are completely

---

[55]Houston, *Inside Roman Libraries*, 87.
[56]Houston, *Inside Roman Libraries*, 120-21.
[57]English translation from Andrew James Carriker, *The Library of Eusebius of Caesarea*, VCSup 67 (Leiden: Brill, 2003), 23n70.
[58]Carriker, *Library of Eusebius of Caesarea*, 25.

useless, not even able to be un-rolled because they have been glued together by decomposition, since the region is both marshy and low-lying, and, during the summer, it is stifling" (*De indolentia* 19).[59]

It is apparent that papyrus bookrolls did not survive well in the humid environment of Rome. Even in the case of the Caesarean library mentioned above, these century-or-more-old books that were still in the library were damaged and in need of replacement. There is no telling how long these books were in this state of disrepair before Euzoius set about making replacements.

Along with wear and tear, natural disasters often proved to be formidable to book collections and libraries. In AD 192, a terrible fire broke out in Rome, which destroyed many storehouses, libraries, and book collections.[60] Galen incurred terrible losses to his collection of books and store of medicines.[61] The eruption of Vesuvius in AD 79 destroyed both Pompeii and Herculaneum in Italy. As was discussed above, this disaster destroyed an extensive collection of books in the Villa of the Papyri in Herculaneum.[62]

Imperial persecution also played a role in the destruction and banning of books, and not just Christian books. The great poet Ovid, who flourished during the reign of Emperor Augustus, was exiled to Tomis on the Black Sea (modern Constanta, Romania), and his books were banned from imperial libraries. He even composed a poem that listed the libraries that banned his works (*Tristia* 3.1.65-72).[63] In the beginning of the first century AD, Titus Labienus's books were burned by a senatorial decree, and the instigator of this decree eventually had his own books burned as well. This practice of book burning culminated in the edict of Diocletian in AD 303 "ordering the confiscation and burning of Christian books."[64]

---

[59]English translation from Rothschild and Thompson, "Galen: 'On the Avoidance of Grief,'" 116.

[60]Dio (*Hist. rom.* 73.24.1-3) and Herodian (*Hist. rom.* 1.14.3-6) also mention this great fire. See also Nicholls, "Galen and Libraries in the *Peri Alupias*," 123-24.

[61]Rothschild and Thompson, "Galen: 'On the Avoidance of Grief,'" 110-11.

[62]See chap. 3 of Houston, *Inside Roman Libraries*, 87-129.

[63]Peter Green, ed., *Ovid, the Poems of Exile: Tristia and the Black Sea Letters* (Berkeley: University of California Press, 2005), xxv, 205; Starr, "Circulation of Literary Texts," 219.

[64]Gamble, *Books and Readers*, 150. There is a long history of book burning in the Roman imperial age; on this, see Joseph A. Howley, "Book-Burning and the Uses of Writing in Ancient Rome: Destructive Practice Between Literature and Document," *JRS* 107 (2017): 213-36. For the incident of Labienus, see 217. See Eusebius's eyewitness testimony to the burning of Christian books in his *Hist. eccl.* 8.2.

When considering the localized persecutions of Christians early on in the first and second centuries, it is no stretch of the imagination to visualize the confiscation, loss, or even destruction of the "autographs and first copies" of the New Testament writings.[65] One must also remember that many of these New Testament manuscripts discovered in the sands of Egypt were cast aside in the trash heaps of Oxyrhynchus, some of them torn to shreds before doing so.[66] This reveals that Christians sometimes threw away biblical manuscripts after a period of use, likely after being replaced with a new copy, rather than being retained for hundreds of years. This is because it was the *text* of the autographs that was important. Once a good copy of the text was produced, the physical autograph could then be discarded.

CONCLUSION

This chapter has given us reason to doubt that the autographs of the New Testament lasted hundreds of years. This obviously challenges Evans's further claim that these long-lasting autographs of, say, Matthew "would have exerted influence on the text of Matthew."[67] Though Evans is confident of the autographs' influence over the transmission of the New Testament writings, it is further evident from the papyri that closeness in proximity to the physical autographs does not necessitate a reliable or more accurately copied text.

A fragment of Julius Africanus's (AD 160–240) work illustrates this point. P.Oxy. 3.412 is a well-known bookroll portion containing Africanus's encyclopedic piece titled *Kestoi*. This work was part of the Oxyrhynchus book collections examined by Houston.[68] Though a good-quality copy of Africanus's work, it was not valued for long by its owners. The work had to be written no later than the AD 220s, and the roll was reused on the reverse for a will dated to AD 275–276. Thus this roll was used for fifty years at most before the material was reused for a will.[69] Though this copy was produced within twenty

---

[65]Evans, "How Long Were Late Antique Books in Use?," 30.

[66]On this phenomena see AnneMarie Luijendijk, "Sacred Scriptures as Trash: Biblical Papyri from Oxyrhynchus," *VC* 64, no. 3 (2010): 217-54. For a list of discarded Christian manuscripts, see the appendix in Luijendijk, "Sacred Scriptures as Trash," 250-54.

[67]Evans, "How Long Were Late Antique Books in Use?," 30.

[68]Bernard P. Grenfell and Arthur S. Hunt, "412. Julius Africanus, Κεστοί," in *The Oxyrhynchus Papyri III*, ed. Grenfell and Hunt, GRM 5 (London: Egypt Exploration Fund, 1903), 36-41; Houston, *Inside Roman Libraries*, 156-58.

[69]Grenfell and Hunt, "412. Julius Africanus, Κεστοί," 36; Houston, *Inside Roman Libraries*, 157.

years or less of the time Africanus's *Kestoi* was first written, "several lines of the incantation especially are clearly corrupt, and one of them is incomplete."[70]

Therefore, both of Evans's assertions—that the autographs may have lasted hundreds of years and that they probably stabilized the textual transmission—fail to take the contrary evidence into consideration. Along these same lines, his argument risks conflating the importance of the autographs as physical artifacts and the *text* of these autographs. In reality, a later manuscript could faithfully reproduce the text of the autograph despite being removed by hundreds of years in time from the physical autograph.[71] Likewise, an earlier manuscript could poorly reproduce the text of the physical autograph, due to scribal error and other issues, despite being directly copied from or close in time to the physical autograph (as noted above with P.Oxy. 3.412). For these reasons, we should not follow Evans's argument for trusting the stable transmission of the New Testament text. Reasons for trusting it do exist, but they lie elsewhere, as detailed in other chapters.

Quite different from Evans's claims are Larsen's, which blur the lines between the composition of the autographs by the author and the alterations made by readers and scribes after the New Testament writings began to circulate. As discussed above, the authors and readers of these accidentally published works still clearly distinguished between the author's version and the alterations and plagiarizing of subsequent versions. In the case of the Gospels themselves, the earliest known reference to both Mark and Matthew, made by Papias of Hierapolis (late first to early second century), views these Gospels as distinct texts rather than "an open textual tradition" (Eusebius, *Hist. eccl.* 3.39.15-16).[72]

From this survey of publication in the Greco-Roman world, then, we should conclude that when the New Testament writings began to circulate is also when the text of these documents was finalized. From that point on, there exists a stream of copying and distribution that is distinguishable from the earlier stages of composition.

---

[70]Grenfell and Hunt, "412. Julius Africanus, Κεστοί," 37.
[71]On this see chapter six below.
[72]Larsen, "Accidental Publication," 379.

Key Takeaways

▶ For the New Testament, the autographs should be conceived of as the completed authorial work that was released by the author for circulation and copying, not earlier draft versions or layers of composition.

▶ Once a work had been circulated in a community, that writing could not be significantly transformed, either by plagiarizing or altering its text, without these actions becoming known.

▶ Once a New Testament writing was completed and released for circulation, there may have been a number of copies made under the control of the author or authors.

▶ It is unlikely that the New Testament autographs still existed and influenced the text by the time of our earliest copies. Even if they did, this alone would not guarantee that the existing manuscripts are reliable.

CHAPTER THREE

MATH MYTHS

HOW MANY MANUSCRIPTS WE HAVE AND WHY MORE ISN'T ALWAYS BETTER

Jacob W. Peterson

NUMBERS ARE BOTH VITAL AND PRONE to manipulation. They are meaningful and trivial, concrete and pliable. Without reliable numbers, humankind never could have reached the moon. Without malleable numbers, companies such as Coca-Cola never could have sold the drink Enviga on the premise it contained "negative calories," causing the consumer to lose weight just by drinking it.[1]

When it comes to the number of manuscripts, the New Testament documents are in rarefied company among the wider world of classical authors. As a general rule there are more of them, many are earlier, and they tend to be more complete. But the bulk, while more complete, are not early. The early ones are typically fragmentary and few in number. What should we make of the numbers? Are they meaningful? Are the numbers useful?

Authors who appeal to the number of New Testament manuscripts often get into trouble because of a lack of nuance or by overstating what the numbers actually mean and represent. Variations of the following quote appear repeatedly in the popular literature: "Two factors are most important in determining the reliability of a historical document: the number of manuscript copies in existence, and the time between when it was first written

---

[1]Coca-Cola and its partners were ultimately taken to court and, as a result of a 2009 decision, had to change their marketing and pay fines. See, for example, the settlement from New Jersey: State of New Jersey Department of Law and Public Safety Division of Consumer Affairs, "Assurance of Voluntary Compliance/Discontinuance Between the State of New Jersey and the Coca-Cola Company, Nestle USA Inc. and Beverage Partners Worldwide North America," February 26, 2009, www.nj.gov/oag/newsreleases09/022609-ENVIGA-AVC-agreement.pdf.

and the oldest existing copy."[2] These authors go on to cite the "24000+" manuscripts of the New Testament as sure proof of its reliability.

Aside from the conflation of *textual* reliability with *historical* reliability, such claims commit the logical fallacy of assuming that a larger number and an earlier date necessarily equate to more reliability. The lack of qualification for the manuscript counts is a recurring issue as well. The problem typically occurs when the New Testament is compared to other classical works with respect to the number of manuscripts and the date of the earliest copy. For the New Testament, numbers from five thousand to twenty-five thousand are given, depending on what the author includes, and a date in the early second century is reported. This is usually followed by a summary, such as that of Norm Geisler: "No other book is even a close second to the Bible on either the *number* or early dating of the copies."[3]

The problem is that, even when the number and dates of the manuscripts are right, the claims typically lack crucial context about the chronological distribution of the manuscripts, the fragmentary nature of the earliest manuscripts, and the unequal representation of some parts of the New Testament in the manuscripts. The goal of this chapter is to provide some of that much-needed context. In doing so, we will look more closely at the number of New Testament manuscripts and the significance attached to that number. First, we will tackle the issue of how manuscripts are counted and who counts them. This is followed by a discussion of all the factors that make counting manuscripts difficult. From there, we will discuss the increasing number of manuscripts by considering what it means for a manuscript to be discovered, how they are discovered, what kinds are being found, and how many may still be out there. The chapter will then shift to discussing the problems associated with talking about the number of manuscripts. In particular, we will uncover why simply counting them is not enough and how the manuscripts are distributed by age, content, and size. The chapter will conclude with a practical turn as we deal with how to talk about the manuscript witness to the New Testament text.

---

[2]Josh McDowell and Bob Hostetler, *Don't Check Your Brains at the Door* (Nashville: Thomas Nelson, 2011). This is not restricted to print literature but occurs online as well; for example, Matt Slick, "Manuscript Evidence for Superior New Testament Reliability," CARM: Christian Apologetics & Research Ministry, December 10, 2008, https://carm.org/manuscript-evidence.

[3]Norman L. Geisler, *Christian Apologetics*, 2nd ed. (Grand Rapids: Baker Academic, 2013), 345. For more on the comparison to other classical works, see chapter four in this volume.

COUNTING MANUSCRIPTS

Making sense of the number of manuscripts first requires understanding how manuscripts are categorized and counted, and who does the counting.

Categories of manuscripts. Most New Testament students are generally familiar with the four categories of manuscripts: papyri, majuscules, minuscules, and lectionaries.[4] These categories are part of the Gregory-Aland (GA) system, devised by Caspar René Gregory and continued by Kurt Aland. In the GA system, papyri are designated by a capital *P* followed by a number (e.g., P100 or $\mathfrak{P}^{100}$), majuscules by a number with a prefixed zero (e.g., 042), minuscules by a plain number (e.g., 1739), and lectionaries by a lowercase *l* followed by a number (e.g., l249 or ℓ249).[5] Gregory created the system to improve on the varied and often confusing conventions of past scholars. The goal was a uniform means of referencing texts scattered around the world without having to remember and keep up with changing library shelf numbers. It is much more efficient to refer simply to "022" than to its nine shelf numbers! Likewise, the designation "P40" does not require remembering that its shelf number changed from "P.Heid. Inv. no. 45" to "P.Heid. Inv. G. 645."

---

[4]Majuscules are often referred to as uncials, which is a term that refers to a particular style of script in Latin manuscripts. Accordingly, *majuscule* is preferred. See D. C. Parker's comments in "The Majuscule Manuscripts of the New Testament," in *The Text of the New Testament in Contemporary Research: Essays on the Status Quaestionis*, 2nd ed., ed. Bart D. Ehrman and Michael W. Holmes, NTTSD 42 (Leiden: Brill, 2013), 41.

Other types of evidence, such as amulets, ostraca, and inscriptions, also contain portions of the New Testament but are not counted as official manuscripts. For an introduction to these, see Peter M. Head, "Additional Greek Witnesses to the New Testament (Ostraca, Amulets, Inscriptions, and Other Sources)," in Ehrman and Holmes, *Text of the New Testament*, 429-60. See also Stanley Porter, "Why So Many Holes in the Papyrological Evidence for the Greek New Testament?," in *The Bible as Book: The Transmission of the Greek Text*, ed. Scot McKendrick and Orlaith Sullivan (New Castle, DE: Oak Knoll, 2003); Porter, "Textual Criticism in the Light of Diverse Textual Evidence for the Greek New Testament: An Expanded Proposal," in *New Testament Manuscripts: Their Texts and Their World*, ed. Thomas J. Kraus and Tobias Nicklas, TENTS 2 (Leiden: Brill, 2006), 305-37. For a detailed study on the textual value of amulets, see Brice C. Jones, *New Testament Texts on Greek Amulets from Late Antiquity*, LNTS 554 (London: Bloomsbury T&T Clark, 2016).

[5]Gregory introduced his system in Caspar René Gregory, *Die griechischen Handschriften des Neuen Testaments* (Leipzig: Hinrichs, 1908).

Some majuscules have retained a letter designation to go along with their number (e.g., א = 01, A = 02, Ψ = 044, etc.). More complicated are letters with multiple references, such as D (05) for Codex Bezae containing the Gospels and Acts, and D (06) for Codex Claromontanus containing the Pauline Epistles. Other letters with this problem are E (07 and 08), F (09 and 010), G (011 and 012), H (013, 014, and 015), K (017 and 018), L (019 and 020), and P (024 and 025). To distinguish these, the letter will often be accompanied by a superscript *e*, *a*, *p*, or *r* where *e* = Gospels, *a* = Acts and the Catholic Epistles, *p* = Paul, and *r* = Revelation.

Despite their many benefits, it is easy to overlook how inconsistent the categories are as a classification system. The first category, papyri, is a material-based category. Majuscule and minuscule are script-based categories, whereas lectionary is a content-based category. Inconsistencies arise from multiple types of overlap. For instance, a lectionary can be either majuscule or miniscule. Papyri feature majuscule script, meaning the difference between them and majuscules is entirely one of material. This division often leads to the incorrect impression that the two categories exist as chronologically distinct points in the transmission of the New Testament text when, in fact, the two overlap for several centuries.[6]

Who counts them and how? As previously mentioned, Kurt Aland continued Gregory's system for cataloguing manuscripts. In 1959, Aland founded the Institute for New Testament Textual Research (INTF), which is now responsible for the official registry of New Testament manuscripts.[7] One of INTF's many projects is maintaining the *Kurzgefaßte Liste der griechischen Handschriften des Neuen Testaments* (or *Concise List of Greek Manuscripts of the New Testament*; *Liste* for short) as a record of all known manuscripts. The *Liste* provides basic information about the manuscript's location, its date, its contents, and various physical features, such as line counts and page dimensions. Thankfully, the *Liste* is now freely available and continually updated online at ntvmr.uni-muenster.de/liste.

INTF is notified when a new manuscript is discovered and provided with images and as much bibliographical detail as possible. Its task then, especially with fragmentary manuscripts, is to ensure that the newly discovered manuscript is not part of some previously identified manuscript.[8] If INTF believes the manuscript is a new one, it is assigned a new GA number and has its information added to the online *Liste*.

WHY COUNTING IS DIFFICULT

Searching the *Liste* reveals the following manuscripts as the most recently added, as of April 2019, in each category: P139, 0323, 2940, and l2483. Adding

---

[6]These problems have long been recognized; see, for example, Kurt Aland and Barbara Aland, *The Text of the New Testament: An Introduction to the Critical Editions and to the Theory and Practice of Modern Textual Criticism*, 2nd ed., trans. Erroll F. Rhodes (Grand Rapids: Eerdmans, 1989), 74; D. C. Parker, *An Introduction to the New Testament Manuscripts and Their Texts* (Cambridge: Cambridge University Press, 2008), 35.

[7]The INTF abbreviation comes from the German Institut für neutestamentliche Textforschung.

[8]Kurt Aland, *Kurzgefaßte Liste der griechischen Handschriften des Neuen Testaments*, 1st ed., ANTF 1 (Berlin: de Gruyter, 1963), 12.

those numbers results in a count of 5,885 manuscripts. Yet the typical approximation for how many Greek New Testament manuscripts we have is a bit north of 5,500.[9] Why the hesitancy by most to provide a precise total? In part, as will be discussed later in this chapter, the number would almost certainly be outdated by the time of publication. A main reason, however, lies with how difficult and laborious it is to come up with an accurate count. The 5,885 total just cited, for instance, is surely incorrect, as will be shown.[10] The following discussion covers a few of the reasons why counting manuscripts is so difficult and why we should be content with approximations rather than worry about having the most precise count.

Double counting. As mentioned, one of INTF's tasks is determining when two samples are from the same manuscript. An unfortunate fact of history is that the papyri have become fragmentary, and some manuscripts were disassembled and sold as pieces. Accordingly, pieces of the same manuscript can turn up in collections all over the world. Matching these pieces is a difficult task, so it is no wonder there are many places in the *Liste* where portions of a manuscript were assigned two or more GA numbers only to have subsequent scholarship reveal them to be from the same manuscript. One of the more famous examples of this concerns P64 and P67, which were revealed to be two parts of the same manuscript of Matthew.[11] Today, you

---

[9]A brief selection of manuscript counts include "over 5800" in Stanley E. Porter, *How We Got the New Testament: Text, Transmission, Translation*, Acadia Studies in Bible and Theology (Grand Rapids: Baker Academic, 2013), 23; "c. 5700" in J. Ed Komoszewski, M. James Sawyer, and Daniel B. Wallace, *Reinventing Jesus: How Contemporary Skeptics Miss the Real Jesus and Mislead Popular Culture* (Grand Rapids: Kregel, 2006), 71; "over 5600" in Peter J. Gurry, "The Number of Variants in the Greek New Testament: A Proposed Estimate," *NTS* 62, no. 1 (2016): 98; "more than 5500" in Eldon J. Epp, "Why Does New Testament Textual Criticism Matter? Refined Definitions and Fresh Directions," *ExpTim* 125, no. 9 (2014): 419; "about 5400" in Greg Gilbert, *Why Trust the Bible?* (Wheaton, IL: Crossway, 2015), 45; "over 5000" in Craig S. Keener, *The IVP Bible Background Commentary: New Testament*, 2nd ed. (Downers Grove, IL: InterVarsity Press, 2014), 14; "approximately 5000" in Parker, *New Testament Manuscripts and Their Texts*, 57.

[10]Josh McDowell and Sean McDowell are to be commended for qualifying why the precise number is incorrect in *Evidence That Demands a Verdict: Life-Changing Truth for a Skeptical World* (Nashville: Thomas Nelson, 2017), 48. They write, "The official number of 5,856 requires some revision, however. One should deduct MSS that have gone missing, those that have been destroyed, and those that have been discovered to be a part of a known MS." However, they return to the inflated number of 5,856 without qualification a few pages later.

[11]This case was made more difficult when P4 was determined to have been copied by the same scribe of P64 and P67. T. C. Skeat proposed they all belonged to a single manuscript of the four Gospels in "The Oldest Manuscript of the Four Gospels?," *NTS* 43, no. 1 (1997); reprinted in T. C. Skeat, *The Collected Biblical Writings of T. C. Skeat*, ed. J. K. Elliott, NovTSup 113 (Leiden: Brill, 2004), 158-92. Recent scholarship, however, favors understanding P4 as a separate codex;

will see this papyrus referenced in any number of ways, such as P64(=67), P64/67, and P[64+67], to indicate they are a single manuscript.

When using the online *Liste*, numbers in parentheses next to an entry identify this issue. The first time part of a manuscript is listed, all of the other parts are in parentheses and preceded by a plus sign. All subsequent entries for that manuscript have only the initial number in parentheses after an equal sign. For example, here's how GA 070 and its constituent parts are presented:

```
070(+0110+0124+0202)
0110(=070)
0124(=070)
0202(=070)
```

However, a scroll through the majuscules reveals several gaps in the numbering, for instance from 0177 to 0181. It is only by consulting the print version of the *Liste* that it becomes clear 0178, 0179, 0180, 0190, 0191, and 0193 are also reported to be part of 070.[12] To confuse matters more, 0194 is reported as being the same as 0124, which we already know to be the same as 070. A complete record of 070, therefore, includes eleven different GA numbers and is properly 070(+0110+0124+0178+0179+0180+0190+0191+0193+0194+0202). Whenever a manuscript is found to be the same as another, INTF does not reuse the old number. This prevents confusion in later scholarship between the new manuscript with that number and the old one.[13]

---

see Peter M. Head, "Is P[4], P[64] and P[67] the Oldest Manuscript of the Four Gospels? A Response to T. C. Skeat," *NTS* 51, no. 3 (2005); S. D. Charlesworth, "T. C. Skeat, P[64+67] and P[4], and the Problem of Fibre Orientation in Codicological Reconstruction," *NTS* 53, no. 4 (2007): 582-604.

[12]Kurt Aland, *Kurzgefaßte Liste der griechischen Handschriften des Neuen Testaments*, 2nd ed., ANTF 1 (Berlin: de Gruyter, 1994).

[13]Aland, *Kurzgefaßte Liste*, 1st ed., 15. Prior to Aland assuming responsibility for the *Liste*, this does not appear to have been a rule. The designation "P25" has referred to three distinct manuscripts. In 1926, Ernst von Dobschütz designated P.Oxy. 1353 as P25 in "Zur Liste der Neutestamentlichen Handschriften. II," *ZNW* 25 (1926): 300. This was subsequently reassigned by von Dobschütz as 0206, since it was parchment and not papyrus, in "Zur Liste der Neutestamentlichen Handschriften. IV," *ZNW* 32 (1933): 192. According to Kenneth Clark, von Dobschütz then listed a papyrus of James as P25; see Kenneth W. Clark, *A Descriptive Catalogue of Greek New Testament Manuscripts in America* (Chicago: University of Chicago Press, 1937), 79. Unfortunately, this same papyrus was listed as P54 by Walther Eltester; see Bruce M. Metzger, "A List of Greek Papyri of the New Testament," *ExpTim* 59, no. 3 (1947): 80. This James papyrus is now known only as P54, and a manuscript of Matthew was assigned the vacated P25 spot, apparently at the suggestion of D. Hans Lietzmann. For this and a comment that von Dobschütz never assigned P25 to the James papyrus, see Georg Maldfeld, "Die griechischen Handschriftenbruchstücke des Neuen

The reverse circumstance has happened several times when two or more manuscripts were assigned the same number. This typically happened when multiple distinct manuscripts were bound together in a single codex. One example is a minuscule from the Vatopedi Monastery in Greece with the shelf number 889. It was entered into the *Liste* with five separate entries featuring the number 2306 followed by the letters *a* through *e*. These five manuscripts now have their own GA numbers: 2306 for 2306a, and 2831-2834 for 2306b-2306e.

There is yet another complication in the seemingly straightforward numbering system in the *Liste*. Some manuscripts have had sections or quires replaced or added in, with the missing material added by a secondary scribe. In the case of Codex Vaticanus (03) a fifteenth-century scribe added the end of Hebrews (from Heb 9:14 on) and Revelation. Quite sensibly, this supplementary material received a new GA number: 1957. In a number of manuscripts, the supplementary material is not given a new GA number but instead is suffixed in the Nestle-Aland text with an *s* (e.g., 032 at Jn 1:1–5:11 and 1241 for sections in Paul and the Catholic Epistles).

It should be clear now that GA 0323 as the most recently catalogued majuscule does not mean there are 323 majuscules. The case of 070 alone demonstrates the number is inflated by at least ten. Yet double counting is not the only reason why getting an accurate total is difficult.

Loss. Another factor affecting our manuscript count is loss. This phenomenon is observable in the *Liste*, with the location or institute listed as "Besitzer unbekannt" ("owner unknown"), which has been attributed to 136 manuscripts. There are a number of ways this happens, ranging from accidental to illegal. It might sound rather farfetched that a manuscript could be lost in the same way that one loses one's keys, yet this seems to be the case with a number of manuscripts found in old library catalogues (e.g., 0174). Naturally, manuscripts have a high value both materially and as religious objects, so it is no surprise that many have been stolen over the years. The problem with the two above scenarios for the task of counting manuscripts is that if the manuscript was not well documented, it could reappear and be

---

Testamentes auf Papyrus," *ZNW* 42, no. 1 (1949): 230-33. One must be careful when consulting publications from this time period when it comes to what manuscript is being referred to with particular designations. As one example, Ellwood M. Schofield uses "P25" to refer to the James papyrus (P54) in his dissertation "The Papyrus Fragments of the Greek New Testament" (PhD thesis, Southern Baptist Theological Seminary, 1936).

recatalogued with a new GA number, resulting in it having two entries in the *Liste*.

Manuscripts are also lost through more natural causes such as fires, floods, and insects. For instance, many manuscripts from Turin are recorded as destroyed by fire.[14] Then there are manuscripts, such as 1257-1259 from a school in Izmir, that are listed as "burnt?" Do these survive and do we count them? An unfortunate result of war has been the loss of several manuscripts as well. From World War II we know that manuscripts were badly damaged or lost completely in the firebombing of Dresden (e.g., 241 and 2039).[15] There are numerous early manuscripts, such as 062, catalogued in Damascus, Syria, that are already listed as "owner unknown." With the ongoing Syrian wars, their location and survival are even more uncertain. Although different from the types of loss above, many manuscripts have been sold to private owners, which makes tracking them more difficult and all but eliminates using them for research (e.g., 0258, a fourth-century copy of John sold by Sotheby's).

Sometimes manuscripts are recorded as lost in the *Liste* when they still exist. This is the case with 0229, which is reported as "zerstört" (destroyed) and formerly located at the Biblioteca Medicea Laurenziana in Florence. However, it turns out the manuscript is housed at the Istituto Papirologico Girolamo Vitelli at the University of Florence and has been known since 1970.[16]

Incorrectly added. Finally, there are some manuscripts that were simply incorrectly added to the *Liste*. In some instances, this was nothing more than

---

[14]Parker reports this as the 1904 fire at the National Library, in *New Testament Manuscripts and Their Texts*, 43. See the surrounding discussion for other examples of lost manuscripts. Although not "lost," many manuscripts were severely damaged by fires like the one in Turin. For instance, GA 338 went from 365 leaves to just four.

[15]The extent of manuscript loss in Dresden, and elsewhere in Europe, is largely unknown. The issue is further complicated by the fact that Russia carried off many manuscripts as war prizes (e.g., 238 and 2837), which they claim to have returned in the 1950s; see Patricia Kennedy Grimsted, ed., *Archives of Russia: A Directory and Bibliographic Guide to Holdings in Moscow and St. Petersburg* (New York: Routledge, 2015), 2:670, 685, 883. See also Grimsted's work on issues of repatriation in Patricia Kennedy Grimsted, F. J. Hoogewoud, and F. C. J. Ketelaar, eds., *Returned from Russia: Nazi Archival Plunder in Western Europe and Recent Restitution Issues*, 2nd rev. ed. (Builth Wells, UK: Institute of Art and Law, 2013).

[16]Iginio Crisci, "La collezione dei papiri di Firenze," in *Proceedings of the Twelfth International Congress of Papyrology*, ed. Deborah H. Samuel, *ASP* 7 (Toronto: Hakkert, 1970), 93. High-resolution images are available at psi-online.it/documents/psi;13;1296. Another example is GA 1799, on which see Tommy Wasserman, *The Epistle of Jude: Its Text and Transmission*, ConBNT 43 (Stockholm: Almqvist & Wiksell, 2006), 119-20n14; and Daniel B. Wallace, "The Demise of Codex 1799," *Daniel B. Wallace* (blog), August 18, 2012, danielbwallace.com/2012/08/18/the-demise-of-codex-1799.

a category mistake or a change in cataloguing procedure. This was the case with 0152 and 0153, which are an amulet and ostracon, respectively. Gregory classified them as majuscules; Ernst von Dobschütz reclassified them as an amulet and ostracon, respectively; and Kurt Aland subsequently removed them from the *Liste*.[17] On more than one occasion, manuscripts have made it into the *Liste* that were not written in Koine Greek. The understandable cases are several manuscripts, such as 2114, that were written in Modern Greek and were initially included. The more confusing cases are those such as 1151 and 1825, written in Slavonic and Syriac, respectively, that made it in.

Sometimes a manuscript is determined to have some dependence on a print edition. These could be either forgeries or just someone with a desire for a handwritten copy; imputing motive in these cases is undoubtedly difficult. It is rare, but occasionally such a copyist fools people and the manuscript is given a GA number. One of the more famous examples is 2427 or "Archaic Mark," which was initially dated to the thirteenth century but was shown by Stephen Carlson in an SBL paper to be a nineteenth-century copy of Philipp Butt-mann's 1860 edition of the New Testament.[18] Again, these are likely very rare, but it remains a possibility that further complicates our cataloguing efforts.

In addition to these types of errors, other manuscripts were once in-cluded in the *Liste* only to be taken out because they were shown to be com-mentaries, homilies, or any other number of types of texts.[19]

Material bias. There are also manuscripts that, for whatever reason, most scholars agree should not be counted but nonetheless maintain a number. This primarily affects the New Testament papyri. For example, P99 is a fourth- or fifth-century manuscript containing what appears to be a school exercise with Latin and Greek vocabulary and phrases taken from the Pauline Epistles.[20] Surely this should not count as a New Testament

---

[17]On this progression, see Jones, *New Testament Texts on Greek Amulets*, 9-12.

[18]A synopsis of Carlson's paper is available at Stephen C. Carlson, "'Archaic Mark' (MS 2427) and the Finding of a Manuscript Fake," SBL Forum, http://sbl-site.org/Article.aspx?ArticleID=577 (accessed March 22, 2019); see also Joseph G. Barabe, Abigail B. Quandt, and Margaret M. Mitchell, "Chicago's 'Archaic Mark' (MS 2427) II Microscopic, Chemical and Codicological Analyses Confirm Modern Production," *NovT* 52, no. 2 (2010): 101-33. For an interesting case combining loss, recovery, and forgery, see Daniel B. Wallace, "Photographing a Forgery?," *The Center for the Study of New Testament Manuscripts* (blog), January 2, 2010, csntm.org/TCNotes /Archive/PhotographingAForgery.

[19]For other examples of mistaken inclusion, see Parker, *New Testament Manuscripts and Their Texts*, 41.

[20]Alfons Wouters, *The Chester Beatty Codex AC 1499: A Graeco-Latin Lexicon on the Pauline*

manuscript. J. K. Elliott describes this general phenomenon as giving "an undue significance to New Testament writings on papyrus, as if the very writing material was itself so important."[21] Part of the problem with really fragmentary papyri is that it is extremely difficult to determine whether it was a continuous text or something that would not count, such as an amulet, a song, or a commentary. Aland, who was responsible for maintaining the *Liste*, observes, "Among the ninety-six items which now comprise the official list of New Testament papyri there are several which by a strict definition do not belong there," and he goes on to ascribe some of these to "the occasionally uncritical attitude of earlier editors of the list."[22] In total, he lists fifteen examples of this among the ninety-six papyri known to him and says, "These peculiarities are on the whole negligible."[23] I am not sure how 15 percent of all papyri being potentially incorrectly categorized counts as negligible, but it shows the generally accepting attitude for papyri despite myriad problems in their classification and inclusion in the *Liste*.

Epistles and a Greek Grammar (Leuven: Peeters, 1988); see also Klaus Junack et al., *Das Neue Testament auf Papyrus II: Die Paulinischen Briefe*, Tiel 1, *Röm, 1 Kor, 2 Kor*, ANTF 12 (Berlin: de Gruyter, 1989), LXVII-LXXIV.

[21] J. K. Elliott, "Absent Witnesses? The Critical Apparatus to the Greek New Testament and the Apostolic Fathers," in *The Reception of the New Testament in the Apostolic Fathers*, ed. Andrew Gregory and Christopher Tuckett (Oxford: Oxford University Press, 2005), 50. Elliott's purposes were different from our own, as he was interested in clearing space in the apparatus for recording the writings of the apostolic fathers, but his point remains true. He offers several other examples of dubiously listed papyri and majuscules on pp. 49-50. See also Thomas J. Kraus, "'Parchment or Papyrus?': Some Remarks About the Significance of Writing Material When Assessing Manuscripts," in *Ad fontes: Original Manuscripts and Their Significance for Studying Early Christianity—Selected Essays*, ed. Thomas J. Kraus, TENT 3 (Leiden: Brill, 2007), 13-24.

[22] Aland and Aland, *Text of the New Testament*, 2nd rev. ed., 85. A similar statement is made on p. 85 in the 1st ed.

[23] Aland and Aland, *Text of the New Testament*, 2nd rev. ed., 85. The fifteen manuscripts are P2, P3, P10, P12, P42, P43, P44, P50, P55, P59, P60, P62, P63, P78, and P80. Interestingly, Kurt Aland was himself responsible for cataloguing as many as seven of these papyri. Von Dobschütz's last entry was P48, in "Zur Liste der NTlichen Handschriften. IV," 188. Numbers 49-54 were assigned in the period between von Dobschütz and Aland by Walther Eltester, although he did not publish a list; for this and a list of the papyri, see Metzger, "List of Greek Papyri of the New Testament," 80-81. The first papyrus Aland catalogues and describes as new ("überhaupt neu") is P55, in "Zur Liste der griechischen neutestamentlichen Handschriften," *TLZ* 75 (1950): 59. The problem is that up to P62 were reported by Georg Maldfeld in "Die griechischen Handschriftenbruchstücke des Neuen Testamentes auf Papyrus." It is therefore unclear how much Aland was involved, if at all, in listing P55-P62. The first papyrus that Aland definitively had a hand in cataloguing was P63, in "Zur Liste der griechischen neutestamentlichen Handschriften," *TLZ* 78 (1953): 468. This perhaps explains the Alands' comment that Kurt revived the system and made his first report in 1953 despite having clearly published a list in 1950; see *Text of the New Testament*, 2nd rev. ed., 74.

Summary. The above discussion serves to illustrate how difficult it is to provide an accurate total for our New Testament manuscripts. An accurate count is clearly not simply a matter of adding up the numbers for the most recently registered manuscripts. A quick look at the majuscules, a comparatively easy group to count, provides plenty of evidence against bean counting. If we just count the number of unique entries in the *Liste*, there are 282 majuscules.[24] This means that of the 323 items given a majuscule number, forty-one have been stricken from the *Liste*; most were to consolidate those that were assigned multiple numbers. This number still includes all of the manuscripts with unknown owners and locations and those whose earlier location was known but are presently doubtful, as with the Damascus manuscripts. The number drops to 261 if all of these are removed. Additional questions are raised about what it means to "have" a manuscript, since thirteen of those were preserved on microfilm. Do we count a manuscript that might not physically exist but is preserved via images?[25] What about 0254? It has microfilm images, but they are totally worthless for reading this palimpsest manuscript. At best, we can say that there are between 261 and 282 majuscules. Arriving at a range this precise for the thousands of minuscules and lectionaries would be a monumental task and one that, as will hopefully become clear in what follows, is not worth undertaking—at least not for apologetic purposes.

DISCOVERING MANUSCRIPTS

Another factor that makes attempts at providing precise counts of New Testament manuscripts difficult is the continued discovery of more manuscripts. While it is certainly nice to have an ever-increasing supply of witnesses to the New Testament text, we must be cognizant of what is behind this increase. Most importantly, we must ask, What does it mean to "discover" a manuscript, and what kinds of manuscripts are being found?

How discoveries happen today. There are a number of possible meanings of *discovery* in play when a new manuscript is announced. Of course, there

---

[24]For a point of comparison, Parker determined the "nominal number of separate majuscule MSS" to be 285 in 2012, in "Majuscule Manuscripts," 48.

[25]My opinion is they do count. Images are a poor substitute for the physical object and the material culture it preserves, but images are better than nothing. Good images preserve the text, which is of primary importance for textual criticism. Recent shifts in digitization have moved toward "archival" copying, which aims to preserve as much of the codex qua codex as possible rather than prioritizing one element (e.g., the text) at the cost of others.

is the traditional sense in which a manuscript that was lost for centuries is found again and thus, more properly, rediscovered. Famous examples of this are the papyri from Oxyrhynchus, the Chester Beatty papyri, and the Bodmer papyri, which for various reasons were buried or discarded only to be unearthed in Egypt in the late nineteenth and early twentieth centuries. Although the excavations have stopped, the Oxyrhynchus collection continues to produce new discoveries as scholars work through the thousands of unidentified fragments. More controversially, New Testament papyri have allegedly been found through dissolving mummy cartonnage to separate the layers of papyrus used in its construction.[26] Another team is working to virtually dissect mummy cartonnage with advanced imaging technology.[27] While no New Testament texts are reported to have been found this way, it is illustrative of new ways that scholars are working to find texts in new places.

Another way that manuscripts are discovered involves working with various libraries around the world to bring to light manuscripts that were previously unknown to Western scholarship. In most cases, New Testament text critics do not know about a manuscript unless it has been catalogued by the previously mentioned INTF. Perhaps the leader in this type of discovery is the Center for the Study of New Testament Manuscripts (CSNTM).[28] In our work cataloguing and digitizing manuscripts at monasteries and libraries around the world, CSNTM often "discovers" New Testament manuscripts that the library has known for centuries in many cases but about which INTF was unaware. In this sense, a "discovery" is the official registration of a manuscript by INTF that was unknown to the wider New Testament scholarly community but was known to its owner or holding library.

There is another type of manuscript discovery that falls in between the two just mentioned that involves New Testament manuscripts hiding in plain sight. Frequently, New Testament manuscripts are found within other known manuscripts, New Testament or otherwise. This can take

---

[26]The most public examples of this practice have been by Josh McDowell and Scott Carroll. I indicate that New Testament papyri have *allegedly* been discovered this way because the scholarly community awaits peer review and publication of any such fragments. Until this happens, their existence is mere hearsay and should not factor into any discussion of textual evidence.

[27]The project is "Deep Imaging Mummy Cases: Non-Destructive Analysis of Multi-Layered Papyrus." Professor Melissa Terras at University College London is leading the project, which features an international team of specialists in a range of disciplines.

[28]For some brief accounts of manuscripts being discovered, see Parker, *New Testament Manuscripts and Their Texts*, 45.

many forms, such as leaves or quires that were replaced for any number of reasons, a leaf being repurposed as binding material or a flyleaf for another manuscript, or New Testament writings being bound together with non-biblical texts, as is often the case with Revelation being found with other liturgical writings. Along the same lines, new discoveries have been made by recognizing biblical texts underneath other writings in palimpsest man-uscripts.[29] The most exciting recent work on this front is the Sinai Palimp-sests Project at St. Catharine's Monastery in Egypt, which is online at http://sinaipalimpsests.org.

Recent discoveries. As someone who has been involved in almost every type of discovery mentioned above, I am acutely aware of just how easy it is to get excited about new finds. New manuscripts *are* exciting because they in-crease our overall witness to the text and, in many cases, you are the first person to see the text in hundreds of years. However, not all discoveries are created equally, so it is important to understand *what* is being discovered today.

On one end of the spectrum for generating interest and excitement, several New Testament papyri have been found in recent years. As men-tioned in this book's introduction, there were 98 papyri listed in NA[27], pub-lished in 1993. That number increased to 127 in the twenty-eighth edition, published in 2012, and since then an additional eleven papyri have been catalogued by INTF.[30] This is a fairly impressive amount of papyri discovered in the past twenty-five years. At the other end of the spectrum is a re-placement leaf I recently discovered inside an eleventh-century lectionary at the University of Edinburgh. Whereas newly discovered papyri are studied intensely and get cited in the next edition of critical texts, this newly discovered lectionary replacement leaf will perhaps only ever be mentioned here. My general impression of the majority of recent discoveries is that they tend to align more with this latter camp of interesting but text-critically unimportant manuscripts than with ones that will contribute greatly to our understanding of the New Testament text.

---

[29]Although it does not count as a discovery of a new manuscript, technology has enabled further discoveries within known texts. In my own work, the images of the Chester Beatty papyri by CSNTM led to discoveries of new letters and a better understanding of the manuscripts. Simi-larly, multispectral imaging by groups such as the Early Manuscripts Electronic Library has enabled new discoveries within palimpsest manuscripts by making lost text visible again. Again, these are not discoveries of new manuscripts but a better understanding of their texts, which can sometimes be more important.

[30]As of April 6, 2019. The last papyrus catalogued is P139.

The reason for this impression is that none of the papyri just mentioned are even remotely close in importance to the great finds of the past. Most of them are small fragments with only portions of a few verses surviving. CSNTM, which was founded in 2002, has discovered almost seventy manuscripts in the intervening seventeen years. The most important manuscript among their finds is 0322, a seventh- to ninth-century palimpsest containing a few chapters from Mark. Its work at the Albanian National Archives in Tirana resulted in their biggest find in terms of content, with dozens of relatively complete medieval manuscripts being discovered. Altogether CSNTM's finds amount to more than twenty thousand pages of text. While these manuscripts should be studied, chances are, the bulk of them are generally representative of the later, abundantly attested Byzantine text. The intention here is not to denigrate any recent discoveries or to suggest the work is unimportant. Rather, the point is to demonstrate that a wide range of texts are being discovered in terms of age, extent, and quality. No one rightly expects every manuscript discovered to be a Codex Sinaiticus, so we should be careful not to give the impression that all new discoveries are of equal significance for textual criticism.

How many are left to be discovered? All of this raises an interesting question about how many manuscripts are left to be discovered. As far as the discoveries from archaeological digs and the like that tend to result in papyri are concerned, it would be impossible and imprudent to venture a guess. As it stands, about one papyrus manuscript has come to light every year since the twenty-seventh edition of the Nestle-Aland text was published in 1993. Of course, there are some years where a handful are published in quick succession, but a one-papyrus-per-year rate is generally reflective of the overall trend since P1 was published in 1898.

Although CSNTM is not the only organization working with manuscripts, its rate of discovery can be used to gain a rough estimate of how many manuscripts might be sitting on the shelves of libraries around the world waiting to be "discovered." CSNTM has digitized 668 manuscripts since 2002, and 67 of those were new discoveries.[31] Assuming that rate continues for the approximately catalogued 5,300 manuscripts, then there are about

---

[31]These numbers are accurate as of April 2019 per Andrew K. Bobo, the research coordinator at CSNTM.

525 manuscripts left to discover.[32] This is an exciting prospect, but we must keep in mind that manuscripts do not have to abide by theoretical calculations, and the rate of discovery could change drastically in either direction. These numbers are little more than a fun thought experiment.

WEIGHING MANUSCRIPTS

With the above caveats and difficulties as a background, we can proceed to discuss some of the issues that come up when talking about the number of manuscripts. As a point of entry, issues arise in discussions of manuscript numbers when there is a failure to nuance the point being made. Yes, there are about fifty-three hundred Greek New Testament manuscripts, but they are not all created equally, and that number should not be used as though they are. It is not sufficient to simply *count* manuscripts; they must be *weighed*. This is the battle cry of text critics when engaging Majority Text advocates, but it also has potency for those who wish to tout the trove of New Testament manuscripts as a death knell for skeptics.

Dates of manuscripts. It is generally well recognized that not all of our manuscripts are early. The relationship between date and manuscript importance will be taken up in more detail in other chapters of this book, dealing specifically with why early manuscripts are not necessarily better and why later ones are not necessarily worse, but I want to take an initial look here at the dates of Greek New Testament manuscripts that survive from the first millennium.

It is important to remember from the outset the earlier points about how difficult it is to count manuscripts with complete precision. Accordingly, the numbers in all that follows should be understood in that light rather than as gospel truth. In particular, manuscripts that are missing without images but are still in the *Liste* are not counted in the following analyses.[33] Further, in this section on manuscript dates, the numbers will be biased toward the early end of the spectrum to avoid doubling. For instance, P3 is dated to the sixth/seventh century but will be counted only for the sixth.[34] With these considerations in mind, the manuscript distribution by century is shown in figure 3.1 below.

---

[32]For the reasoning behind 5,300, see "Use Round Numbers" below.

[33]For example, 0254, mentioned earlier, is not included.

[34]In the more extreme, GA 1684 has a tenth- to thirteenth-century date range but is counted only for the tenth century.

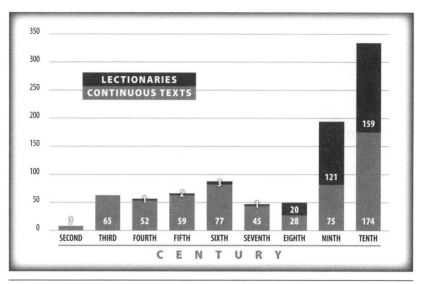

Figure 3.1. Distribution of Greek New Testament manuscripts by century for the first millennium

It is clear from this distribution that although there are a good number of early manuscripts, the bulk are still considerably late, with a sizable percentage being lectionaries. Furthermore, this first-millennium window represents only a fraction of the total amount. If there are approximately fifty-three hundred manuscripts in total, 83 percent of them come from the year 1000 or later. This does not mean the number of manuscripts from the second to tenth centuries is insignificant; clearly the New Testament is well attested in this period. Rather, it is intended to be the first step toward putting the many thousands of manuscripts into proper perspective.

Contents of manuscripts. The next step is to understand what these manuscripts actually contain. There are just over sixty manuscripts of the whole New Testament. This leaves the other 99 percent containing only portions of the text.[35] The standard divisions of the New Testament in the manuscript tradition are the Gospels (represented by *e*), Acts and the Catholic Epistles (*a*), the Pauline Epistles (*p*), and Revelation (*r*). It is very common to find the Gospels transmitted alone and Acts and the Catholic Epistles together with the Pauline Epistles, but these are hardly rules, and almost any combination can be found.[36] The following chart shows how well

---

[35]Parker cites sixty-one in *New Testament Manuscripts and Their Texts*, 70.
[36]See chapter thirteen in this volume for more on this.

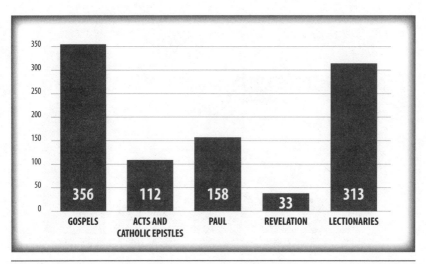

Figure 3.2. Distribution of Greek New Testament manuscripts by contents for the first millennium

the various sections are represented in the first millennium, with a separate column for the lectionary count (see fig. 3.2).

The important point here is that when speaking of the 889 manuscripts from the first millennium, there are not 889 *complete* New Testament manuscripts.[37] Indeed, while the Gospels are numerically well represented, the manuscripts containing other parts, especially Revelation, are a small fraction of the total. Breaking these divisions down by century is also helpful, lest we forget that most of these are not early. As with figure 3.1, the numbers in figure 3.3 are biased toward the earliest possible date for each manuscript.

Differing sizes of manuscripts. Even these numbers need to be put into proper perspective. What does it mean to have *x* number of manuscripts for a particular part of the New Testament? Just as 889 New Testament manuscripts from the first millennium does not mean 889 complete New Testament manuscripts, 158 manuscripts of the Pauline Epistles still does not mean there are 158 manuscripts *of that entire corpus.* Furthermore, it does not mean that even an entire epistle is contained in a manuscript. On the extremes, Codex Sinaiticus contains the whole New Testament, whereas P12 has parts of a single verse from Hebrews.[38]

---

[37] This is my count after factoring in all of the problems discussed in this chapter.

[38] And P12 should probably not count in the first place! See footnote above in the section "Material Bias."

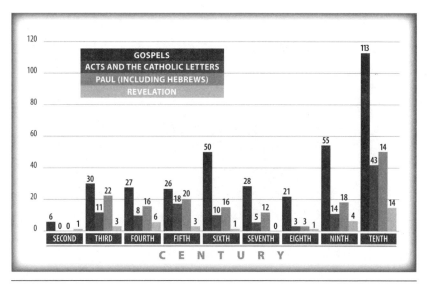

Figure 3.3. Greek New Testament manuscript contents by century

So, how complete is the earliest witness to some books? Of the Gospels, Mark is numerically the least attested, and the following chart in 3.4 shows how much is preserved prior to the fourth century as percentages of each chapter.[39]

The only manuscripts of Mark from this period are P45, which is absent for 78 percent of that Gospel, and P137, which contains only parts of six verses from Mark 1. John, on the other hand, is very well represented in this earliest period.

John is found in several significant early manuscripts (i.e., P45, P66, and P75) that cover the majority of the Gospel and then several smaller ones that fill in the gaps. Only fourteen verses in the whole Gospel do not find a witness in this period as seen in figure 3.5.[40]

Summary. The point here is not to cause despair about books such as Mark but to point out that not all manuscripts are equal when it comes to

---

[39]Data for this is pulled from the online *Liste*. A verse is counted if a single letter from it is present in the manuscript. Mark 16:9-20 is not included in the calculations. This does not affect the Mk 16 count but only the overall percentage.

Making the cutoff at the fourth century, and so prior to the great majuscules 01, 02, 03, etc., comes close to begging the question. However, it is precisely this second- to third-century period that is often under question as the period of least controlled copying; see, for instance, Bart D. Ehrman, *Misquoting Jesus: The Story Behind Who Changed the Bible and Why* (New York: HarperCollins, 2005), 51-52, 129. See the Alands, who began to see a need to change existing perceptions about the earliest period in *Text of the New Testament*, 2nd rev. ed., 59-64, 93-95.

[40]This number does not include the twelve verses of the *pericope adulterae* (Jn 7:53–8:11).

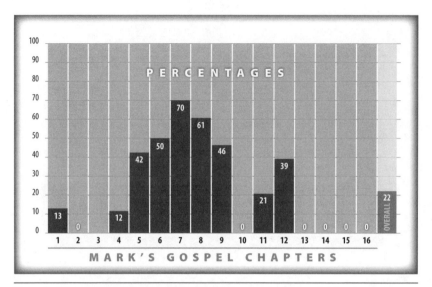

Figure 3.4. Percentage of Mark's Gospel preserved by chapter prior to the fourth century

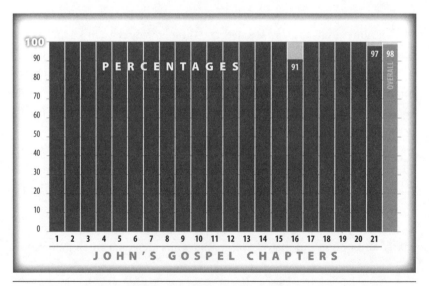

Figure 3.5. Percentage of John's Gospel preserved by chapter prior to the fourth century

early attestation and that even when a section (e.g., the Gospels) has numerous manuscripts, it does not mean that every Gospel has equal representation or that what exists is early and complete. When speaking of the fifty-three hundred manuscripts of the New Testament, these clarifications of the data are the types of things that must be taken into account. The bulk of manuscripts are late, and not everything is represented equally. The Gospels have many manuscripts, while Revelation has very few. Within the textual tradition of each book, some, such as John, have a high percentage preserved early, while some, such as Mark, have considerably fewer in the earliest period. Furthermore, all of the above caveats are secondary to the quality of the manuscripts being counted. Not all of these manuscripts contain texts we would trust or that the scribe necessarily copied well.

CONCLUSION

In concluding this chapter, I want to offer a few points about how to approach and make use of the number of manuscripts in teaching, apologetics, or in any context dealing with nonspecialists. As an overview, the evidence should not be made to say more than it can, and it is crucial to be honest about problem areas in the evidence. If the internet age has taught us anything, it is that people can and will uncover gaps, manipulation, and dishonesty with the data if they are present. Christians, therefore, should be extra careful.

The first point is that bigger numbers do not necessarily equate to better evidence. The reality is that many manuscripts have no noticeable impact on scholarship or critical editions, let alone on, say, English Bibles. It is also true that a very good and reliable text existed with Westcott and Hort's edition published more than a century ago, when there were far fewer manuscripts available.[41]

Don't count noses. There are two ways to interpret the number of manuscripts responsibly when it comes to the reliability of the New Testament text. On the one hand, a large majority of manuscripts are text-critically unnecessary for establishing the original text, producing no more noticeable effect than a pebble dropped in the ocean.[42] On the other hand, it is precisely this lack of effect that is important when judging reliability. If the bulk of the papyri discovered at the beginning of the twentieth century and all other manuscripts since then have not resulted in major revisions of our critical editions, then this attests to a remarkably stable text that can reliably be reconstructed even without them. The typical newly discovered manuscript

---

[41]On the lack of impact the papyri had, especially on altering the text, see Eldon J. Epp, "The Papyrus Manuscripts of the New Testament," in Ehrman and Holmes, *Text of the New Testament*, 16-21.

[42]This is why the Byzantine manuscripts can usually be represented as a single whole in, say, the NA^{28} or UBS^5. There is no need to cite thousands of manuscripts individually when they agree most of the time with one another. The point is not that their shared text does not matter but that their shared text does not improve simply by virtue of being found in so many manuscripts.

is therefore likely to be both statistically insignificant and confirmatory of a reliable text. It is important to note that confirming a text as reliable is distinct from making it *more* reliable. The latter is certainly reliant on the manuscript evidence, but when manuscripts cease contributing new information, it is dependent wholly on method.[43]

Use round numbers. The second point is to be content with round numbers. Using round numbers, such as fifty-three hundred, suggested in this chapter, is prudent for a couple of reasons. All of the complicating factors outlined above make attempts at precision a needlessly tedious task that is almost certain to end in error. Even fifty-three hundred is potentially generous. If the rate of error in cataloguing the majuscules is consistent for every category of manuscripts, then fifty-one hundred is a better approximation.[44] The reason for bumping up the number to fifty-three hundred from fifty-one hundred is that minuscules and lectionaries are less affected than majuscules by the problem of double counting. This is because they tend to be less fragmentary, and therefore there is less likelihood that two or more pieces might be held in different libraries and be given different GA numbers. However, minuscules and lectionaries are still subject to fires and floods, being misplaced, being sold into obscurity, and being incorrectly added to the catalog.[45] Returning to why using a round number is sufficient, it needs to be remembered that finding one more minuscule is not going to convince someone Christianity is true.

Be clear about manuscripts' (limited) apologetic value. This brings us to the final point, which is the importance of understanding what manuscripts can and cannot do. In the negative, manuscripts alone cannot prove the truth of Christianity. What manuscripts can do is provide evidence of a reliable text. A reliable text attested by thousands of manuscripts is just that: a reliable *text*. But a reliable text is not a guarantee of reliable content. Just

---

[43]In particular, new methods, such as the coherence-based genealogical method, that better deal with problems such as contamination in the manuscript tradition theoretically create a more reliable text by more thoroughly understanding the relatively stable evidence available in the manuscripts.

[44]This is arrived at by $(282 \div 323) \times 5885 = 5138$. As a reminder, the 282 includes manuscripts with unknown owners and locations. If those are dropped, the math is $(261 \div 323) \times 5885 = 4755$; see under "Why Counting Is Difficult" above.

[45]It is possible that minuscules and lectionaries are affected more by events such as fires and floods than are majuscules. For instance, the average monastery does not have any majuscules but may have a handful of minuscules and lectionaries. Accordingly, when that monastery's library is damaged or totally lost, the burden is not shared proportionally among all four types of New Testament manuscripts.

as a reliable text of Thucydides's *History of the Peloponnesian War* still requires interpretation and verification to assess its historicity, so does the New Testament.[46] Having a reliable enough text is undoubtedly important, because without it arguing for the accuracy of its material would be impossible. Yet providing arguments for the trustworthiness of a text's actual claims is not something with which textual criticism can help. Those types of important arguments must come from other fields of inquiry.

My hope is that this chapter has been helpful for understanding the challenges faced when dealing with the number of New Testament manuscripts. Textual criticism appears to be more popular than ever and promises to stay at the forefront of many apologetics contexts. Accordingly, anyone working in this area must be aware of the issues and must deal with them honestly and with the required nuance.

Key Takeaways

▶ The official catalogue of Greek New Testament Manuscripts is maintained by the INTF in Münster. The total number of entries in the INTF catalogue is not necessarily the total number of Greek New Testament manuscripts.

▶ New manuscripts continue to be discovered, usually in existing libraries or collections. These, however, are by no means equal in size or significance.

▶ Most manuscripts of the New Testament are only manuscripts of part of the New Testament, and providing an exact count of them is a fool's errand. It is best to say that there are about fifty-three hundred Greek New Testament manuscripts in existence, although fifty-one hundred might be the safer estimate.

---

[46]The speeches recorded by Thucydides provide a great example. Thucydides states in *History of the Peloponnesian War* 1.22: "The speeches are given in the language in which, as it seemed to me, the several speakers would express . . . the sentiments most befitting the occasion, though at the same time I have adhered as closely as possible to the general sense of what was actually said" (Thucydides, *History of the Peloponnesian War*, vol. 1, *Books 1-2*, trans. C. F. Smith, LCL 108 [Cambridge, MA: Harvard University Press, 1919]). See, for instance, Donald Kagan's work in this area, which not once makes reference to the manuscript tradition or its reliability as evidence for the historicity of the speeches, "The Speeches in Thucydides and the Mytilene Debate," in *Studies in the Greek Historians*, ed. Donald Kagan, Yale Classical Studies 24 (Cambridge: Cambridge University Press, 1975). This should make clear the distinction between textual and historical reliability.

CHAPTER FOUR

MYTHS ABOUT CLASSICAL LITERATURE

RESPONSIBLY COMPARING THE NEW TESTAMENT TO ANCIENT WORKS

James B. Prothro

THIS CHAPTER TAKES UP ARGUMENTS that uphold the reliability of the New Testament by comparing the great wealth of manuscripts that attest to its text with the relatively slimmer manuscript attestation for works of the classical canon such as Homer or Suetonius. This argument is rhetorically effective for at least two reasons.

First, it is effective because of the *numerical data*. Many classical works survive in very few manuscripts, and many are dated to several centuries after the original work was composed. By contrast, the New Testament manuscripts number many—often thousands—more. There are, likewise, manuscripts—fragmentary or otherwise—from within a century after the New Testament documents are traditionally thought to have been composed. Likewise, the great number of manuscripts show substantial agreement across the board as to what the text of the New Testament is. These data engender confidence overall in our knowledge of the New Testament text and in our ability, with so many witnesses, to reconstruct it accurately.

Second, the argument is effective because of the *suggestive power of analogy*. A skeptic who understands the process of textual criticism might simply ask, "What if the New Testament, reconstructed to the best of our abilities, is still not what the original authors wrote?" The comparative argument can then suggest that, if you trust that we have anything close to the original texts of authors such as Caesar or Thucydides (whose works often form a significant basis for history textbooks) despite their much poorer manuscript attestation, you should have at least as much credence in the New Testament.

This chapter will not overturn the basic claims of the data or the practical goal of the comparative argument. Indeed, it is precisely because of the argument's value that I hope to clear up some myths and mistakes that make the argument vulnerable to critique or that cover over its value. The primary problem is with the numbers given for classical works, which are often inaccurate. A secondary difficulty is when the argument is presented to prove more than it legitimately can. In this chapter, I will try to illustrate the issues and, more importantly, will try to help future apologetics by demystifying some issues and suggesting some strategies for presenting the argument more strongly.

THE DATA AND THE ARGUMENT

First, we can get a sense of the argument by looking at some representative versions of it. Though it can be found at least as far back as Richard Bentley in the eighteenth century, perhaps the most influential scholar to employ the comparative argument is F. F. Bruce in his apologetic *The New Testament Documents: Are They Reliable?* (1st ed., 1943).[1] Bruce also has the distinction of being a trained classicist himself, having taught classics in his first academic posts, which adds to his ethos as commentator on both fields.[2] We will take Bruce as our major representative and then look at a few recent presentations.

Bruce's book begins by addressing briefly what the New Testament documents are and their estimated dates. He then asks the question, "What is the evidence for their early existence?" He gives as a foil the theories of the old Tübingen school (F. C. Baur and company) that many New Testament books "including the Gospels and the Acts" were written at least a century after Jesus' death, and he counters by appealing to the "greater and more conclusive" evidence available for their early existence. This is where the comparison with classics begins: "The evidence for our New Testament writings is ever so much greater than the evidence for many writings of classical

---

[1]Richard Bentley, *Remarks upon a Late Discourse of Free-Thinking: In a Letter to N. N. by Phileleutherus Lispiensis*, 6th ed. (Cambridge: Cambridge University Press, 1725), 65-68. Here I follow the sixth edition of F. F. Bruce, *The New Testament Documents: Are They Reliable?*, 6th ed. (Grand Rapids: Eerdmans, 1981).

[2]For a biography, see Tim Grass, *F. F. Bruce: A Life* (Grand Rapids: Eerdmans, 2011).

authors, the authenticity of which no one dreams of questioning." He explains, there are "over 5,000 Greek manuscripts of the New Testament in whole or in part," and the "most important" ones (e.g., Vaticanus 03, Sinaiticus 01) date no later than the fourth century.[3]

That Bruce uses Tübingen as a foil illustrates that, at least in part, he wants to show that the New Testament documents were not written so long after the events they relate (note that he addresses the books that purport to relate events—the Gospels and Acts—especially). But he does not yet offer the reader the earlier papyri available to him, such as those in the Chester Beatty or Bodmer collections. Instead, he turns first to compare manuscript attestation for several classical histories:

> Perhaps we can appreciate how wealthy the New Testament is in manuscript attestation if we compare the textual material for other ancient historical works. For Caesar's *Gallic War* (composed between 58 and 50 BC) there are several extant MSS, but only nine or ten are good, and the oldest is some 900 years later than Caesar's day. Of the 142 books of the Roman History of Livy (59 BC–AD 17) only thirty-five survive; these are known to us from not more than twenty MSS of any consequence, only one of which, and that containing fragments of Books iii-vi, is as old as the fourth century. . . . The History of Thucydides (c. 460–400 BC) is known to us from eight MSS, the earliest belonging to c. AD 900, and a few papyrus scraps, belonging to about the beginning of the Christian era. The same is true of the History of Herodotus (c. 488–428 BC). Yet no classical scholar would listen to an argument that the authenticity of Herodotus or Thucydides is in doubt because the earliest MSS of their works which are of any use to us are over 1,300 years later than the originals.[4]

Bruce then contrasts the textual evidence for the New Testament. While any of these classical works may have only a handful of manuscripts, and most relatively very late, the New Testament's major witnesses were copied within only a few centuries after the originals were composed, and several papyri are earlier than that! If any modern reconstruction of an ancient work approximates the text of the original document, it is the New Testament.

One might, of course, object that more manuscripts means more errors to deal with in the manuscript tradition. Here Bruce furthers the data he

---

[3]Bruce, *New Testament Documents*, 9, 10.
[4]Bruce, *New Testament Documents*, 11.

offered in the comparison. With the wealth of manuscripts, combined with the early date of many papyri and quotes from patristic authors, one comes to the conclusion that we could hardly be in a better situation when it comes to ascertaining the original text of the New Testament: "If the great number of MSS increases the number of scribal errors, it increases proportionately the means of correcting such errors, so that the margin of doubt left in the process of recovering the exact original wording is not so large as might be feared; it is in truth remarkably small." He quotes Sir Frederic Kenyon's statement that the chronological proximity of the extant New Testament documents to their times of composition demonstrates definitively "that the Scriptures have come down to us substantially as they were written."[5]

The comparison with classics is used to similar ends in recent apologists and scholars, though the data given sometimes diverge from Bruce (and sometimes do not). Craig Blomberg lays it out methodically: anyone asking whether what the New Testament authors wrote is true must first ask whether we even *have* what those authors actually wrote. His comparison with classics emerges several pages later as an illustration. For the very popular *Iliad* and *Odyssey* of Homer, he says, we have no more than twenty-five hundred manuscripts "of those works put together." Herodotus is attested by only seventy-five, while there are "20 copies of Thucydides, and 27 of the works of the Roman historian Livy." Blomberg also appeals to the relatively late date of classical manuscript attestation: "And the oldest surviving manuscript for any of these authors dates from at least four centuries after the time it was first written, sometimes as many as nine centuries after, versus a gap of only one century, or less, for most of the New Testament books."[6] Blomberg's numbers are not identical to Bruce's, and he adds Homer (whom Bruce does not mention), but the point is the same.

A more popular-level apologetic comes from Amy Orr-Ewing, who upholds the New Testament with "24,000" manuscripts (including versions and other witnesses) against the attestation for classical authors: Caesar with ten manuscripts beginning from the tenth century, Thucydides with eight

[5]Bruce, *New Testament Documents*, 14, 15, citing Frederic Kenyon, *The Bible and Archaeology* (London: G. Harrap, 1940), 288-89.
[6]Craig L. Blomberg, *Can We Still Believe the Bible? An Evangelical Engagement with Contemporary Questions* (Grand Rapids: Brazos, 2014), 13, 35. These numbers appear also in Mark D. Roberts, *Can We Trust the Gospels? Investigating the Reliability of Matthew, Mark, Luke, and John* (Wheaton, IL: Crossway, 2007), 31.

manuscripts beginning from the tenth century, Plato with seven manuscripts from the tenth century, Tacitus with twenty manuscripts beginning from the twelfth century, Suetonius with eight manuscripts from the tenth century, and Homer's *Iliad* with 643 manuscripts from the fifth century BC.[7] Orr-Ewing's figures are closer to Bruce's than to Blomberg's while including more classical authors than both. Nevertheless, the point is the same.

A final example comes not from an apologetics book but a primer for New Testament text criticism by Stanley Porter and Andrew Pitts. They cite Bruce (above) and provide essentially the same data as he on classical authors: Caesar's *Gallic Wars*, eight to nine manuscripts from the ninth century; Livy, twenty fragments (one from the fourth century); Thucydides, eight manuscripts from the tenth century; Herodotus, eight manuscripts from the tenth century. They then offer in comparison the New Testament, for which they claim "over seventy-two hundred Greek manuscripts of various sizes and shapes representing different portions of the NT," *not* including versional evidence. From this they conclude, "When compared with other works of antiquity, the New Testament has far greater (numerical) and earlier documentation than any other book. Most of the available works of antiquity have only a few manuscripts that attest to their existence, and these are typically much later than their original date of composition."[8]

These examples will suffice for now to show the argument's main contours and its use. In each presentation, the argument turns on two data points: (1) the relative wealth of manuscript attestation for the New Testament in comparison with classical authors and (2) the relatively early date of some of these manuscript witnesses. These two points, it should be said now, are *indisputable* overall. They are just true. However, there are some errors and inconsistencies in these (and other) presentations of the argument. Some are simply errors in numbers, some in the fairness of the numbers compared in the argument. In an argument about numbers, errors in numbers make the argument vulnerable to detraction. Before thinking about the argument

---

[7]Amy Orr-Ewing, *Why Trust the Bible? Answers to 10 Tough Questions* (Nottingham, UK: InterVarsity Press, 2005), 43. Describing the number 24,000, she states, "There are more than 5,300 known Greek manuscripts of the New Testament. Add 10,000 Latin manuscripts and 9,300 early portions of the New Testament, and we have around 24,000 extant manuscript copies of portions of the New Testament" (*Why Trust the Bible?*, 42).

[8]Stanley E. Porter and Andrew W. Pitts, *Fundamentals of New Testament Textual Criticism* (Grand Rapids: Eerdmans, 2015), 33, 50.

overall, the following two sections will illustrate some of the errors and offer suggestions as to how to correct them and improve the argument.

PROBLEMS WITH NUMBERS AND DATES

One thing immediately noticeable from the few samples of the comparison above is a basic disagreement about data, particularly regarding the number and dates of manuscripts for the classics. This is true even for those works published within the last decade or so. Porter and Pitts (2015) have only eight manuscripts for Herodotus, but Blomberg (2014) has seventy-five. Orr-Ewing (2005) has eight manuscripts for Thucydides, while Blomberg has twenty. All of these numbers are, of course, lower than those for the New Testament, so the basic points of the comparison stand. But readers interested in the New Testament's reliability who read more than one book might ask themselves which numbers are correct, and apologists looking to make the argument anew might ask themselves the same question.

What this discrepancy introduces us to is, in fact, the deeper problem that many presentations of the comparative arguments are *simply inaccurate* when it comes to these numbers—especially, though not only, when they are reproducing Bruce's figures. This has been pointed out sufficiently by Clay Jones, an apologist at Biola University. Jones devotes a whole article to updating the numbers in the *Christian Research Journal*.[9] Jones rightly finds that classical works often have more manuscripts than are commonly given, and some of these are of considerably earlier dates than given.

Regarding the number of manuscripts themselves, a few examples will suffice. For Caesar's *Gallic Wars*, Jones counts not ten (so Bruce) but 251 manuscripts.[10] Again, it is far less than the manuscript attestation for the Gospels, so the comparison's basic points remain, but 251 is a far cry from ten! Likewise, Orr-Ewing (and others) cite Plato as attested by only seven manuscripts, when there are again over two hundred.[11] Perhaps the biggest gap in terms of numbers comes with Homer. Several writers state that the

---

[9]Clay Jones, "The Bibliographical Test Updated," *CRJ* 35, no. 3 (2012): 32-37, www.equip.org/articles /the-bibliographical-test-updated/. I am thankful to Elijah Hixson for sharing a print copy.

[10]Citing Virginia Brown, "Latin Manuscripts of Caesar's Gallic War," in *Palaeographia diplomatica et archivistica: Studi in onore di Giulio Battelli*, Storia e letteratura 139 (Rome: Edizioni di storia e letteratura, 1979), 1:105-57.

[11]See Nigel G. Wilson, "A List of Plato Manuscripts," *Scriptorium* 16, no. 2 (1962): 386-95. Jones directs us more recently to Robert S. Brumbaugh, "Plato Manuscripts: Toward a Completed Inventory," *Manuscripta* 34 (1990): 114-21.

Iliad has only 643 manuscripts.[12] Jones shows that internet searches (in 2012) reveal this to be a popular statistic on websites defending the New Testament's reliability (though notably not websites devoted to Homer).[13] Where precisely authors have gotten this count is not always transparent; it may have come from Bruce M. Metzger, who in a 1963 essay cited numbers that add up to 643 manuscripts for the *Iliad*.[14]

Though the source is credible and the argument is popular, Metzger's 1963 numbers are now simply inaccurate. Martin West, editor of the most recent Teubner edition of the *Iliad*, discusses 1,569 papyri in his monograph on that epic's text (published 2001).[15] Indeed, since West's monograph, more papyri have been edited and published, some quite old (most dating to the first two centuries on either side of the common era).[16] This, in addition to nearly two hundred nonpapyri (parchment and paper) manuscripts for the *Iliad*, increases the number of manuscripts by well over a thousand. Presumably, Blomberg's happily higher approximation for Homer ("less than 2,500" for the *Iliad* and *Odyssey* together) is an attempt to update these numbers.

If these examples show that our manuscript numbers are often wildly off, other examples show that inaccurate counting also results in inaccurate figures for classical works' earliest manuscript attestation. For Herodotus, Bruce and others give about eight manuscripts; Blomberg gives 75. Jones's update instead gives 109, counting 49 papyri and nearly 60 nonpapyri. But even with these numbers, Jones too errs in reporting that the "earliest surviving manuscript dates from the tenth century AD," over a millennium after Herodotus (d. 425

---

[12]E.g., Orr-Ewing, *Why Trust the Bible?*, 43; Josh McDowell, *The New Evidence That Demands a Verdict* (Nashville: Thomas Nelson, 1999), 34; Norman L. Geisler and William E. Nix, *A General Introduction to the Bible: Revised and Expanded* (Chicago: Moody, 1986), 404; Geisler and Nix, *From God to Us: How We Got Our Bible*, 2nd ed. (Chicago: Moody, 2012), 70.

[13]Jones, "Bibliographical Test Updated," 33.

[14]Bruce Metzger writes, "In 1955 Hans Joachim Mette listed 453 papyri of the *Iliad*. Besides these the *Iliad* is contained in two uncial and 188 minuscule manuscripts," in "Recent Trends in the Textual Criticism of the Iliad and the Mahābhārata," in *Chapters in the History of New Testament Textual Criticism*, NTTS 4 (Leiden: Brill, 1963), 145.

[15]Martin L. West, *Studies in the Text and Transmission of the Iliad* (Berlin: de Gruyter, 2001). Noted by Jones, "Bibliographical Test Updated," 33.

[16]E.g., Sofía Torallas Tovar and Klaas A. Worp, "A Fragment of Homer, *Iliad* 21 in the Newberry Library, Chicago," BASP 46 (2009): 11-14; Charles Bartlett et al., "Six Homeric Papyri from Oxyrhynchus at Columbia University," BASP 48 (2011): 7-26. Much recent work has been done by papyrologist Andrzej Mirończuk: "P.Oxy. 4.755 descr.—a Homeric Papyrus at Princeton (*Iliad* 5.130-174)," BASP 50 (2013): 7-14; Mirończuk, "Three Homeric Papyri at Cleveland," ZPE 183 (2012): 21-26; Mirończuk, "Unpublished Papyri of the Iliad at Yale," ZPE 185 (2013): 18-20.

BC).[17] Unless Jones means to exclude papyri from what he terms "manuscripts" (which would contradict his count), we will have to roll this date back almost *one thousand years*. Papyri from the first or second century AD attest fragments from book 1 and a substantial part of book 2.[18] Books 7 and 8 are attested in the second or third centuries AD.[19] Book 9 was found in a Duke papyrus that was dated to the first or second century AD, but subsequent research suggests it comes from the same roll as another earlier papyrus—putting this fragment of book 9 in the first or perhaps second century BC.[20]

Likewise, Thucydides is given eight manuscripts, with dates beginning AD 900, by Bruce, Orr-Ewing, and Porter and Pitts, and given twenty manuscripts by Blomberg.[21] However, even by 1913 (before Bruce), a whole book was filled with papyri of Thucydides.[22] The 1938 Oxford edition of Thucydides speaks of some thirty papyri and parchments in evidence.[23] Such figures, of course, would require updating in later decades, and recently papyri of Thucydides have been found dating even back to the third or mid-second century BC (long before 900).[24]

The initial point is this: numbers of known manuscripts can change, and relative dates for manuscript attestation can change drastically at the discovery of one papyrus. This is simply an issue of fact checking and updating, and it is expected in any discussion of antiquity. That numbers need updating—especially those found in older books—is not in itself a problem.[25] It *is* a

---

[17]The quote is from Jones, "Bibliographical Test Updated," 33. See also Geisler and Nix, *General Introduction to the Bible*, 405; Porter and Pitts, *Fundamentals of New Testament Textual Criticism*, 50; Bruce, *New Testament Documents*, 11.

[18]Andrzej Mirończuk, "Notes on P.Oxy. XLVIII 3376 (Herodotus II)," *ZPE* 182 (2012): 80-87; Mirończuk, "New Readings in P.Oxy. XLVIII 3372 (Herodotus I 6-9)," *ZPE* 182 (2012): 77-79.

[19]Andrzej Mirończuk, "Notes on Five Herodotean Papyri," *BASP* 49 (2012): 227-32.

[20]See Agostino Soldati, "Due frammenti di un unico rotolo? P.Duke inv. 756 e P.Mil. Vogl. Inv. 1358 (Herodotus IV 144.2-145.1 e 147.4-5)," *BASP* 42 (2005): 101-6.

[21]Bruce, *New Testament Documents*, 11; Orr-Ewing, *Why Trust the Bible?*, 43; Porter and Pitts, *Fundamentals of New Testament Textual Criticism*, 50; Blomberg, *Can We Still Believe the Bible?*, 35.

[22]Friedrich Fischer, *Thucydidis reliquiae in papyris et membranis aegyptiacis servatae* (Leipzig: Teubner, 1913).

[23]H. S. Jones, ed., *Thucydidis historiae*, rev. J. E. Powell, OCT (Oxford: Clarendon, 1938), 1:ix. See also J. U. Powell, "The Papyri of Thucydides and the Translation of Laurentius Valla," *ClQ* 23, no. 1 (1929): 11-14.

[24]Kevin W. Wilkinson, "Fragments of a Ptolemaic Thucydides Roll in the Beinecke Library," *ZPE* 153 (2005): 69-74. See the note on a second-century AD papyrus in P. J. Sijpesteijn, "A New Papyrus Text of Thucydides," *Aeg* 51 (1971): 221-23.

[25]However, as we will see below in our examples from Thucydides and Tacitus, Bruce's numbers were not always as fair and accurate as they could have been in his own day.

problem when modern apologists simply follow old figures without updating—
especially when those apologists are updating their New Testament numbers
to include recent finds. It may not be intentional or underhanded—and one
should remember that proper apologists are required to be up on several fields
(philosophy, archaeology, history, theology) and are stretched thin in their
research time. But, again, in arguments about numbers, bad numbers weaken
the argument.

The primary set of "mistakes" that need to be dealt with have now been
addressed. The rest of the essay now can be more constructive, to help us
understand the number counts and consider the comparative argument's
value and best use.

UNDERSTANDING THE NUMBERS AND COMPARING FAIRLY

It is important to say here that the New Testament apologist may be forgiven
for not having absolute numbers. And one should not assume that apologists have been nefariously skewing data. But, given the above, the interested
reader—not least the apologist hoping to better the argument in the future—
might also wonder why such discrepancies in numbers and dates are found
in the literature at all. If our numbers are wrong, where did they come from?
And how can we avoid this in the future?

These questions open up an important issue relating to the comparative
argument, one that in part clarifies the discrepancies and also should inform
apologists when making the argument: classicists and New Testament scholars
do not always "count" the same way. Especially at the time when many of our
standard editions were written, the classical text critic is actually inclined *not*
to count every possible witness. When working with a family tree or stemma
of manuscripts for a textual tradition, witnesses that share the same distinctive
errors or that are otherwise clearly copied from another known witness are
actually removed from consideration when reconstructing the original text.
This is because their testimony to the original text is considered merely derivative, contributing nothing distinctive. By this process, known as *eliminatio*
(elimination), the critic's task can be significantly streamlined. Consider the
instructions in Paul Maas's famous manual: "It will now be obvious that a
witness is worthless (worthless, that is, *qua* witness) when it depends exclusively on a surviving exemplar or on an exemplar which can be reconstructed
without its help. A witness thus shown to be worthless . . . must be *eliminated*

(*eliminatio codicum descriptorum*)."[26] This results in a *functional* count, which can exclude many witnesses unnecessary for reconstruction.

New Testament text criticism today, by contrast, is far more inclusive. This contrast in method is important. For one, it is itself a result of the larger and more varied textual basis for reconstructing the New Testament; our data set is too different to do it this traditional way. Likewise, because of contamination and scribes potentially checking more than one manuscript in making a copy, even a copy that is late or would otherwise appear derivative overall can preserve an original reading corrupted by earlier manuscripts. For the New Testament, at least ideally, no witness is "worthless." This leads to an important point that the comparative argument can help bring out: New Testament textual critics are updating and improving their methods based on the nature of the data, discovering more appropriate and effective methods to reconstruct the text in light of what might in other methods be an unruly number of witnesses and variants.[27]

This difference in method should help clarify, in part, why the numbers are so divergent. Take the example of Thucydides. For Thucydides, Bruce claimed "eight MSS, the earliest belonging to c. AD 900, and a few papyrus scraps, belonging to about the beginning of the Christian era."[28] Now, as mentioned above, the Oxford text just a few years before spoke of some thirty papyri and parchments and several late manuscripts that aid in reconstructing one of the main witnesses.[29] So on an inclusive count, Bruce is wrong, but on a *functional* count he is on the mark: there are about seven manuscripts from which editions of Thucydides are primarily derived, the others being eliminable or fragmentary (note that Bruce's number explicitly excludes "papyrus scraps").

Such discrepancy in counting can even come up among classicists, with some giving total counts and others functional counts.[30] Regarding Tacitus,

---

[26]Paul Maas, *Textual Criticism*, trans. Barbara Flower (Oxford: Clarendon, 1958), 2 (emphasis original). Maas's first edition is from 1927. For a good introduction to the *eliminatio* method, see Paolo Trovato, *Everything You Always Wanted to Know About Lachmann's Method: A Non-Standard Handbook of Genealogical Textual Criticism in the Age of Post-Structuralism, Cladistics, and Copy-Text*, 2nd ed., Storie e linguaggi (Padova: Libreriauniversitaria.it Edizioni, 2017).

[27]See Tommy Wasserman and Peter J. Gurry, *A New Approach to Textual Criticism: An Introduction to the Coherence-Based Genealogical Method*, SBLRBS 80 (Atlanta: SBL Press, 2017).

[28]Bruce, *New Testament Documents*, 11.

[29]Jones, *Thucydidis historiae*, ix-x.

[30]It is worth noting that this text-critical procedure has received critique. For just one example, see Sebastiano Timpanaro, *The Genesis of Lachmann's Method*, ed. and trans. Glenn W. Most (Chicago: University of Chicago Press, 2005), 154-56.

F. Haverfield reported approximately twenty manuscripts for the second half of the *Annals* and *Histories* in 1916, and in 1941 critic C. W. Mendell reported "thirty known manuscripts" of *Annals* 11-21.[31] Nevertheless, Jones can cite a book from 1999 stating, "Tacitus's historical works descend in two manuscripts, one for books 1-6, another for 11-16 and the surviving portions of the history."[32] This is not because we lost a couple of dozen manuscripts but because of the difference in counting.[33]

This can help explain why some of our numbers look the way they do. The question for those making the comparative argument now, however, becomes a question of which way they will choose to count. Jones, for instance, finds the quote above about only two Tacitus manuscripts but finds another mentioning thirty-one derivative manuscripts. Jones commendably counts inclusively and gives the higher number. Porter and Pitts, however, citing the page where Bruce gives eight Thucydides manuscripts and mentions papyri outside his count, give readers the low number and neglect to mention the existence of the excluded papyri.[34]

Here I would caution apologists to ensure that they are *fair* in their comparison. A fair comparison needs to compare like with like—compare apples to apples, as the saying goes. In comparing the manuscript attestation for two different ancient corpora, we are comparing like with like. But fair comparison also demands a like treatment of both corpora. To further the metaphor, it is not simply enough to be comparing two sets of apples; we need to be sure that we keep our eyeglasses on when analyzing each rather than looking with blurry eyes on one apple and with untrammeled sight on another.

Unfortunately, apologists' numbers often reflect an inclusive count for the New Testament but a functional one for classical works. Porter and Pitts give Bruce's specific and low numbers for classics and then give in comparison

---

[31] F. Haverfield, "Tacitus During the Late Roman Period and the Middle Ages," *JRS* 6 (1916): 196-97; C. W. Mendell, "Tacitus: Yalensis III," *Yale University Library Gazette* 15, no. 4 (1941): 70.

[32] David Potter, *Literary Tests and the Roman Historian* (Oxford: Routledge, 1999), 72 (as quoted in Jones, "Bibliographical Test Updated," 33).

[33] Indeed, even this may be debated. In the case of Tacitus, there has been some argument about whether certain manuscripts are in fact so derivative: see C. W. Mendell, "Manuscripts of Tacitus' Minor Works," *MAAR* 19 (1949): 133-45; C. W. Mendell and Samuel A. Ives, "Ryck's Manuscript of Tacitus," *AJP* 72, no. 4 (1951): 337-45; Kenneth Wellesley, "Was the Leiden MS of Tacitus Copied from the Editio Princeps?," *AJP* 89, no. 3 (1968): 302-20.

[34] Jones, "Bibliographical Test Updated," 33-34. Also better here is Peter M. Head, *Is the New Testament Reliable?*, Grove Biblical Series B 30 (Cambridge: Grove, 2003), 10. Compare Porter and Pitts, *Fundamentals of New Testament Textual Criticism*, 50.

"over seventy-two hundred Greek manuscripts of various sizes and shapes" (a gross overestimate on any count). Orr-Ewing gives the low numbers for classical texts, which we have seen usually does not include even all Greek or Latin manuscripts, and then gives a number for the New Testament (twenty-four thousand) that includes fragments and non-Greek versions.[35] Not only is this unfair comparison, but it risks harming legitimate points of the comparative argument if the tables were turned. Indeed, even our traditional and more modest number of five thousand or more New Testament manuscripts includes all kinds of manuscripts that we hardly use to reconstruct the actual text, some fragmentary but valuable for their early dates. Note Bruce's qualifications to his numbers for classical works: he counts manuscripts that are deemed "good," "of any consequence," or "of any use to us" and does not count early but fragmentary "papyrus scraps."[36] But, we should ask, what if we counted the same for the New Testament? What if our many Byzantine-cluster manuscripts were excluded except for a few stemmatic representatives? What if the fragmentary papyri that are valuable for their early dates but useful to consult for only a handful of verses (or words!) of text were not in our count? I do not know exactly what the number would be, but I know it would be nowhere near five thousand.

New Testament apologists (and critics) need to be sure they are comparing fairly, in view not only of the different numbers one can find but the different ways of counting numbers that might influence what one is reading. If we are going to count the New Testament evidence inclusively, we should do the same for the classical corpus we are comparing. What is so wonderful about the New Testament's textual attestation is that it is better in either case. Even when we are as inclusive as possible in our count of the classical works, the New Testament still has earlier relative attestation, more extensive attestation, and far fewer chronological gaps from the time of composition and the time of the printing press and modern editions.[37] Remembering St. Ambrose of

---

[35]Porter and Pitts, *Fundamentals of New Testament Textual Criticism*, 33, 50; Orr-Ewing, *Why Trust the Bible?*, 42-43.

[36]Bruce, *New Testament Documents*, 11.

[37]One notes R. A. McNeal's statement about the state of Herodotus's text, even with the 100+ manuscripts: "The vital readings, that is those which are apt to be genuine ancient variants or are significant conjectures, can almost always be found in three or sometimes four mss.: A, B, D, and R. Only rarely are any of the others necessary. . . . Apart from a few papyrus fragments and citations in later authors and grammarians, our oldest and best witness to the text is the tenth-century ms. Laurentianus 70.3" ("On Editing Herodotus," *L'Antiquité Classique* 52 [1983]:

Milan's dictum "No man heals himself by wounding another," we should avoid treating this comparison as a competition.[38] Happily, it is not one. To compare our wealth of data to the lowest possible numbers for classics (and consequently to use the late dates of only the "good" manuscripts) is *completely unnecessary*. The health and stability of the New Testament's textual transmission are evident by the data alone. They are put into sharp relief when compared with the best possible numbers for classical works, but the comparison is not necessary to prove that our basis for the New Testament is very strong.

THE VALUE OF THE ARGUMENT

Even with updated numbers and clarification on the counts, the comparative argument still yields its two basic data points: (1) the wealth of manuscript evidence available for the New Testament's text and (2) the relatively early attestation we have for the New Testament in the manuscript record. But, after all this, one might ask whether these points are still worth making. Is the comparative argument a good argument? Yes, I think it is a good argument. But to make the argument well in the future, we need to consider what the argument is good *for*. This will help us know what burden we can and should make the argument bear (or not).

We may say first that the comparison is excellent to illustrate *the state of play in New Testament text criticism*. When instructing people who are learning—in a classroom or elsewhere—about textual criticism for the first time, the comparison is excellent to illustrate the both happy and difficult task of the New Testament text critic. Helmut Köster introduces the comparison by saying that it shows the New Testament's apparently much more favorable basis than most classical texts, while immediately also noting that the complexity of the textual tradition thereby requires more complex methods of editorial analysis.[39] Indeed, it can illustrate why New Testament critics do not

---

111). With the state of the New Testament textual tradition and the benefits of our methodology (especially the advances possible with the coherence-based genealogical method), this can hardly be said even of a corpus so poorly attested as the Catholic Epistles.

[38]"Nemo alium vulerando se sanat" (Ambrose, *Enarrationes in XII Psalmos Davidicos* 37.46 [PL 14:1033]).

[39]Helmut Köster, *Einführung in das Neue Testament im Rahmen der Religionsgeschichte und Kulturgeschichte der hellenistischen und römischen Zeit* (Berlin: de Gruyter 1980), 445-46; similarly Porter and Pitts, *Fundamentals of New Testament Textual Criticism*, 51; Head, *Is the New Testament Reliable?*, 10-11; Stefan Schreiber, "Der Text des Neuen Testaments," in *Einleitung in das*

and cannot simply exclude some manuscripts from consideration, and an apologist noting the classical principle of *eliminatio* can use even such methodological differences between the disciplines to demonstrate the New Testament's very different textual basis and, importantly, introduce the methods we devise to deal carefully and reliably with such a base of evidence.

Relatedly, the comparison also helps people understand *why we have so many variants*, which is especially helpful for the apologist's task. People hear of something like four hundred thousand variant readings in the New Testament and easily become terrified that nothing we have is reliable.[40] In addition to reminding people that most of these are inconsequential changes in orthography or word order, the data in the comparative argument can put this into perspective. Of course there are so many errors to speak of across a textual tradition that has so many handmade copies! Indeed, it should be a testament to the meticulous concern for detail and exactness that New Testament critics mark and consider all the small and unessential variations that they do.[41] The great number of manuscripts, not to mention the general uniformity in most of the manuscripts, can help put an initially shocking number of variants into perspective.

In addition to putting the problem of our many variants into perspective, the numbers given in the comparative argument also suggest that—apart from having the originals themselves—we have the best data imaginable to work with to reconstruct the originals accurately. Here, however, we need to remain circumspect about what the data can and cannot demonstrate. Some suggest simply from the numbers that we can trust that our reconstructed New Testament text represents the original documents.[42] That New Testament scholars have a vast amount of evidence for the text is unquestionable. However, the wealth of textual data is not enough, on its own, to prove that our reconstructed text reliably matches the original compositions;

Neue Testament, ed. Martin Ebner and Stefan Schreiber, 2nd ed., Kohlhammer Studienbücher Theologie 6 (Stuttgart: Kohlhammer, 2013), 53.

[40]See Peter J. Gurry, "The Number of Variants in the Greek New Testament: A Proposed Estimate," *NTS* 62, no. 1 (2016): 97-121.

[41]A similar apologetic point was made long ago by Bentley, *Remarks upon a Late Discourse of Free-Thinking,* 66-68.

[42]See Norman L. Geisler and Patty Tunnicliffe, *Reasons for Belief: Easy-to-Understand Answers to 10 Essential Questions* (Grand Rapids: Bethany House, 2013), 102-3: "With so many manuscripts, we can accurately reconstruct beyond question more than 99 percent of the original text"; similarly Bruce, *New Testament Documents,* 14-15.

to believe that we can reconstruct the original well with all the evidence depends largely on whether one trusts whether we have adequate *methods* for attaining this goal with the evidence we have.[43] This is open to question, logically at least. For those such as atheist objector Robert Price, there will never be proof enough that anything we have corresponds to the original because we do not have the originals against which to check our reconstruction.[44] The gap between the originals and our earliest copies still leaves the logical possibility that all the copies we're working with descend from already corrupted manuscripts.

But if this counterclaim follows logically, the Christian apologist can easily respond that this logical objection is hardly *reasonable*. It is here that the comparative side of the argument adds particular value. The comparison with classics allows one to appeal to what skeptics think they know of ancient extrabiblical history and point to its much thinner textual basis. This is Bruce's move: "The evidence for our New Testament writings is ever so much greater than the evidence for many writings of classical authors, the authenticity of which no one dreams of questioning."[45] In brief, the comparative appeal suggests that if you don't think you can trust the New Testament text, then you *really* can't trust any ancient text.

This suggestion is, I think, fair game. In apologetics, one is trying to mount reasons for *warranted belief* as much as to prove facts. However, we should acknowledge that building warrant for trusting the New Testament on the basis of people's trust in classical texts comes with risks, because its effectiveness depends on the extent to which people trust the accuracy of the classical documents. Those who are unsure that we can know what historical classical authors wrote will hardly be moved by the comparison, even if they admit the New Testament's more reliable transmission.[46] This argumentation also cannot ultimately address theories about postauthorial interpolations in the textual tradition or, as with Homer and others, questions

---

[43]One notes that even New Testament textual critics are not totally united on the goal of the "original" text or its definition.

[44]Robert M. Price, *The Case Against the Case for Christ: A New Testament Scholar Refutes the Reverend Lee Strobel* (Cranford, NJ: American Atheist Press, 2010), 98-99.

[45]Bruce, *New Testament Documents*, 10.

[46]So, e.g., Bart Ehrman, using Plato as an example (Bart D. Ehrman and Daniel B. Wallace, "The Textual Reliability of the New Testament: A Dialogue," in *The Reliability of the New Testament: Bart D. Ehrman and Daniel B. Wallace in Dialogue*, ed. Robert B. Stewart [Minneapolis: Fortress, 2011], 47, 51).

about the notion of a single "author" in the first place (one suspects this is why Bruce compared only histories, not epics).[47]

Finally, we must remember that the comparison cannot ultimately engender confidence in the historicity or theological truth of the New Testament (as happens often in more popular presentations of the argument).[48] Even people who think Herodotus's text is sufficiently reliable and consult it as a historical source still do not think all his information (or his claims about where he got it) is true.[49] At the end of the day, Christian apologists using this argument do not want people to believe classical texts the same way that they want people to believe the Gospels, and using this argument to suggest textual veracity (rather than textual reliability) can implicitly undermine this end by asking people to trust the New Testament in the same way that they trust classical texts. To say this is not to denigrate the value of the comparative argument—it is very effective in illustrating the wealth of New Testament information and suggesting that we are better situated to reconstruct the original of the New Testament than that of any other ancient book—but it is to say that further arguments about the truth of the texts will require more historical, philosophical, and theological tools than comparing manuscripts for the Gospels and Suetonius.[50]

CONCLUDING SUGGESTIONS FOR MAKING THE ARGUMENT WELL

In assessing the comparative argument with classics, this essay has pointed out errors and attempted to contextualize and clarify some reasons why these errors prove to be so common. Still, apologists may come to this point

---

[47]For a helpful overview of the form-critical and authorial debates about Homer, see especially the review of Homer studies and of Martin West's recent reconstruction of the *Iliad* in Gregory Nagy, *Homer's Text and Language* (Urbana: University of Illinois Press, 2004), chap. 3. Those interested in countering form-critical claims about the Gospels should consult Richard Bauckham, *Jesus and the Eyewitnesses: The Gospels as Eyewitness Testimony*, 2nd ed. (Grand Rapids: Eerdmans, 2017).

[48]Technically, this takes us beyond our purposes and into truth and theology. However, as Bruce says in the preface to his fifth edition, "It is, indeed, difficult to restrict a discussion of the New Testament writings to the purely historical plane; theology insists on breaking in" (*New Testament Documents*, xiv), and this is no less true of the comparative argument in several online forums (and, depending on what Bruce means by "authenticity," even in Bruce).

[49]E.g., the episode of Arion and the dolphin (Herodotus, *Historiae* 1.23-24).

[50]See the recent contribution of Matthew J. Ramage, *Jesus Interpreted: Benedict XVI, Bart Ehrman, and the Historical Truth of the Gospels* (Washington, DC: Catholic University of America Press, 2017).

and ask what they should do now. It is a different (and easier) thing to critique from the sidelines—as I have done in this essay—than it is to coach or quarterback! Where should an apologist—who is already stretched for research time and forced to keep up with several fields—go to find better numbers, and is there any way to shore up the comparative argument so that it is more effective or less vulnerable?

The data that emerge in the comparative argument is impressive for the New Testament's textual basis. No matter how the numbers are updated or changed for classics, the New Testament still has more attestation, better attestation, and better early attestation. Indeed, noted classicist Giorgio Pasquali has said as much of the New Testament: "No other Greek text is handed down so richly and credibly."[51] This cannot itself prove that we have exactly what the New Testament authors wrote down, but it does show that the New Testament scholar has better material to work with than scholars of standard classical works. If one has any confidence in our methods of analyzing the text of the New Testament in so many manuscripts (and I think one should!), the data in the comparative argument are an excellent step in engendering confidence in the New Testament. If this is the goal of the comparative argument, let me offer a few practical suggestions about how to make the argument well in the future.

Keep it relative. The comparative argument, by its nature, can only demonstrate that the New Testament has a *better* textual basis for scholars to work with than classical works, not that it has a perfect one. You can argue the latter point, but you'll need to introduce methodology into the mix. The good news about this is that for the comparison to do what it can do, all you need to show are the two basic data points mentioned at the beginning of this paper: the relatively greater number of New Testament manuscripts and the New Testament's relatively early manuscript attestation. What this means, thankfully, is that you only need to prove the relative point, not the exact numbers of manuscripts for classical authors.

Do not be so specific about numbers. It is unnecessary. The comparative argument's basic points are not at all compromised if you say something like "fewer than fifty" instead of "eight." Even if you say something like, "Few of the classical works have more than a couple hundred manuscripts, and most

---

[51]Giorgio Pasquali, *Storia della tradizione e critica del testo*, 2nd ed. (Florence: Le Monnier, 1952), 8. I am grateful to Peter J. Gurry for the citation.

of them have far less," the point is made by the indisputably greater number of New Testament manuscripts. The more specific your number is, the more vulnerable it is to a skeptic who wants to weaken your credibility. Moreover, even if your numbers are immaculate today, new publications or new dates for previously published papyri might make your numbers inaccurate by the time people are engaging your argument. It would be a shame to allow the value of the comparative argument to be occluded in this way.

Check for updated numbers. Of course, you may want some specific numbers to illustrate the comparison. Where should you go? The first and easiest places to check are recent authors who have researched the numbers more closely—especially Clay Jones's article cited above. Another easy place to check is the Leuven Database of Ancient Books (LDAB), accessible at www.trismegistos.org/ldab/. Because of the nature of the site and the evidence (the list also includes quotations), simply counting entries down the page will not render an exact and definitive "count," but it will certainly allow one to check whether another scholar's estimate is close to the mark. Another benefit of the site is that it often links one to secondary literature by classical scholars. For instance, selecting the site's "Advanced Search" option and searching "Homer" in the "Ancient Author" box yields several pages of documents. When one clicks on any one document, details are provided such as estimated date, where it is housed, collections in which it is published, and secondary literature discussing it. This is an excellent place to find pieces discussing the state of the text of any author or work, which the apologist can then use to learn more for comparison.

Cite a classicist. In fact, citing a classicist on the issue has the benefit of showing that you've done your homework and allows you to give the year in which the data were published—which allows you to make your point about the numbers but also allows some wiggle room due to updating over time. Nothing argumentatively is lost, and less is risked, if you say, "In 1971 x scholar counted only y manuscripts of z author; even if those numbers have changed slightly with more recent finds, they hardly compare to the New Testament," rather than making the absolute claim, "There *are y* manuscripts of z author." (This deferral in determining the number can also be achieved by saying, "The LDAB currently lists y manuscripts for z author.") Articles or books by classicists can be found through the references in the LDAB, by checking the introductions to critical editions of classical works (though many are still in Latin), or by standard research methods.[52] I would advise checking more than one source and counting inclusively if you find a disagreement about numbers in the sources such as those shown above.

Be more circumspect. Using the LDAB and reading classicists can be time consuming, especially if you mean to give manuscript data on several classical authors. Another effective tack an apologist could take is to discuss only a few isolated examples. This allows you to research a little more and to summarize the difficulties classicists face in reconstructing these texts (in contrast to the situation with the New Testament). Peter Head's little book on the New Testament text does this well: rather than seeking to give a chart for several classical authors, he focuses only on three—Josephus, Philo, and Tacitus. This technique allows him to summarize more accurately the situation and numbers for each, and it also gives the reader a more vivid contrast between what a textual critic has to work with in these authors versus the New Testament. He is able accurately to arrive at the basic data points of the comparative argument: the New Testament has "more manuscripts" and "more early texts, including possibly half a dozen from the second century," with "basically no chronological gaps in the manuscript record."[53] The point is accurate, made sufficiently and vividly, and with less vulnerability.

Use the data to introduce text-critical method. The comparative data can put the numerous New Testament variants into perspective and suggest that we are in the best position to understand and evaluate the New Testament text. But this also is an excellent occasion to introduce our methods for dealing with the many, many manuscripts. Show that New Testament scholars not only have better material to work with but that their tools for evaluating the material and reconstructing the text are excellent and constantly being tweaked for improvement. Use the other essays in this volume to show some of the developments. This is where the argument about the New Testament's relatively *better* manuscript attestation becomes an argument that what we have for the New Testament is not simply *more* reliable than what we have for Plato but that what we have is simply *reliable*.

---

[52]For the record, most of the footnotes in this essay are gleaned from using the LDAB and a JSTOR account.

[53]Head, *Is the New Testament Reliable?*, 10.

Key Takeaways

▶ Scholars and apologists often count all the manuscripts for the New Testament *that exist* (an inclusive count), whereas classicists generally only count the ones *they need to use* (a functional count). This needs to be considered when comparing numbers.

▶ Apologists' numbers too often reflect this inclusive count for the New Testament but a functional count for manuscripts of classical works and end up comparing apples and oranges. Whichever count is used, one should be consistent on both sides.

▶ When counting manuscripts and giving dates for comparison, scholars and apologists also often give numbers that reflect or exaggerate the most recent discoveries for New Testament manuscripts, but do not check for updated numbers or dates for classical manuscripts. Consistency in comparison should be clear here too.

▶ The comparative argument is valuable but limited; it can demonstrate only that the New Testament has a *better* textual basis than classical works, not that it has a perfect one. Text-critical methods are what give reliability to our use of the manuscripts, not the numbers alone.

▶ The more specific your number is, the more vulnerable it is to a skeptic who wants to weaken your credibility.

▶ Citing a classicist on the issue has the benefit of showing that you've done your homework and allows you to give the year in which the data were published—which allows you to make your point about the numbers but also allows some wiggle room due to updating over time.

CHAPTER FIVE

DATING MYTHS, PART ONE
HOW WE DETERMINE THE AGES OF MANUSCRIPTS

Elijah Hixson

IT IS COMMON WHEN READING a primer on New Testament textual criticism, an apologetic defense of the Bible, or often a New Testament introduction to encounter a list of early manuscripts and their ages. For evangelicals, the attraction of early manuscripts is understandable. As Michael J. Kruger writes, "The less time passed between the original writing and our earliest copies, the less time there was for the text to be substantially corrupted, and therefore the more assured we can be that we possess what was originally written."[1]

The date of a manuscript is indeed important. It can situate that manuscript in a proper historical context, or in some cases, it can require some readjustment to the understanding of some slice of history to account for the presence of a manuscript with that date. To take one common example, commentators often cite the date of P52 (P.Ryl. 457) as "around AD 125" to prove that John's Gospel was written in the first century rather than the second century, as argued by a number of nineteenth- and early twentieth-century scholars.[2]

---

[1]Michael J. Kruger, "Do We Have a Trustworthy Text? Inerrancy and Canonicity, Preservation and Textual Criticism," in *The Inerrant Word: Biblical, Historical, Theological, and Pastoral Perspectives*, ed. John MacArthur (Wheaton, IL: Crossway, 2016), 311.

[2]Raymond Brown describes the discovery of P52, among other early papyri, as "the most conclusive argument against the late dating of John," in *An Introduction to the Gospel of John*, ed. Francis J. Moloney, Anchor Yale Bible Reference Library (New Haven, CT: Yale University Press, 2003), 209. Similarly, D. A. Carson seems to mistake P.Egerton 2 for P52, but he likewise appeals to an early copy of John, writing, "Dates in the second century are now pretty well ruled out of court by the discovery of Papyrus Egerton 2 (cf. §II, above)," in *The Gospel According to John*

Unfortunately—and this seems to be especially the case for some evangelicals—an attraction to early manuscripts can and does lead to a number of problems. The cavalier attitude toward the destruction of mummy masks—artifacts of cultural heritage—in the quest to find early manuscripts of the Bible has earned Scott Carroll and Josh McDowell a good deal of criticism from friend and foe alike.[3] Appeals to P137, alleged to be a first-century fragment of Mark, became so common that when it was finally published, some were disappointed at the earliest fragment of Mark 1.[4]

Early manuscripts of the New Testament are not *always* good witnesses to the original text either. P72 (P.Bodm. VII-VIII) is the earliest substantial manuscript of 1–2 Peter and Jude, but it seems to have been written by a rather careless scribe.[5] A number of scholars even mention that P72 appears to have a noticeable tendency to change the text in order to emphasize the divinity of Jesus. James R. Royse writes of P72, "We seem to be compelled, therefore, to conclude that here too [at Jude 5] the scribe has deliberately introduced a reading in order to ascribe Deity to Christ."[6] Bart Ehrman mentions the same reading in P72 as one of the "orthodox corruptions of Scripture" he writes about.[7] Even if the scribe was not actually responsible

(Grand Rapids: Eerdmans, 1991), 82. Carson does not mention P.Egerton 2 in his §II, but he does mention "Papyrus 52, dating from AD 130" (24). Brent Nongbri is likely correct that "Kurt Aland appears to be the one guilty of popularizing this earlier dating," and asserts that the Alands "(with absolutely no evidence) push the date still earlier" than circa 100–150 to an emphasis on the early half of the already-narrow date range, in Nongbri, "The Use and Abuse of P52: Papyrological Pitfalls in the Dating of the Fourth Gospel," *HTR* 98, no. 1 (2005): 30-31n22.

[3]For a summary, see Candida R. Moss and Joel S. Baden, *Bible Nation: The United States of Hobby Lobby* (Princeton, NJ: Princeton University Press, 2017), 36-40. Peter M. Head describes their destruction of mummy masks as "slapdash, deplorable and not reflective of good practice in Christian scholarship" in the comments on Tommy Wasserman, "Breaking News on the First-Century (?) Fragment of Mark," *Evangelical Textual Criticism* (blog), May 5, 2014, http://evangelical textualcriticism.blogspot.co.uk/2014/05/breaking-news-first-century-fragment-of.html.

[4]Pieter Lalleman, "Oldest Manuscript of Mark Is Nonetheless a Disappointment," *Christian Today*, May 31, 2018, www.christiantoday.com/article/oldest-manuscript-of-mark-is-nonetheless -a-disappointment/129500.htm.

[5]See discussions in James R. Royse, *Scribal Habits in Early Greek New Testament Papyri*, NTTSD 36 (Leiden: Brill, 2008), 549; J. K. Elliott, "The Early Text of the Catholic Epistles," in *The Early Text of the New Testament*, ed. Charles E. Hill and Michael J. Kruger (Oxford: Oxford University Press, 2012), 214.

[6]Royse, *Scribal Habits*, 611. Whereas manuscripts typically read that either "Jesus" or "the Lord" saved a people out of Egypt, P72 has "God Christ" at Jude 5. For a fuller discussion and bibliography on the changes of the scribe of P72, see Royse, *Scribal Habits*, 609-14.

[7]Bart D. Ehrman, *The Orthodox Corruption of Scripture: The Effect of Early Christological Controversies on the Text of the New Testament*, 2nd ed. (Oxford: Oxford University Press, 2011), 100. On theologically motivated changes, see chapter eleven in this volume.

for the "orthodox corruptions," they are in the manuscript, and there are enough of them to form a pattern. It is therefore inadvisable to assume without qualification that earlier is *always* better, more accurate, or less likely to contain "corruptions" when one of the earliest manuscripts of 1–2 Peter and Jude looks as though it was written by a copyist who changed the text in places to make a stronger case that Jesus is God.

When it comes to reporting the dates of manuscripts, some evangelical scholars and apologists often give unjustifiably early or narrow date ranges.[8] By doing so, they leave the door open for criticism that they are misrepresenting the evidence. On early dates for P52, for example, Paul Foster writes, "For some people, having an early NT fragment is perhaps more of an ideological commitment than something that is established on the basis of close analysis."[9] Such appeals to specific or early dates of manuscripts are often inappropriate in light of the uncertainties of paleographical dating, and as we will see, P52 does not automatically rule out a second-century composition of John's Gospel. This chapter seeks to explain the ways manuscripts are dated while explaining limitations of dating methods, to examine a case study of a commonly cited early manuscript whose "early" date has been revised (P52), and to offer some solutions to nonspecialists who discuss early dated manuscripts in their work. The discussion emphasizes early dated manuscripts for two reasons. First, it is more common for such manuscripts to appear (often by name) in apologetic defenses of the New Testament. Second, there are fewer securely dated manuscripts in the earlier centuries, and consequently, paleographic dating is less reliable for early manuscripts than for later manuscripts.

METHODS FOR DATING MANUSCRIPTS

Occasionally a manuscript can be dated with certainty, and here we look at a few examples. Such instances include manuscripts whose scribes recorded the date of their production, with references to particular historical persons

---

[8]Two recent examples are Norman L. Geisler, *Christian Apologetics*, 2nd ed. (Grand Rapids: Baker Academic, 2013), 343-44, and Philip W. Comfort, *A Commentary on the Manuscripts and Text of the New Testament* (Grand Rapids: Kregel Academic, 2015), 45-93.

[9]Paul Foster, "Bold Claims, Wishful Thinking, and Lessons About Dating Manuscripts from Papyrus Egerton 2," in *The World of Jesus and the Early Church: Identity and Interpretation in Early Communities of Faith*, ed. Craig A. Evans (Peabody, MA: Hendrickson, 2011), 200. Foster is certainly no enemy of evangelicals. I wrote my PhD thesis under his supervision, and I am not the only contributor to this volume to have done so.

who can be identified elsewhere, or manuscripts with an archaeological context that settles the date of the manuscript. Even if a date cannot be assigned with complete confidence, historical or archaeological considerations can sometimes provide the earliest possible date, known as the *terminus post quem* (literally "limit after which"), or the latest possible date known, as the *terminus ante quem* (literally "limit before which").

Content. Sometimes the scribe of a manuscript recorded when he or she produced it. One example is the scribe of GA 1415 (Athens, National Library of Greece, Manuscript 123).

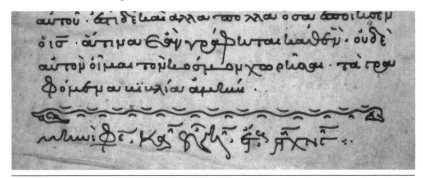

Figure 5.1. The colophon in GA 1415 (Athens, National Library of Greece, Ms. 123), f. 189r telling the precise date on which it was finished

Beneath the decorative line, the scribe wrote μηνὶ φε(βρουαριω) κ̄ᾱ (ινδικτιωνος) η̄ ετ(ους) ͵ϛχν̄γ̄ (*mēni phe[brouariō] 21 [indiktiōnos] 8 et[ous] 6653*), which means, "Month of February, the 21st, in the 8th indiction [i.e., the eighth year in a fifteen-year cycle]; year 6653." Dates were written relative to the creation of the world, which according to the Byzantine system was September 1, 5509 BC, so February 6653 translates to AD 1145.[10]

Even without such a written date, manuscripts might still contain datable information. Sometimes a piece of papyrus was reused by writing another text on the back. If a piece of papyrus lacks a date on one side, a date or a reference to a datable person or event on the other side might still narrow the possible date range by providing a *terminus post quem* or *terminus ante quem*. Eric Turner undertook a study of reused papyri where both sides were

---

[10]Another example is 1402 (Athens, National Library of Greece, Manuscript 180), dated to AD 1089 by its scribe, whose name was Andrew. Daniel B. Wallace mentions this manuscript in a discussion of colophons in Greek New Testament manuscripts in "Medieval Manuscripts and Modern Evangelicals: Lessons from the Past, Guidance for the Future," *JETS* 60, no. 1 (2017): 18.

dated and concluded that official documents such as contracts or deeds were generally reused within one hundred years, with "a slight balance of probability in favour of re-use within 25 years."[11]

Manuscript content can also provide a *terminus post quem*. Turner mentions that P.Bodm. XX, a manuscript of a work describing the martyrdom of a bishop named Phileas, "which on palaeographical grounds might plausibly be assigned to [the third century], cannot be earlier than c. A.D. 306, the year in which its hero-bishop faced his persecutor."[12] Likewise, copies of a book obviously cannot be made before the author finishes writing it. P.Oxy. 3.405 was originally unidentified and dated "not later than the first half of the third century, and might be as old as the latter part of the second."[13] It was later identified as a fragment of Irenaeus's *Adversus haereses* 3.9. Although the hand was judged to be from AD 150–250, the copy could not have been made before Irenaeus wrote the work, around AD 180.

Archaeological indicators. Occasionally, the archaeological context can provide clues for dating. A volcanic eruption, for example, provides a *terminus ante quem* for the Herculaneum papyri. They obviously must have been written before Herculaneum and Pompeii were destroyed by the eruption of Mount Vesuvius in AD 79.

One Greek New Testament papyrus that can be dated from its archaeological context is P10 (P.Oxy. 2.209), a writing exercise that contains Romans 1:1-7.[14] In its *editio princeps*, Bernard Grenfell and Arthur Hunt note that it "was found tied up with a contract dated 316 A.D., and other documents of the same period."[15] AnneMarie Luijendijk made the connection that the contract to which Grenfell and Hunt refer was one they had already published, P.Oxy. 1.103, a lease for a plot of land. More importantly, P.Oxy. 1.103 is part of a larger archive—a collection of papyri compiled by a single individual in

[11]Eric G. Turner, "Recto and Verso," *JEA* 40 (1954): 106.

[12]Eric G. Turner, *Greek Manuscripts of the Ancient World*, 2nd ed., rev. P. J. Parsons, BICS Supplement 46 (London: Institute of Classical Studies, 1987), 22.

[13]Bernard P. Grenfell and Arthur S. Hunt, "405-406. Theological Fragments," in *The Oxyrhynchus Papyri III*, ed. Bernard P. Grenfell and Arthur S. Hunt, GRM 5 (London: Egypt Exploration Fund, 1903), 10.

[14]Admittedly, a writing exercise such as this one should probably not even count as a manuscript of the New Testament. On the difficulties involved with counting manuscripts, see chapter three in this volume.

[15]Bernard P. Grenfell and Arthur S. Hunt, "CCIX. St. Paul's Epistle to the Romans, Chap. I," in *The Oxyrhynchus Papyri II*, ed. Bernard P. Grenfell and Arthur S. Hunt, GRM 2 (London: Egypt Exploration Fund, 1898), 8.

antiquity. This particular individual was one Leonides, son of Theon. Other dated manuscripts in his archive give it the range of AD 315–334.[16] Despite the fact that P10 is a part of Leonides's archive, it is unclear who exactly wrote it. Romans 1:1-7 is written in a different kind of script from the rest of the archive, so it is impossible to prove that the same person wrote both, simply because there is no point of comparison for the style of handwriting used for Romans. (Imagine going through a set of notes from someone that are written entirely in cursive and finding a single page of block-letter writing.) Whether Leonides himself wrote P10 or whether it is the fourth-century Egyptian equivalent of children's refrigerator art, it clearly does seem to be a writing exercise. In any case, we have a twenty-year window for its likely date because of the archive of which it is a part.

Archaeological evidence is not always so certain, however. The St. Cuthbert Gospel (London, British Library, Add Manuscript 89000) was first discovered in 1104, when St. Cuthbert's tomb at Durham Cathedral was opened. It was buried with him, so presumably it would have a *terminus ante quem* of the date of his burial—he died on March 20, AD 687. However, Richard Gameson notes that the manuscript is too late to have been made during Cuthbert's lifetime. Based on several features, Gameson dates the manuscript to AD 710–730.[17] In this case, the discovery of the manuscript in the tomb of St. Cuthbert does not prove that it was written during Cuthbert's lifetime; it proves only that it was placed in his tomb at some point before the tomb was opened in 1104.

Paleographic dating. Though secure dates are ideal, in many cases, ancient manuscripts—especially manuscripts of literary works such as the New Testament—lack any securely datable features and must be dated paleographically. Paleographic dating relies on the appearance of the handwriting to assign a date range during which the manuscript was most likely produced. The general idea is that Greek (or Latin, Coptic, etc.) was typically written in one of a number of given styles, and handwriting within these styles changed over time. Particular styles of handwriting can be anchored

---

[16]AnneMarie Luijendijk, "A New Testament Papyrus and Its Documentary Context: An Early Christian Writing Exercise from the Archive of Leonides (P.Oxy. II 209/P10)," *JBL* 129, no. 3 (2010): 575-96.

[17]Richard Gameson, "Materials, Text, Layout and Script," in *The St. Cuthbert Gospel: Studies on the Insular Manuscript of the Gospel of John*, ed. Claire Breay and Bernard Meehan (London: British Library, 2015), 33.

here and there by securely dated manuscripts.[18] For any given manuscript, a paleographer will first identify the style. Then he or she will decide where in the overall development of that style the hand falls—within a particular style of handwriting, earlier manuscripts have earlier features, and later manuscripts have later features. A date is assigned based on where the hand sits on that early-to-late spectrum. The real situation is of course more complicated than I have presented here, but in general, this is the way dates have been traditionally assigned to manuscripts by paleographers.[19]

Although the method is widely used, it is not perfect. Eric Turner is skeptical of putting too much weight on "styles" of handwriting because "the term 'style of handwriting' suggests an external reality [that may not have existed], or at least an ideal present in the minds of the scribes who wrote it."[20] Even if one assumes that the style theory works, manuscripts can have mixed features within a given style. Sometimes late manuscripts have "early" features, or vice versa. Sometimes two manuscripts written in the same style of hand can be extraordinarily similar, despite having been written decades or even centuries apart. For this reason, responsible paleographers have always been careful with dates, often advocating broad ranges rather than narrow ones. According to INTF, for example, the hand of P94 can be dated to only a two-hundred-year window—fifth or sixth century. Recent studies have placed increased emphasis on caution when assigning narrow date-ranges.[21] Of the commonly given date of "around 125" for P52, Paul Foster writes, "Such a precise date is, of course, nonsense. Paleographical analysis

---

[18]On the problems with paleographic dating due to the dearth of securely dated manuscripts, see Don Barker, "How Long and Old Is the Codex of Which P.Oxy 1353 Is a Leaf?," in *Jewish and Christian Scripture as Artifact and Canon*, ed. Craig A. Evans and H. Daniel Zacharias, SSEJC 13/LSTS 70 (New York: T&T Clark, 2009), 194-96.

[19]See especially Guglielmo Cavallo, *Ricerche sulla maiuscola biblica*, Studi e testi di papirologia editi dall'Istituto Papirologico «G. Vitelli» di Firenze 2 (Florence: Le Monnier, 1967). See also Guglielmo Cavallo and Herwig Maehler, *Greek Bookhands of the Early Byzantine Period A.D. 300–800* (London: Institute of Classical Studies, 1987); Pasquale Orsini, *Manoscritti in maiuscola biblica: Materiali per un aggiornamento*, SAAFLS 7 (Cassino: Edizioni dell'Università degli studi di Cassino, 2005).

[20]Turner, *Greek Manuscripts of the Ancient World*, 20.

[21]See, for example, Brent Nongbri, "The Limits of Palaeographic Dating of Literary Papyri: Some Observations on the Date and Provenance of P. Bodmer II (P66)," *MH* 71, no. 1 (2014): 1-35; Nongbri, "Use and Abuse of P52"; Pasquale Orsini and Willy Clarysse, "Early New Testament Manuscripts and Their Dates: A Critique of Theological Palaeography," *ETL* 88, no. 4 (2012): 443-74. See also Christian Askeland, "Dating Early Greek and Coptic Literary Hands," in *The Nag Hammadi Codices and Late Antique Egypt*, ed. Hugo Lundhaug and Lance Jennott, STAC 110 (Tübingen: Mohr Siebeck, 2018), 457-89.

does not allow such precision for undated texts." Turner warns that for "literary" hands, "a period of 50 years is the least acceptable spread of time."[22]

A comparison of P.Ryl. 16 and scribe A of Codex Sinaiticus illustrates the problem that resulted in Turner's hesitancy to assign any date ranges shorter than fifty years on the basis of paleography alone.[23] These two manuscripts are written in the same general style, called "biblical majuscule," but they were written forty to two hundred years apart from each other. The comparison aims to show why one should not be too eager to accept the earliest possible or even the latest possible dates.

P.Ryl. 16 is a fragment of a comedy that was reused as a letter. The letter on the back can be dated to AD 256, giving this papyrus its *terminus ante quem*, but we do not know how long before AD 256 it was written. In 1967, Guglielmo Cavallo paleographically dated the manuscript to the narrow window of circa 220–225 (!).[24] The manuscript is part of an archive, however, which can shed some additional light on its date. In a study of reused papyri with dates on both sides, Turner suggested that P.Ryl. 16 might be as early as AD 150 because other reused papyri in the archive were about one hundred years old before reuse.[25]

Figure 5.2. P.Ryl. 16 is a fragment of a comedy with a dated letter on the backside

---

[22]Foster, "Bold Claims, Wishful Thinking," 199; Turner, *Greek Manuscripts of the Ancient World*, 20.
[23]Thanks are due to Brent Nongbri, who inspired me to compare P.Ryl. 16 with Codex Sinaiticus.
[24]Cavallo, *Ricerche sulla maiuscola biblica*, 45-46.
[25]Turner, "Recto and Verso," 106. However, there is no guarantee that P.Ryl. 16 was written as early as AD 150. At least one papyrus in this archive was reused after only nine months, and several others after fifteen to thirty years.

The other hand of our comparison is scribe A of Codex Sinaiticus, which has a *terminus post quem* because it was produced with the Eusebian apparatus in the Gospels. It obviously could not have been made before Eusebius had developed this cross-reference system, which probably happened during the window of AD 290–340. Codex Sinaiticus could be *later* but not earlier. On the basis of the handwriting, Cavallo dated Codex Sinaiticus to circa 360 "or a few years later" (!).[26]

Cavallo described the hand he calls "biblical majuscule" as emerging from a "sober and undecorated script." "True biblical majuscule" has a "visible contrast between thin horizontal strokes and fatter vertical ones (particularly gamma, pi, tau), while oblique [i.e., diagonal] strokes appear in between (alpha, delta, lambda)." Cavallo continued, "Among late examples . . . the script shows a stronger contrast between fat and thin strokes and decorative buttons at the extremities of the latter, in particular on the horizontal strokes of gamma, delta, epsilon, pi and tau."[27] In other words, the hand that we are comparing should have thick vertical strokes and thin horizontal strokes. The later the hand is, the more the contrast there will be. Later examples of the hands tend to have decorative serifs on horizontal strokes, but earlier examples tend not to have them.

In the above comparison, we see handwriting from two manuscripts that Cavallo dated 135 to 140 years apart, and to be fair, P.Ryl. 16 *is* earlier than Codex Sinaiticus. There are differences between the two hands, admittedly. The *epsilon* (ε) and *sigma* (c) are not the same—they are slightly more decorative in Codex Sinaiticus. The *phi* (φ) in Codex Sinaiticus is more angled than round. Codex Sinaiticus has generally more difference between the thick vertical strokes of *nu* (N) and the thinner diagonal stroke (but not always; see the ν in μενειν [*menein*]).[28] Still, the two hands bear a remarkable similarity. Additionally, *tau* (T) in P.Ryl. 16 has more prominent serifs, or "hooks," on the ends of the horizontal stroke than *tau* in Codex Sinaiticus—a feature Cavallo considered to be more characteristic of *later* examples of "biblical majuscule." Cavallo himself dated the manuscripts 135 years apart, but this comparison is even more problematic if P.Ryl. 16 is a few decades earlier, as Turner argued.

---

[26]Cavallo, *Ricerche sulla maiuscola biblica*, 58.

[27]Guglielmo Cavallo, "Greek and Latin Writing in the Papyri," in *The Oxford Handbook of Papyrology*, ed. Roger S. Bagnall (Oxford: Oxford University Press, 2009), 128-29.

[28]It is also problematic to look merely at "test letters," so I have reproduced the samples in groups of the same words.

P.Ryl. 16 (AD 220–225, according to Cavallo)	Codex Sinaiticus, Scribe A (ca. AD 360, according to Cavallo)

Figure 5.3. A comparison of P.Ryl. 16 (left) and scribe A of Codex Sinaiticus (right), showing their similar hands

The point of the comparison is to illustrate how difficult it can be to assign a date paleographically. Yes, *something* is different between the two hands, but can we accurately measure it to be 135 years' worth of development? Furthermore, "development" assumes that the styles changed in linear fashion, as Turner noted. But, he said, "If [a particular style] was written in several centres it is likely that cross-influences will have affected this style, as they did other styles."[29] To state it alternatively, do we really see 135 years' worth of linear development between the hands of P.Ryl. 16 and scribe A of Codex Sinaiticus, or are the two similar because the scribes had similar influences? If the latter, we cannot really be confident enough to assign such narrow dates as Cavallo does.

Additionally, it is possible for scribes contemporary with each other to have conflicting features with regard to date. P. J. Parsons mentioned features of Codices Sinaiticus, Vaticanus (03), and Alexandrinus (02), in which a scribe or scribes exhibit later features of handwriting than other scribes working at the same time on the same manuscript.[30] Even a near-perfect

---

[29]Turner, *Greek Manuscripts of the Ancient World*, 22.

[30]P. J. Parsons, "Review of *Ricerche sulla maiuscola biblica* by Guglielmo Cavallo," *Gn* 42, no. 4 (1970): 380.

match with a securely dated manuscript is not enough to assign a secure date paleographically.[31]

Other methods. Other aspects might occasionally provide more information on the date of a manuscript. For example, Turner suggests that the format and dimensions of a codex might shed light on its date.[32] Illuminated manuscripts have an additional layer of available information in their art. If a manuscript has been found with an intact cover, the cover might provide a *terminus post quem*. A deed dated October 7, AD 348, for example, was reused in the cover of Nag Hammadi Codex VII, indicating that the codex had to have been made after that date and suggesting a similar date range for the other Nag Hammadi codices.[33]

Scientific testing could be of some use as well. The York Gospels (York, Minster Library, Add Manuscript 1) have a *terminus ante quem* of around AD 1020 because the manuscript came to York through Wulfstan, the archbishop of York, who died in AD 1023, but it was unclear how long before AD 1020 it was written. DNA analysis revealed that an unusually high percentage of the parchment sampled came from female calves. One would expect male calves to be used for parchment because males are less valuable for maintaining and growing a herd. Cattle numbers in the British Isles suffered in the late tenth century because of a cattle plague that swept through between AD 986 and 988, and female cattle would have been especially valuable to repopulate herds after the plague. The best explanation for the unusually high presence of parchment made from female calves in the York Gospels is that its pages were made from the skins of female calves that died in that plague, which, if correct, suggests a strong possibility for a composition date of the York Gospels around the year AD 990.[34]

---

[31]Brent Nongbri writes of P52, "I have not provided any third-century documentary papyri that are absolute 'dead ringers' for the handwriting of P52, and even if I had done so, that would not force us to date P52 at some exact point in the third century. Paleographic evidence does not work that way" ("Use and Abuse of P52," 46).

[32]E. G. Turner, *The Typology of the Early Codex* (Philadelphia: University of Pennsylvania Press, 1977), 7.

[33]J. W. B. Barns, G. M. Browne, and J. C. Shelton, eds., *Nag Hammadi Codices: Greek and Coptic Papyri from the Cartonnage of the Covers*, NHS 16 (Leiden: Brill, 1981), 57. Stephen Emmel rightly questions *how* much later they were made, however, in "The Coptic Gnostic Texts as Witnesses to the Production and Transmission of Gnostic (and Other) Traditions," in *Das Thomasevangelium: Entstehung-Rezeption-Theologie*, ed. Jörg Frey, Enno Edzard Popkes, and Jens Schröter, BZNW 157 (Berlin: de Gruyter, 2008), 38.

[34]Matthew D. Teasdale et al., "The York Gospels: A 1000-Year Biological Palimpsest," *Royal Society Open Science* 4, no. 10 (2017): 7.

Radiocarbon dating might be a possibility, though it requires the destruction of a small piece of the item dated, and most conservators would probably forbid such destruction. Additionally, scientific testing is often not able to settle historians' questions. R. E. Taylor and Ofer Bar-Yosef write, "Radiocarbon 'warps' create periods throughout the ^{14}C time scale where there are inherent systemic limitations in the precision with which a ^{14}C-based time segment can be expressed."[35] Like paleography, radiocarbon dating can give only a range of most probable dates, but because of these "warps," there are periods within the overall timeline where radiocarbon dating results are less useful than others. For example, as Josephine K. Dru shows, "^{14}C science can often distinguish the 130s from the 40s CE. But it *cannot* distinguish the 130s from the 220s CE—though the time difference is the same!"[36] These specifics mean that, if P52 were to be radiocarbon dated, the best we could hope for (*if* the tests achieved state-of-the-art accuracy and precision) is a better sense of whether its *papyrus* (the material on which the text was written, not the writing itself) originated before 130, between circa 135–225, or later. Carbon-14 analysis could not show whether 135, 150, 175, 200, or 225 is more probable. Is that worth the cost of a slightly smaller P52?

In summary, the process of dating a manuscript often involves a combination of methods and/or sources, and even still, assigned dates must be taken with caution. Turner writes, "Palaeography is neither a science nor an art, but works through a continual interaction of the methods appropriate to both approaches. And in the last resort a judgment has to be made—and judgment [sic] is fallible."[37]

P52: DOES IT DATE TO AROUND 125?

C. H. Roberts and the earliest manuscript. In light of the difficulties of paleographic dating and the fallibility of judgments, we turn to the fragment that holds the distinction of being the most commonly cited early manuscript: P52 (P.Ryl. 457). It is a fragment of John's Gospel about three-and-a-half by

---

[35]R. E. Taylor and Ofer Bar-Yosef, *Radiocarbon Dating: An Archaeological Perspective*, 2nd ed. (Walnut Creek, CA: Left Coast Press, 2014), 59-60, but see a fuller discussion of evaluating radiocarbon dates at 130-71.

[36]Josephine K. Dru, "Radiocarbon Dating for Manuscripts on Papyrus or Parchment: Improving Interpretation Through Interdisciplinary Dialogue," poster presented at ManuSciences, Villa Clythia, Fréjus, France, September 2017 (emphasis original).

[37]Turner, *Greek Manuscripts of the Ancient World*, 20.

two-and-a-half inches in size to which academics and apologists alike frequently appeal as the oldest extant manuscript of the New Testament. When
C. H. Roberts first published P52 in 1935, he assigned it a date on the basis of
its handwriting: "On the whole we may accept with some confidence the first
half of the second century as the period in which P. Ryl. Gr. 457 was most
probably written."[38] Roberts arrived at that date by comparing the handwriting of P52 to that of other known papyri.[39] It is important to note that
Roberts did not say that P52 *was* written between AD 100 and 150 but that it
was most probably written then.

A few considerations provide reason for revising Roberts's early date for
P52 ("*most probably*" AD 100–150). First, Roberts's two closest matches to the
hand of P52 were not themselves securely dated. Second, the securely dated
specimens in general were not close matches. Third, there are now many
more published manuscripts with which to compare P52 than when Roberts
first published it in 1935, such that consensus regarding the paleographic
dates can change. In the case of one of the two "close matches"—P.Egerton
2—it did. Roberts compared P52 to an early dated manuscript that is no
longer considered to be so early.[40] A recent redating of P.Egerton 2 concluded
that it dates to circa AD 150–250 and that "it is not impossible that [P.Egerton
2] was produced sometime at the turn of the third century."[41] In summary,
Roberts assigned the early date to P52 primarily on the basis of problematic
comparisons or manuscripts without secure dates, one of which has recently
been dated much later. In light of the many papyri published since 1935, we
must now consider whether P52 really is as old as is commonly claimed.

Recent rejection of an early date. In 1975, Eric Turner accepted Roberts's
date of circa AD 100–150, but with reservation.[42] Turner mentioned P.Amh.

[38]C. H. Roberts, *An Unpublished Fragment of the Fourth Gospel in the John Rylands Library* (Manchester: Manchester University Press, 1935), 16.
[39]Roberts, *Unpublished Fragment of the Fourth Gospel*, 14-16. Brent Nongbri helpfully provides
images of each of these with discussion of their relative value for dating P52 in Nongbri, "Use
and Abuse of P52."
[40]Nongbri writes, "The problematic nature of paleographically dating thee papyri comes into even
sharper relief when we notice that the principle comparanda for dating Egerton Papyrus 2 are
for the most part *the same as* those later used by Roberts to date P52. The independent value of
Egerton Papyrus 2 for dating P52 is thus minimal," in "Use and Abuse of P52," 34 (emphasis
original).
[41]Peter Malik and Lorne R. Zelyck, "Reconsidering the Date(s) of the Egerton Gospel," *ZPE* 204
(2017): 63.
[42]Turner, *Typology of the Early Codex*, 100.

II 78 as a manuscript with "similarities"—it is a petition firmly dated to AD 184. In 1989, Andreas Schmidt identified two other manuscripts—still only paleographically dated—that exhibit close similarities to P52. Schmidt then suggested that P52 dates to circa AD 170, plus or minus twenty-five years.[43] Sixteen years after Schmidt's study, Brent Nongbri made an even stronger case for adopting a wider date range for P52.

Nongbri began his important article thus: "The thesis of this paper is simple: we as critical readers of the New Testament often use John Rylands Greek Papyrus 3.457, also known as P52, in inappropriate ways, and we should stop doing so." To be perfectly honest, he isn't completely wrong. His work demonstrated that most of Roberts's comparanda (manuscripts with comparable handwriting) are not close matches to P52, and he also introduced several additional securely dated comparanda. Nongbri concluded, "Any serious consideration of the window of possible dates for P52 must include dates in the later second and early third centuries."[44] It is important to note that Nongbri is not suggesting that we abandon the possibility of an early date of P52. Rather, he is arguing that the early date range for P52 should be extended to include later dates.[45]

More recently, other manuscript specialists have rejected the AD 100–150 date for P52. Don Barker, a papyrologist at Macquarie University, writes, "It is difficult to place [P52] in a very narrow time period," and he assigns P52 to anywhere in the second or third centuries.[46] Barker continues, "This may be unsatisfactory for those who would like to locate [P52] in a narrower time frame but the palaeographical evidence will not allow it."[47] Christian Askeland cites Nongbri and Barker's work with approval, condemning "indefensible arguments for ridiculously early dates of various New Testament papyri" in his own article on the difficulties of paleographic dating.[48]

---

[43] Andreas Schmidt, "Zwei Anmerkungen zu P. Ryl. III 457," *APF* 35 (1989): 11-12.

[44] Nongbri, "Use and Abuse of P52," 23, 46.

[45] For example, Nongbri writes, "I think it is safe to say that although a few Christian books *may* be as old as the second century, none of them *must* be that old, not even the celebrated fragment of the fourth gospel in the John Rylands Library [i.e., P52]," in *God's Library: The Archaeology of the Earliest Christian Manuscripts* (New Haven, CT: Yale University Press, 2018), 269 (emphasis original). *God's Library* is an excellent introduction to several important issues regarding early manuscripts.

[46] Don Barker, "The Dating of New Testament Papyri," *NTS* 57, no. 4 (2011): 574-75. In addition to the studies discussed here, see also Foster, "Bold Claims, Wishful Thinking."

[47] Barker, "Dating of New Testament Papyri," 575.

[48] Askeland, "Dating Early Greek and Coptic Literary Hands," specifically, 466.

Whether or not Nongbri and Barker are correct that P52 could be as late as the third century, they are absolutely correct that dates of circa AD 125 or AD 100–150 are too early.[49]

How useful is P52 to apologetics? First, P52 does not and cannot offer definitive proof that John's Gospel is a first-century composition by an eyewitness. Even if P52 were written in the afternoon of April 26, AD 125 (it wasn't), it would prove only that sections from John 18 were in Egypt by AD 125. Technically, such a date does not prove that John's Gospel was in its "final" (canonical) form by then, nor does it prove that the text it contains is any more than a few months old. An early date of P52 might render these possibilities unlikely—even extremely unlikely—but it cannot *disprove* them. Two examples from redaction-critical commentaries demonstrate this point. First, Rudolf Bultmann accepted a date of P52 in the period of AD 100–150 and still argued that as much as forty years could have passed between the original writing of John's Gospel and a final redaction that left it in the canonical form we have today. Second, Walter Schmithals was well aware of the existence of P52, but he still dated a final redaction of John's Gospel to around AD 160–180.[50] Given the uncertain nature of paleographical dating and the fact that P52 has not deterred source-critical scholars from adopting second-century dates of a final redaction to John's Gospel, we quote again Paul Foster's remarks about the usefulness of P52: "Was John's Gospel written before the end of the first century? Yes, probably. Does P52 prove this to be the case? No, probably not."[51]

Second, the occasional absence of P52 in critical editions of the Greek New Testament shows why it is not necessary for reconstructing the original text. The UBS[3] (published in 1975) makes no mention of P52. It is included in the index of manuscripts to the UBS[4] and UBS[5], but neither edition cites P52 for or against any variant in the text. The NA[28] contains eleven variation units for John 18:31-33, 37-38 (the verses for which P52 is extant for at least part), but because the papyrus is so fragmentary, the NA[28] cites P52 only

---

[49]Pasquale Orsini and Willy Clarysse assign P52 a date of circa 125–175 in their important essay "Early New Testament Manuscripts and Their Dates," 470.

[50]Rudolf Bultmann, *The Gospel of John: A Commentary*, trans. G. R. Beasley-Murray, R. W. N. Hoare, and J. K. Riches (Philadelphia: Westminster, 1971), 12; Walter Schmithals, *Johannesevangelium und Johannesbriefe: Forschungsgeschichte und Analyse*, BZNW 64 (Berlin: de Gruyter, 1992), 242. See also his discussion of the date of P52 on pp. 9-11.

[51]Foster, "Bold Claims, Wishful Thinking," 204.

once. The one instance is a variant more or less with respect to word order at John 18:33. The reading of P52 was adopted as the text of John's Gospel against the reading of the majority of manuscripts, but Westcott and Hort had already adopted this reading as the text of John decades before P52 was published. Likewise, P52 makes no appearance in the apparatus of the recent *Greek New Testament Produced at Tyndale House Cambridge*, an edition that emphasizes its dependence and use of early manuscripts and scribal habits not only for the text but even the spelling and paragraphing of the New Testament.[52]

Third, some scholars who are neither trained papyrologists nor paleographers have proposed unusually early or narrow dates for P52, and these dates should not be accepted. Karl Jaroš (AD 80–125), Philip Comfort (AD 110–125), and Carsten Peter Thiede (AD 80–130) are each controversial for their early dates, which have failed to gain scholarly acceptance.[53] Pasquale Orsini and Willy Clarysse criticize Jaroš and Comfort (specifically, the edition of New Testament papyri he cowrote with David Barrett) for their early dates, and they dismiss Thiede altogether.[54] With respect to the date of P52, Orsini and Clarysse note that the comparanda used by Comfort-Barrett and Jaroš are inappropriate because they are not even the same "style" of handwriting as P52. They show that the early dates proposed by Jaroš and Comfort-Barrett are methodologically unsound, concluding, "Biblical scholars should realise that some of the dates proposed by some of their colleagues are not acceptable to Greek palaeographers and papyrologists."[55]

---

[52]Dirk Jongkind et al., eds., *The Greek New Testament, Produced at Tyndale House, Cambridge* (Wheaton, IL: Crossway, 2017), 505-23.

[53]Karl Jaroš, *Die ältesten griechischen Handschriften des Neuen Testaments* (Cologne: Böhlau, 2014), 71; Comfort, *Commentary on the Manuscripts and Text*, 65-66; Carsten Peter Thiede, *The Earliest Gospel Manuscript? The Qumran Fragment 7Q5 and Its Significance for New Testament Studies* (Carlisle, UK: Paternoster, 1992), 21-22.

[54]Orsini and Clarysse, "Early New Testament Manuscripts and Their Dates." On Thiede's claim that P64+67 could date to the late first century, "perhaps (though not necessarily) predating A.D. 70" (Carsten Peter Thiede, "Papyrus Magdalen Greek 17 [Gregory-Aland P⁶⁴]: A Reappraisal," *TynBul* 46, no. 1 [1995]: 38; Carsten Peter Thiede and Matthew D'Ancona, *The Jesus Papyrus* [London: Weidenfeld & Nicolson, 1996]), Klaus Wachtel writes, "Thiedes Argumentation für eine Datierung des P64/67 ins 1. Jahrhundert ist jedoch als methodisch unzulänglich und sachlich falsch zurückzuweisen" ("Thiede's argument for a dating of P64/67 in the first century, however, is rejected as methodologically insufficient and factually wrong"), in "P⁶⁴/⁶⁷: Fragmente des Matthäusevangeliums aus dem 1. Jahrhundert?," *ZPE* 107 (1995): 80. For Comfort and Barrett's edition of New Testament papyri, see Philip W. Comfort and David Barrett, *The Text of the Earliest New Testament Greek Manuscripts*, corrected, enl. ed. (Wheaton, IL: Tyndale House, 2001).

[55]Orsini and Clarysse, "Early New Testament Manuscripts and Their Dates," 462, 466.

Christian Askeland rightly rejects the conclusions of Jaroš, Comfort, and Thiede, describing their respective works under the heading "Paleography Gone Wrong."[56] Craig A. Evans describes "assertions of very early dates for some papyri" by a few scholars including Thiede and Comfort as "especially problematic."[57] Many recent scholars who mention the date of P52 give it a mid-second century or late-second century date.[58]

As it happens, P52 is not the only New Testament manuscript to receive such controversial treatment from these authors and others. In his *Commentary on the Text and Manuscripts of the New Testament*, Comfort cites "manuscripts with certain dating" in defense of his circa 200 date for P45, but none of the manuscripts he cites are dated securely. Two are reused rolls with dates on one side (but not the side relevant to P45), and the other is a paleographic date of a cursive hand—admittedly easier to date than a literary hand but by no means certain. Comfort also mentions E. C. Colwell's famous study of scribal habits, including Colwell's conclusion that the scribe of P75 copied "letter by letter," but he seems unaware of Klaus Junack's study from 1981 criticizing Colwell's conclusions about "letter by letter" copying or Dirk Jongkind's more recent article that touches on the same issue.[59] Comfort cites

---

[56]Askeland, "Dating Early Greek and Coptic Literary Hands," 464-65.

[57]Craig A. Evans, "Christian Demographics and the Dates of Early New Testament Papyri," in *The Language and Literature of the New Testament: Essays in Honor of Stanley E. Porter's 60th Birthday*, ed. Lois K. Fuller Dow, Craig A. Evans, and Andrew W. Pitts, Biblical Interpretation Series 150 (Leiden: Brill, 2016), 201n3.

[58]Mid-second century: David C. Parker, *An Introduction to the New Testament Manuscripts and Their Texts* (Cambridge: Cambridge University Press, 2008), 234; Juan Chapa, "The Early Text of John," in Hill and Kruger, *Early Text of the New Testament*, 141; Orsini and Clarysse, "Early New Testament Manuscripts and Their Dates," 460; Alan Mugridge, *Copying Early Christian Texts: A Study of Scribal Practice*, WUNT 362 (Tübingen: Mohr Siebeck, 2016), 250-51. Late second century: Charles E. Hill, "Did the Scribe of P52 Use the Nomina Sacra? Another Look," *NTS* 48, no. 4 (2002): 592; Roger S. Bagnall, *Early Christian Books in Egypt* (Princeton, NJ: Princeton University Press, 2009), 89. Lonnie D. Bell allows any date in the second century, in *The Early Textual Transmission of John: Stability and Fluidity in Its Second and Third Century Greek Manuscripts*, NTTSD 54 (Leiden: Brill 2018), 38. Barker allows a date for P52 anywhere in the second or third centuries, in "Dating of New Testament Papyri," 575.

[59]Comfort, *Commentary on the Manuscripts and Text*, 60-61. See also E. C. Colwell, "Method in Evaluating Scribal Habits: A Study of P45, P66, P25," in *Studies in Methodology in Textual Criticism of the New Testament*, ed. Bruce M. Metzger, NTTS 9 (Grand Rapids: Eerdmans, 1969), 106-24; Klaus Junack, "Abschreibpraktiken und Schreibergewohnheiten in ihrer Auswirkung auf die Textüberlieferung," in *New Testament Textual Criticism: Its Significance for Exegesis; Essays in Honor of Bruce M. Metzger*, ed. Eldon J. Epp and Gordon D. Fee (Oxford: Clarendon, 1981), 277-95; Dirk Jongkind, "Singular Readings in Sinaiticus: The Possible, the Impossible, and the Nature of Copying," in *Textual Variation: Theological and Social Tendencies? Papers from the Fifth Birmingham Colloquium on the Textual Criticism of the New*

H. J. M. Milne and T. C. Skeat for having "demonstrated that Scribe A of Codex Vaticanus was likely the same scribe as Scribe D of Codex Sinaiticus," but this statement is simply untrue.[60] Milne and Skeat came to the *opposite* conclusion. After a discussion of the similarities between the hands, they write, "It would be hazardous to argue identity of the two hands."[61] Comfort even appeals to Guglielmo Cavallo for a mid-second-century date of P66.[62] Cavallo did accept that date in 1967, but he changed his mind in favor of a later date by 1975, so Comfort's appeal to Cavallo in the present tense is misleading.[63] In general, one gets the impression that Comfort gives emphasis to references that could be used to support his controversial conclusions, and even then he does not always represent them accurately.

CONCLUDING SUGGESTIONS

We do have early manuscripts of the New Testament, and apologists are right to appeal to them. Even if our extant witnesses are not quite as early as we once thought, the number of early manuscripts of Christian Scriptures is a testimony to their importance to early Christians. That we can even identify tiny fragments as New Testament manuscripts by the text they contain is a testimony to the macrostability of the New Testament text. Below are a few practical suggestions for identifying and reporting the dates of early New Testament manuscripts responsibly.

- Always use a full date range for a manuscript rather than the midpoint or early end of a date range. A date of "circa AD 200" might imply either a range of 175–225 or a range of 150–250, and it does not convey the fact that a manuscript dated to 150–250 is just as likely to be written

---

Testament, ed. H. A. G. Houghton and D. C. Parker, TS, Third Series 6 (Piscataway, NJ: Gorgias, 2008), 35-54.

[60]Comfort, *Commentary on the Manuscripts and Text*, 94.

[61]H. J. M. Milne and T. C. Skeat, *Scribes and Correctors of the Codex Sinaiticus* (London: British Museum Press, 1938), 90.

[62]Comfort, *Commentary on the Manuscripts and Text*, 70. Michael J. Kruger also accepts a second-century date for P66, in *Canon Revisited: Establishing the Origins and Authority of the New Testament Books* (Wheaton, IL: Crossway, 2012), 235. Kruger appeals to Herbert Hunger's controversial dating, though more recent scholarship has rejected Hunger's second-century proposal. Herbert Hunger, "Zur Datierung des Papyrus Bodmer II (P66)," AÖAW 4 (1960): 12-33. See, however, Turner, *Greek Manuscripts of the Ancient World*, 108; Nongbri, "Limits of Palaeographic Dating of Literary Papyri," 9-13; Orsini and Clarysse, "Early New Testament Manuscripts and Their Dates," 470.

[63]On Cavallo's change of mind, see Nongbri, "Limits of Palaeographic Dating of Literary Papyri," 13.

in 248 as it is likely to be written in 156, or anywhere in between. We simply cannot be more precise.[64]

- Avoid sensational dates and excessively early or narrow date ranges. If it sounds too good to be true, assume that it is. Remember Eric Turner's assessment that for literary hands (which applies to almost all early New Testament manuscripts), fifty years is the *smallest* acceptable window for a date range assigned on paleographic grounds. A date in the first century for any New Testament manuscript is an immediate red flag—*especially* for an unpublished manuscript.

- Accept the full range of the date given by INTF. This information can be found in the back of NA[28] (pp. 792-819) or via the electronic version of their official register of Greek New Testament manuscripts.[65] The electronic availability of the *Liste* ensures that their information is freely accessible with nothing more than an internet connection, and as they are the keepers of the official register of New Testament manuscripts, no one can fault a nonspecialist for trusting their judgment. INTF dates P52 in the second century. The online *Liste* assigns P52 to the mid-second century (125–175), but NA[28] gives the full second century as the possible date. I suggest adopting the broader range.[66] For P66 and P75, the online *Liste* has dated them to the early third century, with dates of AD 200–225. NA[28] reports "c. 200" for each manuscript. Thus, in these instances, I suggest accepting the broader range of AD 200–225. Turner's objections to a range of fewer than fifty years notwithstanding, again—no one can fault a nonspecialist for accepting the date range adopted by INTF.[67]

---

[64]At this point I must confess my own sins. In 2015, I gave the dates of P46 and P75 as "Around A.D. 200" in a chapter I coauthored with Timothy Paul Jones, "How Was the New Testament Copied?," in *How We Got the Bible*, by Timothy Paul Jones (Torrance, CA: Rose, 2015), 120. If I could do it over again, I would give the date ranges of AD 200–300 for P75 and AD 175–250 for P46.

[65]"Liste," Institut für Neutestamentliche Textforschung, http://ntvmr.uni-muenster.de/liste (accessed January 12, 2018). In the "Manuscript Num." box with the dropdown menu on "GA," type the Gregory-Aland number for a manuscript (e.g., P52, 023, 1739, or l1747) to search for it. If the dropdown menu is set to "ID," manuscripts are identified slightly differently. Each manuscript has a five-digit code beginning with 1, 2, 3, or 4, for papyri, majuscules, minuscules, and lectionaries, respectively. The initial number is followed by the numerical portion of the GA number, preceded by zeros if necessary to fill out five digits. Thus, for the examples given above, the IDs would be 10052, 20023, 31739, and 41747.

[66]As of January 12, 2018, for P52 as well as P66 and P75 below.

[67]Brent Nongbri has suggested that P66 and P75 could possibly be as late as the fourth century.

- Rather than appealing to P52 to rule out a second-century composition of John, appeal to other factors such as its reception in the second century to argue for its authenticity. This approach is admittedly more complex, but Charles E. Hill has written a thorough discussion of its second-century reception that would be helpful in formulating such an argument.[68]

Finally, remember that Christianity is a faith that stood unshaken for centuries while the earliest copies of its texts lay quietly buried in the sands of Egypt. People became Christians long before P52 was discovered, and they will continue to do so even if it is not quite as ancient as was previously thought.[69]

Key Takeaways

▶ Often a manuscript can be dated only by paleography, which is a difficult and imprecise way of assigning the date by means of an assessment of the handwriting.

▶ It is almost always unwise to assign a date range of fewer than fifty years on the basis of paleography; a range of seventy-five to one hundred years is typically more preferable.

▶ The middle year of a date range is no more likely (but also no less likely) to be the "actual date" of a manuscript than any other date in that range. Always try to give the full range; do not assume the earliest date is the right date.

▶ The responsible date range of P52, probably our earliest New Testament manuscript, is AD 100–200, and a few scholars even extend this range into the 200s.

See Nongbri, "Limits of Palaeographic Dating of Literary Papyri"; Nongbri, "Reconsidering the Place of Papyrus Bodmer XIV-XV (P75) in the Textual Criticism of the New Testament," *JBL* 135, no. 2 (2016): 405-37. If researchers at the INTF are persuaded by his arguments, perhaps they will change their entry for these manuscripts.

[68]Charles E. Hill, *The Johannine Corpus in the Early Church* (Oxford: Oxford University Press, 2004).

[69]Several individuals read early drafts of this chapter, and I am especially thankful to Brent Nongbri, Josephine Dru, and Grant Edwards for their helpful feedback. Remaining errors are, of course, my own.

CHAPTER SIX

DATING MYTHS, PART TWO

HOW LATER MANUSCRIPTS CAN BE BETTER MANUSCRIPTS

Gregory R. Lanier

DECADES AGO the introduction to the NA[26] declared that we have moved out of an age of majuscules (nineteenth century) and papyri (early twentieth) and into an "age of the minuscules."[1] Yet for the pastor, student, commentary writer, and even scholar, the temptation remains to focus on the usual suspects (say, 01, 02, 03, 04, 05, P75), for with the discovery and accessibility of an embarrassment of riches in terms of post-ninth-century minuscule manuscripts has come a bewildering sense of staring into the abyss of manuscripts known primarily by their sterile numerical labels. Indeed, one of the key challenges of recent work on the text and transmission of the Greek New Testament is this: What on earth do we make of this "frighteningly large number of manuscripts"?[2]

One common response—in practice, if not also in theory—is to treat these later manuscripts as a black box: that is, an indistinguishable mass of corrupt and secondary manuscripts that, due to their chronological distance from the original/initial text, contribute nothing toward recovering it.[3] The

---

[1]From the introduction to NA[26] (47*); the comment was removed in NA[27] and NA[28], but the sentiments are echoed in Kurt Aland and Barbara Aland, *The Text of the New Testament: An Introduction to the Critical Editions and to the Theory and Practice of Modern Textual Criticism*, 2nd ed., trans. Erroll F. Rhodes (Grand Rapids: Eerdmans, 1989), 129.

[2]Kurt Aland, "The Significance of Papyri for Progress in New Testament Research," in *The Bible in Modern Scholarship*, ed. J. Philip Hyatt (Nashville: Abingdon, 1965), 339. Aland's "appalling number" of minuscules has only worsened in the intervening fifty years; INTF's *Kurzgefasste Liste* currently catalogues 2,936 (as of May 2018).

[3]Barbara Aland and Klaus Wachtel, "The Greek Minuscules of the New Testament," in *The Text*

default setting of this "dating myth" runs thus: a later manuscript is worse *because of its later date*—that is, that the length of time permits more stages of copying and corruption—and an earlier manuscript is better *because of its earlier date*.[4] If so, the thousands of later manuscripts en masse are "corrupt" (seemingly the most common epithet) and useless, and can conveniently be ignored. A nearly opposite response, voiced by a small minority of scholars, is to treat most of these later manuscripts—for a variety of reasons—not as *worse* but rather *better* than the oft-touted but "corrupt" majuscules and papyri.

This apparent stalemate presents a conundrum for our text-critical apologetic, because both responses unintentionally undermine our confidence in the fidelity of the New Testament text and its transmission. *If the former response is right*, then can we really hang our hat on an argument from quantity (e.g., compared to the *Iliad*), since vast numbers of manuscripts that juice the statistics are deemed corrupt and useless?[5] How do we explain the implications of the wildly corrupt state of the text that prevailed throughout most eras of the Christian world? Alternatively, *if the latter response is right*, then how do we account for the apparent early and widespread corruption of these ancient artifacts that, at least according to the Tischendorf/Westcott-Hort tradition, get us closer in time to the era of the authors?

This essay will attempt to put our text-critical apologetic on firmer footing by modifying the default settings in this way: *sometimes later manuscripts*

---

of the New Testament in Contemporary Research: Essays on the Status Quaestionis, 2nd ed., ed. Bart D. Ehrman and Michael W. Holmes, NTTSD 42 (Leiden: Brill, 2013), 88. Frederik Wisse laments, "Every additional minuscule, however high its market price might be, has made the critic's task more confusing and difficult. . . . Either he will try to take all the MS evidence into account without hope of ever finishing his task, or he will ignore the great majority of existing MSS" (*The Profile Method for the Classification and Evaluation of Manuscript Evidence, as Applied to the Continuous Greek Text of the Gospel of Luke*, SD 44 [Grand Rapids: Eerdmans, 1982], 1).

[4]This idea goes back at least to Richard Bentley (*Dr. Bentley's Proposals for the Printing of a New Edition of the Greek New Testament, and St. Hierom's Latin Version with a Full Answer to All the Remarks of a Late Pamphleteer* [London: J. Knapton, 1721]), who comments, "What has crept into any copies since [the fifth century] is of no value or authority." Even the recent *The Greek New Testament, Produced at Tyndale House, Cambridge* (Wheaton, IL: Crossway, 2017) can, indirectly, fuel this misconception due to its focus on pre-sixth-century witnesses.

[5]On this, see the discussion about Peter Gurry's post "On the 'Idle Boast' of Having So Many New Testament Manuscripts," *Evangelical Textual Criticism* (blog), August 16, 2017, http://evangelical textualcriticism.blogspot.com/2017/08/on-idle-boast-of-having-so-many-new.html; Maurice A. Robinson, "Appendix: The Case for Byzantine Priority," in *The New Testament in the Original Greek: Byzantine Textform*, ed. Maurice A. Robinson and William G. Pierpont (Southborough, MA: Chilton, 2005), 568.

are better manuscripts, though not always. To begin, we must clarify what it means to be "better."

DEFINING *BETTER*: WHAT ARE WE REALLY AFTER IN TERMS OF MANUSCRIPT VALUE?

When discussing the textual integrity of the Greek New Testament and the value of the more than five thousand Greek manuscripts (not to mention Latin and others)—none of which perfectly contain the earliest form—there is a need to be clear about what exactly we are aiming for. Put succinctly, what needs to be demonstrated in order to have a high degree of confidence that the wording of the New Testament has been faithfully transmitted from its point of origin throughout the world over the past millennia? Three central considerations come to mind.[6]

(1) *Tradition*: Is the whole textual tradition, including its "later" stages, essentially stable? Is it even right (let alone helpful) to say that one branch of the tradition is hopelessly "corrupt" and essentially useless compared to another? (2) *Text*: To what degree of confidence can we approach the reconstruction of the earliest text? Or, more specifically, how and when do later manuscripts provide us with readings that are earlier and more likely to be original, and how do they help us piece together the history of the text? (3) *Quality controls*: How do scribal features of later manuscripts shed light on the quality of the process as it unfolded over an incredibly long period of time? Are we dealing with scribes who were sloppy or, worse, mindlessly conforming to some standard imposed on them? Or are there reasons to believe that at least some later scribes were able "textual critics"?

The term *better*, then, is not merely a function of whether later manuscripts sometimes help in variant decisions—though that is a big part of it—but also a measure of the overall integrity of the entire process throughout the period of transmission. When positioned this way, later manuscripts often have much to contribute. We will thus proceed by examining the value of later manuscripts in forming an overall view on tradition, text, and quality controls.[7]

---

[6]A fourth is *reception history*, namely, how textual variation, codicology, scribal features, and so forth contribute to our understanding of the development of Christian theology; space does not permit engaging this in detail.

[7]*Later* can be defined in several ways; due to space constraints, we will focus primarily on minuscules (arising in the 800s) and will not, unfortunately, be able to spend time on "later" majuscules and lectionaries.

REFINING OUR APPROACH TO LATER MANUSCRIPTS

Tradition: Appreciating the Byzantine witnesses. The most concrete manifestation of the *later-is-worse* "dating myth" is the long-standing divide over the Byzantine or Majority tradition.[8] Broadly speaking, this is a form of the text found in the lion's share—though not all—of later manuscripts throughout the Christian East and West, a specific iteration of which attained near-universal status in the printing-press era in the form of the *textus receptus*. Since the overthrow of its hegemony in the 1800s (by Lachmann, Tischendorf, Westcott, Hort, and others), the Byzantine tradition has often been pronounced a "secondary kind of text inferior in its value."[9] Whether admitting it or not, most eclectic textual scholars who tend to value earlier manuscripts (and/or internal considerations) over later manuscripts give "no real role to the Byzantine text."[10]

Space does not permit a detailed analysis of the arguments against the Byzantine text-form, nor the recent resurgence of scholarly attempts to reassert a robust, principled defense of it (and shed prior inferior arguments).[11]

---

[8]Terminology here is itself tricky, as this text-form has a long history of confusing labels (Antiochian, Lucianic, Oriental, Asiatic, Constantinopolitan, Syrian, Traditional, *Koine*/K, Alpha, Ecclesiastical) and the sigla Byz and 𝔐, found in modern critical editions, which themselves are not always used consistently. Even "Byzantine" and "Majority" are somewhat misleading, but they are the current consensus labels.

[9] For instance, Larry W. Hurtado describes the intersection of W and Family 13 as "a secondary kind of text inferior in its value . . . [and] well on its way toward the Byzantine text-type." *Text-Critical Methodology and the Pre-Caesarean Text: Codex W in the Gospel of Mark*, SD 43 (Grand Rapids: Eerdmans, 1981), 62. On the overthrow of the dominance of the *textus receptus*, see Aland and Aland, *Text of the New Testament*, 3-19; Bruce M. Metzger and Bart D. Ehrman, *The Text of the New Testament: Its Transmission, Corruption, and Restoration*, 4th ed. (Oxford: Oxford University Press, 2005), 137-94.

[10]Michael W. Holmes, "*The Text of the Epistles* Sixty Years After: An Assessment of Günther Zuntz's Contribution to Text-Critical Methodology and History," in *Transmission and Reception: New Testament Text-Critical and Exegetical Studies*, ed. J. W. Childers and David C. Parker, TS, Third Series 4 (Piscataway, NJ: Gorgias, 2006), 108; he is referring to Bruce M. Metzger's *A Textual Commentary on the Greek New Testament*, 2nd ed. (New York: United Bible Societies, 1994), and Aland and Aland, *Text of the New Testament*, in particular.

[11]See Gregory R. Lanier, "Taking Inventory on the 'Age of the Minuscules': Later Manuscripts and the Byzantine Tradition Within the Field of Textual Criticism," *CBR* 16, no. 3 (2018): 263-308. See also Daniel B. Wallace, "The Majority Text Theory: History, Methods, and Critique," in Ehrman and Holmes, *Text of the New Testament*, 711-44; Maurice A. Robinson, "New Testament Textual Criticism: The Case for Byzantine Priority," *TC* 6 (2001): n.p., later condensed in Robinson, "The Case for Byzantine Priority," in *Rethinking New Testament Textual Criticism,* ed. David Alan Black (Grand Rapids: Baker Academic, 2002), 125-39; Jakob Van Bruggen, "The Majority Text: Why Not Reconsider Its Exile?," in *The Bible as Book: The Transmission of the Greek Text*, ed. Scot McKendrick and Orlaith A. O'Sullivan (London: British Library, 2003), 147-53; Gordon D. Fee, "Modern Textual Criticism and the Revival of the *Textus Receptus*," *JETS* 21, no. 1 (1978): 19-33.

Rather, we will make four observations that bring better balance to the discussion and, for the purposes of text-critical apologetics, actually *strengthen* the entire enterprise regardless of one's overall text-critical method.

The Byzantine tradition is not the same thing as the textus receptus. It is surprising how tenacious this conflation has been, even among scholars who should know better.[12] Yes, the manuscripts used by Erasmus are "late" and broadly from the reservoir of witnesses labeled (in hindsight) "Byzantine." But today's reconstructed Byzantine text differs in nearly two thousand places from the *textus receptus*, which largely underlies the KJV.[13] The problems behind the selection and editing of manuscripts underlying Erasmus's initial work and the ultimate *textus receptus* are well known, but the guilt by association that spills over into the a priori exclusion of the Byzantine text is unwarranted.

The Byzantine text is not monolithic and thus cannot be so easily thrown out en masse. The very fact that there is a debate about the Byzantine text at all presupposes that there is something out there to which we can point and say, *this* is Byzantine and *that* is not. In other words, though Hermann von Soden showed long ago that there is diversity even in "the Byzantine text," there is a latent impression among scholars of all stripes that whatever we call *the* Byzantine text is essentially uniform or monolithic.[14] This text is then regarded with suspicion (i.e., the product of ecclesiastical pressure to conform to a uniform and deficient standard text) or confidence (i.e., the product of near-perfect divine preservation of the text). In this, much of the debate pushes in the direction of rejecting it entirely or accepting it wholesale. However, in recent scholarship, including work done by the more rigorous proponents of Byzantine priority, there has been a renewed appreciation for the internal diversity within the Byzantine tradition itself.[15]

---

[12]E.g., Aland and Aland, *Text of the New Testament*, 19; Fee, "Modern Textual Criticism," 19; Bruce M. Metzger, "The Caesarean Text of the Gospels," *JBL* 64, no. 4 (1945): 477.

[13]As collated by Daniel B. Wallace, "Some Second Thoughts on the Majority Text," *BSac* 146 (1989): 277, though this point was anticipated by the Kirsopp Lake nearly a century earlier. Wallace refers to the 1995 edition of Robinson-Pierpont. For the text of the KJV, see especially Irena D. Backus, *The Reformed Roots of the English New Testament: The Influence of Theodore Beza on the English New Testament*, PTMS 28 (Eugene, OR: Pickwick, 1980); F. H. A. Scrivener, *The Authorized Edition of the English Bible (1611), Its Subsequent Reprints and Modern Representatives* (Cambridge: Cambridge University Press, 1884), 243-63.

[14]See Hermann von Soden, *Die Schriften des neuen Testaments in ihrer ältesten erreichbaren Textgestalt*, 2 vols. (Göttingen: Vandenhoeck & Ruprecht, 1911–1913).

[15]"I have not yet found one manuscript that contains all the majority readings of a NT writing"

For instance, four of the key Byzantine witnesses for Acts and the Catholic Epistles (minuscules 18, 35, 319, 617) vary among themselves—that is, contain more than one reading for a given unit of text—8 percent of the time, representing nearly one thousand textual units; for comparison, 01, 02, and 03 (key majuscules for these New Testament writings) vary among themselves 13 percent of the time.[16] No one would, of course, suggest the latter group is monolithic and undifferentiated, so why the former when the overall variability profile is, all things considered, not *that* different? Moreover, scholars have long pointed out (though they perhaps have been ignored) that the scribes of manuscripts typically deemed "Byzantine" in text-type were by no means uniform in procedure.[17] This lack of homogeneity forces us, then, to reconsider whether its seat at the text-critical table should be revisited.

The entire textual stream—including the Byzantine tradition—is far more stable than typically admitted. As mentioned above, certain scholars tend to privilege the earlier majuscules and papyri (or the so-called Alexandrian text-type) and pit the Byzantine tradition against it as largely corrupt and secondary; the reverse holds among Byzantine proponents. Only recently, however, have we been able to quantify rigorously the overall stability of the textual stream. For Acts and the Catholic Epistles (one-fifth of the Greek New Testament), 15 percent of the text is *completely nonvariant* among the hundreds of collated Greek witnesses, including the Byzantines; an additional 54 percent is likewise *nonvariant* among the most frequently cited sixteen majuscules and minuscules (including four Byzantines) spanning

---

(Klaus Wachtel, "The Byzantine Text of the Gospels: Recension or Process?," paper presented at the Society of Biblical Literature Annual Meeting, 2009, p. 5). Robinson and Pierpont make this point repeatedly in their *New Testament in the Original Greek*, but their edition (esp. the sparse marginal "split" readings) gives the contrary impression of uniformity.

[16]Using collation data published electronically by the INTF. For James, Gerd Mink asserts a slightly different computation of 94 to 98 percent agreement among pairs of Byzantine manuscripts, which naturally decreases when one includes more manuscripts in the cross-comparison ("Problems of a Highly Contaminated Tradition: The New Testament. Stemmata of Variants as a Source of a Genealogy for Witnesses," in *Studies in Stemmatology II*, ed. Pieter van Reenen, August den Hollander, and Margot van Mulken [Amsterdam: John Benjamins, 2004], 22). For details on the method used, see Gregory R. Lanier, "Quantifying New Testament Textual Variants: Key Witnesses in Acts and the Catholic Letters," *NTS* 64, no. 4 (2018): 551-72.

[17]E.g., see Ernest Cadman Colwell's analysis of the "chaotic" editing of 574 ("The Complex Character of the Late Byzantine Text of the Gospels," *JBL* 54, no. 4 [1935]: 211-21). He concludes, "There is no homogeneity in the late medieval text of the gospels. The universal and ruthless dominance of the middle ages by one text-type is now recognized as a myth" (212). Perhaps only a few listened!

over one thousand years.[18] Furthermore, the undivided Byzantine text *fully agrees* with the new Editio Critica Maior (ECM) text of Acts and the Catholics—that is, the form of the text with which it should, as the theory goes, be diametrically opposed—94 percent of the time.[19] For the Gospels, the rate of agreement between the NA[27] and select majority readings is at least 86 percent based on sampling, though the number may adjust upward as fuller collation data becomes available.[20] Put differently, the core tradition remains remarkably stable over time, in that the difference between the two texts usually thought to be most polarized is actually fairly small.

Distinctly Byzantine readings often have ancient roots. For Byzantine proponents, this is a tautology since Byzantine tradition *is* the most ancient one. But even among their opponents, research in the past several decades has demonstrated that hundreds of specific *readings* that have been classified at times as distinctly Byzantine are not, say, secondary conflations or corruptions arising from some later recension, but in fact are already attested by witnesses that are often a millennium older. For instance, P45, P46, and P66 share over one hundred readings with the Byzantine tradition against the early majuscules, and other chronologically earlier witnesses such as 02, 032, and some versions regularly contain what later become classified as Byzantine variants.[21] In fact, the recent ECM editions for Acts and the Catholic Epistles accept Byzantine readings *against* the four major majuscules (01, 02,

---

[18]Lanier, "Quantifying New Testament Textual Variants." By *text* here is meant both places of textual variation in the ECM (i.e., variant units) *and* the space between those.

[19]For variation units (as defined by the ECM), the rate of agreement is 92 percent: 9,684 agreements of 10,512 variant units (92 percent Acts, 93 percent Catholic Epistles). However, the rate increases when one factors in the 15 percent of textual units that have no variation at all (that is, there are no alternative readings in any witness collated in the ECM). For this ECM data on the undivided Byzantine agreements, see Holger Strutwolf et al., eds., *Novum Testamentum Graecum, Editio Critica Maior: III/2, Apostelgeschichte, Begleitende Materialien* (Stuttgart: Deutsche Bibelgesellschaft, 2017), 8; and Barbara Aland et al., eds., *Novum Testamentum Graecum, Editio Critica Maior: IV.2, Die Katholischen Briefe, Begleitende Materialien*, 2nd rev. ed. (Stuttgart: Deutsche Bibelgesellschaft, 2013), 10, 13, 15, 17.

[20]Wachtel, "Byzantine Text of the Gospels," 6 (Wachtel is using *Text und Textwert* and *Parallelperikopen*, which by design prioritizes highly variable passages).

[21]The seminal study is Harry Sturz, *The Byzantine Text-Type and New Testament Textual Criticism* (Nashville: Thomas Nelson, 1984), but his work was already anticipated by Günther Zuntz, *The Text of the Epistles: A Disquisition upon the Corpus Paulinum* (Oxford: Oxford University Press, 1953). Zuntz writes, "A number of Byzantine readings, most of them genuine, which previously were discarded as 'late,' are anticipated by P46" (55). Fee and others have rightly pointed out that many of these agreements could be purely coincidental—but not all of them. Thus, while the Byzantine *text-type* (if we want to call it that) may not have existed in its mature form in the third/fourth centuries, some genuine readings did.

03, 04) ten times.[22] More tellingly, thirty-six of the fifty-two recent modifications to Acts in the ECM were specifically in the Byzantine direction (even if not exclusively Byzantine).[23]

Such findings have led several scholars to argue that what later becomes identifiable as "Byzantine" developed progressively over time; that is, a multitude of Byzantine *readings* go back as far as the 200s, though the mature Byzantine tradition or *text-form* did not clearly solidify until the 900s.[24] From a text-critical perspective, then, the fact that "the Byzantine [tradition] has preserved second-century tradition not preserved by the other text-types" indicates that it should, at least sometimes, be treated as on par with other witnesses and not discarded to the "late" heap.[25] Indeed, a growing chorus of scholars not otherwise part of the Byzantine-priority camp admit that "tenacious negative bias against the Byzantine majority text" is in need of a "reevaluation," such that the Byzantine tradition "is an important witness to the early text."[26]

In sum, when one takes into consideration the entirety of the textual stream and the indications of its stability, one realizes that the long-standing competition between earlier and later manuscripts and the text-forms they represent is overblown: for the vast majority of the Greek New Testament's textual history, "the text is Alexandrian *and* Byzantine *and* every other text-type."[27] In other words, the core textual tradition encompassed by any text-type is both very large and very stable. Granted, scholars will continue debating the major differences represented in the Byzantine tradition, such as

---

[22]My own estimates using INTF's published electronic collations. In the ECM, see Acts 1:10/34-36; 1:26/8; 4:4/28; 7:13/34-36; 16:28/4-14; 17:22/6; 23:10/6-8; 23:30/34-44; 2 Pet 2:4/20; Jas 2:4/2-6. Note: Forward slashes and subsequent numbers represent the "addresses" of variation units in the ECM.

[23]Holger Strutwolf et al., eds., *Novum Testamentum Graecum, Editio Critica Maior: III/1.1 Apostelgeschichte, Text* (Stuttgart: Deutsche Bibelgesellschaft, 2017), 34*-35*.

[24]On this see Klaus Wachtel, *Der Byzantinische Text der Katholischen Briefe: Eine Untersuchung zur Entstehung der Koine des Neuen Testaments* (Berlin: de Gruyter, 1995); Martin Heide, *Der einzig wahre Bibeltext? Erasmus von Rotterdam und die Frage nach dem Urtext*, 5th ed. (Hamburg: VTR, 2006), 170-72.

[25]Sturz, *Byzantine Text-Type*, 64.

[26]Strutwolf et al., *Apostelgeschichte, Text*, 30*-31*; Barbara Aland et al., eds., *Novum Testamentum Graecum, Editio Critica Maior: IV/1 Die Katholischen Briefe, Text*, 2nd rev. ed. (Stuttgart: Deutsche Bibelgesellschaft, 2013), 10 and throughout. See also Tommy Wasserman and Peter J. Gurry, *A New Approach to Textual Criticism: An Introduction to the Coherence-Based Genealogical Method*, SBLRBS 80 (Atlanta: SBL Press, 2017), 107-8.

[27]David C. Parker, "A Comparison Between the *Text und Textwert* and the Claremont Profile Method Analyses of Manuscripts in the Gospel of Luke," *NTS* 49, no. 1 (2003): 137.

the endings of Mark (Mk 16:9-20), the *pericope adulterae* (Jn 7:53–8:11), and miscellaneous readings of some length (Acts 8:37 and the like), but on the whole, such differences are the exception, not the rule. If nothing else, scholars on all sides should admit that "rejection *en bloc* of the 'Byzantine text' . . . tends to rob us of a most helpful instrument" and that its uncritical replacement with a new *textus receptus* based on an earlier-is-better-and-later-is-worse "dating myth" needs to be reexamined.[28] Klaus Wachtel sums up well: "The high agreement rates connecting these witnesses demonstrates that a large body of text was safely transmitted from the very beginning of its transmission through the Byzantine period to today."[29]

TEXT: APPRECIATING THE LATER
CHANNELS OF AN ANCIENT STREAM

The prior discussion on textual traditions more broadly leads to the important question: How can "later" manuscripts contain earlier and often high-quality texts if they are so far removed in time from the earliest sources? The common misconception is that manuscript copying always degrades over time—much like the children's game of Telephone—whereby later manuscripts arise from scribes who copy contemporary ones, which themselves are likewise late and corrupt, and make them worse. But is that the case? Here we will cast our net more broadly and consider how minuscules, including non-Byzantine ones, give us insight into how textual preservation can actually *improve* over time. We will work through two major considerations on this front and then draw some important conclusions about how "late" manuscripts can and should shore up our text-critical apologetic in terms of reconstructing the original/initial text.

Later scribes on occasion self-consciously copied much earlier manuscripts. For many of the thousands of minuscules, we simply know very little about their origins, scribes, exemplars (= manuscript being copied), and so on. But in some cases, we know a bit more, and one thing we find is that,

---

[28]Zuntz, *Text of the Epistles*, 12. For the criticism that NA/UBS have become the new TR, see, e.g., Holmes, "*Text of the Epistles* Sixty Years After," 90; Kurt Aland anticipated this critique in "Ein neuer Textus Receptus für das griechische Neue Testament?," *NTS* 28, no. 1 (1982): 141-53.

[29]Klaus Wachtel, "On the Relationship of the 'Western Text' and the Byzantine Tradition of Acts—A Plea Against the Text-Type Concept," in *Novum Testamentum Graecum: Editio Critica Maior, III/3: Apostelgeschichte, Studien*, ed. Holger Strutwolf et al. (Stuttgart: Deutsche Bibelgesellschaft), 140.

with reasonable frequency, a manuscript produced at a later date has been directly copied, either entirely or in portions (resulting in "block mixture"), from a much older manuscript (which may now be lost) or an intermediate exemplar that itself derives from a much older manuscript. Let us consider a few examples.

The famous minuscule 1739, which is one of the most frequently cited for Paul and the Catholic Epistles, was produced by a scribe named Ephraim in the mid-950s. After more than a century of research on 1739 and its scribe, the general consensus is the following. Ephraim was a quite good scribe whose "vigilant insistence on exact reproduction" extended even to reproducing the column formatting and holes or gaps of his exemplar.[30] Further, the exemplar he copied was produced by a talented scribe or compiler who himself produced a "text-critical production" that, as indicated in marginal notes, was based on two or more manuscripts that date at least to the 400s (maybe earlier), originate most likely in the library at Caesarea, and (at least for portions) reflect the text and/or commentary of Origen.[31] What makes this further significant is that Ephraim appears to have worked in Constantinople in a scriptorium that, as we know from other minuscules copied there, was producing largely "Byzantine" output; Ephraim stands out, then, as one who cuts against the grain and conveys a text that is often dubbed "Alexandrian" despite its provenance in the heart of Byzantium.[32] Furthermore, other minuscules share a similar text with 1739 and form a "family" (primarily 945 and 1891 but also possibly 206, 322, 323, 429, 453, 522, 630, 1704, and 2200), though a precise relationship between Ephraim's work and that of these other scribes is undetermined.[33] In short, 1739 is a tenth-century manuscript that conveys a high-quality text found in manuscript(s) at least

---

[30] Amy S. Anderson, *The Textual Tradition of the Gospels: Family 1 in Matthew*, NTTS 32 (Leiden: Brill, 2004), 42.

[31] See discussions on 1739 in Anderson, *Textual Tradition of the Gospels*, 35-45; Thomas C. Geer, "Codex 1739 in Acts and Its Relationship to Manuscripts 945 and 1891," *Bib* 69 (1988): 27-46; Kwang-Won Kim, "Codices 1582, 1739, and Origen," *JBL* 69, no. 2 (1950): 167-75; Zuntz, *Text of the Epistles*, 71-84; Kirsopp Lake and Silva New, *Six Collations of New Testament Manuscripts*, HTS 17 (Cambridge, MA: Harvard University Press, 1932). The specific makeup of 1739 for Acts, Romans, and the rest of Paul is more complex than can be analyzed in detail here. On "text-critical production," see Aland and Wachtel, "Greek Minuscules of the New Testament," 72.

[32] Anderson, *Textual Tradition of the Gospels*, 46. On the generally "Byzantine" character of the copies done at Ephraim's scriptorium, see Christian-Bernard Amphoux, "La parenté textuelle du sy[h] et du groupe 2138 dans l'épître de Jacques," *Bib* 62 (1981): 267-68.

[33] Thomas C. Geer, *Family 1739 in Acts*, SBLMS 48 (Atlanta: Scholars Press, 1994).

five centuries older and that, in turn, makes its way downstream to other
minuscules:

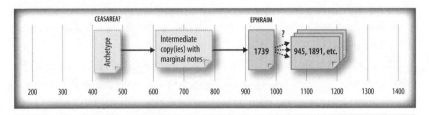

Figure 6.1. The genealogy of minuscule 1739

Family 1 offers another example for the Gospels. Family 1 (f^1 in most apparatuses) is an oft-studied group of minuscules that, at latest tally, includes
at least 1, 22, 118, 131, 205, 209, 872, 1192, 1210, 1278, 1582, 2193, 2542.[34] Of these
minuscules, 1 (ca. 1100s) and 1582 (ca. 900s) are the most prominent, and
several independent studies have shown persuasively that they are independent copies—through one or more intermediate steps—of a much older
shared exemplar (often dubbed "A-1") that is no longer extant. While the text
contained in these manuscripts (and Family 1 as a whole) has much in
common with other fully Byzantine witnesses, it also shares numerous affinities with various non-Byzantine forms of the text as well as church fathers,
thus giving this family high visibility in textual criticism. Moreover, most likely
the scribe of 1582 is the same Ephraim discussed above for 1739, and the ancestor of "A-1" goes back to at least the 500s, yielding the following picture:[35]

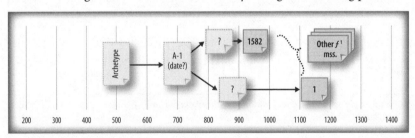

Figure 6.2. The genealogy of 1582

[34] Alison Welsby, *A Textual Study of Family 1 in the Gospel of John*, ANTF 45 (Berlin: de Gruyter,
2014), 3-5.

[35] Anderson, *Textual Tradition of the Gospels*, 72; Amy S. Anderson, "Codex 2193 and Family 1 in
Mark," in *Studies on the Text of the New Testament and Early Christianity: Essays in Honor of
Michael W. Holmes*, ed. Daniel M. Gurtner, Juan Hernández Jr., and Paul Foster, NTTSD 50
(Leiden: Brill, 2015). See also the dated but still seminal Kirsopp Lake, *Codex 1 of the Gospels
and Its Allies*, TS 7 (Cambridge, 1902), especially xxiv.

The early-600s translation of the Greek New Testament known as the Harklean Syriac (syr^h) also aptly illustrates the notion of a later textual tradition with much earlier roots.[36] In 615/6, Thomas of Harqel, the bishop of Mabbug and a participant in the Miaphysite controversy, completed a "scholarly revision of the lost Philoxenian version" of the Syriac New Testament.[37] This Philoxenian version (syr^ph)—completed by Polycarp under the commissioning of Philoxenius in 507/8—itself has earlier roots in both the late fourth-/early fifth-century Syriac Peshitta (syr^p) and the third-century Old Syriac (syr^s or syr^c).[38] But Thomas was less interested in the Syriac tradition itself and more interested in repristinating it toward the Greek. In his Syriac colophons and various marginal notes, most of which have been preserved fairly well in downstream copies, Thomas indicates that he revised the Philoxenian by comparing it to what he considered "accurate" Greek manuscripts to which he had access—two or three for the Gospels, two for Paul, one for Acts/Catholics, and two for Revelation—presumably from at least the 500s.[39] Due to the pronounced way in which Thomas sought to conform the Syriac to his Greek exemplars, we can with some confidence back-translate the Harklean Syriac text (and marginal glosses) into Greek.[40] From these reconstructions we know that the Greek text consulted by Thomas in the 600s is extremely close to that contained in minuscule 2138 (and its "family," including at least ten other minuscules dating from the

---

[36]Of the voluminous materials on the Harklean Syriac, see Samer S. Yohanna, *The Gospel of Mark in the Syriac Harklean Version: An Edition Based upon the Earliest Witnesses*, BibOr 52 (Rome: Gregorian & Biblical Press, 2014); Peter J. Williams, "The Syriac Versions of the New Testament," in Ehrman and Holmes, *Text of the New Testament*, 143-66; Sebastian P. Brock, *The Bible in the Syriac Tradition*, Gorgias Handbooks 7 (Piscataway, NJ: Gorgias, 2006); Andreas Juckel, "Introduction to the Harklean Text," in *Comparative Edition of the Syriac Gospels: Aligning the Sinaiticus, Curetonius, Peshitta, and Harklean Versions*, vol. 1, *Matthew*, ed. George A. Kiraz, NTTS 21.1 (Leiden: Brill, 1996); Barbara Aland and Andreas Juckel, *Das Neue Testament in syrischer Überlieferung: I. Die Grossen Katholischen Briefe*, ANTF 7 (Berlin: de Gruyter, 1986); Bruce M. Metzger, *The Early Versions of the New Testament: Their Origin, Transmission and Limitations* (Oxford: Clarendon, 1977), 63-75; Günther Zuntz, *The Ancestry of the Harklean New Testament* (Oxford: Oxford University Press, 1945).

[37]Yohanna, *Gospel of Mark in the Syriac Harklean Version*, 5.

[38]Williams, "Syriac Versions of the New Testament," 145-55.

[39]On the Harklean colophons and marginalia, see Ian R. Beacham, "The Harklean Syriac Version of Revelation: Manuscripts, Text and Methodology of Translation from Greek" (PhD thesis, University of Birmingham, 1990); John D. Thomas, "The Colophon of the Harclean Syriac Version," *NETR* 3, no. 1 (1980): 16-26; John D. Thomas, "The Harklean Margin: A Study of the Asterisks, Obeli, and Marginalia of the Harklean Syriac Version with Special Reference to the Gospel of Luke" (PhD diss., University of St Andrews, 1973).

[40]Consult the Aland and Juckel volumes in the ANTF series.

tenth to thirteenth centuries), which was produced by a scribe named Michael in 1072, likely at a scriptorium in Constantinople.[41] In other words, the medieval scribes who produced the "family 2138" manuscripts had access to a form of the text that is accurately transmitted from manuscripts at least five centuries older and used by Thomas (who, in turn, was interacting with—even going against—Syriac texts with roots yet another three to four centuries earlier). The complex picture shows, in a pronounced way, how later manuscripts can convey earlier texts:

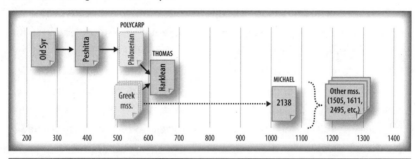

Figure 6.3. The genealogy of 2138 and its close relatives

A final illuminating but more tentative example is Family 13 (f^{13}, also known as the Ferrar Group; nearly twenty minuscules and growing) and particularly one of its best representatives, minuscule 69.[42] The Family 13 text has long been considered important in textual criticism, and while pinning down precise origins is difficult, the current hypothesis is that these minuscules share some sort of genealogical relationship with 038/Θ (Koridethi, 800s), possibly 032/W (Freer Gospel, 400s–500s), and some form of

[41]Amphoux, "La parenté textuelle," 267-68. Aland and Juckel (*Neue Testament in syrischer Über-lieferung*, especially 45-89) first built the hypothesis from the Catholic Epistles but have subsequently confirmed it with other portions of the New Testament. Their results are further developed by Matthew Spencer, Klaus Wachtel, and Christopher J. Howe, "The Greek Vorlage of the Syra Harclensis: A Comparative Study on Method in Exploring Textual Genealogy," *TC* 7 (2002): n.p.; Wachtel, *Byzantinische Text der Katholischen Briefe*, 56, 189-91; Amphoux, "La parenté textuelle"; Christian-Bernard Amphoux, "Quelques témoins grecs des formes textuelles les plus anciennes de Jc: le groupe 2138," *NTS* 28, no. 1 (1982): 91-115.

[42]For more detail, see Jac Perrin, "Family 13 in Saint John's Gospel" (PhD thesis, University of Birmingham, 2012); Didier Lafleur, *La Famille 13 dans l'évangile de Marc*, NTTSD 41 (Leiden: Brill, 2013); Jacob Geerlings, *Family 13 (The Ferrar Group): The Text According to Matthew*, SD 19 (Salt Lake City: University of Utah Press, 1961); Kirsopp Lake and Silva Lake, *Family 13 (The Ferrar Group): The Text According to Mark, with a Collation of Codex 28 of the Gospels*, SD 11 (Philadelphia: University of Pennsylvania Press, 1941).

the Greek text available to Origen.[43] What is more certain is that the Family 13 minuscules at least share a pre-900s archetype (now lost); that the subsequent minuscules over the next several centuries show increasing assimilation toward a Byzantine form of text; but that the latest member of the family, 69 (Leicester Codex), has the most pristine form of text, deriving directly from the much earlier archetype rather than through intermediate copies. Most Family 13 members were copied in southern Italy, but 69 was copied by a very productive scribe named Emmanuel in the late 1400s in England, where he apparently had access to and directly used a much older manuscript.[44] Though the picture is fuzzier than the other examples described above, it still contributes to our broader point:[45]

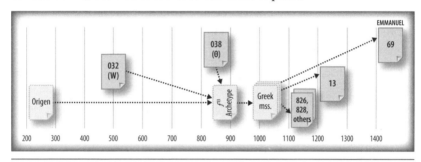

Figure 6.4. The genealogy of Family 13

Later scribes on occasion correct their "later" exemplars using "earlier" manuscripts. As a general rule, "scribes reproduced the manuscripts that were available to them"; that is, they were primarily copyists seeking faithfully to render what they had in front of them, whether a contemporaneous exemplar or (as in the cases outlined above) an older one.[46] However, even "late" copyists sometimes used other manuscripts to make revisions to their base exemplar either in the text itself or in the margins, and, in some cases,

---

[43]On 038/Θ, see Didier Lafleur, "Le Codex de Koridethi (Θ.038) et la Famille 13: Une Nouvelle Collation de l'Évangile de Marc," in *Textual Research on the Psalms and Gospels / Recherches textuelles sur les psaumes et les évangiles: Papers from the Tbilisi Colloquium on the Editing and History of Biblical Manuscripts, Actes du Colloque de Tbilisi, 19-20 septembre 2007*, ed. Christian-Bernard Amphoux and J. Keith Elliott, NovTSup 142 (Leiden: Brill, 2012). On 032/W, see Hurtado, *Text-Critical Methodology*, 61-62.

[44]Lake and Lake, *Family 13*, 11; J. Rendel Harris, *The Origin of the Leicester Codex of the New Testament* (London: C. J. Clay and Sons, 1887); M. R. James, "The Scribe of the Leicester Codex," *JTS* 5 (1904): 445-47.

[45]This diagram is a simplified form of Lafleur, *La Famille 13*, 240.

[46]Aland and Wachtel, "Greek Minuscules of the New Testament," 72.

these other manuscripts are demonstrably much older.[47] For instance, minuscule 424 (ca. 1000s) contains a text in the Epistles that has been corrected from a Byzantine form toward something close to 1739, whose compiler, in turn, not only worked from a much older exemplar (as argued above) but also corrects it against readings found centuries earlier in Irenaeus, Clement, Origen, Eusebius, and Basil.[48] Minuscule 700 (ca. 1000s) shows the influence of numerous earlier forms of the text as well as an extremely rare variant of the Lukan Lord's Prayer that may be as early as the time of Marcion.[49] Minuscule 2464 was produced in the same scriptorium as the Byzantine "Uspenski Gospels" (minuscule 461), but it deviates so markedly at points from its peer that it is likely the scribe was also comparing to a different, and likely much older, exemplar.[50] We could add more, but the point is this: while some scribes evince a tendency to work within a contemporary bubble, so to speak, some go the other way and edit a late exemplar by comparing it to, and integrating readings from, earlier manuscripts. This does not necessarily mean that the result is any closer to the original text, but it does illustrate another mechanism by which later manuscripts may contain earlier forms of text.

In light of the above phenomena, we must maintain a distinction between the age of a *manuscript* (the specific artifact produced on papyrus or parchment by a scribe at a particular time and place) and the age of the *text* it contains. This distinction between an "internal age" (text itself) and "external age" (physical artifact) has been established from at least the time of J. S. Semler (1765).[51] The notion that "the more recent need not be the worse" (*recentiores*

---

[47]See discussion in Georg Gäbel et al., "The CBGM Applied to Variants from Acts: Methodological Background," *TC* 20 (2015): 2.

[48]Geer, "Codex 1739," 27; W. L. Richards, *The Classification of the Greek Manuscripts of the Johannine Epistles*, SBLDS 35 (Missoula, MT: Scholars Press, 1977), 16.

[49]Herman C. Hoskier postulated that the scribe of 700 was working from a majuscule but also examining several other earlier manuscripts, producing a highly mixed text that is "deeply interesting," in *A Full Account and Collation of the Greek Cursive Codex Evangelium 604* (London: David Nutt, 1890), i, xxii. On Marcion's Lord's Prayer variant and its relation to 700, see Dieter T. Roth, "The Text of the Lord's Prayer in Marcion's Gospel," *ZNW* 103, no. 1 (2012): 47-63.

[50]Aland and Wachtel, "Greek Minuscules of the New Testament," 72.

[51]In *Vorbereitung zur theologischen Hermeneutik: Drittes Stück, Erste Abteilung* (Halle: Hemmerde, 1765), 88-89, J. S. Semler distinguishes between *äusserliches* and *innerliches Alter*, though the idea may go back yet further to Johann A. Bengel and Richard Simon (Peter J. Gurry, *A Critical Examination of the Coherence-Based Genealogical Method in New Testament Textual Criticism*, NTTSD 55 [Leiden: Brill, 2017], 38n11; Eldon J. Epp, "Textual Clusters: Their Past and Future in New Testament Textual Criticism," in Ehrman and Holmes, *Text of the New Testament*, 528).

non deteriores, formulated by Pasquali in the 1950s) is not new news, especially for those who subscribe to a Byzantine priority position for which this principle is utterly foundational.[52] But among those who otherwise hold a form of the "later is worse" myth of manuscript dating, this principle is often eclipsed by the radiant light of the majuscules and papyri. An important corrective, then, is this: the *text* of a late manuscript—which, when understood this way, is the true "witness" for textual criticism—"may be considerably older than the manuscript itself."[53] In other words, if we think of the early stages of textual transmission as a river of witnesses in which the original/initial text was carried along (with variation, of course), we clearly see signs of quite pristine channels at much later stages.[54]

What value, then, do "later" channels offer to the task of reconstructing the original/initial text? Several minuscules, at least for certain books of the New Testament, contain "a valuable early text which can compete with even the best of the uncials," often providing significant later (downstream) corroboration of readings already known from earlier manuscripts.[55] But even among lesser-quality minuscules, there is the possibility of finding a "precious stone" hidden among the lesser pebbles of competing variants—that is, a rare variant reading that deserves attention either for reconstructing the original/initial or for shining light on interesting historical and theological factors (even if nonoriginal).[56] Finally, minuscules contribute to fleshing out more fully the overall history of the transmission of the text.[57] All these factors indicate that our text-critical apologetic should be careful not to be dismissive toward (or ignorant of) later minuscules just because they are "late."

QUALITY CONTROLS: APPRECIATING
THE WORK OF THE LATER SCRIBES

While the scribal habits and process controls of earlier scribes have been well documented, there have been few systematic analyses of later scribes, no

---

[52]See Robinson, "Case for Byzantine Priority" (2002), 135.

[53]Mink, "Problems of a Highly Contaminated Tradition," 29; see also Spencer et al., "Greek Vorlage of the Syra Harclensis," §11.3.

[54]Slightly modifying Zuntz's reservoir and river metaphor (*Text of the Epistles*, 110-13).

[55]Aland and Aland, *Text of the New Testament*, 128.

[56]Aland and Aland, *Text of the New Testament*, 339; also Margaret Davies, *The Text of the Pauline Epistles in MS. 2344 and Its Relationship to the Text of Other Known Manuscripts, in Particular to 330, 436 and 462*, SD 38 (Salt Lake City: University of Utah Press, 1968), 149.

[57]On these points, see Aland and Wachtel, "Greek Minuscules of the New Testament," 73-75.

doubt in part due to the sheer number of manuscripts.[58] Filling this void are two competing and equally vague impressions: the later, medieval scribes were either incompetent and thoughtless in their work, or they were subject to a forced march to conform to the Byzantine standard.[59] In either case the dating myth is perpetuated, as the later manuscripts produced by such later scribes are deemed all the worse. But are such impressions well grounded?

One interesting way to get a read on this is to examine some of the most hotly debated "later" passages (particularly between eclectic critics and Byzantine advocates), where we might expect blind conformity or even sloppiness to arise. Is there any evidence that later scribes were exercising careful text-critical judgment even in these passages? Let us take a look at three examples.

The pericope of the adulterous woman (Jn 7:53–8:11). We cannot, of course, get into the innumerable complexities here, but observe the following notes from "later" scribes:[60]

- 565 (800s), at the end of John 21: "The chapter about the adulteress, not being present in the current copies, was omitted; it was located right after 'does not arise.'"

- 1 (1100s), at the end of John 21 (where it inserts the *pericope adulterae*): "The chapter about the adulteress: in the Gospel according to John, this does not appear in the majority of copies; nor is it commented upon by the divine fathers whose interpretations have been preserved—specifically, by John Chrysostom and Cyril of Alexandria; nor is it taken up by Theodore of Mopuestia and the others. For this reason, it was not kept in the place where it is found in a few copies, at the beginning of the 86th chapter [according to Eusebius], following, 'Search and see that a prophet does not arise out of Galilee.'"

---

[58]Though most studies of *individual* manuscripts (Welsby, Anderson, Lake, and several others mentioned above) often include notes about the patterns *for that scribe*. On the scribal habits and process controls of earlier scribes, see especially James R. Royse, *Scribal Habits in Early Greek New Testament Papyri*, NTTSD 36 (Leiden: Brill, 2008); Dirk Jongkind, *Scribal Habits of Codex Sinaiticus*, TS, Third Series 5 (Piscataway, NJ: Gorgias, 2007).

[59]See Anderson's diagnosis of this misconception in *Textual Tradition of the Gospels*, 46.

[60]Good places to start are David Alan Black and Jacob N. Cerone, eds., *The Pericope of the Adulteress in Contemporary Research*, LNTS 551 (London: Bloomsbury T&T Clark, 2016); Chris Keith, "Recent and Previous Research on the *Pericope Adulterae* (John 7.53–8.11)," *CBR* 6, no. 3 (2008): 377-404.

- Mingana Syriac 480 (1700s): "This story is not found in all manuscripts. But Abba Mar Paule found it in one of the Alexandrian [NB: the city] manuscripts and translated it into Syriac as written here from the Gospel of John."[61]

- Family 13: Several members of this minuscule family transfer the *pericope adulterae* to Luke 21:38, and in doing so they typically make some sort of scribal annotation or brief comment, some even showing awareness of the fact that other witnesses include it in John.[62]

Whether such scribal phenomena have a bearing on establishing the authenticity of *pericope adulterae* is a separate question. For our purposes the key point is this: some later scribes knew of the status of this pericope in other Greek manuscripts as well as church fathers and took such information into account in their work.

The ending(s) of Mark (Mk 16:9-20). We also see similar scribal annotations at the ending of Mark, often immediately prior to this disputed passage.[63]

- 1, 205, 209, 1582 (900s–1400s): "In some of the copies the Evangelist is completed to this point, as far as which Eusebius Pamphili also made his canons. But in many these are also present . . ." (or something similar)

- 15, 22, 1110, 1192, 1210 (900s–1100s): "In some of the copies the Evangelist is completed to this point. But in many these are also present . . ." (or something similar)

- 20, 215, 300 (1000s): "From here to the end does not occur in some of the copies, but in the ancient copies it all occurs in full"

- 199 (1100s): "In some of the copies, this does not occur, but it stops here"[64]

---

[61]See Peter J. Gurry, "On the Origin of the Pericope Adulterae in the Syriac NT," *Evangelical Textual Criticism* (blog), October 24, 2016, http://evangelicaltextualcriticism.blogspot .com/2017/03/on-origin-of-pericope-adulterae-in.html, and the discussion there.

[62]See Didier Lafleur, "Which Criteria for Family 13 (F13) Manuscripts?," *NovT* 54, no. 1 (2012): 110-11, 142.

[63]For an introduction to the debate, see David Alan Black, ed., *Perspectives on the Ending of Mark: Four Views* (Nashville: B&H Academic, 2008).

[64]For these notations, see Nicholas P. Lunn, *The Original Ending of Mark: A New Case for the Authenticity of Mark 16:9-20* (Eugene, OR: Pickwick, 2014), 36-37; and David W. Hester, *Does Mark 16:9-20 Belong in the New Testament?* (Eugene, OR: Wipf & Stock, 2015). While both volumes are mixed in terms of overall scholarly quality, they do have helpful discussions of and plates showing these scribal notes.

What we see here—regardless of how much weight such comments should have in deciding on the original/initial ending—is a clear awareness by these scribes (or those of their archetypes) concerning competing readings in other manuscripts, which factored into their decision on how to handle the Markan ending(s).

Sweat like drops of blood (Lk 22:43-44). Several minuscules of Family 13 treat this famous passage in quite an interesting way: some scribes omit it from Luke entirely, and nearly all move it to Matthew 26:39; but in either case, they always give some sort of scribal indication of the linkage between the two locations. This suggests the scribes in this family were aware of competing options among manuscripts available to them and were, for reasons unknown, making a *"conscious transfer of the verses from Luke to Matthew."*[65] They may have been wrong for doing so, but it was by no means random or accidental.

No doubt some scribes were clumsier than others, and there was certainly a tendency toward increasing textual conformity in the medieval era. But these examples—and we could include numerous others for less-contentious passages—indicate that at least some later scribes were by no means lazy, untrustworthy, or mindless. Rather, they appear far more aware as text critics than usually conceded, allowing their awareness of readings from "older" manuscripts, patristic readings, and even competing "later" readings from their own contemporaries to serve as process controls for their copying work. If so, then even if their final output contains nonoriginal/noninitial textual readings, we can nevertheless have a higher degree of confidence in the essential conscientiousness of their efforts.

A PRIMER ON "BETTER" MINUSCULES

What remains is to provide some guidance on a select number of key "later" minuscules of above-average value that should always be a factor in studying the text of the New Testament. Before providing a brief primer, we must offer the caveat that, due in part to some of the scribal processes described above whereby a scribe might consult or correct against other manuscripts than their immediate exemplar, essentially every manuscript (or its ancestor, if it

---

[65]Claire Clivaz, "The Angel and the Sweat like 'Drops of Blood' (Lk 22:43-44): P[69] and f^{13}," *HTR* 98, no. 4 (2005): 434-35 (emphasis original).

is a near identical copy) is to some lesser or greater degree "mixed."[66] Moreover, this mixture is not necessarily uniform across a manuscript, as a scribe might switch exemplars or consult a different manuscript for one epistle versus another, or even switch halfway through a Gospel, and so on. Due to such vicissitudes, some sections—macro collections such as Gospels, or specific books/epistles, or even subsets of chapters within books, and the like—are "better" than others. Such block mixture means that the value of a given minuscule may vary based on where one is within it.

In an effort to quantify this in a helpful way, we will describe the general tendency of each minuscule listed below using as shorthand the two opposed perspectives that dominate modern textual criticism, introduced above. Namely, does the text of the minuscule *lean* in the direction of the eclectic NA text that, on balance, reflects earlier majuscules and papyri (●)? Does it *lean* in the direction of the Byzantine tradition (○)? Or is it somewhere in between (◑)?[67] In this way the table can serve everyone, regardless of one's macro philosophy of the text. We will break down the analysis for each major section of the New Testament, acknowledging the challenge of block mixture.[68] Representative comments on each minuscule will round out this primer.

---

[66]Epp, "Textual Clusters," 522.

[67]Using *Text und Textwert*'s statistics as summarized in Aland and Aland, *Text of the New Testament*, 129-38. Blanks indicate the manuscript does not contain that portion of the New Testament. The "lean" ratings are determined as follows: ○ if 65+ percent of *Teststellen* read 2 (Byz); ● if 65+ percent read 1 (NA) or 1/2 (shared); and ◑ otherwise. Note we are intentionally avoiding assigning text-types (which are increasingly questioned) or I-V categories (as with Aland and Aland).

[68]Excluding Revelation; most of these minuscules do not contain it, and it has its own peculiar textual history.

MS	Century	Gospels	Acts	Catholics	Paul	Comments
1 (f¹)	12th	◐	○	○	○	"Closely knit textual family . . . [texts] share a unique profile of Non-Majority text readings," including numerous singular readings[1]
13 (f¹³)	13th	◐				Launched the debates about a "Caesarean" text-type
33	9th	◐	●	●	●	"Queen of the cursives"[2]
69	15th	◐	○	○	○	Famous for idiosyncratic handwriting; one of few minuscules used in S. P. Tregelles's edition[3]
81	11th		●	◐	●	"One of the most important of all minuscule manuscripts"[4]
579	13th	◐				Most valuable in Mark/Luke
700	11th	◐				"Deeply interesting manuscript," with a peculiar mix of variants[5]
892	9th	●				Arguably the best minuscule of the Gospels; first Greek-only manuscript with *pericope adulterae*
1175	11th		●	◐	◐	Same caliber as 33 and 1739 in portions
1241	12th	◐	○	●	◐	"Interesting text" but all over the board in terms of mixture[6]
1739	10th		◐	●	●	In Paul, it is "comparable, in age and quality, to P46"[7]
1881	14th			◐	●	One of the most consistently cited minuscules in NA28
2344	11th		◐	●	○	Closely related to 33 and 69, but varies per book
2464	9th		●	◐	◐	Least valuable in Romans, but valuable elsewhere

[1] Alison Welsby, *A Textual Study of Family 1 in the Gospel of John*, ANTF 45 (Berlin: de Gruyter, 2014), 3.
[2] As described by Eichhorn in the early 1800s.
[3] Technically it is part of f¹³ but, as it contains more than the Gospels, it deserves to be treated separately.
[4] Bruce M. Metzger and Bart D. Ehrman, *The Text of the New Testament: Its Transmission, Corruption, and Restoration*, 4th ed. (Oxford: Oxford University Press, 2005), 88.
[5] Herman C. Hoskier, *A Full Account and Collation of the Greek Cursive Codex Evangelium 604* (London: David Nutt, 1890), i.
[6] Kirsopp Lake and Silva New, *Six Collations of New Testament Manuscripts* (Cambridge, MA: Harvard University Press, 1932), vii.
[7] Günther Zuntz, *The Text of the Epistles: A Disquisition upon the Corpus Paulinum* (Oxford: Oxford University Press, 1953), 69.

Table 6.1. A primer on the textual tendencies of important minuscule manuscripts

CONCLUSION

We began by articulating how the "dating myth" that assumes a "later" manuscript is *worse because it is later*—and the opposite view that privileges later Byzantine manuscripts—both introduce problems for our text-critical apologetic. In response, we have attempted to clarify the value of later manuscripts by examining the fidelity of the entire textual tradition (namely, restoring some appreciation for the Byzantine tradition while nevertheless acknowledging its shortcomings); illustrating how "later" manuscripts can have "earlier" texts via copying or correcting against older exemplars; and shoring up confidence in the scribal quality controls even in the medieval era. In short, with a well-defined meaning of *better* in place, we can say with confidence that *later manuscripts can be better ones*, though not always, of course.

The net effect is that the unparalleled mass of minuscules—though intimidating indeed—deserves its day in court: "Except in von Soden's inaccurate and unused pages, the minuscules have never been allowed to speak. Once heard, they may well be found wanting, but at least their case will have been presented."[69] Fortunately, the use of computers, indefatigable efforts by text critics around the world to digitize and collate minuscules, and the application of new approaches to the data that do not, at least in principle, prioritize external age over internal age (namely, the coherence-based genealogical method/ECM efforts), are ensuring that "later" minuscules, even the inferior ones, are heard.

Key Takeaways

▶ Although it is often thought that the later a manuscript is, the worse its textual quality will be, this is not always true. Sometimes later manuscripts can have better readings than some earlier manuscripts. Even our latest manuscript can preserve very early readings in isolation.

▶ The core textual tradition of the New Testament remains remarkably stable over time. The difference between the two texts usually thought to be most polarized is actually fairly small.

▶ Later scribes show evidence of conscientious work, seen in their choice of early manuscripts and in their choice to correct their manuscripts.

---

[69]Wisse, *Profile Method*, 5.

CHAPTER SEVEN

MYTHS ABOUT COPYISTS

THE SCRIBES WHO COPIED
OUR EARLIEST MANUSCRIPTS

Zachary J. Cole

ONE OF THE TRICKIEST QUESTIONS about the transmission of the New Testament text is this: in the earliest period, before the time of the Roman emperor Constantine (r. AD 306–337), *who exactly was doing the copying?* Many books about textual criticism offer an answer that goes something like this:

> The copying practices we have considered thus far have been principally those of the first three centuries of Christianity, when most of the copyists of the Christian texts were not professionals trained for the job but simply literate Christians of this or that congregation, able to read and write and so called upon to reproduce the texts of the community in their spare time. Because they were not highly trained to perform this kind of work, they were more prone to make mistakes than professional scribes would have been.[1]

This quotation is from Bart Ehrman's now-famous *Misquoting Jesus*. Later on, he reiterates, "In the early Christian centuries, scribes were amateurs and as such were more inclined to alter the texts they copied—or more prone to alter them accidentally—than were scribes in the later periods who, starting in the fourth century, began to be professionals."[2] Forget the familiar image of medieval monks hunched over writing desks. In the early period, we are told, Christian manuscripts were copied by zealous but passably literate amateurs rather than "professionals." Ehrman is not the

---

[1] Bart D. Ehrman, *Misquoting Jesus: The Story Behind Who Changed the Bible and Why* (New York: HarperCollins, 2005), 71.
[2] Ehrman, *Misquoting Jesus*, 98.

only one to hold this view. In fact, many introductions to the subject seem to agree that the first copyists of the New Testament were insufficiently untrained novices who corrupted the text through their incompetent work and outright tampering with the text.[3] This understanding bears serious implications about the reliability of the text. If the earliest New Testament copyists were energetic but inexperienced, how do we know that the text was not corrupted beyond recovery in this formative stage? This is a sobering thought.

But, strangely enough, other voices sing a different tune. Some scholars assert the exact opposite about early scribes. The impression one gets from reading these scholars is that most early Christian copyists were—on the contrary—actually professional, careful, scrupulous, and well trained, and they studiously avoided making any changes to the text. Much like their Jewish counterparts who painstakingly copied the Hebrew text of the Old Testament with reverence and attention to the minutest detail, so also many early Christian copyists transmitted the text believing it to be the very word of God. After all, the earliest Christians were themselves Jewish, and it would be natural for them to copy New Testament books with the same care as they would Old Testament books.[4]

So which is it? Of these two different portraits of early Christian copyists, which is the right one? Were the early New Testament copyists mostly zealous amateurs, or were they careful professionals? Or were they somewhere in between? In this chapter we will attempt to dispel a few myths about the early scribes, their training, and their handling of the New Testament text. We will take as our focus the first three centuries of Christianity,

---

[3]For example, Léon Vaganay and Christian-Bernard Amphoux, *An Introduction to New Testament Textual Criticism*, rev. ed., trans. Jenny Read-Heimerdinger (Cambridge: Cambridge University Press, 1991), 73 (also 3, 53, 57, 91-92). See also J. Harold Greenlee, *Introduction to New Testament Textual Criticism* (Peabody, MA: Hendrickson, 1995), 51-52; Gordon D. Fee, "Textual Criticism of the New Testament," in *Studies in the Theory and Method of New Testament Textual Criticism*, ed. Eldon J. Epp and Gordon D. Fee, SD 45 (Grand Rapids: Eerdmans, 1993), 9; Robert F. Hull Jr., *The Story of the New Testament Text: Movers, Materials, Motives, Methods, Models* (Atlanta: Society of Biblical Literature, 2010), 15.

[4]See, for example, Philip W. Comfort, *The Quest for the Original Text of the New Testament* (Grand Rapids: Baker Books, 1992), 41-58 (esp. 42-43); Comfort, *Encountering the Manuscripts: An Introduction to New Testament Paleography and Textual Criticism* (Nashville: Broadman & Holman, 2005), 255-88. See also the literature cited there, such as Colin H. Roberts, "Books in the Graeco-Roman World and in the New Testament," in *The Cambridge History of the Bible*, vol. 1, *From the Beginnings to Jerome*, ed. P. R. Ackroyd and C. F. Evans (Cambridge: Cambridge University Press, 1970), 48-66.

the era prior to the emperor Constantine, in order to evaluate what the evidence tells us about the early copyists. To do this we will first examine the competency of early scribes: What do we know about their training or lack thereof? Second, we will examine their attitudes toward the text: Did they faithfully copy it, or did they rewrite it whenever and however they wanted?

ZEALOUS AMATEURS? THE TRAINING
OF EARLY CHRISTIAN SCRIBES

Professionals or not? We begin with the argument that the earliest scribes were zealous but incompetent. Why is this idea popular? One reason goes back to the work of a well-known and important scholar of early Christianity, Colin H. Roberts. In a series of lectures delivered in 1977, Roberts argued that there is a noticeable similarity between early Christian manuscripts and another body of ancient texts known as "documentary papyri."[5] Broadly speaking, documentary papyri (often called just "documents") are the mundane texts left behind by ancient people: personal letters, tax receipts, contracts, grocery lists, business memoranda, and other kinds of functional pieces of writing. Because these were practical documents, the scribes who produced them usually used handwriting that was unpretentious, often quickly written, and sometimes plainly unattractive. This writing is often "cursive" in the sense that letters are joined together for the sake of speed and convenience. The documentary style of writing stands in contrast with the slowly written, carefully executed letters often used in the copying of books of literature, namely, "literary hands." Expensive and luxurious copies of classics such as Homer's *Iliad* and *Odyssey* were often written in the elegant and consistent calligraphy of a literary hand rather than the more ordinary documentary hand.[6] The way that I might scribble down a grocery list on my way to the store will no doubt pale in comparison to the fancy calligraphy found on an opulent wedding invitation.

---

[5]Colin Roberts, *Manuscript, Society and Belief in Early Christian Egypt*, 1977 Schweich Lectures (Oxford: Oxford University Press, 1979). Documentary papyri became known to scholars during the boom of archaeological excavation of Egypt in the late nineteenth century. See Adolf Deissmann, *Light from the Ancient East: The New Testament Illustrated by Recently Discovered Texts of the Graeco-Roman World*, trans. Lionel Strachan (New York: Hodder and Stoughton, 1910).
[6]For more on documentary and literary hands, see Eric G. Turner, *Greek Manuscripts of the Ancient World*, 2nd ed., rev. P. J. Parsons, BICS Supplement 46 (London: Institute of Classical Studies, 1987), 1-23; Colin H. Roberts, *Greek Literary Hands: 350 B.C.–A.D. 400* (Oxford: Clarendon, 1956), xi-xvi.

There can be quite a bit of overlap between literary and documentary handwriting, as they were not rigid and hermetically sealed styles. Some ancient books were written in informal, unpretentious hands, and at the same time some documents were written carefully and slowly.[7] In any case, what Roberts argues is that the earliest manuscripts of the New Testament have more in common with documentary papyri—the practical, everyday texts—rather than literary papyri. In particular, Roberts observes that early Christian manuscripts are more often in codex form rather than roll form, they use abbreviations in the text, their scripts are unpretentious, and they divide the text with punctuation and paragraphing—all of which are features also found in documentary texts. His conclusion: the earliest Christian copyists were trained to make documents, not literature.

Here is Roberts himself on the matter:

> What I think they all [early Christian papyri], in varying degrees, have in common is that, though the writing is far from unskilled, they are the work of men not trained in calligraphy and so not accustomed to writing books, though they were familiar with them; they employ what is basically a documentary hand but at the same time they are aware that it is a book, not a document on which they are engaged. They are not personal or private hands; in most a degree of regularity and of clarity is aimed at and achieved. . . . In none can be traced the work of the professional calligrapher or the rapid, informal hand of the private scholar.[8]

So far, so good. For the most part, scholars today are in agreement with Roberts's assessment. Unfortunately, however, many today misunderstand his actual argument. It is often assumed that the *unpretentious scripts* of early New Testament papyri indicate an *unprofessional standard of copying*. That is, unattractive and unpretentious writing must mean "untrained" scribes and poor standards of transcription. But this is not actually what Roberts argues, nor is it true.

It is simply a mistake to assume that unattractive and workaday handwriting entails a lack of training or a poor standard of copying. Roberts does

---

[7]In fact, one recent study shows that a great many of the literary books discovered in one ancient Egyptian city were actually written with scripts that are "informal and unexceptional" rather than calligraphic: William A. Johnson, *Bookrolls and Scribes in Oxyrhynchus* (Toronto: University of Toronto Press, 2004), 161.

[8]Roberts, *Manuscript, Society and Belief*, 14.

not claim this, nor is it demonstrable from any other study. Style of script is one thing; accuracy in transcription is another. In fact, there is evidence that suggests attractive, literary handwriting often entails *in*accurate copying. For example, in describing a "deluxe" copy of Virgil, Roberts himself comments, "The text itself was both carelessly written and (as is not infrequently the case with éditions *de luxe* [deluxe editions]) of poor quality."[9] Carefully note what Roberts says here: the pretty letters and *de luxe* presentation of this book did not guarantee a high level of care in transcription—and in fact this "is not infrequently the case." Roberts is not alone here; we can see from the comments of many ancient authors that book shops and other professional copying services were frequently unreliable because of their poor standard of copying.[10]

In reality, there is no evidence to assume a necessary connection between *calligraphy* and *care* in transcription—these are separate issues. The textual quality of a manuscript must be determined on its own terms, not on the erroneous assumption that the beauty of its script is the most relevant factor. To return to Roberts's argument about Christians and documentary papyri, he simply makes the point that early Christian copyists appear to have been trained to copy documents rather than works of literature—yet *trained* they were! Scribes who copied documentary papyri were indeed still scribes, and they needed requisite training, competency, and ability to do so. Documentary papyri are not inherently substandard; they serve a different purpose from copies of literature. We should not make the mistake of thinking that works of literature somehow required a higher level of accuracy than did documents. Just ask the business owner whether she needs accurately copied contracts, or the merchant whether he wants accurate receipts, or indeed the government whether it requires accurate tax records.[11]

To put it bluntly, Roberts never argues that early Christian scribes were unprofessional in the sense of untrained or inexperienced. For this reason,

---

[9]Colin H. Roberts, ed., *The Antinoopolis Papyri*, vol. 1, GRM 28 (London: Egypt Exploration Society, 1950), 75 (P.Ant. I 29).

[10]See, for instance, Harry Y. Gamble, *Books and Readers in the Early Church: A History of Early Christian Texts* (New Haven, CT: Yale University Press, 1995), 91, and the references given there.

[11]Consider, for instance, William Warren, "Who Changed the Text and Why? Probable, Possible, and Unlikely Explanations," in *The Reliability of the New Testament: Bart D. Ehrman and Daniel B. Wallace in Dialogue*, ed. Robert B. Stewart (Minneapolis: Fortress, 2011), 113. Here, I think the term *professional* is used in a potentially confusing way because it seems to be equated with "highly trained."

I think the term *professional* can be anachronistic and ultimately misleading. When discussions of early scribes rely on this term, they tend to conjure modern understandings of occupation and vocation. But these modern ideas are likely to distort our perception of ancient copying. Rather than asking whether Christian scribes were "professionals," I prefer to ask whether they were *competent* and *trained*.

Competent and trained? *Recent studies.* Regardless of the attractiveness of early Christian manuscripts, what does the evidence suggest about the training and competency of the scribes themselves? Fortunately, this question can be answered with a great deal of certainty. This is because one simply needs to examine the earliest extant manuscripts to observe the quality of their work. In fact, many scholars have recently done this kind of analysis with a view to discovering the level of training and ability of early Christian scribes. Put simply, what they have found is that most of the early Christian manuscripts are clearly the products of trained and competent copyists, not zealous amateurs.

Two such studies are worth highlighting here. The first is the work of Kim Haines-Eitzen. In her monograph *Guardians of Letters*, Haines-Eitzen asks, "Who were the scribes who copied early Christian literature during the second and third centuries?" To answer this question, she examines the evidence of early Christian scribes found in ancient literature, archaeology, and the papyri themselves. One of her observations is key:

> What is striking about our earliest Christian papyri is that they all exhibit the influences of literary and documentary styles, and they all seem to be located in the middle of the spectrum of experience and level of skill. The scribes who produced these copies fit well into the portrait of multifunctional scribes— both professional and nonprofessional—whose education entailed learning how to write a semicursive style.[12]

Note carefully what she argues here. *All* of the earliest Christian papyri evidence a mix of documentary and literary influence. This means that early Christian papyri, far from looking like the work of "amateurs," actually bear the characteristics of both documentary papyri and literary manuscripts and thus can be located in "the middle of the spectrum of experience and level

---

[12]Kim Haines-Eitzen, *Guardians of Letters: Literacy, Power, and the Transmitters of Early Christian Literature* (Oxford: Oxford University Press, 2000), 75.

of skill." Finally, these papyri exhibit the work of "multifunctional" scribes. Haines-Eitzen uses the term *multifunctional* to describe copyists who were able to produce *both* documentary texts *and* works of literature, not simply one or the other.

Once again, we meet the terminology of *professional* versus *nonprofessional*, and this can lead to confusion. So we should be clear. For Haines-Eitzen the term *professional* simply indicates someone who was *by trade* a scribe or held a scribal title (such as the administrative scribes in Egypt). Importantly, the term is not synonymous with "competent" (in fact, we have evidence of professional yet clearly *incompetent* scribes![13]). Many copyists in the ancient world were slaves, servants, or freedpersons who were trained and fully able to copy texts accurately, even though they may not have been paid for it, and it may not have been their primary task. These individuals often filled the roles of "secretaries, clerks, stenographers, and record keepers" in large households, but they would not necessarily be scribes by trade or by title, or considered "professional" in the modern sense. Thus, one of Haines-Eitzen's key findings is that early Christian literature was circulated and disseminated through informal channels formed on social networks, or "in-house."[14] When seeking to obtain a copy of a New Testament book, early Christians probably did not commission the "professional" scribes of the book shops for their services; rather, they more likely enlisted the help of individuals within their own social circles. But this does not in any way imply that these individuals were insufficiently trained or that they were unskilled amateurs. In fact, the opposite appears to have been the case, and she states this quite clearly:

> The fact that Christian papyri (as well as many classical papyri more generally) all exhibit the influences of documentary and literary styles indicates scribes who were either comfortable with and experienced in both styles or trained in more general styles of writing that could be adapted in rather simple ways to different tasks; it seems to me that the latter scenario is more likely since had these scribes had extensive training in literary book hand, their hands would have manifested this training.[15]

---

[13]Haines-Eitzen discusses one fascinating example of a certain Petaus, who, although he was an official "village scribe" (and thus a "professional"), was functionally illiterate (*Guardians of Letters*, 27-28).

[14]Haines-Eitzen, *Guardians of Letters*, 29, 54.

[15]Haines-Eitzen, *Guardians of Letters*, 68.

In other words, while it is not so clear that many early Christian copyists were professional scribes by trade, there is no doubt that most were competent and experienced.

There is another, more recent study that comes to a similar conclusion. In 2016, Alan Mugridge published an exhaustive analysis of the physical form of early Christian papyri, observing features such as scribal hand, writing material, dimensions, letters per line, lines per page, punctuation, critical signs, and so on. He too comes to the conclusion that most early Christian transcribers were able copyists: "It seems clear that the vast majority of the Christian papyri were copied by trained scribes."[16] He goes on:

> All of this should cast doubt on the view that on the whole Christian manuscripts were copied by unskilled writers during the early centuries, and also suggests that we need to re-examine any implications drawn from this view that the transmission of Christian texts was quite inaccurate. It is true that, as Roberts proposed, many of the papyri show the hand of scribes accustomed to producing documents. Nevertheless, they still exhibit the skill of the trained scribes who produced such documents, including a number of papyri copied to a calligraphic standard, even though we do not know whether they were paid for their efforts or did their work voluntarily.[17]

Here Mugridge generally confirms the argument of Haines-Eitzen and shows that the evidence of the manuscripts themselves exposes a misperception about the early scribes. While it remains true that, in many ways, Christian papyri resemble documentary papyri (as they use the codex book form and abbreviations), it is important to stress that this does not equate to "unprofessional" work in the sense of untrained or inexperienced. As a group, early New Testament manuscripts show the same levels of care, experience, and accuracy that one could reasonably expect of any ancient text. So, to describe the earliest Christian copyists as "nonprofessionals" is misleading because it conjures an impression of the evidence that is warped by modern ideas. While it may well be true that they were not necessarily

---

[16]Alan Mugridge, *Copying Early Christian Texts: A Study of Scribal Practice*, WUNT 362 (Tübingen: Mohr Siebeck, 2016), 147.

[17]Mugridge, *Copying Early Christian Texts*, 148.

scribes by trade or by title (although some probably were), it is quite clear that they were nonetheless capable of high-quality work.[18]

Some examples. At this point, it is worth considering a few specific examples. We can examine, for instance, the manuscript called P45—a papyrus copy of the canonical Gospels and Acts that dates to the third century AD.[19] Thirty folios (or sixty pages, counting front and back) remain of an original 220 folios or so (or 440 pages). The scholar who first edited the manuscript describes its handwriting in this way: "The codex is written throughout in a small and very clear hand. . . . The writing is very correct, and though without calligraphic pretensions, is the work of a competent scribe."[20] Günther Zuntz published one folio from this same codex and describes it in similar terms:

> His hand is on the whole amazingly even, and his practice with regard to orthography, punctuation and the use of *nomina sacra* astonishingly consistent. The beginnings of lines are placed one below the other with great regularity so as to effect, from top to bottom, an almost faultless, straight line running parallel with the fibres of the papyrus. . . . The scribe aims at neatness rather than rigid uniformity.[21]

Far from the scribblings of an amateur, P45 preserves the work of a consistent and practiced scribe. Another example is P46, which is a collection of Paul's letters that dates to the third century AD. Eighty-six folios (or 172 pages) remain of this manuscript. Its editor compares its handwriting to that of P45 (mentioned above):

> The script of the papyrus is in marked contrast with that of the Chester Beatty papyrus of the Gospels and Acts [P45]. It is far more calligraphic in character, a rather large, free, and flowing hand with some pretensions to style and elegance. It is upright and square in formation, and well spaced out both between

---

[18]The presence of stichometric counts in some papyri, such as P46, which were often used to tally the amount of work involved in copying a particular text for the purpose of payment, suggests that some early copyists were professional in the sense of being scribes by trade. See Mugridge, *Copying Early Christian Texts*, 137-38.

[19]Images of P45 and many other New Testament manuscripts can be accessed for free at the Center for the Study of New Testament Manuscripts (www.csntm.org).

[20]Frederic G. Kenyon, ed., *The Chester Beatty Biblical Papyri. Descriptions and Texts of Twelve Manuscripts on Papyrus of the Greek Bible: Fasiculus II: The Gospels and Acts. Text* (London: Emery Walker, 1933), viii-ix.

[21]Günther Zuntz, "Reconstruction of One Leaf of the Chester Beatty Papyrus (Matth. 25, 41-26, 39)," *ChrÉg* 26 (1951): 192.

the letters and between the lines. . . . In general it may be said that the letters are rather early in style and of good Roman formation.[22]

Around the same time, Henry Sanders agreed with this assessment, stating, "The writing is of the book hand type and the letters are carefully formed and well spaced."[23] This characterization can hardly describe the work of an unskilled transcriber.

A third and final example is P75, a substantial copy of Luke and John that dates to the third century AD.[24] Fifty-one folios (or 102 pages) now remain of an original seventy-two. Like the other texts we have seen, it was written in a "clear and generally carefully executed uncial."[25] More recently, Sarah Edwards comments, "The manuscript was written on papyrus of such fine quality that the verso is generally as smooth as the recto. In texture it resembles hand-woven linen. . . . The codex is far more beautiful than the photographs reveal. If I were to describe it with one word, that word would be 'elegant!'"[26] Scholars widely recognize the high-quality work found in P75, and there is not the slightest suspicion it is the work of a zealous but untrained Christian.

Many more examples could be discussed here, but the point should be clear. When we look at the early manuscripts themselves, what we find is that they clearly are not the work of incompetent fanatics. Rather, most of them bear the marks of trained and capable scribes who blended techniques of documentary and literary writing styles. So much for "amateurs."

But we also do not want to overstate the case. Not all of the early Christian papyri we have today can be described in such positive terms. Some of them are indeed sloppily written, carelessly produced, and evidently written by untrained individuals. One good example of this is P72, a third-century copy

---

[22]Frederic G. Kenyon, ed., *The Chester Beatty Biblical Papyri. Descriptions and Texts of Twelve Manuscripts on Papyrus of the Greek Bible: Fasiculus III: Supplement: Pauline Epistles. Text* (London: Emery Walker, 1936), xiii.

[23]Henry Sanders, *A Third-Century Papyrus Codex of the Epistles of Paul*, University of Michigan Studies: Humanistic Series 38 (Norwood, MA: Plimpton, 1935), 12.

[24]This is the consensus view, but one scholar has recently argued that it could also date to the fourth century: Brent Nongbri, "Reconsidering the Place of Papyrus Bodmer XIV-XV (P75) in the Textual Criticism of the New Testament," *JBL* 135, no. 2 (2016): 405-37.

[25]Bruce M. Metzger, "The Bodmer Papyrus of Luke and John," *ExpTim* 73, no. 7 (1962): 201.

[26]Sarah A. Edwards, "P75 Under the Magnifying Glass," *NovT* 18, no. 3 (1976): 195. See also Victor Martin and Rodolphe Kasser, eds., *Papyrus Bodmer XIV: Évangile de Luc chap. 3–24* (Cologny-Geneva: Bibliotheca Bodmeriana, 1961), 13: "The writing is a beautiful upright uncial, elegant and careful."

of 1–2 Peter and Jude. The handwriting of this manuscript is noticeably rough and unclear. Scholars believe that this manuscript was intended for private use (rather than for congregational worship).[27] Another example is P47, a third-century papyrus copy of Revelation. Although its handwriting is readable, the script is somewhat sloppy and inconsistent with things such as letter size. The most recent study of this manuscript puts it bluntly: "We are not dealing with a highly skilled calligraphic hand."[28]

We need to be wary of painting with brushstrokes that are too broad. Just as it is inaccurate to say that all early copyists were untrained amateurs, it is likewise inaccurate to say that they were all experts. Rather, among the early manuscripts we find a wide range of scribal skills and abilities, but still a significant majority appear to be competent transcribers.

The length of New Testament manuscripts. A final point is worth thinking about before we move on. One of the ways that "amateur" copyists are identified is by their inability to maintain a consistent script for extended periods of time. That is, someone who is not trained or sufficiently accustomed to the task of copying a lengthy text will gradually lose the ability to write legibly and consistently. In a fascinating study, Roger Bagnall and Raffaella Cribiore examine more than three hundred ancient letters that were written by women. Their purpose is to learn as much as they can about ancient women from the physical remains of these letters. Interestingly, they note that fatigue is one of the clear indications of a "personal hand;" that is, the person making the document was untrained in transcription: "It happens very often, however, that personal hands produced acceptable results at first but are then betrayed by the length of a text. In contrast to scribal hands, which seem to become more impatient and faster toward the end, personal hands are often overcome by the effort, just as are school hands."[29]

We have all seen this in our own experience: try as we might to maintain some consistency, the fact is that legibility usually lessens as the amount of writing increases. This was evidently true with ancient writers as well. If we

---

[27]James R. Royse, *Scribal Habits in Early Greek New Testament Papyri*, NTTSD 36 (Leiden: Brill, 2008), 546. See also Michel Testuz, *Papyrus Bodmer VII-IX* (Cologny-Geneva: Bibliothèque Bodmer, 1959), 9-10; Tommy Wasserman, "Papyrus 72 and the *Bodmer Miscellaneous Codex*," *NTS* 51, no. 1 (2005): 154.
[28]Peter Malik, *P.Beatty III (P47): The Codex, Its Scribe, and Its Text*, NTTSD 52 (Leiden: Brill, 2017), 47.
[29]Roger S. Bagnall and Raffaella Cribiore, *Women's Letters from Ancient Egypt: 300 B.C.–A.D. 800* (Ann Arbor: University of Michigan Press, 2006), 45.

consider the length of early Christian manuscripts, it is remarkable how consistent the scripts are. As noted above, many of our early manuscripts are extremely lengthy: recall that P45 originally contained around 220 folios, P46 originally contained around 104 folios, and P75 originally contained around 72 folios. What we see in the surviving pages of these manuscripts is a consistent clarity of script. This is a testament to the capability and skill of our earliest transcribers. Moreover, this fact is all the more significant when we consider how short most ancient letters were compared to New Testament books: the average ancient letter was less than one page in length.[30] The prolonged consistency of the hands found in most New Testament manuscripts reflects the work of scribes who were able to maintain legible and consistent scripts for impressive stretches. What this fact demonstrates is experience in transcription.

Thus far we have made some important clarifications about early Christian scribes: they were not all "amateurs" and "nonprofessionals." In fact, the evidence we have suggests that most of the early copyists were competent, trained individuals who were more than capable of doing the work of transcription—whether or not they were scribes by trade or by title. It is easy to assume that, prior to Constantine, Christians must have been deprived, short-staffed, and without access to capable scribes. This idea seems to fit with our understanding of the fledgling church in that era. Nevertheless, an investigation of the actual manuscripts reveals a more nuanced picture that involves scribes of a variety of skills and training, but definitely including many who were capable. When we return once again to Roberts and his original comments and set aside the term *professional*, the point can be seen quite clearly: "The Christian manuscripts of the second century, although not reaching a high standard of calligraphy, generally exhibit a competent style of writing which has been called 'reformed documentary' and which is likely to be the work of experienced scribes, whether Christian or not."[31]

A note on evidence. Before moving on, it is worth admitting what we do not know. Specifically, we do not have the same amount of evidence for the *earliest* period of transmission as we would like. Our material evidence

---

[30]Based on a count of fourteen thousand Greco-Roman letters, Alfred Wikenhauser reports that the average length of a private letter on papyrus is about eighty-seven words, while that of Paul's letters is about thirteen hundred words (*New Testament Introduction*, trans. J. Cunningham [New York: Herder and Herder, 1958], 346-47).

[31]Colin H. Roberts and T. C. Skeat, *The Birth of the Codex* (London: Oxford University Press, 1983), 46.

reaches back well into the third century, but for the second century it is extremely fragmentary, and for the first century it is (at present) nonexistent. We cannot make firm judgments about the training of scribes whose work no longer remains. This fact is worth bearing in mind. Even still, there is little reason to suggest that what we would find in the late first/early second centuries would differ greatly from what we see in the late second/early third centuries.

WILD AND FREE? EARLY SCRIBAL FIDELITY

Now we must turn to our final question. Experienced or not, were the earliest scribes in the habit of changing the text whenever they wanted? Even if we were to establish the competency of early scribes, this does not mean that they always copied with care. Here we must be careful to distinguish *ability* and *attitude*. A scribe might have been capable of producing the most luxurious and accurate of manuscripts yet at the same time display a casual or lax attitude toward the text. Such a situation was in fact hinted at above when we noted Roberts's comments about Greco-Roman *éditions de luxe*—they often are pretty but penned by inattentive scribes. So even if we know that most early Christian scribes were trained and capable, as I have argued above, we still need to consider whether they have been faithful to the text they received.[32]

To anticipate my conclusion, I argue that it is very unlikely that the text has been corrupted beyond retrieval by freewheeling scribes. While there may be instances of some "free" and perhaps wild copying in the early period, we have good reason to believe that original words of the apostles have been faithfully preserved.[33] I offer three points that support this view. First, due to the wealth of our evidence, we have a paradoxical safety in numbers. Second, we have strong evidence that the text has been carefully transmitted in at least one stream of manuscripts. Third, when we look at the nature of our textual variants, they do not appear to be the kind of variants that would arise if scribes were in the habit of writing whatever they wanted.

---

[32]It is also possible that a trained and competent scribe might have faithfully transmitted a text of poor quality (that is, the *previous* scribe might have introduced errors). Such a question is beyond the scope of this chapter.

[33]For another approach to this issue, see the excellent discussion in Andreas J. Köstenberger and Michael J. Kruger, *The Heresy of Orthodoxy: How Contemporary Culture's Fascination with Diversity Has Reshaped Our Understanding of Early Christianity* (Wheaton, IL: Crossway, 2010), 203-31.

The wealth of manuscripts. The first point to consider is the sheer mass of manuscripts we have. Having thousands of New Testament manuscripts helps to mitigate—at least to a certain degree—the effects of those who might tamper with the text. If we had only a handful of New Testament manuscripts, it would be extremely challenging to identify places where the text had been corrupted. But this is not the case; thousands of New Testament manuscripts have come down to us, and they are continually being discovered. This embarrassment of riches poses some challenges for us, but one of its benefits is that errors in transmission can be more easily identified and removed.[34]

David Instone-Brewer describes this idea as a "paradoxical safety in numbers."[35] What he means is that the immense volume of material evidence for the New Testament text entails two important facts. On the one hand, having more manuscripts means having more textual variants; this is simple mathematics. All handwritten documents will have errors in them. On the other hand, more manuscripts at the same time permits more textual stability in the long run. As Instone-Brewer describes it,

> Imagine that two pupils wrote down their teacher's dictation; we could find both contained some errors but it would often be impossible to decide which of the two versions was correct. Now imagine that a class of thirty pupils wrote down the same dictation; there would be many more errors in total, but the correct version would be much easier to work out because only one or two would make the *same* error. With so many New Testament manuscripts we therefore have a strong foundation for discovering the original wording.[36]

This is a helpful analogy. We should not be too concerned about the danger that one sleepy or perhaps heretical scribe has hopelessly corrupted the text for all who followed. Our knowledge of the text of the New Testament is not based on the witness of one or two manuscripts but rather a great many that come from different times, different regions, and even different languages. To be sure, we must keep in mind that it would be misleading to suggest we

---

[34]For the phrase "embarrassment of riches" I credit J. Ed Komoszewski, M. James Sawyer, and Daniel B. Wallace, *Reinventing Jesus: How Contemporary Skeptics Miss the Real Jesus and Mislead Popular Culture* (Grand Rapids: Kregel, 2006), 75-82.

[35]David Instone-Brewer, *Did the Church Change the Bible?*, Grove Biblical Series B 64 (Cambridge, UK: Grove, 2012), 7.

[36]Instone-Brewer, *Did the Church Change the Bible?*, 7.

have thousands of manuscripts that date to the first few centuries of Christianity; in fact, we do not. Rather, from this early period we have about 125 Greek manuscripts of the New Testament. While this may not sound impressive at first, comparison with any other ancient book will demonstrate how this constitutes a richness of evidence.[37]

An example might be beneficial here. Many English Bibles skip John 5:4, going straight from John 5:3 to John 5:5. This is more than simply a mistake in numbering; it signals a text-critical problem. What is missing in the elusive John 5:4? The story is about Jesus healing the lame man at the pool of Bethesda, and John 5:4 explains why the sick and lame were at the pool in the first place: "For an angel of the Lord went down at certain seasons into the pool, and stirred up the water; whoever stepped in first after the stirring of the water was made well from whatever disease that person had" (NRSV). What is significant about this variant is that our knowledge of early manuscripts helps us to see how the verse came to be added later. The earliest Greek manuscript to contain John 5:4 is 02 (Codex Alexandrinus), an important manuscript that dates to the fifth century AD. However, the discovery of several *earlier* manuscripts has shown that the text of John in the third and fourth centuries did not have this verse. Four manuscripts in particular show no sign of this verse: P66, P75, 01, and 03. These manuscripts go straight from John 5:3 to John 5:5. With this early textual evidence, we can see that John 5:4 appears to be an explanatory gloss by a later scribe who tried to add some detail that John appeared to leave out. The point is this: scholars of the New Testament are enormously privileged to have not just one or two but several dozens of manuscripts that date to the earliest centuries of Christianity. This wealth of evidence significantly increases the likelihood that textual aberrations will be identified and removed.

The evidence of careful transmission. The second point to consider relates to evidence that the text has been copied carefully. There is no disputing the fact that many New Testament manuscripts contain corruptions and rewritings. This is simply a fact of all handwritten texts. But it is nonsense

---

[37]On the number of extant New Testament manuscripts, see Jacob Peterson's contribution to this volume (chapter 3), and for a discussion of classical literature, see the chapter by James Prothro (chapter 4).

to suggest that every manuscript is hopelessly corrupt or that the original text is beyond hope of recovery. Text critics widely recognize that many New Testament manuscripts evidence a conscious effort to produce a reliable, accurate text. Some of the best-known manuscripts fit this description, for example, Codex Sinaiticus (01), Codex Vaticanus (03), and P75, but there are many others. Scholars have long recognized that such manuscripts contain high-quality texts and are witnesses of careful, accurate copying of the New Testament. Historically, scholars have seen these manuscripts as representatives of an identifiable textual stream flowing from the ancient Egyptian city of Alexandria, which contrasts with the "Western" tradition, thought to be a separate stream of manuscripts characterized by a freer attitude toward the text. In this regard, we can allow Bruce Metzger and Bart Ehrman to explain:

> It would be a mistake to think that the uncontrolled copying practices that led to the formation of the Western textual tradition were followed everywhere that texts were produced in the Roman Empire. In particular, there is solid evidence that in at least one major see of early Christendom, the city of Alexandria, there was conscious and conscientious control exercised in the copying of the books of the New Testament.[38]

Scholars now tend to avoid speaking of textual "traditions" and "text-types" as such, but this quotation nevertheless captures an important aspect of the transmission of the text.[39] It is not simply evangelicals who recognize 01, 03, and P75 to be accurately copied texts; this is the majority view among text critics across the theological spectrum.[40] This fact confirms for us that while there may have been early copyists who took liberties with the text that they received, the same cannot be said of all or even most of these early transcribers. It is furthermore significant that many of our earliest witnesses illustrate this tendency toward conscientious transcription. For example,

---

[38]Bruce M. Metzger and Bart D. Ehrman, *The Text of the New Testament: Its Transmission, Corruption, and Restoration*, 4th ed. (New York: Oxford University Press, 2005), 277-78.

[39]On the reasons for this development, see Eldon J. Epp, "Textual Clusters: Their Past and Future in New Testament Textual Criticism," in *The Text of the New Testament in Contemporary Research: Essays on the Status Quaestionis*, 2nd ed., ed. Bart D. Ehrman and Michael W. Holmes, NTTSD 42 (Leiden: Brill, 2013), 519-77.

[40]In addition to Metzger and Ehrman, see also Kurt Aland and Barbara Aland, *The Text of the New Testament: An Introduction to the Critical Editions and the Theory and Practice of Modern Textual Criticism*, 2nd ed., trans. Erroll F. Rhodes (Grand Rapids: Eerdmans, 1989), esp. 106.

many early papyri, such as P1, P4, P64+67, and P77+P103, show strong textual affinities with Sinaiticus and Vaticanus. This fact is significant for several reasons, but one worth noting here is that we are able to demonstrate a practice of careful copying over time.[41] That is, scholars are able to track a consistent line of careful copying practices from the second century, with P4 and P64+67, to the third century, with P66 and P75, all the way to the fourth century, with 01 and 03, and beyond, all of which cohere closely in their wording.[42] When these early witnesses all agree in their wording, this allows us to have a high degree of confidence about the state of the text in even *earlier* stages of transmission.[43]

The nature of our textual variants. The third consideration to make relates to the nature of the textual variants we see in the New Testament. If we ask what *sorts* of changes and alterations we find among our manuscripts of the New Testament, the answer is illuminating. Supposing that scribes were in the habit of rewriting verses, adding stories, deleting verses, and writing whatever they wanted, we should expect to see a certain kind of variation in our manuscripts that demonstrates such was the case. We might expect to see, for instance, added paragraphs or chapters and multiple versions of books. But what is striking is that these sorts of changes are noticeably absent from the manuscript record. That is, the kind of textual variation we see in manuscripts affects units of text that are the length of a verse and smaller.

There are, of course, some exceptions to this rule. For example, two units of twelve verses each, in Mark 16:9-20 and John 7:53–8:11, are in doubt. Also, there is a "Western" text of Acts that is a bit longer than the received form, but not because of an added scene or story but because of

---

[41]Eldon J. Epp, "The Significance of the Papyri for Determining the Nature of the New Testament Text in the Second Century: A Dynamic View of Textual Transmission," in *Studies in the Theory and Method of New Testament Textual Criticism*, ed. Eldon J. Epp and Gordon D. Fee, SD 45 (Grand Rapids: Eerdmans, 1993), 289.

[42]As mentioned above, Brent Nongbri has argued that it might well be a fourth-century manuscript, thus dating to the same general time frame as 01 and 03 (Nongbri, "Reconsidering the Place of Papyrus Bodmer XIV-XV"). Even if so, the point can still be made with reference to the early testimony of P4 and P64+67, on which see Tommy Wasserman, "A Comparative Textual Analysis of P4 and P64+67," *TC* 15 (2010): 1-26.

[43]On this, see Daniel B. Wallace, "Laying a Foundation: New Testament Textual Criticism," in *Interpreting the New Testament Text: Introduction to the Art and Science of Exegesis*, ed. Darrell L. Bock and Buist M. Fanning (Wheaton, IL: Crossway, 2006), 39-40.

minor additions within existing verses made throughout.[44] The Gospels and Acts in particular, therefore, demonstrate that while scribes did change the texts they copied, the *nature* of those changes is significant. As Michael W. Holmes describes,

> In short, a very high percentage of the variation evident in the text of the Four Gospels and Acts affects a verse or less of the text. On this level, the fluidity of wording within a verse, sentence, or paragraph is sometimes remarkable. At the same time, however, in terms of overall structure, arrangement, and content, these five documents are remarkably stable. They display simultaneously, in other words, what one may term microlevel fluidity and macrolevel stability.[45]

This is a useful framework with which to work: microlevel fluidity and macrolevel stability. Using this terminology helps to situate the particular task of the New Testament textual critic. For the most part, our concern is not with major portions of text—their (in)authenticity, rewriting, and/or rearrangement—but rather at the level of the verse and smaller.

However, this stands in contrast with the task of many who study other ancient texts, as these are often confronted with comparatively major differences between witnesses. For example, Homer's *Iliad* and *Odyssey* are well-attested works in terms of surviving manuscripts (especially the *Iliad*). However, both texts contain many lengthy passages that are textually uncertain, ranging from single lines to whole paragraphs and to the entirety of a book.[46] A similar example is the early Christian text the Shepherd of Hermas. This work appears to have been written and circulated as two

---

[44]On the "Western" text of Acts, see Bruce M. Metzger, *A Textual Commentary on the Greek New Testament*, 2nd ed. (New York: United Bible Societies, 1994), 222-36; Jenny Read-Heimerdinger, "The «Long» and the «Short» Texts of Acts: A Closer Look at the Quantity and Types of Variation," *RCT* 22 (1997): 245-61. Peter Gurry calculates that 05 (Codex Bezae) is just short of 8 percent longer than 01 (Codex Sinaiticus), in "Just How Much Longer Is Codex Bezae's Text in Acts?," *Evangelical Textual Criticism* (blog), June 27, 2016, http://evangelicaltextualcriticism .blogspot.co.uk/2016/06/just-how-much-longer-is-codex-bezaes.html.

[45]Michael W. Holmes, "From 'Original Text' to 'Initial Text': The Traditional Goal of New Testament Textual Criticism in Contemporary Discussion," in Ehrman and Holmes, *Text of the New Testament*, 674.

[46]For example, according to Sir Maurice Bowra, the entirety of *Iliad* book 10 might be an independent poem added by an unknown poet at a later time. See his "Composition," in *A Companion to Homer*, ed. A. J. B. Wace and F. H. Stubbings (London: Macmillan, 1962), 45-46. For a commentary on some of the interpolations, see George Bolling, *The External Evidence for Interpolation in Homer* (Oxford: Clarendon, 1925).

separate books, which were later combined and supplemented with other passages.[47] For some other ancient books, many portions are simply lost to us. For example, first-century Jewish historian Josephus wrote a number of works that have been preserved, but only imperfectly. Peter Head notes that we have 134 manuscripts with portions of the Greek text of Josephus's works, but in many places these are incomplete, leaving several passages with no extant text at all (though some can be supplemented by surviving Latin translations).[48]

So if indeed the early scribes of the New Testament were in the habit of taking liberties with the text, such activity has been restricted mostly to the level of the verse and smaller. This fact does not by any means solve the many problems that textual critics face in reconstructing the original wording, but it does simplify the task enormously. Rather than worrying about major structural differences and missing portions of text, New Testament scholars work with a body of literature that is stable in its macrostructure and more fluid in its details.[49]

CONCLUSION

In this chapter we have addressed several myths about early scribes and their work. First, it is a myth that the early Christian copyists were all untrained amateurs. Second, it is also a myth that early Christian copyists were all rigorously schooled in the tradition of Jewish scribes. The reality is more complicated: from the evidence of their existing work (the manuscripts themselves), we see that the majority of early Christian copyists were competent and experienced scribes who were more than capable of doing the job of transcription, even if they were not producing luxurious copies of literature. Third, it is a myth that Christian scribes changed the text whenever they saw fit. The kinds of variants that we see in the textual record do not reflect this tendency, and the high number of reliable manuscripts available to us leads most scholars to agree that we have a very good idea of what the apostles originally wrote.

---

[47]Michael W. Holmes, ed., *The Apostolic Fathers: Greek Texts and English Translations*, 3rd ed. (Grand Rapids: Baker Academic, 2007), 446. See also Carolyn Osiek, *The Shepherd of Hermas*, Hermeneia (Minneapolis: Fortress, 1999), 10.

[48]Peter M. Head, *Is the New Testament Reliable?*, Grove Biblical Series B 30 (Cambridge, UK: Grove, 2003), 8-11.

[49]For a good example of this, see Peter M. Head, "Christology and Textual Transmission: Reverential Alterations in the Synoptic Gospels," *NovT* 35, no. 2 (1993): 105-29.

Key Takeaways

▶ The earliest copyists of New Testament manuscripts were neither careless amateurs nor professionals with Xerox-machine accuracy. From the quality of the handwriting, we find a wide range of scribal skills and abilities among the early manuscripts, but a majority appear to be competent transcribers.

▶ As a group, early New Testament manuscripts show the same levels of care, experience, and accuracy that one could reasonably expect of any ancient text. When compared with carefully copied later manuscripts, the earliest scribes do not appear overly careless, as they are often described.

▶ The macrostructure of the New Testament is remarkably stable, especially in comparison to other ancient works. Though textual variation exists, it is usually at the micro rather than macro level.

CHAPTER EIGHT

MYTHS ABOUT COPYING
THE MISTAKES AND CORRECTIONS SCRIBES MADE

Peter Malik

THE MANUAL COPYING OF TEXTS was a laborious, multifaceted task
that involved several simultaneous mental and mechanical processes. The
basic process of transmitting the wording from the exemplar onto the empty
leaf of papyrus, parchment, or paper involved much more than merely
"reading" and "writing." The tedious process of copying entailed many concomitant tasks. To name but a few, scribes had to heed the text layout on
every page and determine the proper word division; they had to check for
and correct possible errors in the exemplar as well as resolve what to do with
corrections or marginal notes that might have been present in the text. At a
material level, copyists had to make sure their writing materials were in
order, which, among other things, included periodically replenishing their
pen with fresh ink and resharpening it to keep the strokes even. It has been
argued, and not without reason, that such processes provided scribes at
various levels with plenty of opportunities for error.[1] In other words, scribes
were busy people, and copying was a demanding job, which inevitably resulted in inaccuracies and blunders of all kinds.

However, the changes that are sometimes thought to be of particular historical significance, because of what they say about either early Christian
beliefs, the origin of the Gospels, or the theological motives of scribes, often

---

[1]Louis Havet, *Manuel de critique verbale appliquée aux textes latins* (Paris: Hachette, 1911), §428,
mentions several disrupting factors in the process of copying, including repositioning of the
hand to begin a new line, turning folios, and reinking the pen. According to Havet, due to these
factors, "Attention [of the copyist] is thus weakened by various and irregular interruptions and
perturbations, which necessarily condition his errors" (my translation).

turn out to be rather more mundane than it seems at first sight. In this, we see that scribes' main goal was not to innovate, and when they did it was often accidental. While many such inaccuracies are still often to be seen in manuscripts, the scribes themselves were not ignorant of their shortcomings. Indeed, we may often observe that they strove to improve and revise their work before they handed it over to posterity. Scribal corrections are the clearest token of that effort.

COPYING AND CORRECTING: EXAMPLES
FROM THE MANUSCRIPT TRADITION

The evidence of corrections is not always easy to interpret. Unlike such phenomena as *nomina sacra* ("sacred names"), numerical abbreviations, readers' notes, or paragraphing, which are typically not transferred to modern editions, corrections are in varying degrees represented in critical apparatuses, hence their textual content can be accessed by such means.[2] Yet corrections are much more than textual changes: their mode, timing, author, and source are important subjects in their own right, subjects that are in turn of vital importance for the accurate appraisal of corrections encountered in an apparatus. Corrections may also disclose scribes' attitudes toward their task and texts they were copying, thus being particularly valuable in the study of ancient book production.[3] Importantly, how corrections are interpreted may significantly alter one's perception of scribes' overall performance. Understandably, then, corrections constitute an important piece in the puzzle of transmission history and as such are well worth closer attention.

At a general level, there is no all-encompassing method for the study of manuscript corrections, as their nature varies from scribe to scribe, from manuscript to manuscript.[4] Hence, the enterprise of this sort is inherently inductive and so requires patient acquaintance with the corrections themselves as well

---

[2]This lack of reproducing in modern editions the phenomena listed above is partly remedied in Dirk Jongkind et al., eds., *The Greek New Testament, Produced at Tyndale House, Cambridge* (Wheaton, IL: Crossway, 2017), where the paragraphing, accentuation, and spelling are more directly informed by the data of manuscripts.

[3]On scribes' attitudes toward their task and texts perhaps being revealed by their corrections, see Larry W. Hurtado, *The Earliest Christian Artifacts: Manuscripts and Christian Origins* (Grand Rapids: Eerdmans, 2006), 186; Kim Haines-Eitzen, *Guardians of Letters: Literacy, Power, and the Transmitters of Early Christian Literature* (Oxford: Oxford University Press, 2000), 109.

[4]See Peter Malik, *P.Beatty III (P47): The Codex, Its Scribe, and Its Text*, NTTSD 52 (Leiden: Brill, 2017), 72n5, for further discussion and references.

as with the broader tendencies of the manuscript where they occur. Not a few early manuscripts contain very sparse corrections or even none at all; in some *de luxe* codices, however, we have centuries of extensive correcting activity by different hands (e.g., Codex Sinaiticus). In some cases, the scribe corrected errors only in the process of copying, never checking his work thereafter; at other times, numerous reviews were conducted, sometimes even by means of two different exemplars. Rather than providing a vague theoretical framework for the study of corrections, then, it might be more useful to work through two specific examples of corrected manuscripts and (hopefully) learn something of the problem's complexity in the process.

P66: The more corrections, the merrier (or messier) the text? There are six early papyrus manuscripts, which may be regarded as "extensive" by the virtue of their substantial state of preservation. The first three of these are P45 (P.Beatty I; LDAB 2980), P46 (P.Beatty II; LDAB 3011), and P47 (P. Beatty III; LDAB 2778). Being part of the famous Chester Beatty biblical papyri, they were acquired by Sir Alfred Chester Beatty in the early 1930s and were published by Sir Frederic G. Kenyon within the following decade.[5] The discovery was nothing short of sensational, for the Beatty manuscripts were in fact the first find of substantially preserved biblical papyri to be published. Thus, these artifacts presented scholars with a unique opportunity to study, on a much larger scale, the remnants of early Christian textual and material culture from Roman Egypt.[6] Some two decades later, Martin Bodmer acquired a sizable lot of extensive papyri with more diverse contents, written in Greek and Coptic.[7] The Bodmer papyri have

---

[5]Frederic G. Kenyon, ed., *The Chester Beatty Biblical Papyri: Descriptions and Texts of Twelve Manuscripts on Papyrus of the Greek Bible*, 16 vols. (London: Emery Walker, 1933–1941).

[6]So emphatically Charles Horton, "The Chester Beatty Biblical Papyri: A Find of the Greatest Importance," in *The Earliest Gospels: The Origins and Transmission of the Earliest Christian Gospels—The Contribution of the Chester Beatty Gospel P45*, ed. Charles Horton, JSNTSup 285 (London: T&T Clark, 2004), 149: "As a group the Chester Beatty Biblical Papyri remain the single most important find of early Christian manuscripts so far discovered and individually they have provided scholarship, and by extension the laity, with direct contact with the formative years of Christianity." For the most recent treatment of the Beatty collection, see Brent Nongbri, *God's Library: The Archaeology of the Earliest Christian Manuscripts* (New Haven, CT: Yale University Press, 2018), 116-56.

[7]*Papyrus Bodmer I-XXXVIII* (Cologny-Geneva: Bibliotheca Bodmeriana, 1954–1991). This publication does not account for all the papyri in the Bodmer collection. The publication information may be conveniently accessed online via Joshua D. Sosin, Roger S. Bagnall, James Cowey, Mark Depauw, Terry G. Wilfong, and Klaas A. Worp, eds., *Checklist of Editions of Greek, Latin, Demotic and Coptic Papyri, Ostraca and Tablets*, June 1, 2011, https://library.duke.edu/rubenstein/scriptorium/papyrus/texts/clist_papyri.html. For a detailed study of the collection's contents and history, see Nongbri, *God's Library*, 157-215.

brought to light many intriguing texts, but for our present purposes they are, besides the Beatty materials, the only other papyrus collection to include extensive early papyri with New Testament texts—namely, P66 (P. Bodm. II; LDAB 2777), P72 (P.Bodm. VII-VIII; LDAB 2565), and P75 (P.Bodm. XIV-XV; LDAB 2895).

The first published Bodmer New Testament papyrus is P66, a (probably) third-century codex containing sizable portions of John's Gospel.[8] Initially, the discovery of P66 was rather quickly overshadowed by the publication of P75, a two-Gospel codex containing parts of Luke and John, owing to the latter's remarkably close affinity with Codex Vaticanus.[9] However, despite the fact that the text of P66 was deemed more "free" and further removed from the earliest recoverable text of John than that of P75, one particular aspect of this papyrus caught scholarly attention very early on. Gordon D. Fee, followed by Erroll F. Rhodes, brought to attention more than four hundred (!) instances of correction in the manuscript—the vast majority penned by the same scribe.[10] Arguably, such a high density of correcting by the original scribe is unparalleled in the New Testament manuscript tradition, and it raises a number of intriguing issues.

In his recent study of scribal habits in P66, James R. Royse presents what is hitherto the most thorough investigation of corrections in this

---

[8]Recently, the relatively wide consensus concerning the early dating of P66 has been called into question by Brent Nongbri, "The Limits of Palaeographical Dating of Literary Papyri: Some Observations on the Date and Provenance of P.Bodmer II (P66)," *MH* 71, no. 1 (2014): 1-35, who suggests that the date range be extended into the fourth century. In contrast, Pasquale Orsini and Willy Clarysse, "Early New Testament Manuscripts and Their Dates: A Critique of Theological Palaeography," *ETL* 88, no. 4 (2012): 470, assign the date in AD 200–250. Incidentally, Orsini has recently entertained the extended date for P66 as well, but based on different grounds (and palaeographical comparanda) from Nongbri. See Orsini's guest post, "Palaeographic Method, Comparison and Dating: Considerations for an Updated Discussion," *Evangelical Textual Criticism* (blog), February 6, 2018, http://evangelicaltextualcriticism.blogspot.de/2018/02/palaeographic-method-comparison-and.html.

[9]Victor Martin and Rodolphe Kasser, eds., *Papyrus Bodmer XIV: Évangile de Luc chap. 3–24* (Cologny-Geneva: Bibliotheca Bodmeriana, 1961); Martin and Kasser, eds., *Papyrus Bodmer XV: Évangile de Jean chap. 1–15* (Cologny-Geneva: Bibliotheca Bodmeriana, 1961). On P75's close affinity with Codex Vaticanus, the classic treatment is Carlo Maria Martini, *Il problema della recensionalità del codice B alla luce del papiro Bodmer XIV*, AnBib 26 (Rome: Pontificio Istituto Biblico, 1966).

[10]Gordon D. Fee, "Corrections of the Papyrus Bodmer II and the Nestle Greek Testament," *JBL* 84, no. 1 (1965): 66-72; Fee, "The Corrections of Papyrus Bodmer II and Early Textual Transmission," *NovT* 7, no. 4 (1965): 247-57; Erroll F. Rhodes, "The Corrections of Papyrus Bodmer II," *NTS* 14, no. 2 (1967): 271-81.

papyrus.[11] Royse counts 465 such places and makes a number of distinctions among them. First, he identifies forty-nine "corrections *in scribendo*"—that is, made by the scribe in the very process of copying.[12] At each such place, the scribe would correct his error in the making before proceeding further. Second, there are 164 "corrections of slips," where the scribe would, again, correct an obvious error, but at some later point rather than in the process of creating it—whether upon completing the error or during a later check of his work.[13] Third, Royse has a group of 126 corrections he refers to as "significant." These are places where the initial reading is not an obvious nonsense or orthographical slip but is still regarded as a scribal error.[14]

Now, without these corrections (excepting the final group), the scribe's performance in his basic task of copying the text of his exemplar could have been regarded as extremely sloppy. Indeed, such is the assessment given by Ernest C. Colwell: "It is hard to believe that [producing a good copy] was the intention of P66." He characterizes the scribe's copying as "careless and ineffective" and even marked by "wildness."[15] But the basis on which Colwell reached this conclusion is the text of P66 *before* correction.[16] How should we then regard the text as the scribe left it *after* all these hundreds of revisions? Royse's appraisal, which follows the latter approach, is rather more positive: except for P75, the error rate reached by the scribe of P66 is "much lower than that of any other papyri" Royse considered (i.e., P45, P46, P47, P72).[17] We see, then, that despite the scribe's initial lack of skill and care in reproducing his exemplar, he was greatly concerned for the accuracy of his copy, and the hundreds of corrections of his initial errors epitomize that concern.[18]

---

[11]James R. Royse, *Scribal Habits in Early Greek New Testament Papyri*, NTTSD 36 (Leiden: Brill, 2008), 409-90. In this vein, one should be on the patient lookout for Peter M. Head's forthcoming magisterial treatment of this and many other aspects of P66.

[12]Royse, *Scribal Habits*, 422-35.

[13]Royse, *Scribal Habits*, 436-43.

[14]Royse, *Scribal Habits*, 444-60. He writes: "We may presume that at all these places the scribe was attempting to reproduce his *Vorlage* [source] but failed. Later he compared his copy with the *Vorlage*, noticed a discrepancy, and altered his first, failed attempt" (461).

[15]Ernest C. Colwell, "Method in Evaluating Scribal Habits: A Study of P45, P66, P75," in *Studies in Methodology in Textual Criticism of the New Testament*, edited by Bruce M. Metzger, NTTS 9 (Grand Rapids: Eerdmans, 1969), 114, 118, 121.

[16]As argued by Royse, *Scribal Habits*, 74.

[17]Royse, *Scribal Habits*, 495.

[18]In this vein, see Peter M. Head's review in Juan Hernández Jr., Peter M. Head, Dirk Jongkind, and James R. Royse, "Scribal Habits in Early Greek New Testament Papyri: Papers from the 2008

The final level of complexity in P66's corrections is reached in a group of (according to Royse) 126 readings where the scribe probably used another exemplar, one with different textual affinities.[19] The practice of using another exemplar was not unheard of in antiquity and was at times followed in book shops that produced copies of literary papyri.[20] Most likely, such usage was not reflective of "text-critical" motivations on the scribe's part per se; rather, consulting a second exemplar was probably meant to facilitate a further check on the work one had already completed. But such intention behind the use of another exemplar need not mean that the intended result was actually achieved. Introducing readings from a different exemplar that exhibited different textual affinities occasions and exacerbates the problem of "contamination" of the text, which is so typical of the New Testament tradition.[21] At places with such corrections, the subsequent scribe using P66 as an exemplar for a further copy of John would have faced the same dilemma as its current readers: Should I follow the reading before or after correction— or both?[22] Be that as it may, P66 offers scholars a rich pool of information for further scrutiny at many different levels.

Codex Montfortianus (GA 61): Traces of Greek philology in the sixteenth century. The early age and the concomitant high sociohistorical value of the papyri often overshadow the manuscripts that constitute the vast majority of the Greek New Testament tradition, namely minuscules. These codices, made of parchment or paper, were written in a cursive Greek script that became widely used chiefly from the tenth century onward. Scholars tend to refer to this mass of materials by the shorthand "Byzantine manuscripts," which might imply a cohesive, stable whole. This, in general, is not entirely incorrect, given the greater similarity of such manuscripts in

---

SBL Panel Review Session," *TC* 17 (2012): 11-12, where he argues that one should consider both sets of data—i.e., the scribe's initial performance as well as his correcting activity—in studying scribal habits.

[19]Royse, *Scribal Habits*, 461-84.

[20]See, e.g., Eric G. Turner, "Review of *The Use of Dictation in Ancient Book-Production* by T. C. Skeat," *JTS*, n.s. 10 (1959): 150; Eric G. Turner, *Greek Papyri: An Introduction* (Oxford: Clarendon, 1980), 93.

[21]For further discussion of this problem as well as some proposed strategies of handling it, see Gerd Mink, "Problems of a Highly Contaminated Tradition: The New Testament. Stemmata of Variants as a Source of a Genealogy for Witnesses," in *Studies in Stemmatology II*, ed. Pieter van Reenen, August den Hollander, and Margot van Mulken (Amsterdam: John Benjamins, 2004), 13-85.

[22]At some places where correctors introduced alternative readings without deleting the originals, one could potentially conflate the readings into one. See, e.g., Turner, *Greek Papyri*, 125-26.

comparison with the papyri and early majuscules. It is far from true, however, at a level of individual manuscripts, which also exhibit their own peculiarities as well as unique scribal characteristics and textual features.[23]

One such a late treasure trove is GA 61, also known as Codex Montfortianus (Trinity College Dublin, Manuscript 30).[24] Probably produced early on in the sixteenth century, this minuscule rose to fame primarily as the first Greek manuscript known to attest the so-called *Comma Johanneum*, a brief trinitarian interpolation at 1 John 5:7-8. It was from this manuscript, in fact, that Desiderius Erasmus introduced the *Comma* into the third edition of his Greek New Testament, thus becoming the standard feature of the *textus receptus* (and so also the Bible translations based on it).[25] The feature for which GA 61 is little known, however, is an abundance of marginal notes, added by two different hands subsequent to its production.

Of particular interest are the corrections made in the book of Revelation. The principal text of Revelation in GA 61 reflects what is commonly known as the "Koine" strand of the Byzantine tradition.[26] Virtually all of some sixty marginalia added by another hand in Revelation 1–4, however, exhibit a shift toward a form of text with much higher proportion of readings of the "Andreas" strand, as well as introducing some other, unique variants. Each

---

[23]For more on the Byzantine manuscripts and their diversity, see chapter six in this volume.

[24]The manuscript's name derives from Thomas Montfort, one (perhaps penultimate) of its several owners before Archbishop James Ussher presented it to Trinity in the seventeenth century. For more information, see the manuscript's entry on the Trinity College website: "New Testament, Codex Monfortianus," Trinity College Dublin, http://digitalcollections.tcd.ie/home/index .php?DRIS_ID=MS30_001 (accessed May 1, 2018).

[25]The readers of the KJV know the rendering of 1 John 5:7-8 thus: "For there are three that bear record *in heaven, the Father, the Word, and the Holy Ghost: and these three are one. And there are three that bear witness in earth*, the Spirit, and the water, and the blood: and these three agree in one" (interpolation italicized). Compare, for instance, the shorter rendering of the ESV, which is based on the critically edited text: "For there are three that testify: the Spirit and the water and the blood; and these three agree." For a thorough history of the *Comma*, see Grantley McDonald, *Biblical Criticism in Early Modern Europe: Erasmus, the Johannine Comma, and Trinitarian Debate* (Cambridge: Cambridge University Press, 2016).

[26]The notion of a stable Byzantine text is even less applicable to the manuscripts of Revelation, where the Byzantine tradition is split into at least three major groups, and even these are far from uniform. The *Text und Textwert* volume for Revelation differentiates between three types of Byzantine readings: Koine, Andreas (i.e., type of text utilized in the Revelation commentary by Andrew of Caesarea), and the Complutensian text (i.e., text utilized in the Complutensian Polyglot). See Markus Lembke, Darius Müller, Ulrich B. Schmid, and Martin Karrer, eds., *Text und Textwert der griechischen Handschriften des Neuen Testaments*, vol. 6, *Die Apokalypse: Teststellenkollation und Auswertungen*, ANTF 49 (Berlin: de Gruyter, 2017), 13*-18*, for the groupings, and 444, 521, and 605, for the textual profile of GA 61.

reading is accompanied by a siglum denoting the Greek word γράφεται (*graphetai*, "it is written"), which is often used to mark off alternative readings in Byzantine manuscripts. Remarkably, one recent study has shown that these marginal corrections are likely to have been made on the basis of one of the first two editions of Erasmus's Greek New Testament.[27] These marginalia, then, are not so much "corrections" meant to remedy prior scribal errors but rather are expressions of philological activity on the part of a careful early modern reader of Revelation. In effect, what we have here are text-critical notations that alert the users of the codex to competing textual traditions at various points in the Greek text. The person who added these marginal notes shows awareness of the numerous differences between this particular copy of the Greek New Testament and another exemplar—in this instance possibly a printed edition—that may have been regarded as equally authoritative.

In the case of GA 61, then, the 61[c] readings found in the apparatuses of our editions are not to be taken as corrections of *scribal slips*.[28] Rather, they constitute something of a separate witness reflecting an alternative text form attested in Erasmus's edition.[29] These editorial interventions are indicative of a critically acute reading and philological sensibility, as well as an interest in and awareness of the variant readings on the part of one of its sixteenth-century users. Given that these readings were made *after* Erasmus consulted the manuscript for his own edition, we may conjecture that the person responsible for them was a scholar resident in the British Isles rather than a native Greek speaker of the Eastern Orthodox background. As such, then, these marginal glosses are tangible traces of careful engagement with Greek Scriptures in the early modern biblical scholarly tradition. Indeed, this type of activity epitomizes the emerging marriage of the humanistic philological approaches and the increasing use of the original languages in Western theological circles. All in all, then, the case of GA 61 is a telling example of

---

[27] See Darius Müller, "Abschriften des Erasmischen Textes im Handschriftenmaterial der Johannesapokalypse: Nebst einigen editionsgeschichtlichen Beobachtungen," in *Studien zum Text der Apokalypse*, ed. Marcus Sigismund, Martin Karrer, and Ulrich Schmid, ANTF 47 (Berlin: de Gruyter, 2015), 242-45.

[28] Note that, to consult the readings of 61[c] in the apparatus, readers will have to consult the ECM (not yet available for Revelation at the time of writing) or one of the earlier editions such as von Soden or Tischendorf, as it is not among the consistently cited witnesses in NA[28]. In contrast, UBS[5] does cite 61 on occasion, but only in the Catholic Epistles.

[29] On the text of Revelation in Erasmus's edition, see Müller, "Abschriften des Erasmischen Textes," 169-74.

how corrections (depending, of course, on their age and nature) can offer useful information concerning the subsequent use of—as well as the socio-historical issues pertaining to—the manuscript in which they appear.

INTERPRETING THE EVIDENCE OF CORRECTIONS: THREE CASE STUDIES

In discussing the above examples, we have encountered two very different manuscripts that display two very different types of correcting activity.

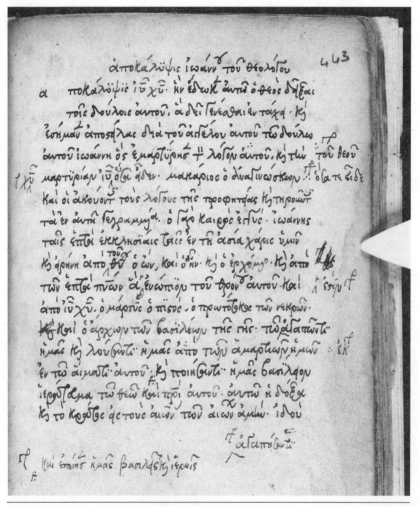

Figure 8.1. Revelation 1 in Codex Montfortianus (Trinity College Dublin MS 30) showing corrections based on Erasmus's printed editions

Those two cases helped us observe corrections more broadly as a type of scribal activity with its own set of general tendencies, peculiarities, and significance. Having illustrated the problem on a broader scale, we now turn to a handful of readings where the evidence of corrections has considerable bearing on one's analysis of the text. We begin again with P66, the much-corrected papyrus of John.

Jesus, the really thirsty, not-a-mere-man kind of God: Ehrman and P66. Few people who have heard about textual criticism at all have not heard the name of Bart D. Ehrman. Although Ehrman is widely known particularly for his *New York Times* bestseller *Misquoting Jesus*, a provocative book meant to introduce textual criticism to the broader public, perhaps the most famous of his scholarly works is *The Orthodox Corruption of Scripture*.[30] In this (no less provocative) work, Ehrman embarks on a quest to unearth what he considers to be one very important, yet hitherto neglected, influence behind textual variation—namely, the various christological controversies in the second and third centuries of the Common Era.[31] This now-classic book has received many a review and critical response— positive and otherwise—and it is not within the scope of this discussion to respond to it in broad terms.[32] For our purposes, however, it might be useful to recall one salient detail raised by Fee in what has been perhaps the most critical of Ehrman's reviews.[33]

Ehrman discusses three readings of the aforementioned P66 (Jn 10:30; 19:5, 28), where the variation involves scribal correction. At the first of these, Ehrman notes that the addition of the article before "God" in P66 enhances "the force of this pronouncement ['I and the Father are one,' Jn 10:30] and the

---

[30]Bart D. Ehrman, *Misquoting Jesus: The Story Behind Who Changed the Bible and Why* (New York: HarperCollins, 2005); Ehrman, *The Orthodox Corruption of Scripture: The Effect of Early Christological Controversies on the Text of the New Testament*, 2nd ed. (Oxford: Oxford University Press, 2011). *Misquoting Jesus* has received a wide array of critical reviews, of which probably most detailed is by Peter J. Williams, "Review of Bart Ehrman, *Misquoting Jesus*," *Evangelical Textual Criticism* (blog), December 31, 2005, http://evangelicaltextualcriticism.blogspot .de/2005/12/review-of-bart-ehrman-misquoting-jesus_31.html.

[31]See chapter eleven in this book.

[32]Besides reviews in scholarly periodicals, an entire collected volume from the fifth Birmingham Colloquium (2007) was dedicated to addressing issues arising from Ehrman's work: H. A. G. Houghton and D. C. Parker, eds., *Textual Variation: Theological and Social Tendencies? Papers from the Fifth Birmingham Colloquium on the Textual Criticism of the New Testament*, TS, Third Series 6 (Piscataway, NJ: Gorgias, 2008).

[33]Gordon D. Fee, "Review of *The Orthodox Corruption of Scripture: The Effect of Early Christological Controversies on the Text of the New Testament* by Bart D. Ehrman," *CRBR* 8 (1995): 203-6.

clarity of the Jews' understanding of it."[34] Now, this is a rather complex argument, not least because it extrapolates a strong semantic link from quite meager variation.[35] What is more, however, this is not so much a reading of "P66" but rather of P66*—that is, a reading *before* the scribal correction.[36] In his work on scribal habits, Royse plausibly suggests that the initial reading arose by simple erroneous "doubling" (dittography) of a syllable at the end of the Greek word *yourself* (σεαυτὸν τόν, *seauton ton*), which the scribe then corrected against the same exemplar.[37]

Even more intriguing, perhaps, is John 19:5, Ehrman's second example. Here he cites P66 as omitting the sentence "Behold the man." He further asserts that the support furnished by the "otherwise unrelated" Old Latin and Lycopolitan (a dialect of Coptic) versions "should alert us to the possibility of a deliberate modification of the text." Following this line of reasoning, Ehrman then interprets the omission as reflecting the "troubling" implications of the sentence: Jesus cannot have been a "mere mortal."[38] Again, it is uncertain whether the scribe of P66 would have been so troubled by the utterance of Pilate, who was in the end responsible for Jesus' execution.[39] From a text-critical point of view, however, Ehrman's argument is considerably weakened by the fact that the omission seems to have been corrected: although the page in question is partly defective, the place of omission involves correction marks, and one can possibly even make out some traces of the correction in the lower margin area.[40] This, of course, does not explain the presence of the variant in the aforementioned versions, but if an error like this could happen in the Greek, there is no a priori reason why it cannot have occurred independently in Latin and/or Coptic. More troubling still is the fact that Ehrman never seems to show awareness that

---

[34]Ehrman, *Orthodox Corruption*, 98-99.

[35]In this vein, Peter M. Head, "Scribal Behaviour and Theological Tendencies in Singular Readings in P. Bodmer II (P66)," in Houghton and Parker, *Textual Variation*, argues pertinently: "If the scribe of P66 were particularly concerned to enhance the doctrine of the deity of Christ we might expect to see clearer evidence than this" (p. 67).

[36]The point highlighted by Fee, "Review of *The Orthodox Corruption of Scripture*," 205.

[37]For a further discussion of this reading, see Royse, *Scribal Habits*, 444, 459.

[38]Ehrman, *Orthodox Corruption*, 110, 111.

[39]According to Head, "Scribal Behaviour," 70, another difficulty with Ehrman's suggestion is "that ascribing motives to omissions is even more difficult than for other alterations." Without clear cumulative evidence, of course, ascribing motives to any scribal alterations runs the risk of arbitrariness.

[40]For further discussion, see Royse, *Scribal Habits*, 448n278, 459-60. Incidentally, NA28 also cites P66* for the omission, thus interpreting the variation in quite the same way.

the reading of P66 was corrected by the same scribe, in each of the above cases against the very exemplar he used to copy the text in the first place.

Both of Ehrman's abovementioned examples are meant to lend support for his argument concerning "anti-adoptionistic corruption" in the New Testament textual transmission. The third instance is of "anti-docetic" type and concerns variation at John 19:28. In this case, the scribe of P66 initially omitted the phrase "in order that the Scripture might be fulfilled."[41] Again, Ehrman argues that the reading does not appear to have originated by accident, since it does not involve an omission due to similar endings (homoioteleuton) or beginnings (homoioarcton) of the words and since P66 is not, in his view, "particularly prone to omissions of entire phrases or clauses."[42] In accounting for the omission's origin, then, Ehrman warns us, "We would be remiss in this case to overlook the theological possibilities of the corruption." In particular, he posits that the presence of this clause may have struck the scribe as implying that Jesus was not genuinely thirsty: he said it only in order to fulfill the scriptural mandate.[43] Whether Ehrman's explanation squares with the scribe's exegetical sensibilities is a moot point, however.[44] For, as above, the omission was rectified by means of scribal correction. That the scribe would do away with such a conscious intervention into the text as Ehrman envisages seems most unlikely. Rather, we have an error—possibly an omission by skipping over a line in the exemplar or

---

[41]Unlike in the previous case, here it is the initial reading that is lacunose and the marginal correction that is extant.

[42]Ehrman, *Orthodox Corruption*, 227, citing Colwell, "Method in Evaluating Scribal Habits," 115-18. Ehrman's reference to Colwell seems somewhat mistaken, however. The page range that he refers to concerns "influence of similar forms" (i.e., scribal errors occasioned by visual confusion), so of course errors that do not involve doubling, visually similar phenomena, or similar endings will not have been discussed there. On 118, however, Colwell in fact says that, despite his intention to make a good copy, the scribe of P66 was "careless and ineffective." It is not inconceivable, then, that the scribe with such copying behavior may have omitted an entire phrase without prior intention to do so. Whether, on the other hand, we could expect this scribe to have engaged in such intricate exegesis as Ehrman suggests is far from certain. For the most extensive, as well as the most recent, discussion of scribal habits in P66, see Royse, *Scribal Habits*, 399-544. In this vein, one particular point of Royse's discussion worth highlighting here is that, toward the end of his transcription, the scribe's performance seems to deteriorate (*Scribal Habits*, 495). If this is the case, then we have yet another contributing factor to the omission at Jn 19:28: the scribe's increasingly wavering attention. The same line of argument is picked up in Head, "Scribal Behaviour," 71.

[43]Ehrman, *Orthodox Corruption*, 227, 228.

[44]See Head, "Scribal Behaviour," 71, who notes, "Here the speculative element is, to say the least, rather uncontrolled. The situation and intentional action required goes way beyond the available evidence."

simply by oversight—that at some point the scribe noticed and corrected so as to restore the wording of the exemplar.[45]

As noted above, it was Fee who first noticed that Ehrman failed to distinguish between corrected and uncorrected readings in P66. His response to Ehrman's aforementioned interpretations is worth quoting in full:

> The deliberate "corruption," therefore, does not exist at all, since the *correction* in each case, which aligns the text with the rest of the MS tradition, was made *by the original scribe himself* (among hundreds of such). This scribe's "corrections" are what are clearly deliberate—and these show no interest in christology.... Significantly, this scribe stands squarely in the middle (ca. 200 CE) of the two centuries of Ehrman's interest. If Ehrman's case for "christological corruption" so clearly fails in our one *certain* piece of evidence for deliberate variation, then one might rightly question the degree of deliberation in a large number of other variations as well, which seem to have equally good, if not better, explanations of other kinds for their existence.[46]

Whatever one makes of Fee's critique, it seems clear that the way in which the critic evaluates (or fails to evaluate) the evidence of these corrections has noticeable impact on her analysis of variants, including their reception-historical significance.

Who was in the beginning (of Mark's Gospel in Codex Sinaiticus)? Our next example comes from the famous Codex Sinaiticus (01; LDAB 3478), without doubt one of the most splendid expressions of Christian literary culture.[47] One of the distinguishing features of Sinaiticus is the vast number of corrections made at various points of its initial production as well as its subsequent use. The first layer of corrections was made in the scriptorium by the very scribe who penned the codex, and the Codex Sinaiticus website designates

---

[45]So already Kurt Aland, "Neue neutestamentliche Papyri III: Walther Eltester zum 75. Geburtstag," *NTS* 20, no. 4 (1974): 378, who asserts that the omission "does not denote a textual variant, but only a momentary lapse of the scribe (or the corrector) who added the text back in the lower page-margin" (my translation).

[46]Fee, "Review of *Orthodox Corruption*," 205 (italics original).

[47]The images are available online via the Codex Sinaiticus website: http://codexsinaiticus.org. For an accessible overview of the manuscript's features and history, see David C. Parker, *Codex Sinaiticus: The Story of the World's Oldest Bible* (London: British Library, 2010). For the most important treatment of the Sinaiticus's codicology, paleography, and scribal features, written shortly after the British Library's acquisition of a major portion of the manuscript, see H. J. M. Milne and T. C. Skeat, *Scribes and Correctors of the Codex Sinaiticus* (London: British Museum Press, 1938).

these with the "S1" label.[48] There are a good number of such cases (varying in extent from book to book), but not nearly as many as those made by the so-called C group, some two centuries later.[49] Besides reflecting some measure of production care on the scribes' part, these corrections spark special interest because, in some biblical books, they have been shown to reflect the use of another exemplar.[50] At such places, the manuscript in fact becomes a textual witness to *both* readings in question. Yet it is not always easy to distinguish a correction made against another ex-emplar from a mere correction of prior error, as we shall see in the following (somewhat notorious) example.

Figure 8.2. The correction involving "Son of God" in Mark 1:1 in Codex Sinaiticus

The abrupt opening of the Gospel of Mark has long fascinated its interpreters, not least thanks to a pressing textual problem in its very first verse: Did the author intend to open his narrative with "the beginning of the gospel of Jesus Christ" or with "the beginning of Jesus Christ, son of God"?[51] A brief look at the critical appa-ratus in NA[28] reveals that Sinaiticus is cited for *both* the omission and in-clusion of the term "son of God" (υἱοῦ θεοῦ, *huiou theou*). For omission, the apparatus cites ℵ*, a reading of the manuscript before the correction, whereas for the inclusion the siglum used is ℵ[1], the earliest layer of correc-tions. Both the initial reading and the subsequent correction event have been interpreted variously. On the one hand, the scribe may have omitted the words "son of God" by homoioteleuton, which seems plausible given that each of the consecutive words would have had the same ending and given that such omissions are ubiquitous in the manuscript tradition.[52] On

---

[48]"The Transcription," Codex Sinaiticus, http://codexsinaiticus.org/en/project/transcription_detailed.aspx (accessed May 1, 2018). This procedure is followed unless there are clear distin-guishing features, which would enable a more specific attribution. The most detailed treatment of the scriptorium correctors is still Milne and Skeat, *Scribes and Correctors*, 40-46.

[49]See Milne and Skeat, *Scribes and Correctors*, 46-50.

[50]Dirk Jongkind, *Scribal Habits of Codex Sinaiticus*, TS, Third Series 5 (Piscataway, NJ: Gorgias, 2007), 144, 167-69, 203-4, 222, posits the presence of another exemplar in Lukan and Pauline portions of the manuscript, but not in 1 Chronicles and the Psalter.

[51]See Tommy Wasserman, "The 'Son of God' Was in the Beginning (Mark 1:1)," *JTS* 62, no. 1 (2011): 20n1, for detailed bibliographical information. On interpretation of the passage, see, e.g., Adela Yarbro Collins, *Mark: A Commentary*, Hermeneia (Minneapolis: Fortress, 2007), 130-32.

[52]In Sinaiticus, as in most other early Christian manuscripts, each of the words in question would have appeared as a *nomen sacrum*, i.e., a contracted form with an overline written above. So, in Greek, the words "of Jesus Christ, son of God" would look something like I̅Y̅X̅Y̅Y̅Y̅Θ̅Y̅. Some have argued that visual confusion in such a chain of abbreviated words is to be expected. For

that interpretation, the correction may have been affected by the same scribe, who simply restored the reading of his exemplar.[53] In that case Sinaiticus's support for the shorter reading is considerably weakened.

On the other hand, it is not impossible that, at this point, the scribe transmitted the reading of his exemplar accurately, such that the alteration was made by means of another exemplar at a later review in the scriptorium. That the correction was not made in the process of copying seems clear from a different, lighter-colored ink as well as from thinner pen strokes, which are characteristic of subsequent scriptorium corrections.[54] Furthermore, the letter formation is reminiscent of corrections made by the scribe's "senior" colleague (termed "scribe D").[55] Interestingly, in several other places in Mark where scribe D can be identified as the author of a correction, he seems to have consulted a different exemplar.[56] As noted above, similar evidence may be found in other New Testament books.[57] If this analysis holds, then Sinaiticus provides genetic support for both the omission *and* the inclusion of the title "son of God" in the beginning of Mark's Gospel. Deciding on which of the two readings is to be preferred, however, is not the matter for our discussion, and it does not hinge solely on one's assessment of this variation in Sinaiticus.[58]

---

this line of argument, see esp. Wasserman, "'Son of God' Was in the Beginning," 45-50. While in general Wasserman's analysis holds up to scrutiny—there demonstrably are manuscripts that omit *nomina sacra* by parablepsis (see chapter five in this volume), even in book openings—I am not inclined to agree this applies to Sinaiticus. See my response in Peter Malik, "The Earliest Corrections in Codex Sinaiticus: A Test Case from the Gospel of Mark," BASP 50 (2013): 214-19, and Wasserman's rejoinder in Tommy Wasserman, "Historical and Philological Correlations and the CBGM as Applied to Mark 1:1," *TC* 20 (2015): 5-6. I still think I'm right, though. Sorry, Tommy! On scribal habits in Sinaiticus, see Jongkind, *Scribal Habits*, esp. pp. 131-246.

[53]So Wasserman, "'Son of God' Was in the Beginning," 46, although he duly acknowledges the possibility of another exemplar as well.

[54]Malik, "Earliest Corrections," 212.

[55]Parker, *Codex Sinaiticus*, 50: "It is arguable that D was in some ways senior, perhaps supervising the other two. The evidence for this is that his work is of a higher quality than theirs, and that he quite often corrects it, sometimes even writing replacement leaves."

[56]As argued in Malik, "Earliest Corrections," 252.

[57]A rare exception appears to be Revelation, where it seems impossible to detect either the correcting work of scribe D or the use of another exemplar. In fact, all the S1 corrections in that portion of Sinaiticus may have been made by scribe A in the copying phase. See further Peter Malik, "The Earliest Corrections in Codex Sinaiticus: Further Evidence from the Apocalypse," *TC* 20 (2015): 9-12.

[58]Needless to say, the way one handles this textual problem does affect one's exegesis of the Markan narrative. In this vein, see David E. Garland, *A Theology of Mark's Gospel: Good News About Jesus the Messiah, the Son of God*, BTNT (Grand Rapids: Zondervan, 2015), 195-98.

The Egerton Gospel: "Our fathers" are "your fathers." So far, all of our examples have concerned manuscripts with texts from the New Testament canon. In order to illustrate that such issues are not constrained to "biblical" texts, we shall take a look at P.Egerton 2 + P.Köln VI 255 (LDAB 4736), a manuscript with noncanonical contents.[59] Named by its principal editors as an "unknown gospel" and now widely known as the Egerton Gospel (GEgerton), this text has attracted considerable scholarly attention, not least because of some conspicuous similarities with Jesus traditions found in the New Testament, especially in the Fourth Gospel.[60] Upon its publication, most scholars argued variously for GEgerton's familiarity with or even literary dependence on the relevant New Testament texts, with only a few occasional dissenting voices.[61]

The most recently published portion of GEgerton, housed in the Papyrus Collection of the University of Köln, contains a saying that bears close similarity to John 5:39: "For if you believed Moses, you would believe me; for concerning me he wrote to your fathers" (frag. 1v, lines 20-23). Despite rather close correspondence, GEgerton does deviate from the canonical account by adding the phrase "to *your* fathers," which too may well reflect Johannine influence (see Jn 6:49). Although typically papyrological details are not at the forefront of debates concerning literary dependence, Francis

---

[59]The images are available online on the websites of the respective holding institutions. For the London fragment, see http://bl.uk/manuscripts/FullDisplay.aspx?ref=Egerton_Papyrus_2; the Cologne fragment may be viewed at https://papyri.uni-koeln.de/stueck/tm63527.

[60]H. I. Bell and T. C. Skeat, eds., *Fragments of an Unknown Gospel and Other Early Christian Papyri* (London: British Museum Press, 1935). The Köln fragment of GEgerton was published later as "Unbekanntes Evangelium oder Evangelienharmonie" ("Unknown gospel or a gospel harmony") by Michael Gronewald (*Kölner Papyri [P.Köln] VI*, Pap.Colon. VII.6 (Opladen: Westdeutcher Verlag, 1987], 136-45). The Egerton papyri are a group of manuscripts acquired by the British Library, thanks to the generous bequeathal of funds by Francis Henry Egerton in 1829. See "Manuscripts and Archives," British Library, www.bl.uk/reshelp/findhelprestype/manuscripts/ongoingcoll/ongoingcollections.html#egerton (accessed May 1, 2018).

[61]Perhaps the first major proponent of GEgerton's dependence on John was C. H. Dodd, *New Testament Studies* (Manchester: Manchester University Press, 1953), 12-55. Among others, Dodd was followed by C. K. Barrett, *The Gospel According to St. John: An Introduction with Commentary and Notes on the Greek Text*, 2nd ed. (London: SPCK, 1978), 110. It should be noted that the principal editors did not commit to this explanation but rather discussed it as one of the possibilities, along with John's dependence on GEgerton and both of them drawing on another source independently (Bell and Skeat, *Fragments of an Unknown Gospel*, 37-38). Among notable examples of dissenting voices are John D. Crossan, *Four Other Gospels: Shadows on the Contours of Canon* (New York: Harper & Row, 1985), 41-57; Helmut Koester, *Ancient Christian Gospels: Their History and Development* (London: SCM Press, 1990), 205-16.

Watson has recently used just this datum as the point of departure for his argument for GEgerton's being something of a "Johannine source."[62]

But let us return to the reading of our papyrus. It appears that the scribe first began to write "our fathers" (πατράσιν ἡμῶν, *patrasin hēmōn*) but then changed the reading to "your fathers" (πατράσιν ὑμῶν, *patrasin hymōn*), practically by altering just one letter. Watson criticizes Michael Gronewald, the fragment's editor, for preferring the corrected reading in the main text of his edition.[63] According to Watson, once this "dubious editorial decision" has been abandoned, the Egerton saying may be seen as reflecting a "Mosaic stratum," that is, a tradition reflective of a Jewish-Christian setting before the expulsion of Christians from the synagogue.[64] Watson, however, does not present clear *papyrological* reasons for either preferring the reading prior to correction or judging Gronewald's editorial decision as "dubious." In effect, he commits the same fallacy.

While there are several ways in which this reading may be interpreted, a few conclusions can be made with a good measure of confidence.[65] For one

Figure 8.3. P.Köln VI 255; PA fragment of the Egerton Gospel, showing the correction in line 5 from "our fathers" (πατράσιν ἡμῶν, *patrasin hēmōn*) to "your fathers" (πατράσιν ὑμῶν, *patrasin hymōn*)

---

[62]Francis Watson, *Gospel Writing: A Canonical Perspective* (Grand Rapids: Eerdmans, 2013), 286-340.

[63]Watson, *Gospel Writing*, 295.

[64]Watson, *Gospel Writing*, 330-31. This (reconstructed) historical situation is often regarded as underlying the conflict of the Johannine Jesus with "the Jews."

[65]For various options, see Peter Malik, "Whose Fathers? A Note on the (Un-)Johannine Echo in the Egerton Gospel," *EC* 9 (2018): 201-11.

thing, it seems clear that the correction was made by the scribe himself and that there are no indications in GEgerton of a secondary correction by any other scribal hand(s). Moreover, neither the extent of the corrections in the papyrus nor the text's apparent lack of wider circulation suggests the possibility that the initial scribe would have used another exemplar with variant readings, with which he would have altered the "correct" reading to an alternative, competing one. Indeed, all the corrections in our papyrus are just that, corrections of prior scribal errors; and in each case, the correction was quite possibly made shortly after the initial error.[66]

In view of the foregoing, we can conclude that, even in such a short text without wide distribution or a history of authoritative use as GEgerton, the scribe took care to transmit the wording of his text with a good measure of accuracy. We have also seen, however, that interpretation of a corrected reading must rest on careful evaluation of evidence rather than on unfounded assumptions in either direction—not to mention one's exegetical preferences. Rather, GEgerton seems to show awareness of the Johannine account at this point yet still further reinforcing Jesus' distancing from his Jewish interlocutors (called "lawyers" in GEgerton; compare "Jews" in Jn 6:41, 52). Even though we might not have a definitive confirmation of GEgerton's dependence on John here, this reading creates doubt about Watson's argument to the contrary.

CONCLUSIONS

Biblical manuscripts have a lot to offer if we are willing to pay close attention to their details and interact with them on their own terms. Nowhere has this principle been expressed clearer than in F. J. A. Hort's famous dictum: "Knowledge of documents should precede final judgement upon readings."[67] Knowledge of documents entails knowledge of their general tendencies as well as their particular details. One such detail (namely, scribal corrections) occupied us in the preceding discussion.

We have seen that the scribal task was demanding, and so is the task for those of us who have undertaken to make sense of its results. The fact that the scribes were often willing (and at times eager) to improve on the results

---

[66]See further Malik, "Whose Fathers?," 204n11.

[67]B. F. Westcott and F. J. A. Hort, *The New Testament in the Original Greek: Introduction, Appendix*, 2nd ed. (London: Macmillan, 1896), 31.

of their—occasionally sloppy—end products makes our task even more
challenging but also all the more intriguing. It is hoped that a closer acquaintance with this particular aspect of the manuscript tradition will help us to
be more alert to intricacies involved within and behind the variants we
might encounter.

Key Takeaways

▶ Corrections in manuscripts show that scribes strove to improve and
revise their work before they handed it to posterity. The corrections
in P66, for instance, show that despite its scribe's initial lack of skill
and care in reproducing his exemplar, he was greatly concerned for
the accuracy of his copy.

▶ Corrections added later in the life of a manuscript can show how its
readers interacted thoughtfully with its text. They can even shed light on
whether a scribe made any intentional, theologically motivated changes.

▶ Careful attention to corrections plays a role in debates about the
origin of the Gospels. In the case of the so-called Egerton Gospel, a
reading thought to support its use in writing John's Gospel turns out
to be unlikely.

CHAPTER NINE

MYTHS ABOUT TRANSMISSION

THE TEXT OF PHILEMON FROM BEGINNING TO END

S. Matthew Solomon

FOR TOO LONG, TEXTUAL SCHOLARS have had to study the transmission of the Greek text of the New Testament with incomplete data.[1] More than twenty years ago, Thomas Geer pleaded, "For too long in our discipline, too much has been based on too little. The time has come for full collations of manuscripts to enable us to write confidently about the history of the New Testament text."[2] The primary goal of this chapter is to describe and analyze the text of Philemon as found in the *entire* Greek manuscript tradition.[3] One of the outcomes of this chapter is to demonstrate that more work is needed, showing why work to establish the text of the New Testament continues. The eighteenth- and nineteenth-century pioneers in New Testament textual criticism would have taken full advantage of the access to images currently

---

[1] One of the major exceptions currently is Tommy Wasserman, *The Epistle of Jude: Its Text and Transmission*, ConBNT 43 (Stockholm: Almqvist & Wiksell, 2006), who transcribed all extant manuscripts of Jude. See also the work of M. Bruce Morrill, "A Complete Collation and Analysis of All Greek Manuscripts of John 18" (PhD thesis, University of Birmingham, 2012); and Herman C. Hoskier, *Concerning the Text of the Apocalypse*, 2 vols. (London: Quaritch, 1929).

[2] Thomas C. Geer Jr., "Analyzing and Categorizing New Testament Greek Manuscripts: Colwell Revisited," in *The Text of the New Testament in Contemporary Research: Essays on the Status Quaestionis*, ed. Bart D. Ehrman and Michael Holmes, SD 46 (Grand Rapids: Eerdmans, 1995), 265. In the essay revised in 2014 by Jean-François Racine in the second edition of *The Text of the New Testament in Contemporary Research*, François added that sophisticated familiarity with manuscripts is a goal yet to be achieved (Thomas C. Geer Jr. and Jean-François Racine, "Analyzing and Categorizing New Testament Greek Manuscripts," in *The Text of the New Testament in Contemporary Research: Essays on the Status Quaestionis*, 2nd ed., ed. Bart D. Ehrman and Michael W. Holmes, NTTSD 42 [Leiden: Brill, 2013], 497).

[3] This is possible by using data from my doctoral dissertation. See S. Matthew Solomon, "The Textual History of Philemon" (PhD diss., New Orleans Baptist Theological Seminary, 2014).

enjoyed by contemporary scholars, had images been available. They were hindered, however, by the cost of travel and the time it took to examine manuscripts in their individual settings—usually libraries and monasteries.[4] Contemporary scholars are now able to use critical apparatuses as jumping-off points for further research because they can view textual variants in images of manuscripts made widely available.

A legitimate question at this point is, If we basically have the original text of the New Testament, why should we investigate more manuscripts in more detail? The best answer is that the story of textual variants in the text of the New Testament is only beginning to be told. While major variation units are covered in the Greek New Testaments that most scholars, seminarians, pastors, and laypeople use, exponentially more textual variants exist.[5] To demonstrate this point, it is important to note that a comprehensive comparison of all Greek manuscripts of Philemon has revealed at least 330 new textual variants (i.e., new readings, not necessarily new variation units) compared to major editions dating back to the 1800s.[6] For a letter that is only 335 words long in NA[28]/UBS[5], this number demonstrates that there is much more going on in the manuscript tradition than appears. The UBS apparatus presents only four variation units, and the NA apparatus presents only twenty-three. The reality, however, is that hundreds of places of textual variation exist for the small letter of Philemon.[7]

I hope that by the end of this chapter, you will see how important complete examinations of all New Testament manuscripts are to the continuing study of New Testament textual criticism and how the text was transmitted throughout the years. We must remember that every single handwritten

---

[4]A good example of the difficulties in accessing manuscript data can be seen in access to Codex Vaticanus in the 1800s, one of the oldest and best witnesses to the text of the New Testament. When Constantin von Tischendorf wanted to examine the manuscript in Rome, he was restricted to three hours a day for only two days. See Eldon J. Epp, "Codex Sinaiticus: Its Entrance into the Mid-Nineteenth Century Text-Critical Environment and Its Impact on the New Testament Text," in *Codex Sinaiticus: New Perspectives on the Ancient Biblical Manuscript*, ed. Scot McKendrick et al. (Peabody, MA: Hendrickson, 2015), 64-65.

[5]Variation units are places in the text of manuscripts where two or more individual related variations occur.

[6]The number 330 here is only an approximation, as I've tried to isolate new readings not available in other apparatuses to the best of my ability. This tally has been difficult to compile in some ways because different apparatuses handle variation units differently. My comparison is to NA[28], UBS[5], Tischendorf, Tregelles, and von Soden.

[7]These numerous variation units should not be alarming, as most are quite innocuous. The point remains: the 570+ manuscripts of Philemon differ with each other at many places.

copy of the Bible was *someone's* Bible—whether personal or church copies (more likely). Since this is the case, we can look at every single one of these copies in a quest both for the original reading and for how churches and individuals have interpreted the text over the years. Sometimes, textual variation can act as commentary on the text of the New Testament, a fact to which we will return below.

COLLATING PHILEMON

Textual scholars read and compare manuscripts so they can piece together the "original text" and understand better the people who copied those texts. The job of the New Testament textual critic is incredibly difficult, however, because of the vast wealth of data available (fifty-three-hundred-plus manuscripts). One tool that textual critics across the centuries have used is called collation, wherein two or more texts are compared to each other to reveal and catalog the differences between them.[8]

To date, a large number of manuscripts of the New Testament have not been examined in detail. While the oldest witnesses to the text of the New Testament (as well as the most important newer ones) have been studied, much work remains to be done. Never in the history of the world have scholars had access to more data than is currently available. In the blossoming world of digital humanities, people involved in New Testament textual studies have experienced unprecedented access to manuscript images. Libraries and museums around the world are digitizing their collections, allowing access to manuscripts that was previously costly to the viewer in both time and money. The INTF is in the process of making available online images of New Testament manuscripts that were previously available only in microfilm format on site. The CSNTM has photographed manuscripts in high-resolution digital format.[9] Previous generations of scholars worked well with the information that was available, often using collations compiled by others who studied particular manuscripts in person. Access to the manuscripts themselves was

---

[8]In this chapter I will mainly use the term *collation*, although the preferred method of data gathering has now shifted to digital transcriptions, as used by the INTF in the Virtual Manuscript Room, among others. A collation records the differences between two texts, so in theory a full transcription of a manuscript could be re-created from the data gathered by a collation. In other words, the result of either a digital transcription or a collation is easily usable data.

[9]In the process of digitizing manuscripts, Dan Wallace and CSNTM have been introduced to manuscripts that were previously unknown to New Testament text critics. For details about how CSNTM has "discovered" previously unknown manuscripts, see chapter three in this volume.

limited. Thankfully, the world is now ready for comprehensive study of individual books and manuscripts of the New Testament.

For my dissertation, I collated every available Greek manuscript of Philemon against the modern text of UBS[4]/NA[27].[10] After the collations, I input all the differences into a textual apparatus, where all textual variants for the entire Greek tradition of the text of Philemon are presented. But, before we go any further, I will explain the basics of what it is textual critics actually *do* in collation.

Paper collations. Traditionally, the process of collating manuscripts included comparing a particular manuscript to a standardized base text. For many, this standard was the *textus receptus* because it largely represented the text of the New Testament in the majority of manuscripts, leaving fewer differences to record. The collator would compare the text of a manuscript with the text of the *textus receptus*, and when the two texts disagreed, the collator would record the differences.

Let us look at an example. At Philemon 1 in the *textus receptus*, Paul identifies himself as δέσμιος (*desmios*, "prisoner"). In GA manuscript 945, Paul identifies himself as δοῦλος (*doulos*, "slave"). So, when a collator came across the reading in 945, he or she would record as follows:

Verse: base text reading] manuscript reading
Philm 1: δεσμιος] δουλος

In this way, the textual critic is recording only the differences between that particular manuscript and the *textus receptus*. Where there are no differences between the two, the text of the manuscript can be assumed to contain the text of the *textus receptus*. In other words, the collation represents the entire text of the manuscript in an abbreviated space that allows scholars to access data easily.[11]

Another way to produce a paper collation is to print the base text and then write in the differences between the manuscript and the base text. In this way, one step is removed: the collator does not need to record the base text reading every time there is a difference between the two. The collator produces what amounts to a paper transcription of the manuscript, producing

---

[10]These were the most up-to-date, widely used critical editions available at the time of my project.
[11]For more details, see David C. Parker, *An Introduction to the New Testament Manuscripts and Their Texts* (Cambridge: Cambridge University Press, 2008), 95-107.

the text exactly as it appears. The Center for New Testament Textual Studies produced its electronic critical apparatus using the latter paper transcription method described above, the results of which were then manually entered into an electronic document.[12]

The work of the collator is laborious. The collator records every single difference between the manuscript and the base text, a process that requires many hours of work. For several reasons, collation is especially difficult. First, the goal of producing a collation is to be perfect. For this reason, at least two collations should be completed. The difficulty with achieving perfection should be apparent. When comparing two documents and recording the differences, the collator could easily miss differences between the texts in the act of looking back and forth between the two documents.[13] So the collator in most instances should read letter by letter in order to avoid errors. A further challenge to the collator is avoiding fatigue. The collator must take breaks regularly to avoid undue eye strain.

Electronic transcriptions. Despite the advent of computers, textual critics should still master the ability to complete a paper collation, as some libraries and other settings may not allow for the use of electronics when inspecting a manuscript. Contemporary textual critics, though, prefer to transcribe manuscripts electronically, which has advantages over paper transcriptions. These electronic transcriptions are made by changing a digital base text to match as closely as possible what is displayed in a manuscript. Electronic transcriptions provide data that can be used in a variety of ways by anyone. A transcriber can also add paratextual data in the form of markup languages such as XML tagging. What this means is that not only is the manuscript text itself recorded but many of the codicological features as well. These paratextual features include paragraph markers, punctuation, column and page breaks, illuminations, decorations, titles, and postscripts, among other things. A comprehensive electronic transcription allows for a manuscript to be published as it appears but in electronic format.[14]

---

[12]This is the same method I used, since I was familiar with the process and had the resources of the Center for New Testament Textual Studies available at my disposal at the time. Also, the entire microfilm library at INTF had not yet been digitized and uploaded to the Virtual Manuscript Room, so I could not use the transcription editor in the same capacity as someone could presently.

[13] Interestingly, this same phenomenon has produced textual variants in manuscripts, as copyists would sometimes produce errors due to a slip of the eye.

[14]For an excellent example, see www.codexsinaiticus.org, where Codex Sinaiticus has been reproduced electronically alongside digital images of the manuscript.

The INTF, the Institute for Textual Scholarship and Electronic Editing, the Museum of the Bible Scholars Initiative, the Center for New Testament Textual Studies, and the International Greek New Testament Project now transcribe texts of the New Testament electronically, which allows for unprecedented levels of collaboration. Collators compare images of manuscripts to digital base texts, making changes to the electronic text. The result is an exact digital transcription of the text of the manuscript, complete with tagging of paratextual features.

Philemon collation process. The process of comparing every single manuscript of Philemon to one another began with several decisions. First, I decided to use the same process of collating as the Center for New Testament Textual Studies (as described above).[15] Also, I decided that I would record every difference found in the manuscripts, including the minor differences discussed above. That way, once a paper transcription was completed, I would not have to consult the manuscript for the text (although some paratextual features might need to be revisited).

A practical example can illustrate why it is important to record seemingly meaningless differences. One of the major textual variants in the New Testament can be found in Romans 5:1. Here, two different readings are found in the manuscripts: ἔχομεν (*echomen*, "we have peace") and ἔχωμεν (*echōmen*, "let us have peace"), where the difference between the two types of verbs is one single vowel. *Omega* and *omicron* sound very similar when read out loud. Normally, this type of difference would be overlooked, except that in this instance the difference in vowels changes the mood of the verb from a concrete thought (indicative) to a more contingent thought (subjunctive) in a moment when Paul is discussing justification by faith. Potential theological ramifications might be found in the textual variant found in Romans 5:1. One of the best witnesses to the text of Paul's letters is 33, which reads ἔχωμεν (*echōmen*, "let us have"). This manuscript, though, repeatedly changes between *omicron* and *omega* throughout its text of the New Testament. Given this tendency, is 33 a witness to "let us have" or to "we have"? Although 33 has an *omega* in Romans 5:1, the answer is ambiguous. When

---

[15]I began working at the Center for New Testament Textual Studies in 2007 as the administrative assistant and served as senior project director by the time I began work on my dissertation. So I used the method I was familiar with to complete the work. In the future, I will digitally transcribe the manuscripts I've already collated using the tools of the INTF, making the data available to any interested users.

viewing the NA^{28} apparatus, one would not be immediately aware that vowel interchange occurs frequently in 33.

The research process was laborious. Not only did I have to sift through the 750-plus Pauline manuscripts to determine which of them contained Philemon, I had to arrange access to those manuscripts, whether through images online, through the microfilms and photographs stored at research centers such as the Center for New Testament Textual Studies or INTF, or by visiting libraries to see the manuscripts in person.[16] Only then could I begin collating. The entire process lasted one and a half years. Since accuracy is valued over a completed product, the work of a textual critic moves slowly. The smallest details, the smudging of ink, a hole in the manuscript—everything is closely examined to determine what text the manuscript contains. This focus on 100 percent accuracy explains why the entire New Testament has not been analyzed in this comprehensive way. Philemon is 335 words long in NA^{28}/ UBS^5, making it one of the smallest books in the New Testament. Many other New Testament books are much longer and therefore require more time and energy.

THE TEXT OF PHILEMON

The process of transcribing and collating manuscripts allows scholars to track how ancient texts morphed and changed throughout the copying process over approximately fifteen hundred years.[17] In this section, I will provide a general overview of the text of Philemon in the Greek manuscript tradition. Also, I will consider what the text of Philemon would look like if we did not have the earliest manuscripts that we do.

The text of Philemon before AD 900. Paul's letter to Philemon can be found in more than 570 Greek manuscripts. This number can be deceiving, though. Only twenty-three out of the 570-plus manuscripts of

---

[16]At one point I had a friend photograph a manuscript that I would not have had access to otherwise. The reason I first had to determine which manuscripts include Philemon is that the official register of Greek New Testament manuscripts, the *Kurzgefaßte Liste*, which is now available online at http://ntvmr.uni-muenster.de/liste, currently does not tell which books are in a manuscript, only which groups of books (i.e., Gospels, Pauline epistles, etc.). An indexing process is currently ongoing by the online community on the Virtual Manuscript Room, wherein the contents of every page of the entire Greek New Testament manuscript corpus will be identified, allowing for easy electronic searches even on the level of chapters and verses of New Testament manuscripts.

[17]This is not to say that the initial text of the New Testament became completely indiscernible at any point in the transmission process, only that textual changes have occurred in the copying process.

Philemon. date before AD 900.[18] The earliest witnesses include P61 (ca. 700), P87 (third century), P139 (fourth century), 01 (fourth century), 02 (fifth century), 04 (fifth century), 06 (sixth century), 016 (fifth century), and 048 (fifth century). The earliest Greek witness to Philemon, P87, is a small scrap containing little text, fewer than one hundred letters. P139, too, is a small scrap containing portions of a handful of verses. A later papyrus manuscript of Philemon, P61, also is fragmentary and contains very little text. Manuscript 04 is lacking the first two verses; 016 is fragmentary, having suffered burns; and 048 is a palimpsest in which the undertext has been written over and is very difficult to see, leading to deficient portions for Philemon. In other words, of the nine manuscripts containing Philemon before circa AD 700, only three contain the entire text of Philemon: 01, 02, and 06.[19] Fourteen extant manuscripts of Philemon date to the ninth century AD: 010, 012, 018, 020, 025, 044, 0150, 0278, 0319, 33, 1424, 1841, 1862, and 1900. These manuscripts represent different textual clusters and signify a period of some textual diversity. In addition, thirty-six extant manuscripts of Philemon date to the tenth century, and these contain texts very similar to the Majority Text. So, while we have many manuscripts of Philemon, it is important to note that the majority of those manuscripts represent a later text. Only about 4 percent of the manuscripts we have for Philemon date to before the year 900, and that number climbs to only about 10 percent when including manuscripts from the 900s.

The text of Philemon in later manuscripts. While scholars try to use representatives of all manuscripts and principles of textual criticism to reconstruct the initial text, many manuscripts from the second millennium AD are not consulted because their texts are so similar. We need to consult all the manuscripts in order to determine which, if any, manuscripts are representative of the majority of later, similar manuscripts (i.e., the majority

---

[18]Around this time, the majority of manuscripts being copied contained a distinctly later form of the text of the New Testament. While minor differences occurred among manuscripts in this style, the majority of the manuscripts contained remarkably similar texts and are referred to as the Majority Text or the Byzantine Text. For more on the Majority Text, see Gordon D. Fee, "The Majority Text and the Original Text of the New Testament," in *Studies in the Theory and Method of New Testament Textual Criticism*, ed. Eldon J. Epp and Gordon D. Fee, SD 45 (Grand Rapids: Eerdmans, 1993), 183-208; Daniel B. Wallace, "The Majority Text Theory: History, Methods, and Critique," in Ehrman and Holmes, *Text of the New Testament*, 2nd ed., 711-44; and chapter six in this volume.

[19]Even 02 is deficient in the top left corner of the folio on which Philemon is found.

text). This may also be the case with Philemon, minus a few instances. So how would the text of Philemon read if we did not have manuscripts that dated before the year 900?[20] In this section we will examine the differences between the majority text of Philemon and the initial text as represented in the UBS/NA texts.

If the earliest witnesses to Philemon did not exist, a couple of familiar readings might be different in modern Greek New Testaments and English translations. One of the differences found between the NA/UBS text and the majority text can be found in Philemon 2, where the letter is addressed to Apphia as ἀδελφῇ (*adelphē*, "sister") in the NA/UBS and ἀγαπητῇ (*agapētē*, "beloved") in the majority text. The vast majority of later manuscripts and early printed critical editions of the Greek New Testament do not contain what is believed to be the initial text of Philemon in Philemon 2. This is not to say that no one would have had access to this reading in the time period after the year 900. On the contrary, "sister" can be found in twenty manuscripts after AD 900.[21] Without the earlier witnesses from a key period in the transmission of Philemon, we might adopt the wrong reading as original. In other words, if we did not possess the eleven other manuscripts before the year 900 that have the reading "sister," we would more than likely not consider it a viable option for the initial text.

Another reading that would be different without the earliest Greek manuscripts of Philemon can be found in Philemon 7, where Paul states that he prays "because I have great joy." In the majority of Greek manuscripts, especially those after 900, Paul states that it is "because we are very thankful." If the earliest manuscripts did not exist, then the reading "I have great joy" would probably be seen as secondary because only about 10 percent of the manuscripts that date from the tenth to the sixteenth centuries contain that reading. The rest read "we are very thankful."

The prime example of how different Philemon might be without the earliest Greek witnesses comes in Philemon 12, where the initial text reads, "whom I sent to you, him, this one is my heart." In this syntactically difficult sentence, the initial text states that Paul is sending Onesimus, who is very

---

[20]Of course, early evidence exists in other witnesses to the text of the New Testament, such as the church fathers and the early New Testaments translated into different languages. This section will concentrate on Greek witnesses solely, though.

[21]That is, manuscripts 81, 104, 442, 459, 628c, 636c, 676, 1678, 1721, 1739, 1840, 1881, 1889, 1984c, 2523, 2544, 2625, 2690, 2739, and 2805.

dear to him, back to Philemon. Out of the entire Greek manuscript tradition, only five manuscripts contain this initial text: 01*, 02, 010, 012, and 33.[22] The remaining Greek witnesses to the text of Philemon add the verb *receive*, so the verse reads "whom I have sent to you, him, this one is my heart, *receive him,*" looking forward, perhaps, to the idea of Paul's command to receive Onesimus as himself in Philemon 17. Scribes added the verb in Philemon 12 in multiple places, further suggesting it is not part of the initial text of Paul's letter. The problem with adding this warm welcome prematurely is that it goes against Paul's logic in this part of the letter. Paul describes his feelings solely for Onesimus and does not want to give Philemon hope that Onesimus will return for good.[23]

TYPES OF VARIANTS IN PHILEMON

Whereas some places in the New Testament manuscript tradition seem to contain textual variants that are conscious changes to the text made by either copyists or readers, most of the variants present in Philemon seem to be introduced simply to make the text clearer. In the ancient world, most reading was done aloud in public settings, so many variants no doubt crept into the textual tradition to make the text communicate clearly. In this section I will present examples of these types of variants that occur frequently throughout the text of Philemon. Examples of variants that seem to be conscious changes to the meaning of the text will be handled in the next section.

Before turning attention to specific examples, a brief introduction to the types of textual variants found in manuscripts is needed. Textual critics have observed both major and minor variants over the years. Major variants include additions or omissions, replacements, and differences in word order.[24] These are the types of variants that appear in the apparatuses of critical editions.

[22]In addition to this very small number of readings attesting to the absence of the command to receive Onesimus, only three witnesses (01, 02, and 33) contain Philem 12 exactly as it is presented in the UBS/NA text. This number is surprising and demonstrates how Paul's letter to Philemon might have been read in a slightly different manner without these earlier manuscripts.

[23]Markus Barth and Helmut Blanke, *The Letter to Philemon*, Eerdmans Critical Commentary (Grand Rapids: Eerdmans, 2000), 351-60 (see also 107-8), thoroughly examine the structure of this verse and the variant readings.

[24]Of course, these differences are all a matter of perspective when it comes to their labeling. We can only suggest that a variant is an addition if we believe the "original" composition did not contain the word. The same goes with omissions, replacements, and changes of word order. Generally speaking, these textual variants are framed in comparison to the UBS/NA critical texts, and my analysis will be no different.

Minor variants, on the other hand, include spelling differences that do not change the meaning of words, movable *nu* endings, obvious errors, differences in how proper names are spelled, errors in sight where text is added or removed due to a slip of the eye, and sometimes different types of abbreviations. These minor variations are prolific in the manuscript tradition, wherein almost every word of the text of the New Testament can be found in a variation unit of some sort (whether major or minor).[25] The idea that the UBS/NA editions represent basically the entire manuscript tradition minus the variants listed in their apparatuses is one that needs to be eliminated.

Additions and omissions. Let us now consider a few examples from Philemon. The first category is additions and omissions. Sometimes copyists or readers added text that made the meaning clearer. Examples of this can be observed in Philemon 10 and Philemon 25. In Philemon 8, Paul begins his appeal on behalf of Onesimus, and in Philemon 9 he introduces the main verb παρακαλῶ (*parakalō*, "I appeal"). In Philemon 10, this same verb is used, and some manuscripts insert different coordinating conjunctions in different positions. For example, 075 along with thirty-four other manuscripts adds οὐν (*oun*, "therefore"), connecting the second instance of "I appeal" back to the first. A handful of other manuscripts at this point add either καί (*kai*, "and") or δέ (*de*, "even") to make the connection. These conjunctions were added to aid both readers and hearers in the public reading of the text. In most cases, there are no major exegetical implications and the change in meaning is insignificant, especially since most of these types of readings are secondary. Another example in Philemon 10 is the addition of the pronoun μου (*mou*, "my") after the prepositional phrase ἐν τοῖς δεσμοῖς (*en tois desmois*, "in bonds"). This is an unnecessary clarifying feature of the majority of manuscripts of Philemon, seeming to be a move on the part of scribes to ensure that the reader understood that Paul is the one imprisoned, not Onesimus.[26]

Another type of addition may be liturgical in nature. In Philemon 25, which is a benediction of sorts, reading "may the grace of the Lord Jesus Christ be with your spirits," two examples can be observed. First, most manuscripts of

---

[25] This is certainly the case for Philemon and is more than likely the case for the rest of the text of the New Testament.

[26] Barth and Blanke, *Philemon*, 336, argue that the presence of the article itself before δεσμοῖς provides the sense of "these chains" or "my chains."

Philemon have added the pronoun ἡμῶν (hēmōn, "our") to the phrase τοῦ κυρίου (tou kyriou, "of the Lord"). Most manuscripts have also added the familiar ἀμήν (amēn, "amen") to the end of the phrase. These additions do not affect meaning in any significant way but may have arisen due to the liturgical nature of Philemon 25 and the letter's use in worship.[27]

Replacements. In the second category, copyists and/or readers sometimes replaced or substituted words in the text with little to no effect on meaning, usually making the text slightly clearer. Examples of this concept can be observed in Philemon 5 and Philemon 20. In Philemon 5, Paul is fleshing out why he is thankful for Philemon, because he has heard of his love and faith that he has πρός (pros, "toward") the Lord Jesus and εἰς (eis, "for") all the saints. The language here can be seen as awkward for Paul, as the use of πρός with "faith" in reference to "Lord Jesus" is not found elsewhere in the New Testament.[28] Some copyists, then, have changed the prepositions to correspond to normal usage, with some changing πρός to εἰς and/or εἰς to πρός in the verse. More than likely, these decisions stem from a desire to normalize the syntax in this verse with the rest of Paul's writings.

Another example of a replacement is found in Philemon 20, where we can observe where some manuscripts read ἐν χριστῷ (en christō, "in Christ"), while most read ἐν κυρίῳ (en kuriō, "in the Lord"), and a few omit the phrase altogether. This variation unit is unique in that the difference between the two main readings is a difference of one very similar-looking letter. In Christian manuscripts, copyists used a convention scholars call *nomina sacra* or "sacred names," wherein they abbreviated certain divine and otherwise significant words, adding a line above the abbreviation. The difference between these two readings is a single letter: χ (chi) versus κ (kappa). These two letters are easily confused, and the difference in meaning is not very significant in the context of Philemon 20. Although this counts as a major variation unit, the difference in meaning is not significant, and the rise of different readings is mechanically explainable.

---

[27]Bruce M. Metzger, *A Textual Commentary on the Greek New Testament*, 2nd ed. (New York: United Bible Societies, 1994), 589; Roger L. Omanson, *A Textual Guide to the Greek New Testament: An Adaptation of Bruce M. Metzger's Textual Commentary for the Needs of Translators* (Stuttgart: Deutsche Bibelgesellschaft, 2006), 451; Joseph A. Fitzmyer, *The Letter to Philemon: A New Translation with Commentary and Introduction*, AB (New Haven, CT: Yale University Press, 2000), 126.

[28]Bonnie B. Thurston and Judith M. Ryan, *Philippians and Philemon*, SP 10 (Collegeville, MN: Liturgical Press, 2005), 223.

Transpositions. In the third category, copyists and/or readers sometimes changed the word order in the text with little to no effect on meaning. Examples of this can be observed in Philemon 1 and Philemon 13. In Philemon 1, Paul includes his typical letter greeting, including the phrase "a prisoner of Christ Jesus." The textual tradition is split almost fifty-fifty here between manuscripts that read "Christ Jesus" and manuscripts that read "Jesus Christ." This transposition is curious considering that Romans, 1 and 2 Corinthians, Ephesians, Philippians, Colossians, and 1 and 2 Timothy all read "Christ Jesus," while Galatians, 1 and 2 Thessalonians, and Titus read "Jesus Christ."[29] Even though this counts as a major variation, there is no major difference in meaning. Similarly, in Philemon 13, the majority of manuscripts reverse the order of μοι διακονῇ (*moi diakonē*, "he might serve me"). This change does not affect the meaning of Philemon 13, but the move was more than likely done to aid in reading. In its original word order, two pronouns are read one after the other: σοῦ (*sou*, "of you"), then μοι (*moi*, "to me"). It appears that many readers of Greek manuscripts preferred not to read these pronouns in sequence, breaking them up with a change in word order that does not affect meaning at all due to the inflectional nature of the Greek language, wherein word order is not the most important factor in the grammatical function of words.

While viewing the apparatus of NA[28] or UBS[5], one might come to the conclusion that the text of Philemon contains few textual variants. This is certainly not the case. Major variants, such as the examples just discussed, and minor variants, explained above, can be found throughout the text of Philemon. In fact, almost every word in Philemon is included in a variation unit wherein at least one manuscript contains a textual variant. Most of the variants do not greatly affect meaning, nor do they tell the story of the history of the textual transmission. For this reason, most textual variants are left out of apparatuses.[30] An examination of all Greek witnesses to the text of Philemon has revealed that the textual tradition contains more variants than some might expect, even if most have no serious merit.

---

[29]Variations of the order also appear in all of Paul's letters, so this variation is not unique to Philemon.

[30]The exception more recently has been the International Greek New Testament Project and ECM volumes, which include many more variants. Even so, the manuscript selection process for ECM leaves out a good many manuscripts and their variants.

TEXTUAL VARIANTS AS COMMENTARY

If most textual variants do not affect meaning in any significant way, should we still study them? At some point, every ancient and medieval Greek manuscript was used in a real church in a real community. Each of these manuscripts was *someone's Bible*. Over the years, though, textual variants arose through the copying process. Regardless of how these variants arose, churches that read from these manuscripts may not have known of any different readings. Our question, then, becomes: Once the task of establishing the original text is satisfactorily complete, what are we to do with the leftover variants? Additionally, can textual variants shed light on how an ancient community understood the text of the New Testament? In the same way, can textual variants help in modern interpretation of the text of the New Testament? This section will explore a selection of exegetically significant variants from Philemon that can shed light on meaning and interpretation throughout the centuries.

From "participation" to "ministry." Philemon 6 is by far the most difficult verse in the book to understand in terms of vocabulary and syntax. As Paul continues his thanksgiving section, he provides a purpose clause that gives an object to his ambiguous prayer from the second half of Philemon 4, stating, "so that the participation of your faith may become effective in the knowledge of every good thing which is in us in Christ." Most manuscripts in the Greek tradition read κοινωνία (*koinōnia*, "participation"). Some manuscripts (01c, 0150, 1874, 1881, and others), though, read διακονία (*diakonia*, "ministry") in place of "fellowship" or "participation." The overwhelming support of early and reliable witnesses gives precedent to "participation" over "ministry," making the second reading the focus of our discussion here.

Scribal considerations must be examined as well. The specific meaning of κοινωνία here has been the subject of some debate. Modern scholars have provided a range of meanings for the term: "association," "communion," "sharing," "participation," "partnership," "contributions," "fellowship," and others.[31] Modern difficulties in understanding the meaning of κοινωνία may shed light on why διακονία can be found in some manuscripts. Perhaps

---

[31]Eduard Lohse, *Colossians and Philemon: A Commentary on the Epistles to the Colossians and to Philemon*, trans. W. R. Poehlmann and R. J. Karris, Hermeneia (Philadelphia: Fortress, 1971), 193; Thurston and Ryan, *Philippians and Philemon*, 223; Fitzmyer, *Philemon*, 97; Barth and Blanke, *Philemon*, 281.

ancient and medieval readers and scribes shared the same difficulty and sought to clarify the verse by changing κοινωνία to διακονία to avoid ambiguity.

Another important aspect to consider is strictly a letter issue: the two terms share several common letters in Greek. A careless scribe initially could have made the change from *participation* to *ministry* unintentionally. In this case, *ministry* could have stayed in the tradition, as the noun makes sense in the flow of Paul's letter. Whichever way the variant arose, the presence of *ministry* in the textual tradition points to difficulties in interpretation throughout the centuries. Perhaps this variant reading can help us in interpretation. In this particular instance, past readers struggled with the meaning of the word *participation*. Some readers, though, were comfortable with the term *ministry* or *service* of faith here. This variant reading helps us to understand that this activity of faith that Paul was praying would become effective was certainly connected to the church and involved an act of service or ministry, not simply a passive type of fellowship.

The addition of **work.** Continuing in Philemon 6, Paul prays that the participation of Philemon's faith will be effective "in the knowledge of every good thing." The ambiguous use of ἀγαθοῦ (*agathou*, "good thing") here led to the addition of a clarifying noun, ἔργου (*ergou*, "work"). In this case, "every good" became "every good *work*." Once the reading made its way into the tradition, it remained, being found in more than 120 manuscripts.[32] Although found in all these manuscripts, the addition appears to be secondary in light of external evidence.

Scribal and authorial considerations must be examined as well. In terms of inscriptional probabilities (i.e., what Paul might have written), the addition of *work* might appear to go against the grain in terms of what Paul usually communicated to his congregations. Although Paul emphasizes salvation being free from "works of the law," good works more broadly is not a concept foreign to his teaching. Paul uses a form of the phrase ἔργον ἀγαθόν (*ergon agathon*, "good work") twelve times in his letters, each time in a positive sense (Rom 2:7; 2 Cor 9:8; Eph 2:10; Phil 1:6; Col 1:10; 1 Tim 2:10, 5:10; 2 Tim 2:21; 3:17; Titus 1:16; 3:1).[33] In this instance, therefore, it is possible that Paul could have penned "every good work."

---

[32]In their discussion on the variant, Barth and Blanke comment that a very small group of manuscripts added the noun. That the noun has been added to more than 120 Greek manuscripts demonstrates the need for full collations of the entire Greek tradition.

[33]The only letters lacking the phrase are 1 Corinthians, Galatians, and 1 and 2 Thessalonians.

In terms of transcriptional probabilities, scribes might have added *work* to clarify the somewhat ambiguous *good*. "Of all good" or "of every good thing" is open ended, which could have led some scribes to insert a clarifying noun. Conversely, if *work* were present initially, its deletion (thus creating a more ambiguous phrase at the end of an already awkward verse) seems less likely. Also, six of the twelve instances of the phrase "good work" occur in the Pastoral Epistles, located right before Philemon in most manuscripts. Due to close proximity, scribes could have added *work* to *good* to correct the perceived error of its absence because they were accustomed to seeing the phrase.

The secondary nature of the phrase "every good work" makes it a prime candidate for a variant that can be used as commentary for this particular verse. The original text "every good" by itself cries out for something to complete the thought. In this case, scribes inserted *work*, giving the otherwise ambiguous phrase some kind of tangible action or result. Paul's prayer was that the participation of Philemon's faith would become effective in the knowledge of not just all goodness but specifically good deeds and actions. That this reading found staying power in about 20 percent of the Greek manuscript tradition indicates its acceptance as a legitimate way to understand the text here.

"In us" or "in you." The second-to-last phrase in Philemon 6 includes the phrase "in us" in the text portion of modern Greek critical editions. The textual tradition, though, is split about two-thirds to one-third in total number of manuscripts that read ἡμῖν (*hēmin*, "in us") and ὑμῖν (*humin*, "in you [plural]"), respectively, which is an unusual split percentage for this letter.[34] Important manuscripts also are split almost evenly in number: 02, 04, 06, 044, 048, 81, and the majority text read "in us," while P61, P139, 01, 010, 012, 025, 0278, 33, 1739, and 1881 read "in you." One manuscript, 38, reads "in me," which is just a strange reading. Only considering external evidence, the edge belongs to "in you," as the manuscripts that contain the reading are of slightly better quality, especially with the fourth-century witness of P139.[35]

---

[34]For most of the variants that center on a difference between first-person and second-person pronouns, the mass quantity of manuscripts support one over the other, which suggests an orthographical shift.

[35]P139 was recently published in the eighty-third Oxyrhynchus volume: David Lincicum, "5347. Philemon 6-8, 18-20," in *The Oxyrhynchus Papyri LXXXIII*, ed. P. J. Parsons and N. Gonis (London: Egypt Exploration Society, 2018), 11-14.

With external evidence slightly favoring one reading over another, scribal and authorial evidence must be considered as perhaps a deciding force. As far as authorial considerations are concerned, Paul uses "in you (plural)" 164 times and used "in us" only thirty-five times in his letters, which is a split of about 80 percent to 20 percent. Interestingly, he uses first-person personal pronouns 826 times in his letters and second-person personal pronouns 841 times, which is nearly an even split. When he uses personal pronouns in the dative case, he prefers to use "in you (plural)." So Paul more than likely would have used "in you (plural)" in this instance. As far as scribal considerations are concerned, scribes would have been more likely to change "in us" to "in you (plural)" because of the presence of "of you" earlier in the verse. If "in you (plural)" were present initially, the shift to "in us" is difficult to explain.[36] Authorial and scribal considerations in this case are inconclusive.[37]

This variant is often discussed in commentaries. The general consensus favors "in us" as original, mostly due to assimilation. Bruce Metzger argues that "in us" is original due to its expressive nature and the fact that scribes would have been more likely to assimilate the text to other second-person personal pronouns in the surrounding verses.[38] Barth and Blanke devote one and a half pages of their commentary to discussing the implications of both readings, which is far more coverage than any other commentary. They argue that "in you" should be the adopted reading based on intrinsic grounds. Referencing Ernst Lohmeyer, they point out that in Paul's thanksgiving sections, he normally does not lump himself with the congregation to which he is writing. Further, they argue that Paul never thanks God for granting him love and faithfulness to an outstanding degree. To this end, all good things would be experienced in the congregation, not simply in an ideal and abstract manner.

---

[36]Of course, not a few of the variant readings more than likely arose because the two words are differentiated only by a letter that was eventually pronounced almost identically. This similarity makes the originality of either reading even more difficult to determine.

[37]For a lengthier discussion on Paul's use of first-, second-, and third-person personal pronouns, see C. E. B. Cranfield, "Changes of Person and Number in Paul's Epistles," in *Paul and Paulinism: Essays in Honour of C. K. Barrett*, ed. M. D. Hooker and S. G. Wilson (London: SPCK, 1982), 280-89.

[38]Metzger, *Textual Commentary*, 588. See also Omanson, *Textual Guide*, 449-50; Thurston and Ryan, *Philippians and Philemon*, 224; Peter T. O'Brien, *Colossians, Philemon*, WBC (Waco, TX: Word Books, 1982), 275; Lohse, *Colossians and Philemon*, 194; Fitzmyer, *Philemon*, 98.

Based on manuscript, scribal, and authorial considerations, both readings deserve to be considered by interpreters. In other words, here is a place where no major exegetical point should be made solely on this particular word. Both readings have compelling evidence, and neither can be completely settled. Both readings are adapted by good scholars. Both readings, therefore, should be considered when completing the exegetical task of Philemon 6. This particular place of variation among the Greek manuscript tradition is not simply a place where we decide the original and throw out the variant. In the text of Philemon, we have a place where we cannot say for certain which reading is initial to the text of Paul's letter.

Summary. While we have the luxury of examining nearly two millennia of manuscripts and critical editions of the Greek New Testament, churches throughout the centuries used the texts they had for the public reading of Scripture. In some instances, awareness of different readings existed (especially in the early period). For the most part, though, texts with variations were read and accepted as authoritative in churches. For Philemon, we can see several places where textual variation can act as commentary. Textual variations can help us to understand how the text was understood in some settings. As such, textual variations that have been deemed as completely secondary should not be jettisoned completely by scholars, pastors, and laypeople but should be seen as a part of the interpretive Technicolor tapestry of the church being woven for nearly two thousand years now.

CONCLUSION

The text of Philemon, like most of the New Testament, enjoys a complicated history, more so than many realize. Through the painstaking process of reading and examining every single letter and mark of every single extant Greek manuscript, the picture becomes somewhat clearer. Paul's letter to Philemon survives in 570-plus extant Greek manuscripts to which we currently have access. Of those, only twenty-three survive from the period before the standardization of the Majority Text. Even among those, only three contain the entire text of Philemon from the earliest period of the copying process.

Upon comprehensive examination of the text to Philemon, at least 330 new readings have been discovered that are not currently published in critical editions from the past three hundred years, when serious study of textual criticism began in earnest. All variant readings help in understanding not only the transmission of the text but also how churches and communities understood these texts throughout the years. It is safe to say that we have the entire initial text of Paul's letter, even if we have two places where the initial text may be uncertain between two words. We do not know which reading is original—"to us" or "to you (plural)" in Philemon 6, and the presence or absence of *and* in Philemon 11.[39] For these places, which reading is original really does not matter for interpretation. It does not matter because it did not matter to the early church. We cannot hold ancient manuscript culture to the same standard as our modern print culture. This is not to say that we cannot have confidence in the text—may it never be! While we do not possess many early copies of Philemon, most textual variation is easily explainable in terms of correcting awkward syntax. In fact, Philemon 14-17 contains relatively little textual variation.

The question of the text of the New Testament is not settled. More research and analysis needs to be completed. The study of manuscripts goes beyond the reconstruction of the initial text. Textual variants themselves can be windows into beliefs, or at the very least into how readers have read the text across the centuries. As more and better images become available, more data can be mined than has ever before been possible. The field of New Testament textual criticism is alive and well, with more detailed study to be done. The manuscripts are plentiful, but the laborers are few.

Key Takeaways

▶ There are more than 570 manuscripts of Philemon, and only three of them are complete manuscripts written before circa AD 700. If we had only manuscripts copied more than nine hundred years after Paul wrote Philemon, our text of Philemon would change very little.

▶ An examination of all Greek witnesses to the text of Philemon has revealed that the textual tradition contains more variants than some might expect, even if most of them have no serious merit.

---

[39]Due to space concerns, the presence or absence of *and* was not covered in this essay. Even so, the internal and external considerations are inconclusive, and either position could be argued convincingly, leading to editors putting the conjunction in brackets in NA[28] and UBS[5].

▶ There are really only two places where the initial text may be uncertain: "to us" or "to you" in Philemon 6, and the presence or absence
of *and* in Philemon 11.

▶ Textual variations that aren't original can still help us to understand
how the text was understood in some settings.

CHAPTER TEN

MYTHS ABOUT VARIANTS

WHY MOST VARIANTS ARE INSIGNIFICANT
AND WHY SOME CAN'T BE IGNORED

Peter J. Gurry

THE NEW TESTAMENT TEXT has come down to us in thousands of copies with many more thousands of textual differences between them. No one disputes this basic fact. It presents an apparent problem, however, for those of us who believe that the New Testament is foundational for faith in Jesus Christ. After all, what we know of Jesus we know primarily through the New Testament writings.[1] If we cannot know something as basic as *what* those writings say about Jesus, then there is little point in further debating whether what they say is true. Because of this, the textual differences between our witnesses to the New Testament text have been a recurring concern in debates about Christianity's viability.[2]

Reading the recent literature, however, brings one into contact with two very different opinions of how many and how important the differences between our New Testament manuscripts are. Take, for instance, Bart Ehrman, who began to think in seminary that the New Testament cannot

---

[1]For a survey of the evidence from beyond the New Testament, see Robert E. van Voorst, *Jesus Outside the New Testament: An Introduction to the Ancient Evidence* (Grand Rapids: Eerdmans, 2000).

[2]We might note that Dale B. Martin has recently argued that this problem is circumvented when Christians recognize that "Scripture is any text of the Bible brought to Christians by the holy spirit and read by Christians in faith and by the leading of the holy spirit" (*Biblical Truths: The Meaning of Scripture in the Twenty-First Century* [New Haven, CT: Yale University Press, 2017], 75). As valid as his general point about the Bible's existence in multiple forms is, even this statement assumes some way of knowing when "any text" is "of the Bible." For more of Martin's view, see his "The Necessity of a Theology of Scripture," in *The Reliability of the New Testament: Bart D. Ehrman and Daniel B. Wallace in Dialogue*, ed. Robert B. Stewart (Minneapolis: Fortress, 2011), 81-93.

be God's word because "even if God had inspired the original words, we don't have the original words." From this he concluded, "The doctrine of inspiration was in a sense irrelevant to the Bible as we have it, since the words God reputedly inspired had been changed and, in some cases, lost."[3] In short, Ehrman concluded that there are too many variants to believe the Bible's claims about its own inspiration.

On the other hand, it is common to find Christian authors who believe that textual variation poses no threat to Christian belief in the inspiration of Scripture since "for over 99 percent of the words of the Bible, we *know* what the original manuscripts said" and "for most practical purposes, then, the current published scholarly texts of the Hebrew Old Testament and Greek New Testament *are the same as the original manuscripts*."[4] Sometimes this near-perfect percentage is applied in the reverse so that it is 99 percent of all the *variants* that are unimportant rather than 99 percent of the original *words* that are known accurately, a slightly different metric.[5] Either way, the impression is that, despite Ehrman's doubts, textual variants present no real challenge at all to Christian confidence in the Bible. In the words of Matthew Barrett, any textual uncertainties raised by our disparate manuscripts are "always in matters insignificant, never having to do with Christian doctrine or the credibility of the biblical text."[6]

Which of these competing views is true? Is the Bible's inspiration a moot point because the original text is lost in the mists of time, or do we have nothing to worry about because our modern editions match the original text in 99 percent of cases? In this chapter, we will show why both claims are overstated. In the first case, it is true that a large majority of our vast number

[3]Bart D. Ehrman, *Misquoting Jesus: The Story Behind Who Changed the Bible and Why* (New York: HarperCollins, 2005), 211; similar statements are found on 7, 69. It may be worth noting that this problem is a frequent one for Muslims in their encounter with Christianity.
[4]Wayne Grudem, *Systematic Theology: An Introduction to Biblical Doctrine* (Grand Rapids: Zondervan, 1994), 96 (emphasis original). In personal communication, Grudem was clear that he believes some variants, such as the ones discussed below, do matter; they are just relatively rare. For an older but similar view, see the introductory volume in Louis Berkhof, *Systematic Theology: New Combined Edition* (Grand Rapids: Eerdmans, 1996), 159, originally published in 1932.
[5]For example, Timothy Paul Jones, *Misquoting Truth: A Guide to the Fallacies of Bart Ehrman's Misquoting Jesus* (Downers Grove, IL: InterVarsity Press, 2007), 44. In some cases, the 99 percent rate of irrelevance is applied both to individual variants and to places of variation, a distinction text critics are keen to distinguish. See Ron Rhodes, *The Big Book of Bible Answers: A Guide to Understanding the Most Challenging Questions* (Eugene, OR: Harvest House, 2001), 27-28.
[6]Matthew Barrett, *God's Word Alone: The Authority of Scripture: What the Reformers Taught . . . and Why It Still Matters*, The 5 Solas (Grand Rapids: Zondervan, 2016), 267.

of variants really are trivial for modern Bible readers; but we also hope to show why giving the impression that *no* variants matter for Christian doctrine gives an equally false impression. Some variants, despite being tucked away in Bible footnotes or commentaries, really do touch on important doctrines and so cannot be ignored by Christians who treasure the Bible as the Word of God.

The first matter of concern, then, is to consider what seem like wild claims about the number of variants in our manuscripts and some helpful (and not so helpful) ways to put this estimated number in context. Next, we consider whether these variants affect Christian doctrine and practice before concluding with some reflections on how these variants do matter.

THE NUMBER OF VARIANTS

The first point to consider when thinking about whether textual variants affect the Christian faith is how many we have. Over the centuries, New Testament scholars have given many suggestions about how many variants there are in our manuscripts. Some of the earliest printed editions of the Greek New Testament marked variants in the margin, but the number recorded was kept quite small. This changed most dramatically with the publication of John Mill's momentous edition of 1707, a work of thirty years that recorded something like 30,000 textual variants.[7] A century after Mill and Richard Bentley, Frederick Nolan could claim that further works since Mill's day had added another 100,000 variants to our knowledge.[8] Another century would add yet another 100,000 estimated variants, until our own day, when the most common number is given as 400,000. At least one noted textual critic has even suggested a number as high as 750,000.[9] To put this in perspective, some like to note that there are only around 138,020 words in the

---

[7]This caused a controversy, which Mill did not live to see; he died within a fortnight of his edition's publication. Instead, it fell to a man from Cambridge, classicist Richard Bentley, to defend his Oxford colleague's work from attacks. See Adam Fox, *John Mill and Richard Bentley: A Study of the Textual Criticism of the New Testament, 1675–1729* (Oxford: Basil Blackwell, 1954), 105-15; Grantley McDonald, *Biblical Criticism in Early Modern Europe: Erasmus, the Johannine Comma and Trinitarian Debate* (Cambridge: Cambridge University Press, 2016), 181-85, 218-28.

[8]Frederick Nolan, *An Inquiry into the Integrity of the Greek Vulgate or Received Text of the New Testament* (London: F. C. & J. Rivington, 1815), 2.

[9]For a chronological list of proposed estimates, see Peter J. Gurry, "The Number of Variants in the Greek New Testament: A Proposed Estimate," *NTS* 62, no. 1 (2016): 118-21. For the suggestion of 750,000, see Eldon J. Epp, "Why Does New Testament Textual Criticism Matter? Refined Definitions and Fresh Directions," *ExpTim* 125, no. 9 (2014): 419.

standard Greek New Testament, leaving us with more variants than actual words from which they vary.[10]

A better estimate. The problem with all these estimates is that we are not told where they come from. Ehrman, for example, is the first prominent scholar to raise the number to 400,000, but when it comes to telling us how he arrived at this number he, like others, attributes the number to nameless "scholars" and offers no further detail.[11] If we take the most comprehensive collections of variants available, however, it is possible to arrive at a more responsible estimate.

We now have nearly complete and accessible collations of our Greek manuscripts for at least three sections of the New Testament: John 18, Philemon, and Jude.[12] If we count the number of variants in these sections and divide by the number of words in the standard Greek New Testament, we arrive at the rate of variation. The results are 3.86 individual variants per word for John 18, 3.53 for Philemon, and 3.67 for Jude.[13] Multiply these rates by the 138,020 words in the same standard Greek New Testament, and you arrive at between 488,220 and 533,584 variants. Since we are dealing with an estimate here, it is probably best to leave it as a round half-million non-spelling variants in our Greek manuscripts.

Each qualification matters. This estimate does *not* include spelling differences, or variants found only in other sources, such as patristic citations of the New Testament or early translations into Syriac, Latin, and the like. This is due to limitations both in our source data and in the very nature of these other witnesses. Versions, for example, can be notoriously difficult to translate back into the Greek, and the varied ways in which the church fathers cite the New Testament makes cataloging and counting their variants

---

[10]Ehrman, *Misquoting Jesus*, 89; Bart D. Ehrman and Daniel B. Wallace, "The Textual Reliability of the New Testament: A Dialogue," in *The Reliability of the New Testament: Bart D. Ehrman and Daniel B. Wallace in Dialogue*, ed. Robert B. Stewart (Minneapolis: Fortress, 2011), 21.

[11]Ehrman, *Misquoting Jesus*, 89; for others, see Gurry, "Proposed Estimate," 102. The only earlier and higher estimate I have found is 500,000, given in Matthew S. DeMoss, *Pocket Dictionary for the Study of New Testament Greek*, IVP Pocket Reference (Downers Grove, IL: IVP Academic, 2001), 127. But I have not found anyone who references his number.

[12]Michael Bruce Morrill, "A Complete Collation and Analysis of All Greek Manuscripts of John 18" (PhD thesis, University of Birmingham, 2012); S. Matthew Solomon, "The Textual History of Philemon" (PhD diss., New Orleans Baptist Theological Seminary, 2014); Tommy Wasserman, *The Epistle of Jude: Its Text and Transmission*, ConBNT 43 (Stockholm: Almqvist & Wiksell, 2006). For more detail on Solomon's work, see chapter nine in this volume.

[13]For numbers behind these, see Gurry, "Proposed Estimate," 110.

difficult too. We should also note that our estimate counts "variants" that could be the original reading. This is because it counts variants *among* our manuscripts rather than variants *from* the original text, since the latter is, after all, the very thing we are trying to identify in the first place.[14]

Interpreting the estimate. Now that we have a reliable estimate, the question remains as to what to make of it. Like any good statistic, the estimated number of variants requires context, and several have been offered. Many of those, however, are more than a little problematic. In our introduction, we saw that some scholars compare the total estimated variants in all our manuscripts to the total number of words in some particular edition of the Greek New Testament. While this makes for a dramatic comparison, it actually tells us very little because it uses a fixed number on one side of the equation (words in one particular New Testament) with a variable one on the other (variants in all our manuscripts). Others have instead tried comparing the number of variants to the number of manuscripts to provide perspective. Here again, we have a weak comparison since manuscripts vary widely in terms of their size and contents. Some of our New Testament manuscripts are, after all, hundreds of pages long and contain the entire New Testament (such as Sinaiticus), while others are mere fragments containing a single verse (such as P12).[15] A comparison that suggests that both manuscripts have the same number of variants is pretty unhelpful.

What both of these comparisons miss is that scribes create variants from a text only by making additional copies of it. The more copying, the more variants, generally speaking. But wrapped in this curse is a blessing because, counterintuitively, more manuscripts mean the potential for more data with which to resolve their differences. Such was the point made already by Richard Bentley in response to concerns about Mill's estimated thirty thousand variants published in 1707. Bentley noted that the more manuscripts the better since "by a joint and mutual help all the faults may be mended; some copy preserving the true reading in one place, and some in another."[16] In other words, the very cause of the problem (copying) can also supply us with its solution (more copies).

---

[14]On this point, see Gurry, "Proposed Estimate," 105-6. Based on my data, if we assume the original reading survives at every point of variation, then about 17 to 25 percent of these estimated variant readings are *also* original readings.

[15]For more on this variety and on P12 in particular, see chapter three in this volume.

[16]Richard Bentley, "Remarks upon a Late Discourse of Free-Thinking," in *The Works of Richard Bentley*, ed. Alexander Dyce (London: Robson, Levey, and Franklyn, 1838), 3:349-50.

Fortunately, we can go well beyond Bentley's general principle because we have far more—and far more precise—data available than in his day. For example, if we compare the number of variants in the Greek continuous-text manuscripts of John 18 with the number of estimated words *in those same manuscripts*, then we get a good picture of just how many unique variants scribes created for each word that they hand copied. Since we have 3,058 variants in 1,659 manuscripts of John 18, and since the average copy of John 18 has roughly eight hundred words, then the result is just one distinct variant per 434 words copied, or 3,058 distinct variants out of 1,300,000 words.[17] If we cut out the 1,360 of these variants that are nonsensical, we are left with 1,698 meaningful textual variants.[18] That, of course, is still a large number for professional textual critics to wade through when deciding which of these are original in the hundreds of places where a decision needs to be made. (Most of them will be quite easy to decide, of course, either because they are attested by so few manuscripts or because they are such obvious corruptions.) But, from the scribes' perspective, only one new variant per 434 words copied is pretty good when you realize that every one of these came with the opportunity to create a new, otherwise unattested reading.

Even with these variants, we still need to ask just how many of these variants in John 18 are important to the meaning. To gain some sense of that, consider that the NA[28] edition, which is designed for academic study, includes 154 variant readings in this chapter of John. The UBS[4] edition, designed specifically for Bible translators, includes just ten. The more recent Tyndale House Greek New Testament lists twelve variant readings. If we consider a few well-regarded commentators on John, we note that D. A. Carson discusses just three variants, and C. K. Barrett eight.[19] How many of

---

[17]The figure of 3,058 is just over 0.2 percent of 1.3 million. This percentage, however, is imperfect because we are counting each variant only once but counting words copied each time they occur in a manuscript. Ultimately, measuring scribal fidelity accurately *across the whole tradition* would require us to measure each manuscript against its own exemplar, something we cannot do. In lieu of that, I have elsewhere used coherence to help determine how often the same variant may have been made independently. See Peter J. Gurry, *A Critical Examination of the Coherence-Based Genealogical Method in New Testament Textual Criticism*, NTTSD 55 (Leiden: Brill, 2017), 114-41. On the number eight hundred for John 18, most of our manuscripts are Byzantine, and eight hundred words is one word shy of what is in the Robinson-Pierpont Byzantine text.

[18]For these numbers, see Gurry, "Proposed Estimate," 108.

[19]D. A. Carson, *The Gospel According to John*, PNTC (Grand Rapids: Eerdmans, 1991), 576, 579-80; C. K. Barrett, *The Gospel According to St. John*, 2nd ed. (London: SPCK, 1978), 517, 520, 522, 524, 531, 536, 539.

these deserve the notice of typical English Bible readers? Based on the major modern translations, the answer is zero. Not a single note about any variant in John 18 is to be found in the ESV, NIV, NRSV, or even the richly foot-noted NET. The translators of these versions are right in this since all of the major variants in John 18 are easily resolved, do not significantly affect the meaning, or both.

Naturally, other chapters of John and other books will differ, but this example illustrates the basic point that only a tiny sliver of the total number of variants are really worth a translator's time, let alone the average Bible reader's.[20] By my calculations, only about 0.3 to 2.8 percent of all our esti-mated variants are in the UBS[4] edition designed for translators.[21] And while some of these are left out from editorial oversight or out of sheer necessity, the number of variants that might meaningfully affect translation cannot be far from this.

Conjecture. Before we consider some specific variants, it is worth men-tioning how rarely editors of the Greek New Testament have to guess or "conjecture" what the original text is—in other words, how rarely editors have concluded that *all* our manuscripts are wrong and the original text is simply not to be found in any of them. Such conjecture is fairly common practice among editors of classical works and, it should be said, has long been practiced by New Testament editors too.[22] Yet when we consider the mainstay scholarly edition of the Greek New Testament, the NA, we see a decreasing use of conjecture over time. In the thirteenth edition published in 1927, editor Erwin Nestle (son of Eberhard Nestle) introduced eighteen conjectures in the apparatus that he thought "must be considered original."[23]

---

[20]For a translator's perspective, see chapter fifteen in this volume.

[21]See Peter J. Gurry, "How Many Variants Make It into Your Greek New Testament?," *Evangelical Textual Criticism* (blog), May 10, 2016, http://evangelicaltextualcriticism.blogspot.com/2016/05/how-many-variants-make-it-into-your.html.

[22]For a fine introduction to conjecture and its history, see Jan Krans, "Conjectural Emendation and the Text of the New Testament," in *The Text of the New Testament in Contemporary Research: Essays on the Status Quaestionis,* 2nd ed., ed. Bart D. Ehrman and Michael W. Holmes, NTTSD 42 (Leiden: Brill, 2013), 613-35; Krans, *Beyond What Is Written: Erasmus and Beza as Conjectural Critics of the New Testament,* NTTS 35 (Leiden: Brill, 2006). A remarkable—and remarkably large—catalog is available in the Amsterdam Database of New Testament Conjectural Emenda-tion at http://ntvmr.uni-muenster.de/nt-conjectures.

[23]Eberhard Nestle and Erwin Nestle, eds., *Novum Testamentum Graece cum apparatu critico,* 13th ed. (Württemberg: Württembergische Bibelanstalt, 1927), 12*. These are found at Mt 2:6; 6:16; 12:33; 15:5; Mk 7:11; Acts 7:38; 16:12; Rom 13:3; 1 Cor 2:4; 6:5; 14:38; 16:22; 2 Cor 3:3; 7:8; 8:12; 1 Tim 4:3; 5:13; Rev 2:13 and are marked by a diamond in the apparatus. Some of these have since

Contrast that to the NA[28], released in 2012, where we find only two conjectures the editors think are original (one at Acts 16:12 and one at 2 Pet 3:10).[24]
Other editors, such as those of the Tyndale House edition, reject all conjectures on principle, although there remains debate about the justification for
this.[25] Still, even the eighteen conjectures in Nestle's thirteenth edition bear
witness to the remarkable reliability of the New Testament text. The original
reading is usually, if not always, there somewhere in our witnesses; the challenge, where such exists, is in settling convincingly on where exactly it is.[26]

SOME DIFFICULT AND IMPORTANT VARIANTS

Despite what has been said, many protest that merely counting variants does
not tell the whole story. Kenneth Clark, for example, writes, "Counting words
is a meaningless measure of textual variation, and all such estimates fail to
convey the theological significance of variable readings."[27] Likewise, Ehrman
says of his self-styled "orthodox corruptions" that their "significance cannot
simply be quantified; it is pointless, for example, to calculate the numbers of
words of the New Testament affected by such variations or to determine the
percentage of known corruptions that are theologically related."[28]

To be sure, we do not need to go so far as to say that counting is meaningless, especially when such statistics are put in proper context. But it is
true that variants, like manuscripts, should be weighed and not merely
counted. In light of this, let us sample the most difficult and important
variants in the New Testament. This should provide us with a more realistic

been found in manuscripts, and a few might be categorized as editorial alternatives (e.g., μαράνα
θά versus μαρὰν ἀθά in 1 Cor 16:22). On these conjectures and conjectures in the Nestle(-Aland)
tradition more generally, see Krans, "Conjectural Emendation," 620.

[24]The ECM for Acts has removed the conjecture at Acts 16:12 but added one at Acts 13:33.

[25]For the justification, see Dirk Jongkind et al., eds., *The Greek New Testament Produced at Tyndale
House, Cambridge* (Wheaton, IL: Crossway, 2017), 505. For a contrary view, see Ryan D. Wettlaufer, *No Longer Written: The Use of Conjectural Emendation in the Restoration of the Text of
the New Testament, the Epistle of James as a Case Study*, NTTSD 44 (Leiden: Brill, 2013).

[26]For the underappreciated role of rhetorical argument in textual criticism, see R. J. Tarrant, *Texts,
Editors, and Readers: Methods and Problems in Latin Textual Criticism*, Roman Literature and
Its Contents (Cambridge: Cambridge University Press, 2016), 30-48; Gary Taylor, "The Rhetoric
of Textual Criticism," *Text* 4 (1988): 39-57.

[27]Kenneth W. Clark, "The Theological Relevance of Textual Variation in Current Criticism of the
Greek New Testament," *JBL* 85, no. 1 (1966): 5.

[28]Bart D. Ehrman, *The Orthodox Corruption of Scripture: The Effect of Early Christological Controversies on the Text of the New Testament*, 2nd ed. (Oxford: Oxford University Press, 2011), 322.
For more on this type of variant, see chapter eleven in this volume.

sense of whether textual variants pose a serious threat to the Christian faith in general or inspiration in particular.

Definitions. When thinking about the significance of textual variants, it is helpful to keep two categories in mind. The first is whether the variant is important for interpretation. By all accounts, most variants do not affect the meaning of the text. This obviously applies to spelling differences (does it change the meaning if we spell John's name with one or two *nus* in Greek?), but it also applies to many other smaller variants, which merely make the implicit explicit or the ambiguous clear. These types of variants occur throughout our manuscripts, and any major edition of the Greek New Testament will bear this out on page after page.[29] These types of variants pose no threat to the Christian faith or to the Bible's inspiration. They merely show that scribes or readers were at times willing to make the text read more clearly.

An example may help. In Acts 13:33, there is a knotty problem in Paul's speech at Pisidian Antioch. There Paul refers to the fulfillment of God's promises in Jesus by saying that "what God promised to the fathers" has now been fulfilled in the resurrection. But the people to whom that promise is fulfilled is not so clear. It is either "to us, their children," or "to our children," or perhaps "to us, the children."[30] The first and last of these make the most sense in context. The second is altogether awkward since we wouldn't expect the fulfillment of this promise to be among the *children* of Paul's audience. The problem is that the first reading is the latest attested, the second is the earliest, and the third is not attested at all—it's a conjecture.[31] Regardless of how we resolve this particular issue, this variant is one that does affect Paul's precise meaning, but also one that in no way affects the *importance* of the resurrection, still less the *fact* of the resurrection. No one would be foolish enough to suggest that because this verse has a variant, the truth of the resurrection itself is in peril.

---

[29]One could consult Constantin von Tischendorf's famed eighth edition (*Novum Testamentum graece, editio octava critica maior*, 2 vols. [Leipzig: Giesecke & Devrient, 1869–1872]) to see this in practice, or the volumes of the more recent ECM, published by the German Bible Society.

[30]The Greek readings are, respectively, τοῖς τέκνοις αὐτῶν ἡμῖν (*tois teknois autōn hēmin*), τοῖς τέκνοις ἡμῶν (*tois teknois hēmōn*), and the conjecture τοῖς τέκνοις ἡμῖν (*tois teknois hēmin*).

[31]For discussion of this variant, see B. F. Westcott and F. J. A. Hort, *The New Testament in the Original Greek: Introduction, Appendix*, 2nd ed. (London: Macmillan, 1896), 65; Bruce M. Metzger, *A Textual Commentary on the Greek New Testament*, 2nd ed. (New York: United Bible Societies, 1994), 362; Klaus Wachtel, "Text-Critical Commentary," in *Novum Testamentum Graecum: Editio Critica Maior III: The Acts of the Apostles, Part 3; Studies*, ed. Holger Strutwolf et al. (Stuttgart: Deutsche Bibelgesellschaft, 2017), 20.

What we are interested in, then, is variants that are genuinely difficult to resolve *and* that have some level of bearing on the text in a way that might affect Christian claims. Let us now turn to a few illustrative examples.

Mark 1:1. In the very first verse of what is thought by most to be the very first Gospel, we find a difficult and significant variant. The Gospel opens with what reads like the title to the whole book: "The beginning of the gospel of Jesus Christ, Son of God." The variant involves the words "Son of God," as some important witnesses omit them.[32] In Mark's Gospel, Jesus' sonship is an important theme, highlighted at his baptism (Mk 1:11), then again when he confronts unclean spirits (Mk 3:11), at the transfiguration (Mk 9:7), at his trial before the Sanhedrin (Mk 14:61), and climactically on the lips of a Gentile centurion (Mk 15:39). The issue, then, is *not* whether Mark presents Jesus as the Son of God but whether Mark wants us to read his account of the good news about Jesus with this in mind from the first line on.

In the standard critical editions (the UBS[5] and NA[28]), the words are placed in brackets indicating that "textual critics today are not completely convinced of the authenticity of the enclosed words."[33] This scholarly uncertainty is confirmed when we consider the two other most recent critical editions. The SBL Greek New Testament omits the words completely, whereas the Tyndale House Greek New Testament has them without brackets. Within the UBS, the rating given to this reading is a C, indicating that the editors had difficulty deciding. The reason is easy to see by going no further than the first manuscript listed in our apparatus, Codex Sinaiticus (01). This important manuscript has *both* readings, the shorter reading found as the first-written text (01*), with the longer reading found there too as a correction by one of the original scribes of the manuscripts.[34] Both readings can also be found in early Christian authors. Origen, for example, attests the shorter reading and Irenaeus the longer on several occasions. Our earliest witness to this portion of Mark is actually an amulet from the late third or fourth century (P.Oxy. 76.5073), and it does not have the longer

---

[32]There are a number of other minor variants here too, but only these two deserve serious consideration. For studies of this variant, see especially Peter M. Head, "A Text-Critical Study of Mark 1.1: 'The Beginning of the Gospel of Jesus Christ,'" *NTS* 37, no. 4 (1991): 621-29; Tommy Wasserman, "The 'Son of God' Was in the Beginning (Mark 1:1)," *JTS* 62, no. 1 (2011): 20-50; Ehrman, *Orthodox Corruption*, 85-88.

[33]NA[28], 54*.

[34]For a thorough and careful assessment of this correction, see Peter Malik, "The Earliest Corrections in Codex Sinaiticus: A Test Case from the Gospel of Mark," *BASP* 50 (2013): 214-19.

reading.[35] Most of the manuscript and versional evidence, it must be said, comes down on the side of the longer reading.

What makes this variant particularly difficult is the contradictory evidence for how each reading might have originated in the first instance. On the one hand, it is not hard to imagine scribes copying the shorter reading and, either out of reverence for Jesus or knowledge of Mark's Gospel, adding the words "Son of God."[36] On the other hand, the series of letters in this first verse of Mark make an accidental omission easy to explain because six of the words end in the same letter. When the names for Jesus are written as abbreviations, or *nomina sacra*, and without spaces (ΙΥΧΥΥΥΘΥ), it is quite easy to imagine two of them being dropped by accident. Scholars call such an omission homoioteleuton (literally, "similar endings") because the similar endings were the cause.

Some have objected to this explanation, however, because they note how the *nomina sacra* are designed to give words special attention. Moreover, since this is the start of the book, the suggestion is that a scribe would be most alert at just this point, probably having taken a break just before starting here.

While this may have been true in some cases, we actually have clear examples of just this omission happening at the start of Mark's Gospel in some later manuscripts.[37] One such example is a manuscript housed in Ferrara, Italy. GA 582 (or Manuscript Biblioteca Comunale Cl. II, 187, III) is a fourteenth-century complete New Testament copied by a scribe with a particularly bad penchant for leaving things out by accident. When I visited the manuscript in July 2016, I counted more than 130 omissions that were subsequently added in the margin. These were places where the scribe had left text out only to later discover his error and correct it. Of these 130 omissions, nearly 60 percent are cases where homoioteleuton is an obvious cause. Not surprisingly, we find two such cases on the very first page of Mark, one in the very first line, where the phrase "son of God" (υἱοῦ τοῦ θεοῦ, *huiou tou theou*) is clearly omitted from the main text and just as clearly added back

---

[35]G. S. Smith and A. E. Bernhard, "5073. Mark 1:1-2. Amulet," in *The Oxyrhynchus Papyri LXXVI*, ed. D. Colomo and Juan Chapa (London: Egypt Exploration Society, 2011), 19-23.

[36]While the particular addition of this title for Jesus has yet to be identified elsewhere in a manuscript (see Wasserman, "'Son of God' Was in the Beginning," 49), this does not remove it from the realm of possibility here.

[37]For additional examples, see Wasserman, "'Son of God' Was in the Beginning," 46-47.

in the margin. In other words, neither the use of *nomina sacra* nor the start of a book was enough to keep this scribe from accidental omission. And what happened in this manuscript could certainly explain the omission in 01* and other manuscripts.[38]

Whatever the original reading is here (and I think the evidence points toward the longer reading), this variant is, by all accounts, a difficult *and* important variant. Certainly it is one that English translations should continue to note for their readers. Furthermore, it is one that Christians cannot ignore when closely reading Mark's Gospel even if, in the full analysis, the sonship of Jesus is not what's at stake.

Luke 23:34. A second and even more difficult and important variant than Mark 1:1 involves one of the Bible's best-known sayings. In Luke 23:34, as Jesus is crucified between two criminals, he utters words that are as astonishing as they are famous, "Father, forgive them, for they know not what they do." With these words, Jesus models the response to persecution that he commands for his followers (Lk 6:28) and that his followers will later emulate (Acts 7:60) and further commend (1 Pet 2:21-23).[39]

The problem, textually, is that in some very early and important manuscripts, Jesus does not pray this remarkable prayer at all; the words are simply not there. This is true in our earliest manuscript, P75 (second to third century) and in Codex Vaticanus (fourth century), which, when agreeing with P75, likely attests a text that reaches back to the second century or earlier. Here, however, the omission is not explainable by similar endings, as in Mark 1:1. Once again Codex Sinaiticus attests both readings. In this case, the original scribe wrote the longer reading, a second scribe marked the prayer for erasure, and a third tried to erase the erasure! Codex Bezae (fifth century) shows a correction too, with the first scribe omitting the prayer and a later, sixth-century scribe adding it in the bottom margin of the page.[40]

---

[38]Evidence from the coherence-based genealogical method also supports the longer reading as original. See Tommy Wasserman and Peter J. Gurry, *A New Approach to Textual Criticism: An Introduction to the Coherence-Based Genealogical Method*, SBLRBS 80 (Atlanta: SBL Press, 2017), 43-50.

[39]For the influence on later Christians, see Ignatius, *To the Ephesians* 10.2-3; Justin, *First Apology* 14; Eusebius, *Hist. eccl.* 5.2.5.

[40]Curiously, the NA[27] (p. 48*) ascribes the addition in Bezae to a ninth-century corrector, whereas the NA[28] (p. 59*) ascribes it to one from the twelfth. The change is inexplicable, but the sixth-century date should be followed here, per David C. Parker, *Codex Bezae: An Early Christian Manuscript and Its Text* (Cambridge: Cambridge University Press, 1992), 41-43; Parker, *The Living Text of the Gospels* (Cambridge: Cambridge University Press, 1997), 162.

The reading is not found in the Latin text of 05 either originally or by correction. This along with several other majuscules (032, 038, 070, 0124), two minuscules (579, 1241), and then some of the earliest Syriac, Latin, and Coptic translations amounts to all the evidence for the omission of the prayer. On the other side of the ledger, the prayer is found in most of our witnesses, of which the earliest and most important Greek manuscripts are 01*, 02, and 04.

The evidence from the second century shows that the verse was known in its longer form by Irenaeus (*Haer.* 3.18.5), while it is not clear whether Marcion's version of Luke contained it.[41] There is also a tantalizing statement of the same prayer attributed to James the brother of Jesus at his martyrdom, by a second-century church father named Hegesippus. The account is recorded for us only later in the fourth century by Eusebius (*Hist. eccl.* 2.23.16). The problem is that we do not know whether this was the source for Luke 23:34 or whether Luke 23:34 was the source for the prayer that Hegesippus (per Irenaeus) attributes to James.[42]

The manuscript evidence is somewhat split, although the agreement of P75, 03, and 05* weighs heavily in most text critics' minds. No doubt, this explains the double brackets in NA[28]/USB[5] and the confidence of the UBS committee in giving their decision an A rating. The strongest argument in favor of the prayer's omission was stated as long ago as 1881, when Westcott and Hort wrote, "Wilful excision, on account of the love and forgiveness shown to the Lord's own murderers, is absolutely incredible: no various reading in the New Testament gives evidence of having arisen from any such cause."[43] In addition, it is often pointed out that without the prayer, the text flows smoothly from the soldiers crucifying Jesus (Lk 23:33) to casting lots for his garments (Lk 23:35).

On the other hand, Jesus' prayer sits comfortably with Luke's second volume, wherein Stephen prays a similar but not identical prayer as he is

---

[41]Dieter T. Roth, *The Text of Marcion's Gospel*, NTTSD 49 (Leiden: Brill, 2015), 407-8. The verse is also referenced in Ephrem's *Commentary on the Diatessaron* 21.3; for the English, see Carmel McCarthy, trans., *Saint Ephrem's Commentary on Tatian's Diatessaron: An English Translation of Chester Beatty Syriac MS 709 with Introduction and Notes*, JSSSup 2 (Oxford: Oxford University Press, 1994), 318.

[42]Compare the competing views of D. Daube, "'For They Know Not What They Do': Luke 23,34," in *Augustine, Post Nicene Latin Fathers, Orientalia, Nachleben of the Fathers*, ed. F. L. Cross, StPatr 4 (Berlin: de Gruyter, 1961), 58; and Joël Delobel, "Luke 23.34a: A Perpetual Text-Critical Crux?," in *Sayings of Jesus: Canonical and Noncanonical: Essays in Honor of Tjitze Baarda*, ed. William L. Petersen, Johan S. Vos, and Henk J. de Jonge (Leiden: Brill, 1997), 34n30.

[43]Westcott and Hort, *Appendix*, 68.

stoned (Acts 7:60). If Luke 23:34 were added under the influence of Stephen's prayer, we might expect their wording to agree more closely.[44] In
addition, the theme of ignorance that we see in Jesus' prayer ("for they know
not what they do") is one that Luke returns to multiple times in Acts (Acts
3:17-19; 13:27; 17:30).[45] Such ignorance does not imply innocence, since the
prayer is for forgiveness. Rather, the point seems to be that the soldiers (and
the Jews?) do not realize the significance of who they are crucifying or how
God intends to reverse their evil for a far greater good (see Chrysostom,
Homiliae in epistulam i ad Corinthios 7.5).[46]

Ultimately, the decision must be made based on which reading best explains the origin of the other. (This is the fundamental principle of all New
Testament textual criticism.) If the prayer is *not* original, then where did it
come from? If the prayer *is* original, why would anyone want to remove it?
One answer to the first question is that it comes from Stephen's prayer. But
we have already noted that the wording is not as close as we would expect if
that were the case. On the other hand, it could be suggested that the prayer
is authentic to Jesus but not to Luke. In this scenario, the saying was a
"floating tradition" that eventually found its way into Luke.[47] But, if that were
the case, we are left to explain why it was only ever added to Luke and not
to any of the other Gospels.

To the second question—why it would be removed—many answers have
been given, all having to do with the prayer's apparent theological problems.[48] The theological problems in question, we must remember, are not

[44]Jason A. Whitlark and Mikeal C. Parsons argue in "The 'Seven' Last Words: A Numerical Motivation for the Insertion of Luke 23.34a," *NTS* 52, no. 2 (2006): 188-204, that the prayer was
added after the four Gospels were collected in order to bring Jesus' final words from the cross
to a symbolically significant seven, but I do not find this especially convincing.

[45]See, for example, Eldon J. Epp, "The 'Ignorance Motif' in Acts and Anti-Judaic Tendencies in
Codex Bezae," *HTR* 55, no. 1 (1962): 51-62.

[46]On the question of whom Jesus asks the Father to forgive, see Raymond E. Brown, *The Death of
the Messiah: From Gethsemane to the Grave; A Commentary on the Passion Narratives in the Four
Gospels* (New York: Doubleday, 1994), 2:973; Delobel, "Luke 23:34a," 32-33.

[47]Whitlark and Parsons, "'Seven' Last Words," 201-4.

[48]For defenses of one or more of these explanations, see Nathan Eubank, "A Disconcerting Prayer:
On the Originality of Luke 23:34a," *JBL* 129, no. 3 (2010): 521-36; Shelly Matthews, "Clemency
as Cruelty: Forgiveness and Force in the Dying Prayers of Jesus and Stephen," *BibInt* 17, no. 1
(2009): 118-46, reprinted in *Violence, Scripture, and Textual Practices in Early Judaism and
Christianity*, ed. Ra'anan Boustan, Alex Jassen, and Calvin Roetzel (Leiden: Brill, 2010), 117-44;
David E. Garland, *Luke*, ZECNT 3 (Grand Rapids: Zondervan, 2011), 922-23; Brown, *Death of
the Messiah*, 2:979-80.

ours but those of the early church. They range from the fact that (1) the prayer seems to go unanswered given that God judged the Jews by destroying Jerusalem in AD 70, (2) Jesus offers forgiveness to the unrepentant, (3) the verse implies unfairness to those acting in innocence, or (4) that anti-Semitism made some early Christians dislike such mercy being offered to the Jews. Christian writers certainly did write about these larger issues in general, and in some cases these concerns are even hinted at when discussing this particular prayer.[49] It must be said, however, that these very same discussions show that Christian writers could easily address their concerns about the prayer without excising it from Luke. In other words, what these explanations for excision forget is that actual commentary—rather than textual editing—was the Christians' method of choice (then as now) for dealing with problem passages.[50]

In the end, a decision on this variant is extremely difficult. The early and weighty support of P75, 03, and 05 is hard to ignore on the one side. On the other side, it really is difficult to explain where this prayer in this context came from if not from Luke himself. Whichever the original reading, this is another case of a variant like Mark 1:1 that Christian readers cannot ignore.

John 1:18. Having discussed two difficult and important variants, perhaps we might balance our discussion with the less interesting—but, just for that reason, important—places where no difficult variants are found in the New Testament. Take, for instance, the famous beginning of John's Gospel, where the deity of Christ is set forth with unique clarity and power. In this passage, we get one famous textual variant in John 1:18 concerning whether Jesus is called the "only-begotten God" (μονογενὴς θεός, *monogenēs theos*) or the "only-begotten Son" (μονογενὴς υἱός, *monogenēs huios*) who is at the Father's side. The difference is one letter when written as *nomina sacra* (ΘΣ vs. ΥΣ).

In isolation, this variant is quite significant, as it seems to be a choice between Jesus' divinity and his unique sonship. But, of course, this variant does not occur in isolation. It comes only after John's rich theological introduction, in which he makes clear that the preexistent Logos is divine (Jn 1:1) and became incarnate (Jn 1:14). In none of these first fourteen verses is there

---

[49]Many of these are helpfully given in Eubank, "Luke 23:34a," 528-35.

[50]Contra Eric W. Scherbenske (*Canonizing Paul: Ancient Editorial Practice and the Corpus Paulinum* [Oxford: Oxford University Press, 2013], 229, 231, 236), I am not convinced that there is a discernable shift by the fourth century from controlling interpretation by changing the text itself to controlling it by changing the paratextual material.

a theologically significant variant. In fact, these verses are so textually stable that they agree word-for-word between the very first published Greek New Testament (Erasmus's, published in 1516) right up to the most recent (the Tyndale House edition published in 2017). There is not even a single letter different between them.[51] These two editions span hundreds of years and are based on very different manuscripts and editorial principles. Whichever reading is original, then, Jesus is clearly divine in the introduction to John's Gospel. Numerous other nonvariant passages that we might call theologically load-bearing could be cited.[52]

These three variants are certainly not the only ones in the Gospels, but they are illustrative. It is important to stress that most books of the New Testament have only a handful of variants that combine this level of importance *and* difficulty. Others we could mention in the Gospels occur at Matthew 12:47; 19:9; 21:29-31; 24:36; 26:28; Mark 1:2; 16:9-20; Luke 2:14; 10:1, 17; 11:1-4; 22:43-44; and John 5:3-4; 7:53–8:11. Moving outside the Gospels, we find such variants in Acts 20:28; Romans 5:1; 14:23/16:25-27; Ephesians 1:1; 2 Thessalonians 2:7; 1 Timothy 3:16; Hebrews 2.9; 2 Peter 3:10; and Jude 5. It is worth noting that there is no attempt to hide these variants.[53] They are plainly visible right in the footnotes of most any modern English translation of the Bible. Additionally, their merits are discussed in places such as Bruce Metzger's textual commentary cited above, the "TC" notes of the NET Bible, and, of course, in the more detailed Bible commentaries. In other words, there is no conspiracy of silence about them; they are well known.

VARIANTS AND DOCTRINE

These examples along with the data about the estimated number of variants in our manuscripts illustrate the problem we face in discussing them fairly. On the one hand, it is clear that most variants really are easily resolved or ignored. On the other hand, we have seen examples in Mark 1:1 and Luke 23:34 where variants simply cannot be ignored. How, then, should we best present the evidence?

---

[51]See Peter J. Williams, *Can We Trust the Gospels?* (Wheaton, IL: Crossway, 2018), 119-20.

[52]For other variants dealing with the deity of Christ, see Brian J. Wright, "Jesus as ΘΕΟΣ: A Textual Examination," in *Revisiting the Corruption of the New Testament: Manuscript, Patristic, and Apocryphal Evidence*, ed. Daniel B. Wallace, TCNT (Grand Rapids: Kregel, 2011), 229-66.

[53]One thinks of the subtitle to Bart Ehrman's *Jesus, Interrupted: Revealing the Hidden Contradictions in the Bible (and Why We Don't Know About Them)* (New York: HarperOne, 2009).

Sometimes the impression from the apologetic literature is that variants do not matter at all. Others are more careful to claim only that *"no orthodox doctrine or ethical practice of Christianity depends solely on any disputed wording."*[54] Daniel Wallace is even more precise, admitting that some "noncentral" beliefs or practices seem to be affected by viable variants but that "no viable variant affects any *cardinal* truth of the New Testament."[55] Both qualifications ("viable" and "cardinal") are important and match what we have here called difficult and important variants. In this sense, Wallace is surely right that no core Christian doctrine (e.g., the resurrection, the deity of Christ, salvation, the Trinity) is based solely on a textually difficult passage. Even Bart Ehrman grants that his own view is not a problem for this conclusion. He has said publicly that his view is not at odds with that of his mentor, Bruce Metzger, which is that "essential Christian beliefs are not affected by textual variants in the manuscript tradition of the New Testament."[56]

That is not to say, however, that no passage that *addresses* or *touches on* core doctrines is textually suspect. Some certainly are, such as 1 John 5:7-8, which says in the King James Version, "There are three that bear record in heaven, the Father, the Word, and the Holy Spirit, and these three are one." That is as explicit a definition of the Trinity as one finds in the Bible. Yet no serious textual critic today accepts this reading as authentic, and neither do evangelical theologians, who are still quite able to make a biblical case for the doctrine of the Trinity.[57] In other words, the fundamental doctrine of the Trinity in no way *depends* on this variant reading even though the variant in

---

[54]Craig L. Blomberg, *Can We Still Believe the Bible? An Evangelical Engagement with Contemporary Questions* (Grand Rapids: Brazos, 2014), 127 (emphasis original). D. A. Carson likewise says that "no doctrine and no ethical command is affected by the 'probability' passages, but only the precise meaning of specific passages" (*The King James Version Debate: A Plea for Realism* [Grand Rapids: Baker, 1979], 73).

[55]J. Ed Komoszewski, M. James Sawyer, and Daniel B. Wallace, *Reinventing Jesus: How Contemporary Skeptics Miss the Real Jesus and Mislead Popular Culture* (Grand Rapids: Kregel, 2006), 114 (emphasis added).

[56]This is found in an interview in the paperback edition of Ehrman, *Misquoting Jesus*, 252-53. He goes on to say that "most textual variants . . . have no bearing at all on what a passage means. But there are other textual variants . . . that are crucial to the meaning of a passage. And the theology of entire books of the New Testament are [*sic*] sometimes affected by the meaning of individual passages." He expands further on this in *Jesus, Interrupted*, 183-89.

[57]Fred Sanders, for example, writes that this text "should not be used as biblical support for Trinitarian theology, though it has some value as early Christian commentary on John's letter" (*The Triune God*, NSD [Grand Rapids: Zondervan, 2016], 164). For a richly detailed survey of the debate over 1 Jn 5:7, see McDonald, *Biblical Criticism in Early Modern Europe*.

question certainly addresses that doctrine. As for variants touching on
matters of Christian practice, we might mention the text-critical debates
over Romans 16:7 and 1 Corinthians 14:34-35 and the bearing they have for
some on the question of women's ordination.[58]

In light of such cases, we cannot claim without qualification that variants
never affect texts that touch on Christian doctrine or practice. Sometimes
they clearly do. Yet no one would claim that an issue such as the Trinity or
the ordination of women is hanging in the balance because of these disputed
texts. It would be better to say, then, that no Christian doctrine or practice—
major or minor—is *determined* by a textually difficult passage.

The reason for this will be obvious to anyone with even a basic
knowledge of Christian theology. That reason is that Christians do not
base their theology on a single verse here or there, let alone a single word
or two within them. Instead, theology at its best is built on a web of biblical evidence—that is to say, on the "whole counsel of God" (Acts 20:27).
As theologian John Frame notes in discussing the impact of textual
variants on theology, "Scripture is highly redundant, in a good way," such
that "the doctrines of the Christian faith are never derived from a single
text."[59] In this way, when one passage on the Trinity is suspect, many
others rush in to take its place. The thick web of theology is not destroyed
for lack of one strand that turns out not to be silk. In the case of 1 John 5:7,
for example, it is helpful to realize that the church's most important doctrinal statements of the Trinity, such as the Nicene Creed, were produced
completely without reference to this text for the simple reason that it did
not exist in Greek manuscripts when these statements were formulated.[60]
Richard Bentley noted exactly this point as far back as 1717, writing that if
1 John 5:7 is not original, then it follows that "Arianism in its Height was
beat down without the Help of that Verse: And let the *Fact* prove as it will,
the *Doctrine* [of the Trinity] is unshaken."[61]

---

[58]See, for example, Philip B. Payne, "Vaticanus Distigme-Obelos Symbols Marking Added Text,
Including 1 Corinthians 14.34-35," *NTS* 63, no. 4 (2017): 604-25; Eldon J. Epp, *Junia: The First
Woman Apostle* (Minneapolis: Fortress, 2005); David Shaw, "Is Junia Also Among the Apostles?
Romans 16:7 and Recent Debates," *Churchman* 1 (2013): 105-18.

[59]John M. Frame, *The Doctrine of the Word of God*, A Theology of Lordship 4 (Phillipsburg, NJ:
P&R, 2010), 248. Frame's whole chapter on the transmission of Scripture, from which this quote
is taken, is in my view the best treatment of the theological issues. See further 251-52.

[60]On this point see Komoszewski, Sawyer, and Wallace, *Reinventing Jesus*, 113-14.

[61]A letter to J. Craven on Jan. 1, 1717, quoted in McDonald, *Biblical Criticism in Early Modern
Europe*, 223.

Having said this, few if any would go on to claim that Jesus' prayer from the cross in Luke 23:34 has *no* effect whatsoever on our theology or practice. To be sure, it does not change the *fact* that Jesus teaches us to love our enemies (Mt 5:43-48) and to forgive them (see Mt 6:14-15; 18:21-35). But just as certainly it does have some effect on how we think about this truth, how we apply it, and how we teach it. Likewise, we may be content to say that the story of the woman caught in adultery (Jn 7:53–8:11) is not the only place where we see Jesus' mercy on full display or that the key elements in Mark 16:9-20 are recorded elsewhere, but would any go so far as to say that these texts have *no* effect on our teaching, preaching, or Christian living? The very fact that they continue to draw so much interest tells against such a conclusion. Clearly, then, they have *some* effect, even if it is small when put in perspective of the whole of Christian faith and practice.

CONCLUSION

In the final analysis, it is best to admit that, in relatively rare cases, variants really *do* have some bearing on some doctrines and ethical practices of the Christian faith, but none of these doctrines or ethical practices is *established* from these disputed texts. Nor are any of them in jeopardy because of these disputed texts. Mark 1:1 is a good example where the variant matters for how we read Mark's Gospel, but the Sonship of Jesus himself is not riding on this variation, not even in Mark. The same could be said of Jesus' ethical teaching on forgiveness with respect to Luke 23:34 and on his divinity in the case of John 1:18. Jesus clearly wants us to forgive our enemies in the New Testament, and he is just as clearly presented as divine with or without these important readings. Furthermore, as we saw in John 18, the vast majority of variants, upward of 99 percent, are awfully boring for most Bible readers, are easily resolved, or both. The exceptions, which do exist and should not be ignored, are nevertheless few and far between.

We are safe, then, to claim that neither the Christian faith nor the Bible's inspiration is threatened by textual variants. The words of Stephen Neill from a half-century ago remain true: "Indeed, I think it is no exaggeration to say that the very worst Greek manuscript now in existence . . . contains enough of the Gospel in unadulterated form to lead the reader into the way of salvation."[62] If the very *worst* manuscript can do this, then we are that

---

[62]Stephen Neill, *The Interpretation of the New Testament: 1861–1961*, The Firth Lectures, 1962 (London: Oxford University Press, 1964), 63-64.

much more secure in having New Testaments based on the very *best* of our Greek manuscripts.

It is true that our Bibles could change slightly in the future as more research sheds greater light or as methods of textual criticism change. It is also true that knotty and important textual decisions remain and we should not ignore these. Yet because of the overall fidelity of scribes over fifteen hundred years and because of the Herculean efforts of textual scholars for hundreds beyond that, we can sing the words of the eighteenth-century hymn:

How firm a foundation, ye saints of the Lord,
is laid for your faith in His excellent Word!
What more can He say than to you He hath said,
to you who for refuge to Jesus have fled?[63]

Key Takeaways

▶ The estimated number of variants in just our Greek manuscripts is around half a million, not including spelling differences. Nearly half of these are meaningless mistakes.

▶ Only a tiny fraction of the known variants are ever discussed by commentators. Fewer still deserve a footnote in a modern translation. In John 18, not one of the more than three thousand variants makes it into a footnote of the ESV, NIV, NRSV, or even the NET.

▶ It is true, then, that most variants do not affect the meaning of the text or the Christian faith in general. A few dozen do, however, and some of these are theologically important, as in Mark 1:1; Luke 23:34; and John 1:18.

▶ We should not give the impression that New Testament variants do not matter at all for Christian theology or practice; we can and should, however, recognize that no doctrine is in jeopardy because of a serious variant.

---

[63]It is unclear who wrote this hymn.

CHAPTER ELEVEN

MYTHS ABOUT
ORTHODOX CORRUPTION
WERE SCRIBES INFLUENCED BY THEOLOGY,
AND HOW CAN WE TELL?

Robert D. Marcello

WHEN DEALING WITH ANY DEBATED TOPIC, it is easy to discuss it in terms that favor a certain position. The same is true when it comes to the reliability of the text of the New Testament. Almost everyone who is critically engaged in the topic now has access through online and text resources to the same data. However, the packaging of that data often changes how one perceives the details. And the fact is, packaging matters. With the proliferation of interest in this topic, particularly among those not engaged in critical study, packaging matters even more. It matters because many misappropriate this information and draw conclusions that are unjustifiable given the evidence. One particular example of this is the area of scribal changes or corruptions of the text. A common saying is, "We can't trust the text of the New Testament, because scribes edited it." As Kurt Eichenwald puts it, "Scribes added whole sections of the New Testament, and removed words and sentences that contradicted emerging orthodox beliefs."[1]

Yes, scribes did introduce corruptions, or intentional changes of the text for theological reasons, into the manuscript tradition of the text. There is ample evidence to support that conclusion. However, what about the first part of that slogan? Is the corruption that we find in the New Testament manuscript tradition so pervasive that it renders the text untrustworthy?

---

[1]Kurt Eichenwald, "The Bible: So Misunderstood It's a Sin," *Newsweek*, January 2015, newsweek.com/2015/01/02/thats-not-what-bible-says-294018.html.

Are these corruptions that significant? These later implications are often a
part of the packaging of the data. If the data are presented in certain ways,
it is easy to draw such conclusions. At the same time, it is also easy for the
data to be dismissed by apologists who also have theological motivations to
tamper with the reality of the text's history. This chapter will investigate just
that issue by showing some real examples of theologically motivated textual
changes (or "orthodox corruptions") along with some not-so-real examples
of such corruptions. In working through these examples, hopefully one can
gain an accurate appreciation for the history of the text along with the ability
to articulate what is at stake in this discussion so that the packaging matches
the facts.

BACKGROUND TO THE QUESTION

When it comes to corruptions, one of the most significant commentators on
the topic was scholar F. J. A. Hort, who deals with the subject briefly in the
appendix of his classic work, coauthored with B. F. Westcott, *The New Testament in the Original Greek*. Here he states,

> It will not be out of place to add here a distinct expression of our belief that
> even among the numerous unquestionably spurious readings of the New Tes-
> tament there are no signs of deliberate falsification of the text for dogmatic
> purposes. The licence of paraphrase corruption, where scribes allowed them-
> selves to change language which they thought capable of dangerous miscon-
> struction; or attempted to correct apparent errors which they doubtless as-
> sumed to be due to previous transcription; or embodied in explicit words a
> meaning which they supposed to be implied . . . in a word, they bear witness
> to rashness, not to bad faith.[2]

The opinion that scribes did not change the text for dogmatic purposes, here
summarized by Hort, became a common perspective in determining textual
decisions within the New Testament.[3] Westcott and Hort's position became
even more important because of the publication of their Greek New Testament, which was a standard text and used widely by subsequent scholars.
However, Hort also clarifies, "It is true that dogmatic preferences to a great

---

[2]B. F. Westcott and F. J. A. Hort, *The New Testament in the Original Greek: Introduction, Appendix*
(London: Macmillan, 1881), 282-83.
[3]One such example is D. Bludau, *Die Schriftfälschungen der Häretiker: Ein Beitrag zur Textkritik
der Bibel*, NTAbh 11 (Münster: Aschendorff, 1925).

extent determined theologians, and probably scribes, in their choice between rival readings *already in existence.*[4] The distinction seems to be that scribes did not invent new readings for dogmatic purposes but may have been inclined to favor an already existing reading that corresponded with an orthodox interpretation of the text. While Hort did not see a role for intentional dogmatic changes, many others have seen that as a possible feature of transmission and argued against Hort's view in particular.[5]

It appears Hort's view on this issue was short-lived among specialists even though his text continued to be widely used. In fact, many scholars came to the conclusion that scribes did in fact alter the text for doctrinal purposes.[6] Even with this change in course, most scholars still come short of ascribing motive to the scribes—a key distinction. In fact, some go in the opposite direction and indicate a positive motive on the part of scribes. For example, Metzger comments on a specific change in his *Textual Commentary on the Greek New Testament*, saying that at times some changes were "introduced from a sense of reverence for the person of Jesus."[7] As such, the debate began a slow transition from the belief that scribes did not *invent* readings for dogmatic purposes to a growing body of evidence that indicates that scribes may have in fact done just that.

Kenneth W. Clark's comments on the concept of intentional corruption are significant here because he distinguishes between the scribes' actions and their intentions. Here he states,

> We can agree with Hort that "perceptible fraud" is not evident in textual alteration, that "accusations of wilful tampering . . . prove to be groundless," and

---

[4]Westcott and Hort, *Introduction, Appendix*, 283 (emphasis added).

[5]Frederick C. Conybeare, "Three Early Doctrinal Modifications upon the Text of the Gospels," HibJ 1, no. 1 (1902): 96-113; J. Rendel Harris, *Side-Lights on New Testament Research: Seven Lectures Delivered in 1908, at Regent's Park College, London* (London: Kingsgate Press; James Clarke, 1908), 29-35; Wilbert F. Howard, "The Influence of Doctrine upon the Text of the New Testament," *London Quarterly and Holborn Review* 6, no. 10 (1941): 1-16; Kirsopp Lake, *The Influence of Textual Criticism on the Exegesis of the New Testament* (Oxford: Parker and Son, 1904).

[6]J. Harold Greenlee, *Introduction to New Testament Textual Criticism* (Peabody, MA: Hendrickson, 1995), 60-61; Maurice Goguel, *Le Texte et Les Éditions Du Nouveau Testament Grec* (Paris: E. Leroux, 1920), 64-67; Kirsopp Lake, *The Text of the New Testament*, 6th ed., rev. by Silva New (London: Rivingtons, 1928), 6; D. Plooij, *Tendentieuse Varianten in den Text der Evangeliën* (Leiden: Brill, 1926); Léon Vaganay, *Initiation à la critique textuelle néotestamentaire* (Paris: Bloud & Gay, 1934), 53-54; C. S. C. Williams, *Alterations to the Text of the Synoptic Gospels and Acts* (Oxford: Blackwell, 1951), 5.

[7]Bruce M. Metzger, *A Textual Commentary on the Greek New Testament*, 2nd ed. (New York: United Bible Societies, 1994), 200. See his note on Jn 11:33.

that dogma has not motivated "deliberate falsification." But these are heinous faults such as we should never allege, and these are not the terms that we should employ. Willful and deliberate, yes. But not tampering, falsification, and fraud. Alteration, yes; but not corruption. Emendation, yes; but not in bad faith. These denials of evil or unethical intention can well be sustained, but such intention is not a proper allegation by the textual critic. He must analyze the text constructively to understand the theological value of any variation, and its place in historical theology.[8]

Clark indicates that the type of alteration found within the New Testament is not of a malicious nature, intended to invent a specific reading. While it is true that dogmatic preferences inclined scribes to prefer the textual option that they deemed most orthodox from among the available readings, the nature of that influence was not intended to create a knowingly false text but rather a good-faith clarification. Thus, Clark distinguished the falsification of readings from good-faith choices, thereby vindicating the scribes' motives for most scribal alterations.

Others have argued that there is indeed clear-cut dogmatic influence within the text, and it was intentional. Eldon Epp provided a thorough study of Codex Bezae in Acts. There he showed that in 40 percent of the variants there was "the unmistakable result—a clearly anti-Judaic tendency in the D-text of Acts."[9] More and more, the motivation of the scribe came into question, since now there were clear examples of a theological influence on textual alteration.[10] This changed the subsequent landscape of research into the text of the New Testament in general and scribal alterations in particular.[11] Bart Ehrman, in his landmark work *The Orthodox Corruption of*

[8]Kenneth W. Clark, "The Theological Relevance of Textual Variation in Current Criticism of the Greek New Testament," *JBL* 85, no. 1 (1966): 5.

[9]Eldon J. Epp, *The Theological Tendency of Codex Bezae Cantabrigensis in Acts*, SNTSMS 3 (Cambridge: Cambridge University Press, 1965), 171.

[10]Bruce M. Metzger and Bart D. Ehrman, *The Text of the New Testament: Its Transmission, Corruption, and Restoration*, 4th ed. (New York: Oxford University Press, 2005), 284: "The sensible inference is that the scribe himself, or his tradition, was anti-Jewish (in some sense) and that this prejudice came to be embodied in the transcription of the text."

[11]Alexander Globe, "Some Doctrinal Variants in Matthew 1 and Luke 2, and the Authority of the Neutral Text," *CBQ* 42, no. 1 (1980): 52-72; Bart D. Ehrman and Mark A. Plunkett, "The Angel and the Agony: The Textual Problem of Luke 22:43-44," *CBQ* 45, no. 3 (1983): 401-16; Peter M. Head, "Christology and Textual Transmission: Reverential Alterations in the Synoptic Gospels," *NovT* 35, no. 2 (1993): 105-29; Mikeal C. Parsons, "A Christological Tendency in P^{75}," *JBL* 105, no. 3 (1986): 463-79; Tommy Wasserman, "Papyrus 72 and the *Bodmer Miscellaneous Codex*," *NTS* 51, no. 1 (2005): 137-54; Wasserman, "Misquoting Manuscripts? The Orthodox Corruption

Scripture, took this issue head-on and then popularized much of the information in *Misquoting Jesus*.[12] In his study he presents four key christological issues of orthodoxy—antiadoptionistic corruptions, antiseparationist corruptions, antidocetic corruptions, and antipatripassianist corruptions. Through these categories, he demonstrates how theological controversies found their way into the transmission history of the text. He argues, "Scribes occasionally altered the words of their sacred texts to make them more patently orthodox and to prevent their misuse by Christians who espoused aberrant views."[13] Basing his argument on the thesis of Walter Bauer about early Christianity, which states that there were multiple forms of Christianity competing for what would later be considered orthodoxy, Ehrman situates the scribes within the same framework.[14] In so doing, he provided the first lengthy study of theologically motivated alterations and demonstrated that such alterations were a legitimate category for understanding the transmission of the text.

One voice providing further entry into this topic is Wayne Kannaday. He was a student of Ehrman and provides a study outlining pagan criticisms along with the rebuttals of early apologists. He then compares those with scribal alterations in early Christianity. Kannaday concludes, "In the course of defending their text, their faith, and their Lord against pagan assault the scribes engaged in what I have termed 'scribal apologetics.' In so doing, they repaired and renovated the Gospel handed down to them, making it to pagan readers and critics more palatable, on the one hand, and more resistant to challenge, on the other."[15] Kannaday's point is to demonstrate that scribes were agents in defending orthodoxy—not only those contemporary apologists.

---

of Scripture Revisited," in *The Making of Christianity: Conflicts, Contacts, and Constructions: Essays in Honor of Bengt Holmberg*, ed. M. Zetterholm and S. Byrskog, ConBNT 47 (Winona Lake, IN: Eisenbrauns, 2012), 325-50.

[12]Bart D. Ehrman, *The Orthodox Corruption of Scripture: The Effect of Early Christological Controversies on the Text of the New Testament*, 2nd ed. (Oxford: Oxford University Press, 2011); Bart D. Ehrman, *Misquoting Jesus: The Story Behind Who Changed the Bible and Why* (New York: HarperCollins, 2005).

[13]Ehrman, *Orthodox Corruption*, xi.

[14]Walter Bauer, *Rechtgläubigkeit und Ketzerei im ältesten Christentum* (Tübingen: Mohr Siebeck, 1934); Walter Bauer, *Orthodoxy and Heresy in Earliest Christianity*, ed. Robert A. Kraft and Gerhard Krodel (Philadelphia: Fortress, 1971).

[15]Wayne C. Kannaday, *Apologetic Discourse and the Scribal Tradition: Evidence of the Influence of Apologetic Interests on the Text of the Canonical Gospels*, TCSt 5 (Atlanta: Society of Biblical Literature, 2004), 139.

David C. Parker is another voice who has gone further in describing the scribal contributions to the text of the New Testament. Parker provided a provocative thesis when he stated, "There is no definitive text to be discovered."[16] By declaring that it would be a fruitless—even unattainable—enterprise to determine an early definitive text, he shifts the focus of the text-critical endeavor to an emphasis on scribal habits rather than the original text. In doing so, he focuses on explaining why scribes would come up with certain readings, since the text was not a fixed document but a "living" entity. As such, Parker removes the concept of an original text from the equation and indicates that scribes, within a theological community, produced variants, and all variants were products of their community. Thus, as he states elsewhere, the pursuit to find a "pure tradition" is unsuccessful, as both heretical and orthodox corruptions were introduced into the text.[17] The text critic's task ought to be understanding the scribes within their context over against the pursuit of an original text form.

All of these scholars have contributed to the conversation about theologically motivated corruptions in one form or another. They provide the foundation for understanding how the discussion has evolved and why certain claims about the reliability of the text are currently circulating. Equally important is a discussion of method. In order to have a robust understanding of the text's reliability, one must have a fair method that accounts for all the evidence in the manuscript tradition. The following section will address this issue specifically.

METHOD MATTERS

Ascertaining a motive for anyone's actions from their writing is difficult even when considering contemporary authors. Doing so for someone living in a time and place in history with unknown influences, unknown sources, and an often-unknown identity makes the task even bleaker. It is true that some have been able to offer helpful observations on a scribe's *tendency* throughout a manuscript.[18] However, at times there seems to be a general assumption

---

[16]David C. Parker, *The Living Text of the Gospels* (Cambridge: Cambridge University Press, 1997), 6.
[17]David C. Parker, "Textual Criticism and Theology," *ExpTim* 118, no. 12 (2007): 587.
[18]Epp, *Theological Tendency of Codex Bezae Cantabrigensis*; Juan Hernández Jr., *Scribal Habits and Theological Influences in the Apocalypse: The Singular Readings of Sinaiticus, Alexandrinus, and Ephraemi*, WUNT 2/218 (Tübingen: Mohr Siebeck, 2006); Wasserman, "Papyrus 72 and the Bodmer Miscellaneous Codex."

among scholars that scribes were well intentioned even in the midst of adopting a theological reading.[19] When apologetic intentions are declared, such claims are met with ample caution since those claims often are simply lacking in sufficient evidence for such a historical claim.[20] This is especially true when variant readings are read in isolation from the scribe's general tendency throughout an entire manuscript. Certainly, reconstructing the social context of a scribe becomes helpful since understanding contemporary debates provides a further window into the reason for a scribe's actions.

However, many questions arise out of such an endeavor. Did a reading arise because a scribe was influenced by apologetic purposes for orthodoxy *or* for heresy?[21] Without studying the scribe's actions throughout a manuscript, it is difficult at best to make a claim one way or the other.[22] Does the scribe consistently alter the manuscript or demonstrate any pattern of alteration? Is there a consistent theological tendency, or is the author picking data points to undergird a thesis?[23] The latter seems to be the case when it comes to Ehrman's method. One of the key weaknesses of his study is that his examples of scribal corruptions are often isolated from discussions about the manuscript in which they are contained. As Wallace notes regarding Ehrman's *Misquoting Jesus*, "First, there is next to no discussion about the various manuscripts. It is *almost* as if external evidence is a non-starter for Ehrman. Further, as much as he enlightens his lay readers about the discipline, the fact that he does not give them the details about which manuscripts are more trustworthy, older, and so on, allows him to control the

---

[19]For some examples, see Head, "Christology and Textual Transmission," 129; Metzger, *Textual Commentary*, 68.

[20]One example of such claims is Kannaday, *Apologetic Discourse and the Scribal Tradition*, 240. He states, "These readings attest to alterations of the canonical Gospels effected by copyists who, in their work of transmitting them, edited their exemplars with apologetic interests clearly and consciously in mind." Both Kim Haines-Eitzen and Jennifer Knust push back against this type of claim in their reviews of Kannaday's work, respectively, in Kim Haines-Eitzen, "Review of *Apologetic Discourse and the Scribal Tradition: Evidence of the Influence of Apologetic Interests on the Text of the Canonical Gospels*," *JBL* 124, no. 2 (2005): 383; Jennifer Wright Knust, "Review of *Apologetic Discourse and the Scribal Tradition: Evidence of the Influence of Apologetic Interests on the Text of the Canonical Gospels*," *JR* 86, no. 4 (2006): 672.

[21]Parker, "Textual Criticism and Theology," 587.

[22]Ulrich Schmid, "Scribes and Variants—Sociology and Typology," in *Textual Variation: Theological and Social Tendencies? Papers from the Fifth Birmingham Colloquium on the Textual Criticism of the New Testament*, ed. D. C. Parker and H. A. G. Houghton, TS, Third Series 3 (Piscataway, NJ: Gorgias, 2008), 8.

[23]Wasserman, "Misquoting Manuscripts?," 349.

information flow."[24] This pattern creates a false understanding of the scribal actions and raises doubts about Ehrman's conclusions in general.[25] One clear issue of method is that one must have a good understanding of the quality and nature of the manuscripts containing the alteration.

This leads to another methodological issue, which can often be seen as a basic element of Ehrman's *Orthodox Corruption*. Consistently, the least orthodox reading is thought to be original, and the orthodox reading is deemed the corruption.[26] While it may be the case that the orthodox reading was the corruption, using that assumption for one's method presupposes what the original text was, what the reading was in the manuscript's ancestor, that the scribe had intention to alter the text and implemented it, and many other factors. All of these dynamics are largely unknown in the majority of available manuscripts—resulting in a real lack of evidence to support such a premise. If one does not note the scribe's tendency throughout a witness, and if one consistently views the orthodox reading as the corruption, then the conclusions one is likely to draw are questionable. Again, this does not deny that there are real cases of dogmatic influences on the text; however, the issue here is one of method and how one is able to determine such influences. Accordingly, the implicit working notion—that the least orthodox reading is preferred—is flawed due to lack of historical evidence to support such a claim.[27]

Furthermore, a truism of textual criticism by Westcott and Hort, which has stood the test of time, is that "knowledge of documents should precede final judgment on readings."[28] Knowing the ancestor from which a manuscript was

---

[24]Daniel B. Wallace, "The Gospel According to Bart: A Review Article of *Misquoting Jesus* by Bart Ehrman," *JETS* 49, no. 2 (2006): 329-30.

[25]This is not to say that many of the individualized conclusions found within *Orthodox Corruption* are invalid or that the work in general does not provide a valuable contribution to the understanding of the textual transmission. In fact, Ehrman ought to be credited with opening wide the door to the discussion of orthodox corruption, and in doing so, he demonstrates that many past assumptions were overly simplistic. Nevertheless, by using such a methodology, some of his examples of corruption have been justly criticized (see Wallace, "Gospel According to Bart"; Wasserman, "Misquoting Manuscripts?").

[26]Adam G. Messer, "Patristic Theology and Recension in Matthew 24.36: An Evaluation of Ehrman's Text-Critical Methodology," in *Revisiting the Corruption of the New Testament: Manuscript, Patristic, and Apocryphal Evidence*, ed. Daniel B. Wallace, The Text and Canon of the New Testament (Grand Rapids: Kregel, 2011), 127-88; Wasserman, "Misquoting Manuscripts?," 349.

[27]Philip M. Miller, "The Least Orthodox Reading Is to Be Preferred: A New Canon for New Testament Textual Criticism," in Wallace, *Revisiting the Corruption*, 57-90; Wasserman, "Misquoting Manuscripts?," 349.

[28]Westcott and Hort, *Introduction, Appendix*, 31.

copied would, of course, tell us whether a variant was simply adopted from its exemplar or whether it was generated by the scribe.[29] Obviously, one is rarely privy to such information in the manuscript tradition; however, claims about dogmatic motivation at a point in history should be held to the same strict standard of historiography as other historical claims. This strict standard does not always seem to be followed consistently in discussions of scribal motivations or claims regarding corruption.[30] Knowing a scribe's source provides invaluable information for reconstructing part of the reason for a variant. Without such knowledge, in particular when we are missing other pieces of evidence, strong claims of probability are thereby weakened considerably. This is the reason that a robust method that takes into account a multitude of factors such as those discussed above is essential when claiming that a scribe corrupted the text.

While one must admit that there are specific examples of corruption within the manuscript tradition of the New Testament, the way scholars have determined whether a text is corrupt and the level of probability of that corruption is often overplayed. As one can see, certain data and methodological considerations must be taken into account to provide a more accurate picture of scribal activity. Without such data or when an investigation lacks such considerations, the results are also open to criticism. Ehrman, while not alone in his claims of corruption, provides an example of this type of investigation, since there are some weaknesses in his method. That he has popularized the concept and delivered it in a well-packaged book opens his work up to specific criticism, as it is the work with which most readers are familiar. Nevertheless, an honest discussion also acknowledges that, while his claims may be too broad and his methodology at times weak, the central thesis that there are indeed orthodox corruptions within the manuscript tradition remains true. Therefore, the following will examine both aspects of this—pointing out real and not-so-real examples of corruption.

EXAMPLES OF VARIOUS KINDS OF CORRUPTIONS

As has been said, there are good examples within the available manuscripts, and that reality has allowed certain scholars to find highly likely examples

---

[29]Wasserman, "Misquoting Manuscripts?," 350.
[30]Wasserman, "Misquoting Manuscripts?," 341.

of individual dogmatic changes. This section is not meant to provide an exhaustive list of examples but to demonstrate what textual corruptions look like and how they affect our understanding of the text. Also, while it is true that scribes changed the text of the New Testament for dogmatic reasons, the practice was not nearly as widespread or prevalent as some indicate. Therefore, it is important to look at some good examples that have been called corruptions but that have compelling counterexplanations.

Cases of real corruption and their significance. It is easy to dismiss a concept that makes theology messy or more difficult. If scribes corrupted and not merely preserved the text, then can anything really be trusted? Apologists, pastors, teachers, and academics may struggle with how to deal with this question, and in doing so, some have dismissed the concept of scribal corruptions prematurely and without all the evidence.[31] What follows are two examples of well-accepted corruptions within the manuscript tradition. They provide a window into the world of ancient scribes and show how they were motivated by theological influences and adjusted their texts accordingly.

Scribal corruption in Codex Bezae. One of the clear examples of dogmatic influence on the text of a manuscript comes from Eldon Epp's groundbreaking work on Codex Bezae. Within this work, Epp explains how what he calls the Western D-text of Acts is a prime sample to mine for theological tendency.[32] Furthermore, the study's method is good because it restrains itself to a single early manuscript—one that has long been known for its unique character and textual makeup of the so-called Western text.[33] One of the reasons Epp chose this text as a key one to mine for examples was the

---

[31]While admitting that theologically motivated alterations exist, McDowell dismisses them too easily based on the number of extant manuscripts and that single variants don't alter cardinal doctrines of the faith. Such alterations are not irrelevant based on either argument. Just because cardinal doctrines of Christianity are not affected by a single verse does not dismiss the fact that scribes at time changed the text of the New Testament for dogmatic reasons. See Josh McDowell and Sean McDowell, *Evidence That Demands a Verdict: Life-Changing Truth for a Skeptical World* (Nashville: Thomas Nelson, 2017), 66.

[32]Eldon J. Epp, "Text-Critical Witnesses and Methodology for Isolating a Distinctive D-Text in Acts," *NovT* 59, no. 3 (2017): 225-96.

[33]Epp, *Theological Tendency of Codex Bezae Cantabrigensis*, 7. Epp's study is considered a valuable contribution to our understanding of the theologically motivated changes within the text. Certainly, some take issue with various examples within the text; nevertheless, the work as a whole has been widely accepted as not only a valuable study but one that has opened doors to future research.

work of P. H. Menoud, who stressed that the Western text's emphasis is "the newness of the Christian faith as regards Judaism."[34]

Epp picks up on this and takes the variant tradition of the Western "D" text of Acts further than the "more notable variants" and also considers smaller variants "in an effort to determine whether or not they support the interests discerned in the larger and better-known D-readings." As noted, his conclusion is that 40 percent of the variants taken into consideration have an "anti-Judaic" bias. He clarifies what is meant by the term *anti-Judaic* by saying that it is used broadly to describe

> that religious complex out of which Christianity arose and contemporary with the earliest period of the new faith. . . . [It] involves the concept of Israel as the distinctive and exclusive people of God and also, at times, refers to the official religious system, including the regulations, customs, and institutions of both "Palestinian" and "Diaspora" Judaism, though cult does not largely figure into this study.

His study finds that these variants "reveal this tendency directly, are contributory to it, or at least comport with such a viewpoint."[35] Metzger notes, "Some of the evidence Epp adduces is certainly impressive. . . . [Acts] 2.23; 3.13-14; 13.28-29, involve more or less plain examples of variant readings in which the Jews' relationship to the condemnation of Jesus to death is more sharply described in the Bezan text, which places greater emphasis on the Jews' responsibility and on their hostile attitude toward him."[36]

These examples are just some of the numerous instances evaluated by Epp demonstrating this recurring theme. Here, not only do the variants seem to contain a specific bias but also considering (1) the amount of them, (2) the fact that both significant and insignificant variants function the same way, and (3) the universal nature of the bias throughout the manuscript, one is hard-pressed to argue that the scribe of Bezae does not have such a bias. This example is a clear illustration of a study demonstrating scribal corruption at work within a specific manuscript and by a specific scribe.

---

[34]P. H. Menoud, "The Western Text and the Theology of Acts," *Studiorum Novi Testamenti Societas*, Bulletin II (1951): 27.

[35]Epp, *Theological Tendency of Codex Bezae Cantabrigensis*, 23, 167-68.

[36]Bruce M. Metzger, "Review of *The Theological Tendency of Codex Bezae Cantabrigiensis in Acts* by Eldon Jay Epp," *Gn* 40, no. 8 (1968): 33.

P72 and theological tendencies. P72, or what has been referred to as the Bodmer Miscellaneous Codex because of its multiple seemingly unrelated works bound together in the same codex, is a late third- to-mid-fourth-century codex.[37] The codex has been discussed with regard to its theological tendencies and the significance of those tendencies in recent years.[38] These examinations have shown that there is good reason to view its variants as having a high Christology and stressing the divinity of Jesus. It seems that these changes also reflect some of the contemporaneous dialogue happening within proto-orthodox circles in regards to heretical claims. Therefore, not only do the variants consistently demonstrate a high Christology, and do so across books (Jude and 1–2 Pet), but they also do so right in line with what would be expected within their communities given the concurrent theological discussions.

One such example is a reading from 2 Peter 1:2, where the scribe omits the conjunction *and* (καί, *kai*) between "of God and Jesus our Lord" (τοῦ θεοῦ καὶ Ἰησοῦ τοῦ κυρίου ἡμῶν, *tou theou kai Iēsou tou kyriou hēmōn*). In doing so, the scribe creates a reading where the syntax now equates Jesus and God. Earlier in the codex, at 1 Peter 5:1, the scribe also substitutes the word *God* where every other manuscript except for one uses the word *Jesus*.[39] Such cases make it clear that the scribe of this manuscript is undoubtedly providing a high Christology. The combination of a scribe's tendency throughout an entire manuscript along with solid specific examples and ample social implications offer a clear illustration that models an effective method.

Cases of not-so-real corruption. While there are some clear examples of corruption, the practice is easily exaggerated when it comes to actually demonstrating instances of corruption. In what follows one can see two not-so-real examples illustrating various reasons to question the claim that they model theologically motivated corruptions.

---

[37]Wasserman, "Papyrus 72 and the *Bodmer Miscellaneous Codex*," 137.

[38]For multiple specific examples of variants that demonstrate these theological tendencies, see Wasserman, "Papyrus 72 and the *Bodmer Miscellaneous Codex*"; Tobias Nicklas and Tommy Wasserman, "Theologische Linien im Codex Bodmer Miscellani?," in *New Testament Manuscripts: Their Texts and Their World*, ed. Thomas J. Kraus (Leiden: Brill, 2006); David G. Horrell, "The Themes of 1 Peter: Insights from the Earliest Manuscripts (The Crosby-Schøyen Codex MS 193 and the Bodmer Miscellaneous Codex Containing P72)," *NTS* 55, no. 4 (2009): 502-22.

[39]Nicklas and Wasserman, "Theologische Linien im Codex Bodmer Miscellani?," 183-85.

Matthew 24:36 and the ignorance of the Son. One commonly cited example of orthodox corruption is the exclusion of the phrase "nor the Son" in Matthew 24:36 in a discussion on who knows the time of Jesus' return.[40] The inclusion of the phrase has been widely accepted as being original, due in large part to its being well attested in some of the earliest manuscripts.[41] Also, with the phrase removed there are grammatical issues, and some have argued that a scribe would be more likely to delete the phrase than to add it based on theological reasons.[42] A phrase that would seem to question the omniscience of Christ would obviously be suspect to a scribe. Some argue that this theological bias would have driven scribes to remove the phrase from the text, thereby eliminating the dilemma.

However, this raises significant questions regarding scribal motivations and actions. First, why would scribes remove the phrase "nor the Son" but leave the word "alone" in Matthew's text? The two cases functionally accomplish the same thing in regard to meaning.[43] If the Father *alone* knows the time of Christ's return, then tacitly the Son does not. Second, in almost all instances where the text is found in a manuscript containing both Matthew and Mark, Mark's text is left unaltered, whereas Matthew is missing the phrase. Why wouldn't the same scribe omit a christologically significant phrase from *both* Gospels if the purpose of the alteration were theological? Further, the longer reading suffers from grammatical and redactional issues as well.[44] These problems raise significant questions about the originality of the longer reading. Even if it were original, the assumption that the shorter reading was theologically motivated becomes suspect considering the presence of the phrase in Mark and the use of "alone" in the same verse. Wallace has demonstrated that it is most likely Matthew, not a later scribe,

---

[40]Metzger, *Textual Commentary*, 51-52; Ehrman, *Orthodox Corruption*, 108.

[41]01*, 03, 05, 038, 13, 28, 124, 346, 788, *f*[13], a, b, c, f, ff2, h, q.

[42]Metzger, *Textual Commentary*, 51-52; Ehrman, *Orthodox Corruption*, 107-8; Bart D. Ehrman, "Text and Transmission: The Historical Significance of the 'Altered' Text," in *Studies in the Textual Criticism of the New Testament*, NTTS 33 (Leiden: Brill, 2006), 333.

[43]Daniel B. Wallace, "The Son's Ignorance in Matthew 24.36: An Exercise in Textual and Redaction Criticism," in *Studies on the Text of the New Testament and Early Christianity: Essays in Honour of Michael W. Holmes*, ed. Daniel M. Gurtner, Juan Hernández Jr., and Paul Foster, NTTSD 50 (Leiden: Brill, 2015), 200. Wallace points out that grammatically Matthew's tendency is not to use a pair of conjunctions but rather only include a single "not even." He also demonstrates that Matthew has a clear tendency to preserve a higher Christology when dealing with passages parallel to Mark.

[44]Wallace, "Son's Ignorance in Matthew 24.36," 196, 199, 201-4.

who removed the phrase and added μόνος (*monos*, "only"), thereby soft-
ening the concept of the Son's ignorance. This follows the general pattern of
how Matthew uses Mark's Gospel.[45] The point is that this text, while pur-
ported to be a significant example of theologically motivated corruption,
does not marshal the support often attributed to it.

"God" or the "Son" in John's prologue? Another important text for this discussion is John 1:18. This text has been used to support the concept of a
theologically motivated corruption created to combat the belief that Jesus
was adopted as God's son at some point during his life, or what is referred
to as adoptionism.[46] Here the question revolves around which variant was
original—either μονογενὴς θεός (*monogenēs theos*, "the only God") or
μονογενὴς υἱός (*monogenēs huios*, "the only son").[47] In some witnesses, the
form of the text with θεός (*theos*, "God") also can be found with the article.[48]
Ehrman has argued that "the only Son" was original and that the alternate
variants were "created to support a high Christology in the face of widespread claims, found among adoptionists."[49] The debate on the original
reading largely boils down to the question of whether "God" or "Son" is the
correct reading. The inclusion of the article seems to be a scribal clarification
since the lack of the Greek article is a harder reading. The inclusion of the
article could have been due to a harmonization with other passages (Jn 3:16,
18), and the shorter reading has strong support.[50] Central to claims of corruption is the idea that the text was changed to support a specific theological
point of view.

However, reconstructing that social context is difficult at best with little
literature to support such claims. If one is going to claim that a scribe was
making an intentional change to combat a specific heresy in the early
church, then one must demonstrate the contemporary relevance of that
heresy within the cultural or theological dialogue of that specific scribe. Just
because a heresy existed at the time of writing, it does not mean a scribe
both had it in mind and was arguing against it. It is this point Benjamin

---

[45]Wallace, "Son's Ignorance in Matthew 24.36," 204.

[46]Ehrman, *Orthodox Corruption*, 96.

[47]μονογενὴς θεός (*monogenēs theos*, "the only God"): P66, 01*, 03, 04*, 019, sy^{p.hmg}, Or^{pt}, Did;
ὁ μονογενὴς υἱός (*ho monogenēs huios*, "the only son"): 02, 03³, 017, 036, 037, 038, 044, f^{1.13}, 565,
579, 700, 892, 1241, 1424, 𝔐, lat, sy^{c.h}, Cl^{pt}, Cl^{exThd. pt}.

[48]ὁ μονογενὴς θεός (*ho monogenēs theos*, "the only God"): P75, 01¹, 33, Cl^{pt}, Cl^{exThd pt}, Or^{pt}.

[49]Ehrman, *Orthodox Corruption*, 96.

[50]Wasserman, "Misquoting Manuscripts?," 343.

Burkholder's work addresses by demonstrating that the early church did not use this verse in the manner that Ehrman describes. Rather,

> It was employed to substantiate their notion that God was transcendent and the one in his bosom made the knowledge of God possible. When μονογενὴς θεός [*monogenēs theos*, "only God"] does become a litmus test for orthodoxy, it occurs at such a late date that it cannot aid in determining how the reading came into existence.

He further shows that the way in which the verse *was* used in early church writings would not entice a scribe to make an alteration to the text, thereby undercutting the claim for a theologically motivated corruption.[51]

Not only does this specific claim of corruption struggle on social-historical grounds, it also struggles to provide the best explanation of the internal evidence. One key issue here is a grammatical one. Ehrman argues that an insurmountable issue for the "the only God" reading is what it could mean in the first century. Particularly, he addresses the "entirely implausible" understanding that the adjective μονογενής (*monogenēs*, "only") is being used as a noun, which would produce the reading "the only one, himself God."[52] Nevertheless, this seemingly impossible situation is entirely possible for the New Testament writers. Wallace provides numerous examples of the very construction Ehrman claims does not happen. In doing so, the internal argument for μονογενὴς θεός (*monogenēs theos*, "only God") becomes stronger. This is particularly true when viewed in light of the fact that (1) μονογενής is used as a noun a few verses earlier (Jn 1:14) and (2) the reading "unique God" makes little sense in both the immediate content of the prologue—equating Jesus and the Father's divine status in John 1:1—and John's broader content in the Gospel.[53] Finally, John's return to referring to the Father from John 1:1 would form an *inclusio*, bracketing the prologue and providing focus for his readers.[54] All of these internal clues provide further

---

[51]Benjamin J. Burkholder, "Considering the Possibility of a Theological Corruption in Joh 1,18 in Light of Its Early Reception," *ZNW* 103, no. 1 (2012): 83, 67.

[52]Ehrman, *Orthodox Corruption*, 93, 95-96.

[53]Wallace, "Gospel According to Bart," 344-46 (see Jn 6:70; Rom 1:30; Gal 3:9; Eph 2:20; 1 Tim 1:9; 1 Pet 1:1; 2 Pet 2:5 for the construction in question).

[54]C. K. Barrett, *The Gospel According to St. John: An Introduction with Commentary and Notes on the Greek Text*, 2nd ed. (London: SPCK, 1978), 169; Craig S. Keener, *The Gospel of John: A Commentary* (Peabody, MA: Hendrickson, 2003), 1:425; contra Peter J. Williams, "Not the Prologue of John," *JSNT* 33, no. 4 (2011): 375-86, who argues that one should break up the beginning of John differently. Nevertheless, the internal continuity remains even if these verses belong to a different section within the text, since either way John's theological consistency is in support of the proposed reading.

support to the manuscript evidence that "the only God" is the reading that best explains the evidence. As such, the claim that this text is a good example of orthodox corruption is severely undercut.

CONCLUSION

The text of the New Testament does not come down to our generation without years of history. That history, like all of history, has aspects of corruption in it, which many would like to forget. When packaging this history and presenting it to interested audiences, we do them no service by denying or whitewashing these facts. Equally, by overblowing the significance of corruptions or the prevalence of the practice, we do no service either. The reality is that there are some clear instances of corruption within the text's history that can be determined with a responsible method. Also, there are instances where individuals have claimed that the text is corrupt when there is ample evidence to the contrary. These claims do not accurately reflect a text that, while it does have certain instances of corruption, has a history that is remarkably stable. The actual facts do not need to be whitewashed for claims of the text's reliability to stand. In fact, it is with a solid methodology that we are able to determine that corruptions *do* exist. If we can determine an intentional change has been made by some theologically motivated scribe, then we can conversely also determine what the text looked like *prior to* that change by evaluating the alternate readings.

We are not, then, left wondering whether such corruptions have happened everywhere; we can pinpoint where they did and why they arose. We are not left with a hopelessly corrupt text but a textual tradition that, while including corruptions, includes the genuine text. We need to be fair to the data and to our audiences by not creating a perception that the history of the text is unscathed. When such statements are easily debunked, the result is often to throw out the good with the bad. Likewise, by packaging the data as a hopeless enigma, we overstate the severity and pervasiveness of the theological influence within the manuscript tradition. Both extremes must be avoided, and those who are charged with packaging this data for audiences must be faithful to the facts.

While it is true that the text was sometimes changed for theological reasons, instances of this practice are few and far between. What is more important is that, by the same process that we are able to identify such changes, we are also able to identify the original text. While some packaging may make this task appear bleak, the reality is the ability to uncover the original text enables us to continue to trust the reliability of the text of the New Testament.

Key Takeaways

▶ Scribes did sometimes change the text for theologically motivated reasons; however, not a few textual variants that might appear to be theologically motivated are better explained by other factors.

▶ Determining the intention behind textual variants is much more difficult than some surmise. This means we should be appropriately skeptical about bold claims of theologically motivated variation or "orthodox corruption."

▶ The best approaches to determining when this happened are based on a knowledge of an entire manuscript and the context in which it was made, not simply on isolated occurrences from otherwise unrelated manuscripts.

CHAPTER TWELVE

MYTHS ABOUT PATRISTICS
WHAT THE CHURCH FATHERS THOUGHT ABOUT TEXTUAL VARIATION

Andrew Blaski

IN THEIR NOW-CLASSIC WORK *The Text of the New Testament*, Bruce Metzger and Bart Ehrman put forth the following proposition regarding the use of patristic scriptural quotations in the field of textual criticism:

> Besides the textual evidence derived from New Testament Greek manuscripts and from early versions, the textual critic has available the numerous scriptural quotations included in the commentaries, sermons, and other treatises written by early church fathers. Indeed, so extensive are these citations that if all other sources for our knowledge of the text of the New Testament were destroyed, they would be sufficient alone for the reconstruction of practically the entire New Testament.[1]

Of these two sentences, the first is certain, while the second is wholly ambiguous. What, after all, constitutes an "early" church father? What constitutes a "citation"? What does "practically" the entire New Testament entail? In recent decades, variations of this argument have made their way into countless Christian apologetic books aimed at defending the integrity of the New Testament text, but to what degree is the claim true? To what degree is it helpful? We will explore these questions and more in this chapter, ultimately exposing what has become one of the longest-standing myths in the field of text criticism.

---

[1]Bruce M. Metzger and Bart D. Ehrman, *The Text of the New Testament: Its Transmission, Corruption, and Restoration*, 4th ed. (New York: Oxford University Press, 2005), 126.

A MYTH OF EPIC PROPORTIONS: LORD DALRYMPLE
AND THE MISSING ELEVEN VERSES

Despite their statement's problems, Metzger and Ehrman have actually presented the tamer version of a much bolder and far more prevalent claim. To this we turn first. In the *Baker Encyclopedia of Christian Apologetics*, under the heading "New Testament Manuscripts," Norman Geisler states, "If we compile the 36,289 quotations by the early church fathers of the second to fourth centuries, we can reconstruct the entire New Testament minus 11 verses."[2] Contrary to the ambiguity we saw above, it is precisely the specificity of this claim that lends it its apparent validity. But where did the claim originate? Geisler was not the first to employ it, nor was he the last. The greatest challenge in assessing its veracity is therefore locating its source. It can be found in a multitude of popular-level apologetic volumes, but if one is fortunate enough to find an accompanying citation at all, the citation will lead typically to yet another popular-level apologetic putting forth the same unsubstantiated declaration.[3] There appears to be no hard data whatsoever. Yet the claim has become so widely accepted and so frequently employed by apologists in recent decades that very few have ever stopped to ask the obvious question: Is it true?

Perpetuating the problem is the peripheral nature of the claim. Rarely, if ever, has it been used as a central argument for establishing the trustworthiness of the New Testament text. Rather, apologists consistently employ it as a kind of add-on argument, as if to say, "Even if these other impressive arguments don't convince you, we could also reconstruct the entire New Testament text (minus eleven verses) from patristic quotations alone." Perhaps for this reason above all the claim has gone unchecked over

---

[2]Norman L. Geisler, "New Testament Manuscripts," in *The Baker Encyclopedia of Apologetics*, ed. Norman L. Geisler (Grand Rapids: Baker, 1999), 532.

[3]For a very small sampling, see Dan Story, *Defending Your Faith: Reliable Answers for a New Generation of Seekers and Skeptics* (Grand Rapids: Kregel, 1997), 38-39; Pamela Ewan, *Faith on Trial: An Attorney Analyzes the Evidence for the Death and Resurrection of Jesus* (Nashville: Broadman & Holman, 1999), 31; Norman L. Geisler and Ravi Zacharias, *Who Made God? And Answers to over 100 Other Tough Questions of Faith* (Grand Rapids: Zondervan, 2003), 146; Judson Polling, *How Reliable Is the Bible?* (Grand Rapids: Zondervan, 2003), 54; Chad Meister, *Building Belief: Constructing Faith from the Ground Up* (Grand Rapids: Baker, 2006), 147; Dean Hardy, *Stand Your Ground: An Introductory Text for Apologetics Students* (Eugene, OR: Wipf & Stock, 2007), 133; Michael Sherrard, *Relational Apologetics: Defending the Christian Faith with Holiness, Respect, and Truth* (Brooks, GA: Hill Harrow Books, 2012), 127; George Seber, *Can We Believe It? Evidence for Christianity* (Eugene, OR: Wipf & Stock, 2015), 157.

the years. It tends to serve as more of a buffer for other, better arguments than as a key argument in its own right. Where *did* the claim originate, then? The story is a fascinating one and is itself a prime example of how easy it is to misconstrue or misremember a person's words or deeds over time.

In 1841 Scottish author Robert Philip published a book titled *The Life, Times, and Missionary Enterprises of the Rev. John Campbell,* which, as suggested, narrates the life of John Campbell (1766–1840), a prominent Scottish philanthropist and missionary to South Africa. In his book Philip includes a number of lengthy and detailed quotations from Campbell's personal journals and correspondences, giving it an overall autobiographical quality and a wealth of firsthand accounts. The importance of this lies in the fact that one of the many journal entries reveals the origins of our "myth." In a section titled "Anecdote of Lord Hailes," Campbell narrates an event that, in Philip's words, "had much influence in satisfying [Campbell's] own mind upon the perfection of the New Testament."[4] It is worth reading in full:

I remember distinctly an interesting anecdote referring to the late Sir David Dalrymple, (better known to literary men abroad by his title of Lord Hailes,) a Scotch judge. I had it from the late Rev. Walter Buchanan, one of the ministers of Edinburgh. I took such interest in it, that though it must be about fifty years since he told it, I think I can almost relate it in Mr. Buchanan's words:

"I was dining some time ago with a literary party at old Mr. Abercrombie's, (father of General Abercrombie who was slain in Egypt, at the head of the British army), and spending the evening together. A gentleman present put a question, which puzzled the whole company. It was this: 'Supposing all the New Testaments in the world had been destroyed at the end of the third century, could their contents have been recovered from the writings of the first three centuries?' The question was novel to all, and no one even hazarded a guess in answer to the inquiry.

"About two months after this meeting, I received a note from Lord Hailes, inviting me to breakfast with him next morning. He had been of the party. During breakfast he asked me, if I recollected the curious question about the possibility of recovering the contents of the New Testament from the writings of the three first centuries? 'I remember it well, and have thought of it often without being able to form any opinion or conjecture on the subject.'

[4]Robert Philip, *The Life, Times, and Missionary Enterprises of the Rev. John Campbell* (London: John Snow, 1841), 215.

"'Well,' said Lord Hailes, 'that question quite accorded with the turn or taste of my antiquarian mind. On returning home, as I knew I had all the writers of those centuries, I began immediately to collect them, that I might set to work on the arduous task as soon as possible.' Pointing to a table covered with papers, he said, 'There have I been busy for these two months, searching for chapters, half chapters, and sentences of the New Testament, and have marked down what I have found, and where I have found it; so that any person may examine and see for themselves. I have actually discovered the whole New Testament from those writings, except seven or eleven verses (I forget which), which satisfies me that I could discover them also. Now,' said he, 'here was a way in which God concealed, or hid the treasures of this world, that Julian, the apostate emperor, and other enemies of Christ who wished to extirpate the gospel from the world, never would have thought of; and though they had, they never could have effected their destruction.'

"The labor in effecting this feat must have been immense; for the gospels and epistles would not be divided into chapters and verses as they are now. Much must have been effected by the help of a concordance. And having been a judge for many years, a habit of minute investigation must have been formed in his mind."[5]

Here we have the origin of our myth, and quite a myth it is. By Campbell's own account, Lord Dalrymple, a local judge engaging in a bit of amateur biblical research, communicated the results of that research to Walter Buchanan over breakfast, who then (sometime later) passed on a version of those results to John Campbell, who proceeded to record them in his journal fifty years after the fact. This is, of course, not to mention that the journal entry itself comes to us via Robert Philip's book (yet another degree of separation). Remarkably, Campbell is not even certain about the number of "missing" verses (seven or eleven)—one of two critical pieces of information that have successfully made their way into modern apologetic texts.

As for the other, is it true that there are exactly 36,289 quotations of the New Testament in the works of the second- to fourth-century fathers? This number, it seems, did not originate with Dalrymple but rather from the work of another nineteenth-century figure: John William Burgon, dean of Chichester Cathedral. In a quest not altogether different than Dalrymple's own, Burgon created a sixteen-volume index of patristic biblical quotations taken

---

[5]Philip, *Life, Times, and Missionary Enterprises of the Rev. John Campbell*, 215-16.

from Christianity's first three to four centuries, which is now held in the British Museum. Though the work has not been published, Frederic Kenyon included the numerical results of Burgon's study in his own *Handbook to the Textual Criticism of the New Testament*. Taken together, the number of quotations he separately lists for Justin Martyr, Irenaeus, Clement of Alexandria, Origen, Tertullian, Hippolytus, and Eusebius add up to exactly 36,289 (hence the very specific number).[6] However, Kenyon himself is highly critical of Burgon, noting that the editions Burgon relies on are "comparatively uncritical texts of the Fathers."[7] Indeed, the majority of editions at that time were reliant on a few comparatively late manuscripts.

The claim, then, appears to be a conflation of two unsubstantiated, unpublished nineteenth-century studies, and yet it has appeared in literally dozens of *current* apologetic texts, with even the most basic questions left unanswered: Which editions of the fathers were these men using? Which edition of the New Testament? How did they define a quotation? Why did they focus on those particular writers and not others? Where can I find the original studies? Still, what is perhaps most striking about this myth, or rather the prevalence of this myth, is that it stands in direct opposition to what biblical scholars have long known and taught regarding the attestation (or lack thereof) of entire *books* of the New Testament in the first two to three centuries of Christianity's growth. The epistle of James is a prime example. James was rarely cited in the earliest centuries, was not included in the famous Muratorian Canon (second to third century), and was even listed as a "disputed" book by Eusebius of Caesarea as late as the mid-fourth century (*Hist. eccl.* 3.25.1-6). This was due in part to its apparent lack of influence in the Christian literature of the time. Though there is evidence that it inspired portions of the Shepherd of Hermas, it is not until the third century that we find *any* direct quotations.[8] Yet the claim that the entirety of the New Testament can be reconstructed from the writings of this period alone (minus eleven verses) still circulates with regularity.

As far back as 1905, a committee of the Oxford Society of Historical Theology set out to "prepare a volume exhibiting those passages of early Christian

---

[6]Frederic G. Kenyon, *Handbook to the Textual Criticism of the New Testament* (London: Macmillan, 1901), 224.
[7]Kenyon, *Handbook to the Textual Criticism*, 206.
[8]See Pseudo-Clementine, *Two Epistles Concerning Virginity* 1.11.4.

writers which indicate, or have been thought to indicate, acquaintance with any of the books of the New Testament."[9] The committee limited its search to the authors sometimes called the "Apostolic Fathers" (a loosely given title generally signifying the second generation of Christian writers after the apostles), and employed a four-tiered grading system of A, B, C, and D to indicate the degree of probability that an author was citing or even referring to a New Testament text. Between the twenty-seven books of the New Testament and the eight works chosen by the committee (the Epistle of Barnabas, the "two ways" portion of the Didache, the remainder of the Didache, 1 Clement, 2 Clement, the letters of Ignatius, the writings of Polycarp, and the Shepherd of Hermas), there were 216 points of possible overlap. The results were telling. Out of those 216 possibilities, less than 3 percent were given an A rating, indicating certain knowledge of a New Testament book. Conversely, more than 60 percent of the possible points of overlap received no rating, indicating no (visible) knowledge whatsoever.[10] The point is not that these writers must have been unaware of any works they did not explicitly mention but rather that it is often highly difficult to *positively* prove that they were aware (making Campbell's anecdote all the more impossible).[11]

---

[9]Oxford Society of Historical Theology, *The New Testament in the Apostolic Fathers* (Oxford: Clarendon, 1905), iii.

[10]Oxford Society of Historical Theology, *New Testament in the Apostolic Fathers*, 137. These conclusions are not meant to be final. Ranking systems such as this one are by nature subjective, which the committee itself readily admits. It should also be noted that in 2005, Oxford University Press published another study intended "to update, to develop, and to widen the scope" of the issues treated by the 1905 committee. See Andrew F. Gregory and Christopher M. Tuckett, eds., *The Reception of the New Testament in the Apostolic Fathers* (Oxford: Oxford University Press, 2005), v. In the words of the editors, "Some of these studies reach conclusions not dissimilar to those of the Oxford Committee . . . whereas others find more . . . or less evidence for the use of the New Testament in the Apostolic Father whom they discuss than did the authors of the corresponding discussion in 1905" (2).

[11]Granted, the majority of biblical quotations in the first three centuries come well after the apostolic fathers. For example, the book of James (discussed above) actually has a good deal of attestation in the latter part of the third century. Yet even a cursory glance at a modern index of patristic biblical citations will reveal that "eleven verses" is far too low a number for the entirety of the New Testament. For an accessible, up-to-date, and reliable index of patristic biblical quotations (both Eastern and Western), we can look to the Biblindex Project (www.biblindex .mom.fr). Originally published as the seven-volume Biblia Patristica series, the project now exists as a free searchable online database, supported by Sources Chrétiennes. The index contains not only direct citations but also biblical adaptations and allusions from Christianity's earliest centuries (eventually expanding into the early Middle Ages). If, then, we search for all patristic references (including adaptations and allusions) to the book of James up to the year 300, Biblindex still shows a total of *forty-seven* missing verses (out of 108 total).

Christian apologists must remember that perpetuating baseless claims such as the one above will ultimately only provide their critics with additional ammunition. In 2006, for example, an Islamic apologetic organization known as Islamic Awareness took it on themselves to get to the bottom of Campbell's anecdote. Not surprisingly, they found hard evidence that the claim had become greatly exaggerated throughout the course of its transmission. Beginning with the assumption that Dalrymple had indeed recorded the results of his research (as suggested by Campbell), they discovered that a multitude of Dalrymple's unpublished papers were being held at the National Library of Scotland. Among those papers, they found catalogued thirteen notebooks on the Greek New Testament, as well as a number of loose-leaf folios, which collectively serve to reveal the exact timing and extent of Dalrymple's work. What they ultimately uncovered was evidence of a study that spanned a time period of about four years (1780–1784), consisting of at least four different attempts (in three collations) to discover which portions of the New Testament could be reconstructed using only the patristic writings of the first three centuries. Each attempt appears to draw from different sources (with some overlap), to contain different emphases, and in some cases to examine different books of the New Testament. Presumably, Dalrymple intended eventually to synthesize the totality of his results into a single work worthy of publication, but this synthesis never came to fruition.

A number of these findings stand in contrast to Campbell's report, including the timespan of Dalrymple's work (four years rather than two months), but chief among them is the number of "missing verses." After methodically charting the number and percentage of missing verses in each of Dalrymple's efforts (available for viewing online), members of Islamic Awareness came to the conclusion, "Even if we admit the best-case scenario of the least number of missing verses in each of the books of the New Testament as seen in the three collations, we obtain 4336 verses (~54%) absent in the Patristic citations of the New Testament."[12]

---

[12]"Sir David Dalrymple (Lord Hailes), the Patristic Citations of the Ante-Nicene Church Fathers and the Search for Eleven Missing Verses of the New Testament," *Islamic Awareness*, May 2007, www.islamic-awareness.org/Bible/Text/citations.html. This article includes a much lengthier and much more detailed analysis of Campbell's anecdote, including charts and photographs of his original work. It also analyzes the edition of the Greek New Testament Dalrymple used as his standard, itself an important and problematic element of his research.

Regardless of the accuracy of their numbers, these apologists knew that the "eleven missing verses" claim had no basis in reality (and they showed it). The irony in what they found, of course, is palpable. In transmitting Dalrymple's claim that the original wording of the New Testament is partially attainable through patristic quotations, Campbell ended up altering the original wording of the claim itself. It seems we can put this form of our myth to rest.

QUALIFYING THE ARGUMENT

What, then, if the argument is modified, or better defined? Daniel Wallace, for example, has made claims similar to those above but adds that the patristic quotations at our disposal "date as early as the first century and continue through the *thirteenth* century."[13] At first glance, this seems far more promising. Surely, adding a full millennium of Christian writings onto the question posed to Lord Dalrymple helps its overall cause. However, Wallace's more realistic argument demands an additional inquiry: If the title of "ancient church father" can be applied to writers living as late as Thomas Aquinas (ca. 1225–1274), what meaning or importance does the argument even retain? Surely, the only reason the claim was ever compelling was that the writings of the earliest fathers were composed within a few generations of the apostles themselves and that they were contemporaneous with some of the earliest extant New Testament manuscripts.[14] Indeed, more time elapsed between Jesus and Thomas Aquinas than between Thomas Aquinas and Daniel Wallace. While Wallace's argument is therefore more realistic, it is simultaneously less valuable. Herein lies the fundamental problem with the argument as a whole, whether as expressed by Metzger, Wallace, or anyone else. As soon as we begin to give actual content to the terms of the argument, such as "early," "church fathers," "practically," or even "quotations," the argument ceases to function.

The word *quotations* is a prime example. Textual critics must be able to recognize a quotation *as* a quotation in order to make use of it. How, then, is a quotation defined? One of the more traditional methods has been to divide patristic scriptural references into one of three categories: *citations*

---

[13]Lee Strobel, *The Case for the Real Jesus: A Journalist Investigates Current Attacks on the Identity of Christ* (Grand Rapids: Zondervan, 2007), 83 (emphasis added).

[14]Of course, Wallace would be correct to state that Christian writings as late as the thirteenth century can be *helpful* in the field of New Testament textual criticism. The argument loses its punch, however, when speaking about *total* New Testament reconstruction.

(direct quotations, perhaps with a very small degree of variation), *adaptations* (significantly modified scriptural references), and *allusions* (references containing only reminiscences of the original wording). As an example, we can look to Origen of Alexandria (ca. 185–254) and his famous *Commentary on the Gospel of John*. In the course of that work, Origen refers to John 14:9 ("He who has seen me has seen the Father") multiple times, and in more than one context. The following are three examples:

> It is through this mirror that Paul and Peter and their contemporaries see God, because [the Savior] says, "He who has seen me has seen the Father who sent me." (13.153)

> And perhaps because they saw the image of the invisible God, since he who has seen the Son has seen the Father, they have been recorded to have seen God and to have heard him, in that they have perceived God and heard God's words in a manner worthy of God. (6.19)

> On the one hand, insofar as he who has seen the Son has seen the Father who sent him, one sees the Father in the Son. (20.47)[15]

In their analysis of these passages, Bart Ehrman, Gordon Fee, and Michael Holmes have determined that the first example is a citation, the second is an adaptation, and the third is an allusion.[16] But how? The only way for them to be certain (aside from instances in which the writer explicitly states that he is quoting from a manuscript) is to *compare* these references to what is found in the manuscript tradition. Of course, scholars may disagree with Ehrman, Fee, and Holmes over the definition of a quotation, or over the number of possible categories (some include categories such as *locution*, or even *lemma*), but by necessity, any method of identification must rely at least in part on comparison.[17] As the editors of the *Editio Critica Maior* recognize,

---

[15]Ronald Heine, trans., *Origen: Commentary on the Gospel of John*, 2 vols., FC 80, 89 (Washington, DC: Catholic University of America Press, 1989, 1993).

[16]Bart D. Ehrman, Gordon D. Fee, and Michael W. Holmes, *The Text of the Fourth Gospel in the Writings of Origen*, SBLNTGF 3 (Atlanta: Society of Biblical Literature, 1992), 1:299. The New Testament in the Greek Fathers series is one of the most important tools in the ongoing effort to reconstruct early New Testament texts through the writings of the fathers. Each volume attempts to construct a particular Greek father's known New Testament text (or portions of it), along with scholarly commentary and analysis.

[17]A lemma is the scriptural passage that appears as the text or object of a patristic commentary. See Carroll D. Osburn, "Methodology in Identifying Patristic Citations in NT Textual Criticism," *NovT* 47, no. 4 (2005): 313-43.

"A true quotation is one where the wording of the Father's text is identical with a reading found in the manuscript tradition."[18] If, then, we were to attempt a reconstruction of the entire New Testament using only the scriptural "quotations" of the church fathers, we would first have to determine which of those quotations are in fact actual quotations, or citations, rather than adaptations, allusions, or other types of references.[19] Doing so requires a trustworthy point of comparison, and so the original argument falls flat once more. A line is judged to be crooked because it fails to conform to a straight line. Similarly, the chief way to determine that a scriptural quotation *is* a quotation (or not) is to compare it to the New Testament manuscripts we already possess.

We can see that, on further reflection, each of the terms of the original argument breaks down. However, we may wish to ask one further question: *Why* are there so many inexact quotations and references in the writings of the Fathers? Why is it so difficult to identify an actual quotation? Certainly, faulty memory and a scarcity of accessible manuscripts played an enormous role, but is there more to it than that? As we shall see, there are certain fundamental differences between modern Christian perceptions of the New Testament (and its interpretation) and the perceptions held by some of the early Christian writers mentioned above. Those differences affect the very

---

[18]Barbara Aland et al., eds., *Novum Testamentum Graecum, Editio Critica Maior: IV/1. Die Katholischen Briefe, Text* (Stuttgart: Deutsche Bibelgesellschaft, 1997), 13*. It is notable that in the above passages, from Origen's *Commentary on John*, the "citation" does not actually conform exactly to the text of Jn 14:9. Rather, Origen seems to conflate Jn 14:9 ("He who has seen me has seen the Father") with Jn 12:45 ("he who sees me sees him who sent me"). Yet the example is still considered a "citation" because Origen consistently quotes it in this manner (see *Contra Celsum* 7.43; *Homiliae in Lucam* 1.4). Indeed, it seems this was the form he knew (whether through mental conflation or an actual variant).

[19]Of course, even this can prove difficult. Before relying on a patristic quotation with any sense of confidence, the textual critic must ask a series of fundamental questions that are often quite difficult to answer: Was the patristic text itself copied accurately over the centuries? If it was translated, was it translated properly? Did a later copyist "correct" the scriptural citation in question to better reflect the form of the text known in his own time? Did a *theological* opponent—or ally—intentionally alter the patristic text in order to harm or preserve the author's reputation? If they point out a textual variant, is it because they examined the manuscript evidence themselves or because they were passing on something they learned from another author? Did they change locations at any point in their lifetime, and if so, do we know in which setting the quotation in question was written? Was the patristic text even written by the listed author, or did someone simply use that author's name in order to grant legitimacy to his/her own work? Given the right resources, these questions can often be answered with a certain degree of confidence, but questions such as these make the overall use of patristic quotations in textual criticism something of a risk.

manner in which the church fathers quoted Scripture and therefore equally affect our ability to make use of their quotations.

A PATRISTIC THEOLOGY OF QUOTATIONS

Among the major conceptual differences between early and modern Christians is the very notion of a concrete and precisely defined "something" called "the New Testament."[20] This is not to say that patristic writers did not recognize the existence of authoritative apostolic texts or that they did not perceive these authoritative texts to be "Scripture" or "canonical" from a very early date.[21] Rather, in Christianity's earliest centuries, the New Testament did not exist as a set of twenty-seven authoritative books in a definitively closed *list*. There was a certain fluidity, even within the boundaries Christians increasingly came to recognize. On the face of it, this may not seem relevant to the way in which an early Christian writer would cite Scripture, but contrasted with today's norms (especially among evangelical Protestants), the relevance soon becomes clear.

When a canon is closed, particularly in a religious context, the totality of texts within that canon can eventually come to be regarded as *itself* the object of contemplation. The impact of this process differs from tradition to tradition, but a closed canon by definition engenders a greater mental divide

---

[20]For the sake of brevity, I must paint in very broad strokes. Early Christian theology and exegetical practice was highly diverse, involving multiple eras, geographical regions, controversies, traditions, and individuals. However, in contrast to modern practices (themselves highly diverse), the distinguishing features and commonalities of this period do make themselves known. Though I will outline elements of those features in what follows, nothing should be taken as universal. For accessible treatments of early Christian exegetical practice (as well as early Christian theologies of Scripture), see James Kugel and Rowan Greer, *Early Biblical Interpretation*, LEC 3 (Philadelphia: Westminster, 1986); Manlio Simonetti, *Biblical Interpretation in the Early Church: An Historical Introduction to Patristic Exegesis*, trans. John Hughes (Edinburgh: T&T Clark, 1994); Frances Young, *Biblical Exegesis and the Formation of Christian Culture* (Cambridge: Cambridge University Press, 1997); John O'Keefe and R. R. Reno, *Sanctified Vision: An Introduction to Early Christian Interpretation of the Bible* (Baltimore: Johns Hopkins University Press, 2005); Hans Boersma, *Scripture as Real Presence: Sacramental Exegesis in the Early Church* (Grand Rapids: Baker, 2017).

[21]The writings of Paul are referred to as "scripture" even within the books of the New Testament (2 Pet 3:15-16). By the end of the first century and the beginning of the second, writers such as Clement of Rome, Ignatius of Antioch, and Polycarp of Smyrna were alluding to and loosely quoting some of the Gospels and Pauline epistles as authoritative. In the late second century, Irenaeus of Lyons famously declared that there could be no more and no fewer than four Gospels, just as there are only four corners of the earth and four winds (*Haer.* 3.11.8). And Tertullian, a contemporary of Irenaeus, was already using the designation "New Testament" nearly two hundred years before the canon had "closed" (*Against Praxeas* 15). Yet, as we shall see, patristic perceptions of this "new" Testament were not identical to certain modern perceptions.

between oneself and the canonical texts. The canonical texts become equivalent to the whole of the truth rather than the authoritative set of lenses through which one enters into a larger truth. As a result, one often ceases the attempt to carry on in the same tradition as the authoritative books, or to use those books as authoritative tools, and begins instead to seek out ways to penetrate the *barrier* between oneself and the canonized books, whether historical, geographical, cultural, or linguistic.[22]

The point, simply, is this: for Christianity's earliest thinkers, the mental divide between text and interpreter was not as great as it tends to be today, which (as we shall see) allowed those thinkers to be more free and even playful with the text itself. Such things cannot be reduced purely to the "closing" of the canon, but because many early Christians lacked a totality *of* authoritative words, the object of Christian contemplation in the earliest centuries tended to be Christ *the* authoritative Word.[23] He is clothed in language but not bound by it. Though stated in overly simplistic terms, this distinction between text and person is arguably visible even within the pages of the New Testament. John Behr, a prominent patristics scholar, puts it this way:

> Thus, in the material which comes to be collected together as the canonical New Testament, reflection on Christ is an exegetical enterprise. But, it is very important to note that it is Christ who is being explained through the medium of Scripture, not Scripture itself that is being exegeted: the object is not to understand the "original meaning" of an ancient text, as in modern historical-critical scholarship, but to understand Christ himself, who, by being explained "according to the Scriptures" becomes the sole subject of Scripture throughout—he is the Word of God.[24]

---

[22]For many of the Fathers, the writings of the New Testament were authoritative, and indeed "canonical," not because they provided the final and complete word on all points of Christian practice and belief (as the later controversies and councils would demonstrate) but because they provided the final word on the interpretive method and lens by which to rightly reflect on *the* Word of God, who is Christ. Of course, this mindset did not suddenly disappear after the fourth century. There is a sense in which it was not fully challenged until the beginnings of the Protestant Reformation, when it became necessary for those involved to point to an *unchanging* and *complete* source of truth distinctive from the church.

[23]It is important also to keep in mind that many of the Fathers were breathing the same cultural, linguistic, and philosophical air as the apostles. As inhabitants of the twenty-first century, we simply do not breathe that same air, and as a result we approach the text differently. I have chosen here to focus on the issue of the closed canon, however, because it is so central to the way in which evangelicals in particular view and defend the New Testament, and because it is necessary to discuss what "the New Testament" *was* in this period if we intend to "reconstruct it" using the writings of that same period.

[24]John Behr, "The Paschal Foundations of Christian Theology," *SVTQ* 45, no. 2 (2001): 123.

Regardless of the accuracy of Behr's statement (no doubt many biblical scholars would object), this is an accurate depiction of what the *Fathers* perceived in the apostolic writings. The object of interpretation is Christ *the* Word, and all other words conform themselves to him, thereby serving to reveal him. When the Fathers encountered Paul, for example, they tended not to see a man concerned with demonstrating the "original intent of the author" or even the "exact words" of the author. Rather, they saw a man perfectly comfortable conforming biblical passages, and indeed entire biblical narratives, to the christological tradition he had received. It is Paul, after all, who teaches that the story of Sarah and Hagar is an "allegory" (Gal 4:24) of the two covenants, corresponding to the "children of slavery" (Gal 4:25) and the "children of promise" (Gal 4:28). It is Paul who teaches that Christ is the true "paschal lamb" (1 Cor 5:7) and that Adam was a "type of the one who was to come" (Rom 5:14). It is Paul who states that the rock from which the Israelites drank in the desert "was Christ" (1 Cor 10:4) and that the marital union of husband and wife "refers to Christ and the church" (Eph 5:32).

The examples go on, and though the degree to which one finds such figural readings varies from book to book (and though modern interpreters would no doubt explain each of those passages differently), the Fathers saw in these passages an underlying interpretive principle that is no less present in the Gospels and the other apostolic writings. In John 5:39, Jesus is recorded as saying, "You search the Scriptures because you think that in them you have eternal life; and it is they that bear witness about me" (ESV). Then, in Luke's account, he appears to apply this principle personally with two of his disciples on the road to Emmaus, where, "Beginning with Moses and all the Prophets, he interpreted to them in all the Scriptures the things concerning himself" (Lk 24:27 ESV).

If the apostles interacted with the biblical texts in such a creative manner, their successors saw no barrier to prevent them from doing the same. If, as Paul states, "The letter kills, but the Spirit gives life" (2 Cor 3:6), then the "letter" always kills, and the "spirit" always gives life. For the fathers, this notion manifested itself practically in a multitude of ways, including the very nature and shape of their scriptural citations. In short, there is a very close parallel between the manner in which the New Testament writers interacted with the Old Testament and the manner in which the church fathers interacted with the New Testament. Quite often, those interactions do not conform to modern standards of quotation. Could we, then, reconstruct the entire New Testament using *only* the quotations of the earliest church fathers? We ought perhaps to respond in the form of another question: Could we reconstruct even a significant portion of the Old Testament text using *only* the quotations of the New Testament? The two questions are deeply connected, and taken in conjunction, they provide a helpful framework for what follows.

Composite citations. To show that the Scriptures *theologically* conform to Christ and his teachings, Christian writers occasionally ensured that they were *physically* conformed to him as well. That is, at times, these authors carefully selected, shifted, and paired together the phrases and passages of Scripture in order to make more explicit the manner in which they reveal Christ or a central element of Christian belief. We find, for instance, numerous examples of composite citations throughout the pages of the New Testament, wherein two or more Old Testament passages are fused together and conveyed as though they are one.[25] In Romans 3:9-18, Paul unites a number of different passages, drawn from the Psalms, Proverbs, and Isaiah in order to underscore the point that all people are "under sin":

> What then? Are we Jews any better off? No, not at all; for I have already charged that all men, both Jews and Greeks, are under the power of sin, as it is written:
>
> > "None is righteous, no, not one;
> > no one understands, no one seeks for God.
> > All have turned aside, together they have gone wrong;
> > no one does good, not even one [Ps 14:1-3; 53:1-3]."
> > "Their throat is an open grave,
> > they use their tongues to deceive" [Ps 5:9].
> > "The venom of asps is under their lips" [Ps 140:3].

---

[25]In a recent volume on the phenomenon of composite citations in antiquity, Sean A. Adams and Seth M. Ehorn define a composite citation as "when literary borrowing occurs in a manner that includes two or more passages (from the same or different authors) fused together and conveyed as though they are only one." See Adams and Ehorn, eds., *Composite Citations in Antiquity*, vol. 1, *Jewish, Graeco-Roman, and Early Christian Uses*, LNTS 525 (London: Bloomsbury T&T Clark, 2015), 4. It should be noted that composite citations are *not* unique to the authors of the New Testament, or to Christian writers in general, nor are they reducible purely to theological conviction. Theology, however, does play a central role for the *manner* in which a Christian writer might construct such a citation.

Their mouth is full of curses and bitterness [Ps 10:7].

Their feet are swift to shed blood,

in their paths are ruin and misery [Prov 1:16],

and the way of peace they do not know [Is 59:8].

There is no fear of God before their eyes [Ps 36:1]. (RSV)

Nowhere does this text, in this form, appear in the Old Testament, and yet Paul seems perfectly comfortable declaring, "It is written." Of course, these words *were* "written" in the straightforward sense of the word, but the real point is that we would find ourselves sorely disappointed if we attempted to use Paul's "quotation" to reconstruct an original Old Testament text. Such a text does not exist. In continuity *with* the apostles, then, some early Christian writers applied the same methods in their interpretation *of* the apostles. One of the more prominent examples is Justin Martyr (ca. 100–165), a second-century philosopher and apologist who spent the majority of his career teaching in Rome. In one of his best-known works, the *First Apology*, Justin consistently uses composite citations in order to deliver his message concisely and effectively. In a section detailing Christ's central moral teachings, for example, Justin writes,

[Jesus] said, "Give to everyone who asks and turn not away from him who wishes to borrow [Lk 6:30]. For if you lend to those from whom you hope to receive, what new thing do you do? Even the publicans do this [Lk 6:34]. Lay not up for yourselves treasure upon earth, where moth and rust corrupt and thieves break in; but lay up for yourselves treasure in heaven, where neither moth nor rust corrupts [Mt 6:19]. For what will it profit a man, if he should gain the whole world, but lose his own soul? Or what will he give in exchange for it? [Mt 16:26]. Lay up treasure therefore in heaven, where neither moth nor rust corrupts [Mt 6:20]." (*First Apology* 15)[26]

Again, nowhere in the Gospels does Jesus say these exact words in this exact order, and using them for the reconstruction of a New Testament passage would prove highly problematic without a solid point of reference. To the modern critic, such methods may seem reckless. Indeed, ancient Christian writers understood the potential dangers involved, warning against the ways in which such a principle might be abused. Irenaeus of Lyons (second

---

[26]Translations of *First Apology* come from Leslie William Barnard, trans., *Saint Justin Martyr: The First and Second Apologies*, ACW 56 (New York: Paulist Press, 1997).

century), for example, lambasts the Valentinian "gnostics" for disregarding the "order and connection" of the Scriptures by "transferring passages, and dressing them up anew, and making one thing out of another." He compares the oracles of Scripture to a collection of precious jewels, which a skilled artist has carefully constructed into the mosaic of a king. The Valentinians, he complains, "rearrange the gems, and so fit them together as to make them into the form of a dog or of a fox" (*Haer* 1.8.1).[27] They then go about tricking the ignorant into believing that the image of the dog or the fox was the image originally crafted by the artist.

Despite his complaint, it cannot be that Irenaeus intrinsically objects to the rearranging of passages, for aside from Paul and the other New Testament writers, he himself does so in the context of this very same work.[28] Indeed, the assumption is that the jewels (or "oracles") within the mosaic do actually conform to *some* image, and that this image is not one that can always be discovered simply by reading the text in a straightforward, linear manner. As he goes on, he reveals that the fundamental problem is not the rearranging of passages itself but that the Valentinians "adapt the oracles of God *to their baseless fictions*" (*Haer.* 1.8.1). That is, their starting point is faulty and erroneous. The "hypothesis" with which they begin is without warrant, and as a result they only compound the problem and deceive others by forcing the scriptural evidence to fit their defective assumptions.

For Irenaeus, the proper starting point is what some refer to as the "rule of faith," or the "canon of truth."[29] This "canon," remarkably similar in order and content to the later creeds, is nothing less than the apostolic "hypothesis" required to see rightly the image of the king. It is a verbal expression of Christ himself, crucified, risen, and preached "according to the Scriptures" (meaning the Old Testament). It is the canon (rule or standard) that precedes, underlies, and gives shape to what would become the more concrete

---

[27]Translations of *Against Heresies* come from Dominic J. Unger, trans., *Against the Heresies*, ACW 55 (New York: Paulist Press, 1992).

[28]For example, Irenaeus later rearranges the order of two of John the Baptist's proclamations in the Gospel of John, and moreover he makes it appear as though they both originate from a single speech (as opposed to two separate encounters on two separate days). He writes, "For the knowledge of salvation which was wanting to them was that of God's Son, which John gave them when he said, 'Behold the Lamb of God, who takes away the sin of the world [Jn 1:29]. This is he of whom I said, "After me comes a man who ranks before me, for he was before me, and from his fullness have we all received [Jn 1:15-16]""" (*Haer.* 3.10.3).

[29]For Irenaeus's articulation of the rule, see *Haer.* 1.10.1.

canon (list) of New Testament books. Provided, then, that the words of Scripture were arranged in such a way that they served to demonstrate and reveal this hypothesis, rearranging them was not inherently problematic. Indeed, it was often beneficial for the purposes of communicating one's exegetical, theological, or apologetic point.[30]

Ultimately, this could affect even the way in which a writer approached textual variation. Occasionally, provided a textual variant reading did not explicitly run contrary to the apostolic deposit of faith, patristic writers were happy to allow multiple readings to stand in their interpretations. In his *Commentary on Romans*, for example, Origen notes that there are two possible readings of Romans 3:5. It is either "Is God unjust who inflicts wrath against men?" or "Is God unjust who inflicts wrath? I am speaking according to man." Yet he appears to make no effort to determine which was the "original." Rather, he simply goes on to accept and explain the meaning of both textual variants in a manner consistent with his theology (*Commentary on Romans* 3.1).

Augustine of Hippo (ca. 354–430), when faced with a similar problem in the various Latin translations, remarks, "Which of these two followed the original words one cannot tell, unless one reads copies of the original language. But all the same, for those who are shrewd readers, something important is being suggested by each version" (*Doctr. chr.* 2.12.17).[31] Of course, both Origen and Augustine were known for urging their students to familiarize themselves with the original texts (where they could be known), and yet they did not always perceive variants as inherently problematic. Provided that the variant words speak truly about the invariant Word, they felt free to accept multiple readings.

"In other words." As we have already begun to see, many early Christian writers believed that while one finds meaning *through* the words of Scripture,

---

[30]For Irenaeus, however, this hypothesis or "rule of faith" is not superior to that of his opponents simply because it is *his* hypothesis. For him, it is the true apostolic rule of faith because it has both respected the "order and connection" of the Scriptures and because it has been passed down through apostolic succession. On the authoritative dynamic between Scripture, the rule of faith, tradition, and apostolic succession in Irenaeus's work, see especially chap. 2 of John Behr's *The Mystery of Christ: Life in Death* (Crestwood, NY: St. Vladimir's Seminary Press, 2006), 45-72. Behr also notes how for Irenaeus, as for other patristic writers, Christ is like the "treasure," hidden in the Scriptures (or the "treasure hidden in the field"), ultimately making Scripture a "treasury" or "thesaurus" of words and images with which to articulate the mystery of Christ (55).

[31]Translations of *On Christian Doctrine* are from Edmund Hill, trans., *Teaching Christianity* (Hyde Park, NY: New City Press, 1996).

meaning is not necessarily equivalent *to* the words of Scripture. Granted, no one today would suggest that the mere possession of the words guarantees correct interpretation, but many would suggest that if one understands the basic historical contexts and definitions of the words, a correct interpretation will be well within reach. In other words, the literal sense dominates. This was not necessarily so in the ancient world. No early figure better personifies the difference than Origen, arguably Christianity's first great scriptural commentator and by far its most prolific. In his most famous and controversial work, *On First Principles*, Origen teaches the following: "The weakness of our understanding cannot discover the deep and hidden thoughts in every sentence; for the treasure of divine wisdom is concealed in vessels of poor and humble words, as the apostle points out when he says: 'We have this treasure in earthen vessels, that the greatness of the divine power may shine forth the more' (2 Cor 4:7)" (*On First Principles* 4.1.7).[32]

For Origen, the primary error of Jewish interpretation is its insistence on taking the text at face value, or too literally, such that the Messiah ought "actually and visibly to have 'proclaimed release to captives.'" The same holds true for the "heretics," such as Marcion, who took the notion of God's "anger" or "jealousy" in the plain sense, and ended up rejecting the "Creator God" in favor of a "more perfect God" revealed in Jesus Christ (*On First Principles* 4.2.1). By contrast, Origen teaches that every passage of Scripture must be interpreted in a *pneumatic*, or spiritual sense. Even with regard to the Gospels, he asks, "Is there not also hidden in them an inner meaning which is the Lord's meaning, and which is only revealed through the grace that was given to him who said, 'We have the mind of Christ, that we may know the things that were freely given to us by God'?" (4.2.3). For Origen, Scripture is a historical, literal text only in the most superficial sense. It is important to understand the history, but it is far more important to understand the *meaning* (and unlike certain streams of modern thought, the two are not equivalent).

The natural outcome of such a mindset, in contrast to certain modern norms, is a greater propensity for putting things into "other words." This includes a greater propensity for adaptations and allusions that skillfully communicate Christian truth. In this, too, the Fathers were not without biblical warrant. One of the more prominent examples of a New Testament

---

[32]Translations of *On First Principles* are from George Butterworth, trans., *On First Principles* (New York: Harper & Row, 1966).

author intentionally adapting an Old Testament text to his christological convictions is found in Hebrews 10:5-7, which draws on Psalm 40:6-8. The text begins, "Consequently, when Christ came into the world, he said, 'Sacrifices and offerings you have not desired, but a body have you prepared for me'" (Heb 10:5 ESV). Remarkably, the original psalm does not include any form of the phrase "a body you have prepared for me" but rather reads "ears you have dug for me." Many seeming "misquotations" in the New Testament are merely the result of the text having been translated into Greek, but in this case, the author appears to have intentionally put the text into other words to better communicate one of his overarching points (the importance of the sacrifice of "the body of Jesus Christ" in Heb 10:10). Furthermore, the author attributes the words of the psalmist directly to Jesus, adding an additional layer of intrigue. Do these changes dramatically affect the meaning or intention of the psalmist? Perhaps not, but this in fact illustrates the overarching point. Even in the ESV Study Bible, for example, one finds the following commentary: "NT quotations of OT texts are not always precise; NT authors often reword them or adapt them to suit their own purposes, yet always in a way that is compatible with their original meaning."[33] Unlike certain patristic writers, however, we would be highly uncomfortable replicating something like this today.

For the Fathers, this overall mindset also resulted in a greater openness to the use of translations that effectively communicate Christian theology in their choice of language. Translations were commonplace and were often considered spiritually authoritative in their own right. Even among the authors of the New Testament, the Septuagint was the most common source of Old Testament quotations (yet another reason why it would be difficult to reconstruct the Old Testament from the New). This alone suggests that for some, lacking the "original words" of the text was not an inherent obstacle to right interpretation. With few exceptions, this conviction grew stronger in the earliest centuries of Christianity, when the Septuagint remained dominant and few Christians possessed the capacity to read Hebrew.

As Christianity began to spread throughout the ancient world, the Scriptures (including what would become the New Testament) were gradually translated into languages such as Latin, Syriac, and Coptic, resulting in a

---

[33]David W. Chapman, "The Letter to the Hebrews," in *The ESV Study Bible*, ed. Lane T. Dennis et al. (Wheaton, IL: Crossway, 2008), 2377.

multitude of differences between manuscripts and versions. This made it increasingly more difficult to ascertain what the "original" text said. In response, Augustine of Hippo (among others) urged translators to familiarize themselves with Greek and Hebrew, being troubled by the "infinite variety of Latin translations." In his classic work *On Christian Doctrine*, Augustine states that the "proper meaning of a passage, which several translators attempt to express . . . can only be definitely ascertained from an examination of it in the language they are translating from" (2.13.19). Clearly, Augustine understood the importance of the original languages, yet, despite his strict instructions, he retained the belief that the Septuagint version of the Old Testament has "greater authority" than the Hebrew. Why? Because the translation was inspired by the Holy Spirit: "And for correcting any Latin versions at all, Greek ones should be employed, among which, as regards the Old Testament, that of the Seventy Translators has the greatest authority. These are said, throughout all the more learned Churches, to have been so directed by the Holy Spirit in their translations, that while being so many they had but a single mouth" (2.15.22).

Translations are nothing less than extended interpretations, or controlled articulations of meaning. They are not equivalent to saying "in other words," but they are quite literally in *other* words. Augustine, like many early Christians, believed that the Septuagint was "inspired" or "directed" by the Holy Spirit, not because the original Hebrew wording was somehow inadequate or "less inspired" but because inspiration must be located also in the mind of the interpreter(s).[34] Origen states this point succinctly, writing, "On this point the entire Church is unanimous, that while the whole law is spiritual, the inspired *meaning* is not recognized by all, but only by those who are gifted with the grace of the Holy Spirit in the word of wisdom and knowledge" (*On First Principles*, preface 8). In short, uninspired interpretations of inspired texts will not get you very far, even if you possess the original words.

For many early Christian writers, then, translations and adaptations/ allusions (as well as adapted translations) were not always perceived as being inadequate or even limiting. They were often considered an inspired means

---

[34]This is not to say that recognizing such inspired readings is an easy task. Augustine seems only to affirm the inspiration of the Septuagint because he is inclined to believe the story attached to it (that the seventy translators were kept in separate rooms and that when they had finished their work, each of them had produced a translation identical to the others).

of communicating inspired meaning. The point here is not that the Fathers all played fast and loose with the Scriptures (though some might be worthy of the accusation). Many were in fact quite precise with their quotations. The point, rather, is that one's very theology of Scripture and scriptural interpretation affects the way in which one quotes and uses it.

We therefore ask yet again, Could we reconstruct virtually the entire New Testament using *only* the quotations of the earliest church fathers? In response, we also ask yet again, Could we reconstruct even a significant portion of the Old Testament text using *only* the quotations of the New Testament? Between all the adaptations, allusions, composite citations, and Greek translations common among the New Testament authors (partially resulting from their very theology *of* Scripture), the answer must be a definitive no. That is, we could not do so without the Old Testament manuscript tradition as a point of reference. Without that manuscript tradition, one would simply be left guessing. Because the Fathers tended to imitate the New Testament authors in their interpretation and style of quotation, the same generally holds true for their writings.[35]

Does all of this suggest that the original wording did not matter to early Christian writers? Certainly not. Many (perhaps most famously Jerome) insisted on the primacy of the Hebrew with regard to the Old Testament, and most Christians understood the importance of reading the apostolic writings in Greek. Even Origen, who explicitly taught that one must move beyond the bare words (or plain meaning) of Scripture, was a forerunner to modern textual criticism. He tended to be more precise in his quotations and is famous for having gathered together not only the Hebrew text(s) of the Old Testament but also the recognized Septuagint of his day along with a variety of other Greek translations such as those of Aquila, Symmachus, and Theodotion. Origen placed each of these versions, along with a Greek transliteration of the Hebrew, into side-by-side parallel columns. This monumental work came to be known as the Hexapla ("six-columned thing") and was preserved in the library of Caesarea for centuries before its likely destruction. This is hardly the work of a man indifferent to the original wording of Scripture. But again, it is crucial to understand that his concern to possess

---

[35]Of course, the sheer volume of patristic writings (and thus quotations) does allow for more comparison than the New Testament writings can offer. Yet, without the manuscript tradition, endless quotations can end up complicating just as many things as they resolve.

the original wording does not, for him, suggest that attaining the original wording was his ultimate goal. Rather, the original wording best *enabled* him to discover the meaning hidden within the wording (the treasure hidden in "earthen vessels").

THE SILVER LINING

It seems that we can finally put this myth to rest. But despite everything we have seen in this chapter, it is important to recognize that the quotations of the church fathers can and do play an important role in New Testament textual criticism. Specifically, they can be helpful in determining when and where a certain textual variant became prevalent or was being read.

Take, for example, the letters of Cyprian (ca. 210–258), bishop of Carthage in the mid-third century.[36] The scriptural quotations in those letters appear almost always to agree with the text preserved in the Old Latin manuscript known as VL 1 (Codex Bobiensis; *k*). The manuscript itself does not date until the fourth or fifth century, at least a century *after* Cyprian's time. As Cyprian could not possibly have consulted a copy produced after his own death, scholars have theorized that VL 1 must have descended from an earlier copy located somewhere in the proximity of North Africa in the mid-third century. In cases such as this, patristic quotations are enormously helpful.

Another example relates to the establishment of the oldest form of a text, as in the case of Luke 3:22. The majority of witnesses, including P4 (late second/early third century), record that at the baptism of Jesus, the voice from heaven declared, "You are my beloved Son, in you I am well pleased," while other witnesses, beginning with Codex Bezae (fifth century) have the voice proclaiming, "You are my Son, today I have begotten you." Judging by the Greek manuscript evidence alone, one might conclude that the latter reading was a later innovation, or at least a minority reading. However, the patristic evidence suggests otherwise. Justin Martyr, Clement of Alexandria, Origen, Methodius, the Gospel according to the Hebrews, the Gospel according to the Ebionites, and the Didascalia all make use of the latter reading, serving to flip the conclusion on its head. As Metzger and Ehrman put it, "This means that, with the exception of P4, *all* of the surviving witnesses of the second and third centuries appear to have known

---

[36]This example and the next are summarized in Metzger and Ehrman, *Text of the New Testament*, 126-27.

this alternative form of the text."[37] Again, without access to these patristic witnesses, our knowledge of the transmission history of this text would be greatly diminished.

Finally, there are a multitude of instances in which a church father explicitly comments on a textual variant in the context of one of his commentaries, homilies, letters, or other theological or apologetic works. These have been thoroughly documented in recent years, and so one brief example should suffice.[38] In Irenaeus's great work *Adversus Haereses* (*Against Heresies*), while discussing the antichrist and the great apostasy to come, he offers up an explanation of the number of the beast, which is famously 666 in Revelation 13:18. However, he notes that he is aware of a variant reading of this passage that instead has the number 616. His rejection of this variant is absolute, and his reasoning is as follows: First and foremost, he states that 666 is found in "all the most approved and ancient copies." Second, he notes that this reading has been upheld by "those men who saw John face to face." Finally, he comments on the internal meaning and logic of 666. Six, the number of apostasy, is repeated three times, specifically indicating an apostasy "which occurred at the beginning, during the intermediate periods, and which shall take place at the end." He appears to attribute the variant to the error of a copyist but explicitly warns against intentionally perpetuating it, as it might lead the faithful into error regarding the identity of the beast (*Haer.* 5.30.1). Though Irenaeus is not the sole witness to this variant (the third-century P115 is the earliest manuscript witness), his commentary provides additional insight into its date, location, and prevalence. Furthermore, examples such as this one offer a special glimpse into the way early Christians thought about textual variation, including why some variants were accepted while others were rejected, or why certain manuscripts were considered more reliable than others.

While we may not, therefore, be able to reconstruct the entire New Testament text using only the quotations of the church fathers, textual critics can certainly do a great deal of important work with them, given the right set of circumstances and resources.[39]

---

[37]Metzger and Ehrman, *Text of the New Testament*, 128 (emphasis added).

[38]See especially Amy M. Donaldson, "Explicit References to New Testament Variant Readings Among Greek and Latin Church Fathers," 2 vols. (PhD diss., University of Notre Dame, 2009).

[39]For two helpful essays on the topic, see Gordon D. Fee (revised by Roderic L. Mullen), "The Use of the Greek Fathers for New Testament Textual Criticism," in *The Text of the New Testament in*

CONCLUSION

The myth at the heart of this chapter has proven to be exactly that, but there is a sense in which the Fathers themselves would have affirmed the underlying sentiment it represents. What would we do if every single copy of the New Testament were suddenly destroyed? To what (or whom) would we turn? We would no doubt turn to the Fathers of the church. Not because they possess the original wording of the New Testament text within their writings, but because they possess Truth. At least, that is how Irenaeus would have answered the question. Indeed, he poses a variation of that same question in *Adversus haereses*, asking, "What if the apostles had not left us the Scriptures?" That is, what if there were no writings available to us at all? (Note how the question itself presupposes the supreme importance of Scripture.) Irenaeus replies, "Ought we not, then, to follow the disposition of tradition, which they handed down to those to whom they entrusted the churches?" (*Haer.* 3.4.1). The churches, and those to whom they have been entrusted, carry within them that which (or he whom) the Scriptures were always meant to articulate. At the heart of our myth, then, is the desire to know that Christianity would survive, in possession of the truth, even if it turned out that all the New Testament manuscripts were inaccurate. This hypothetical situation naturally stretches and pushes us, and Christians of different theological stripes may respond to it in different ways (with some taking offense at the very proposition). Yet thanks to the many great scribes and text critics who have worked tirelessly over the centuries, such a hypothetical has never become reality. We do not need to reconstruct the New Testament text without manuscripts. In fact, thanks to them, the myth deconstructed in this chapter was never really necessary in the first place.

Key Takeaways

▶ The argument that we can reconstruct all but eleven verses of the New Testament from 36,289 quotations by the church fathers is not only false but it is a conflation of two different arguments that are both riddled with problems. It should not be used.

Contemporary Research: Essays on the Status Quaestionis, 2nd ed., ed. Bart D. Ehrman and Michael W. Holmes, NTTSD 42 (Leiden: Brill, 2013), 351-73; H. A. G. Houghton, "The Use of the Latin Fathers for New Testament Textual Criticism," in Ehrman and Holmes, *Text of the New Testament*, 375-405.

▶ Even if true, the argument fails because it is viciously circular: we have to know what the text of the New Testament is before we can identify patristic quotations of it.

▶ In general, patristic theology of Scripture affected the value of patristic quotations of Scripture. For instance, when a variant reading did not run contrary to the rule of faith, patristic writers were sometimes happy to allow multiple readings to stand in their interpretations.

▶ Many early Christian writers believed that while one finds meaning *through* the words of Scripture, meaning is not necessarily equivalent *to* the words of Scripture. Consequently, many patristic writers felt free to be more fluid in their wording when they "quoted" Scripture than many Christians today would be.

CHAPTER THIRTEEN

MYTHS ABOUT CANON

WHAT THE CODEX CAN AND CAN'T TELL US

John D. Meade

THE ANCIENT CODEX (the precursor to the modern book form) was invented around the turn of the era and perhaps was in use by the middle of the first century.[1] Before the codex, the primary writing medium was the roll or scroll. Why did early Christians adopt the codex form? Some scholars believe that the development from scroll to codex caused the concept of canon to become more concrete, for with this new book technology scribes could now organize many works in order, and for the first time choices over what books to include and exclude were made.[2] The idea is that codex implies canon, so that the multibook codex creates or at least corresponds with the development of the canon. In considering just what the codex can and cannot tell us about the New Testament canon, we must (1) consider how early Christians described their religious literature and (2) summarize the contents of our codices, paying close attention to their contents. The following lines of evidence show that the canon lists reveal the New Testament canon, and that while the codices sometimes correspond to the New Testament canon, more often they simply reflect what books Christians were reading. Thus, if one wants to know the contours of the early canon, one should consult the lists. If one wants to become acquainted with the early Christian's repository or library, one should consult the contents of manuscripts.

---

[1]Graham N. Stanton, *Jesus and Gospel* (Cambridge: Cambridge University Press, 2004), 190.

[2]Armin Lange, "Canonical History of the Hebrew Bible," in *Textual History of the Bible: The Hebrew Bible*, vol. 1A, *Overview Articles*, ed. Armin Lange and Emanuel Tov (Leiden: Brill, 2016), 35-81, esp. 74-75 and the literature cited.

CANON LISTS AND THEIR IMPORTANCE

Before turning to the codices, we need to supply the early context for canon, the canon lists. These lists are exclusive lists of authoritative books, and their importance lies in that they provide rather specific information on the contents and boundaries of the canon of Scripture. The lists can be partial (e.g., only Gospels, as in Irenaeus's *Haer.* 3.1.1) or complete (e.g., the entire New Testament, Old Testament, or both). Furthermore, the church fathers' or scribe's commentary in and around the list of books often provides crucial information that a crude reproduction of the list cannot convey (see the tables at the end of this chapter).[3]

Canon lists represent the culmination of a process—not the beginning of one. Therefore, the presence of lists does not establish a canon but rather evinces a time when the complete canon crystallized. For example, even though Athanasius in 367 was the first to include all twenty-seven New Testament books into one canon list (though see Origen below), he did not invent this list. He compiled a complete list of books that were *already* recognized as canonical (four Gospels, Acts, fourteen epistles of Paul, seven Catholic Epistles) and included Revelation—a book at the edges, that is, a book that most but not all churches would have recognized as canonical.

The number of lists and what they are. From the early period (up to ca. AD 400), early Christians drafted eighteen canon lists and presented them as complete and exclusive lists of New Testament books—nine in Greek, eight in Latin, and one in Syriac.[4] The lists and their dates are as follows:

---

[3]For a full representation of the sources in original language and English translation with commentary, see Edmon L. Gallagher and John D. Meade, *The Biblical Canon Lists from Early Christianity: Texts and Analysis* (Oxford: Oxford University Press, 2018).

[4]These numbers omit the two disputed, partial lists of Origen that Eusebius combined and included in *Historia ecclesiastica* 6.25.3-10 as *testimonia* to Gospels, Epistles, and Apocalypse. Geoffrey Mark Hahneman, *The Muratorian Fragment and the Development of the Canon* (Oxford: Oxford University Press, 1992), 133, lists fifteen undisputed catalogues, which overlap largely with my own. I have included Origen's list in *Homiliae on Josuam* 7.1, the Laodicean canon 59, and the Muratorian Fragment as part of my data set, noting some difficulties with these lists. Furthermore, there are some thirteen later lists of New Testament books that are also of great interest. See also B. F. Westcott, *A General Survey of the History of the Canon of the New Testament*, 7th ed. (New York: Macmillan, 1896), 548-95. Michael E. Stone has also published seven articles on the Armenian canon lists in the *Harvard Theological Review* (1973–2011); these lists are later in time and sometimes include only Old Testament books. Although outside the purview of this study, they are of great interest.

- Origen (ca. 250; *Hom. Jos.* 7.1)[5]

- Eusebius (ca. 325; *Hist. eccl.* 3.25)

- Cyril of Jerusalem (ca. 350; *Catechetical Lectures* 4.36)

- Athanasius (367; *Festal Letters* 39.18)

- Synod of Laodicea 59 (343–380)[6]

- Apostolic Canons 85 (375–380)

- Gregory of Nazianzus (381–390; *Carmen* 12)

- Amphilochius (ca. 380; *Epistula Iambica ad Seleucum* lines 280–319)

- Epiphanius (ca. 376; *Panarion* 76.22.5)

- Muratorian Fragment (second, third, or fourth century)[7]

- Codex Claromontanus (ca. 300–350)

- Mommsen Catalogue (before 365)

- Jerome (395; *Ep.* 53)

- Rufinus (ca. 404; *Commentarius in symbolum apostolorum* 35)

- *Breviarium Hipponense* (ca. 393)

- Augustine (397; *Doctr. chr.* 2.8.13.29)

- Pope Innocent I (405; *Ep.* 6.7)

- Syriac List of St. Catherine's Monastery (350–400)

Canonical books. These lists agree on the four Gospels, on Acts, and mostly on the fourteen epistles of Paul (Hebrews is omitted in the Muratorian Fragment, Mommsen, and perhaps Claromontanus, although textual corruption may be the cause of the omission of some books in this list). This core canon was anticipated already in the second century. If the Muratorian

---

[5]Origen's original Greek list was lost, and only Rufinus's Latin translation remains. Recent analysis shows that although Rufinus may have altered Origen's text in subtle ways to reflect a fourth-century situation, the list in its Latin dress is still faithful to the original list Origen produced in the third century. See Edmon L. Gallagher, "Origen *via* Rufinus on the New Testament Canon," *NTS* 62, no. 3 (2016): 461-76.

[6]The list of books was added before the Council of Chalcedon (451) but may have also been part of the original fourth-century synod. See the discussion in Gallagher and Meade, *Biblical Canon Lists*, 129-34.

[7]See Gallagher and Meade, *Biblical Canon Lists*, 175-83, for commentary on the debates about the purpose of the Fragment and its date.

Fragment belongs to the second century, then the Gospels, Acts, and thirteen epistles of Paul are clearly listed, though our evidence of this core canon does not depend on the early dating of the Fragment.[8] Around 180, Irenaeus speaks of the established four Gospels by his time (*Haer.* 3.1.1; 3.11.8). From the late second century, Christians such as Irenaeus (*Haer.* 3.13.3), Tertullian (*Against Marcion* 5.1-4), and Clement of Alexandria (*Stromata* 5.12.82) recognized Acts as part of their Scriptures. The church had Paul's fourteen letters by 200, since Tertullian describes Paul's thirteen letters (Hebrews omitted) and treats them as a collection of his epistles (*Against Marcion* 5), and Clement of Alexandria (d. ca. 215) attributes them to Paul and cites all fourteen letters except Philemon (perhaps due to its brevity).[9]

On the other hand, our canon lists reveal dispute over the Catholic Epistles. In Greek and Latin traditions, twelve lists contain the traditional seven Catholic Epistles, which shows most of the churches recognized their canonicity, probably from an earlier time than the fourth century; only Eusebius, Amphilochius, Apostolic Canons, the Muratorian Fragment, and Mommsen deviate from this pattern. Eusebius says only 1 Peter and 1 John are recognized and places the other five among the disputed books. Amphilochius accepts James, 1 Peter, and 1 John but notes disputes over 2 Peter, 2–3 John, and Jude. The Muratorian Fragment lists Jude and the letters of John (1–2 John or 1–3 John?) and lacks the others. Mommsen lacks James and Jude. Although the tendency was to reduce the number of these letters, the Apostolic Canons *adds* 1–2 Clement among them. The Syriac list of St. Catherine's Monastery does not include the Catholic Epistles, showing the early disputes over these books within the Syriac church.[10] Cyril of Jerusalem (ca. 350) is the first to list all seven Catholic Epistles without dispute.[11]

---

[8]Joseph Verheyden has shown the probability of the late second- or early third-century date of the Fragment, while also showing the improbability of the fourth-century date, in "The Canon Muratori: A Matter of Dispute," in *The Biblical Canons*, ed. J.-M. Auwers and H. J. de Jonge (Leuven: Leuven University Press, 2003), 487-556. For the alternate view, see Clare Rothschild, "The Muratorian Fragment as Roman Fake," *NovT* 60, no. 1 (2018): 55-82, who argues that the Fragment represents a fictitious attempt to provide a venerable second-century precedent for a later position on canon. She eventually settles on an early fourth-century date for the composition of the Fragment.

[9]The debate over a pre-Marcionite ten-letter collection (omitting the Pastorals and Hebrews) continues; see Gallagher and Meade, *Biblical Canon Lists*, 42, and the literature cited there.

[10]On the Syriac reception of these books, see Bruce M. Metzger, *The Canon of the New Testament: Its Origin, Development, and Significance* (Oxford: Oxford University Press, 1987), 220.

[11]See Gallagher and Meade, *Biblical Canon Lists*, 44-48, and the literature cited there.

Of the eighteen canon lists, Revelation is omitted or disputed in Origen, Eusebius, Cyril of Jerusalem, Synod of Laodicea, Apostolic Canons, Gregory of Nazianzus, Amphilochius, and the Syriac list—that is, most of the Eastern lists. However, even among these lists, the situation is complex. Gregory may include an allusion to the book of Revelation in his list, while Amphilochius lists it but notes, "The majority say it is spurious." The textual transmission of Origen's *Homiliae on Josuam* has some textual witnesses that include Revelation, while others do not.[12] Eusebius lists it twice, once among his "recognized (= canonical) books" and again among his "disputed-spurious books," while Cyril, the Synod of Laodicea, and Apostolic Canons omit it (though the Ethiopic version of Apostolic Canons includes it). The complex reception of Revelation has been documented elsewhere.[13]

Books at the edges of the canon. The Greek lists of Eusebius and Athanasius place other books in secondary lists that were not finally included in the twenty-seven-book New Testament. The Apostolic Canons includes extra books within its primary list. Eusebius includes in his list the following books as "disputed-spurious": the Acts of Paul, the Shepherd of Hermas, the Apocalypse of Peter, the Epistle of Barnabas, the Didache, and a Gospel According to the Hebrews. In his secondary list, Athanasius lists the Shepherd and the Didache as part of his "books to be read to catechumens." The Apostolic Canons includes 1–2 Clement among the canonical books.

The Latin lists of the Muratorian Fragment, Claromontanus, and Rufinus also contain more books than those associated with the traditional New Testament. The Muratorian Fragment includes the Epistle to the Laodiceans ("forged"), the Epistle to the Alexandrians ("forged"), the Apocalypse of Peter ("private reading according to some"), and the Shepherd of Hermas ("private reading only"). Claromontanus includes Barnabas, the Shepherd of Hermas, the Acts of Paul, and the Apocalypse of Peter with an *obelus* or lance (→), usually used in ancient manuscripts to indicate misplaced text.[14]

---

[12]Gallagher, "Origen *via* Rufinus," 473n38.

[13]Gallagher and Meade, *Biblical Canon Lists*, 49-52, and the literature cited there.

[14]I am indebted to Elijah Hixson for the following suggestion. The *obeli* were probably added secondarily to the manuscript, after the folios were bound. The strokes are thinner and in a different color ink. Furthermore, the opposite pages contain ink transfer from the marks, showing that the scribe likely did not wait for the ink to dry before turning the page. Thus, the *obeli* represent a different writing event from the list of books, but we do not know how long an interval occurred between the list and the marks. The *obeli* next to these books is consistent with a mid-fourth-century date for the canon list.

In his list of ecclesiastical books, Rufinus includes the Shepherd, the Two Ways (the Didache?), and the Judgment of Peter.

Early Christian description of religious literature. The preceding section raises the question about how early Christians described their religious literature. Generally, they did not describe books in a binary way: canonical and noncanonical. Rather, they employed a tri-fold description of religious literature: canonical scripture, useful/intermediate scripture, and apocryphal. In *Festal Letters* 39.20-21, for example, Athanasius describes this literature as follows:

> But for the sake of greater accuracy, I add this, writing from necessity. There are other books, outside of the preceding, which have not been canonized (κανονιζόμενα, *kanonizomena*), but have been prescribed by the ancestors to be read (ἀναγινώσκεσθαι, *anaginōskesthai*) to catechumens wanting to be instructed in the word of piety. . . . Nevertheless, beloved, the former books are canonized (κανονιζομένων, *kanonizomenōn*); the latter are (only) read (ἀναγινωσκομένων, *anaginōskomenōn*); and there is no mention of the apocryphal books (ἀποκρύφων, *apokryphōn*).[15]

In accordance with the ancestors, Athanasius lists the canonical books of Old and New Testament, several books that are to be read (e.g., Tobit, the Shepherd, the Didache), and the category of apocryphal books but does not list them. Other early Christian fathers who presented a similar tri-fold description include Amphilochius (*Epistula Iambica ad Seleucum* 251-260), Epiphanius (*De mensuris* 4), Jerome (*Preface to the Books of Solomon*), and Rufinus (*Commentarius in symbolum apostolorum* 36).[16] For example, in the context of a canon list, Jerome says the Shepherd is "not in the canon" (*Prologus Galeatus*), but in another context, he calls it "useful" and says many ancient writers quoted it authoritatively (*Vir. ill.* 10). Therefore, early Christians had an intermediate category of books—books considered somewhere between canonical and apocryphal; specifically, these books were considered useful for instruction in piety but not for establishing ecclesiastical doctrine.

---

[15]Adapted from Gallagher and Meade, *Biblical Canon Lists*, 124-26.

[16]The history of the tri-fold description is not altogether clear. The first clear evidence of tiers within religious literature is Josephus (*Against Apion* 1.38, 41; after AD 94), who presents Jewish literature in two tiers: (1) the twenty-two books "rightly trusted" and (2) other books "not deemed worthy of the same trust." His second tier of books may have included the Maccabean literature, which he used extensively but was not among the twenty-two books.

Would early Christians refer to these books that were useful but not canonical as "Scripture" or as "inspired"? Would they cite them as Scripture
alongside canonical texts? They did. For example, Irenaeus calls the Shepherd
ἡ γράφη (*hē graphē*), usually translated "Scripture" (*Haer.* 4.20.2).[17] Clement
of Alexandria believed the Shepherd to be a genuine revelation, thus making
Hermas "technically a prophet."[18] Origen refers to the Shepherd as very
useful and divinely inspired (*Commentarii in Romanos* 10.31) but does not
include it in his canon list (*Hom. Jos.* 7.1). Athanasius cites the Shepherd 26.1
alongside Genesis 1:1 (*De incarnatione* 3.1), indicating to some scholars that
he considered it canonical, at least earlier in his career.[19] However, in *De
decretis* 18.3.2 and his canon list he says clearly the book is not in the canon,
showing that he referred to the book earlier as "useful" but not as "canonical."

Therefore, patristic biblical theory included a tri-fold description of religious literature. An ancient author's canon list did not include all the books
that he considered to be Scripture, and the scope of scriptural books was
often wider than his canon list. Although patristic biblical theory included
distinctions between canonical and useful scriptures, a church father's exegetical practice sometimes appears to blur his theoretical distinctions, as in
the case of Origen's use of the Shepherd (though his early third-century
context must be remembered). Athanasius also says that the Shepherd is
useful and quotes it authoritatively. Yet neither Father included the book in
his canon list.

---

[17]This translation is debated. Charles E. Hill thinks that Irenaeus considered the Shepherd a ge-
neric writing and not Scripture ("'The Writing Which Says . . .': The *Shepherd of Hermas* in the
Writings of Irenaeus," in *Papers Presented at the Sixteenth International Conference on Patristic
Studies Held in Oxford 2013*, ed. Markus Vinzent, StPatr 65 [Leuven: Peeters, 2013], 138), whereas
Dan Batovici concludes that Irenaeus understood Hermas as Scripture and not just a neutral
writing ("'Hermas' Authority in Irenaeus' Works: A Reassessment," *Aug* 55, no. 1 [2015]: 29-30).
Batovici does not decide whether Irenaeus would have placed Hermas in the canonical or useful
category, though (30). D. Jeffrey Bingham concludes that Irenaeus's scriptural hierarchy of the
top-tier prophets and the apostles and the lower-tier profitable early Christian texts (e.g.,
1 Clement) would have accounted for the scriptural status of Hermas (similar to the Muratorian
Fragment), but Bingham doubts Irenaeus knew Hermas, since he refers only to Mandate 1.1, i.e.,
Shepherd 26.1 ("Senses of Scripture in the Second Century: Irenaeus, Scripture, and Noncanonical Christian Texts," *JR* 97 [2017]: 53-54).

[18]Dan Batovici, "Hermas in Clement of Alexandria," in *Papers Presented at the Sixteenth International Conference on Patristic Studies Held in Oxford 2011*, ed. Markus Vinzent, StPatr 66 (Leuven: Peeters, 2013), 51.

[19]Bart D. Ehrman, "The New Testament Canon of Didymus the Blind," *VC* 37 (1983): 1-21, esp.
18-19; James D. Ernest, *The Bible in Athanasius of Alexandria*, The Bible in Ancient Christianity
2 (Leiden: Brill, 2004), 80-81n51.

Conclusions. From these data, we see that in the second century there was already a core New Testament canon consisting of the four Gospels, Acts, and thirteen or fourteen epistles of Paul. By the mid-fourth century (though see Origen's canon list from the mid-third century), probably some churches recognized seven Catholic Epistles, with others recognizing only two or three, and others, as seen in Apostolic Canons, recognizing more. The Revelation of John was recognized early, but later doubts about its authorship caused it to be omitted from many Eastern lists in the fourth century. By the end of the fourth century, these disputes appear to have subsided as the twenty-seven-book New Testament canon crystallized. This major formative stage did not cause the secondary lists of other important books to disappear, since they continued to be listed well after the fourth century.

These other important books circulated from the late first and second century AD. Church fathers referred to them and cited them in ways similar to how they cited canonical books. But their biblical theory accounts for this phenomenon. In the third- and fourth-century fathers, canon lists did not exhaust all scriptural works, and other scriptural works spilled over the canonical boundaries, as evidenced by the secondary lists of scriptural books. The debate over whether a tiered view of New Testament Scripture existed in the second century continues, but recent scholarship shows its plausibility.

As we turn to the material evidence of our manuscripts, we need to remember that the New Testament canon is clearly observed from the early Christian lists. We also need to heed the early Christian statements on specific books and their overall biblical theory to avoid committing historical anachronism by assigning canonical significance to works found in codices that the ancient Christians would not have recognized as canonical.

THE CONTENTS OF OUR NEW TESTAMENT MANUSCRIPTS

Bearing in mind that the canon lists and other such explicit statements provide the evidence for the New Testament canon, in this section we look at the evidence of codices—single and multiple books—from AD 100 to 700 and include several relevant Latin and Coptic multibook codices (each is clearly labeled in the tables below).[20] Most studies limit the evidence to

---

[20]The LDAB (www.trismegistos.org/ldab/) provides the data for this section. Once the thirty entries for "magical" texts are removed from the "literary" texts, there are about 270 relevant entries. This study does not attempt an exhaustive analysis of manuscripts in Latin and Coptic. However, LDAB yielded some relevant evidence of multibook codices for this study, and they have been included below.

Greek and manuscripts dated to the end of the third century, but this study expands the date range and the languages, attempting to show whether the codex format helped determine the canon or at least reflected it. Some scholars have argued that it did. For example, J. K. Elliott writes,

> Canon and codex go hand in hand in the sense that the adoption of a fixed canon could be more easily controlled and promulgated when the codex was the means of gathering together originally separate compositions. . . . We must assume that the authorities behind Codex Sinaiticus and Codex Alexandrinus considered these works canonical [the Shepherd, Barnabas, 1–2 Clement] and wished to promote them as such. Certainly, the user of these codices would have accepted all the texts in their Bible codex as having equal status.[21]

Elliott thus holds that what is in the codex is what was believed to be in the canon. In explaining why Christians preferred the codex, Michael Kruger agrees with Elliott that there is a relationship of some kind between the two, writing, "The most plausible suggestions [for why Christians preferred the codex over the roll] link the codex with the early development of the New Testament canon."[22] Next, he tells us what two distinctive functions the codex performed: "(1) Positively, it allowed certain books to be physically grouped together by placing them in the same volume; and (2) negatively, it provided a natural way to limit the number of books to those contained within the codex; that is, it functioned as a safeguard."[23]

Larry Hurtado is somewhat broader but still thinks there is a connection between "scripture" and codex, writing, "In any case, it is clear that Christians

---

[21]J. K. Elliott, "Manuscripts, The Codex and the Canon," *JSNT* 63 (1996): 111. Similarly, Greg Lanier, *A Christian's Pocket Guide to How We Got the Bible* (Ross-shire, Scotland: Christian Focus, 2018), 82, says, "And in some sense, we could say that codex=canon, at least for the group that assembled the codex, since book covers by definition rule things 'in' or 'out.'" Also, Daryl D. Schmidt, "The Greek New Testament as a Codex," in *The Canon Debate*, ed. Lee Martin McDonald and James A. Sanders (Peabody, MA: Hendrickson, 2002), 479, says, "The extant manuscripts surely tell us something about the 'sense' of canon in believing communities." For these scholars, the physical codex in some way is indicative of canon.

[22]Michael J. Kruger, *Canon Revisited: Establishing the Origins and Authority of the New Testament Books* (Wheaton, IL: Crossway, 2012), 249. I am thankful to Dr. Kruger for corresponding with me about his view on this matter (personal correspondence, April 16, 2018). I am still not sure how closely he relates codex with canon, but in his view codex either implies canon and points to it or it develops it in some way.

[23]Kruger, *Canon Revisited*, 250. On 259, Kruger summarizes his view, "No doubt the adoption of the codex is *closely linked to* the origins of the New Testament canon and the desire to place multiple books inside the confines of a single manuscript" (emphasis added). He does not tell us in what way the codex is linked to the origins of the New Testament canon.

favored the codex particularly for the writings that they treated as scripture." A little later, he offers this important caveat:

> We should, however, be wary of simplistic conclusions. For example, in light of the clear preference for the codex generally, it would be unsound to assume that if a text was copied in a codex this signals that the text was used as scripture. On the other hand, given this general Christian preference for the codex, particularly for scriptures, plus a noteworthy readiness to use the roll for a variety of other Christian texts, it is reasonable to judge that the use of a roll to copy a text signals that the copyist and/or user for whom the copy was made did not regard that text (or at least that copy of that text) as having scriptural status.[24]

Thus, not every literary work copied in codex form implies its scriptural status. But in the case of multibook codices, Hurtado does suggest that the codex form reflects a connection between the works included. As he writes, "I suggest specifically that the physical linkage of texts in one manuscript probably reflects a view of them as sharing *some common or related subject matter or significance* for readers."[25] Therefore, on this view, the physical grouping of books helped to determine or develop scriptural collections or a canon in a binary manner: a book is either included between the covers or it is not. But around the same time that many of these codices were produced and read, Christians had already developed the tri-fold description of literature with its middle category of useful books that could be placed alongside those books they acknowledged as canonical. Therefore, it will be difficult to interpret the data of the codices presented below according to the statements of the early Christians given above, for early Christians maintained conceptual distinctions between their books (useful and canonical books) that physical linkages between them in codices could not maintain.

In what follows, I argue that the codex did not serve to demarcate the Christian canon, nor did it help it develop in any notable way, even though at times the contents of our codices overlap with the canon lists. Thus, the codex does not furnish a rule that would only generate exceptions. The early New Testament canon can be observed from the early statements and lists, and furthermore, that evidence should help us interpret the material evidence of the codices.

Single-book codices. Work has been undertaken on the interpretation of the fragmentary remains of codices. From one extant page, can we know

---

[24]Larry W. Hurtado, *The Earliest Christian Artifacts: Manuscripts and Christian Origins* (Grand Rapids: Eerdmans, 2006), 59, 81.

[25]Hurtado, *Earliest Christian Artifacts*, 35 (emphasis added).

whether that codex contained more than one book? An even further question is, What would the fragmentary evidence reveal about the putative early collections of books in one codex?

Michael Dormandy recently wrote an article in which he has placed the Greek codices from the second to the sixth century in six categories: (1) certainly collection-evident; (2) plausibly collection-evident; (3) certainly or plausibly one work; (4) plausibly multiwork, indeterminably collection-evident; (5) plausibly not collection-evident; and (6) definitely not collection-evident. His third category is relevant for our study. In this category Dormandy includes the fragments of codices deemed to contain one book, and it is significant that in each century (second to sixth) the majority of manuscripts were categorized as containing one work. Part of Dormandy's conclusion captures the difficulties involved in this interpretation: "Although the number of single-work manuscripts identified by this study is high, this is partly due to my decision, discussed above, to assume that a manuscript is single-work, unless there is evidence to the contrary."[26] But he finally concludes that single-book codices were "common enough," and this datum calls into question that "the works of the NT very commonly circulated together." Indeed, Dormandy refers to the analysis of Francis Watson that, if the four-Gospel codex were the norm, we might expect an equal number of fragments of each Gospel, but fragments from Matthew and John far outnumber fragments from Mark and Luke.

As we will see below, multibook codices did exist, but these were probably not the norm or very common in the patristic period. However, if the single-book codex was the norm, it would be a challenge to see the correspondence between canon and codex. But what do multibook codices tell us? We turn to that evidence next.

Multiple-book codices. There are some sixty New Testament multiple-book codices, that is, codices that have one book joined to another. Most of these types preserve only two books but some more than two.[27] Once again, we will

---

[26]Michael Dormandy, "How the Books Became the Bible: The Evidence for Canon Formation from Work-Combinations in Manuscripts," *TC* 23 (2018), http://jbtc.org/v23/TC-2018-Dormandy.pdf.

[27]Outside the immediate purview of this study but relevant to the subject are the several Old Testament codices (AD 100–800; excluding S, B, A, C, Q, which contain deuterocanonical and canonical books) that combine canonical and other books: LDAB 3120 (Proverbs + Wisdom + Sirach), 3491 (Ecclesiastes + Song of Songs + Sirach + Sentences of Sextus), 5715 (quotes from Wisdom + Sirach + Psalms), 9221 (palimpsest with underwriting from Proverbs + Song of Songs + Sirach; overwriting Euclid's *Elements*). In Coptic we have: 107730 (Proverbs + Sirach), 107762 (Joshua + Judges + Ruth + Judith + Esther), 108321 (Job + Proverbs + Ecclesiastes + Song of Songs + Wisdom + Sirach), 108391 (Ecclesiastes + Sirach), and 108537 (Joshua + Tobit).

examine the evidence according to the collections established from the canon lists above, treating evidence of codices with two or more books. We will examine the pandects (complete New Testament) in their own section below.

Gospels. Most of the evidence of multiple-book codices is from the Gospels. Matthew is joined with other Gospels thirteen times and once with Acts, as follows:

LDAB	GA	Date	Contents
2899	064 + 074 + 090	500–599	Matthew + Mark
2901	043	500–599	Matthew + Mark
2987	0104	600–699	Matthew + Mark
2988	0107	650–699	Matthew + Mark
2990	042	500–599	Matthew + Mark
128512	067	400–499	Matthew + Mark
2936	P4 + P64 + P67	150–250	Matthew + Luke
2982	0171	175–225	Matthew + Luke
2978	1276	500–599	Matthew + John
2979	P44[1]	500–699	Matthew + John
2989	087 + 092b	500–599	Matthew + Mark + John
62323	1601	400–599	Matthew + Mark + John
2984	078	500–599	Matthew + Luke + John
2981	P53	350–399	Matthew + Acts

[1] P44 is said to be a lectionary containing Mt 17:1-3, 6-7; 18:15-17, 19; 25:8-10; Jn 10:8-14, although the John portions appear to be in a different hand. The portions previously assigned to P44 but containing Jn 9:3-4; 12:16-18 are from a different manuscript altogether and have since been reassigned as P128.

Table 13.1. Manuscripts with Matthew and other Gospels or Acts

Three times Matthew is grouped with Old Testament and other books:

LDAB	GA	Date	Contents
8942 (Latin)[1]		425–499	Acts of Pilate + Matthew + Infancy Gospel of Jesus
2993 (Greek + Coptic)	P62	300–399	Matthew + Daniel 3:51-53 (= Ode 8)
3315	035	500–599	Isaiah + Matthew

[1] H. A. G. Houghton, *The Latin New Testament: A Guide to Its Early History, Texts, and Manuscripts* (Oxford: Oxford University Press, 2016), 230, says the work is *Gospel of Thomas* whereas LDAB calls it "childhood gospel of Thomas." But according to the most recent, close analysis it is actually the *Infancy Gospel of Jesus.* See Anne-Catherine Baudoin, "Le premier temoin manuscrit des *Actes de Pilate* (ONB, cod. 563): antiquite et autorite de la traduction latine d'un texte grec," REG tome 129 (2016/2), 349-68, esp. 351. She notes that the underwriting from the fifth century contains Acts of Pilate (i.e. what became in later centuries chapters 1–16 of the Gospel of Nicodemus), Gospel of Matthew 26–28, and Infancy Gospel of Jesus.

Table 13.2. Manuscripts with Matthew and books outside the New Testament

Mark + John occurs once:

LDAB	GA	Date	Contents
2927	P84	550–599	Mark + John

Table 13.3. Manuscript with Mark and John

Luke appears with John and other material:

LDAB	GA	Date	Contents
2895	P75	275–325	Luke + John
2896 (Coptic + Greek)	P2	500–699	Luke + John
2897 (Coptic + Greek)	070 + 0110 + 0124 + 0178 + 0179 + 0180 + 0190 + 0191 + 0193 + 0194 + 0202	550–650	Luke + John
2898 (Coptic + Greek)	029 + 0113 + 0125 + 0139	500–599	Luke + John
2932	026	400–499	Luke + John
107965 (Coptic)		300–399	Exodus + Luke + Shepherd of Hermas

Table 13.4. Manuscripts with Luke and John or Luke and books outside the New Testament

In addition to the above, John appears in multiple-book codices three times without any of the other Gospels:

LDAB	GA	Date	Contents
2806 (Greek + Coptic)	P6	400–450	1 Clement (Coptic) + John (Greek-Coptic) + James (Coptic)
777		500–699	John + Commentaries on Psalms
2763 (Coptic + Greek)		275–350	John + mathematical school exercise

Table 13.5. Manuscripts with John and books outside the New Testament

The four Gospels appear together four times and with Acts two times (though not always in the same order):

LDAB	GA	Date	Contents
2904	024	500–599	Matthew + Mark + Luke + John
2905	022	550–599	Matthew + Mark + Luke + John
2986	1043	400–499	Matthew + Mark + Luke + John
10657		500–599	Matthew + Mark + Luke + John
2980	P45	200–250	Matthew + Mark + Luke + John + Acts
2929	05	400–450	Matthew + Mark + Luke + John + Acts + 2 John (Latin)

Table 13.6. Manuscripts with the four Gospels (and Acts)

Most of these multiple-book codices contain only two or three books. A relative few codices evince the four-Gospel collection or a Gospel collection with Acts. Matthew was grouped with the Infancy Gospel of Jesus and the Acts of Pilate. Luke was grouped with material including the Shepherd of Hermas. John was grouped with 1 Clement and some commentarial literature and school exercises. Thus, the evidence both comports and contrasts with the early evidence for the New Testament canon presented above. Christians had already acknowledged the four-Gospel collection by 180, as Irenaeus says. The canon lists indicate no disputes over this collection. Thus, the relative few codices that incorporate the four Gospels comport with the evidence above. But some codices did contain a Gospel with some unexpected material. In Greek, there was no evidence of the canonical Gospels being grouped with apocryphal Gospels such as the Gospel of Thomas. But in Latin, Matthew was joined to the Infancy Gospel of Jesus and the Acts of Pilate (!), and in Greek and Coptic, Luke and John were grouped with the Shepherd and 1 Clement, respectively.

Pauline Letters. What do the multiple-book codices show us about the Pauline letters? I present the evidence from shortest to longest collections.

Paul's letters were probably formed into a collection by AD 200, according to the statements of early Christians. The material evidence coheres with the early *testimonia* since these codices appear almost exclusively to include traditional Pauline material, even though no one codex includes all of them except the pandects (see below).

LDAB	GA	Date	Contents
3060	P34	500–699	1 Corinthians + 2 Corinthians
3008	P92	250–350	Ephesians + 2 Thessalonians
3002	0208	400–499	Colossians + 1 Thessalonians
3017	P30	175–225	1 Thessalonians + 2 Thessalonians
3054 (Coptic + Greek)	P205	500–599	Titus + Philemon
3016	P15 + P16	300–399	1 Corinthians + Philippians
3001	088	400–599	1 Corinthians + Titus
3007	0209	600–699	Romans + 2 Corinthians + 2 Peter
3063	P61	600–699	Romans + 1 Corinthians + Colossians + Philippians + 1 Thessalonians + Titus + Philemon
7312	0285 + 081	500–599	Romans + 1–2 Corinthians + Ephesians + 1 Timothy + Hebrews + Philippians
3011[1]	P46	200–250	Romans + Hebrews + 1–2 Corinthians + Ephesians + Galatians + Philippians + Colossians + 1 Thessalonians
7152	015	500–550	1–2 Corinthians + Galatians + Colossians + 1–2 Thessalonians + Hebrews + 1–2 Timothy + Titus
3044	016	500–599	1–2 Corinthians + Galatians + Ephesians + Philippians + Colossians + 1–2 Thessalonians + Hebrews + 1–2 Timothy + Titus + Philemon

[1] The codex probably contained 2 Thessalonians. Debates ensue over whether it originally contained Philemon and the Pastorals; see Edmon L. Gallagher and John D. Meade, *The Biblical Canon Lists from Early Christianity: Texts and Analysis* (Oxford: Oxford University Press, 2018), 41, and the literature cited there.

Table 13.7. Manuscripts with the Pauline Epistles

There were two other groupings:

LDAB	GA	Date	Contents
2844	0296	500–599	1 John + 2 Corinthians
3030[1]	P99	400–499	Glossary on 2 Corinthians + Galatians + Ephesians; Greek verb conjugations + alphabet

[1] This codex does not contain "literary" material; it contains grammatical commentary on these three books.

Table 13.8. Manuscripts with Pauline Epistles and non-Pauline books or material

Acts. In addition to Acts joined to the Gospels above, it is also joined with the following books:

LDAB	GA	Date	Contents
2893	0166	450–550	Acts + James
2894	P74	500–699	Acts + James + 1–2 Peter + 1–3 John + Jude
2907	093	550–599	Acts + 1 Peter
2906	048	400–499	Acts + James + 1–2 Peter + 1–3 John + Romans + 1–2 Corinthians + Ephesians + Philippians + Colossians + 1 Thessalonians + 1–2 Timothy + Titus + Philemon + Hebrews

Table 13.9. Manuscripts with Acts and the Catholic Epistles

The book of Acts appears in single-book codices and is joined with the Gospels and Catholic Epistles. Interestingly, the material evidence does not reflect a joining of Acts to the Pauline Epistles.

Catholic Epistles. In addition to being joined with Acts, these books are also joined to the following:

LDAB	GA	Date	Contents
3070	0247	400–599	1–2 Peter
2840	0251	400–599	3 John + Jude
2565 + [220465]	P72 (= Jude + 1–2 Peter)	310–350 [325–399]	Nativity of Mary / Protoevangelium of James + 3 Corinthians + Ode of Solomon 11 + Jude + Melito's *Peri Pascha* + 1–2 Peter + [Apology of Phileas + Psalms 33–34]
107771 (Coptic)		300–399	*Peri Pascha* (Melito) + 2 Maccabees + 1 Peter + Jonah + Pachomian homily on Easter
108050 (Coptic)		600–699	Psalms + Hebrews + James + end of a martyrium

Table 13.10. Manuscripts with the Catholic Epistles or Catholic Epistles and non-New Testament books

LDAB 2565 (includes P72, P.Bodm. VII [Jude] + P.Bodm. VIII [1–2 Peter]) is a fourth-century composite codex with an array of contents and an unusual compilation and codicology. Although most New Testament scholars treat P72 (Jude and 1–2 Peter) as a "single-papyrus continuous" manuscript, recent codicological analysis shows that "P.Bodmer VIII was only joined to this unit and the other quires of the composite codex at a later time," even if P.Bodm. VII and P.Bodm. VIII are considered to be from the same copyist.[28] Brent Nongbri concludes that it appears that the interval between the production of these two works was not long, but his study does call into question the notion of P72 as one continuous manuscript. Thus, 1–2 Peter (P.Bodm. VIII) were together added secondarily to the codex that already contained, with continuous pagination, P.Bodm. V (Protoevangelium of James) + P.Bodm. X (3 Corinthians) + P.Bodm. XI (Ode of Solomon 11) + Jude (P.Bodm. VII), along with the other books in the codex. Therefore, Jude and 1–2 Peter were not part of the same manuscript originally, even though the current form of the codex reveals that they were eventually joined together. But, of course, the final compilation of the codex reveals that these Catholic Epistles were joined together along with many other noncanonical works as well.

Perhaps this situation does justify the claim that "this manuscript seems to be an oddity in that it also includes a number of noncanonical works. . . . Thus P72 appears to be the exception that proves the rule" or "that it was made for private use and not to be taken as typical of early Christian manuscripts."[29] But since the primary compilation had already included Jude with noncanonical books, some scribes clearly had no issue with combining canonical and noncanonical material together. Even when scribes made a secondary compilation, they had no issue with adding 1–2 Peter to this codex that contained works of mixed status. Therefore, we cannot claim, as Kruger does, that in P72 "we do have 1 and 2 Peter and Jude preserved in the same third-century manuscript," unless we mean in a secondary, later compilation. Its "oddity" lies in its complicated compilation history, not necessarily in its inclusion of noncanonical books, since both the primary and later compilations attest to a codex with mixed contents.

Revelation. Revelation is not joined with any other New Testament book in Greek except in the pandects (see below).[30] The scribe of LDAB 2786 (includes P18; dated to 200–299), which includes Revelation 1:4-7, used the blank side of LDAB 3477 (Ex 40:26-38; dated to 200–299).

---

[28]Brent Nongbri, "The Construction of P.Bodmer VIII and the Bodmer 'Composite' or 'Miscellaneous' Codex," *NovT* 58, no. 4 (2016): 394-410, esp. 410. On 410n33, Nongbri notes that the decorative elements at the beginning and ending of Jude are different from those used in 1–2 Peter, thus suggesting they did not come from the same scribe.

[29]Kruger, *Canon Revisited*, 246.

[30]See LDAB 107887 (450–499; Coptic) for the following combination: Revelation + 1 John + Philemon.

Significance. The codices from 100 to 700 reveal a tendency for the surviving evidence most commonly to be single pages from manuscripts of unknown length. Presumably, these copies would be more portable and user-friendly than the scroll or larger codices in which many books were joined together. But if this conclusion is true, then what might it mean for the theory that early Christians adopted the codex for a canonical purpose? Would it not suggest that early Christians did not use the codex for this purpose?

The relatively fewer examples of multiple-book codices from the same period reveal some interesting features. First, most of the multiple-Gospel codices have only two or three Gospels; some have all four. In Greek manuscripts, there is no evidence of a noncanonical Gospel being joined to a canonical Gospel. Second, no codex contains all the traditional letters of Paul, but codices containing Paul's letters usually contain only Pauline letters—not other works (see discussion of pandects below). Third, some early evidence of the Catholic Epistles remains, but there is almost no evidence of an early collection of these letters (LDAB 2894 is dated between 500 and 699). Fourth, Revelation is never joined to other New Testament books from this period in Greek except for the pandects (discussed below). Fifth, some codices show that early Christians did join books from the traditional twenty-seven-book New Testament with other important works such as 1 Clement and the Shepherd, and even works such as Protoevangelium of James, the Infancy Gospel of Jesus, and the Acts of Pilate. Therefore, without the canon lists, the material evidence could be used to show a fluid New Testament canon: (1) single-book codices could be used to show an open canon and (2) the codices containing books of mixed status could be used to show that the New Testament was in constant flux. But we have the canon lists, and they do help us interpret the contents of our manuscripts.

We now need to examine the early pandects. Given this background, these codices stand out in several ways.

The early pandects. Finally, we turn to the early pandects, that is, the megacodices that contained the Old and New Testament. Because Codex Vaticanus's fourth-century text breaks off at Hebrews 9:14, we will leave it aside in this discussion; its original contents are simply too uncertain. The contents of Codex Sinaiticus (fourth century) and Codex Alexandrinus (fifth century) will be considered.

Codex Sinaiticus (01) has Gospels, Paul, Acts and the Catholic Epistles, Revelation, Barnabas, and the Shepherd, while Codex Alexandrinus (02) has Gospels, Acts and the Catholic Epistles, Paul, Revelation, and 1–2 Clement.[31] Both manuscripts have books added to the end of the traditional twenty-seven-book New Testament. How did the person who ordered these codices esteem these books? We have already seen that 1 Clement and the Shepherd were joined to other New Testament books above in 2806 (400–450) and 107965 (300–399), respectively.[32] Second Clement is found elsewhere only in Codex Hierosolymitus and a Syriac version, while Barnabas is preserved in Hierosolymitus, nine late Greek manuscripts, a papyrus fragment, and a Latin version.[33] Therefore, what does their inclusion in a biblical codex mean? Did early Christians believe that, by including books in these codices, each book was canonical, as Elliott says? Since we have the early Christian canon lists and, in some cases, specific statements on these books, we are able to evaluate the less clear evidence of their appearance in the pandects with the more explicit statements from these lists.[34]

Codex and canon: differences between them. In this final section, we describe the differences between canon and codex and suggest a theory for interpreting the contents of early Christian codices. The codex is a material document that contains one book or many. The Gospels and Pauline letters, respectively, were sometimes grouped together into one codex, but more often were not. In unusual cases, collections of the Gospels, Paul, Acts and

---

[31]In the contents of books at the beginning of 02, the Psalms of Solomon are listed as the last book of the manuscript. Either the book fell out or the plan to include it was never executed in the first place.

[32]First Clement is in Greek, attested only in 02 and Codex Hierosolymitus (AD 1056) but known from Latin, Syriac, and Coptic versions. See Michael W. Holmes, ed., *The Apostolic Fathers: Greek Texts and English Translations*, 3rd ed. (Grand Rapids, Baker Academic, 2007), 39.

The Shepherd was a very popular book, as the other eighteen Greek manuscripts show (LDAB numbers): 1094 (dated 150–250), 1095 (dated 150–225), 1097 (dated 250–299), 1098 (dated 200–250), 1099 (dated 200–299), 1101 (dated 200–399), 1102 (dated 350–399), 1103 (dated 300–350), 1104 (dated 300–399), 1105 (dated 300–399), 1106 (dated 400–450), 1108 (dated 400–499), 1109 (dated 300–499), 1110 (dated 350–499), 1111 (dated 400–499), 1112 (dated 450–550), 1113 (dated 500–599), 1115 (dated 475–525). Thomas A. Wayment, *The Text of the New Testament Apocrypha (100–400 CE)* (New York: Bloomsbury T&T Clark, 2013) includes images and transcriptions of many of these manuscripts.

[33]Holmes, *Apostolic Fathers*, 135-36, 375-76.

[34]Dan Batovici, "The Apostolic Fathers in Codex Sinaiticus and Codex Alexandrinus," *Bib* 97, no. 4 (2016): 581-605, esp. 583-84, has helpfully summarized the lines of interpretation according to scholars who believe the additional books were canonical and those who think the books are appendixes to these codices.

Catholics Epistles, and Revelation and other books could be combined into one pandect along with the Old Testament books. Thus, we might compare an ancient pandect to a library or a collection of books.[35] Early Christians read many kinds of books, and this is reflected in the remains of their codices.

A canon list, on the other hand, represents a church father's or scribe's list of authoritative books. The list may be presented as final, closed, and exclusive, as in the case of Gregory of Nazianzus, or as a simple, exclusive list of books, as in the case of Origen. The list is exclusive and contains books recognized by most or all churches as authoritative for church doctrine. Therefore, one would expect to discover differences between the contents of a codex and the canon. But do the differences amount to different canons, one represented by the codex and another represented by the canon list? I propose that the early Christian tri-fold description of religious literature accounts not only for the exclusive canon lists but also for the inclusion of useful books from the middle category of books in the codex. Thus, when we compare early Christian canon lists with the Christian pandects, we see useful books alongside canonical books, and this picture agrees with their own description.[36]

The canon lists as key. When we examine the evidence of the pandects, we cannot forget what we learned from the canon lists previously. Only one late fourth-century canon list, Apostolic Canons 85, includes some of these four extra books in its canon: 1–2 Clement.[37] But this one list shows that only a sector of churches in Syria thought 1–2 Clement were in the New Testament

---

[35]Although a little later in time, the pandect codices of the fifth and sixth centuries were considered "a sacred library/collection" (*sacra bibliotheca*); see Frans van Liere, *An Introduction to the Medieval Bible* (Cambridge: Cambridge University Press, 2014), 26. Similarly, Peter J. Williams has shown how the singular term *Bible*, with its focus on the material object, has obscured the older designation "the Scriptures," which implied a collection of works; see Peter J. Williams, "The Bible, the Septuagint, and the Apocrypha: A Consideration of Their Singularity," in *Studies on the Text and Versions of the Hebrew Bible in Honour of Robert Gordon*, ed. Geoffrey Khan and Diana Lipton (Leiden: Brill, 2012), 169-72.

[36]In the discussion of the New Testament canon, it is easy to lose sight of the fact that the Old Testament sections of these manuscripts contained canonical and useful books (e.g., Wisdom of Solomon and Tobit), as defined by early Christian canon lists, alongside one another. Thus, this proposal helps to explain not only the New Testament situation but also the Old Testament one.

[37]Batovici ("Apostolic Fathers," 598) suggests that, since the Apostolic Canons is part of the larger work of the Apostolic Constitutions, canon 85 was not intended to be "a definite list of the biblical books," but rather the list of books was included to self-legitimize an ecclesial regulation. As such, this list of books represents only a list of scriptures. But this conclusion is difficult to reconcile with how the list begins, "Now let the venerated and holy books be for all of you, clerics and laypeople." Furthermore, since the rest of the list corresponds to the other lists from the fourth century, the drafter of this list appears to consider 1–2 Clement canonical.

canon; that is, 1–2 Clement enjoyed a very limited canonical reception.[38] It should be noted that 02 places 1–2 Clement at the end and does not join them to the Catholic Epistles, as in the Apostolic Canons; thus, 02 is probably not following the Apostolic Canons. Therefore, given the other canon lists and the tri-fold description of religious literature, whoever ordered Codex Alexandrinus probably considered 1–2 Clement as useful but not canonical scripture. That is, early Christians placed the two kinds of scripture between the same covers but kept them conceptually distinct.

The Shepherd was the most popular book of these four works, given its manuscript attestation and citations. But church fathers never recognized it as canonical. Athanasius describes it as "rather useful" but does not include it in the canon (*De decretis* 18.3.2) and later relegated it to books that are to be read but are not canonical (*Festal Letters* 39). Jerome states it is not in the canon (*Prologus Galeatus*) but still useful (*Vir. ill.* 10). Rufinus includes the Shepherd among his "ecclesiastical" books that may be "read in the churches but appeal should not be made to them on points of faith" (*Commentarius in symbolum apostolorum* 36). Eusebius includes the Shepherd among his disputed-spurious books—not his "acknowledged" books (*Hist. eccl.* 3.25). Codex Claromontanus includes the Shepherd in its list with an *obelus*, probably indicating that it is not canonical. Although Origen describes the book as "very useful" and "divinely inspired" (*Commentarii in Romanos* 10.31), he does not include the work in his list of New Testament books (*Hom. Jos.* 7.1), probably because he knew that not all Christians recognized its canonicity. Finally, the Muratorian Fragment designated the Shepherd for private, not public, reading. Thus, the case of the Shepherd shows that a book may enjoy great popularity and even be cited as divinely inspired scripture but not be included in the canon. Given this context, the person who ordered Sinaiticus probably considered the Shepherd an important and useful book but not a canonical one, especially in the fourth century.

The Epistle of Barnabas was also a popular book. Clement of Alexandria wrote a commentary on it (according to Eusebius, *Hist. eccl.* 6.14.1) and

---

[38]On the reception of the Clementine letters, see Gallagher and Meade, *Biblical Canon Lists*, 54, 263-64. Eusebius describes 1 Clement as "recognized by all" (*Hist. eccl.* 3.38.1) but, significantly, he does not include it in his major discussion of the recognized and disputed books of the New Testament canon in *Historia ecclesiastica* 3.25. He knows of 2 Clement, but it enjoyed even less of a reception than 1 Clement.

mentions "the apostle Barnabas" several times in his *Stromata*. Origen calls it a "catholic epistle" (*Contra Celsum* 1.63).[39] However, once again, church fathers do not include the book in their canon lists. Eusebius lists the book among his disputed-spurious books (*Hist. eccl.* 3.25), and Codex Claromontanus includes it with an *obelus*. Jerome calls the work an *apocryphon* (*Vir. ill.* 6). Therefore, Barnabas may have been considered useful scripture, like the Shepherd, but there is no clear evidence that early Christians reckoned it among the canonical books. Its presence alongside the canonical books in a fourth-century codex only enhances the point that the codex was a sacred library or collection of scriptural books, not the concretization of the closed, biblical canon.

CONCLUSION: WHAT HATH CANON TO DO WITH CODEX?

If, as has been argued, the canon lists are the key to interpreting the contents of our codices, why have these lists not been used this way before? The reason may be that the twentieth century saw a wonderful advance in knowledge of the history of the Bible. The field of archaeology matured, and many biblical manuscripts were discovered for the first time. Now, *realia* could be esteemed more than the "cultural memory" enshrined in texts. In this same spirit, the manuscripts themselves could now be viewed as artifacts and their material remains could be evaluated accordingly. What could they tell us? Helpfully, they do provide wonderful evidence of the biblical text, and they have long been used as such by textual critics. Beyond that, they may tell us which copies were for private or public use. The codex form perhaps reveals what books were scriptural both according to the quantity of manuscripts and the physical linkages between books. Conversely, a book written on media other than the codex (e.g., the scroll) could perhaps reveal a work's unscriptural status, keeping in mind that not all "scriptural" texts were canonical for the early Christians. Although these advances in the field are welcomed, we need to interpret the material data primarily according to early Christian views of their own literature, a warning that sometimes appears to go unheeded.

But the matter need not end there. Manuscripts provide for us the textual form of the biblical books, such as longer and shorter versions of

---

Mark, and sometimes, the multibook codex agrees with Christian statements (e.g., a four-Gospel codex could be interpreted as corresponding to Christian testimony on the matter). However, as we saw, there are codices, which reflect a more open and fluid canon—but only if we think there is a strong or indicative connection or correspondence between codex and canon. This is because of the manuscripts that show that early Christians copied and promulgated other books not considered to be in their canon. But once we realize that the canon of Christian scripture is to be discovered among the many canon lists *and not in manuscripts*, the picture is clarified, and we see that the codex was primarily a repository of the varied and many books that Christians read. The canon lists can be used to interpret the various contents of the manuscripts according to the actual early Christian categories used to describe their own literature. In short, Christians did prefer the codex form, perhaps for convenience or portability or other factors, but they did not do so primarily as a means of determining or developing the canon. That important function was reserved for a much more explicit means—namely, the canon lists we find in early Christianity.

Key Takeaways

▶ Early Christians preferred the codex form over the bookroll or scroll form.

▶ Early Christians had a category for books that they considered useful and good but not canonical. Sometimes early Christians placed the two kinds of scripture (canonical and noncanonical-but-still-useful) between the same covers but kept them conceptually different.

▶ Early Christian canon lists provide the best way to interpret the varied contents of the early Christian codices.

▶ Just because a book was in the codex does not mean it was therefore deemed canonical.

Origen	Eusebius	Athanasius	Cyril	Laodicea	Apostolic Canons	Epiphanius	Syriac List	Gregory of Nazianzus	Amphilochius
Matthew–John	4 Gospels	Matthew–John	4 Gospels	Matthew–John	Matthew–John	4 Gospels	Matthew–John	Matthew–John	Matthew–John
1–2 Peter	Acts	Acts	Acts	Acts	14 of Paul	14 of Paul	Acts	? Revelation ?	Acts
James	14 of Paul's letters	James	James	James	James	Acts	Galatians	Acts	Romans
Jude	1 John	1–2 Peter	1–2 Peter	1–2 Peter	1–3 John	James	1–2 Corinthians	14 of Paul's letters	1–2 Corinthians
Letters of John	1 Peter	1–3 John	1–3 John	1–3 John	Jude	1–2 Peter	Romans	James	Galatians
Acts	? Revelation ?	Jude	Jude	Jude	1–2 Peter	1–3 John	Hebrews	1–2 Peter	Ephesians
14 of Paul's letters		Rom	14 of Paul's letters	Rom	1–2 Clement	Jude	Colossians	1–3 John	Philippians
(Revelation)	Disputed:	1–2 Corinthians		1–2 Corinthians	Acts	Revelation	Ephesians	Jude	Colossians
	James	Galatians		Galatians			Philippians		1–2 Thessalonians
	Jude	Ephesians		Ephesians			1–2 Thessalonians		1–2 Timothy
	2 Peter	Philippians		Philippians			[1]–2 Timothy		Titus
	2–3 John	Colossians		Colossians					Philemon
	Spurious:	1–2 Thessalonians		1–2 Thessalonians			Titus		Hebrews
	Acts of Paul	Hebrews		Hebrews			Philemon		James
	Shepherd of Hermas	1–2 Timothy		1–2 Timothy					1–2? Peter
	Apocalypse of Peter	Titus		Titus					1–2–3? John
	Barnabas	Philemon		Philemon					? Jude ?
	Didache	Revelation							? Revelation ?
	? Revelation ?	To be read:							
	? Gospel according to Hebrews ?	Didache							
		Shepherd of Hermas							

Table 13.11. Eastern canon lists up to AD 400

Muratorian Fragment	Claromontanus	Mommsen Catalog	Jerome	Rufinus	Breviarum Hipponensis	Augustine	Innocent I
Matthew–John	Matthew	Matthew	Matthew–John	Matthew–John	4 Gospels	Matthew–John	4 Gospels
Epistles of John	John	Mark	14 of Paul	Acts	Acts	Romans	14 of Paul's letters
Acts	Mark	John	Acts	14 of Paul's letters	14 of Paul's letters	1–2 Corinthians	1–3 John
1–2 Corinthians	Luke	Luke	James	1–2 Peter	1–2 Peter	Galatians	1–2 Peter
Ephesians	Romans	13 of Paul's letters	1–2 Peter	James	1–3 John	Ephesians	Jude
Philippians	1–2 Corinthians	Acts	1–3 John	Jude	Jude	Philippians	James
Colossians	Galatians	Revelation	Jude	1–3 John	James	1–2 Thessalonians	Acts
Galatians	Ephesians	1–3 John	Revelation	Revelation	Revelation	Colossians	Revelation
1–2 Thessalonians	1–2 Timothy	1–2 Peter		Ecclesiastical:		1–2 Timothy	
Romans	Titus			Herm.		Titus	
Philemon	Colossians			Two Ways		Philemon	
Titus	Philemon			Judgement of Peter		Hebrews	
1–2 Timothy	1–2 Peter					1–2 Peter	
Epistle to the Laodiceans (forged)	James					1–3 John	
Epistle to the Alexandrians (forged)	1–3 John					Jude	
Jude	Jude					James	
2 epistles of John	→ Barnabas					Acts	
Wisdom	Revelation					Revelation	
Revelation	Acts						
Apocalypse of Peter (private reading)	→ Shepherd of Hermas						
Shepherd of Hermas (private reading)	→ Acts of Paul						
	→ Apocalypse of Peter						

Table 13.12. Latin canon lists up to AD 400

CHAPTER FOURTEEN

MYTHS ABOUT EARLY TRANSLATIONS

THEIR NUMBER, IMPORTANCE, AND LIMITATIONS

Jeremiah Coogan

TRANSLATIONS OF THE NEW TESTAMENT have consistently been part of Christian worship and mission. Over the centuries, Christians have worshiped in languages as diverse as Latin, Syriac, Ethiopic, Hindi, and Mandarin, to name only a few. In this chapter I discuss the earliest translations ("versions") of the New Testament: those in Latin, Syriac, and Coptic.

My objective in this chapter is not to advance novel claims but to summarize the current state of scholarship. I begin by discussing how translation works and what this means for responsibly using evidence from a translation ("receptor text") to reconstruct the text from which it was translated ("source text" or *Vorlage*). I then briefly survey the translations of the New Testament in Latin, Syriac, and Coptic. I focus on major translations and revisions, on manuscript evidence, and on how language and translation technique affect use of these translations for textual criticism of the Greek New Testament.

A particular concern will be to make clear what we know about the total numbers of New Testament manuscripts in each language. This is crucial because, while there is a rich body of manuscript evidence for the text of the New Testament in a number of early translations, apologetic and popular literature is filled with unguarded overstatement on this point. For example, James MacDonald says that there are "nearly 25,000 early manuscripts of the Bible," and he is not alone in claiming this large number. Craig Blomberg also says there are twenty-five thousand, although he does not claim they are all early.[1] In fact, as we will see, while exact numbers for the versions cannot be attained, these estimates are far too large and thus give a misleading picture.

Finally, as the conclusion of the chapter, I briefly discuss early translations of the New Testament as witnesses to Christian worship, reading, teaching, and devotion. Translations of the New Testament are not, in the first instance, tools for textual criticism of the Greek New Testament. Their primary function has always been to enable Christians to encounter Scripture as the living Word of God.

USING TRANSLATIONS FOR TEXTUAL CRITICISM OF THE GREEK NEW TESTAMENT

Every language is different. Those who have undertaken the difficult task of learning a modern language know this well. Idioms confuse, grammatical structures diverge, articles and prepositions are notoriously tricky. For example, if I wanted to tell someone that I am hungry in German, I might say, "Ich habe Hunger." Woodenly, someone might translate this as "I have hunger." But no one who really knows both English and German would translate the expression that way. Instead, someone seeking to communicate my statement in good English might simply say, "I'm hungry." The two expressions perform the same communicative task, but structurally they do not quite match up.

Such challenges increase with longer and more complicated texts. Moreover, English and German are rather closely related to each other. Even readers who do not know German probably recognize cognates (German *Hunger* and English *hunger*, for example).[2] By comparison, Greek is much further separated from Syriac (a Semitic language) or Coptic (an Afro-Asiatic language). Even a relatively close cousin such as Latin poses difficulties. For example, while Greek has a definite article (ὁ/ἡ/τό, *ho/hē/to*, only

---

[1]James MacDonald, *God Wrote a Book* (Wheaton, IL: Crossway, 2004), 18; Craig L. Blomberg, *Can We Still Believe the Bible? An Evangelical Engagement with Contemporary Questions* (Grand Rapids: Brazos, 2014), 16-17, 21. Blomberg gets his number from Daniel B. Wallace, who states that "between fifteen and twenty thousand texts of the ancient versions of the New Testament remain," although he rightly adds that "there are no exact numbers because not all the manuscripts have been carefully catalogued" (J. Ed Komoszewski, M. James Sawyer, and Daniel B. Wallace, *Reinventing Jesus: How Contemporary Skeptics Miss the Real Jesus and Mislead Popular Culture* [Grand Rapids: Kregel, 2006], 79-81). A similar problem of overcounting the numbers occurs with Greek manuscripts as well. See chapter three in this volume.

[2]Of course, as someone who has learned a modern foreign language knows, there are also "false friends." A classic example is German *Gift* (poison) and English *gift*. This challenge extends beyond vocabulary; the apparent familiarity of grammatical structures can mislead us as well.

roughly corresponding to English "the"), Latin does not. Translation requires adaptation in order to convey the source text within the vocabulary and grammar of the receptor language.

Often early translations do not offer clear evidence for deciding between two or more Greek readings. This does not mean that Latin, Syriac, Coptic, or other versions of the New Testament are bad translations. Limitations for reconstructing the text of the Greek New Testament result from inevitable differences between the source language (Greek) and the receptor language. It would be similarly difficult to reconstruct the exact Greek source text used for even the most wooden modern translations of the New Testament.

We might summarize the challenges in using a translation to perform textual criticism of the Greek New Testament under four headings.

Linguistic differences. First, there are the linguistic differences I have just discussed. Because languages do not line up perfectly, some languages are not well suited to reflect certain features in a source text.[3] To return to the previous example, Latin translations are not a reliable guide for the presence or absence of the Greek article, since there is no corresponding feature in Latin.

Translation technique. This leads to a second challenge: translation technique (often discussed under the German name *Übersetzungsweise*). We must attend not only to what the receptor language *can* do but also to what the translator *actually does.* Sometimes this works in our favor. Translators occasionally go out of their way to reflect vocabulary, grammatical constructions, or syntactical features from the Greek source text consistently in Latin, Syriac, or Coptic translation. For example, while Latin does not have a definite article (roughly equivalent to English "the" or Greek ὁ/ἡ/τό, *ho/hē/to*), translators sometimes sought to indicate the presence of the Greek article using the Latin demonstrative *hic* (roughly equivalent to English "this"). The Greek ὁ κόσμος (*ho kosmos,* "the world") is often translated *hic mundus* ("this world"). We would be mistaken to conclude that the Latin *hic mundus* translates a Greek source text including the demonstrative pronoun οὗτος (*houtos,* "this"); the Latin translation *hic mundus* does, however, offer strong evidence for the Greek article in the source text.[4]

---

[3]Bruce M. Metzger's *The Early Versions of the New Testament: Their Origin, Transmission and Limitations* (Oxford: Clarendon, 1977) includes valuable contributions on "The Limitations of [Language] in Representing Greek," authored by specialists in each language discussed.

[4]See H. A. G. Houghton, *The Latin New Testament: A Guide to Its Early History, Texts, and Manuscripts* (Oxford: Oxford University Press, 2016), 147, for discussion and bibliography.

Often, however, even when the receptor language could have reflected a given feature in a way that would enable us to reconstruct the Greek source text, the translator chose not to do this. Often it is clear that the Latin text resembled the textual tradition of the Greek New Testament, but specific points of variation are impossible to discern. The translator might not think it necessary to represent a word in the source text independently by its own word in the translation. Conversely, the translator may add one or several words in order to render the Greek effectively in the receptor language.

Likewise, a given word in Greek can have multiple translation equivalents in the receptor language, or vice versa. In such cases we are aided by studies of translation technique, but these often leave multiple Greek readings as possibilities. As a result of such translation decisions, it is frequently difficult to reconstruct the source text. Many scholars thus prefer to use translations for *confirmation* rather than for *reconstruction*, but even here we must be careful. As a rule, we are on firmest ground when using early translations as evidence for additions, omissions, and transpositions of a phrase or more. For example, the absence of Mark 16:9-20 is quite clear in the fifth-century Codex Bobiensis (VL 1; *k*).[5]

Figure 14.1. Codex Bobiensis (Turin, Biblioteca Nazionale Universitaria, 1163 [G.VII.15]; Gregory-Aland *k*; Vetus Latina (1) preserves the second half of Mark, followed by the first half of Matthew. The rest of the manuscript is lost. The "longer ending" of Mark (16:9-20) was not included in this manuscript, which was copied in Africa in the fourth or fifth century. It offers our earliest manuscript evidence for the New Testament in Latin.

---

[5]Houghton, *Latin New Testament*, 160-61. While Mk 16:9-20 is a classic example, the same can be said for any variation that includes an addition or omission of a phrase or more.

Reconstructing smaller-scale readings in the Greek source text requires caution and restraint. As a general tendency, we observe that within a given language, translation tendencies shift over time from being oriented to the idiom and grammar of the receptor language to being oriented to the idiom and grammar of the source language.[6] This tendency toward revision demonstrates ongoing concern for both the authoritative status of a Greek New Testament text and the accuracy of the translation.

These first two considerations relate directly to the problem of translation. Languages differ from one another, and translators choose various approaches in order to navigate these differences. These two challenges, however, intersect with two other considerations, related to the nature of textual transmission.

Determining the version's initial text. A third challenge is the question of the initial text in the receptor language. A sixth-century Latin manuscript or a tenth-century Syriac one will not exactly preserve the initial translation into that language. All the mishaps that affect the Greek New Testament also affect a translation. Scribes make mistakes by skipping or repeating text. Parallel Gospel passages are harmonized, and Old Testament citations are modified. Translations sometimes also undergo stylistic revisions (especially in Latin) or dialectal shifts (Coptic). Before they can be used for textual criticism of the Greek New Testament, then, translations must themselves be studied and edited. If, for example, we lack a critical edition for a biblical book in the Sahidic dialect of Coptic, then it is problematic to use "the Sahidic version" for reconstructing a Greek text of that book. Textual criticism thus involves not only the New Testament in Greek but also the New Testament in translation. Despite major contributions over the past century, much remains to be done in this area.

Further contact with the Greek. Finally, contact with the Greek New Testament did not cease after an initial moment of translation. There were intentional revisions toward the Greek in a number of languages (for example, the Latin Vulgate, the Syriac Peshitta, the Philoxenian Syriac, the Harklean Syriac), bilingual manuscripts, and Christian contexts where the Greek New Testament was used alongside the New Testament in other

---

[6]See Sebastian P. Brock, "Aspects of Translation Technique in Antiquity," *GRBS* 20, no. 1 (1979): 69-87.

languages.[7] Each complicates matters. Which Greek text is reflected in a given translational reading? For example, does a given Latin reading reflect a second-century Greek source text of the Old Latin Gospels, or does it reflect Jerome's revision in the late fourth century, using a different Greek source text?

Using early translations of the New Testament as witnesses to the Greek New Testament requires caution and hard work. Sometimes a translation does not clearly support a single Greek reading. In other cases, the state of scholarship on a translation or the translation's complicated transmission history do not permit confidence about what Greek source text a reading in the translated language renders.

Why study the versions? Given these challenges, why study the versions at all? Prior to twentieth-century manuscript discoveries in Egypt, early translations (completed before most then-known manuscript witnesses) narrowed the chronological gap between textual composition and extant evidence. Translations from the second or third century offered a way to push back the date of the earliest evidence. Yet in light of recent manuscript finds, some of which themselves date back to the second and third centuries, this reason is less compelling.

The early translations consistently represent a New Testament text quite similar to what we find in Greek. Yet, as translations, they are limited. Contemporary New Testament textual criticism focuses on relatively minor differences in the Greek New Testament text. Many of these are inaccessible through translation, as a result of either linguistic difference or translation technique. It is true that some translations tend to agree more with certain streams of Greek textual transmission than with others (for example, Coptic translations tend to be similar to the Greek papyri also largely originating in Egypt, while Gothic translations more closely resemble the Byzantine text). Nonetheless, at relatively few points do translations shift the balance of evidence in favor of a particular Greek reading or plausibly attest a lost Greek reading. It is in the case of the exceptions, longer variation units such as Mark 16:9-20 or John 7:53–8:11, that translations play their most important role in the study of the Greek New Testament text.

---

[7]Beyond the scope of this chapter, moreover, are cases in which the New Testament is influenced not only by contact with Greek but also by contact with other languages (for example, influence on Armenian by Syriac and vice versa).

In a broader sense, however, the versions attest the remarkable integrity with which the New Testament text was transmitted across time and geography. If the versions reflected more extensive variation, they would be more central to textual criticism of the Greek New Testament. Their relative lack of significance for determining specific readings reflects the remarkable similarity between the Greek New Testament and early translations.

A SURVEY OF EARLY TRANSLATIONS

The earliest and most important translations of the Greek New Testament are those in Latin, Syriac, and Coptic (listed in likely order of antiquity).[8] These are the best attested in manuscript evidence, have been studied most thoroughly, and are cited regularly in editions of the Greek New Testament. Other translations, however, quickly followed these first three. By the late fourth century, most or all of the New Testament had been translated into Gothic, Ethiopic, and Armenian.[9] Still other translations followed in late antiquity and the early Middle Ages, including Georgian, Slavonic, Christian Palestinian Aramaic, and Arabic.[10] By discussing the value and challenges of using the three earliest translations, I hope that the reader will be equipped to explore others as well.

Latin. Latin is the best-attested and best-studied early translation of the New Testament, so it is a natural place to begin.[11] At least some New Testament

[8]Important introductions to the New Testament versions include Kurt Aland, ed., *Die alten Über-setzungen des Neuen Testaments, die Kirchenväterzitate und Lektionare,* ANTF 5 (Berlin: de Gruyter, 1972); Metzger, *Early Versions*; Peter J. Williams, "'Where Two or Three Are Gathered Together': The Witness of the Early Versions," in *The Early Text of the New Testament,* ed. Charles E. Hill and Michael J. Kruger (Oxford: Oxford University Press, 2012), 239-59.

[9]See S. Peter Cowe, "The Armenian Version of the New Testament," in *The Text of the New Testament in Contemporary Research: Essays on the Status Quaestionis,* 2nd ed., ed. Bart D. Ehrman and Michael W. Holmes, NTTSD 42 (Leiden: Brill, 2013), 253-92; Carla Falluomini, "The Gothic Version of the New Testament," in Ehrman and Holmes, *Text of the New Testament,* 329-50; Curt Niccum and Rochus Zuurmond, "The Ethiopic Version of the New Testament," in Ehrman and Holmes, *Text of the New Testament,* 231-52.

[10]Jeff W. Childers, "The Georgian Version of the New Testament," in Ehrman and Holmes, *Text of the New Testament,* 293-328; Metzger, *Early Versions,* 182-214 (Georgian), 394-442 (Slavonic), 75-83 (Christian Palestinian Aramaic), 257-68 (Arabic).

[11]The indispensable introduction to the Latin New Testament is now Houghton, *Latin New Testament*; for a shorter, recent introduction, see Philip Burton, "The Latin Version of the New Testament," in Ehrman and Holmes, *Text of the New Testament,* 167-200. For older discussions, see Bruce Metzger, *Early Versions,* 285-374; J. K. Elliott, "The Translation of the New Testament into Latin: The Old Latin and the Vulgate," in *ANRW* 2.26.1, ed. H. Temporini and W. Haase (Berlin: de Gruyter, 1992), 198-245; Jacobus H. Petzer, "The Latin Version of the New Testament," in *The Text of the New Testament in Contemporary Research: Essays on the Status Quaestionis,* 1st ed., ed. Bart D. Ehrman and Michael W. Holmes, SD 46 (Grand Rapids: Eerdmans, 1995), 113-30.

books may have been translated by the end of the second century, including the Gospels and Paul. The remaining books were translated by the end of the third century. These translations experienced later revisions, the most important of which is known as the Vulgate.

Old Latin. The early Latin translations are known simply as the Old Latin (or *Vetus Latina*) and attest a form of the New Testament text going back to the second century.[12] Within the Old Latin New Testament, however, we find significant textual diversity. At one time it was thought that multiple independent translations might lie behind this diversity, but this appears unlikely in light of recent research. If multiple independent translations of individual books were made, they left few identifiable traces.[13] Theories of regional text-types have experienced a similar fall from scholarly favor. For much of the twentieth century, scholars distinguished between "African" and "European" texts, each divided into further regional text-types. More recent scholarship has been less enthusiastic about this model; as Philip Burton suggests, a theory of regional text-types oversimplifies complex textual evidence. While early citations of the New Testament locate certain text-forms with particular geographic regions, a number of texts traveled widely, and some regions had more than one circulating text.[14] Furthermore, while clusters of witnesses often exhibit patterns of textual agreement with one another, clearly differentiated text-types seem hard to maintain. While parallel independent translations no longer provide a satisfactory model to explain textual diversity in the Old Latin New Testament, this diversity indicates ongoing contact with and revision toward Greek manuscripts.

Ongoing revision of the Old Latin New Testament makes sense in light of both social dynamics, which frequently included bilingual Christian communities, and the early Latin approach to translation. The first of these points is illustrated by bilingual manuscripts that place Latin alongside Greek (most famously Codex Bezae, 05).[15]

---

[12]This is especially true for books of the New Testament with comparatively limited early evidence in Greek. For an example in which the Old Latin agrees against Greek witnesses in offering a reading that may be original, we might consider Mk 9:15; for discussion, see Houghton, *Latin New Testament*, 12.

[13]Houghton, *Latin New Testament*, 12-14, 143-44.

[14]See Burton, "Latin Version"; Houghton, *Latin New Testament*, likewise avoids regional nomenclature for textual clusters.

[15]On Latin-Greek bilingual manuscripts of the New Testament, see Houghton, *Latin New Testament*, 27-31.

Here, however, we focus on the second: the Old Latin translation is oriented toward the idiom of Latin rather than the vocabulary and grammar of the Greek source text. Later revisions, starting as early as the third century, introduce a greater formal equivalence between the Latin and Greek.[16]

What does this mean in practice? On the one hand, idiomatic tendencies in the Old Latin mean that one must be careful about assuming that small-scale features of the Latin translation reflect particular features of the Greek source text. Studies of translation technique continue to explore translation tendencies that might assist in reconstructing the Greek source text. Furthermore, different books of the Bible and different points of revision demonstrate different tendencies, so we must not impose more unity on the texts we call "the Old Latin" than they actually exhibit. A side effect of such later revisions was to introduce more diversity from the Greek tradition into the Latin New Testament by using slightly different Greek texts from those that formed the basis for earlier Latin translation. As a result, multiple Latin readings for a given variation unit occasionally reflect different Greek readings. In practice, however, it is difficult to discern when a given Latin reading reflects contact with a different Greek text and when it simply reflects an inner-Latin variation.

These complexities are not unique to the Old Latin; Syriac, Coptic, and other languages also exhibit a general tendency toward idiomatic early translations and later revisions, with greater focus on formal equivalence of vocabulary and grammar. As in the case of the Old Latin, these revisions in Syriac and Coptic introduce further textual diversity from the Greek tradition. In Latin, the overall movement toward formal equivalence continues in the later revision known as the Vulgate.

Vulgate. While the Vulgate is traditionally associated with Jerome of Stridon (347–420), he is responsible only for the Gospels (completed 383/384 at the behest of Pope Damasus). Rather than producing a new translation, Jerome revised the Old Latin Gospels.[17] He began with a Latin text that circulated in Italy and revised it toward a Greek text with strong similarities to Codex Sinaiticus (01). Others in the fourth and fifth centuries followed Jerome in revising the Latin New Testament. These revisions are

---

[16]For the movement from free to formal, see Houghton, *Latin New Testament*, 11-14, 145.

[17]On Jerome and the Vulgate, see Houghton, *Latin New Testament*, 31-35; Burton, "Latin Version," 182.

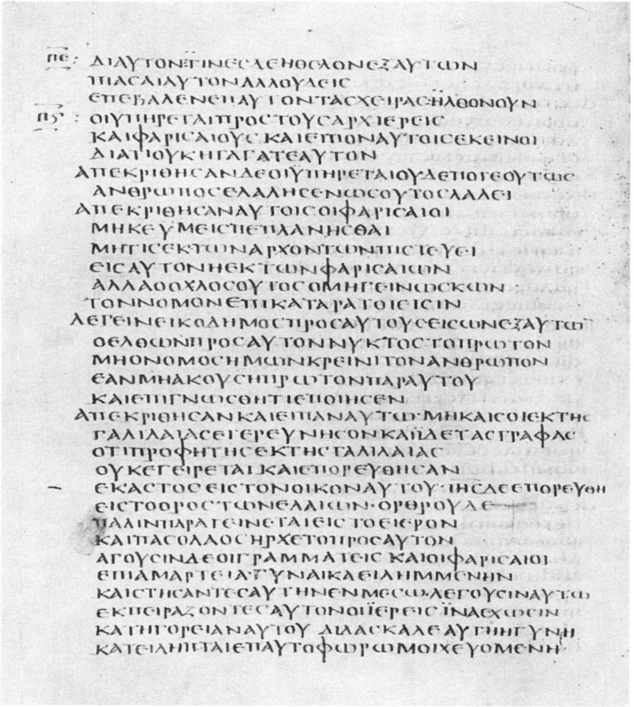

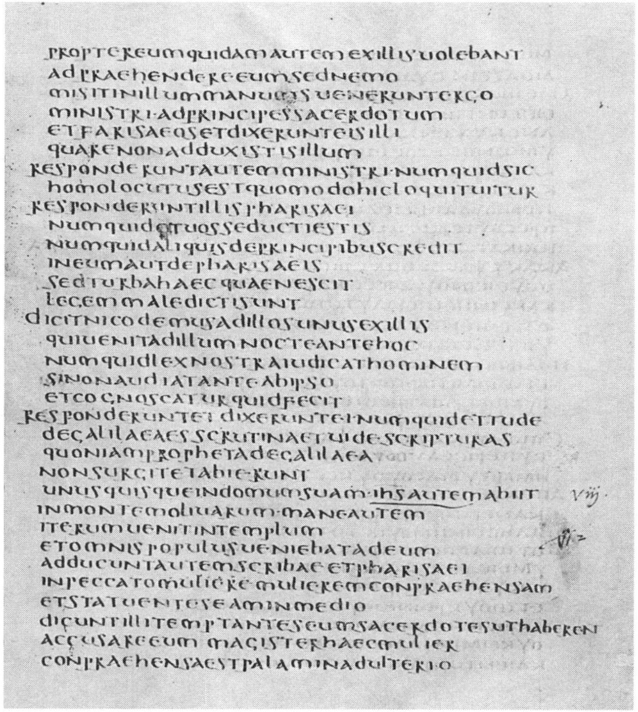

Figures 14.2 and 14.3. Codex Bezae (Gregory-Aland 05; Vetus Latina 5) is a bilingual manuscript containing the Gospels (Matthew–John–Luke–Mark), 3 John, and Acts. The manuscript dates from ca. AD 400 and may have been produced in Berytus (modern-day Beirut). The *pericope adulterae* (John 7:53–8:11) is included in the manuscript, as seen in part here with John 7:44–8:4.

anonymous, but they may be the work of one or more Pelagian scholars.[18] Jerome continues the trend of revising earlier translations toward greater conformity with Greek vocabulary and grammar. With varying degrees of consistency, other Vulgate revisers also mirror the grammar and vocabulary of their Greek base texts more closely than the Old Latin did. This means that, on the whole, the Vulgate is more suited to studying its Greek source text than is the Old Latin.

The Vulgate did not immediately replace the Old Latin.[19] On the contrary, the Vulgate took several centuries to establish itself as a widespread text, and the Old Latin flourished well into the Middle Ages. The texts we possess always reflect mixture between earlier and later translations; there are no "pure" manuscripts of either the Vulgate or the Old Latin. Not only might the text of a given book mingle Old Latin and Vulgate readings, but different parts of a manuscript might reflect different textual traditions. For example, a manuscript in which the Gospels primarily reflect the Old Latin might contain the Pauline letters in a form that primarily reflects the Vulgate (or vice versa). Furthermore, the Vulgate developed its own internal diversity, much of which did not result from direct contact with Greek.[20]

Manuscripts and citations. The earliest extant Latin New Testament manuscripts date from the fourth and fifth centuries. These are primarily parchment codices, many more or less intact. Unlike in Greek and Coptic, there are few papyrus fragments of the Latin New Testament. Unfortunately, there is no comprehensive list of Latin New Testament manuscripts corresponding to the list of Greek New Testament manuscripts kept by the INTF, so we have no reliable estimate of the total number. For the Old Latin, Houghton lists 111 manuscripts containing the New Testament.[21] For the Vulgate, precision is

---

[18]Houghton, *Latin New Testament*, 40-41.

[19]For problems with the traditional account of the Vulgate replacing the Old Latin, see Houghton, *Latin New Testament*, vii.

[20]On later revisions of the Vulgate associated with the eighth- and ninth-century scholars Alcuin and Theodulf, see Houghton, *Latin New Testament*, 104-5.

[21]For Latin editions used in NA[28], see 68*-69* and discussion below. For description and discussion of the most important Latin New Testament manuscripts, see Houghton, *Latin New Testament*, 209-96. Important lists of Old Latin manuscripts are kept by the Vetus-Latina-Institut in Beuron. Most recently published are Roger Gryson and H.-J. Frede, *Altlateinische Handschriften = Manuscrits vieux-latins: Répertoire descriptive: Deuxième partie: Mss 1-275: D'après un manuscrit inachevé de Hermann Josef Frede*, VL 1/2A (Freiburg: Herder, 1999); Roger Gryson, *Altlateinische Handschriften = Manuscrits vieux-latins: Répertoire descriptive: Deuxième partie: Mss 300-485 (manuscrits du psautier)*, VL 1/2B (Freiburg: Herder, 2004).

harder to attain; Metzger's reference to over ten thousand manuscripts of the Vulgate is often cited, but it is imprecise and possibly inaccurate.[22]

Even early and extensive manuscript evidence, however, still leaves a gap of several centuries between the initial Latin translations and the first physical evidence. As a result, citations of the Latin New Testament play a key role in the study of its textual development, especially the geographic and chronological use of particular text-forms.[23] This poses challenges, however, because some Latin authors have eclectic citation habits and because later scribes sometimes modified biblical citations in the works they copied. Using citations to study the Greek New Testament thus requires both critical editions of early Christian writings and careful attention to citation habits.[24] (While citations are less central to reconstructing the development of the New Testament in Coptic and Syriac, we find the same methodological concerns there as well.)

Standing somewhere between the categories of manuscript and citation are other phenomena that enrich our understanding of the Latin New Testament. Paratexts such as prefaces, chapter lists, and the Eusebian Gospel apparatus are important for the history and transmission of the New Testament.[25] Lectionaries and other noncontinuous manuscripts are similarly significant, though often neglected. These sources illuminate how audiences encountered the New Testament in Latin. (These features are relevant in other translations of the New Testament as well.)

Latin translations and textual criticism of the Greek New Testament. In perhaps every way, the Latin is the easiest version to use in studying the Greek New Testament.[26] There is a rich manuscript tradition in Latin. Due to the indefatigable efforts of scholars over the course of the last century, both the Old Latin and the Vulgate exist in careful critical editions, although the Old

---

[22]Metzger, *Early Versions*, 293. A full list of manuscripts is now being compiled at the Institute for Textual Scholarship and Electronic Editing (ITSEE) in Birmingham, UK.

[23]For an introduction, see H. A. G. Houghton, "The Use of the Latin Fathers for New Testament Textual Criticism," in Ehrman and Holmes, *Text of the New Testament*, 2nd ed., 375-406. As an example of responsible method, see H. A. G. Houghton, *Augustine's Text of John: Patristic Citations and Latin Gospel Manuscripts*, OECS (Oxford: Oxford University Press, 2008).

[24]For ancient citations of the Latin Bible, see Roger Gryson, *Répertoire général des auteurs ecclésiastiques latins de l'antiquité et du haut moyen-âge*, 5th ed., 2 vols. (Freiburg: Herder, 2007). See chapter twelve in this volume for more on such citations.

[25]These are discussed thoroughly by Houghton, *Latin New Testament*, 194-204.

[26]On the use of Latin translations for textual criticism of the Greek New Testament, see Burton, "Latin Version," 190-93; Houghton, *Latin New Testament*, 143-53.

Latin project is not quite complete.[27] Early Christian texts that cite the Latin New Testament are also generally well served with critical editions. Studies of Latin translation technique and of citation habits of Latin authors are available in many cases, although there are still many open avenues of research.

Latin New Testament tradition exhibits diverse approaches to translation technique, multiple revisions against different Greek New Testament texts, and mixture between major textual clusters in Latin as well as all the possibilities for textual corruption that result from manuscript copying. Latin itself, moreover, has limitations in reflecting features of the Greek New Testament.[28] These complexities require caution when using the Latin New Testament for the textual criticism of the Greek New Testament. While it is frequently impossible to decide which of two or more Greek readings a given Latin phrase renders, the Latin textual tradition reflects a New Testament text quite similar to those transmitted in Greek. As we will see, many of the challenges and complexities that we find in the Latin New Testament are similar to those in Syriac and Coptic.

Syriac. Syriac is a Semitic language that flourished across the Middle East and central Asia during late antiquity and the Middle Ages. As a result of the rich and ongoing Syriac Christian tradition and the comparatively arid climates where some Syriac Christians live, the Syriac New Testament is well preserved. Indeed, through the seventh century alone there are some 120 manuscripts of the Syriac New Testament.[29]

---

[27]The major editorial project for the Old Latin in both Old and New Testaments has been undertaken by the Vetus-Latina-Institut in Beuron. The Beuron project has completed editions for the entire New Testament except the Gospels and Romans–Galatians. The INTF has prepared editions of the Old Latin Gospels based on the work of Adolf Jülicher. For the Vulgate, two major editions are available, known by their places of publication in Stuttgart and Oxford. The Stuttgart edition is the standard Vulgate text, but the more extensive apparatus of the Oxford edition remains essential. For description and assessment, see Houghton, *Latin New Testament*, 115-25 (Beuron *Vetus Latina*), 125-27 (Jülicher), 127-29 (Stuttgart Vulgate), 129-31 (Oxford Vulgate).

[28]On linguistic challenges of reflecting a Greek text in Latin translation, see Bonifatius Fischer, "Limitations of Latin in Representing Greek," in Metzger, *Early Versions*, 362-74.

[29]For a recent introduction to the Syriac New Testament, see Peter J. Williams, "The Syriac Versions of the New Testament," in Ehrman and Holmes, *Text of the New Testament*, 2nd ed., 143-66. Important older discussions include Bruce Metzger, *Early Versions*, 3-98; Tjitze Baarda, "The Syriac Versions of the New Testament," in *Text of the New Testament*, 1st ed., 97-112.

The most up-to-date list of Syriac New Testament manuscripts is David G. K. Taylor, "Répertoire des manuscrits syriaques du Nouveau Testament," in *Le Nouveau Testament en syriaque*, ed. Jean-Claude Haelewyck (Paris: Geuthner, 2017), 291-313. For the Peshitta, this list includes only manuscripts through the thirteenth century. It also excludes Syriac lectionaries. Many Syriac manuscripts remain to be catalogued in libraries, churches, and monasteries, so this list is provisional.

The richness of Syriac New Testament translations is remarkable. The earliest translations date to the second century. The scholar Tatian (fl. ca. 160–180) wove together multiple Gospel narratives into a work known as the Diatessaron, which circulated widely in Syriac for centuries.[30] Since we lack a text of Tatian's project, it seems better to begin with the Old Syriac Gospels. The subsequent history of the Syriac includes at least three major revisions, known as the Peshitta, the Philoxenian, and the Harklean. In some books (especially those with a more tenuous place in the Syriac tradition, such as 2 Peter, 2–3 John, Jude, and Revelation) it is difficult to associate extant translations with any of these reliably. In our discussion of the Latin New Testament, we noted two major points of translation or revision (the Old Latin and the Vulgate); by contrast, Syriac has *four* major textual forms in some books.

Old Syriac. The Old Syriac Gospels may have been translated as early as the second century, although the third century is equally plausible.[31] Parts of three manuscripts remain. Two have been known for more than a century: the fourth-century Sinai palimpsest (Sy^s = Sinai syr. 30) and the fifth-century fragmentary Curetonian manuscript (Sy^c = BL Add MS 14,451 + Berlin syr. 8 + Deir al-Surian syr. frag. 9).[32] Recently, a third manuscript, a sixth-century palimpsest with portions of all four canonical Gospels (including passages not previously extant in the Old Syriac), was discovered as part of the New Finds at Saint Catherine's Monastery (Sinai syr. NF 37 + 39).[33]

The Sinaitic and the Curetonian descend from the same initial translation, but both show signs of later revision toward the Greek New Testament. The two are sufficiently different that scholars generally cite them separately. We

---

[30]The problems posed by Tatian's project are legion. The term *Diatessaron* may not derive from Tatian himself; for a number of Syriac authors (for example, Ephrem), Tatian's composition was known simply as "the Gospel." Tatian may not have used precisely four Gospels (Matthew, Mark, Luke, John). The original language of the project (Greek or Syriac) remains debated. We lack any extensive text of Tatian's work in the original language, and scholars continue to debate the appropriate methodology for reconstructing it. In light of these issues, it is problematic to use "the Diatessaron" as a straightforward witness to the Greek New Testament. Peter Williams suggests that it should instead be approached with the methodology and caution appropriate to the use of ancient citations (Williams, "Syriac Versions of the New Testament," 145).

[31]On the Old Syriac Gospels, see Metzger, *Early Versions*, 36-48. On the possible influence of the Diatessaron, see William L. Petersen, "The Diatessaron of Tatian," in Ehrman and Holmes, *Text of the New Testament*, 1st ed., 77-96; Sebastian P. Brock, "Limitations of Syriac in Representing Greek," in Metzger, *Early Versions*, 97.

[32]For editions of the Old Syriac Gospels used in NA^{28}, see 70*-71*.

[33]See Sebastian P. Brock, "Two Hitherto Unattested Passages of the Old Syriac Gospels in Palimpsests from St Catherine's Monastery, Sinai," Δελτίο Βιβλικών Μελετών 31A (2016): 7-18. A full edition will be published by David G. K. Taylor.

await further study of the New Finds manuscript and its textual relationship
to the other manuscripts of the Old Syriac Gospels.

While we have no pre-Peshitta manuscripts of Acts and Paul, citations by
fourth-century Syriac authors such as Ephrem, Aphrahat, and the anonymous author of the *Liber Graduum* ("Book of Steps") attest that these also
circulated.[34] Unfortunately, it is difficult to reconstruct these books since we
do not have any extensive texts. Even still, it is likely that—as in the case of
the Gospels—the Peshitta revised these translations rather than starting
anew. These citations pose challenges, but they offer valuable evidence for
the early Syriac transmission of the New Testament.[35] It is possible that the
Catholic Epistles and Revelation circulated in Syriac before the Peshitta, but
no identifiable traces of this remain.

Peshitta. The majority of New Testament manuscripts in Syriac are from
the version known as the Peshitta (sy[p]). The Peshitta has been the primary
Bible of Syriac Christianity for the past fifteen hundred years, although it
exhibits internal variation over time, across regions, and among Syriac
Christian communities.[36] The Peshitta also served as the source for translations into other languages in the Middle East and central Asia, including
Arabic, Middle Persian, and Sogdian.

The Peshitta New Testament was probably translated around the beginning of the fifth century, although parts may have been translated as early
as the fourth. Since the earliest extant Peshitta manuscripts date from the
fifth century, the gap between the initial production of the Peshitta text and
the earliest manuscript evidence is relatively small.[37]

---

[34]There is some debate about whether these translations should be called "Old Syriac." Peter Williams ("Syriac Versions of the New Testament," 149-50) notes that these translations are not necessarily part of the same translation as the Old Syriac Gospels and may not exhibit the same translation technique. For this reason, Williams suggests that only the Old Syriac Gospels should be
referred to as "Old Syriac." Whether one accepts this terminological suggestion, it is important to
recognize that the evidence reflects a number of different points of translation and revision rather
than a single unified collection, and to avoid imposing an undeserved unity on these different texts.

[35]See Sebastian P. Brock, "The Use of the Syriac Fathers for New Testament Textual Criticism," in
Ehrman and Holmes, *Text of the New Testament*, 2nd ed., 407-28.

[36]On the Peshitta, see Metzger, *Early Versions*, 48-63. For editions of the Peshitta used in NA[28],
see 71*. Taylor's 2017 catalogue of Syriac manuscripts includes 333 manuscripts of the Peshitta
up through the thirteenth century. Caspar Gregory (*Textkritik des Neuen Testaments* [Leipzig:
Hinrichs, 1900], 2:508-23) knew over three hundred Peshitta manuscripts, many of them later
than those catalogued by Taylor.

[37]The most securely dated fifth-century manuscript is Paris, BnF manuscript 296, no. 1°, which is
written by a hand that also produced a manuscript dated to 463/464 (Metzger, *Early Versions*,

Differences in translation technique suggest that multiple revisers are responsible for the creation of the Peshitta. Except perhaps for the "major" Catholic Epistles (James, 1 Peter, 1 John), the Peshitta is a revision rather than a new translation.[38] (This parallels the relationship of the Vulgate to the Old Latin.) The original translation did not include the "minor" Catholic Epistles (2 Peter, 2–3 John, Jude) or Revelation—or if it did, no identifiable traces remain. Peshitta manuscripts are sometimes supplemented with these books using later translations. The *pericope adulterae* (Jn 7:53–8:11) is likewise not part of the original Peshitta, but it is frequently supplemented from a later Syriac translation. The Peshitta shows a stronger orientation to the Greek source language and text than the earlier Old Syriac translations. It often resembles a Byzantine form of the Greek New Testament. Further editorial work on the Peshitta New Testament is desperately needed.

Philoxenian and associated translations. In the sixth and seventh centuries, two major projects revised

Figure 14.4. Sinai syr. NF 37, f. 2v. This sixth-century manuscript of the Old Syriac Gospels contains portions of all four canonical Gospels

the Peshitta in order to produce greater fidelity to the Greek text.[39] The first of these is known as the Philoxenian (sy[ph]) because it was commissioned by Philoxenus of Mabbug (d. 523); colophons indicate that the version was

---

49-50). Metzger discusses six further manuscripts that may date from the fifth century (49-51). Taylor identifies a total of nineteen manuscripts that may plausibly date from the fifth century (of these, eleven may instead be from the sixth century).

[38] On multiple revisers, see Williams, "Syriac Versions of the New Testament," 151 and n33; Baarda, "Syriac Versions," 108. Rather than "1 Peter" and "1 John," these two letters are simply known as "Peter" and "John" in many Peshitta manuscripts.

[39] Williams, "Syriac Versions of the New Testament," 152-53; Metzger, *Early Versions*, 63-75. For editions of the Philoxenian Syriac used in NA[28], see 71*.

Figure 14.5. BnF ms. syr. 296, no. 1º is among the oldest extant Peshitta manuscripts. While it lacks a dated colophon, the same scribe also produced BL Add. MS 14,425, a manuscript containing Genesis and Exodus dated by a colophon to 463/464. Shown here is the end of Acts and the beginning of James

completed in 507/508. This translation was designed for christological controversy; apparently the Peshitta was seen as insufficiently precise at key textual cruxes. While the Philoxenian was intended to reflect the twenty-seven-book edition of the Greek New Testament (presumably by a careful revision of the Peshitta), only the minor Catholic Epistles and Revelation are preserved for us today.[40] This was the first Syriac translation of the minor Catholic Epistles and Revelation, which were absent in the earlier Peshitta. A number of manuscripts circulated with the Peshitta in most books but the Philoxenian translation for the four minor epistles. The Syriac translation of the *pericope adulterae* (Jn 7:53–8:11) is also sometimes attributed to the Philoxenian. The limited manuscript attestation of the Philoxenian tradition may result in part from the fact that it circulated primarily in the Miaphysite Syriac church. In any case, it was mostly eclipsed by the Harklean version.[41]

Harklean. A second revision of the Peshitta was completed in 615/616 and includes the whole New Testament. Named after the bishop and scholar Thomas of Harqel (ca. 570–640), the Harklean version (sy[h]) aspires to maximal equivalence between Greek source text and Syriac translation. Indeed, it regularly defies the grammar and idiom of Syriac in order to imitate its Greek source text. As a result, the Harklean is especially valuable for reconstructing the Greek base text once one has identified the translation techniques used to render Greek into Syriac. The source text for this revision seems close to the Byzantine text except in the Catholic Epistles. The Harklean left a significant manuscript footprint, especially in the Gospels.[42]

Syriac translations and textual criticism of the Greek New Testament. Idiomatic Syriac is quite different from Greek.[43] As a result of linguistic difference, the Old Syriac and Peshitta frequently do not provide reliable evidence for many features in Greek, including word order or case, the

---

[40]Some debate exists over whether these translations are the Philoxenian, as opposed to some other anonymous version, but this is unduly skeptical. It is my judgment that the "Crawford" version of the Apocalypse is also part of the Philoxenian project. Taylor lists twenty-four manuscripts containing the Philoxenian version of the minor Catholic Epistles; the earliest is BL Add. MS 14,623, which dates to the year 823.

[41]The Harklean tradition revises the Peshitta more rigorously than the Philoxenian does; whether it revises the Peshitta as revised by the Philoxenian is harder to discern. See Williams, "Syriac Versions of the New Testament," 154-55.

[42]For editions of the Harklean Syriac in NA[28], see 71*-72*. According to Williams ("Syriac Versions of the New Testament," 154), there are more than 125 manuscripts of the Harklean version, most of them manuscripts of the Gospels. Taylor's 2017 catalogue lists only sixty-seven.

[43]Brock, "Limitations of Syriac in Representing Greek," 83-98.

presence or absence of articles, conjunctions and other small words, and verbal constructions.[44]

As an example, we might think about Mark 15:45. Here some Greek manuscripts (notably 01, 03, 019, 038, 565, followed by NA[28]) read τὸ πτῶμα (*to ptōma*, "the corpse"), while most others read τὸ σῶμα (*to sōma*, "the body").[45] 05 reads τὸ πτῶμα αὐτοῦ (*to ptōma autou*, "his corpse"). Sy[s] reads ܫܠܕܗ (*šaldeh*, "his corpse"); sy[p] reads ܦܓܪܗ (*phagreh*, "his body"). NA[28] cites sy[s] in support of τὸ πτῶμα αὐτοῦ (= 05) and sy[p] in support of τὸ σῶμα (with the majority of manuscripts). But a closer look at Syriac idiom and vocabulary makes this problematic. Both Syriac nouns appear with an affixed possessive ("his"). Since the suffix is idiomatically obligatory in Syriac, however, this does not offer evidence for the presence of the Greek possessive αὐτοῦ (*autou*) in the source text for either Syriac rendering. Thus, there is no reason why ܫܠܕܗ (*šaldeh*, noun with possessive) in sy[s] should support τὸ πτῶμα αὐτοῦ (*to ptōma autou*) rather than simply τὸ πτῶμα (*to ptōma*). Furthermore, there is no tidy way to link πτῶμα (*ptōma*) to ܫܠܕܐ (*šaldā*) and σῶμα (*sōma*) to ܦܓܪܐ (*phagrā*). The first two nouns are used only to refer to dead bodies, while the last two can refer to bodies living or dead. Yet in the narrative context, Jesus' body *is* dead. Since the body on the cross is a corpse, the Syriac translator of Mark 15:45 might reasonably use ܫܠܕܐ (*šaldā*, "corpse") to translate σῶμα (*sōma*). In short, the Sy[s] reading ܫܠܕܐ (*šaldā*) might support any of the three Greek readings. The Syriac noun ܦܓܪܐ (*phagrā*, "body") likewise has a sufficiently broad range that it can translate either πτῶμα (*ptōma*) or σῶμα (*sōma*). The Sy[p] reading ܦܓܪܗ (*phagreh*, noun with possessive) might thus also support any of the three Greek readings.

Even in the case of the Old Syriac, however, certain aspects of translation technique (for example, the transliteration of proper names) offer reliable evidence even for small-scale features of the Greek source text. Further studies of translation technique are needed. Subsequent revisions of the Syriac New Testament sought increasingly formal parallels with the Greek

---

[44]On these limitations, see Peter J. Williams, *Early Syriac Translation Technique and the Textual Criticism of the Greek Gospels*, TS, Third Series 2 (Piscataway, NJ: Gorgias, 2004); Peter J. Williams, "Some Problems in Determining the *Vorlage* of Early Syriac Versions of the NT," *NTS* 47, no. 4 (2001): 537-43; Williams, "'Where Two or Three Are Gathered Together.'"

[45]We find a similar case in Mk 15:43. For discussion of both, see Williams, "'Where Two or Three Are Gathered Together,'" 251-52.

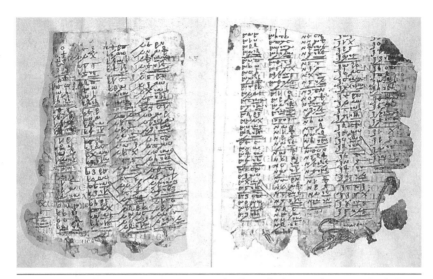

Figure 14.6. London, BL Or. MS 5707 (Gregory-Aland 086; fa 6) is a sixth-century Greek-Coptic bilingual manuscript of John's Gospel with Greek in the left column of each page and Fayumic Coptic in the right. It was later erased and over-written. Shown here is John 3:5-7 in Fayumic partially visible underneath a later Arabic text

source text. For example, while the Old Syriac regularly rearranges the word order of its Greek source, the Peshitta does so less often, and the Harklean attempts maximal correspondence, even to the detriment of comprehensibility. Numerous other characteristics reflect a similar pattern of increasingly formal relationship between Syriac and Greek.

On the whole, New Testament textual critics have focused on reconstructing the second- or third-century Greek source text of the Old Syriac; they have been comparatively less interested in the later Greek texts toward which later Syriac versions were revised. It is this early source text, however, that is hardest to reconstruct. Continued research, both on the transmission history of the Syriac New Testament in its various versions and on Syriac sources that cite the New Testament, is still needed.

Coptic. Coptic is a stage of the Egyptian language that flourished in the third through tenth centuries.[46] Egypt's arid climate preserved numerous

---

[46]A full-length introduction to the Coptic New Testament remains to be written. For an excellent shorter introduction, see Christian Askeland, "The Coptic Versions of the New Testament," in Ehrman and Holmes, *Text of the New Testament*, 2nd ed., 201-30; on method and for examples, see also Williams, "'Where Two or Three Are Gathered Together.'" In older scholarship, see Metzger, *Early Versions*, 99-152; Frederik Wisse, "The Coptic Versions of the New Testament," in Ehrman and Holmes, *Text of the New Testament*, 1st ed., 131-41.

Greek and Coptic manuscripts on papyrus and parchment in city dumps from late antiquity.[47] For all Coptic dialects except Bohairic (which continues to be used as a liturgical language by the Coptic church), this is the primary source of manuscript evidence.[48]

Paleographic dating of Coptic manuscripts is notoriously difficult, but physical evidence for the New Testament begins in the third century at the earliest. Significant manuscript finds datable to the fourth century suggest that the bulk of initial translation was completed in the later third and fourth centuries, although revision toward the Greek New Testament continued.[49]

While we know nothing about the Coptic translators or the initial contexts for translation, it is plausible that the development of Coptic writing systems and the translation of early Christian texts accompanied the rise of Egyptian monasticism.

Coptic refers to a continuum of related dialects distributed along the length of the Nile; these dialects had slightly different writing systems. New Testament texts were translated directly into a number of dialects.[50] In other

---

[47]Coptic offers many noncontinuous manuscripts with portions of the New Testament (for example, amulets and writing exercises). These pose methodological challenges but are an important part of the textual evidence and should not be ignored; see Peter M. Head, "Additional Greek Witnesses to the New Testament (Ostraca, Amulets, Inscriptions and Other Sources)," in Ehrman and Holmes, *Text of the New Testament*, 2nd ed., 429-60. For a list of Coptic magical texts from late antiquity (although not exclusively those with biblical citations), see Roxanne Bélanger Sarrazin, "Catalogue des textes magiques coptes," *APF* 63, no. 2 (2017): 367-408.

[48]There is no standard list of Coptic New Testament manuscripts, and it is difficult to estimate the total number. INTF has a collection of collations and manuscript images for Sahidic and Bohairic. The *Liste* available through the Virtual Manuscript Room includes 178 Sahidic manuscripts, but only four in Bohairic (http://ntvmr.uni-muenster.de/liste [accessed January 2, 2018]). This does not reflect extant numbers of Bohairic and Sahidic manuscripts. The International Greek New Testament Project at the University of Birmingham collated the minor Coptic versions of John (that is, dialects other than Sahidic and Bohairic) for the ECM (see www.iohannes. com; as of April 11, 2018, these collations include fourteen manuscripts in four dialects). The important Biblia Coptica series has so far focused on the Sahidic Old Testament and catalogues New Testament manuscripts only when they also contain portions of the Old Testament. All manuscripts in the Biblia Coptica series are also catalogued in the *Liste*. Many Sahidic and (especially) Bohairic manuscripts have never been transcribed or studied. The Biblia Coptica Patristica project identifies biblical citations in Coptic literature; see Karlheinz Schüssler, "Das Projekt 'Biblia Coptica Patristica,'" *OrChr* 79 (1995): 224-28.

[49]On fourth-century evidence, see Frank Feder, "Die koptische Übersetzungen des Alten und Neuen Testaments im 4. Jahrhundert," in *Stabilisierung und Profilierung der Koptischen Kirche im 4. Jahrhundert: Internationale Hallesche Koptologentagung*, ed. Jürgen Tubach and Sophia G. Vashalomidze, Halleschen Beiträgen zur Orientalwissenschaft 44 (Halle: Martin-Luther-Universität, 2007).

[50]On the development of the Coptic language and features of individual dialects, see Askeland, "Coptic Versions," 201-11, and cited literature. As Askeland notes (pp. 201-2), it is sometimes

cases, New Testament texts were not freshly translated from Greek but instead reflect adaptation of translations in a neighboring Coptic dialect (dialectal transposition). In some cases, debate continues about whether direct translation or dialectal transposition better explains the evidence. Even in the case of direct translation, interference from existing translations in other dialects is possible. In cases of dialectal transposition, moreover, revision toward the Greek and bilingual use alongside it continued throughout late antiquity.

Sahidic. The Sahidic dialect (sa) was the most influential in late ancient Egyptian Christianity. The entire New Testament is preserved in Sahidic, although some books are attested better than others. As one might expect, manuscript evidence is strongest for the Gospels. Compared with Bohairic, there are relatively few Sahidic manuscripts. The manuscripts derive primarily from excavations of late ancient trash heaps. While a comprehensive list does not exist, Christian Askeland suggests that there are between 350 and 700 manuscripts of the Sahidic New Testament.[51] As a result of significant manuscript finds during the twentieth century, new critical editions are needed for parts of the Sahidic New Testament, although recent editions of the Gospels, Acts, the Catholic Epistles, and the Apocalypse have moved the state of scholarship forward.[52]

Bohairic. Following the Arabicization of Egypt in the ninth and tenth centuries, the Bohairic dialect (bo) of Coptic continued as a liturgical language. As a result, the Bohairic New Testament has far more manuscript attestation than the other Coptic versions. (As in the case of Sahidic, however, there is no comprehensive list of manuscripts.) Unlike other dialects of Coptic, most Bohairic evidence dates from the eleventh century and after,

---

unclear when the different written conventions reflect different orthography and when they represent genuine phonetic or dialectal difference. These questions are beyond the scope of this chapter, but those interested in further exploring Coptic translations of the New Testament should be aware of them.

On relationships between Coptic versions, see Askeland, "Coptic Versions," 211-12, and cited literature. John's Gospel is particularly well attested in a number of versions and has been the basis of discussion, although one should extrapolate the case of John without confirmation.

[51] Askeland, "Coptic Versions," 207.

[52] For editions of the Sahidic used in NA[28], see 75*. For the Apocalypse, see Christian Askeland, "An Eclectic Edition of the Sahidic Apocalypse of John," in *Studien zum Text der Apokalypse II*, ed. Markus Sigismund and Darius Müller, ANTF 50 (Berlin: de Gruyter, 2017), 33-79.

although a number of manuscripts exist from as early as the fifth and sixth centuries.[53] In part this is because Bohairic was initially the dialect of the Nile Delta, where the soil was too damp to preserve manuscript remains. The Bohairic tradition reflects direct translation from Greek, and it is likely that the later Bohairic tradition was further revised toward both Greek and Arabic.[54] The only full edition of the Bohairic is that of Horner (1898–1905).[55] Especially in light of twentieth-century manuscript discoveries, further editorial work is needed.

Other dialects. In addition to translations of the New Testament in Sahidic and Bohairic, parts of the New Testament are preserved in "minor" Coptic dialects, including Akhmimic (ac), Lycopolitan (ly), Middle Egyptian (mae), and Fayumic (fa). Manuscripts of these minor versions come from archaeological excavations of late ancient papyrus and parchment, and they date between the third and eighth centuries.[56] Finds in the Akhmimic dialect include fragments of Matthew, Luke, John, Romans, Galatians, James, and Jude. This version probably reflects dialectal transposition from Sahidic rather than a fresh translation. The Lycopolitan dialect offers two manuscripts of John. While these resemble the translation of John in the closely related Sahidic dialect, the Lycopolitan does not seem to be a dialectal transposition.[57] Middle Egyptian preserves significant portions of Acts and two different versions of Matthew. While it has been suggested that one or both translations of Matthew reflect different Greek source texts than are otherwise known, these arguments have not been widely persuasive.[58] The Middle Egyptian version of Acts may be related to a text like that of Codex

---

[53]On Bohairic New Testament manuscripts from before the sixth century, see Askeland, "Coptic Versions," 206.

[54]For example, Askeland argues that the *pericope adulterae* was absent in the early Coptic versions; its presence in a number of Bohairic manuscripts is probably explained by influence from Arabic manuscripts (*John's Gospel: The Coptic Translations of Its Greek Text*, ANTF 44 [Berlin: de Gruyter, 2012], 176-77).

[55]For editions of the Bohairic used in NA[28], see 75*.

[56]For editions of the minor Coptic versions used in NA[28], see 75*-76*. For all of those discussed below, see further discussion and bibliography in Askeland, "Coptic Versions."

[57]Askeland, "Coptic Versions," 202-4.

[58]On this point, focusing primarily on one of the two Coptic Matthew manuscripts, see James M. Leonard, *Codex Schøyen 2650: A Middle Egyptian Coptic Witness to the Early Greek Text of Matthew's Gospel: A Study in Translation Theory, Indigenous Coptic, and New Testament Textual Criticism*, NTTSD 46 (Leiden: Brill, 2014).

Bezae (05).[59] The Fayumic exists only in relatively small fragments. Fayumic is closely related to its northern neighbor Bohairic, and some portions of the New Testament in Fayumic may reflect transposition from Bohairic rather than fresh translation.[60] The Fayumic New Testament certainly experienced direct contact with Greek, however, as is attested in the Greek-Fayumic bilingual manuscript 086, the Coptic portion of which is known by the siglum "fa 6."

Coptic translations and textual criticism of the Greek New Testament. Coptic translations play an important role in the textual criticism of the Greek New Testament, but caution is again required. As with Latin and Syriac, Coptic translations of the Greek New Testament are limited in reflecting their source text.[61] Coptic has a verbal structure quite different from Greek, which makes one-to-one correspondence with Greek moods and tenses problematic. Coptic generally does not allow us to identify the Greek preposition + case construction used in the source text; for the same reasons, it is often difficult to use the Coptic text in support of a Greek verb with a prepositional prefix. Coptic, like Syriac, does not have grammatical case and relies on word order and prepositions to relate the components of a sentence. For example, the Greek witnesses to Matthew 4:3 attest conflicting locations for αὐτῷ (*autō*, "to him"). Sahidic of Matthew 4:3 reads ⲁϥϯⲡⲉϥⲟⲩⲟⲉⲓ ⲉⲣⲟϥ (*aftipefouoei erof*, "he-approached to-him"), placing the equivalent of Greek αὐτῷ directly after the verb. This, however, does not support any particular location for αὐτῷ, since this is simply the standard grammatical location for this element of the sentence. These are only some of the many difficulties in reconstructing the Greek source text.

While Coptic is grammatically and syntactically different from Greek, Coptic dialects absorbed a significant number of Greek loanwords.[62]

---

[59]Eldon J. Epp, "Coptic Manuscript G67 and the Rôle of Codex Bezae as a Western Witness in Acts," *JBL* 85, no. 2 (1966): 197-212; see also Askeland, "Coptic Versions," 204-5, esp. n7.

[60]Askeland, "Coptic Versions," 205-6; see also P. E. Kahle, *Bala'izah: Coptic Texts from Deir el-Bala'izah in Upper Egypt*, 2 vols. (Oxford: Oxford University Press, 1954), 279-90.

[61]On translation technique and responsible use of Coptic translations, see Gerd Mink, "Die koptischen Versionen des Neuen Testaments: Die sprachlichen Probleme bei ihrer Bewertung für die griechische Textgeschichte," in Aland, *Alten Übersetzungen*, 160-299; J. Martin Plumley, "Limitations of Coptic (Sahidic) in Representing Greek," in Metzger, *Early Versions*, 141-52; Peter J. Williams, "On the Representation of Sahidic Within the Apparatus of the Nestle-Aland *Novum Testamentum Graece*," *Journal of Coptic Studies* 8 (2006): 123-25; Askeland, "Coptic Versions," 214.

[62]Borrowing occurred during the centuries of Ptolemaic and Roman rule, when Egypt was administered largely in Greek; it continued with Christian translation. In the later Bohairic tradition there is a shift back to indigenous Coptic vocabulary and away from Greek lexical items.

(Syriac and Latin, too, have Greek loanwords, although a comparatively lower proportion of them.) Sometimes these carry the same nuances in Greek and Coptic (functioning as true loanwords); at other points they exhibit semantic drift or stretch. This means that often a Greek loanword in Coptic translation provides evidence for that word in Greek source text, but not always; sometimes a different, more familiar Greek loanword is used instead.

As in Latin and Syriac, we are on firmest ground when citing Coptic translations for the presence or absence of large variation units (such as the *pericope adulterae*, Jn 7:53–8:11, which is absent from all Coptic translations except some late Bohairic manuscripts). In the case of smaller variations, the Coptic versions often simply do not provide a reliable basis. Careful studies of translation technique, however, continue to reveal particular patterns of correspondence between Greek and Coptic. More methodologically problematic for the use of Coptic translations in textual criticism of the Greek New Testament is a lack of adequate critical editions, especially in Bohairic.

CONCLUSION: SCRIPTURE IN TRANSLATION

In this chapter I have surveyed the main features of the New Testament as translated into Latin, Syriac, and Coptic. Although we do not have reliable total numbers of manuscripts in any of the early versions—and the total number of manuscripts is probably not as large as it often claimed—the early versions are nonetheless attested by a rich manuscript tradition that attests to the care and devotion of Christian communities who read the New Testament in translation.

Throughout the chapter I have suggested that early translations are not as useful as we might assume for reconstructing small-scale differences in their Greek base text. Further studies of translation technique may, of course, aid us in a more precise understanding of how these various translations reflect the Greek New Testament.

Yet we must remember that we are working toward different ends from those communities that translated, revised, and transmitted these early translations of the New Testament. By the fourth century, the majority of Christians no longer encountered the New Testament in Greek but in an ever-growing number of other languages. Early translations were not created primarily to aid ancient biblical scholars in reconstructing a Greek text but to serve as *Scripture*.[63] Translations are not simply witnesses for reconstructing the text of the Greek New Testament. They are witnesses to Christian theology and practice in a more robust way, as a window into how the early church studied, prayed, and worshiped.

Key Takeaways

▶ In the second to fourth centuries, the New Testament was translated from Greek into other languages such as Latin, Syriac, and Coptic. Many other translations followed later.

▶ Manuscripts of the New Testament in these versions sometimes shed light on the Greek text used by the translators, but using the translation for textual criticism of the Greek New Testament is difficult and often too fraught with problems to be useful in the details.

▶ There are probably not ten thousand Latin manuscripts, and claiming twenty-five thousand New Testament manuscripts beyond the Greek is an exaggeration too big to keep using. It is better to say there are a few thousand versional manuscripts and leave it at that.

▶ The versions are not simply of value for reconstructing the Greek text; they are immensely valuable in their own right as the Scriptures for the communities that produced them. In some cases, communities continue to use them as their only Bible.

[63]There are partial exceptions to this (for example, the Harklean Syriac), but they are later revisions that circulated alongside existing liturgical translations. See Bart D. Ehrman, "The Text as Window: New Testament Manuscripts and the Social History of Early Christianity," in Ehrman and Holmes, *Text of the New Testament*, 2nd ed., 803-29. While Ehrman focuses on the Greek New Testament, the insight applies equally to translations.

CHAPTER FIFTEEN

MYTHS ABOUT MODERN TRANSLATIONS
VARIANTS, VERDICTS, AND VERSIONS

Edgar Battad Ebojo

I DID IT MY WAY: THE TRANSMISSION OF THE NEW TESTAMENT TEXT AND THE FACE OF MODERN SCRIPTURE TRANSLATION

In its December 31, 2017, translation report, the United Bible Societies highlighted that the New Testament has now been translated into 2,189 languages worldwide.[1] For evangelical Christians, this is something to praise God for, as this means that more and more people have been provided access to the transforming Word of God in their heart languages. The other side of the coin is getting the assurance that these New Testament copies are a faithful replication of the message of the original. But how can this be achieved given that there are now many competing Greek text editions readily available in the market? How should Bible translators choose from these? Or do Bible translators even use these Greek text editions in the first place? Ultimately, how should Bible users, especially Christians who have a very high view of the Scriptures, treat textual decisions undertaken by translators, which may or may not agree with their theological convictions?

My goal here is to sketch a broad landscape of how New Testament translators worldwide perform their task, specifically when confronted with

---

[1]See "2017 Global Scripture Access Report—Gathering Momentum," United Bible Societies, March 12, 2018, www.unitedbiblesocieties.org/2017-global-scripture-access-report-gathering -momentum/. For an insightful historical narrative of the movement of the Christian Scriptures across ages and continents, see Philip A. Noss, *A History of Bible Translation* (New York: American Bible Society, 2007).

textual variations reflected in the critical apparatus of a given printed Greek text. Furthermore, since most of those who use the New Testament today read it from a particular translation, understanding the relationship that exists between textual criticism and Bible translation is a must. As such, part of my project here is to situate the theories and praxis of textual criticism in a more pragmatic scenario—in conversation with Bible translation—and see how textual criticism, as an interested discipline, is affecting (or not) those who are using the text that textual critics have reconstructed.

Textual criticism and Bible translation are not unrelated. In fact, Bible translation can become the most vital expression of textual criticism.[2] For one, many of the documentary sources examined by textual critics are themselves translations in languages such as Coptic, Latin, Syriac, and so on, intended to faithfully transmit the message of their Greek source texts. Lest we become too dogmatic about a purist approach, it is worth remembering that many, if not most, of the early Christians read *their New Testament* in a language translation that they understood best. As such, the search for the "original text" (or the *Ausgangstext*), however elusive it might seem, will always include a thorough examination of these ancient translations. The construction of a list of New Testament variants, as represented in the critical apparatuses of New Testament Greek text editions or even in more exhaustive online databases, will always take into account a comparative analysis with these ancient translations. Hence, the value of the ancient versions and translations to the text-critical discipline is indispensable in this regard.[3]

Second, while there are now comparatively more evangelicals inclined to appreciate better the intricacies of textual criticism in the source language of the New Testament, most evangelicals still encounter text-critical issues via modern translations available to them. This hiatus needs to be bridged if textual critics are to make the discipline relevant to a broader spectrum of users. It is, therefore, incumbent on evangelical textual critics to take evangelicals to another level—even if they use only modern translations. This is

---

[2]On this inviolable relationship, see Harold P. Scanlin, "Bible Translation as a Means of Communicating New Testament Textual Criticism to the Public," *BT* 39, no. 1 (1988): 101-13.

[3]On the recognition of the value of the ancient versions for New Testament textual criticism, see pertinent articles in Bart D. Ehrman and Michael W. Holmes, eds., *The Text of the New Testament in Contemporary Research: Essays on the Status Quaestionis*, 2nd ed., NTTSD 42 (Leiden: Brill, 2013), esp. 143-350.

a clarion call for relevance. But this raises the question: Can we trust the work of modern translators?

JUST DO IT: THEORIES AND PRAXES OF MODERN SCRIPTURE TRANSLATION

There are essentially two types of translation approaches employed in New Testament translations projects worldwide, with varying degrees of theoretical and methodological affinities and dissimilarities: *form-based* and *meaning-based* translations.[4] From these two approaches Bible translators choose to prepare their drafts, and their choice will determine greatly whether their drafts closely reflect the form or the meaning of their source Greek text.

This, of course, assumes that Bible translators really use Greek text editions when translating. But do they always? This is a very important question that touches the very core of a translation team, and the answer lies in the sociocultural makeup of the community where the translation is being undertaken.

The English-speaking world (as well as French, Spanish, and German-speaking) is blessed to have translators who are well equipped in the original languages of the Bible and the facility to understand and analyze them. This is not the case in most parts of the world, however. Many translation projects worldwide, especially in the Global South, employ as translators native speakers who do not have direct access to or the expertise in the original biblical languages.[5] This may come as a surprise, but this is the reality on the ground. However, many evangelicals would concur that the absence of local

---

[4]On this distinction, see Eugene A. Nida and Charles R. Taber, *The Theory and Practice of Translation*, Help for Translators 8 (Leiden: Brill, 1969) as well as Jan de Waard and Eugene Nida, *From One Language to Another: Functional Equivalence in Bible Translating* (Nashville: Thomas Nelson, 1986). But see also Stanley E. Porter, "Assessing Translation Theory: Beyond Literal and Dynamic Equivalence," in *Translating the New Testament: Text, Translation, and Theology*, ed. Stanley E. Porter and Mark J. Boda (Grand Rapids: Eerdmans, 2009), 117-45; D. A. Carson, "The Limits of Functional Equivalence in Bible Translation—and Other Limits, Too," in *The Challenge of Bible Translation: Communicating God's Word to the World—Essays in Honor of Ronald F. Youngblood*, ed. Glen G. Scorgie, Mark L. Strauss, and Steven M. Voth (Grand Rapids: Zondervan, 2003), 65-114. From a translation-studies critique, see Katharina Reiss, *Translation Criticism—The Potentials and Limitations: Categories and Criteria for Translation Quality Assessment*, trans. Erroll F. Rhodes (New York: St. Jerome, 2000), esp. 15-48; Lawrence Venuti, *The Translator's Invisibility: A History of Translation* (London: Routledge, 1995).

[5]There are also cases like this outside the Global South. Andrei Desnitsky, for instance, has passionately shared similar situations in many translation projects in Russia; see "Training Translation Teams," *BT* 56, no. 2 (2005): 98-105.

"Bible experts" must not deter the translation of the Scriptures into the heart languages of the people in need of encountering God. Scripture poverty should not be allowed to perpetuate because the community cannot offer qualified local personnel; there must be ways to address this. How do Bible publishers bridge this gap to ensure the faithful transmission of the New Testament text?

To address this grassroots reality, many Bible translation teams employ the base-model approach to translation, wherein intermediate translations (usually from the languages of wider communication) are used to check and hopefully satisfy the requirements of form, structure, and meaning of the source text in the target language to produce translations with optimum intelligibility and acceptability.[6] Furthermore, in these translation contexts the absence of local "Bible experts" is addressed through the appointment of a translation consultant assigned to a project. The translation consultant, who is usually a nonnative speaker, is a professionally qualified member of the team who can give translators advice on how best to deal with translation issues and problems, including text-critical concerns.[7]

A third safeguard in the translation process is the availability of translation tools. One of these tools is the Translator's Handbook series, a kind of translation commentary with special focus on exegesis and linguistic analyses of each book of the Bible, with various examples from around the world on how a particular passage might be translated best. This handbook series is also a good resource for discussion of text-critical problems from a decidedly translation perspective.

A handy companion to this handbook series is Roger Omanson's *A Textual Guide to the Greek New Testament*.[8] If students (and experts) of textual criticism find help in Bruce Metzger's *Textual Commentary*, New Testament translation teams are in the same way informed of the intricacies

---

[6]On this practice, see H. W. Fehderau, "The Role of Bases and Models in Bible Translations," *BT* 30, no. 4 (1979): 401-14; Robert Bascom, "Bases and Models Revisited: The Importance of Using Different Types of Reference Translations," *BT* 68, no. 1 (2017): 3-10.

[7]On the role and responsibilities of a translation consultant within a translation project, see William D. Reyburn, "The Task and Training of Translation Consultants," *BT* 20, no. 4 (1969): 168-76. It is interesting to note that some translation consultants, in a kind of a reverse scenario, have assisted (and continue to assist) textual critics involved in preparing Greek text editions designed for Bible translators. In fact, the *segmentation apparatus* integrated in the UBS editions was undertaken by a team of translation consultants spearheaded by Roger Omanson. This textual critic–translation consultant partnership continues in the preparation of the sixth edition of the UBS.

[8]Roger Omanson, *A Textual Guide to the Greek New Testament: An Adaptation of Bruce M. Metzger's Textual Commentary for the Needs of Translators* (Stuttgart: Deutsche Bibelgesellschaft, 2006).

of textual variations through Omanson's book. While Metzger's *Textual Commentary* is the basis of Omanson's *Textual Guide*, it dispenses with the technical jargon of the latter and is easier for readers whose primary language is not English.

These three component practices have proven their worth in most New Testament translation projects worldwide and need not be elaborated here except to note that, even with these safeguards, translators still cannot completely escape questions of textual integrity. This reality is betrayed by the footnotes produced alongside the published texts.

TAKE ME AS I AM: GREEK EDITIONS AND THEIR ROLE IN TRANSLATION

Choosing the Greek textual base for translation projects. The presence or absence of a text-critical footnote in any modern translation of the New Testament is largely determined by the *textual base* that the translators and/or the publisher decide to use up front. In many cases, publishers decide on the textual base to satisfy either their personal preferences or the expressed preferences of their target users.

There are now more New Testament Greek editions available to students of New Testament and to Bible translators than ever before. The most recent is the Tyndale House edition, produced under the oversight of Dirk Jongkind and Peter J. Williams. Also fairly recent is Michael Holmes's *SBL Greek New Testament*, the apparatus of which shows comparative readings of four major editions of the Greek New Testament.[9]

The underlying Greek text for the New English Bible (and also REB) was R. V. G. Tasker's *The Greek New Testament*. The subsequent revisers of the 1978 NIV ostensibly used the text now found in *A Reader's Greek New Testament*, first published by Zondervan in 2003 and now on its third edition.[10]

---

[9]Dirk Jongkind et al., eds., *The Greek New Testament, Produced at Tyndale House, Cambridge* (Wheaton, IL: Crossway, 2017); Michael Holmes, *The Greek New Testament: SBL Edition* (Atlanta: Society of Biblical Literature, 2010). The four major editions are Samuel Prideaux Tregelles, *The Greek New Testament, Edited from Ancient Authorities, with Their Various Readings in Full,* 7 vols. (London: S. Bagster & Sons, 1857–1879); B. F. Westcott and F. J. A. Hort, *The New Testament in the Original Greek*, vol. 1, *Text*; vol. 2, *Introduction, Appendix* (London: Macmillan, 1881); Richard J. Goodrich and Albert L. Lukaszewski, eds., *A Reader's Greek New Testament* (Grand Rapids: Zondervan, 2003); and Maurice A. Robinson and William G. Pierpont, eds., *The New Testament in the Original Greek: Byzantine Textform* (Southborough, MA: Chilton, 2005).

[10]R. V. G. Tasker, *The Greek New Testament, Being the Text Translated in the New English Bible* (Oxford; Oxford University Press; Cambridge: Cambridge University Press, 1964); Goodrich and Lukaszewski, *Reader's Greek New Testament.*

On the other hand, those who prefer something in the KJV tradition use the editions of the *textus receptus* published and distributed most widely by the Trinitarian Bible Society. Other KJV adherents consult Robinson and Pierpont's *The New Testament in the Original Greek* as well as Hodges and Farstad's Majority Text edition.[11]

But while these Greek text editions are available and have been market-positioned based on the strengths their publishers feature, it is yet to be seen how translators in the field will respond and use them in their translation projects. The jury is still out.

Greek text editions of the United Bible Societies. The Greek edition most widely used as base for translating the New Testament is the shared text of the United Bible Societies' *Greek New Testament* (UBS) and the Nestle-Aland *Novum Testamentum Graece* (NA), now in their fifth and twenty-eighth editions, respectively. These two editions, both published by the German Bible Society on behalf of the UBS, are a product of an interconfessional editorial committee, essentially depicting the inter-confessional ethos of the UBS.

This shared text is extensively distributed in both its printed and electronic formats. Without reducing the serious scholarship behind its conception and production, the prominence this common text receives derives largely from the global presence of national Bible societies affiliated with the UBS in more than two hundred countries. Unless there is a strong clamor from the churches they serve, the default is always the UBS-NA text.[12] The reason for this, unknown to many, is a document jointly agreed on in 1968

---

[11]Zane C. Hodges and Arthur Farstad, eds., *The Greek New Testament According to the Majority Text*, 2nd ed. (Nashville: Thomas Nelson, 1985); Robinson and Pierpont, *New Testament in the Original Greek*.

[12]Being the default text does not mean that translators follow the decisions of the editors of the UBS editions in toto. Divergence from UBS within UBS translation projects also exists; on this, see Robert G. Bratcher, "The TEV New Testament and the Greek Text," *BT* 18, no. 4 (1967): 167-74. Daniel King, "The Textual History of the New Testament and the Bible Translator," *BT* 68, no. 1 (2017): 32, carefully noting the principle of translation acceptability, writes, "Thus even if in principle a particular translation project has chosen to make UBS text its base-text, this principle will inevitably be compromised from time to time." Of course, this is equally true in any translation initiatives with an expressed textual base for a targeted audience; see Florian Voss and Roger Omanson, "The Textual Base for Modern Translations of the New Testament," *RevExp* 108, no. 2 (2011): 253-61. Interestingly, with the UBS[5], divergence of modern translations (English, French, German, and Spanish) from the common text of UBS-NA can now be easily detected by looking at the critical apparatus, which shows the putative reading chosen by modern translations different from that of the common text's adopted reading.

(revised in 1987) by the UBS and the Vatican's Secretariat for Promoting Christian Unity. This historic document is known in the Bible Society circle as the Guidelines for Interconfessional Cooperation in Translating the Bible; it states in 1.1.1.1, "For joint translation programs, teams should base their work on the critical edition of the Greek New Testament published by the United Bible Societies, which is itself a joint effort of scholars representing Roman Catholic and other Christian constituencies."[13]

The document not only specifies UBS's recommended textual base; it also intimates the sensitive challenges translators face in rendering textual judgment, especially when there is already a long tradition of Bible translation in a particular language community, as is the case for English, German, French, Spanish, and within the Orthodox circles. In such a context, Bible translation is deliberately conservative when it comes to the issue of a textual base. This is because the translator is both *an intermediary between communities* (i.e., his publisher-employer vis-à-vis his community) and *a member of that speech community*, expected to be an objective representative of the academic community but at the same time expected to represent also the interests of his faith community. Received tradition, therefore, plays a game-changing role in this context. This sensitive nature of translation is best expressed in this statement in the guidelines:

> Though a critical text [i.e., UBS] must form the basis of any adequate translation, it is recognized that in some situations certain constituencies may require that some passages of the New Testament found in the Byzantine tradition (as largely represented by the *Textus Receptus*) should be noted in the translation. When this is the case, such material may appear in footnotes with an appropriate marker in the text. The extent of textual adjustment will depend, of course, upon the local situation, and will need to be covered carefully by clear and detailed principles.

This statement touches on one of the central goals of modern translation: acceptability. Bible translators are very sensitive to this aspect of the work.

---

[13]First published in *The Bible Translator*, titled "Guiding Principles for Interconfessional Cooperation in Translating the Bible," *BT* 19, no. 3 (1968): 101-10. On how this document came about despite many hurdles, see Eugene A. Nida, *Fascinated by Languages* (Amsterdam: John Benjamins, 2003), 95-98. To a large extent, Nida was instrumental in bringing Protestants, Roman Catholics, and Orthodox together toward interconfessional initiatives in translating the Bible globally.

The guidelines further state, "Translators should normally follow this text for readings rated as A or B in *The Greek New Testament* but may choose other well attested readings when the text has a C rating." The letters *A, B, C* (and *D*) refer to the rated apparatus of UBS, which has been an integral feature of this Greek text edition since its conception, indicating the relative degree of (un-)certainty of the text adopted by the UBS Editorial Committee vis-à-vis the other existing variants. UBS is certainly not the originator of this device, but it fulfils certain functions that translators require, lest they get utterly lost in the forest of textual minutiae.[14]

This guideline recognizes the reality in the field that many communities do not have native speakers well equipped to handle the original languages of the Bible, much less to decide confidently on questions of textual integrity. Hence, a rated apparatus, with some prescriptive instructions, comes in handy. The presence of translation consultants is then reinforced by the rated apparatus in assisting native translators to make informed decisions when confronted with textual questions.

Although there has been intense critique of this system, its value for Bible translators in the field cannot be underestimated.[15] Translators often do not have direct access to textual scholarship in the same way that textual critics (mostly in North America and Europe) do. Despite this, Bible translators are committed to ensuring the accurate and faithful but also natural and meaningful transmission of the biblical text, based on the mutually agreed-on textual base. Admittedly, this decision is deliberate and does not always depend on the best methodical criteria for the choice of reading that textual critics might use.

Excluding the included: when textual tradition meets church tradition. Note must also be made of the single and double brackets in the UBS-NA and other editions, which present certain translation challenges too. Strictly speaking, brackets are part of the text rather than the apparatus, and

---

[14]On the role of the rated apparatus vis-à-vis the adopted text, see Robert P. Markham, "The Bible Societies' Greek New Testament: The End of a Decade or a Beginning of an Era?," *BT* 17, no. 3 (1966): 106-13, esp. 109-10; see also Tommy Wasserman, "Proposal for a New Rating System in Greek New Testament Editions," *BT* 60, no. 3 (2009): 140-57. On the use of this rating system in the earlier Greek text editions, see Kurt Aland and Barbara Aland, *The Text of the New Testament: An Introduction to the Critical Editions and to the Theory and Practice of Modern Textual Criticism*, 2nd ed., trans. Erroll F. Rhodes (Grand Rapids: Eerdmans, 1989), 9.

[15]Perhaps the most intense is that of Kent D. Clarke, *Textual Optimism: A Critique of the United Bible Societies' Greek New Testament*, JSNTSup 138 (Sheffield: Sheffield Academic Press, 1997).

therefore the enclosed text becomes part of the domain of the translator as well. Bracketing, in the context of New Testament textual criticism, is a necessary editorial device used when (1) it proves difficult to render a clear decision on the question of "original reading" and/or (2) an editorial committee cannot reach a satisfactory consensus.[16]

UBS and NA explain that single-bracketed entries "may be regarded as part of the text . . . but cannot be taken as completely certain."[17] Double-bracketed passages, on the other hand, are "known not to be part of the original text" but are included in the text because of their importance to the history of the church.[18] Double-bracketed passages present special challenges for translators. There are five double-bracketed passages in the UBS-NA text (Mk 16:9-20, 21, aka the shorter ending of Mark; Lk 22:43-44; 23:34a; Jn 7:53–8:11), but only two are usually marked in most translations.[19]

Almost all modern translations include John 7:53–8:11 in the main text, and it is printed immediately after John 7:52, with corresponding brackets and a marginal note.[20] This shows the tenacity of this tradition in the global translation history. It is recognized by subsequent and contemporary church tradition as not only inherently part of the New Testament but also as part of the Johannine Gospel. This has nothing to do directly with the decision

---

[16]Reviews on the practice of bracketing in UBS-NA editions include J. K. Elliott, "The United Bible Societies' Greek New Testament: An Evaluation," *NovT* 15, no. 4 (1973): 288-90; Elliott, "The Third Edition of the United Bible Societies' Greek New Testament," *NovT* 20, no. 4 (1978): 255-61; Elliott, "The United Bible Societies' Greek New Testament: A Short Examination of the Third Edition," *BT* 30, no. 1 (1979): 137; Elliott, "The New Testament in Greek: Two New Editions," *TLZ* 119 (1994): 493-96; Elliott, "The Fourth Edition of the United Bible Societies' Greek New Testament," *TRev* 90 (1994): cols. 9-20; Moises Silva, "Modern Critical Editions and Apparatuses of the Greek New Testament," in *The Text of the New Testament in Contemporary Research: Essays on the Status Quaestionis*, ed. Bart D. Ehrman and Michael W. Holmes, SD 46 (Grand Rapids: Eerdmans, 1995), 287-88; and Reider Aasgaard, "Brothers in Brackets? A Plea for Rethinking the Use of [ ] in NA/UBS," *JSNT* 26, no. 3 (2004): 301-21.

[17]UBS[5], 7*. NA[28], 54*, states that single brackets "indicate that textual critics today are not completely convinced of the authenticity of the enclosed words. . . . Square brackets always reflect a great degree of difficulty in determining the text."

[18]NA[28], 55*, and UBS[5], 7*-8*.

[19]NRSV single-brackets all these passages. While most translations single-bracket Mk 16:9-20 and Jn 7:53–8:11, the ESV and NET Bibles place these passages in double brackets. Only the NET Bible places Lk 22:43-44 and Lk 23:34a in single brackets. ASV brackets Jn 7:53–8:11 only. NIV (1984) single-brackets Mk 16:9-20 and Jn 7:53–8:11 only, but in the TNIV Mk 16:9-20 and Jn 7:53–8:11 are set in italics.

[20]Holmes, *Greek New Testament*, 208, did not include the *pericope adulterae* in the main text but printed it in the apparatus. However, Mk 16:9-20 (and the shorter ending), though equally a text-critical hotspot, was printed in the text. This raises questions about the methodological criteria for exclusion versus inclusion.

of the UBS-NA Editorial Committee but relates to the preference of the churches that have historically used translations/versions (or even manuscripts!) that included the *pericope adulterae* at this point of the Gospel.

Here is an observation worth noting. No one seems to have seriously noted this fact of praxis in translation vis-à-vis the trend of research in textual criticism. If including this passage after John 7:52 has been part of the translation tradition for as long as one can remember, what pragmatic value is there to translators and the communities they represent in the note about other locations it has been placed in the New Testament (i.e., after Jn 7:36 or Jn 21:25, or after Lk 21:38 or Lk 24:53)?

The conclusion of the Gospel of Mark presents another interesting translation case. While textual critics continue to present arguments in favor of inclusion or exclusion of passages after Mark 16:8, translators are interested in another matter—which ending to print in the main text. While textual critics continue to produce interesting treatises on the original ending of this Gospel, translators (and the faith communities they represent) seem to have decided long ago that the Gospel of Mark must not end with Mark 16:8! Their question is which of the six narrative endings to conclude with, and the answer might just be found within the four corners of their churches.[21]

TO HAVE OR NOT TO HAVE FOOTNOTES? ALTERNATIVE RENDERINGS AND ALTERNATIVE READINGS

Types of footnotes. There are aesthetic features in modern translations intended to appeal to Bible buyers, such as beautiful and colorful covers with titles in elegant and catchy type, with socially segmented product lines depending on the target audience; introductory materials to a given edition highlighting its marketing edge over the others; informative book introductions; columniation with varying degrees of sophistication; attractive section headings; impressively informative footnotes that may even threaten to upstage the main text; and others.

What many people do not realize is that several of these features have been part of the transmitted manuscripts. These include page numbers, which we see distinctly from codex manuscripts, written on the top middle

---

[21]On the six narrative endings, see David. C. Parker, *The Living Text of the Gospels* (Cambridge: Cambridge University Press, 1997), 124-47.

area of a page (e.g., P46, 01, 02, 03, etc.); book titles rendered in calligraphic and exquisite rubrications at every beginning (and sometimes also ending) of a book; capacious columniation; chapter and verse divisions, which are not features of our earliest extant manuscripts, though their concepts are represented in some ways other than numbers; a cross-referencing system, which may have been the goal of Eusebius's Canons, at least for the books of the Gospels; and many others.[22] The salient point to be underscored here is that these paratextual features were meant primarily to facilitate ease of reading of the Scriptures in a liturgical context.[23]

Of these modern aesthetic features, footnotes are perhaps the best source for giving text-critical information because many footnotes provide an immediate way to increase the reader's appreciation for the earliest recoverable text. For our present purposes, it is enough to discuss only the *textual* footnotes, of which there are two types, generally distinguished by translators as "alternative rendering" and "alternative reading" footnotes.[24]

Alternative rendering footnotes offer another way of interpreting a word or group of words because of inherent ambiguities in the source text or (seldom) because there is another way of expressing this in the receptor language. The manuscript tradition shows no (significant?) variation, but the text, as it is, can be translated in more than one possible way, which may or may not open up a whole new gamut of exegetical possibilities. Footnotes like this abound in the translations and are usually identifiable with the marker "or" (an abbreviation for the phrase "or can be translated as . . .").

---

[22]On the interesting phenomenon of chapter and verse divisions indicated by means other than numbers, see Edgar Battad Ebojo, "When Non-sense Makes Sense: Scribal Habits in the Space-Intervals, Sense-Pauses, and Other Visual Features in P46," *BT* 64, no. 2 (2013): 128-50, especially those that deal with space intervals; see also Charles E. Hill, "Rightly Dividing the Word: Uncovering an Early Template for Textual Division in John's Gospel," in *Studies on the Text of the New Testament and Early Christianity: Essays in Honour of Michael W. Holmes*, ed. Daniel M. Gurtner, Juan Hernández Jr., and Paul Foster, NTTSD (Leiden: Brill, 2015), 217-38.

[23]On the early structural markers, see David Trobisch, "Structural Markers in New Testament Manuscripts, with Special Attention to Observations in Codex Boernerianus (G 012) and Papyrus 46 of the Letters of Paul," in *Layout Markers in Biblical Manuscripts and Ugaritic Tablets*, ed. Marjo Korpel and Josef M. Oesch, Pericope 5 (Assen: Van Gorcum, 2005), 177-90; see also Larry W. Hurtado, "Manuscripts and the Sociology of Early Christian Reading," in *The Early Text of the New Testament*, ed. Charles E. Hill and Michael J. Kruger (Oxford: Oxford University Press, 2012), 49-62.

[24]Note, however, that there are other types of footnotes, such as cultural, historical, wordplay, proper-name, and textual footnotes.

One example is sufficient for the moment: the phrase ὁ δὲ δίκαιος ἐκ πίστεως ζήσεται (*ho de dikaios ek pisteōs zēsetai*) in Romans 1:17. Many evangelicals memorize this passage by heart by way of the KJV's "The just shall live by faith" (also NKJV). In effect, this is also the rendition of many early twentieth-century translations, such as the ASV (except that δίκαιος [*dikaios*] is translated as "righteous" rather than "just" [Goodspeed and JB render it as "upright"]). Conversely, translators of the 1952 RSV rendered this, "He who through faith is righteous shall live," with a footnote, "Or *The righteous shall live by faith.*"

This seems to be the first break from the KJV translation tradition, showing that this Habakkuk 2:4 quotation (also quoted in Gal 3:11; Heb 10:38) is open to two translation possibilities. The RSV's strategy (i.e., main text *cum* the alternative rendering note) is reflected by the TEV, CEV, and NABre, but many still reflect the KJV rendition plus a footnote of the alternative (CEB, CSB, ESV, HCSB, NASB, etc.), including the NRSV! Interestingly, some translations adopted one of the renditions without any footnote at all (NIV, NKJV).

In instances such as this, the transmission of the text is not at issue, but the ability of the translators to present the broad spectrum of proposed interpretations across history is nonetheless put to the limits. Ultimately, translators still have to make a choice, which obviously will support one exegetical position and relegate the other as an alternative—not an enviable position to be in.

The second type of textual footnote is the alternative reading. Unlike the alternative rendering, the manuscript tradition itself is divided in this instance, offering two or more sensible and meaningful variants. And a choice of one over the other(s) may tip the balance of interpretation toward a particular line. The textual tradition, therefore, is at issue here. It is this kind of variation that characterizes many of the textual footnotes in our modern translations, as profiled in the critical apparatuses of many Greek text editions.

Footnotes as indicators of textual integrity. Not all variations noted in the Greek base text, by virtue of the nature of language and/or the requirement of the receptor culture, need to be footnoted. Many are simply irrelevant to translation. For example, a variation unit may be linguistically relevant in the source language (or in the model text language such as

English, Spanish, or French) but not relevant at all to the receptor language.[25] Variation units that are orthographic in nature or those that have to do with word order may not always be relevant in some translation contexts, especially if they do not affect the meaning of the passage to be translated.[26]

Furthermore, and perhaps more importantly in the context of Bible translation, the end-users' sociocultural context also plays a critical factor in the choice of which variation unit to include and reject. As such, a textual critic, who is an "outsider" in a translation scenario, should not expect to see all the variation units in, say, UBS reflected in a local translation; selectivity in choices will always exist. In fact, some communities in Asia-Pacific and Africa, for example, prefer their translations of the New Testament without footnotes at all, as the presence of a footnote is perceived to reduce the "sacredness" of the translation; they believe that footnotes may encourage "uncertainty" about the firmness and immutability of God's Word. Of course, while this scenario may be theologically desirable, the history of New Testament transmission paints a more complex picture than this.

Intelligibility of the footnotes. But even footnotes that have long been present in the translation tradition are not always intelligible in the way they are structured in many English translations, which in turn are being carried over to other translations that used them as model texts.[27] Let me use the disputed portion of Luke 23:34 to illustrate this point. "And Jesus said, 'Father, forgive them because they do not know what they are doing'" (ὁ δὲ Ἰησοῦς ἔλεγεν πάτερ, ἄφες αὐτοῖς, οὐ γὰρ οἴδασιν τί ποιοῦσιν), one of the so-called Seven Last Words of Jesus, is double-bracketed in UBS, and this decision is rated A.

Most English translations print the disputed text of Luke 23:34 in the main text, enclosed in single brackets (double brackets for ESV), plus a footnote calling into question its authenticity. One's curiosity is aroused, however, once footnotes are set side by side. The ASV notes, "Some ancient authorities

---

[25] An excellent example of this is the presence or absence of prepositions (ἀπό [*apo*, "from"], ἐν [*en*, "in"], εἰς [*eis*, "into"], etc.), which can be otherwise assimilated by the definite article (ὁ [*ho*] and its derivatives) or vice versa. In some Southeast Asian countries this linguistic phenomenon in the source language does not have any significant bearing on translation.

[26] For a wide range of examples to this effect, see Roger L. Omanson, "A Critical Appraisal of the *Apparatus Criticus*," *BT* 49, no. 3 (1998): 301-23.

[27] On the unintelligibility of footnotes in English translations, see Holger Szesnat, "'Some Witnesses Have . . .': The Representation of the New Testament Text in English Bible Versions," *TC* 12 (2007): 1-18.

omit the sentence . . . ," while the RSV has "Other ancient authorities omit. . . ." A beginning Bible reader will be at a loss as to what "ancient authorities" means, whether it refers to a person in antiquity or people in the government. The use of the phrase "ancient authorities" is clearly acceptable in text-critical circles, referring to the manuscript evidence, but it can be confusing to many in the translation context.

It might seem that the term *manuscripts* is a better choice than *authorities*. Maybe, but not always. In contexts where the New Testament translation project is the first written document ever in that community (i.e., a highly oral culture), the concept of "manuscript" as a written document or artifact will prove to be cognitively challenging. In some translation projects in Vietnam and in the Philippines, translators need a descriptive phrase in reference to manuscripts (that is, "old books with old writings") to make it meaningful.

ALL THE WRONG PLACES TO BE: SOME PARATEXTUAL FEATURES IN MANUSCRIPTS THAT HAVE AFFECTED THE FACE OF SCRIPTURE TRANSLATION

There are variation units in Greek editions that have grown out of the paratextual domains of the manuscript tradition. These include indentation, paragraph segmentation, orthography, punctuation, itacism, *nomina sacra*, accents, and others. Some of these features can have implications for translations.

Nomina sacra. Mark 1:1, in the manuscript tradition, attests the readings "The beginning of the good news of Jesus Christ, the Son of God" and "The beginning of the good news of Jesus Christ."[28] Here the variation was most likely caused by the series of abbreviations for names associated with the divine, or the so-called *nomina sacra*.[29] The omission or the addition of the phrase "Son of God" could have been influenced by the optical sequence of *nomina sacra* in this sentence, involving six (or four) final *upsilon*s in a series,

---

[28]Other variants include "The beginning of the Good News of Jesus Christ, Son of the God"; "The beginning of the Good News of Jesus Christ, Son of the Lord"; and "The beginning of the Good News of Jesus."

[29]On this phenomenon, see Ludwig Traube, *Nomina Sacra: Versuch einer Geschichte der Christlichen Kurzung*, Quellen und Untersuchungen zur lateinischen Philologie des Mittelalters 2 (Munich: Beck, 1907); A. H. R. E. Paap, *Nomina Sacra in the Greek Papyri of the First Five Centuries A.D.: The Sources and Some Deductions*, Papyrologica Lugduno-Batava 8 (Leiden: Brill, 1959). Larry Hurtado's article "The Origin of the Nomina Sacra: A Proposal," *JBL* 117, no. 4 (1998): 665-73, has been updated in his *The Earliest Christian Artifacts: Manuscripts and Christian Origins* (Grand Rapids: Eerdmans, 2006), 95-134.

all written in capital (majuscule) scripts, without any spaces in between words (*scriptio continua*), that is:

ΑΡΧΗΤΟΥΕΥΑΓΓΕΛΙΟΥΙΥΧΥΥΥΘΥ

Almost all the modern translations render the first reading, either putting the appositional phrase "the Son of God" in single brackets (NABre) or simply marking it with a footnote about the other variant. Of interest is the rendition of the Lexham English Bible (LEB), which reflects the shortest reading: "The beginning of the gospel of Jesus Christ."

Itacism. Variations in the source text caused by itacism (a linguistic phenomenon in Greek wherein two different letters had been pronounced similarly) may also affect translation, at least from an exegetical point of view. Romans 5:1 is a good case in point.[30]

Manuscript evidence is divided between the subjunctive ἔχωμεν (*echōmen*, "let us have peace [with God]") and the indicative ἔχομεν (*echomen*, "we have peace [with God]"); most Greek text editions (Bengel, Tischendorf, UBS[5]/NA[28], SBL Greek New Testament, Robinson-Pierpont, Hodges-Farstad, etc.) reflect the indicative.[31] The hermeneutical question is whether Christians have peace with God already on account of Christ's vicarious sacrifice on the cross or whether Christians must still actively do something to experience peace with God.

Insofar as English translations are concerned, most reflect the indicative reading (RSV, NRSV, NABre, TEV, CEV, NLT, etc.) over the subjunctive (RV, Philips). There is some variety in the translation tradition, however. Some simply print one reading as if there is no variation in the manuscript tradition. Conversely, NIV agrees with the majority translation, but NIV 1984's footnote ("Or *let us*") is baffling, making it appear as though this is a simple case of *alternative rendering* and not a text-critical issue. HCSB's reading is even more surprising—it has in the main text, "Therefore, since we have been declared righteous by faith, we have peace with God," but the footnote interestingly says, "Other mss read *faith, let us have peace*, which can also be

---

[30]Another good example would be variation units involving the pronouns ὑμεῖς (*humeis*, "you" plural) and ἡμεῖς (*hēmeis*, "we") and their derivative forms. This text-critical question can sometimes be further compounded by the linguistic characteristics of some language communities where the first-person plural "we" is either exclusive or inclusive.

[31]Tregelles, Westcott and Hort, Nestle-1904, Tasker, and Tyndale House Greek New Testament reflect the subjunctive.

translated *faith, let us grasp the fact that we have peace*," which conflates the two readings, producing a reading witnessed by no manuscript.

Accents. Full employment of accents in the manuscript tradition was a later development, although they are used sparingly in some of the earlier extant manuscripts. They were intended primarily as optical aids to Scripture readers. But some text-critical variations involving accents may also affect the translation of the New Testament, and some may even stir heated hermeneutical discussions on the gender question.[32] Romans 16:7 is one such case, dealing with the gender of a person identified in the manuscript tradition as Ἰουνιαν (*Iounian*).

The accusative Ἰουνιαν can be translated either as feminine ("Junia") or masculine ("Junias"), and the choice is largely dependent on how this rare Greek name is accented. The manuscript tradition is divided between the acute accent (Ἰουνίαν, *Iounian*, "Junia"), the unaccented (which can then be read as Ἰουνιᾶν [*Iounian*, "Junias"; reflected by Tasker]), and the variant Ἰουλίαν (*Ioulian*, "Julia," supported primarily by P46; see Rom 16:15). Most Greek text editions prefer the first of these (Bengel, Westcott and Hort, UBS[5]-NA[28], Holmes, Hodges-Farstad, Robinson-Pierpont, etc.).

The current state of translation is equally interesting. The KJV reflects the feminine "Junia." Interestingly, the RV rendered the masculine "Junias" even though Westcott and Hort reflected the feminine form Ἰουνίαν. The ASV, RSV, NIV, JB, the Spanish Dios Habla Hoy, the German Lutherbibel, the French La Nouvelle Bible Segond, and the Traduction Oecumenique de la Bible also reflect "Junias." On the other hand, GNT, NKJV, NRSV, CEV, NLT, ESV, and others reflect the feminine "Junia."

The footnote in the NLT is a bit misleading, as it states, "Junia is a feminine name. Some late manuscripts accent the word so it reads Junias, a masculine name." This note suggests that the feminine reading results from the absence of accent, which is contrary to the manuscript evidence. The NET Bible, while supporting a feminine reading, has a long note containing

---

[32]Sometimes the issue is more translational than text-critical. For instance, the second part of Jn 14:1 has no variation in the manuscript tradition, but the accented verb πιστεύετε (*pisteuete*, either an indicative ["you believe"] or imperative ["believe!"]) opens up three translation possibilities: (1) "believe in God, believe also in me!" (imperative . . . imperative [ASV, CEV, CEB, ESV, TEV, HCSB, NLT, RSV, NRSV, TNIV, etc.]); (2) "you believe in God, you also believe in me" (indicative . . . indicative); and (3) "you believe in God, believe also in me" (indicative . . . imperative [NKJV, NABre, NET Bible, NIV, etc.]).

an intriguing comment: "In Greek only a difference of accent distinguishes between Junias (male) and Junia (female). If it refers to a woman, it is possible (1) that she had the gift of apostleship (not the office)." This type of note makes one wonder whether apostleship in the New Testament time was a matter of gifting when apostleship is associated with a woman, but an office when a masculine figure is in view.

There is a growing voice that *Iounian* here is feminine (possibly the wife of Andronicus, who had made herself equally notable among the apostles, i.e., more notable than others in the apostolic band).[33] This point is of fundamental importance because if a feminine reading of the name is right, and the subsequent clause, οἵτινές εἰσιν ἐπίσημοι ἐν τοῖς ἀποστόλοις (*hoitines eisin episēmoi en tois apostolois*), is translated as "who are prominent among the apostles," then Junia is the first woman apostle *unequivocally* mentioned in the New Testament—a thought that thrusts this text-critical issue to the center of gender studies.[34]

VARIANTS, VERDICTS, AND VERSIONS: THE CONTINUING EVOLUTION OF THE NEW TESTAMENT TEXTS IN THE CONTEXT OF BIBLE TRANSLATION

Bible translation is a viable avenue for conveying text-critical discoveries, albeit in a limited and deliberately selective way. As such, we must not expect modern translations to be the ultimate venue to exhaustively deal with text-critical concerns, the way textual critics do. The variables at play within the translation context are equally as dynamic as recovering the "original text" from ancient artifacts. In the context of evangelicalism, translation is fundamentally perceived as communicating clearly the biblical message and therefore must be judged along that primary intent.

This challenges everyone to look at translation beyond the rigidities of the text but also at the idiosyncrasies of its transmission context, to take into account the various factors at work all at the same time. What modern translators can offer is the motivation and commitment to faithfully and

---

[33]For the most extensive analysis of this variant thus far, see Eldon J. Epp, *Junia: The First Woman Apostle* (Minneapolis: Fortress, 2005), who prefers a feminine reading.

[34]For other New Testament variations with possible gender-critical resonances, see Edgar Battad Ebojo, "Sex, Scribes, and Scriptures: Engendering the Texts of the New Testament," *JBTR* 39 (2016): 367-94.

meaningfully translate the sacred Scriptures of the early church for the use of modern churches, for their own nurture, growth, and maturity. Translation settings for this commitment are not always ideal, but all safety nets, within the capabilities and limited resources of Bible-translating agencies and the target communities they serve, are put in place to arrive at this goal. Yet at the end of the day, translators, especially those concerned with clarity and meaningfulness in the receptor language, will always be found to have "altered" in some ways the form of the source text, and sometimes even the perceived meaning of the source text, in the same way that scribes of old have intimated their preferences, theological or otherwise, through the various text forms they construed to be the Word of God *for them.*

It will not escape our notice that translations do not always agree—translational diversities abound. It is sobering to note, however, that this diversity of translations reflects also the rich diversities that existed in the early church. These diversities exist because translators do not work in a theological and sociocultural vacuum; their target audience is always in front of them when they prepare their drafts. In such contexts, new "readings" will indubitably emerge, conditioned by the linguistic and sociocultural requirements of the target communities for whom the translations are being prepared. Some of these readings may surprisingly be found to have the support of some least-known manuscripts of old; but perhaps more will not enjoy any manuscript support at all.

We use various descriptive categories (e.g., omission, addition, substitution, harmonization) to describe the scribal alterations in the manuscript tradition. We may note that many of these alterations are not directionless, and not necessarily simply intended to distort God's Word either. It is more likely that these were deliberately and selectively undertaken because it made sense to the scribes and to the communities they represented. As such, if the transmission history witnesses to these deliberate alterations, it stands to reason that translators in the field also become deliberately selective in their choice of which reading to reflect as their main text and which reading to relegate as a marginal (alternative) reading in their printed Bible.

Accordingly, not all variants printed in the critical apparatuses of Greek text editions have any significant bearing for translations. Selectivity in the choices between variant readings and how alternative readings are represented is present in any translation, and the degree to which they differ is largely dictated by their target audience. While some variants have potential for their theological resonance, in many cases they are not significant for translation.

This raises a whole new set of questions for editions of the Greek New Testament intended for translators in the field concerning whether variants that do not make any difference in actual translation work at all truly warrant inclusion in the critical apparatus. Many of these are still in the variation units of UBS[5]. But the point is not only for UBS editions. This will continue to challenge any editor or editorial committee of any Greek New Testament, especially if they want to market their edited text as one prepared for Bible translators in the field.

Textual critics desiring to prepare a Greek text edition for Bible translators would do well to intently listen to Bible translators in the field, especially those who do not have direct access to the original biblical languages, to patiently probe and know from them how they are transmitting the "original text" through their translation drafts. The truth of the matter is that most modern translators outside the confines of North America and Europe work on their translation drafts daily, knowing that they are not accessing the "original text" but consciously working from model translations of scientifically reconstructed editions of the New Testament text. This is a humble recognition of the hard and painstaking labors and contributions of committed textual critics. But this similarly underscores the question of how the concept of the "original text" is to be appreciated afresh in changing, diverse contexts, in the same way that what we now call variations in the transmission history first emerged at one point in the history of the early Christians who wanted to make *their* received Scriptures relevant to *their* own contexts, without severing their connections from their spiritual forebears who passed on to them the Word of God.[35] Indeed, verdicts on variants will certainly witness the continuing evolution of the New Testament texts through the versions of God's Word used today (and in the future) in different churches worldwide.

---

[35]An emerging area of new challenges for Bible translators is "translating" the Bible for the millions of deaf communities around the world, whose language is neither written nor oral but visual (i.e., signed). How is fidelity to the "original text" to be understood in this context?

Key Takeaways

▶ Many Bible translation teams employ the base-model approach, which uses intermediate translations to guide the translators.

▶ Translators' concerns and needs do not always line up with those of modern textual critics, and in many cases the community receiving the translation will determine key questions of textual base, notation, and so on.

▶ Footnotes are where most Bible readers come into contact with textual variants. Yet translators are faced with a host of questions when thinking about when and how to use footnotes. In some translations, footnotes are not acceptable to the readers and so are not used at all.

▶ Even the paratextual features of our manuscripts can affect modern translations.

▶ Bible translation is a viable avenue for conveying text-critical information but only in a limited way, and we should not expect modern translations to be the main place for explaining text-critical issues.

BIBLIOGRAPHY

"2017 Global Scripture Access Report—Gathering Momentum." United Bible Societies. March 12, 2018. www.unitedbiblesocieties.org/2017-global-scripture-access-report-gathering-momentum/.

Aasgaard, Reider. "Brothers in Brackets? A Plea for Rethinking the Use of [ ] in NA/UBS." *JSNT* 26, no. 3 (2004): 301-21.

Adams, Sean A., and Seth M. Ehorn, eds. *Composite Citations in Antiquity*. Vol. 1, *Jewish, Graeco-Roman, and Early Christian Uses*. LNTS 525. London: Bloomsbury T&T Clark, 2015.

Aland, Barbara, Kurt Aland, Johannes Karavidopoulos, Carlo M. Martini, and Bruce M. Metzger, eds. *The Greek New Testament*. 4th rev. ed. New York: United Bible Societies, 1993.

Aland, Barbara, Kurt Aland, Gerd Mink, and Klaus Wachtel, eds. *Novum Testamentum Graecum, Editio Critica Maior: IV/1. Die Katholischen Briefe, Text*. Stuttgart: Deutsche Bibelgesellschaft, 1997.

Aland, Barbara, and Andreas Juckel. *Das Neue Testament in syrischer Überlieferung: I. Die Grossen Katholischen Briefe*. ANTF 7. Berlin: de Gruyter, 1986.

Aland, Barbara, and Klaus Wachtel. "The Greek Minuscules of the New Testament." Pages 69-91 in Ehrman and Holmes, *Text of the New Testament in Contemporary Research*, 2nd ed.

Aland, Barbara, et al., eds. *Novum Testamentum Graecum, Editio Critica Maior: IV/1. Die Katholischen Briefe, Text*. 2nd rev. ed. Stuttgart: Deutsche Bibelgesellschaft, 2013.

Aland, Barbara, et al., eds. *Novum Testamentum Graecum, Editio Critica Maior: IV.2, Die Katholischen Briefe, Begleitende Materialien*. 2nd rev. ed. Stuttgart: Deutsche Bibelgesellschaft, 2013.

Aland, Kurt, ed. *Die alten Übersetzungen des Neuen Testaments, die Kirchenväterzitate und Lektionare*. ANTF 5. Berlin: de Gruyter, 1972.

———. "Ein Neuer Textus Receptus für das Griechische Neue Testament?" *NTS* 28, no. 1 (1982): 141-53.

———, ed. *Kurzgefaßte Liste der griechischen Handschriften des Neuen Testaments*. 1st ed. ANTF 1. Berlin: de Gruyter, 1963.

———, ed. *Kurzgefaßte Liste der griechischen Handschriften des Neuen Testaments*. 2nd ed. ANTF 1. Berlin: de Gruyter, 1994.

———. "Neue neutestamentliche Papyri III: Walther Eltester zum 75. Geburtstag." *NTS* 20, no. 4 (1974): 357-81.

———. "The Significance of Papyri for Progress in New Testament Research." Pages 325-46 in *The Bible in Modern Scholarship*, edited by J. Philip Hyatt. Nashville: Abingdon, 1965.

———. "Zur Liste der griechischen neutestamentlichen Handschriften." *TLZ* 75 (1950): 58-60.

———. "Zur Liste der griechischen neutestamentlichen Handschriften." *TLZ* 78 (1953): 465-96.

Aland, Kurt, and Barbara Aland. *The Text of the New Testament: An Introduction to the Critical Editions and to the Theory and Practice of Modern Textual Criticism*. 2nd ed. Translated by Erroll F. Rhodes. Grand Rapids: Eerdmans, 1989.

Amphoux, Christian-Bernard. "La parenté textuelle du sy[h] et du groupe 2138 dans l'épître de Jacques." *Bib* 62 (1981): 259-71.

———. "Quelques témoins grecs des formes textuelles les plus anciennes de Jc: le groupe 2138." *NTS* 28, no. 1 (1982): 91-115.

Anderson, Amy S. "Codex 2193 and Family 1 in Mark." Pages 100-133 in *Studies on the Text of the New Testament and Early Christianity: Essays in Honor of Michael W. Holmes*, edited by Daniel M. Gurtner, Juan Hernández Jr., and Paul Foster, NTTSD 50. Leiden: Brill, 2015.

———. "Review of *Fundamentals of New Testament Textual Criticism*." *JETS* 59, no. 4 (2016): 846-49.

———. *The Textual Tradition of the Gospels: Family 1 in Matthew*. NTTS 32. Leiden: Brill, 2004.

Askeland, Christian. "The Coptic Versions of the New Testament." Pages 201-30 in Ehrman and Holmes, *Text of the New Testament in Contemporary Research*, 2nd ed.

———. "Dating Early Greek and Coptic Literary Hands." Pages 457-89 in *The Nag Hammadi Codices and Late Antique Egypt*, edited by Hugo Lundhaug and Lance Jennott, STAC 110. Tübingen: Mohr Siebeck, 2018.

———. "An Eclectic Edition of the Sahidic Apocalypse of John." Pages 33-79 in *Studien zum Text der Apokalypse II*, edited by Markus Sigismund and Darius Müller, ANTF 50. Berlin: de Gruyter, 2017.

———. *John's Gospel: The Coptic Translations of Its Greek Text*. ANTF 44. Berlin: de Gruyter, 2012.

Augustine. *Teaching Christianity*. Translated by Edmund Hill. Hyde Park, NY: New City Press, 1996.

Baarda, Tjitze. "The Syriac Versions of the New Testament." Pages 97-112 in Ehrman and Holmes, *Text of the New Testament in Contemporary Research*, 1st ed.

Backus, Irena D. *The Reformed Roots of the English New Testament: The Influence of Theodore Beza on the English New Testament*. PTMS 28. Eugene, OR: Pickwick, 1980.

Bagnall, Roger S. *Early Christian Books in Egypt*. Princeton, NJ: Princeton University Press, 2009.

Bagnall, Roger S., and Raffaella Cribiore. *Women's Letters from Ancient Egypt: 300 B.C.–A.D. 800*. Ann Arbor: University of Michigan Press, 2006.

Barabe, Joseph G., Abigail B. Quandt, and Margaret M. Mitchell. "Chicago's 'Archaic Mark' (MS 2427) II Microscopic, Chemical and Codicological Analyses Confirm Modern Production." *NovT* 52, no. 2 (2010): 101-33.

Barker, Don. "The Dating of New Testament Papyri." *NTS* 57, no. 4 (2011): 571-82.

———. "How Long and Old Is the Codex of Which P.Oxy 1353 Is a Leaf?" Pages 192-202 in *Jewish and Christian Scripture as Artifact and Canon*, edited by Craig A. Evans and H. Daniel Zacharias, SSEJC 13/LSTS 70. New York: T&T Clark, 2009.

Barnard, Leslie William, trans. *Saint Justin Martyr: The First and Second Apologies*. ACW 56 (New York: Paulist Press, 1997).

Barns, J. W. B., G. M. Browne, and J. C. Shelton, eds. *Nag Hammadi Codices: Greek and Coptic Papyri from the Cartonnage of the Covers*. NHS 16. Leiden: Brill, 1981.

Barrett, C. K. *The Gospel According to St. John: An Introduction with Commentary and Notes on the Greek Text*. 2nd ed. London: SPCK, 1978.

Barrett, Matthew. *God's Word Alone: The Authority of Scripture: What the Reformers Taught . . . and Why It Still Matters*. The 5 Solas. Grand Rapids: Zondervan, 2016.

Barth, Markus, and Helmut Blanke. *The Letter to Philemon*. Eerdmans Critical Commentary. Grand Rapids: Eerdmans, 2000.

Bartlett, Charles, Susan Boland, Lauren Carpenter, Stephen Kidd, Inger Kuin, and Melanie Subacus. "Six Homeric Papyri from Oxyrhynchus at Columbia University." BASP 48 (2011): 7-26.

Bascom, Robert. "Bases and Models Revisited: The Importance of Using Different Types of Reference Translations." *BT* 68, no. 1 (2017): 3-10.

Batovici, Dan. "The Apostolic Fathers in Codex Sinaiticus and Codex Alexandrinus." *Bib* 97, no. 4 (2016): 581-605.

———. "*Hermas*' Authority in Irenaeus' Works: A Reassessment." *Aug* 55, no. 1 (2015): 5-31.

———. "Hermas in Clement of Alexandria." Pages 41-51 in *Papers Presented at the Sixteenth International Conference on Patristic Studies Held in Oxford 2011*, edited by Markus Vinzent, StPatr 66. Leuven: Peeters, 2013.

Bauckham, Richard. *Jesus and the Eyewitnesses: The Gospels as Eyewitness Testimony*. 2nd ed. Grand Rapids: Eerdmans, 2017.

Baudoin, Anne-Catherine. "Le premier temoin manuscript des *Actes de Pilate* (ONB, cod 563): antiquite et autorite de la traduction latine d'un texte grec." REG tome 129, 2016.

Bauer, Walter. *Orthodoxy and Heresy in Earliest Christianity*. Edited by Robert A. Kraft and Gerhard Krodel. Philadelphia: Fortress, 1971.

———. *Rechtgläubigkeit und Ketzerei im ältesten Christentum*. Tübingen: Mohr Siebeck, 1934.

Beacham, Ian R. "The Harklean Syriac Version of Revelation: Manuscripts, Text and Methodology of Translation from Greek." PhD thesis, University of Birmingham, 1990.

Behr, John. *The Mystery of Christ: Life in Death*. Crestwood, NY: St. Vladimir's Seminary Press, 2006.

———. "The Paschal Foundations of Christian Theology." *SVTQ* 45, no. 2 (2001): 115-36.

Bélanger Sarrazin, Roxanne. "Catalogue des textes magiques coptes." *APF* 63, no. 2 (2017): 367-408.

Bell, H. I., and T. C. Skeat, eds. *Fragments of an Unknown Gospel and Other Early Christian Papyri*. London: British Museum Press, 1935.

Bell, Lonnie D. *The Early Textual Transmission of John: Stability and Fluidity in Its Second and Third Century Greek Manuscripts*. NTTSD 54. Leiden: Brill, 2018.

Bengel, J. A. "Introductio ad universam lectionis varietatem dilucidandem." In *Novum Testamentum Graecum*. Tübingen: George Cott, 1734.

Bentley, Richard. *Dr. Bentley's Proposals for the Printing of a New Edition of the Greek New Testament, and St. Hierom's Latin Version with a Full Answer to All the Remarks of a Late Pamphleteer*. London: J. Knapton, 1721.

———. "Remarks upon a Late Discourse of Free-Thinking." Pages 287-474 in vol. 3 of *The Works of Richard Bentley*, edited by Alexander Dyce. London: Robson, Levey, and Franklyn, 1838.

———. *Remarks upon a Late Discourse of Free-Thinking: In a Letter to N. N. by Phileleutherus Lispiensis*. 6th ed. Cambridge: Cambridge University Press, 1725.

Berkhof, Louis. *Systematic Theology: New Combined Edition*. Grand Rapids: Eerdmans, 1996.

Bingham, D. Jeffrey. "Senses of Scripture in the Second Century: Irenaeus, Scripture, and Noncanonical Christian Texts." *JR* 97 (2017): 26-55.

Black, David Alan, ed. *Perspectives on the Ending of Mark: Four Views*. Nashville: B&H Academic, 2008.

Black, David Alan, and Jacob N. Cerone, eds. *The Pericope of the Adulteress in Contemporary Research*. LNTS 551. London: Bloomsbury T&T Clark, 2016.

Blomberg, Craig L. *Can We Still Believe the Bible? An Evangelical Engagement with Contemporary Questions*. Grand Rapids: Brazos, 2014.

Bludau, D. *Die Schriftfälschungen der Häretiker: Ein Beitrag zur Textkritik der Bibel*. NTAbh 11. Münster: Aschendorff, 1925.

Bock, Darrell L. "Is the New Testament Trustworthy?" Pages 1452-53 in *The Apologetics Study Bible*, edited by Ted Cabal. Nashville: Holman, 2007.

Boersma, Hans. *Scripture as Real Presence: Sacramental Exegesis in the Early Church*. Grand Rapids: Baker, 2017.

Bolling, George. *The External Evidence for Interpolation in Homer*. Oxford: Clarendon, 1925.

Bowman, Alan K., Revel A. Coles, N. Gonis, Dirk Obbink, and P. J. Parsons, eds. *Oxyrhynchus: A City and Its Texts*. GRM 93. London: Egypt Exploration Society, 2007.

Bowra, Maurice. "Composition." Pages 38-74 in *A Companion to Homer*, edited by A. J. B. Wace and F. H. Stubbings. London: Macmillan, 1962.

Bratcher, Robert G. "The TEV New Testament and the Greek Text." *BT* 18, no. 4 (1967): 167-74.

Brock, Sebastian P. "Aspects of Translation Technique in Antiquity." *GRBS* 20, no. 1 (1979): 69-87.

———. *The Bible in the Syriac Tradition*. Gorgias Handbooks 7. Piscataway, NJ: Gorgias, 2006.

———. "Limitations of Syriac in Representing Greek." Pages 83-98 in *The Early Versions of the New Testament: Their Origin, Transmission, and Limitations*, by Bruce M. Metzger. Oxford: Oxford University Press, 1977.

———. "Two Hitherto Unattested Passages of the Old Syriac Gospels in Palimpsests from St Catherine's Monastery, Sinai." Δελτίο Βιβλικών Μελετών 31A (2016): 7-18.

———. "The Use of the Syriac Fathers for New Testament Textual Criticism." Pages 407-28 in Ehrman and Holmes, *Text of the New Testament in Contemporary Research: Essays on the Status Quaestionis*, 2nd ed.

Brogan, John J. "Can I Have Your Autograph? Uses and Abuses of Textual Criticism in Formulating an Evangelical Doctrine of Scripture." Pages 93-111 in *Evangelicals and Scripture: Tradition, Authority and Hermeneutics*, edited by Vincent E. Bacote, Laura Miguelez Quay, and Dennis L. Okholm. Downers Grove, IL: IVP Academic, 2004.

Brooke, George J. "Review of *Kein Markustext in Qumran: Eine Untersuchung der These: Qumran-Fragment 7Q5 = Mk 6,52-53*, by Stefan Enste." *DSD* 8, no. 3 (2001): 312-15.

Brown, Raymond E. *The Death of the Messiah: From Gethsemane to the Grave; A Commentary on the Passion Narratives in the Four Gospels*. Vol. 2. New York: Doubleday, 1994.

———. *An Introduction to the Gospel of John*. Edited by Francis J. Moloney. Anchor Yale Bible Reference Library. New Haven, CT: Yale University Press, 2003.

Brown, Virginia. "Latin Manuscripts of Caesar's Gallic War." Pages 105-57 in vol. 1 of *Palaeographia diplomatica et archivistica: Studi in onore di Giulio Battelli*, Storia e letteratura 139. Rome: Edizioni di storia e letteratura, 1979.

Bruce, F. F. *The New Testament Documents: Are They Reliable?* 5th ed. Grand Rapids: Eerdmans, 1960.

———. *The New Testament Documents: Are They Reliable?* 6th ed. Grand Rapids: Eerdmans, 1981.

———. *Tradition: Old and New*. Grand Rapids: Zondervan, 1970.

Brumbaugh, Robert S. "Plato Manuscripts: Toward a Completed Inventory." *Manuscripta* 34 (1990): 114-21.

Bultmann, Rudolf. *The Gospel of John: A Commentary*. Translated by G. R. Beasley-Murray, R. W. N. Hoare, and J. K. Riches. Philadelphia: Westminster, 1971.

Burkholder, Benjamin J. "Considering the Possibility of a Theological Corruption in Joh 1,18 in Light of Its Early Reception." *ZNW* 103, no. 1 (2012): 64-83.

Burton, Philip. "The Latin Version of the New Testament." Pages 167-200 in Ehrman and Holmes, *Text of the New Testament in Contemporary Research: Essays on the Status Quaestionis*, 2nd ed.

Carlson, Stephen C. "'Archaic Mark' (MS 2427) and the Finding of a Manuscript Fake." SBL Forum. http://sbl-site.org/Article.aspx?ArticleID=577. Accessed March 22, 2019.

Carriker, Andrew James. *The Library of Eusebius of Caesarea*. VCSup 67. Leiden: Brill, 2003.

Carson, D. A. *The Gospel According to John*. PNTC. Grand Rapids: Eerdmans, 1991.

———. *The King James Version Debate: A Plea for Realism*. Grand Rapids: Baker, 1979.

———. "The Limits of Functional Equivalence in Bible Translation—and Other Limits, Too." Pages 65-114 in *The Challenge of Bible Translation: Communicating God's Word to the World—Essays in Honor of Ronald F. Youngblood*, edited by Glen G. Scorgie, Mark L. Strauss, Steven M. Voth. Grand Rapids: Zondervan, 2003.

Cavallo, Guglielmo. "Greek and Latin Writing in the Papyri." Pages 101-48 in *The Oxford Handbook of Papyrology*, edited by Roger S. Bagnall. Oxford: Oxford University Press, 2009.

———. *Ricerche sulla maiuscola biblica*. Studi e testi di papirologia editi dall'Istituto Papirologico «G. Vitelli» di Firenze 2. Florence: Le Monnier, 1967.

Cavallo, Guglielmo, and Herwig Maehler. *Greek Bookhands of the Early Byzantine Period A.D. 300–800*. BICS Supplement 47. London: Institute of Classical Studies, 1987.

Chapa, Juan. "The Early Text of John." Pages 140-56 in *The Early Text of the New Testament*, edited by Charles E. Hill and Michael J. Kruger. Oxford: Oxford University Press, 2012.

Chapman, David W. "The Letter to the Hebrews." Pages 2357-86 in *The ESV Study Bible*, edited by Lane T. Dennis, Wayne Grudem, J. I. Packer, C. John Collins, Thomas R. Schreiner, and Justin Taylor. Wheaton, IL: Crossway, 2008.

Charlesworth, S. D. "T. C. Skeat, P^{64+67} and P^4, and the Problem of Fibre Orientation in Codicological Reconstruction." *NTS* 53, no. 4 (2007): 582-604.

Child, Lee. *Nothing to Lose*. New York: Bantam Dell, 2008.

Childers, Jeff W. "The Georgian Version of the New Testament." Pages 293-328 in Ehrman and Holmes, *Text of the New Testament in Contemporary Research: Essays on the Status Quaestionis*, 2nd ed.

Clark, Kenneth W. *A Descriptive Catalogue of Greek New Testament Manuscripts in America*. Chicago: University of Chicago Press, 1937.

———. "The Theological Relevance of Textual Variation in Current Criticism of the Greek New Testament." *JBL* 85, no. 1 (1966): 1-16.

Clarke, Kent D. *Textual Optimism: A Critique of the United Bible Societies' Greek New Testament*. JSNTSup 138. Sheffield: Sheffield Academic Press, 1997.

Clivaz, Claire. "The Angel and the Sweat like 'Drops of Blood' (Lk 22:43-44): P^{69} and f^{13}." *HTR* 98, no. 4 (2005): 419-40.

Collins, Adela Yarbro. *Mark: A Commentary*. Hermeneia. Minneapolis: Fortress, 2007.

Colwell, Ernest Cadman. "The Complex Character of the Late Byzantine Text of the Gospels." *JBL* 54, no. 4 (1935): 211-21.

———. "Method in Evaluating Scribal Habits: A Study of P^{45}, P^{66}, P^{75}." Pages 106-24 in *Studies in Methodology in Textual Criticism of the New Testament*, edited by Bruce M. Metzger, NTTS 9. Grand Rapids: Eerdmans, 1969.

Comfort, Philip W. *A Commentary on the Manuscripts and Text of the New Testament*. Grand Rapids: Kregel Academic, 2015.

———. *Encountering the Manuscripts: An Introduction to New Testament Paleography and Textual Criticism*. Nashville: Broadman & Holman, 2005.

———. *The Quest for the Original Text of the New Testament*. Grand Rapids: Baker Books, 1992.

Comfort, Philip W., and David Barrett. *The Text of the Earliest New Testament Greek Manuscripts*. Corrected, enlarged ed. Wheaton, IL: Tyndale House, 2001.

Conybeare, Frederick C. "Three Early Doctrinal Modifications upon the Text of the Gospels." *HibJ* 1, no. 1 (1902): 96-113.

Cowe, S. Peter. "The Armenian Version of the New Testament." Pages 253-92 in Ehrman and Holmes, *The Text of the New Testament in Contemporary Research: Essays on the Status Quaestionis*, 2nd ed.

Cranfield, C. E. B. "Changes of Person and Number in Paul's Epistles." Pages 280-89 in *Paul and Paulinism: Essays in Honour of C. K. Barrett*, edited by M. D. Hooker and S. G. Wilson. London: SPCK, 1982.

Crisci, Iginio. "La collezione dei papiri di Firenze." Pages 89-95 in *Proceedings of the Twelfth International Congress of Papyrology*, edited by Deborah H. Samuel, *ASP* 7. Toronto: Hakkert, 1970.

Crossan, John D. *Four Other Gospels: Shadows on the Contours of Canon*. New York: Harper & Row, 1985.

Crossway. "Crossway Statement on the ESV Bible Text." September 28, 2016. www.crossway.org /articles/crossway-statement-on-the-esv-bible-text/.

Daube, D. "'For They Know Not What They Do': Luke 23,34." Pages 58-70 in *Augustine, Post Nicene Latin Fathers, Orientalia, Nachleben of the Fathers*, edited by F. L. Cross. StPatr 4. Berlin: de Gruyter, 1961.

Davies, Margaret. *The Text of the Pauline Epistles in MS. 2344 and Its Relationship to the Text of Other Known Manuscripts, in Particular to 330, 436 and 462.* SD 38. Salt Lake City: University of Utah Press, 1968.

Deissmann, Adolf. *Light from the Ancient East: The New Testament Illustrated by Recently Discovered Texts of the Graeco-Roman World.* Translated by Lionel Strachan. New York: Hodder and Stoughton, 1910.

Delobel, Joël. "Luke 23.34a: A Perpetual Text-Critical Crux?" Pages 25-36 in *Sayings of Jesus: Canonical and Noncanonical: Essays in Honor of Tjitze Baarda,* edited by William L. Petersen, Johan S. Vos, and Henk J. de Jonge. Leiden: Brill, 1997.

DeMoss, Matthew S. *Pocket Dictionary for the Study of New Testament Greek.* IVP Pocket Reference. Downers Grove, IL: IVP Academic, 2001.

Desnitsky, Andrei. "Training Translation Teams." *BT* 56, no. 2 (2005): 98-105.

Dobschütz, Ernst von. "Zur Liste der Neutestamentlichen Handschriften. II." *ZNW* 25 (1926): 299-306.

———. "Zur Liste der Neutestamentlichen Handschriften. IV." *ZNW* 32 (1933): 185-206.

Dodd, C. H. *New Testament Studies.* Manchester: Manchester University Press, 1953.

Donaldson, Amy M. "Explicit References to New Testament Variant Readings Among Greek and Latin Church Fathers." 2 vols. PhD diss., University of Notre Dame, 2009.

Dormandy, Michael. "How the Books Became the Bible: The Evidence for Canon Formation from Work-Combinations in Manuscripts." *TC* 23 (2018), http://jbtc.org/v23/TC-2018-Dormandy.pdf.

Dru, Josephine K. "Radiocarbon Dating for Manuscripts on Papyrus or Parchment: Improving Interpretation Through Interdisciplinary Dialogue." Poster presented at ManuSciences, Villa Clythia, Frejus, France, September 2017.

Ebojo, Edgar Battad. "Sex, Scribes, and Scriptures: Engendering the Texts of the New Testament." *JBTR* 39 (2016): 367-94.

———. "When Non-sense Makes Sense: Scribal Habits in the Space-Intervals, Sense-Pauses, and Other Visual Features in P[46]." *BT* 64, no. 2 (2013): 128-50.

Edwards, Brian H. *Why 27? How Can We Be Sure That We Have the Right Books in the New Testament?* Darlington, UK: Evangelical Press, 2007.

Edwards, Sarah A. "P75 Under the Magnifying Glass." *NovT* 18, no. 3 (1976): 190-212.

Ehrman, Bart D. "First-Century Copy of Mark?—Part 1." *The Bart Ehrman Blog: The History & Literature of Early Christianity.* April 6, 2012. https://ehrmanblog.org/first-century-copy-of-mark-part-1-members.

———. *Jesus, Interrupted: Revealing the Hidden Contradictions in the Bible (and Why We Don't Know About Them).* New York: HarperOne, 2009.

———. *Misquoting Jesus: The Story Behind Who Changed the Bible and Why.* New York: HarperCollins, 2005.

———. "The New Testament Canon of Didymus the Blind." *VC* 37 (1983): 1-21.

———. *The Orthodox Corruption of Scripture: The Effect of Early Christological Controversies on the Text of the New Testament.* 2nd ed. Oxford: Oxford University Press, 2011.

———. "Text and Interpretation: The Exegetical Significance of the 'Original' Text." Pages 307-24 in *Studies in the Textual Criticism of the New Testament,* NTTS 33. Leiden: Brill, 2006.

———. "Text and Transmission: The Historical Significance of the 'Altered' Text." Pages 325-42 in *Studies in the Textual Criticism of the New Testament,* NTTS 33. Leiden: Brill, 2006.

———. "The Text as Window: New Testament Manuscripts and the Social History of Early Christianity." Pages 803-29 in Ehrman and Holmes, *Text of the New Testament in Contemporary Research: Essays on the Status Quaestionis,* 2nd ed.

———. "Would a First-Century Fragment of Mark Matter?" *The Bart Ehrman Blog: The History & Literature of Early Christianity.* January 24, 2015. http://ehrmanblog.org/would-a-first-century-fragment-of-mark-matter/.

Ehrman, Bart D., Gordon D. Fee, and Michael W. Holmes. *The Text of the Fourth Gospel in the Writings of Origen.* Volume 1. SBLNTGF 3. Atlanta: Society of Biblical Literature, 1992.

Ehrman, Bart D., and Michael W. Holmes, eds. *The Text of the New Testament in Contemporary Research: Essays on the Status Quaestionis.* 1st ed. SD 46. Grand Rapids: Eerdmans, 1995.

———. *The Text of the New Testament in Contemporary Research: Essays on the Status Quaestionis.* 2nd ed. NTTSD 42. Leiden: Brill, 2013.

Ehrman, Bart D., and Mark A. Plunkett. "The Angel and the Agony: The Textual Problem of Luke 22:43-44." *CBQ* 45, no. 3 (1983): 401-16.

Ehrman, Bart D., and Daniel B. Wallace. "The Textual Reliability of the New Testament: A Dialogue." Pages 13-60 in *The Reliability of the New Testament: Bart D. Ehrman and Daniel B. Wallace in Dialogue,* edited by Robert B. Stewart. Minneapolis: Fortress Press, 2011.

Eichenwald, Kurt. "The Bible: So Misunderstood It's a Sin." *Newsweek.* January 2015. www.newsweek .com/2015/01/02/thats-not-what-bible-says-294018.html.

Elliott, J. K. "Absent Witnesses? The Critical Apparatus to the Greek New Testament and the Apostolic Fathers." Pages 47-58 in *The Reception of the New Testament in the Apostolic Fathers,* edited by Andrew Gregory and Christopher Tuckett. Oxford: Oxford University Press, 2005.

———. *A Bibliography of Greek New Testament Manuscripts.* 3rd ed. Leiden: Brill, 2015.

———. *Codex Sinaiticus and the Simonides Affair: An Examination of the Nineteenth Century Claim That Codex Sinaiticus Was Not an Ancient Manuscript.* Analecta Vlatadon 33. Thessaloniki: Patriarchal Institute for Patristic Studies, 1982.

———. "The Early Text of the Catholic Epistles." Pages 204-24 in *The Early Text of the New Testament,* edited by Charles E. Hill and Michael J. Kruger. Oxford: Oxford University Press, 2012.

———. "The Fourth Edition of the United Bible Societies' Greek New Testament." *TRev* 90 (1994): cols. 9-20.

———. "Manuscripts, the Codex and the Canon." *JSNT* 63 (1996): 105-23.

———. "The New Testament in Greek: Two New Editions." *TLZ* 119 (1994): 493-96.

———. "Review of *The Earliest Gospel Manuscript: The Qumran Fragment 7Q5 and Its Significance for New Testament Studies.*" *NovT* 36, no. 1 (1994): 98-100.

———. "Review of *The Jesus Papyrus* by Carsten Peter Thiede and Matthew d'Ancona and *Gospel Truth* by Graham Stanton." *NovT* 38, no. 4 (1996): 393-99.

———. "The Third Edition of the United Bible Societies' Greek New Testament." *NovT* 20, no. 4 (1978): 255-61.

———. "The Translation of the New Testament into Latin: The Old Latin and the Vulgate." Pages 198-245 in *ANRW* 2.26.1, edited by H. Temporini and W. Haase. Berlin: de Gruyter, 1992.

———. "The United Bible Societies' Greek New Testament: A Short Examination of the Third Edition." *BT* 30, no. 1 (1979): 135-38.

———. "The United Bible Societies' Greek New Testament: An Evaluation." *NovT* 15, no. 4 (1973): 278-300.

Emmel, Stephen. "The Coptic Gnostic Texts as Witnesses to the Production and Transmission of Gnostic (and Other) Traditions." Pages 33-49 in *Das Thomasevangelium: Entstehung-Rezeption-Theologie,* edited by Jörg Frey, Enno Edzard Popkes, and Jens Schröter, BZNW 157. Berlin: de Gruyter, 2008.

Epp, Eldon J. "Codex Sinaiticus: Its Entrance into the Mid-Nineteenth Century Text-Critical Environment and Its Impact on the New Testament Text." Pages 53-89 in *Codex Sinaiticus: New Perspectives on the Ancient Biblical Manuscript,* edited by Scot McKendrick, David Parker, Amy Myshrall, and Cillian O'Hogan. Peabody, MA: Hendrickson, 2015.

———. "Coptic Manuscript G67 and the Rôle of Codex Bezae as a Western Witness in Acts." *JBL* 85, no. 2 (1966): 197-212.

————. "The 'Ignorance Motif' in Acts and Anti-Judaic Tendencies in Codex Bezae." *HTR* 55, no. 1 (1962): 51-62.

————. *Junia: The First Woman Apostle*. Minneapolis: Fortress, 2005.

————. "New Testament Textual Criticism in America: Requiem for a Discipline." *JBL* 98, no. 1 (1979): 94-98.

————. "The Papyrus Manuscripts of the New Testament." Pages 1-39 in Ehrman and Holmes, *Text of the New Testament in Contemporary Research: Essays on the Status Quaestionis*, 2nd ed.

————. "The Significance of the Papyri for Determining the Nature of the New Testament Text in the Second Century: A Dynamic View of Textual Transmission." Pages 274-97 in *Studies in the Theory and Method of New Testament Textual Criticism*, by Eldon J. Epp and Gordon D. Fee, SD 45. Grand Rapids: Eerdmans, 1993.

————. "Text-Critical Witnesses and Methodology for Isolating a Distinctive D-Text in Acts." *NovT* 59, no. 3 (2017): 225-96.

————. "Textual Clusters: Their Past and Future in New Testament Textual Criticism." Pages 518-77 in Ehrman and Holmes, *Text of the New Testament in Contemporary Research: Essays on the Status Quaestionis*, 2nd ed.

————. *The Theological Tendency of Codex Bezae Cantabrigensis in Acts*. SNTSMS 3. Cambridge: Cambridge University Press, 1965.

————. "Why Does New Testament Textual Criticism Matter? Refined Definitions and Fresh Directions." *ExpTim* 125, no. 9 (2014): 417-31.

Ernest, James D. *The Bible in Athanasius of Alexandria*. The Bible in Ancient Christianity 2. Leiden: Brill, 2004.

Eubank, Nathan. "A Disconcerting Prayer: On the Originality of Luke 23:34a." *JBL* 129, no. 3 (2010): 521-36.

Evans, Craig A. "Christian Demographics and the Dates of Early New Testament Papyri." Pages 201-17 in *The Language and Literature of the New Testament: Essays in Honor of Stanley E. Porter's 60th Birthday*, edited by Lois K. Fuller Dow, Craig A. Evans, and Andrew W. Pitts, Biblical Interpretation Series 150. Leiden: Brill, 2016.

Evans, Craig A. "How Long Were Late Antique Books in Use? Possible Implications for New Testament Textual Criticism." *BBR* 25, no. 1 (2015): 23-37.

Ewan, Pamela. *Faith on Trial: An Attorney Analyzes the Evidence for the Death and Resurrection of Jesus*. Nashville: Broadman & Holman, 1999.

Fackelmann, Anton. "Präsentation christlicher Urtexte aus dem ersten Jahrhundert geschrieben auf Papyrus: Vermutlich Notizschriften des Evangelisten Markus?" *Anagennesis* 4 (1986): 25-36.

Falluomini, Carla. "The Gothic Version of the New Testament." Pages 329-50 in Ehrman and Holmes, *Text of the New Testament in Contemporary Research: Essays on the Status Quaestionis*, 2nd ed.

Feder, Frank. "Die koptische Übersetzungen des Alten und Neuen Testaments im 4. Jahrhundert." Pages 65-93 in *Stabilisierung und Profilierung der Koptischen Kirche im 4. Jahrhundert: Internationalle Hallesche Koptologentagung*, edited by Jürgen Tubach and Sophia G. Vashalomidze, Halleschen Beiträgen zur Orientalwissenschaft 44. Halle: Martin-Luther-Universität, 2007.

Fee, Gordon D. "The Corrections of Papyrus Bodmer II and Early Textual Transmission." *NovT* 7, no. 4 (1965): 247-57.

————. "Corrections of the Papyrus Bodmer II and the Nestle Greek Testament." *JBL* 84, no. 1 (1965): 66-72.

————. "The Majority Text and the Original Text of the New Testament." Pages 183-208 in *Studies in the Theory and Method of New Testament Textual Criticism*, edited by Eldon J. Epp and Gordon D. Fee, SD 45. Grand Rapids: Eerdmans, 1993.

――――. "Modern Textual Criticism and the Revival of the *Textus Receptus*." *JETS* 21, no. 1 (1978): 19-33.

――――. "Review of *The Orthodox Corruption of Scripture: The Effect of Early Christological Controversies on the Text of the New Testament* by Bart D. Ehrman." *CRBR* 8 (1995): 203-6.

――――. "Some Dissenting Notes on 7Q5=Mark 6:52-53." *JBL* 92, no. 1 (1973): 109-12.

――――. "Textual Criticism of the New Testament." Pages 3-16 in *Studies in the Theory and Method of New Testament Textual Criticism*, edited by Eldon J. Epp and Gordon D. Fee, SD 45. Grand Rapids: Eerdmans, 1993.

Fee, Gordon D., and Roderic L. Mullen. "The Use of the Greek Fathers for New Testament Textual Criticism." Pages 351-73 in Ehrman and Holmes, *Text of the New Testament in Contemporary Research: Essays on the Status Quaestionis*, 2nd ed.

Fehderau, H. W. "The Role of Bases and Models in Bible Translations." *BT* 30, no. 4 (1979): 401-14.

Fichtner, Gerhard. *Corpus Galenicum: Bibliographie der galenischen und pseudogalenischen Werke.* Berlin: Berlin-Brandenburgische Akademie der Wissenschaften, 2012.

Fischer, Bonifatius. "Limitations of Latin in Representing Greek." Pages 362-74 in *The Early Versions of the New Testament: Their Origin, Transmission, and Limitations*, by Bruce M. Metzger. Oxford: Oxford University Press, 1977.

Fischer, Friedrich. *Thucydidis reliquiae in papyris et membranis aegyptiacis servatae.* Leipzig: Teubner, 1913.

Fitzgerald, William. *Martial: The World of the Epigram.* Chicago: University of Chicago Press, 2007.

Fitzmyer, Joseph A. *The Letter to Philemon: A New Translation with Commentary and Introduction.* AB. New Haven, CT: Yale University Press, 2000.

Förster, Hans. "7Q5 = Mark 6.52-53: A Challenge for Textual Criticism?" *JGRChJ* 2 (2001): 27-35.

Foster, Paul. "Bold Claims, Wishful Thinking, and Lessons About Dating Manuscripts from Papyrus Egerton 2." Pages 193-211 in *The World of Jesus and the Early Church: Identity and Interpretation in Early Communities of Faith*, edited by Craig A. Evans. Peabody, MA: Hendrickson, 2011.

Fox, Adam. *John Mill and Richard Bentley: A Study of the Textual Criticism of the New Testament, 1675-1729.* Oxford: Basil Blackwell, 1954.

Frame, John M. *The Doctrine of the Word of God.* A Theology of Lordship 4. Phillipsburg, NJ: P&R, 2010.

Gäbel, Georg, Annette Hüffmeier, Gerd Mink, Holger Strutwolf, and Klaus Wachtel. "The CBGM Applied to Variants from Acts: Methodological Background." *TC* 20 (2015): 1-3.

Galen. *Selected Works.* Translated by P. N. Singer. Oxford: Oxford University Press, 1997.

Gallagher, Edmon L. "Origen *via* Rufinus on the New Testament Canon." *NTS* 62, no. 3 (2016): 461-76.

Gallagher, Edmon L., and John D. Meade. *The Biblical Canon Lists from Early Christianity: Texts and Analysis.* Oxford: Oxford University Press, 2018.

Gamble, Harry Y. *Books and Readers in the Early Church: A History of Early Christian Texts.* New Haven, CT: Yale University Press, 1995.

Gameson, Richard. "Materials, Text, Layout and Script." Pages 13-39 in *The St Cuthbert Gospel: Studies on the Insular Manuscript of the Gospel of John*, edited by Claire Breay and Bernard Meehan. London: British Library, 2015.

Garland, David E. *Luke.* ZECNT 3. Grand Rapids: Zondervan, 2011.

――――. *A Theology of Mark's Gospel: Good News About Jesus the Messiah, the Son of God.* BTNT. Grand Rapids: Zondervan, 2015.

Geer, Thomas C., Jr. "Analyzing and Categorizing New Testament Greek Manuscripts: Colwell Revisited." Pages 253-67 in Ehrman and Holmes, *Text of the New Testament in Contemporary Research*, 1st ed.

――――. "Codex 1739 in Acts and Its Relationship to Manuscripts 945 and 1891." *Bib* 69 (1988): 27-46.

――――. *Family 1739 in Acts.* SBLMS 48. Atlanta: Scholars Press, 1994.

Geer, Thomas C., Jr., and Jean-François Racine. "Analyzing and Categorizing New Testament Greek Manuscripts." Pages 497-518 in Ehrman and Holmes, *Text of the New Testament in Contemporary Research: Essays on the Status Quaestionis*, 2nd ed.

Geerlings, Jacob. *Family 13 (The Ferrar Group): The Text According to Matthew*. SD 19. Salt Lake City: University of Utah Press, 1961.

Geisler, Norman L. *Christian Apologetics*. 2nd ed. Grand Rapids: Baker Academic, 2013.

———. "New Testament Manuscripts." Pages 531-37 in *The Baker Encyclopedia of Apologetics*, edited by Norman L. Geisler. Grand Rapids: Baker, 1999.

Geisler, Norman L., and William E. Nix. *From God to Us: How We Got Our Bible*. 2nd ed. Chicago: Moody, 2012.

———. *A General Introduction to the Bible: Revised and Expanded*. Chicago: Moody, 1986.

Geisler, Norman L., and Patty Tunnicliffe. *Reasons for Belief: Easy-to-Understand Answers to 10 Essential Questions*. Minneapolis: Bethany House, 2013.

Geisler, Norman L., and Ravi Zacharias. *Who Made God? and Answers to over 100 Other Tough Questions of Faith*. Grand Rapids: Zondervan, 2003.

Gilbert, Greg. "Debunking Silly Statements About the Bible: An Exercise in Biblical Transmission." The Gospel Coalition. February 8, 2016. www.thegospelcoalition.org/article/debunking-silly -statements-about-the-bible.

———. *Why Trust the Bible?* Wheaton, IL: Crossway, 2015.

Globe, Alexander. "Some Doctrinal Variants in Matthew 1 and Luke 2, and the Authority of the Neutral Text." *CBQ* 42, no. 1 (1980): 52-72.

Goguel, Maurice. *Le Texte et Les Éditions Du Nouveau Testament Grec*. Paris: E. Leroux, 1920.

Goodrich, Richard J., and Albert L. Lukaszewski, eds. *A Reader's Greek New Testament*. Grand Rapids: Zondervan, 2003.

Grass, Tim. *F. F. Bruce: A Life*. Grand Rapids: Eerdmans, 2011.

Green, Peter, ed. *Ovid, the Poems of Exile: Tristia and the Black Sea Letters*. Berkeley: University of California Press, 2005.

Greenlee, J. Harold. *Introduction to New Testament Textual Criticism*. Peabody, MA: Hendrickson, 1995.

Gregory, Andrew F., and Christopher M. Tuckett, eds. *The Reception of the New Testament in the Apostolic Fathers*. Oxford: Oxford University Press, 2005.

Gregory, Caspar René. *Die griechischen Handschriften des Neuen Testaments*. Leipzig: Hinrichs, 1908.

———. *Textkritik des Neuen Testaments*. Leipzig: Hinrichs, 1900.

Grenfell, Bernard P., and Arthur S. Hunt. "405-406. Theological Fragments." Pages 10-12 in *The Oxyrhynchus Papyri III*, edited by Bernard P. Grenfell and Arthur S. Hunt, GRM 5. London: Egypt Exploration Fund, 1903.

———. "412. Julius Africanus, Κεστοί." Pages 36-41 in *The Oxyrhynchus Papyri III*, edited by Bernard P. Grenfell and Arthur S. Hunt, GRM 5. London: Egypt Exploration Fund, 1903.

———. "CCIX. St. Paul's Epistle to the Romans, Chap. I." Pages 8-9 in *The Oxyrhynchus Papyri II*, edited by Bernard P. Grenfell and Arthur S. Hunt, GRM 2. London: Egypt Exploration Fund, 1898.

Grimsted, Patricia Kennedy, ed. *Archives of Russia: A Directory and Bibliographic Guide to Holdings in Moscow and St. Petersburg*. Vol. 2. New York: Routledge, 2015.

Grimsted, Patricia Kennedy, F. J. Hoogewoud, and F. C. J. Ketelaar, eds. *Returned from Russia: Nazi Archival Plunder in Western Europe and Recent Restitution Issues*. 2nd rev. ed. Builth Wells, UK: Institute of Art and Law, 2013.

Gronewald, Michael. *Kölner Papyri [P.Köln] VI*. Pap.Colon. VII.6. Opladen: Westdeutcher Verlag, 1987.

Gronewald, M., B. Kramer, K. Maresch, M. Parca, and C. Römer, eds. *Kölner Papyri (P.Köln) VI*. Papyrologica Coloniensia VII.6. Opladen: Westdeutcher Verlag, 1987.

Grudem, Wayne. *Systematic Theology: An Introduction to Biblical Doctrine*. Grand Rapids: Zondervan, 1994.

Gryson, Roger. *Altlateinische Handschriften = Manuscrits vieux-latins: Répertoire descriptive: Deuxième partie: Mss 300-485 (manuscrits du psautier)*. VL 1/2B. Freiburg: Herder, 2004.

———. *Répertoire general des auteurs ecclésiastiques latins de l'antiquité et du haut moyen-âge*. 5th ed. 2 vols. Freiburg: Herder, 2007.

Gryson, Roger, and H. J. Frede. *Altlateinische Handschriften = Manuscrits vieux-latins: Répertoire descriptive: Deuxième partie: Mss 1-275: D'après un manuscrit inachevé de Hermann Josef Frede*. VL 1/2A. Freiburg: Herder, 1999.

"Guiding Principles for Interconfessional Cooperation in Translating the Bible." *BT* 19, no. 3 (1968): 101-10.

Gurd, Sean Alexander. *Work in Progress: Literary Revision as Social Performance in Ancient Rome*. New York: Oxford University Press, 2012.

Gurry, Peter J. *A Critical Examination of the Coherence-Based Genealogical Method in New Testament Textual Criticism*. NTTSD 55. Leiden: Brill, 2017.

———. "Gary Habermas on First-Century Mark." *Evangelical Textual Criticis*m (blog). February 24, 2018. http://evangelicaltextualcriticism.blogspot.co.uk/2018/02/gary-habermas-on-first -century-mark.html.

———. "How Many Variants Make It into Your Greek New Testament?" *Evangelical Textual Criticism* (blog). May 10, 2016. http://evangelicaltextualcriticism.blogspot.com/2016/05/how-many -variants-make-it-into-your.html.

———. "Just How Much Longer Is Codex Bezae's Text in Acts?" *Evangelical Textual Criticism* (blog). June 27, 2016. http://evangelicaltextualcriticism.blogspot.co.uk/2016/06/just-how-much-longer -is-codex-bezaes.html.

———. "The Number of Variants in the Greek New Testament: A Proposed Estimate." *NTS* 62, no. 1 (2016): 97-121.

———. "On the 'Idle Boast' of Having So Many New Testament Manuscripts." *Evangelical Textual Criticism* (blog). August 16, 2017. http://evangelicaltextualcriticism.blogspot.com/2017/08/on -idle-boast-of-having-so-many-new.html.

———. "On the Origin of the Pericope Adulterae in the Syriac NT." *Evangelical Textual Criticism* (blog). October 24, 2016. http://evangelicaltextualcriticism.blogspot.com/2017/03/on-origin-of -pericope-adulterae-in.html.

Hahneman, Geoffrey Mark. *The Muratorian Fragment and the Development of the Canon*. Oxford: Oxford University Press, 1992.

Haines-Eitzen, Kim. *Guardians of Letters: Literacy, Power, and the Transmitters of Early Christian Literature*. Oxford: Oxford University Press, 2000.

———. "Review of *Apologetic Discourse and the Scribal Tradition: Evidence of the Influence of Apologetic Interests on the Text of the Canonical Gospels*." *JBL* 124, no. 2 (2005): 381-83.

Hanson, Ann Ellis. "The Archive of Isidoros of Psophthis and P. Ostorius Scapula, Praefectus Aegypti." BASP 21 (1984): 77-87.

———. "Two Copies of a Petition to the Prefect." *ZPE* 47 (1982): 233-43.

Hardy, Dean. *Stand Your Ground: An Introductory Text for Apologetics Students*. Eugene, OR: Wipf & Stock, 2007.

Harris, J. Rendel. *The Origin of the Leicester Codex of the New Testament*. London: C. J. Clay and Sons, 1887.

———. *Side-Lights on New Testament Research: Seven Lectures Delivered in 1908, at Regent's Park College, London*. London: Kingsgate Press; James Clarke, 1908.

Hatzilambrou, Rosalia. "Appendix: P. Oxy. XVIII 2192 Revisited." Pages 282-86 in *Oxyrhynchus: A City and Its Texts*, edited by Alan K. Bowman, Revel A. Coles, N. Gonis, Dirk Obbink, and P. J. Parsons, GRM 93. London: Egypt Exploration Society, 2007.

Haverfield, F. "Tacitus During the Late Roman Period and the Middle Ages." *JRS* 6 (1916): 196-201.

Havet, Louis. *Manuel de critique verbale appliquée aux textes latins.* Paris: Hachette, 1911.

Head, Peter M. "Additional Greek Witnesses to the New Testament (Ostraca, Amulets, Inscriptions, and Other Sources)." Pages 429-60 in Ehrman and Holmes, *Text of the New Testament in Contemporary Research: Essays on the Status Quaestionis*, 2nd ed.

———. "Christology and Textual Transmission: Reverential Alterations in the Synoptic Gospels." *NovT* 35, no. 2 (1993): 105-29.

———. "Is P⁴, P⁶⁴ and P⁶⁷ the Oldest Manuscript of the Four Gospels? A Response to T. C. Skeat." *NTS* 51, no. 3 (2005): 450-57.

———. *Is the New Testament Reliable?* Grove Biblical Series B 30. Cambridge, UK: Grove, 2003.

———. "Scribal Behaviour and Theological Tendencies in Singular Readings in P. Bodmer II (P⁶⁶)." Pages 55-74 in *Textual Variation: Theological and Social Tendencies? The Fifth Birmingham Colloquium on New Testament Textual Criticism*, edited by H. A. G. Houghton and D. C. Parker, TS, Third Series 6. Piscataway, NJ: Gorgias, 2008.

———. "A Text-Critical Study of Mark 1.1: 'The Beginning of the Gospel of Jesus Christ.'" *NTS* 37, no. 4 (1991): 621-29.

Head, Peter M., and Philip Satterthwaite. *Method in New Testament Textual Criticism: 1700–1850.* New York: Peter Lang, forthcoming.

Heide, Martin. *Der einzig wahre Bibeltext? Erasmus von Rotterdam und die Frage nach dem Urtext.* 5th ed. Hamburg: VTR, 2006.

Heine, Ronald, trans. *Origen: Commentary on the Gospel of John.* 2 vols. FC 80, 89. Washington, DC: Catholic University of America Press, 1989, 1993.

Hernández, Juan, Jr. *Scribal Habits and Theological Influences in the Apocalypse: The Singular Readings of Sinaiticus, Alexandrinus, and Ephraemi.* WUNT 2/218. Tübingen: Mohr Siebeck, 2006.

Hernández, Juan, Jr., Peter M. Head, Dirk Jongkind, and James R. Royse. "Scribal Habits in Early Greek New Testament Papyri: Papers from the 2008 SBL Panel Review Session." *TC* 17 (2012): 1-22.

Hester, David W. *Does Mark 16:9-20 Belong in the New Testament?* Eugene, OR: Wipf & Stock, 2015.

Hill, Charles E. "Did the Scribe of P⁵² Use the Nomina Sacra? Another Look." *NTS* 48, no. 4 (2002): 587-92.

———. *The Johannine Corpus in the Early Church.* Oxford: Oxford University Press, 2004.

———. "Rightly Dividing the Word: Uncovering an Early Template for Textual Division in John's Gospel." Pages 217-38 in *Studies on the Text of the New Testament and Early Christianity: Essays in Honour of Michael W. Holmes*, edited by Daniel M. Gurtner, Juan Hernández Jr., and Paul Foster, NTTSD 50. Leiden: Brill, 2015.

———. *Who Chose the Gospels? Probing the Great Gospel Conspiracy.* New York: Oxford University Press, 2010.

———. "'The Writing Which Says . . . ': The *Shepherd of Hermas* in the Writings of Irenaeus." Pages 127-38 in *Papers Presented at the Sixteenth International Conference on Patristic Studies Held in Oxford 2013*, edited by Markus Vinzent, StPatr 65. Leuven: Peeters, 2013.

Hixson, Elijah. "Despite Disappointing Some, New Mark Manuscript Is Earliest Yet." *Christianity Today*, May 30, 2018. www.christianitytoday.com/ct/2018/may-web-only/mark-manuscript -earliest-not-first-century-fcm.html.

———. "'First-Century Mark,' Published at Last? [Updated]." *Evangelical Textual Criticism* (blog). May 23, 2018. http://evangelicaltextualcriticism.blogspot.com/2018/05/first-century-mark -published-at-last.html.

Hixson, Elijah, and Timothy Paul Jones. "How Was the New Testament Copied?" Pages 104-23 in *How We Got the Bible*, by Timothy Paul Jones. Torrance, CA: Rose, 2015.

Hodges, Zane C., and Arthur Farstad, eds. *The Greek New Testament According to the Majority Text.* 2nd ed. Nashville: Thomas Nelson, 1985.

Holmes, Michael W., ed. *The Apostolic Fathers: Greek Texts and English Translations.* 3rd ed. Grand Rapids: Baker Academic, 2007.

———. "From 'Original Text' to 'Initial Text': The Traditional Goal of New Testament Textual Criticism in Contemporary Discussion." Pages 637-88 in Ehrman and Holmes, *Text of the New Testament in Contemporary Research: Essays on the Status Quaestionis*, 2nd ed.

———. *The Greek New Testament: SBL Edition.* Atlanta: Society of Biblical Literature, 2010.

———. "*The Text of the Epistles* Sixty Years After: An Assessment of Günther Zuntz's Contribution to Text-Critical Methodology and History." Pages 89-113 in *Transmission and Reception: New Testament Text-Critical and Exegetical Studies*, edited by J. W. Childers and David C. Parker, TS, Third Series 4. Piscataway, NJ: Gorgias, 2006.

Horrell, David G. "The Themes of 1 Peter: Insights from the Earliest Manuscripts (The Crosby-Schøyen Codex MS 193 and the Bodmer Miscellaneous Codex Containing P^{72})." *NTS* 55, no. 4 (2009): 502-22.

Horton, Charles. "The Chester Beatty Biblical Papyri: A Find of the Greatest Importance." Pages 149-60 in *The Earliest Gospels: The Origins and Transmission of the Earliest Christian Gospels—The Contribution of the Chester Beatty Gospel P^{45}*, edited by Charles Horton, JSNTSup 285. London: T&T Clark, 2004.

Hoskier, Herman C. *Concerning the Text of the Apocalypse.* 2 vols. London: Quaritch, 1929.

———. *A Full Account and Collation of the Greek Cursive Codex Evangelium 604.* London: David Nutt, 1890.

Houghton, H. A. G. *Augustine's Text of John: Patristic Citations and Latin Gospel Manuscripts.* OECS. Oxford: Oxford University Press, 2008.

———. *The Latin New Testament: A Guide to Its Early History, Texts, and Manuscripts.* Oxford: Oxford University Press, 2016.

———. "The Use of the Latin Fathers for New Testament Textual Criticism." Pages 375-406 in Ehrman and Holmes, *Text of the New Testament in Contemporary Research: Essays on the Status Quaestionis*, 2nd ed.

Houghton, H. A. G., and D. C. Parker, eds. *Textual Variation: Theological and Social Tendencies? Papers from the Fifth Birmingham Colloquium on the Textual Criticism of the New Testament.* TS, Third Series 6. Piscataway, NJ: Gorgias, 2008.

Houston, George W. *Inside Roman Libraries: Book Collections and Their Management in Antiquity.* Chapel Hill: University of North Carolina Press, 2014.

Howard, Wilbert F. "The Influence of Doctrine upon the Text of the New Testament." *London Quarterly and Holborn Review* 6, no. 10 (1941): 1-16.

Howley, Joseph A. "Book-Burning and the Uses of Writing in Ancient Rome: Destructive Practice Between Literature and Document." *JRS* 107 (2017): 213-36.

Hull, Robert F., Jr. *The Story of the New Testament Text: Movers, Materials, Motives, Methods, Models.* Atlanta: Society of Biblical Literature, 2010.

Hunger, Herbert. "Zur Datierung des Papyrus Bodmer II (P66)." *AÖAW* 4 (1960): 12-33.

Hurtado, Larry W. *The Earliest Christian Artifacts: Manuscripts and Christian Origins.* Grand Rapids: Eerdmans, 2006.

———. "Manuscripts and the Sociology of Early Christian Reading." Pages 49-62 in *The Early Text of the New Testament*, edited by Charles E. Hill and Michael J. Kruger. Oxford: Oxford University Press, 2012.

——. "The Origin of the *Nomina Sacra*: A Proposal." *JBL* 117, no. 4 (1998): 665-73.

——. *Text-Critical Methodology and the Pre-Caesarean Text: Codex W in the Gospel of Mark*. SD 43. Grand Rapids: Eerdmans, 1981.

Iddeng, Jon W. "*Publica aut peri!* The Releasing and Distribution of Roman Books." SO 81 (2006): 58-84.

Instone-Brewer, David. *Did the Church Change the Bible?* Grove Biblical Series B 64. Cambridge, UK: Grove, 2012.

Irenaeus of Lyons. *Against the Heresies*. Translated by Dominic J. Unger. ACW 55. New York: Paulist Press, 1992.

James, M. R. "The Scribe of the Leicester Codex." *JTS* 5 (1904): 445-47.

Jaroš, Karl. *Die ältesten griechischen Handschriften des Neuen Testaments*. Cologne: Böhlau, 2014.

——. "Zur Textüberlieferung des Markusevangeliums nach der Handschrift P.Chester Beatty I (P⁴⁵), zu 7Q5 und zum 'Geheimen Markusevangelium.'" *Aeg* 88 (2008): 71-113.

Jarus, Owen. "Mummy Mask May Reveal Oldest Known Gospel." *Live Science*. January 18, 2015. www.livescience.com/49489-oldest-known-gospel-mummy-mask.html.

Johnson, William A. "The Ancient Book." Pages 256-77 in *The Oxford Handbook of Papyrology*, edited by Roger S. Bagnall. Oxford: Oxford University Press, 2009.

——. *Bookrolls and Scribes in Oxyrhynchus*. Toronto: University of Toronto Press, 2004.

——. *Readers and Reading Culture in the High Roman Empire: A Study of Elite Communities*. Classic Culture and Society. New York: Oxford University Press, 2010.

Jones, Brice C. *New Testament Texts on Greek Amulets from Late Antiquity*. LNTS 554. London: Bloomsbury T&T Clark, 2016.

Jones, Clay. "The Bibliographical Test Updated." *CRJ* 35, no. 3 (2012): 32-37.

Jones, H. S., ed. *Thucydidis historiae*. Vol. 1. Revised by J. E. Powell. OCT. Oxford: Clarendon, 1938.

Jones, Timothy Paul. *Misquoting Truth: A Guide to the Fallacies of Bart Ehrman's Misquoting Jesus*. Downers Grove, IL: InterVarsity Press, 2007.

Jongkind, Dirk. *Scribal Habits of Codex Sinaiticus*. TS, Third Series 5. Piscataway, NJ: Gorgias, 2007.

——. "Singular Readings in Sinaiticus: The Possible, the Impossible, and the Nature of Copying." Pages 35-54 in *Textual Variation: Theological and Social Tendencies? Papers from the Fifth Birmingham Colloquium on the Textual Criticism of the New Testament*, edited by H. A. G. Houghton and D. C. Parker, TS, Third Series 6. Piscataway, NJ: Gorgias, 2008.

Jongkind, Dirk, Peter J. Williams, Peter M. Head, and Patrick James, eds. *The Greek New Testament, Produced at Tyndale House, Cambridge*. Wheaton, IL: Crossway, 2017.

Juckel, Andreas. "Introduction to the Harklean Text." Pages xxxi-lxxvi in *Comparative Edition of the Syriac Gospels: Aligning the Sinaiticus, Curetonius, Peshitta, and Harklean Versions*, vol. 1, *Matthew*, edited by George A. Kiraz. NTTS 21.1. Leiden: Brill, 1996.

Junack, Klaus. "Abschreibpraktiken und Schreibergewohnheiten in ihrer Auswirkung auf die Textüberlieferung." Pages 277-95 in *New Testament Textual Criticism: Its Significance for Exegesis; Essays in Honor of Bruce M. Metzger*, edited by Eldon J. Epp and Gordon D. Fee. Oxford: Clarendon, 1981.

Junack, Klaus, Eberhard Güting, Ursula Nimtz, and Klaus Witte. *Das Neue Testament auf Papyrus II: Die Paulinischen Briefe*. Tiel 1, *Röm, 1 Kor, 2 Kor*. ANTF 12. Berlin: de Gruyter, 1989.

Justin Martyr. *The First and Second Apologies*. Translated by William Leslie Barnard. ACW 56. New York: Paulist Press, 1997.

Kagan, Donald. "The Speeches in Thucydides and the Mytilene Debate." Pages 71-94 in *Studies in the Greek Historians*, edited by Donald Kagan, Yale Classical Studies 24. Cambridge: Cambridge University Press, 1975.

Kahle, P. E. *Bala'izah: Coptic Texts from Deir el-Bala'izah in Upper Egypt.* 2 vols. Oxford: Oxford University Press, 1954.

Kannaday, Wayne C. *Apologetic Discourse and the Scribal Tradition: Evidence of the Influence of Apologetic Interests on the Text of the Canonical Gospels.* TCSt 5. Atlanta: Society of Biblical Literature, 2004.

Keener, Craig S. *The Gospel of John: A Commentary.* Vol. 1. Peabody, MA: Hendrickson, 2003.

———. *The IVP Bible Background Commentary: New Testament.* 2nd ed. Downers Grove, IL: Inter-Varsity Press, 2014.

Keith, Chris. "Recent and Previous Research on the *Pericope Adulterae* (John 7.53–8.11)." *CBR* 6, no. 3 (2008): 377-404.

Kenyon, Frederic G. *The Bible and Archaeology.* London: G. Harrap, 1940.

———, ed. *The Chester Beatty Biblical Papyri. Descriptions and Texts of Twelve Manuscripts on Papyrus of the Greek Bible.* 16 vols. London: Emery Walker, 1933–1941.

———. *Handbook to the Textual Criticism of the New Testament.* London: MacMillan, 1901.

Kim, Kwang-Won. "Codices 1582, 1739, and Origen." *JBL* 69, no. 2 (1950): 167-75.

King, Daniel. "The Textual History of the New Testament and the Bible Translator." *BT* 68, no. 1 (2017): 20-37.

Klauck, Hans-Josef. *Ancient Letters and the New Testament: A Guide to Context and Exegesis.* Translated by Daniel P. Bailey. Waco, TX: Baylor University Press, 2006.

Knust, Jennifer Wright. "Review of *Apologetic Discourse and the Scribal Tradition: Evidence of the Influence of Apologetic Interests on the Text of the Canonical Gospels.*" *JR* 86, no. 4 (2006): 671-72.

Koester, Helmut. *Ancient Christian Gospels: Their History and Development.* London: SCM Press, 1990.

———. *Einführung in das Neue Testament im Rahmen der Religionsgeschichte und Kulturgeschichte der hellenistischen und römischen Zeit.* Berlin: de Gruyter, 1980.

Komoszewski, J. Ed, M. James Sawyer, and Daniel B. Wallace. *Reinventing Jesus: How Contemporary Skeptics Miss the Real Jesus and Mislead Popular Culture.* Grand Rapids: Kregel, 2006.

Köstenberger, Andreas J., and Michael J. Kruger. *The Heresy of Orthodoxy: How Contemporary Culture's Fascination with Diversity Has Reshaped Our Understanding of Early Christianity.* Wheaton, IL: Crossway, 2010.

Krans, Jan. *Beyond What Is Written: Erasmus and Beza as Conjectural Critics of the New Testament.* NTTS 35. Leiden: Brill, 2006.

———. "Conjectural Emendation and the Text of the New Testament." Pages 613-35 in Ehrman and Holmes, *Text of the New Testament in Contemporary Research: Essays on the Status Quaestionis,* 2nd ed.

Kraus, Thomas J. "'Parchment or Papyrus?': Some Remarks About the Significance of Writing Material When Assessing Manuscripts." Pages 13-24 in *Ad fontes: Original Manuscripts and Their Significance for Studying Early Christianity—Selected Essays,* edited by Thomas J. Kraus, TENT 3. Leiden: Brill, 2007.

Kruger, Michael J. *Canon Revisited: Establishing the Origins and Authority of the New Testament Books.* Wheaton, IL: Crossway, 2012.

———. "Do We Have a Trustworthy Text? Inerrancy and Canonicity, Preservation and Textual Criticism." Pages 304-16 in *The Inerrant Word: Biblical, Historical, Theological, and Pastoral Perspectives,* edited by John MacArthur. Wheaton, IL: Crossway, 2016.

Kugel, James, and Rowan Greer. *Early Biblical Interpretation.* LEC 3. Philadelphia: Westminster, 1986.

Lafleur, Didier. *La Famille 13 dans l'évangile de Marc.* NTTSD 41. Leiden: Brill, 2013.

———. "Le Codex de Koridethi (Θ.038) et la Famille 13: Une nouvelle collation de l'Évangile de Marc." Pages 89-112 in *Textual Research on the Psalms and Gospels / Recherches textuelles sur les psaumes et les évangiles: Papers from the Tbilisi Colloquium on the Editing and History of Biblical Manuscripts, Actes du Colloque de Tbilisi, 19-20 septembre 2007*, edited by Christian-Bernard Amphoux and J. Keith Elliott, NovTSup 142. Leiden: Brill, 2012.

———. "Which Criteria for Family 13 (F13) Manuscripts?" *NovT* 54, no. 1 (2012): 105-48.

Lake, Kirsopp. *Codex 1 of the Gospels and Its Allies*. TS 7. Cambridge, 1902.

———. *The Influence of Textual Criticism on the Exegesis of the New Testament*. Oxford: Parker and Son, 1904.

———. *The Text of the New Testament*. 6th ed. Revised by Silva New. London: Rivingtons, 1928.

Lake, Kirsopp, and Silva Lake. *Family 13 (The Ferrar Group): The Text According to Mark, with a Collation of Codex 28 of the Gospels*. SD 11. Philadelphia: University of Pennsylvania Press, 1941.

Lake, Kirsopp, and Silva New. *Six Collations of New Testament Manuscripts*. HTS 17. Cambridge, MA: Harvard University Press, 1932.

Lalleman, Pieter. "Oldest Manuscript of Mark Is Nonetheless a Disappointment." *Christian Today*. May 31, 2018. www.christiantoday.com/article/oldest-manuscript-of-mark-is-nonetheless -a-disappointment/129500.htm.

Lange, Armin. "Canonical History of the Hebrew Bible." Pages 35-81 in *Textual History of the Bible: The Hebrew Bible*, vol. 1A, *Overview Articles*, edited by Armin Lange and Emanuel Tov. Leiden: Brill, 2016.

Lanier, Gregory R. "Quantifying New Testament Textual Variants: Key Witnesses in Acts and the Catholic Letters." *NTS* 64, no. 4 (2018): 551-72.

———. "Taking Inventory on the 'Age of the Minuscules': Later Manuscripts and the Byzantine Tradition Within the Field of Textual Criticism." *CBR* 16, no. 3 (2018): 263-308.

———. *A Christian's Pocket Guide to How We Got the Bible*. Ross-shire, Scotland: Christian Focus, 2018.

Larsen, Matthew D. C. "Accidental Publication, Unfinished Texts and the Traditional Goals of New Testament Textual Criticism." *JSNT* 39, no. 4 (2017): 362-87.

Latacz, Joachim, and Frank Pressler. "Homerus." Pages 450-63 in vol. 6 of *Brill's New Pauly: Encyclopaedia of the Ancient World*, edited by Hubert Cancik and Helmuth Schneider. Leiden: Brill, 2005.

Lefèvre, Eckard. *Vom Römertum zum Ästhetizismus: Studien zu den Briefen des jüngeren Plinius*. Berlin: de Gruyter, 2009.

Lembke, Markus, Darius Müller, Ulrich B. Schmid, and Martin Karrer, eds. *Text und Textwert der griechischen Handschriften des Neuen Testaments*. Vol. 6, *Die Apokalypse: Teststellenkollation und Auswertungen*. ANTF 49. Berlin: de Gruyter, 2017.

Leonard, James M. *Codex Schøyen 2650: A Middle Egyptian Coptic Witness to the Early Greek Text of Matthew's Gospel: A Study in Translation Theory, Indigenous Coptic, and New Testament Textual Criticism*. NTTSD 46. Leiden: Brill, 2014.

Liere, Frans van. *An Introduction to the Medieval Bible*. Cambridge: Cambridge University Press, 2014.

Lightfoot, Neil R. *How We Got the Bible*. Grand Rapids: Baker, 1963.

———. *How We Got the Bible*. 3rd ed. Grand Rapids: Baker, 2003.

Lim, Timothy H. *The Dead Sea Scrolls: A Very Short Introduction*. 2nd ed. Very Short Introductions 143. Oxford: Oxford University Press, 2017.

Lincicum, David. "5347. Philemon 6-8, 18-20." Pages 11-14 in *The Oxyrhynchus Papyri LXXXIII*, edited by P. J. Parsons and N. Gonis. London: Egypt Exploration Society, 2018.

Lohse, Eduard. *Colossians and Philemon: A Commentary on the Epistles to the Colossians and to Philemon*. Translated by W. R. Poehlmann and R. J. Karris. Hermeneia. Philadelphia: Fortress, 1971.

Luijendijk, AnneMarie. "A New Testament Papyrus and Its Documentary Context: An Early Christian Writing Exercise from the Archive of Leonides (P.Oxy. II 209/P[10])." *JBL* 129, no. 3 (2010): 575-96.

———. "Sacred Scriptures as Trash: Biblical Papyri from Oxyrhynchus." *VC* 64, no. 3 (2010): 217-54.

Lunn, Nicholas P. *The Original Ending of Mark: A New Case for the Authenticity of Mark 16:9-20.* Eugene, OR: Pickwick, 2014.

Maas, Paul. *Textual Criticism.* Translated by Barbara Flower. Oxford: Clarendon, 1958.

MacDonald, James. *God Wrote a Book.* Wheaton, IL: Crossway, 2004.

Maldfeld, Georg. "Die griechischen Handschriftenbruchstücke des Neuen Testamentes auf Papyrus." *ZNW* 42, no. 1 (1949): 228-53.

Malik, Peter. "The Earliest Corrections in Codex Sinaiticus: A Test Case from the Gospel of Mark." *BASP* 50 (2013): 207-54.

———. "The Earliest Corrections in Codex Sinaiticus: Further Evidence from the Apocalypse." *TC* 20 (2015): 1-12.

———. *P.Beatty III (P^{47}): The Codex, Its Scribe, and Its Text.* NTTSD 52. Leiden: Brill, 2017.

———. "Whose Fathers? A Note on the (Un-)Johannine Echo in the Egerton Gospel." *EC* 9 (2018): 201-11.

Malik, Peter, and Lorne R. Zelyck. "Reconsidering the Date(s) of the Egerton Gospel." *ZPE* 204 (2017): 55-71.

"Manuscripts and Archives." British Library. www.bl.uk/reshelp/findhelprestype/manuscripts/ongo ingcoll/ongoingcollections.html#egerton. Accessed May 1, 2018.

Markham, Robert P. "The Bible Societies' Greek New Testament: The End of a Decade or a Beginning of an Era?" *BT* 17, no. 3 (1966): 106-13.

Martial. *Epigrams, Volume I: Spectacles, Books 1-5.* Translated by D. R. Shackleton Bailey. LCL 94. Cambridge, MA: Harvard University Press, 1993.

Martin, Dale B. *Biblical Truths: The Meaning of Scripture in the Twenty-First Century.* New Haven, CT: Yale University Press, 2017.

———. "The Necessity of a Theology of Scripture." Pages 81-93 in *The Reliability of the New Testament: Bart D. Ehrman and Daniel B. Wallace in Dialogue,* edited by Robert B. Stewart. Minneapolis: Fortress, 2011.

Martin, Victor, and Rodolphe Kasser, eds. *Papyrus Bodmer XIV: Évangile de Luc chap. 3–24.* Cologny-Geneva: Bibliotheca Bodmeriana, 1961.

———, eds. *Papyrus Bodmer XV: Évangile de Jean chap. 1–15.* Cologny-Geneva: Bibliotheca Bodmeriana, 1961.

Martini, Carlo Maria. *Il problema della recensionalità del codice B alla luce del papiro Bodmer XIV.* AnBib 26. Rome: Pontificio Istituto Biblico, 1966.

Mattern, Susan P. *Galen and the Rhetoric of Healing.* Baltimore, MD: Johns Hopkins University Press, 2008.

Matthews, Shelly. "Clemency as Cruelty: Forgiveness and Force in the Dying Prayers of Jesus and Stephen." *BibInt* 17, no. 1 (2009): 118-46.

———. "Clemency as Cruelty: Forgiveness and Force in the Dying Prayers of Jesus and Stephen." Pages 117-44 in *Violence, Scripture, and Textual Practices in Early Judaism and Christianity,* edited by Ra'anan Boustan, Alex Jassen, and Calvin Roetzel. Leiden: Brill, 2010.

McCarthy, Carmel, trans. *Saint Ephrem's Commentary on Tatian's Diatessaron: An English Translation of Chester Beatty Syriac MS 709 with Introduction and Notes.* JSSSup 2. Oxford: Oxford University Press, 1994.

McDonald, Grantley. *Biblical Criticism in Early Modern Europe: Erasmus, the Johannine Comma and Trinitarian Debate.* Cambridge: Cambridge University Press, 2016.

McDowell, Josh. *More Evidence That Demands a Verdict: Historical Evidences for the Christian Scriptures.* Arrowhead Springs, CA: Campus Crusade for Christ, 1975.

———. *The New Evidence That Demands a Verdict.* Nashville: Thomas Nelson, 1999.

McDowell, Josh, and Bob Hostetler. *Don't Check Your Brains at the Door.* Nashville: Thomas Nelson, 2011.

McDowell, Josh, and Sean McDowell. *Evidence That Demands a Verdict: Life-Changing Truth for a Skeptical World.* Nashville: Thomas Nelson, 2017.

McNeal, R. A. "On Editing Herodotus." *L'Antiquité Classique* 52 (1983): 110-29.

Meister, Chad. *Building Belief: Constructing Faith from the Ground Up.* Grand Rapids: Baker, 2006.

Mendell, C. W. "Manuscripts of Tacitus' Minor Works." *MAAR* 19 (1949): 133-45.

———. "Tacitus: Yalensis III." *Yale University Library Gazette* 15, no. 4 (1941): 70-77.

Mendell, C. W., and Samuel A. Ives. "Ryck's Manuscript of Tacitus." *AJP* 72, no. 4 (1951): 337-45.

Menoud, P. H. "The Western Text and the Theology of Acts." *Studiorum Novi Testamenti Societas,* Bulletin II (1951): 19-32.

Messer, Adam G. "Patristic Theology and Recension in Matthew 24.36: An Evaluation of Ehrman's Text-Critical Methodology." Pages 127-88 in *Revisiting the Corruption of the New Testament: Manuscript, Patristic, and Apocryphal Evidence,* edited by Daniel B. Wallace, The Text and Canon of the New Testament. Grand Rapids: Kregel, 2011.

Metzger, Bruce M. "The Bodmer Papyrus of Luke and John." *ExpTim* 73, no. 7 (1962): 201-3.

———. "The Caesarean Text of the Gospels." *JBL* 64, no. 4 (1945): 457-89.

———. *The Canon of the New Testament: Its Origin, Development, and Significance.* Oxford: Oxford University Press, 1987.

———. *The Early Versions of the New Testament: Their Origin, Transmission and Limitations.* Oxford: Clarendon, 1977.

———. "A List of Greek Papyri of the New Testament." *ExpTim* 59, no. 3 (1947): 80-81.

———. "Recent Trends in the Textual Criticism of the Iliad and the Mahābhārata." Pages 142-54 in *Chapters in the History of New Testament Textual Criticism,* NTTS 4. Leiden: Brill, 1963.

———. "Review of *The Theological Tendency of Codex Bezae Cantabrigiensis in Acts* by Eldon Jay Epp." *Gn* 40, no. 8 (1968): 831-33.

———. *A Textual Commentary on the Greek New Testament.* 2nd ed. New York: United Bible Societies, 1994.

Metzger, Bruce M., and Bart D. Ehrman. *The Text of the New Testament: Its Transmission, Corruption and Restoration.* 4th ed. New York: Oxford University Press, 2005.

Miller, Philip M. "The Least Orthodox Reading Is to Be Preferred: A New Canon for New Testament Textual Criticism." Pages 57-90 in *Revisiting the Corruption of the New Testament: Manuscript, Patristic, and Apocryphal Evidence,* edited by Daniel B. Wallace, The Text and Canon of the New Testament. Grand Rapids: Kregel, 2011.

Milne, H. J. M., and T. C. Skeat. *Scribes and Correctors of the Codex Sinaiticus.* London: British Museum Press, 1938.

Mink, Gerd. "Die koptischen Versionen des Neuen Testaments: Die sprachlichen Probleme bei ihrer Bewertung für die griechische Textgeschichte." Pages 160-299 in *Die alten Übersetzungen des Neuen Testaments, die Kirchenväterzitate und Lektionare,* edited by Kurt Aland, ANTF 5. Berlin: de Gruyter, 1972.

———. "Problems of a Highly Contaminated Tradition: The New Testament. Stemmata of Variants as a Source of a Genealogy for Witnesses." Pages 13-85 in *Studies in Stemmatology II,* edited by Pieter van Reenen, August den Hollander, and Margot van Mulken. Amsterdam: John Benjamins, 2004.

Mirończuk, Andrzej. "New Readings in P.Oxy. XLVIII 3372 (Herodotus I 6-9)." *ZPE* 182 (2012): 77-79.

———. "Notes on Five Herodotean Papyri." *BASP* 49 (2012): 227-32.

———. "Notes on P.Oxy. XLVIII 3376 (Herodotus II)." *ZPE* 182 (2012): 80-87.

———. "P.Oxy. 4.755 descr.—a Homeric Papyrus at Princeton (*Iliad* 5.130-174)." BASP 50 (2013): 7-14.

———. "Three Homeric Papyri at Cleveland." *ZPE* 183 (2012): 21-26.

———. "Unpublished Papyri of the Iliad at Yale." *ZPE* 185 (2013): 18-20.

Mitchell, Timothy N. "What Are the NT Autographs? An Examination of the Doctrine of Inspiration and Inerrancy in Light of Greco-Roman Publication." *JETS* 59, no. 2 (2017): 287-308.

Montgomery, John Warwick. *History and Christianity*. Downers Grove, IL: InterVarsity Press, 1974.

Morrill, Michael Bruce. "A Complete Collation and Analysis of All Greek Manuscripts of John 18." PhD thesis, University of Birmingham, 2012.

Moss, Candida R., and Joel S. Baden. *Bible Nation: The United States of Hobby Lobby*. Princeton, NJ: Princeton University Press, 2017.

Mugridge, Alan. *Copying Early Christian Texts: A Study of Scribal Practice*. WUNT 362. Tübingen: Mohr Siebeck, 2016.

Müller, Darius. "Abschriften des Erasmischen Textes im Handschriftenmaterial der Johannesapokalypse: Nebst einigen editionsgeschichtlichen Beobachtungen." Pages 165-268 in *Studien zum Text der Apokalypse*, edited by Marcus Sigismund, Martin Karrer, and Ulrich Schmid, ANTF 47. Berlin: de Gruyter, 2015.

Nagy, Gregory. *Homer's Text and Language*. Urbana: University of Illinois Press, 2004.

Neill, Stephen. *The Interpretation of the New Testament: 1861–1961*. The Firth Lectures, 1962. London: Oxford University Press, 1964.

Nestle, Erwin. "How to Use a Greek New Testament." *BT* 2, no. 2 (1951): 49-55.

Nestle, Eberhard, and Erwin Nestle, eds. *Novum Testamentum Graece cum apparatu critico*. 13th ed. Württemberg: Württembergische Bibelanstalt, 1927.

"New Testament, Codex Monfortianus." Trinity College Dublin. http://digitalcollections.tcd.ie /home/index.php?DRIS_ID=MS30_001. Accessed May 1, 2018.

Niccum, Curt, and Rochus Zuurmond. "The Ethiopic Version of the New Testament." Pages 231-52 in Ehrman and Holmes, *Text of the New Testament in Contemporary Research: Essays on the Status Quaestionis*, 2nd ed.

Nicholls, Matthew C. "Galen and Libraries in the *Peri Alupias*." *JRS* 101 (2011): 123-42.

Nicklas, Tobias, and Tommy Wasserman. "Theologische Linien im Codex Bodmer Miscellani?" Pages 161-88 in *New Testament Manuscripts: Their Texts and Their World*, edited by Thomas J. Kraus, TENTS 2. Leiden: Brill, 2006.

Nida, Eugene A. *Fascinated by Languages*. Amsterdam: John Benjamins, 2003.

Nida, Eugene A., and Charles R. Taber. *The Theory and Practice of Translation*. Help for Translators 8. Leiden: Brill, 1969.

Nolan, Frederick. *An Inquiry into the Integrity of the Greek Vulgate or Received Text of the New Testament*. London: F. C. & J. Rivington, 1815.

Nongbri, Brent. "Anton Fackelmann: Conservator and Seller of Antiquities." *Variant Readings* (blog). September 13, 2017. https://brentnongbri.com/2017/09/13/anton-fackelmann-conservator-and -seller-of-antiquities/.

———. "The Construction of P.Bodmer VIII and the Bodmer 'Composite' or 'Miscellaneous' Codex." *NovT* 58, no. 4 (2016): 394-410.

———. "A First-Century Papyrus of Mark (Probably Not the One You Think)." *Variant Readings* (blog). July 21, 2017. https://brentnongbri.com/2017/07/21/a-first-century-papyrus-of-mark -probably-not-the-one-you-think/.

———. *God's Library: The Archaeology of the Earliest Christian Manuscripts*. New Haven, CT: Yale University Press, 2018.

———. "The Limits of Palaeographic Dating of Literary Papyri: Some Observations on the Date and Provenance of P. Bodmer II (P66)." *MH* 71, no. 1 (2014): 1-35.

———. "Reconsidering the Place of Papyrus Bodmer XIV-XV (P75) in the Textual Criticism of the New Testament." *JBL* 135, no. 2 (2016): 405-37.

———. "Some Answers on Fackelmann's 'First-Century Mark' Papyrus." *Variant Readings* (blog). August 3, 2017. https://brentnongbri.com/2017/08/03/some-answers-on-fackelmanns-first-century-mark-papyrus/.

———. "The Use and Abuse of P^{52}: Papyrological Pitfalls in the Dating of the Fourth Gospel." *HTR* 98, no. 1 (2005): 23-48.

Noss, Philip A. *A History of Bible Translation.* New York: American Bible Society, 2007.

Nutton, Vivian. "Galen *ad multos annos.*" *Dynamis* 15 (1995): 25-39.

Obbink, Dirk, and Daniela Colomo. "5345. Mark I 7-9, 16-18." Pages 4-7 in *The Oxyrhynchus Papyri LXXXIII,* edited by P. J. Parsons and N. Gonis, GRM 104. London: Egypt Exploration Society, 2018.

O'Brien, Peter T. *Colossians, Philemon.* WBC 44. Waco, TX: Word Books, 1982.

O'Callaghan, José. "¿1 Tim 3,16; 4,1.3 En 7Q4?" *Bib* 53, no. 3 (1972): 362-67.

———. "¿Papiros neotestamentarios en la cueva 7 de Qumrān?" *Bib* 53, no. 1 (1972): 91-100.

O'Keefe, John, and R. R. Reno. *Sanctified Vision: An Introduction to Early Christian Interpretation of the Bible.* Baltimore: Johns Hopkins University Press, 2005.

Olson, Roger E. *The Westminster Handbook to Evangelical Theology.* Louisville: Westminster John Knox, 2004.

Omanson, Roger L. "A Critical Appraisal of the *Apparatus Criticus.*" *BT* 49, no. 3 (1998): 301-23.

———. *A Textual Guide to the Greek New Testament: An Adaptation of Bruce M. Metzger's Textual Commentary for the Need of Translators.* Stuttgart: Deutsche Bibelgesellschaft, 2006.

Origen. *On First Principles.* Translated by George Butterworth. New York: Harper & Row, 1966.

Orr-Ewing, Amy. *Why Trust the Bible? Answers to 10 Tough Questions.* Nottingham, UK: Inter-Varsity Press, 2005.

Orsini, Pasquale. *Manoscritti in maiuscola biblica: materiali per un aggiornamento.* SAAFLS 7. Cassino: Edizioni dell'Università degli studi di Cassino, 2005.

———. "Palaeographic Method, Comparison and Dating: Considerations for an Updated Discussion." *Evangelical Textual Criticism* (blog). February 6, 2018. http://evangelicaltextualcriticism.blogspot.de/2018/02/palaeographic-method-comparison-and.html.

Orsini, Pasquale, and Willy Clarysse. "Early New Testament Manuscripts and Their Dates: A Critique of Theological Palaeography." *ETL* 88, no. 4 (2012): 443-74.

Osburn, Carroll D. "Methodology in Identifying Patristic Citations in NT Textual Criticism." *NovT* 47, no. 4 (2005): 313-43.

Osiek, Caroline. *The Shepherd of Hermas.* Hermeneia. Minneapolis: Fortress, 1999.

Oxford Society of Historical Theology. *The New Testament in the Apostolic Fathers.* Oxford: Clarendon, 1905.

Paap, A. H. R. E. *Nomina Sacra in the Greek Papyri of the First Five Centuries A.D.: The Sources and Some Deductions.* Papyrologica Lugduno-Batava 8. Leiden: Brill, 1959.

Parker, David C. *Codex Bezae: An Early Christian Manuscript and Its Text.* Cambridge: Cambridge University Press, 1992.

———. *Codex Sinaiticus: The Story of the World's Oldest Bible.* London: British Library, 2010.

———. "A Comparison Between the *Text und Textwert* and the Claremont Profile Method Analyses of Manuscripts in the Gospel of Luke." *NTS* 49, no. 1 (2003): 108-38.

———. *An Introduction to the New Testament Manuscripts and Their Texts.* Cambridge: Cambridge University Press, 2008.

———. *The Living Text of the Gospels.* Cambridge: Cambridge University Press, 1997.

———. "The Majuscule Manuscripts of the New Testament." Pages 41-68 in Ehrman and Holmes, *Text of the New Testament in Contemporary Research: Essays on the Status Quaestionis,* 2nd ed.

———. "Textual Criticism and Theology." *ExpTim* 118, no. 12 (2007): 583-89.

Parsons, Mikeal C. "A Christological Tendency in P⁷⁵." *JBL* 105, no. 3 (1986): 463-79.

Parsons, P. J. "Review of *Ricerche sulla maiuscola biblica* by Guglielmo Cavallo." *Gn* 42, no. 4 (1970): 375-80.

Pasquali, Giorgio. *Storia della tradizione e critica del testo.* 2nd ed. Florence: Le Monnier, 1952.

Payne, Philip B. "Vaticanus Distigme-obelos Symbols Marking Added Text, Including 1 Corinthians 14.34-5." *NTS* 63, no. 4 (2017): 604-25.

Perrin, Jac. "Family 13 in Saint John's Gospel." PhD thesis, University of Birmingham, 2012.

Perrin, Nicholas. *Lost in Transmission? What We Can Know About the Words of Jesus.* Nashville: Thomas Nelson, 2007.

Petersen, William L. "The Diatessaron of Tatian." Pages 77-96 in Ehrman and Holmes, *Text of the New Testament in Contemporary Research*, 1st ed.

Petzer, Jacobus H. "The Latin Version of the New Testament." Pages 113-30 in Ehrman and Holmes, *Text of the New Testament in Contemporary Research*, 1st ed.

Philip, Robert. *The Life, Times, and Missionary Enterprises of the Rev. John Campbell.* London: John Snow, 1841.

Piper, John. *A Peculiar Glory: How the Christian Scriptures Reveal Their Complete Truthfulness.* Wheaton, IL: Crossway, 2016.

Pliny. *Letters.* Translated by William Melmoth and W. M. L Hutchinson. 2 vols. LCL. New York: Macmillan, 1915.

Plooij, D. *Tendentieuse Varianten in den Text der Evangeliën.* Leiden: Brill, 1926.

Plumley, J. Martin. "Limitations of Coptic (Sahidic) in Representing Greek." Pages 141-52 in *The Early Versions of the New Testament: Their Origin, Transmission, and Limitations*, by Bruce M. Metzger. Oxford: Oxford University Press, 1977.

Polling, Judson. *How Reliable Is the Bible?* Grand Rapids: Zondervan, 2003.

Porson, Richard. *Letters to Mr. Archdeacon Travis, in Answer to His Defence of the Three Heavenly Witnesses, 1 John v.7.* London: T. & J. Egerton, 1790.

Porter, Stanley E. "Assessing Translation Theory: Beyond Literal and Dynamic Equivalence." Pages 117-45 in *Translating the New Testament: Text, Translation, and Theology*, edited by Stanley E. Porter and Mark J. Boda. Grand Rapids: Eerdmans, 2009.

———. *How We Got the New Testament: Text, Transmission, Translation.* Acadia Studies in Bible and Theology. Grand Rapids: Baker Academic, 2013.

———. "Textual Criticism in the Light of Diverse Textual Evidence for the Greek New Testament: An Expanded Proposal." Pages 305-37 in *New Testament Manuscripts: Their Texts and Their World*, edited by Thomas J. Kraus and Tobias Nicklas, TENTS 2. Leiden: Brill, 2006.

———. "Why So Many Holes in the Papyrological Evidence for the Greek New Testament?" Pages 167-86 in *The Bible as Book: The Transmission of the Greek Text*, edited by Scot McKendrick and Orlaith Sullivan. New Castle, DE: Oak Knoll, 2003.

Porter, Stanley E., and Andrew W. Pitts. *Fundamentals of New Testament Textual Criticism.* Grand Rapids: Eerdmans, 2015.

Post, Darrell. "An Analysis of the Newly Catalogued Gospels Minuscule, GA 2907." ThM thesis, Central Baptist Theological Seminary, 2012.

Potter, David. *Literary Tests and the Roman Historian.* Oxford: Routledge, 1999.

Powell, J. U. "The Papyri of Thucydides and the Translation of Laurentius Valla." *CIQ* 23, no. 1 (1929): 11-14.

"P.Oxy LXXXIII 5345." Egypt Exploration Fund. June 4, 2018. www.ees.ac.uk/news/poxy-lxxxiii-5345.

Price, Robert M. *The Case Against the Case for Christ: A New Testament Scholar Refutes the Reverend Lee Strobel.* Cranford, NJ: American Atheist Press, 2010.

Quinn, Kenneth. "The Poet and His Audience in the Augustan Age." Pages 75-180 in *ANRW* 30.1, edited by Wolfgang Haase. Berlin: de Gruyter, 1982.

Quintilian. *The Orator's Education.* Vol. 1, *Books 1-2.* Translated by Donald A. Russell. LCL 124. Cambridge, MA: Harvard University Press, 2002.

Ramage, Matthew J. *Jesus Interpreted: Benedict XVI, Bart Ehrman, and the Historical Truth of the Gospels.* Washington, DC: Catholic University of America Press, 2017.

Read-Heimerdinger, Jenny. "The «Long» and the «Short» Texts of Acts: A Closer Look at the Quantity and Types of Variation." *RCT* 22 (1997): 245-61.

Reiss, Katharina. *Translation Criticism—The Potentials and Limitations: Categories and Criteria for Translation Quality Assessment.* Translated by Erroll F. Rhodes. New York: St. Jerome, 2000.

Reyburn, William D. "The Task and Training of Translation Consultants." *BT* 20, no. 4 (1969): 168-76.

Rhodes, Erroll F. "The Corrections of Papyrus Bodmer II." *NTS* 14, no. 2 (1967): 271-81.

Rhodes, Ron. *The Big Book of Bible Answers: A Guide to Understanding the Most Challenging Questions.* Eugene, OR: Harvest House, 2001.

Richards, W. L. *The Classification of the Greek Manuscripts of the Johannine Epistles.* SBLDS 35. Missoula, MT: Scholars Press, 1977.

Roberts, Colin H. "2192. Letter About Books." Pages 150-52 in *The Oxyrhynchus Papyri XVIII,* edited by Edgar Lobel, Colin H. Roberts, and E. P. Wegener, GRM 26. London: Egypt Exploration Society, 1941.

———, ed. *The Antinoopolis Papyri.* Vol. 1. GRM 28. London: Egypt Exploration Society, 1950.

———. "Books in the Graeco-Roman World and in the New Testament." Pages 48-66 in *The Cambridge History of the Bible,* vol. 1, *From the Beginnings to Jerome,* edited by P. R. Ackroyd and C. F. Evans. Cambridge: Cambridge University Press, 1970.

———. *Greek Literary Hands: 350 B.C.–A.D. 400.* Oxford Palaeographical Handbooks. Oxford: Clarendon, 1956.

———. *Manuscript, Society and Belief in Early Christian Egypt.* 1977 Schweich Lectures. Oxford: Oxford University Press, 1979.

———. *An Unpublished Fragment of the Fourth Gospel in the John Rylands Library.* Manchester: Manchester University Press, 1935.

Roberts, Colin H., and T. C. Skeat. *The Birth of the Codex.* London: Oxford University Press, 1983.

Roberts, Mark D. *Can We Trust the Gospels? Investigating the Reliability of Matthew, Mark, Luke, and John.* Wheaton, IL: Crossway, 2007.

Robinson, Maurice A. "Appendix: The Case for Byzantine Priority." Pages 533-86 in *The New Testament in the Original Greek: Byzantine Textform,* edited by Maurice A. Robinson and William G. Pierpont. Southborough, MA: Chilton, 2005.

———. "The Case for Byzantine Priority." Pages 125-39 in *Rethinking New Testament Textual Criticism,* edited by David Alan Black. Grand Rapids: Baker Academic, 2002.

———. "New Testament Textual Criticism: The Case for Byzantine Priority." *TC* 6 (2001): n.p.

Robinson, Maurice A., and William G. Pierpont. *The New Testament in the Original Greek: Byzantine Textform.* Southborough, MA: Chilton, 2005.

Roth, Dieter T. *The Text of Marcion's Gospel.* NTTSD 49. Leiden: Brill, 2015.

———. "The Text of the Lord's Prayer in Marcion's Gospel." *ZNW* 103, no. 1 (2012): 47-63.

Rothschild, Clare. "The Muratorian Fragment as Roman Fake." *NovT* 60, no. 1 (2018): 55-82.

Rothschild, Clare K., and Trevor W. Thompson. "Galen: 'On the Avoidance of Grief.'" *EC* 2, no. 1 (2011): 110-29.

Royse, James R. *Scribal Habits in Early Greek New Testament Papyri.* NTTSD 36. Leiden: Brill, 2008.

Sanders, Fred. *The Triune God.* NSD. Grand Rapids: Zondervan, 2016.

Sanders, Henry. *A Third-Century Papyrus Codex of the Epistles of Paul.* University of Michigan Studies: Humanistic Series 38. Norwood, MA: Plimpton, 1935.

Scanlin, Harold P. "Bible Translation as a Means of Communicating New Testament Textual Criticism to the Public." *BT* 39, no. 1 (1988): 101-13.

Scherbenske, Eric W. *Canonizing Paul: Ancient Editorial Practice and the Corpus Paulinum.* Oxford: Oxford University Press, 2013.

Schmid, Ulrich. "Scribes and Variants—Sociology and Typology." Pages 1-23 in *Textual Variation: Theological and Social Tendencies? Papers from the Fifth Birmingham Colloquium on the Textual Criticism of the New Testament,* edited by D. C. Parker and H. A. G. Houghton, TS, Third Series 3. Piscataway, NJ: Gorgias, 2008.

Schmidt, Andreas. "Zwei Anmerkungen zu P. Ryl. III 457." *APF* 35 (1989): 11-12.

Schmidt, Daryl D. "The Greek New Testament as a Codex." Pages 469-484 in *The Canon Debate,* ed. Lee Martin McDonald and James A. Sanders. Peabody, MA: Hendrickson, 2002.

Schmithals, Walter. *Johannesevangelium und Johannesbriefe: Forschungsgeschichte und Analyse.* BZNW 64. Berlin: de Gruyter, 1992.

Schofield, Ellwood M. "The Papyrus Fragments of the Greek New Testament." PhD diss., Southern Baptist Theological Seminary, 1936.

Schreiber, Stefan. "Der Text des Neuen Testaments." Pages 53-67 in *Einleitung in das Neue Testament,* 2nd ed., edited by Martin Ebner and Stefan Schreiber, Kohlhammer Studienbücher Theologie 6. Stuttgart: Kohlhammer, 2013.

Schüssler, Karlheinz. "Das Projekt 'Biblia Coptica Patristica.'" *OrChr* 79 (1995): 224-28.

Scrivener, F. H. A. *The Authorized Edition of the English Bible (1611), Its Subsequent Reprints and Modern Representatives.* Cambridge: Cambridge University Press, 1884.

Seber, George. *Can We Believe It? Evidence for Christianity.* Eugene, OR: Wipf & Stock, 2015.

Semler, J. S. *Vorbereitung zur theologischen Hermeneutik: Drittes Stück, Erste Abteilung.* Halle: Hemmerde, 1765.

Shaw, David. "Is Junia Also Among the Apostles? Romans 16:7 and Recent Debates." *Churchman* 1 (2013): 105-18.

Sherrard, Michael. *Relational Apologetics: Defending the Christian Faith with Holiness, Respect, and Truth.* Brooks, GA: Hill Harrow Books, 2012.

Sherwin-White, A. N. *The Letters of Pliny: A Historical and Social Commentary.* Oxford: Clarendon, 1966.

Sijpesteijn, P. J. "A New Papyrus Text of Thucydides." *Aeg* 51 (1971): 221-23.

Silva, Moises. "Modern Critical Editions and Apparatuses of the Greek New Testament." Pages 283-96 in Ehrman and Holmes, *Text of the New Testament in Contemporary Research,* 1st ed.

Simonetti, Manlio. *Biblical Interpretation in the Early Church: An Historical Introduction to Patristic Exegesis.* Translated by John Hughes. Edinburgh: T&T Clark, 1994.

Simonides, Constantine. *Fac-Similes of Certain Portions of the Gospel of St. Matthew and of the Epistles of Ss. James & Jude Written on Papyrus in the First Century and Preserved in the Egyptian Museum of Joseph Mayer, Esq. Liverpool.* London: Trübner, 1862.

"Sir David Dalrymple (Lord Hailes), the Patristic Citations of the Ante-Nicene Church Fathers and the Search for Eleven Missing Verses of the New Testament." *Islamic Awareness.* May 2007. www .islamic-awareness.org/Bible/Text/citations.html.

Skeat, T. C. *The Collected Biblical Writings of T. C. Skeat.* Edited by J. K. Elliott. NovTSup 113. Leiden: Brill, 2004.

———. "The Oldest Manuscript of the Four Gospels?" *NTS* 43, no. 1 (1997): 1-34.

Slick, Matt. "Manuscript Evidence for Superior New Testament Reliability." CARM: Christian Apologetics & Research Ministry. December 10, 2008. https://carm.org/manuscript-evidence.

Smith, G. S., and A. E. Bernhard. "5073. Mark 1:1-2. Amulet." Pages 19-23 in *The Oxyrhynchus Papyri LXXVI,* edited by D. Colomo and Juan Chapa. London: Egypt Exploration Society, 2011.

Soden, Hermann von. *Die Schriften des neuen Testaments in ihrer ältesten erreichbaren Textgestalt.* 2 vols. Göttingen: Vandenhoeck & Ruprecht, 1911–1913.

Soldati, Agostino. "Due frammenti di un unico rotolo? P.Duke inv. 756 e P.Mil. Vogl. Inv. 1358 (Herodotus IV 144.2–145.1 e 147.4–5)." BASP 42 (2005): 101-6.

Solomon, S. Matthew. "The Textual History of Philemon." PhD diss., New Orleans Baptist Theological Seminary, 2014.

Sosin, Joshua D., Roger S. Bagnall, James Cowey, Mark Depauw, Terry G. Wilfong, and Klaas A. Worp, eds. *Checklist of Editions of Greek, Latin, Demotic and Coptic Papyri, Ostraca and Tablets.* June 1, 2011. https://library.duke.edu/rubenstein/scriptorium/papyrus/texts/clist_papyri.html.

Spencer, Matthew, Klaus Wachtel, and Christopher J. Howe. "The Greek Vorlage of the Syra Harclensis: A Comparative Study on Method in Exploring Textual Genealogy." TC 7 (2002): n.p.

Stanton, Graham. *Gospel Truth? New Light on Jesus and the Gospels.* London: HarperCollins, 1995.

———. *Jesus and Gospel.* Cambridge: Cambridge University Press, 2004.

Starr, Raymond J. "The Circulation of Literary Texts in the Roman World." CIQ 37, no. 1 (1987): 213-23.

Stone, Michael E. "Armenian Canon Lists I—The Council of Partaw (768 C.E.)." HTR 66, no. 4 (1973): 479-86.

———. "Armenian Canon Lists II—The Stichometry of Anania of Shirak (c. 615–c. 690 C.E.)." HTR 68, nos. 3-4 (1975): 253-60.

———. "Armenian Canon Lists III—The Lists of Mechitar of Ayrivankʿ (c. 1285 C.E.)." HTR 69, nos. 3-4 (1976): 289-300.

———. "Armenian Canon Lists IV—The List of Gregory of Tatʿew (14th Century)." HTR 72, nos. 3-4 (1979): 237-44.

———. "Armenian Canon Lists V—Anonymous Texts." HTR 83, no. 2 (1990): 141-61.

———. "Armenian Canon Lists VI—Hebrew Names and Other Attestations." HTR 94, no. 4 (2001): 477-91.

———. "Armenian Canon Lists VII: The Poetic List of Aṙakʿel of Siwnikʿ (d. 1409)." HTR 104, no. 3 (2011): 367-79.

Story, Dan. *Defending Your Faith: Reliable Answers for a New Generation of Seekers and Skeptics.* Grand Rapids: Kregel, 1997.

Strobel, Lee. *The Case for the Real Jesus: A Journalist Investigates Current Attacks on the Identity of Christ.* Grand Rapids: Zondervan, 2007.

Strutwolf, Holger, et al., eds. *Novum Testamentum Graecum, Editio Critica Maior: III/1.1 Apostelgeschichte, Text.* Stuttgart: Deutsche Bibelgesellschaft, 2017.

Strutwolf, Holger, et al., eds. *Novum Testamentum Graecum, Editio Critica Maior: III/2, Apostelgeschichte, Begleitende Materialien.* Stuttgart: Deutsche Bibelgesellschaft, 2017.

Sturz, Harry. *The Byzantine Text-Type and New Testament Textual Criticism.* Nashville: Thomas Nelson, 1984.

Szesnat, Holger. "'Some Witnesses Have . . . ': The Representation of the New Testament Text in English Bible Versions." TC 12 (2007): 1-18.

Tarrant, R. J. *Texts, Editors, and Readers: Methods and Problems in Latin Textual Criticism.* Roman Literature and Its Contexts. Cambridge: Cambridge University Press, 2016.

Tasker, R. V. G. *The Greek New Testament, Being the Text Translated in the New English Bible.* Oxford: Oxford University Press; Cambridge: Cambridge University Press, 1964.

Taylor, David G. K. "Répertoire des manuscrits syriaques du Nouveau Testament." Pages 291-313 in *Le Nouveau Testament en syriaque,* edited by Jean-Claude Haelewyck. Paris: Geuthner, 2017.

Taylor, Gary. "The Rhetoric of Textual Criticism." Text 4 (1988): 39-57.

Taylor, R. E., and Ofer Bar-Yosef. *Radiocarbon Dating: An Archaeological Perspective*. 2nd ed. Walnut Creek, CA: Left Coast Press, 2014.

Teasdale, Matthew D., Sarah Fiddyment, Jiří Vnouček, Valeria Mattiangeli, Camilla Speller, Annelise Binois, Martin Carver, et al. "The York Gospels: A 1000-Year Biological Palimpsest." *Royal Society Open Science* 4, no. 10 (2017): 1-11.

Testuz, Michel. *Papyrus Bodmer VII-IX*. Cologny-Geneva: Bibliothèque Bodmer, 1959.

Thiede, Carsten Peter. *The Earliest Gospel Manuscript? The Qumran Fragment 7Q5 and Its Significance for New Testament Studies*. Carlisle, UK: Paternoster, 1992.

———. "Papyrus Magdalen Greek 17 (Gregory-Aland P⁶⁴): A Reappraisal." *TynBul* 46, no. 1 (1995): 29-42.

Thiede, Carsten Peter, and Matthew D'Ancona. *The Jesus Papyrus*. London: Weidenfeld & Nicolson, 1996.

Thomas, John D. "The Colophon of the Harclean Syriac Version." *NETR* 3, no. 1 (1980): 16-26.

———. "The Harklean Margin: A Study of the Asterisks, Obeli, and Marginalia of the Harklean Syriac Version with Special Reference to the Gospel of Luke." PhD diss., University of St. Andrews, 1973.

Thucydides. *History of the Peloponnesian War*. Vol. 1, *Books 1-2*. Translated by C. F. Smith. LCL 108. Cambridge, MA: Harvard University Press, 1919.

Thurston, Bonnie B., and Judith M. Ryan. *Philippians and Philemon*. SP 10. Collegeville, MN: Liturgical Press, 2005.

Timpanaro, Sebastiano. *The Genesis of Lachmann's Method*. Edited and translated by Glenn W. Most. Chicago: University of Chicago Press, 2005.

Tischendorf, Constantin von. *Novum Testamentum graece, editio octava critica maior*. 2 vols. Leipzig: Giesecke & Devrient, 1869–1872.

Tovar, Sofía Torallas, and Klaas A. Worp. "A Fragment of Homer, *Iliad* 21 in the Newberry Library, Chicago." BASP 46 (2009): 11-14.

"The Transcription." Codex Sinaiticus. http://codexsinaiticus.org/en/project/transcription_detailed .aspx. Accessed May 1, 2018.

Traube, Ludwig. *Nomina Sacra: Versuch einer Geschichte der Christlichen Kurzung*. Quellen und Untersuchungen zur lateinischen Philologie des Mittelalters 2. Munich: Beck, 1907.

Tregelles, Samuel Prideaux. *The Greek New Testament: Edited from Ancient Authorities, with Their Various Readings in Full*. 7 vols. London: S. Bagster & Sons, 1857–1879.

Trobisch, David. "Structural Markers in New Testament Manuscripts, with Special Attention to Observations in Codex Boernerianus (G 012) and Papyrus 46 of the Letters of Paul." Pages 177-90 in *Layout Markers in Biblical Manuscripts and Ugaritic Tablets*, edited by Marjo Korpel and Josef M. Oesch, Pericope 5. Assen: Van Gorcum, 2005.

Trovato, Paolo. *Everything You Always Wanted to Know About Lachmann's Method: A Non-Standard Handbook of Genealogical Textual Criticism in the Age of Post-Structuralism, Cladistics, and Copy-Text*. 2nd ed. Storie e linguaggi. Padova: Libreriauniversitaria.it Edizioni, 2017.

Turner, Eric G. *Greek Manuscripts of the Ancient World*. 2nd ed. Revised by P. J. Parsons. BICS Supplement 46. London: Institute of Classical Studies, 1987.

———. *Greek Papyri: An Introduction*. Oxford: Clarendon, 1980.

———. "Recto and Verso." *JEA* 40 (1954): 102-6.

———. "Review of *The Use of Dictation in Ancient Book-Production* by T. C. Skeat." *JTS* n.s. 10 (1959): 148-50.

———. *The Typology of the Early Codex*. Philadelphia: University of Pennsylvania Press, 1977.

Vaganay, Léon. *Initiation à la critique textuelle néotestamentaire*. Paris: Bloud & Gay, 1934.

Vaganay, Léon, and Christian-Bernard Amphoux. *An Introduction to New Testament Textual Criticism*. Rev. ed. Translated by Jenny Read-Heimerdinger. Cambridge: Cambridge University Press, 1991.

Van Bruggen, Jakob. "The Majority Text: Why Not Reconsider Its Exile?" Pages 147-53 in *The Bible as Book: The Transmission of the Greek Text*, edited by Scot McKendrick and Orlaith A. O'Sullivan. London: British Library, 2003.

Van Groningen, B. A. "ΕΚΔΟΣΙΣ." *Mnemosyne* 16 (1963): 1-17.

Venuti, Lawrence. *The Translator's Invisibility: A History of Translation*. London: Routledge, 1995.

Verheyden, Joseph. "The Canon Muratori: A Matter of Dispute." Pages 487-556 in *The Biblical Canons*, edited by J.-M. Auwers and H. J. de Jonge. Leuven: Leuven University Press, 2003.

Voorst, Robert E. van. *Jesus Outside the New Testament: An Introduction to the Ancient Evidence*. Grand Rapids: Eerdmans, 2000.

Voss, Florian, and Roger Omanson. "The Textual Base for Modern Translations of the New Testament." *RevExp* 108, no. 2 (2011): 253-61.

Waard, Jan de, and Eugene A. Nida. *From One Language to Another: Functional Equivalence in Bible Translating*. Nashville: Thomas Nelson, 1986.

Wachtel, Klaus. "The Byzantine Text of the Gospels: Recension or Process?" Paper presented at the Society of Biblical Literature Annual Meeting, 2009.

———. *Der Byzantinische Text der Katholischen Briefe: Eine Untersuchung zur Entstehung der Koine des Neuen Testaments*. ANTF 24. Berlin: de Gruyter, 1995.

———. "On the Relationship of the 'Western Text' and the Byzantine Tradition of Acts—A Plea Against the Text-Type Concept." Pages 137-48 in *Novum Testamentum Graecum: Editio Critica Maior, III/3: Apostelgeschichte, Studien*, edited by Holger Strutwolf et al. Stuttgart: Deutsche Bibelgesellschaft, 2017.

———. "p64/67: Fragmente des Matthäusevangeliums aus dem 1. Jahrhundert?" *ZPE* 107 (1995): 73-80.

———. "Text-Critical Commentary." Pages 1-38 in *Novum Testamentum Graecum: Editio Critica Maior III: The Acts of the Apostles, Part 3: Studies*, edited by Holger Strutwolf, Georg Gäbel, Annette Hüffmeier, Gerd Mink, and Klaus Wachtel. Stuttgart: Deutsche Bibelgesellschaft, 2017.

Wallace, Daniel B. "7Q5: The Earliest NT Papyrus?" *WTJ* 56, no. 1 (1994): 173-80.

———. "The Demise of Codex 1799." *Daniel B. Wallace* (blog). August 18, 2012. https://danielbwallace.com/2012/08/18/the-demise-of-codex-1799.

———. "Earliest Manuscript of the New Testament Discovered?" *DTS Magazine*. February 9, 2012. www.dts.edu/read/wallace-new-testament-manscript-first-century.

———. "First-Century Fragment of Mark's Gospel Found!?" *Daniel B. Wallace* (blog). March 22, 2016. https://danielbwallace.com/2012/03/22/first-century-fragment-of-marks-gospel-found.

———. "The Gospel According to Bart: A Review Article of *Misquoting Jesus* by Bart Ehrman." *JETS* 49, no. 2 (2006): 327-49.

———. "Laying a Foundation: New Testament Textual Criticism." Pages 33-56 in *Interpreting the New Testament Text: Introduction to the Art and Science of Exegesis*, edited by Darrell L. Bock and Buist M. Fanning. Wheaton, IL: Crossway, 2006.

———. "The Majority Text Theory: History, Methods, and Critique." Pages 711-44 in Ehrman and Holmes, *Text of the New Testament in Contemporary Research: Essays on the Status Quaestionis*, 2nd ed.

———. "Medieval Manuscripts and Modern Evangelicals: Lessons from the Past, Guidance for the Future." *JETS* 60, no. 1 (2017): 5-34.

———. "The Number of Textual Variants—An Evangelical Miscalculation." *Daniel B. Wallace* (blog). September 9, 2013. https://danielbwallace.com/2013/09/09/the-number-of-textual-variants-an-evangelical-miscalculation/.

———. "Photographing a Forgery?" *The Center for the Study of New Testament Manuscripts* (blog). January 2, 2010. csntm.org/TCNotes/Archive/PhotographingAForgery.

———. "Some Second Thoughts on the Majority Text." *BSac* 146 (1989): 270-90.

———. "The Son's Ignorance in Matthew 24.36: An Exercise in Textual and Redaction Criticism." Pages 178-205 in *Studies on the Text of the New Testament and Early Christianity: Essays in Honour of Michael W. Holmes*, edited by Daniel M. Gurtner, Juan Hernández Jr., and Paul Foster, NTTSD 50. Leiden: Brill, 2015.

Warfield, B. B. *An Introduction to the Textual Criticism of the New Testament*. London: Hodder & Stoughton, 1889.

Warren, William. "Who Changed the Text and Why? Probable, Possible, and Unlikely Explanations." Pages 105-23 in *The Reliability of the New Testament: Bart D. Ehrman and Daniel B. Wallace in Dialogue*, edited by Robert B. Stewart. Minneapolis: Fortress, 2011.

Wasserman, Tommy. "Breaking News on the First-Century (?) Fragment of Mark." *Evangelical Textual Criticism* (blog). May 5, 2014. http://evangelicaltextualcriticism.blogspot.co.uk/2014/05 /breaking-news-first-century-fragment-of.html.

———. "A Comparative Textual Analysis of P⁴ and P⁶⁴⁺⁶⁷." *TC* 15 (2010): 1-26.

———. *The Epistle of Jude: Its Text and Transmission*. ConBNT 43. Stockholm: Almqvist & Wiksell, 2006.

———. "Historical and Philological Correlations and the CBGM as Applied to Mark 1:1." *TC* 20 (2015): 1-11.

———. "Misquoting Manuscripts? The Orthodox Corruption of Scripture Revisited." Pages 325-50 in *The Making of Christianity: Conflicts, Contacts, and Constructions: Essays in Honor of Bengt Holmberg*, edited by M. Zetterholm and S. Byrskog, ConBNT 47. Winona Lake, IN: Eisenbrauns, 2012.

———. "Papyrus 72 and the *Bodmer Miscellaneous Codex*." *NTS* 51, no. 1 (2005): 137-54.

———. "Proposal for a New Rating System in Greek New Testament Editions." *BT* 60, no. 3 (2009): 140-57.

———. "The 'Son of God' Was in the Beginning (Mark 1:1)." *JTS* 62, no. 1 (2011): 20-50.

Wasserman, Tommy, and Peter J. Gurry. *A New Approach to Textual Criticism: An Introduction to the Coherence-Based Genealogical Method*. SBLRBS 80. Atlanta: SBL Press, 2017.

Watson, Francis. *Gospel Writing: A Canonical Perspective*. Grand Rapids: Eerdmans, 2013.

Wayment, Thomas A. *The Text of the New Testament Apocrypha (100–400 CE)*. New York: Bloomsbury T&T Clark, 2013.

Wegner, Paul D. *The Journey from Texts to Translations: The Origin and Development of the Bible*. Grand Rapids: Baker, 1999.

———. *A Student's Guide to Textual Criticism of the Bible*. Downers Grove, IL: IVP Academic, 2006.

Wellesley, Kenneth. "Was the Leiden MS of Tacitus Copied from the Editio Princeps?" *AJP* 89, no. 3 (1968): 302-20.

Welsby, Alison. *A Textual Study of Family 1 in the Gospel of John*. ANTF 45. Berlin: de Gruyter, 2014.

West, Martin L. *Studies in the Text and Transmission of the Iliad*. Berlin: de Gruyter, 2001.

Westcott, B. F. *A General Survey of the History of the Canon of the New Testament*. 7th ed. New York: Macmillan, 1896.

Westcott, B. F., and F. J. A. Hort. *The New Testament in the Original Greek: Introduction, Appendix*. London: Macmillan, 1881.

———. *The New Testament in the Original Greek: Introduction, Appendix*. 2nd ed. London: Macmillan, 1896.

———. *The New Testament in the Original Greek: Text*. London: Macmillan, 1881.

Wettlaufer, Ryan D. *No Longer Written: The Use of Conjectural Emendation in the Restoration of the Text of the New Testament, the Epistle of James as a Case Study*. NTTSD 44. Leiden: Brill, 2013.

Whitaker, William. *Disputatio de sacra scriptura contra huius temporis papistas*. Cambridge: Thomas, 1588.

———. *A Disputation on Holy Scripture: Against the Papists*. Translated by William Fitzgerald. Cambridge: Cambridge University Press, 1849.

White, Peter. "Bookshops in the Literary Culture of Rome." Pages 268-87 in *Ancient Literacies: The Culture of Reading in Greece and Rome*, edited by William A. Johnson and Holt N. Parker. Oxford: Oxford University Press, 2009.

Whitlark, Jason A., and Mikeal C. Parsons. "The 'Seven' Last Words: A Numerical Motivation for the Insertion of Luke 23.34a." *NTS* 52, no. 2 (2006): 188-204.

Wikenhauser, Alfred. *New Testament Introduction.* Translated by J. Cunningham. New York: Herder and Herder, 1958.

Wilkinson, Kevin W. "Fragments of a Ptolemaic Thucydides Roll in the Beinecke Library." *ZPE* 153 (2005): 69-74.

Williams, C. S. C. *Alterations to the Text of the Synoptic Gospels and Acts.* Oxford: Blackwell, 1951.

Williams, Peter J. "The Bible, the Septuagint, and the Apocrypha: A Consideration of Their Singularity." Pages 169-72 in *Studies on the Text and Versions of the Hebrew Bible in Honour of Robert Gordon,* edited by Geoffrey Khan and Diana Lipton. Leiden: Brill, 2012.

——. *Can We Trust the Gospels?* Wheaton, IL: Crossway, 2018.

——. *Early Syriac Translation Technique and the Textual Criticism of the Greek Gospels.* TS, Third Series 2. Piscataway, NJ: Gorgias, 2004.

——. "Ehrman's Equivocation and the Inerrancy of the Original Text." Pages 389-406 in *The Enduring Authority of the Christian Scriptures,* edited by D. A. Carson. Grand Rapids: Eerdmans, 2016.

——. "Not the Prologue of John." *JSNT* 33, no. 4 (2011): 375-86.

——. "On the Representation of Sahidic Within the Apparatus of the Nestle-Aland *Novum Testamentum Graece.*" *Journal of Coptic Studies* 8 (2006): 123-25.

——. "Review of Bart Ehrman, *Misquoting Jesus.*" *Evangelical Textual Criticism* (blog). December 31, 2005. http://evangelicaltextualcriticism.blogspot.de/2005/12/review-of-bart-ehrman-mis quoting-jesus_31.html.

——. "Some Problems in Determining the *Vorlage* of Early Syriac Versions of the NT." *NTS* 47, no. 4 (2001): 537-43.

——. "The Syriac Versions of the New Testament." Pages 143-66 in Ehrman and Holmes, *Text of the New Testament in Contemporary Research: Essays on the Status Quaestionis,* 2nd ed.

——. "'Where Two or Three Are Gathered Together': The Witness of the Early Versions." Pages 239-59 in *The Early Text of the New Testament,* edited by C. E. Hill and M. J. Kruger. Oxford: Oxford University Press, 2012.

Wilson, Nigel G. "A List of Plato Manuscripts." *Scriptorium* 16, no. 2 (1962): 386-95.

Wisse, Frederik. "The Coptic Versions of the New Testament." Pages 131-41 in Ehrman and Holmes, *Text of the New Testament in Contemporary Research: Essays on the Status Quaestionis,* 1st ed.

——. *The Profile Method for the Classification and Evaluation of Manuscript Evidence, as Applied to the Continuous Greek Text of the Gospel of Luke.* SD 44. Grand Rapids: Eerdmans, 1982.

Wolf, Gary. "The Church of the Non-believers." *Wired.* November 1, 2006. www.wired.com/2006/11 /atheism.

Wouters, Alfons. *The Chester Beatty Codex AC 1499: A Graeco-Latin Lexicon on the Pauline Epistles and a Greek Grammar.* Leuven: Peeters, 1988.

Wright, Brian J. *Communal Reading in the Time of Jesus: A Window into Early Christian Reading Practices.* Minneapolis: Fortress, 2017.

——. "Jesus as ΘΕΟΣ: A Textual Examination." Pages 229-66 in *Revisiting the Corruption of the New Testament: Manuscript, Patristic, and Apocryphal Evidence,* edited by Daniel B. Wallace, TCNT. Grand Rapids: Kregel, 2011.

Yohanna, Samer S. *The Gospel of Mark in the Syriac Harklean Version: An Edition Based upon the Earliest Witnesses.* BibOr 52. Rome: Gregorian & Biblical Press, 2014.

Young, Frances. *Biblical Exegesis and the Formation of Christian Culture.* Cambridge: Cambridge University Press, 1997.

Youngblood, Ronald, ed. *Evangelicals and Inerrancy: Selections from the Journal of the Evangelical Theological Society.* Nashville: Thomas Nelson, 1984.

Zuntz, Günther. *The Ancestry of the Harklean New Testament*. Oxford: Oxford University Press, 1945.

———. "Reconstruction of One Leaf of the Chester Beatty Papyrus (Matth. 25, 41-26, 39)." *ChrÉg* 26 (1951): 191-211.

———. *The Text of the Epistles: A Disquisition upon the Corpus Paulinum*. 1946 Schweich Lectures. Oxford: Oxford University Press, 1953.

LIST OF CONTRIBUTORS

Andrew Blaski (PhD, University of Edinburgh) is assistant professor of theology and philosophy at Holy Apostles College & Seminary in Cromwell, Connecticut. He has published essays and reviews in *Vigiliae Christianae, Studia Patristica, Origeniana Duodecima,* and the *Expository Times.*

Zachary J. Cole (PhD, University of Edinburgh) is lecturer in biblical studies at Union Theological College, Belfast. He is the author of *Numerals in Early Greek New Testament Manuscripts Text-Critical, Scribal, and Theological Studies* (Brill) along with several journal articles on early Christian manuscripts. He is also a graduate of Dallas Theological Seminary and serves as an ordained minister in the Presbyterian Church in Ireland.

Jeremiah Coogan is a PhD candidate in New Testament and early Christianity at the University of Notre Dame. His work focuses on intersections between Gospel reading, material texts, and literary theory. His dissertation considers how the Eusebian apparatus reconfigures the Gospels as a fourfold unity. His work has been published in a number of venues, including the *Journal of Early Christian Studies* and the *Journal of Late Antiquity.*

Edgar Battad Ebojo (PhD, University of Birmingham) is a global translation adviser (GTA) of the United Bible Societies (UBS) assigned in the Asia-Pacific region. He is also one of the translation consultants for the Philippine Bible Society, where he served for many years as its translations department manager until his present appointment with the UBS. He first served PBS as a Bible translator.

Peter J. Gurry (PhD, University of Cambridge) is assistant professor of New Testament and codirector of the Text & Canon Institute at Phoenix Seminary. He is the author of *A New Approach to Textual Criticism* (SBL; with Tommy Wasserman) and *A Critical Examination of the Coherence-Based Genealogical Method in New Testament Textual Criticism* (Brill).

Elijah Hixson (PhD, University of Edinburgh) is a junior research associate in New Testament text and language at Tyndale House, Cambridge, where he is working with Dirk Jongkind to produce a textual commentary on the Greek New Testament. He is the author of *Scribal Habits in Sixth-Century Greek Purple Codices* (Brill) and numerous articles on textual criticism in publications such as the *Journal of Theological Studies, Novum Testamentum,* and *New Testament Studies.*

Gregory R. Lanier (PhD, University of Cambridge) is associate professor of New Testament at Reformed Theological Seminary (Orlando). His publications include *Septuaginta: A Reader's Edition* (Hendrickson; edited with William A. Ross), *How We Got the*

Bible: Old and New Testament Canon and Text (Christian Focus), and *Old Testament Conceptual Metaphors and the Christology of Luke's Gospel* (T&T Clark) as well as various articles on textual criticism, Christology, and the Septuagint in academic journals. He also serves as associate pastor of River Oaks Presbyterian Church.

Peter Malik (PhD, University of Cambridge) is a research associate at Kirchliche Hochschule Wuppertal/Bethel, where he works on the *Editio Critica Maior* of Revelation. He is the author of *P.Beatty III (P^{47}): The Codex, Its Scribe, and Its Text* (Brill) and is presently engaged on a new edition of the Greek biblical texts of Codex Climaci Rescriptus, a Sinaitic palimpsest.

Robert D. Marcello is assistant executive director of the Center for the Study of New Testament Manuscripts (CSNTM) and a PhD candidate at Dallas Theological Seminary.

John D. Meade (PhD, The Southern Baptist Theological Seminary) is associate professor of Old Testament and codirector of the Text & Canon Institute at Phoenix Seminary. He is the author of *The Biblical Canon Lists from Early Christianity* (Oxford University Press; with Edmon Gallagher) and the forthcoming book *A Critical Edition of the Hexaplaric Fragments of Job 22–42* (Peeters). He is also a member at large of the International Organization for Septuagint and Cognate Studies and cochairs the Steering Committee for the Septuagint Studies section at the Evangelical Theological Society.

Timothy N. Mitchell is a PhD student at the University of Birmingham (UK). His research focuses on the writing and book culture of early Christianity and the textual transmission of the Gospel of Mark in the Π group of manuscripts. He has published articles in *Bibliotheca Sacra*, *Journal of the Evangelical Theological Society*, and *Journal for the Study of the New Testament*.

Jacob W. Peterson is a PhD candidate in New Testament language, literature, and theology at the University of Edinburgh and a research fellow at the Center for the Study of New Testament Manuscripts (CSNTM). His research and writing focus on manuscripts of the Pauline Epistles, and his doctoral thesis is on the Pauline text of GA 1739.

James B. Prothro (PhD, University of Cambridge) is assistant professor of theology at Ave Maria University and studied classics at Washington University in St. Louis. He is a subeditor at *The Religious Studies Review* and the author of *Both Judge and Justifier: Biblical Legal Language and the Act of Justifying in Paul* (Mohr Siebeck).

S. Matthew Solomon (PhD, New Orleans Baptist Theological Seminary) has done extensive collation and research in the text of Philemon. He has presented his research at numerous Society of Biblical Literature meetings, and his academic interests range across New Testament textual criticism, papyrology, early Christianity, and interpretive methods.

Daniel B. Wallace (PhD, Dallas Theological Seminary) is the executive director of the Center for the Study of New Testament Manuscripts (CSNTM) and senior research professor of New Testament studies at Dallas Theological Seminary. He is a past president of the Evangelical Theological Society, a consultant for several Bible translations, and the author of numerous journal articles and books, including *Greek Grammar Beyond the Basics*.

IMAGE CREDITS

1.1. P.Oxy. 83.5345. Courtesy of Egypt Exploration Society

1.2. 7Q5. Used by permission of The Leon Levy Dead Sea Scrolls Digital Library; Israel Antiquities Authority, photo: Shai Halevi

2.1. P.Oxy. 18.2192. Courtesy of Egypt Exploration Society

2.2. P.Mich.inv. 1436. Image digitally reproduced with the permission of the Papyrology Collection, Graduate Library, University of Michigan

2.3. P.Mich.inv. 1440. Image digitally reproduced with the permission of the Papyrology Collection, Graduate Library, University of Michigan

5.1. GA 1415 (Athens, National Library of Greece, Ms. 123), f. 189r. Image used by permission of the National Library of Greece

5.2. P.Ryl. 16. Used by permission of The University of Manchester Library

5.3. Comparison of P.Ryl. 16 and scribe A of Codex Sinaiticus. P. Rly. 16 used by permission of The University of Manchester Library. All others used by permission © The British Library Board BL Add. MS 43725

8.1. Revelation 1 in Codex Montfortianus. Used by permission of Trinity College Dublin

8.2. Mark 1:1 in Codex Sinaiticus. © The British Library Board BL Add. MS 43725

8.3. P.Köln VI 255. Courtesy of © Institute for Ancient History at the University of Cologne

14.1. Codex Bobbiensis. Il codice evangelico k della Biblioteca universitaria nazionale, public domain

14.2. GA 05, MS Nn.2.41; Codex Bezae f. 133v. Image courtesy of Cambridge University Library

14.3. GA 05, MS Nn.2.41; Codex Bezae f. 134r. Image courtesy of Cambridge University Library

14.4. Sinai syr. NF 37, f. 2v. Courtesy of sinai.library.ucla.edu, a publication of St. Catherine's Monastery of the Sinai in collaboration with EMEL and UCLA

14.5. BnF ms. syr. 296, no. 1º. Courtesy of National Library of France, Department of Manuscripts

14.6. BL Or. MS 5707. © The British Library Board BL Or. MS 5707

NAME INDEX

SUBJECT INDEX

SCRIPTURE INDEX

ANCIENT WRITINGS INDEX
(BY AUTHOR)

MANUSCRIPT INDEX

By Rahlfs' sigla